ARCHITECTING WITH RM-ODP

ISBN 0-13-019116-7

90000

9 780130 191168

SOFTWARE ARCHITECTURE SERIES

Thomas J. Mowbray, Ph.D., Series Editor

WWW.WWISA.ORG

The Worldwide Institute of Software Architects (WWISA) is a non-profit professional organization dedicated to establishing a formal profession of software architecture and providing information and services to software architects and their clients—analogous to the formation of the American Institute of Architects roughly 140 years ago. The essential tenet of WWISA is that there is a perfect analogy between building and software architecture, and that the classical role of the architect needs to be introduced into the software construction industry.

The architect, whether designing structures of brick or computer code, forms the bridge between the world of the client and that of the technical builders. This critical bridge has been missing from the software industry, resulting in a decades-long software crisis. Entire software structures are dysfunctional or have been scrapped entirely—before seeing a single "inhabitant." We have simply been building huge, complex structures without architects, and without blueprints.

WWISA was established in 1998 and now has over 1,000 members in 37 countries. Membership is open to practicing and aspiring software architects, professors, students, CIOs, and CEOs. Members participate to promote training and degree programs, develop architectural standards and guiding principles, and work toward creating a standard body of shared knowledge. We are our client advocates; clients are our driving force. We hope to become the clients' bridge to successful software construction by helping them leverage the full range of technology.

ARCHITECTING WITH RM-ODP

JANIS PUTMAN

PH PTR

PRENTICE HALL PTR
UPPER SADDLE RIVER, NJ 07458
WWW.PHPTR.COM

Library of Congress Cataloging in Publication Data

Putman, Janis.
   Architecting with RM-ODP / Janis Putman.
     p. cm.
   ISBN 0-13-019116-7
     I. Computer architecture. 2. Electronic data processing—Distributed processing. I.
   Title.

QA76.9A73 P87 2000
004'.362--dc21

                         00-058866

Editorial/Production Supervisor: *Vanessa Moore*
Acquisitions Editor: *Paul Petralia*
Editorial Assistant: *Justin Somma*
Marketing Manager: *Bryan Gambrel*
Manufacturing Manager: *Alexis R. Heydt*
Cover Design Director: *Jerry Votta*
Cover Designer: *Anthony Gemmellaro*
Interior Formatter: *Sean Donahue*
Project Coordinator: *Anne Trowbridge*

© 2001 Prentice Hall PTR
Prentice-Hall, Inc.
Upper Saddle River, New Jersey 07458

Prentice Hall books are widely used by corporations and government agencies
for training, marketing, and resale.

The publisher offers discounts on this book when ordered in bulk quantities. For more information, contact:
   Corporate Sales Department
   Prentice Hall PTR
   1 Lake Street
   Upper Saddle River, NJ 07458
   Phone: 800-382-3419; FAX: 201-236-7141
   E-mail: corpsales@prenhall.com

All products or services mentioned in this book are the trademarks or service marks of their respective companies
or organizations.

Printed in the United States of America
10 9 8 7 6 5 4 3 2 1

ISBN 0-13-019116-7

Prentice-Hall International (UK) Limited, *London*
Prentice-Hall of Australia Pty. Limited, *Sydney*
Prentice-Hall Canada Inc., *Toronto*
Prentice-Hall Hispanoamericana, S.A., *Mexico*
Prentice-Hall of India Private Limited, *New Delhi*
Prentice-Hall of Japan, Inc., *Tokyo*
Pearson Education Asia Pte. Ltd.
Editora Prentice-Hall do Brasil, Ltda., *Rio de Janeiro*

*To my Mom and in memory of my Dad,
for their love and devotion, and my inspiration.*

CONTENTS

PART ONE   ARCHITECTING DISTRIBUTED PROCESSING SYSTEMS PRIMER

PART TWO   RM-ODP CONCEPTS AND RULES, AND THEIR USES

5   RM-ODP Architecture Model   159

PART THREE PATTERNS FOR DISTRIBUTED PROCESSING CONCERNS

LIST OF FIGURES

LIST OF TABLES

FOREWORD

Every information technology product that you acquire comes with an architecture. Whether you can find it or not, or whether the IT developers thought about it or not, it's in there. It is defined by the nature of the product's components, and the principles and mechanisms by which the components relate to and interact with each other. It is primarily the architecture that determines the degree to which the product will furnish the levels of service you wish to enjoy: last response; easy access; protected access; dependable service; scalability to large distributed operations and heavy workloads.

Some IT architectures are relatively easy to change, but many are not. So if you acquire an IT product that gives you the wrong levels of service and has a hard-to-change architecture, you are in big trouble. If you marry an IT architecture in haste, you will repent at leisure—if you are lucky. If you're living in Internet time, you may not even have the leisure time to repent.

The critical importance of IT architecture became increasingly appreciated during the 1990s, and a number of significant books have established good foundations for software and systems architecture. Also, several organizations have begun to establish standards and guidelines for good IT architectural practice. What is most needed at this point is a thorough treatment of IT architecture principles and practices that covers:

▶ Integration of IT architecture elements with business objectives, rules, and operations
▶ Relations to leading architectures—relevant standards, guidelines, languages, and tools
▶ Process guidelines for concurrently engineering business, architecture, and technology considerations into a viable system definition and implementation
▶ An in-depth example showing how the principles and guidelines apply to a representative IT application system

Janis Putman's book, *Architecting with RM-ODP*, is the best treatment available for covering all of these needs. It is based on a major international standard, the Reference Model of Open Distributed Processing (RM-ODP), which integrates IT and business system definition. It shows how to apply complementary standards, processes and tools, such as the Unified Modeling Language (UML), Zachman viewpoints, USC's WinWin, Spiral Model, and Model-Based (System) Architecting and Software Engineering (MBASE) guidelines; advanced architectural description languages; and domain-specific software architectures. It is clearly written, with careful definitions and distinctions among key terms (e.g., architecture, model, view, open, interoperability, integration), which are consistently used throughout the book. And it illustrates the principles and guidelines with detailed examples from a representative hospital IT system application.

RM-ODP's organizing framework is built around five relatively orthogonal but consistently defined viewpoints:

- ▶ An *Enterprise Viewpoint*, which defines the business perspective of the system: its purpose and scope; its operations, roles, and policies; including such terms as enterprise object, role, interaction, process, take, and policy.
- ▶ An *Information Viewpoint*, which defines the semantics of and relations among the system's information elements; including such terms as information object, static schema, dynamic schema, and invariant schema.
- ▶ A *Computational Viewpoint*, which defines the system functionality and its partitioning into components; including such terms as computational object, interface, interaction, client, server, producer, and consumer.
- ▶ An *Engineering Viewpoint*, which defines the system's distribution; including such terms as engineering object, channel, node, protocol, interface, replicate, and checkpoint/recovery.
- ▶ A *Technology Viewpoint*, which defines the system's technology and products, such as commercial packages and developed code; including conformance points for testing the conformance of code to its specification.

Consistency among these viewpoints is facilitated by sets of basic rules, object model rules, structuring rules, specification rules, and conformance rules. The "openness" of RM-ODP is facilitated by a set of *distribution transparencies* covering access, failure, location, migration, relocation, replication, persistence, and transaction consistency. These basically hide implementation details, enabling multiple product implementations to be used interchangeably.

This book provides extensive elaborations of these concepts and frameworks. It also includes detailed treatments of interoperability, heterogeneous component composition, fault tolerance, quality of service, node management, federation, and policy specification. These are also extensively illustrated via the hospital system example.

The near-term importance of the contributions in this book derives greatly from the book's ability to enable IT architects to operate more efficiently and effectively. Our COCOMO II data analyses have shown that "Architecture and Risk Resolution" is a statistically significant cost driver, whose effect on project productivity ranges from a factor of 1.18 on small projects to 1.63 on very large projects. This is after normalizing out the effects of such other factors as use of tools, process maturity, and component reuse, whose interaction with the architecture factor can produce considerably larger productivity gains.

The long-term importance of the book's contributions derives from the book's ability to help us resolve a dilemma encountered in a recent National Science Foundation workshop summarized in my article with Victor Rasili "Gaining Intellectual Control of Software Development," in *IEEE Software*, May 2000. The dilemma is that one would like clean, build-from-scratch architectural guidelines that would avoid the problems encountered in current poorly architected systems; but that these poorly-architected systems include components that economic necessities require the use of in current systems, making the clean, build-from-scratch guidelines inapplicable.

The most encouraging possibility provided by RM-ODP and the concepts in this book is that they can provide a framework for coping with current-component deficiencies and incompatibilities in the near-term while providing a way to avoid such deficiencies and incompatibilities in the future. I heartily recommend your assimilating and applying the concepts and practices in this book as a step toward achieving both of these goals.

— *Barry Boehm, USC*

PREFACE

To understand anything, you should not try to understand everything.
— Aristotle

*The whole is greater than the sum of the parts; the part is greater than
a fraction of the whole.*
— Aristotle

*Architecting is a challenging process of abstraction, composition,
modularity, and simplification to create an architecture specification.
An architecture specification captures the essence and definition of
the system: understanding, parts, and the relationships among the
parts. An architecture specification defines how a system solves a
business problem within the scope of the business.*
— Putman

*Leave the beaten track occasionally and dive into the woods. You will
be certain to find something that you have never seen before.*
— Alexander Graham Bell

There are large gaps in the theory and practice of software architecture and engineering. Much is published about the representation of a software architecture, such as the Unified Modeling Language (UML), but little is available about the specification for a software architecture. Software engineering methods of domain engineering, process modeling languages, and well-formed patterns of reasoning aid in the specification of an architecture.

The Reference Model of Open Distributed Processing (RM-ODP) defines the standard reference model for distributed software systems architectures, based on object-oriented techniques, accepted at the international level. RM-ODP is a standard adopted by the International Standards Organization (ISO) and the International Telecommunications Union (ITU). RM-ODP is embedded and used actively in mission-critical systems industries such as in telecommunications, in health care, on Wall Street (financial services industry), in various Government systems (Logistics), in European Government Agencies such as UK Aviation control systems, as a foundation for the Object Management Group (OMG) Object Management Architecture (OMA), for defining enterprise architectures, and for defining software architectures.

The software systems architecture work that is emerging, and is focused either at the component level or at the systems level, provides a key resource for architecting. This is enhanced by the architecting techniques of RM-ODP. This book assembles these great ideas, explains what they mean, and shows how to use them for practical benefit, along with real-world case study examples. By using the RM-ODP specification constructs, associated languages, architecture patterns of reasoning, semantic behavior specification, and conformance testing abilities, readers will be able to architect their specific systems based on the RM-ODP specification foundations, and specify architectures that work.

One of the purposes of this book is to provide the approach to using the RM-ODP foundations in architecting and specifying a distributed processing system that addresses such key properties as interoperability, dependability, portability, integration, composability, scalability, transparency, behavior specification, quality of service, policy management, federation, and conformance validation.

Another purpose of this book is to explain the underlying foundations for creating an architectural specification. These foundations come not only from RM-ODP, but also from the current work in software systems architecture.

Another purpose is to guide the reader to understand the importance and benefits of creating an architecture specification for an enterprise.

Yet another purpose is to provide the reader with the principles to construct software systems architecture (at both introductory and in-depth levels).

By applying the proven techniques of RM-ODP for what makes a good architecture, readers will be able to build their own tailored architectures, and clearly represent them in UML or some other tool, with an understanding of the underlying principles.

Practitioners of RM-ODP have found that the standard is extremely beneficial in guiding architecture definition and providing standard terminology/principles for distributed object applications and infrastructures from an enterprise perspective.

OUTSTANDING FEATURES

This book is intended to provide valuable insight into successful architecture specification by describing an unprecedented foundation to accomplish this task, describing the use of the foundation, explaining the relationships of the concepts of architecting, explaining the relationships of the concepts of distributed processing, and identifying the right methods and possible tools for architecting.

All material for the book has been derived from actual experiences. A medical case study is used throughout the book in ever increasing detailed specification. This medical case study is based on actual experience of the author. In addition, many metamodels are provided to represent the concepts of RM-ODP. All of these metamodels are contributions from the author. This is information that readers can use and apply in their architecting today.

RM-ODP provides a reference framework, grammars, methods of abstraction and composition, and separation of concerns to achieve an architecture specification of the system. RM-ODP provides a framework for this separation, using viewpoints, as well as separating out certain decisions (e.g., product decisions) until later. Further, the reference model provides a set of definitions, which always aids in communicating with others.

There is little in the literature about RM-ODP or architecture specification, and certainly not a book dedicated as a tutorial of these subjects. Now there is. In summary, this book offers the following:

- How to manage the architecting process in the lifecycle of a system
- How to solve many architecture reuse and cost-effectiveness problems
- How to create a business specification
- How to understand and use the concepts of distributed processing in an architecture
- How to architect effectively
- How to specify an architecture
- How to understand and specify semantic behavior and nonfunctional properties of a system (the "ilities")
- How to provide the right level of detail in an architecture specification
- How to ensure the implementation conforms to the architecture specification
- How to use RM-ODP effectively
- How to use popular tools, such as UML, to describe an architecture
- A definitive tutorial of RM-ODP

AUDIENCE

This book is designed for:

- Those in the Distributed Software Systems Architecture community who are interested in a methodology for using proven architecture principles.
- Professional software architects who are looking for new ideas about architecting a system. Within this book, the reader will find discussions of the techniques for architecting, for creating an architecture specification, and RM-ODP's relationship to other architecture frameworks.
- Program managers interested in how to create a cost-effective architecture within their enterprise that focuses on the needs of the enterprise and solves an enterprise problem. They will learn how do to do this through an overview of RM-ODP, the program benefits for using it, and where RM-ODP fits in the system lifecycle process.
- Systems engineers interested in the lifecycle approach to enterprise architecture specification.
- Experienced engineers interested in expanding their understanding of how to create a valid architecture specification and gain an understanding of the distributed processing system concepts, why certain constructions are valid and why some are not, what is to be specified and how, and some new ideas and approaches to architecting a system. The reader will be able to develop a collection of useful distributed processing architecting techniques that expand upon the current software systems architecture capabilities.
- Developers interested in the practice of architecture specification and aligning current technology to achieve a workable system, while allowing evolutionary changes in technology solutions.
- Researchers interested in solutions and aids for furthering the research work in architecture specification.
- Individuals in the software community who are generally interested in the application of an architecture method. Readers will find examples of the applications of RM-ODP and specific analysis techniques.

The expected audience will be novice and mid-level program managers, software engineers, those in the IEEE, DoD, research communities, consortia, and general architecture readers.

This book can be used as a textbook and reference book for studies in the methods of architecture; for graduate studies in software architecture specification; for training information about software architecture and RM-ODP; for further education of consultants, integration specialists, and acquisition managers who need to approve and fund such work; and for researchers who are expanding the discipline of software architecture.

The inclusion of RM-ODP will bring to the U.S., principally, the outstanding work that was accomplished by the international standards working group. In brief, the RM-ODP principles form a solution set and foundation for all software architecting endeavors. It is *the* formalized framework for this topic, and at the International Standard (IS) level of acceptance. It forms a solution set and foundation for reuse of design patterns to provide cost-effective software architecture. It is *the* process for this topic, but has never before been described in a book. Many program managers (who typically set the stage as to the methodology of choice for a project), software engineers, and researchers in academia and in DARPA are unaware of the power and solutions provided by the standard, or the process of identifying and instantiating reuse of all the expensive assets of architecture. Many do not realize that there is a language for specifying software-intensive distributed processing, and that language is precisely and rigorously defined in RM-ODP for reuse. Those debating definitions for architecture, system, interface, and others can reuse the internationally agreed upon definitions.

Finally, with the inclusion of RM-ODP and its relationship to other architecture frameworks, it is expected that many software engineers will benefit from reading this work, since it will be the first time these subjects are discussed in print.

HOW TO USE THIS BOOK

This book is divided into four parts, aimed at increasing levels of detail.

▶ Part One provides an overview of the field of software architecture, an RM-ODP primer for managers, and an RM-ODP primer for architects.

▶ Part Two provides an in-depth study of RM-ODP and how to use it. Areas of importance and utility from RM-ODP are highlighted. Ambiguity in RM-ODP is highlighted. Warnings in the use of RM-ODP are highlighted.

▶ Part Three provides a discussion of the principal architecture patterns of use, arranged by topic. Several of these patterns of use come from emerging work under the initiative of RM-ODP, as well as lessons learned from the practice of RM-ODP. These patterns of reasoning used by the architect are founded on the principals of RM-ODP, as discussed in Part Two of the book.

▶ Part Four concludes with relating RM-ODP to other architecture methods. It also provides emerging technologies to further the patterns of reasoning for use in architecting, and a set of architecting heuristics.

The information contained in this book is organized in a manner that provides clear insight into the world of distributed software-intensive processing architecture for designers and developers who are familiar with information systems technology, but want to know more about how to build a good architecture.

Starting with a tutorial about software architecture, and then a tutorial about the standard for software architecture, the reader need not be an expert in the area of international standards, RM-ODP, software architecture, or specific technologies. The book goes on to address the needs of the variety of readers for which it is intended.

Each chapter in the book provides an overview of the subject of the chapter, as well as a summary. For those who wish a broad brush exposure to RM-ODP, the primers of Part One provide this, as well as the overviews and summaries in each chapter of interest.

As each chapter progresses, in Parts Two and Three, more and more in-depth detail is provided. The readings of these chapters are aimed at those who wish to know the technical details of a topic.

There are two case studies used throughout the book, at various levels of detail. The primary case study is a Hospital enterprise, based upon the author's experience with the medical profession. A secondary case study is an airline reservation system, also based upon the author's experience. These case studies are used to describe the concepts of RM-ODP, and to show how they might be used.

CONVENTIONS USED IN THIS BOOK

The conventions used in this book are as follows:

▶ A Point identifies some important aspect being discussed, and is denoted with the following icon:

▶ A Note is typically used to callout the RM-ODP definition, and is denoted with the following icon:

▶ A Warning identifies some ambiguity in RM-ODP, or a warning to the reader of its use. A warning is also used to identify some current day practice that may benefit from using RM-ODP. It is denoted with the following icon:

▶ A Sidebar either provides an example, or relates discussions together, that can be later referred to.

▶ The case studies are often shown in terms of the Unified Modeling Language constructs. In particular, the author used the Rational Rose™ tool to produce and edit the UML diagrams in this book.

▶ Finally, many of the figures use the following conventions:

Icons for Use

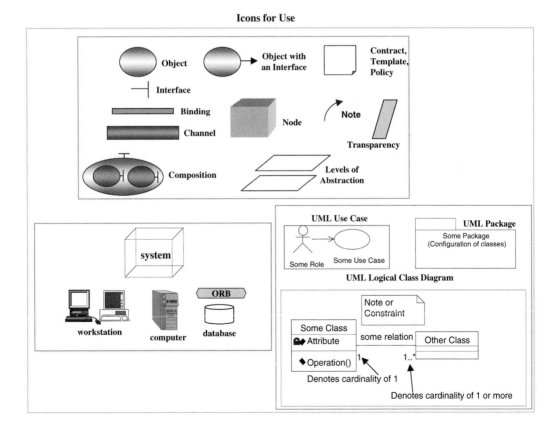

ACKNOWLEDGMENTS

This book would not exist without the extraordinary work accomplished by the creators of RM-ODP. Through their long, arduous, often seemingly impossible task of bringing together the principles of open distributed processing, and coming to agreement, the work stands as a hallmark to the architecting process of a system. Key persons involved in the RM-ODP work include Peter Linington, Andrew Herbet, Ed Stull, John Nicol, Haim Kilov, Kerry Raymond, Tom Rutt, Joaquin Miller, Miriam Bearman, Tom Mowbray, Andrew Watson, Bryan Wood, Sandy Tyndale-Biscoe, Chris Sluman, Kevin Tyson, and many others. It is truly an honor to be associated with this elite group.

The work of Professor Barry Boehm at USC, Professor Mary Shaw at CMU, Professor David Garlan at CMU, Jeanette Wing, Assoc. Dean for Academic Affairs at CMU, Dr. Robert Balzer as USC's Information Sciences Institute, Dr. Alex Wolf at University of Colorado, Dr. Leon Osterweil at UMass, Dr. John Salasin at DARPA, Dr. David Luckham at Stanford, Dr. Daniel Jackson at MIT, and so many others are all formulating and creating the emerging discipline on software architecture. Their work has made architecting the discipline it is today and referenced in this book.

A very special thanks goes to Steven Litvintchouk who helped in so many ways from the technical input, to focusing the topic of discussion, to clarifying the discussion, to encouraging more tutorial detail in the discussion, and then laughing at the autobiographical examples used. He is a great supporter and special friend.

A very special thanks goes to Guy Rosefelt who kept the drive and perseverance alive, helped me out of tough spots, provided some wonderful security and quality of service comments, and continues to be a great supporter and special friend.

A warm special thanks goes to Debbie Harris who reviewed much of this work from a manager's viewpoint, and provided enormous encouragement and support throughout the seemingly constant perturbations.

A special thanks goes to Karen Wells who quickly provided so many great comments and additions that were included.

A special thanks goes to Haim Kilov and Joaquin Miller who answered so many questions, clarifying certain issues.

A special thanks goes to those who reviewed and provided numerous comments to strengthen the work: Debbie Harris, Karen Wells, Judy Peach, Joaquin Miller, Haim Kilov, Guy Rosefelt, Heidi Singleton, Linda Scannell, Steve Wagner, Lorna Estep, Kirstie Bellman, Tom Mowbray, Trish Dunn, and many others.

Thanks also goes to Prentice Hall executive editor Paul Petralia and publisher Jeffrey Pepper who believed in the topic of this book, and offered great support in difficult times.

And special thanks goes to Debbi Harris, Heidi Singleton, Guy Rosefelt, and Steve Litvintchouk who kept saying "you can do it—it's important."

PART ONE

ARCHITECTING DISTRIBUTED
PROCESSING SYSTEMS PRIMER

OPEN, DISTRIBUTED PROCESSING, ARCHITECTURE, AND ARCHITECTING

Everyone deals with information every day. Unfortunately, dealing with lots of information means there are problems. Why is that? A person has to use software and hardware to manage the information, and the software and hardware aren't all built the same way or for the same purpose. So, they don't always "play" well together and, as a result, the person doesn't always "work" very well because the information can lose a lot in the translation and movement between computer systems. This chapter will help one understand the problems faced in this wonderful world of information.

User needs, coupled with real-world mandates and constraints of timely and accurate information, drive the distribution of information and systems. Information is the principal asset for the successful operation of any business. The software systems that process such information need to work together (interwork): a software tool needs to interwork with the operating system; an organization system needs to interwork with other organization systems in an enterprise; and multiple enterprises need to interwork to form a virtual enterprise.[1] Information captures the purpose, policies, objectives, resources, semantics, and constructs of the business that the software system processes. Consistency of this information across the business is a major determinant of the success of the business.

---

1. "A virtual enterprise is a consortium of companies or organizations that come together to share resources (cost, personnel, equipment) to achieve common objectives, foster collaborative efforts, and share engineering and information, while retaining autonomy over those resources." [Putman]

Locations where information is available, rules by which information is accessible, and constructs defining the meaning of the information will generally be different across the software systems of a business, an organization within a business, an enterprise of business organizations, or even a software vendor's product or tool. The need to share information assets and accurate processing of those assets across software is a real need of users of computer systems today.

Software applications (or tools) are available in unprecedented numbers to provide some processing functionality for the home, office, organization, or enterprise computer system. They span the end-to-end needs of the user, at all levels of functionality. There are often multiple vendors providing the "same" functionality in a software tool, when in reality the software tool reflects some value-added capability of a particular vendor. Choices among these dissimilar software tools become a consideration for the organization. And among those choices the user must take into account how well these software products will work together to create a single cohesive computer system. This ability is a challenge for the user in light of the many software tools available, especially considering the rate of technology advancement and additional tools that emerge in the marketplace.

As virtual enterprises become more the norm, information sharing and processing across an enterprise becomes a business requirement. Not only are the individual enterprise organization systems constructed with different software, but they typically use different hardware and networking as well. The ability to combine enterprise systems to achieve a virtual enterprise becomes a challenge in light of the many system dissimilarities: software (either commercial products or developed code), hardware, and networks.

In addition, information is represented differently in different systems. One system may indicate "inches" and another system may indicate "millimeters." For example, the Mars Climate Orbiter failed because one team used English units (e.g., inches) while the other used metric units for a key spacecraft operation. Since this was critical information for the spacecraft positioning and maneuverability, it led to the loss of the spacecraft. [MARS]

Distributed computing is a reaction to the real-world business needs of shared information and systems that interwork. Businesses today believe that distributed computing should evolve to keep up with dynamically changing technological advances coupled with business requirement changes to keep the business competitive. The ability to interwork among organizational units in a business, among enterprises in a virtual enterprise, and among the systems in each requires a plan to include a well-laid–out software architecture for distributed processing, using open system techniques, that in turn plans for the system to achieve the sharing, interworking, and dynamic changes discussed above.

A distributed business environment for communicating multimedia information is represented in Figure 1.1.

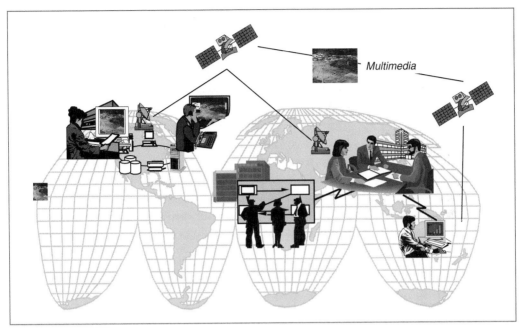

FIGURE 1.1   Global Dynamic Business Information Needs

The complete collection of all such information and processing assets, then, will most likely be distributed and dissimilar. Yet somehow all of these assets must work together seamlessly as a single business system.

This introductory chapter discusses what is meant by "open," "distributed processing," "architecture," and "architecting," and how the Reference Model of Open Distributed Processing (RM-ODP) fits into the picture to aid in solving the issues of information sharing and interworking across distributed software systems.

1.1   OPEN SYSTEM

Current businesses depend upon a plethora of complex computer systems that must work together to support a business. Typically, these systems are built from multiple architectures, multiple designs, different vendor products, and different versions of those products, across all aspects of a computer system. Computer systems are generally developed in parts and possibly placed on different computers. These dissimilar software parts need to interact together in order to enable the construction and execution of the single business system—whether that system is a single computer or a group of computers—that is able to share information in support of business needs. Figure 1.2 represents this concept identifying two different

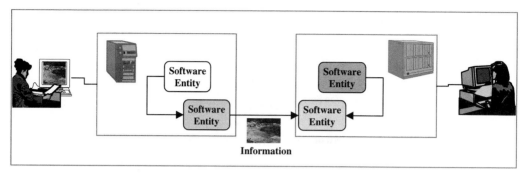

FIGURE 1.2   Interacting Software Entities

computers, each with different software entities that need to interact to exchange information for the end users. In this chapter, there is deliberately no intention of defining what a software entity is. It can be a tool, a software module, a component of a component-based framework, or an object. A software entity reflects some software capability that needs to interwork with some other software.

An *open system* is a system that provides portability and interoperability, whether or not the software entities are on the same computer or reside on different computers. *Portability* allows the software entity to operate on different computer systems. *Interoperability* allows the software entities to exchange information in a way that can be "understood."

Interoperability is about agreement. It is a system capability that supports information sharing, as well as coordinated operation of the multiple applications on a common task. Application interoperability requires that all the layers of software also interoperate; this includes the networks and any hardware entities involved in the communication. [Nutt-92, Edwards-94]

The way one software entity talks, or communicates, with another software entity is through an interface. In addition, a software system is often constructed in layers, in which each layer hides more and more details of capabilities and complexities. Capabilities are functions that the software entity provides. Complexity deals with difficulty: more software entities that have to work together, differences in products that have to work together, differences in information formats that have to be shared, all the software that manages an interface, all the software that manages enforcement of a business rule, and how all of this works together. "The more elements and interconnections, the more complex the architecture and the more difficult the system-level problems." [Rechtin-97] When there are layers of software, not only must the software within a layer interwork, but the software across the layers must also interwork. This is shown in Figure 1.3.

Software Computer System

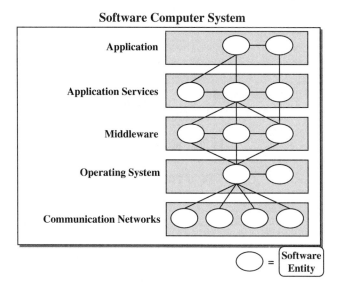

FIGURE 1.3   Representative Software Layers of a Software Computer System

Layers of software communicate using interfaces, not necessarily using network protocols. The implementation details of the software in a layer, or a product in a layer, are not generally revealed, because it may be a vendor product that does not disclose these details. Architects and designers must then anticipate how to interwork one software entity with another, based only on the interface, and perhaps some idea of how the "black box" software entity functions.

In order to use a software entity interface, the interface needs to be *published*. Publish in this case means "to make generally known; to disseminate to the public; to produce or release for distribution; to issue the work of (an author)." [Webster's] If the interface is published, the interface is considered open. This is the first step in an open system, where open means "completely free from concealment: exposed to general view or knowledge." [Webster's]

There are different kinds of openness, three of which are represented in Figure 1.4. These are discussed below.

A *proprietary*, but published, interface comes from a vendor that publishes an interface to a software entity, publishes how that software works, and is in sole control and management of the way the software, architecture, and design works, as well as its published interface (change, delete, and support, configuration management, etc.). The idea is that an organization that wishes to make use of the vendor's product will use the vendor's interface to the product. This kind of openness is generally called "de facto." A published interface is offered by vendors to their proprietary product; e.g., windows vendor, database management system vendor, tool vendor.

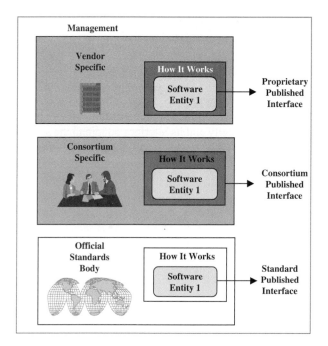

FIGURE 1.4   Kinds of Openness

A *consortium* published interface comes from a consortium that publishes a capability and an interface to that capability. The interface provides another software entity to access some functionality, as specified by the consortium. In this case, the architecture is often published, how the software entity behaves is published, and the interface to the software entity is published. A popular example is the World Wide Web Consortium (W3C). Another popular example is the Object Management Group (OMG). In the case of consortium openness, the consortium may limit the membership of the group. Only the consortium is able, through its defined process, to change the interface specification, cease support of it, or manage the specification. In some consortia, especially those with a small membership, this kind of openness is not dissimilar to vendor-specific openness, except that there are more members involved in the definition and management of the software entity's capabilities and interface definition.

A *standard* published interface results from a group that represents a standard (an IEEE, ANSI, or international standard, such as ISO[2]). In this case, membership is made available to all. Only the members of the group can change a standard. Once the standard becomes an official standard, representing the final

---

2. IEEE is the Institute of Electrical and Electronics Engineers; ANSI is the American National Standards Institute; and ISO is the International Organization for Standardization.

definition for that standard, the capabilities of the software entity are published, the behavior the software is to exhibit is published, and the interface to the software entity is published. The publication of the software entity's characteristics and its interface definition are maintained by the standards organization. A standards organization publishes a capability, not a software product. Different vendors provide the software product in their own way. Although the standard is not based on a particular vendor, the implementation is vendor-specific. The degree to which the software entity and its interface adhere to the standard is called *compliance*. The vendor's product, then, may or may not be in full compliance with the standard. If the vendor's product is compliant with the standard, then that product has achieved the greatest degree of openness.

What is meant, then, by *open* is the use of published concepts, rules, and interfaces, which can be used by any other software entity and combined in a system of such software entities. Openness supports interoperable distributed processing in heterogeneous environments of computers and software.

A layered computer system is represented in Figure 1.5. Sometimes the application consists of dissimilar products, as do the application services (e.g., decision-making tools). "Infrastructure" here encompasses the middleware products supporting one or more applications (e.g., World Wide Web (WWW) browser, security services, or electronic mail). This is particularly riddled with multiple dissimilar product offerings today. Database technology, for example, not only represents different vendors, but also different versions produced by the same vendor. And of course there are different operating systems, different communication protocols, and different networks. Yet all of these possibly dissimilar products comprise a system (or a system of systems, or even a software tool) that needs to work together in support of the business needs.

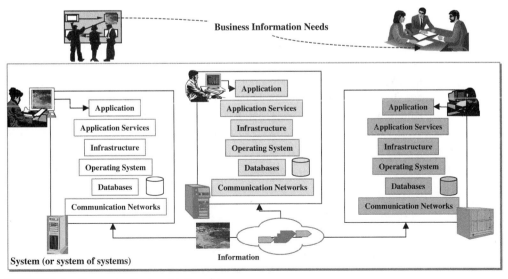

FIGURE 1.5 Computer System Notional Layers

Building distributed systems is not easy. Building distributed systems of different parts, as discussed above, or even of different versions of the same part (such as a new version of an Oracle® database management system) is challenging. Services provided by software entities may differ across computers, provide different products for the same service (e.g., a database management system provided by different vendor products), provide different versions of the same product, provide different middleware services, provide different forms of data representation, or provide different types of architecture of the software topology (e.g., client/server, 3-tier, 4-tier, stand-alone computer). With all these possible differences, and more, the ability to construct systems that have software entities interacting appropriately relies upon knowing and understanding how the software behaves and how the interface is used to gain access to the software. The open system is designed to enable the software (and hardware) parts of a computer system to communicate, without the need to understand how the part is developed.

Interfaces between a software entity requesting a service and a software entity providing the service must be agreed to. Interoperability between a software entity requesting a service and a software entity providing a service deals with agreement not only on the interfaces but on the functioning of all the software entities. An example is a software entity making a request for a network connection. Interoperability between peer software entities deals with interoperability between each set of software entities in the chain of communication, from the software originating a request to the software providing the request; for example, a Web client requesting services of a Web server. Both the client and server must be supported by interoperable software entities at the infrastructure, communications, operating system, and networks layers.

Hence, an *open system* is a system that is designed to enable portability of the software, and allow other software entities to interoperate with it across dissimilar software and systems.

Achieving data, applications, and infrastructure interoperability continues to be a challenge. Networking across multiple distributed processing systems, applications executing in different software environments, and different software products all make it challenging to create a system of interoperable parts that will interoperate with other systems, evolve to new technologies, and maintain the system. Adopting open system standards means that the inter-relationships among the software entities are fully defined by their interfaces, are made available to the public, and are maintained by group consensus. An open system may often be a target objective for a customer, accepting that the initial increment of the system will be only partially open. If this is the case, investing in current technologies, such as the Common Object Request Broker Architecture (CORBA) or Java™, will give a higher degree of software openness and platform independence (portability).

The advantage of an open system is to allow the customer to create a computer system from dissimilar parts. If a system is proprietary, the customer generally must use all parts from that same vendor, and does not generally have the ability to find the best functionality, the best cost, the best performing product, or a product that meets some other business objective. Furthermore, the customer is then typically locked into a single vendor, and must adhere to the business objectives of that vendor. These objectives may include changing a version, stopping support of a product, changing the cost of purchase or maintenance, and so forth. The vendor might even go out of business altogether! The customer must be cognizant that once a single-vendor solution is chosen, the ability of that proprietary computer system to interoperate with another system is compromised.

From a vendor business perspective, the vendor has added value to the product when that product adds features not specified, such as interoperating with other software, thereby creating additional capability for the customer. This capability may meet the needs to configure a system in a particular way, to provide certain functionality in support of business needs, and to compete for the best value-to-cost ratio.

A complete open system requires an architecture that features a non-proprietary (open) interface to the software, an open specification of the software services to be used, and supporting formats sufficient to enable dissimilar software to meet the open system objectives of portability and interoperability. When an architecture is open, all the parts are well-defined to allow the parts to interconnect. This does not mean that all parts of the software are developed to openness; only those parts made accessible to other software are so developed.

"Standardized interfaces within an overall system tend to complicate designs with respect to performance. ...A major challenge of open systems designers is to carefully study the interfaces defined in the open systems specifications, then to proceed with a design that will operate as effectively as possible in the constrained environment" [Nutt-92]. However, the effort to reuse an open interface or an open architecture tends to offset the limitations, and "is usually worth the effort to work in open systems" [Nutt-92].

If an open system allows different software to access the system, so can other systems. This leads to the ability to construct a system from software entities, a system from parts of a system (subsystems), and a system of systems from multiple systems.

Of course, there are also drawbacks to an open system. The cost associated with constructing an open system is generally more. An open interface generally has a front part to describe the standard, the format used, and other related information. An open standard usually has a format of the message that identifies one part of the message from another part (much like the title of a book, the chapter of a book, the section of a book), so that the computer system can process it correctly. Sometimes the format of the message is in user-readable format (ASCII). These are drawbacks in terms of overhead of processing, overhead on networks, and overhead for a developer in designing and developing software entities. Alternatively, a business may know exactly how the message is structured, and can use a business-specific fixed set of fields in a fixed order, eliminating the overhead of the special fields and the readable format.

Another drawback is the reliance on another organization for defining an open interface. This may be risky, depending on the maturity of the organization. If it is a new vendor that has published a brand-new interface, the business should assess the risk of using an immature interface, despite the fact it is open.

Another drawback to an open interface is that it may include a number of options of no importance to the business, and may also require the business to handle these options. Alternatively, a business-specific interface can be developed to include only the parts of the interface important to the business.

Yet another drawback is that an open interface used in a system may still change. The proprietary vendor may decide to change and re-publish the interface. The consortium-published interface may also change. Even the standards bodies may decide a change is needed in the open interface, and change the standard. The business must be cognizant of these potential changes and make a business decision to adopt the newest open interface, or keep the current open interface. Over time, however, the newer open interfaces will dominate the market, resulting in newer open systems. If a business system has not kept up with the changes, that business system may no longer be able to interoperate with another system without incurring the cost to upgrade to the newer standards.

1.2	DISTRIBUTED PROCESSING

Modern-day businesses tend to be composed of physically separated organizations. This leads to information in different locations. Businesses need to share both information and processing, with information moved among geographically disparate locations. The different locations of processing by different systems in the organization make up the computer systems supporting the enterprise. This distribution of information and processing systems is a consequence of today's businesses.

Distributed processing means processing performed by hardware and software entities that are physically separated. Software processing by the computer system can be distributed within the computer system or across multiple distributed computing systems, or both. Distribution means different locations, whether the hardware and software are next to each other or across the world. Distributed systems are a reaction to the complex needs of the business world: geographically distributed organizations require information across geographically disparate locations.

A *distributed processing system* is a system composed of separate processing systems that interwork for the purpose of sharing information and processing.

1.2.1 KINDS OF DISTRIBUTED PROCESSING

Some of the kinds of distributed processing systems are represented in Figure 1.6. The commonplace concept of 2-tier, 3-tier, and n-tier architecture is representative of how the software is distributed to different hardware. This model does not necessarily dictate how the software entities are distributed within a hardware device, nor what software entities support a particular architecture tier. Processing on the client provides end-user functionality. Processing on the server provides support for the client requests. Processing on the database server provides support for the data services. When the n-tier architecture is used, servers interwork with servers, database servers interwork with database servers, and everything interworks with each other.

Software can be distributed independently from hardware. Software distribution relies upon the needs of the client, server, and database server, not so much on the placement or distribution of the hardware. A notion of what software entities might comprise a client is shown in Figure 1.6. The services in support of, in this case, three separate servers that execute the application are shown. Though each application server is independent and could reside on its own hardware plat-

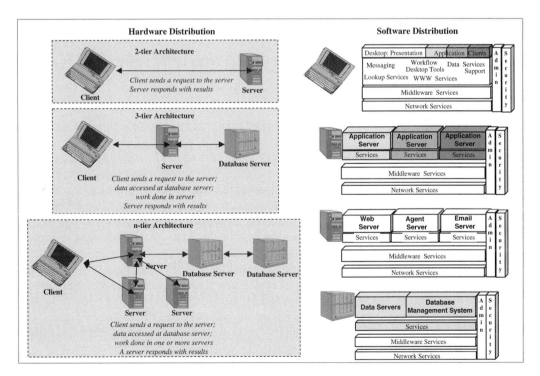

FIGURE 1.6 Representative Distributed Processing Systems

form, this need not be the case. Furthermore, the servers need not be "application" servers. Examples of servers today would include a Web server, an application server, a CORBA server, a component server, a virtual enterprise control server [Goldschmidt-98], and many others.

The software entities in support of a database server are also shown in Figure 1.6. In this case the actual database co-resides on the same hardware device.

What is important to recognize is that the distribution of hardware does not necessarily reflect the distribution of software in a distributed computing system. Furthermore, within a given hardware system, the software that comprise that system need to interwork, at least across the different layers. If a distributed system consists of a security system, for example, that security system may be distributed across all the hardware platforms. The software comprising the security system needs to interwork, no matter what hardware it resides on.

1.2.2 IMPORTANCE

Distributed processing systems are important because they interconnect the distribution and processing of information across business domains; this supports the exchange of information (interoperability) across organizations in the enterprise and groups within the organization. A distributed processing system, then, consists of independent software entities that interact with each other.

Why consider distributed processing? One reason is reliability. Through the use of replication or redundancy, a more reliable system can be realized. A backup is used to take over in case of failure. Another reason is performance. Placing processing and information closer to users improves the timeliness of both. The user perceives immediate access, or close to immediate access. Another reason is to support user needs at multiple sites, which is a priority in businesses today.

The consequences of distributed processing are interoperability, complexity, and concurrency. Distributing processing and enabling distant users to use the system means that the parts of the system must interoperate. However, distribution is complex; there are more discrete parts to the system, some duplicated. These parts must somehow tie together into a single cohesive system and be made available and visible to the end users. When users interact with the system, their interactions need to be managed so that simultaneous access to some processing or information (concurrency) is managed so as not to violate the integrity of the system or information. User-initiated transactions that require guaranteed delivery and order of processing, such as a banking transaction, need to be managed. If the transactions do not fully complete, they may need to be undone (rollback). In a distributed processing environment where the processing of the transactions can be accomplished anywhere, concurrency management across the system is complex.

To realize application interoperability means that each layer of software must also interoperate. Interoperability achieves a seamless system for the business, thereby meeting the information sharing and processing needs of today's business enterprise.

To connect business domains, differences need to be mitigated. These differences can occur as organizational boundaries and objectives; as administration boundaries of security, naming, membership, system administration, etc.; or as technical boundaries of service offerings (application), communication, information representation, data representation, infrastructure support, etc.

The interoperability of distributed processing systems needs to address the differences in hardware, software, networks, operating systems, multiple vendor products, multiple versions of those products, and other heterogeneity challenges. The business need that drives the interoperability need of disparate distributed processing systems is represented in Figure 1.7.

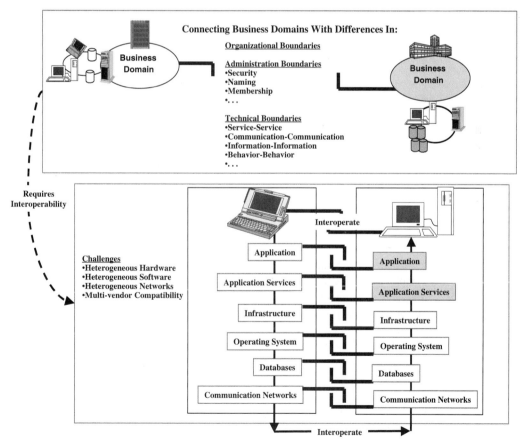

FIGURE 1.7 Connecting Business Domains: Interoperable Distributed Processing Systems

1.2.3 USE OF DISTRIBUTED PROCESSING

Distributed processing is used when the processing of information located in different places is required. Examples of such include:

▶ Telecommunications, which has one of the largest distributed processing systems in the world to support all of the software systems required to process a telephone call

▶ Medical systems that tie together processing within a medical organization, to process across organizations that form a medical care enterprise

▶ Financial systems that process banking, loans, etc.

▶ Office systems that support multiple users, each processing some aspect of information in a collaborative manner

▶ Defense systems, such as command-and-control or combat support, which must process geographically distributed information

▶ Department stores that process transactions, stock inventory, cost of goods, etc.

▶ Real-time embedded systems that must process distributed information within a guaranteed quality of service

▶ Multimedia systems that consist of equipment such as video cameras, speakers, and microphones, plus image, graphical, and textual information, all possibly stored on different storage systems, and the computers that link together all these disparate parts, transmitting or receiving information continuously

Organizations today already have distributed processing systems to support their activities. For example, a medical system may have a distributed system to admit patients for treatment at a hospital, a system to manage the patient care records, a system for billing, a system to perform radiology tests, and so forth. All or some of these individual systems may be interconnected to provide the ability to access the distributed information, resulting in a more effective organization. Perhaps such a system is also interconnected with a physician practice processing system. Such a system, for example, may allow the patient to provide his or her patient history information just once, allowing the system to share that information across all parts that need it, instead of requiring the patient to continually provide patient history information. These are some of the business advantages to be gained from integrating these separate distributed processing systems into a single, distributed processing system.

Use of a distributed processing system may also include bridging separate systems between separate organizations, or within a single organization. The current trend toward electronic commerce supported by the Internet leads to distributed systems spanning different customers, providers, and credit card agencies. This level of integration of distributed systems must maximize the independence of each organization, the ability to interoperate, and the ability to manage their own concerns. That is, a distributed system consists of independent computing systems that interact with each other.

1.2.4 DISTRIBUTED PROCESSING PRINCIPLES

Architecting, designing, and developing a distributed system is complex. It is more difficult to create a distributed system than a central system. In constructing distributed processing systems, organizations need to address certain distribution principles. These principles are identified in the following list.

▶ **Interoperability:** Software entities in distributed systems need to communicate information in a mutually agreed-upon manner in order to understand and process that information correctly. Interoperability is a key consideration for a distributed processing system to enable it to be used as a single virtual system. Interoperability provides the mechanism for the communication and coordination of the distributed information in support of the business needs, providing a consistent view of that information, and its processing. Open systems facilitate interoperability.

▶ **Portability:** A software entity may be used in multiple locations in the distributed processing system. As such, portability allows that software entity to be used in different locations, in different environments, and on different computing resources. Portability of software to such different computing resources is a consideration for the architecture, design, and choice of technology to implement the system. Without portability of the software entity, the organization will need to address different kinds of software to accomplish the same functionality (e.g., different electronic mail systems, instead of one that is portable; different database management systems, instead of one that is portable), or address the requirement that all such environments be the same in order to accommodate the ability for the same software entity be used. Once again, open systems facilitate portability.

▶ **Integration:** An integrated set of software entities and systems provide the end user with a seamless interface to the system, making the system look like one cohesive cooperative set of information and processing. To integrate a set of software means presentation, behavior, and software functionality is consistent and acts as a single system. For example, the operation "access" should be the same whether the access is to a file, a database element, or some processing capability. The same logical operation is used in each integrated application. Further, the software entities that are integrated appear as subparts of the same software system, instead of different software entities requiring different methods of use. "For a set of applications to be integrated, they must exist in an open systems environment, since independent vendors can only produce consistent applications by conforming to an open specification." [Nutt-92]

▶ **Remoteness:** Software entities, systems, and information are distant from each other in location. Communication among these elements may be local or remote. The distributed processing system should hide the remote characteristics from any other processing and from the end user. This requires visible location and visible open interfaces.

▶ **Concurrency:** Any software entity can be executed in parallel with another software entity in a distributed system. Coordinating the results and control of such computation across remote locations should be addressed.

▶ **Heterogeneity:** Software entities and systems can be developed from different technologies, different vendor products, or different versions of the same product. Over time, changes in technology solutions may occur and may be incorporated into a part of the distributed processing system. Heterogeneity can appear in the services supporting the software entity (e.g., security services, communication services, protocols, and component-based frameworks); hardware; networks; and even different architectures and designs. The distributed system, then, must be able to interconnect and interoperate in light of this dissimilarity.

▶ **Autonomy:** Distributed processing systems tend to have their own (autonomous) control authority. Different management controls manage different parts of the distributed system, with no single central management control. Distributed processing systems should account for consistency across the different control authorities. These control authorities manage such things as location, naming of the software entities, naming of users, interface definitions, security policies for access control, resource sharing (e.g., processing, storage, printers, devices, etc.), information access and updates, and so forth. The degree of autonomy supported by a distributed processing system should be considered.

▶ **Evolution:** Over time, an organization may wish to update its distributed processing system to include changes in technology enabling better cost-performance, changes in requirements, changes in strategic directions, and changes in new and better applications. The distributed processing system architecture should consider possible changes and accommodate changes at minimal impact to the distributed processing system.

▶ **Scale:** Over time, additional users, additional distributed processing, and additional resources may be added to the distributed processing system to accommodate the increasing demands of the organization. In addition, some action in time may require that the distributed processing system dramatically increase its resource and processing capability, or re-prioritize its available resources and processing (e.g., surge of activity based on war, or on determining a cause of failure that needs an immediate response). In such cases, the architecture and design of the system should accommodate surge and scale capabilities, with minimum impact on the system.

▶ **Failure recovery:** Any part of the distributed processing system may fail. The failure may be catastrophic to the business. If a distributed processing system fails, a duplication of the processing or information is possible (because it's distributed), leading to the ability for continued operation. Fault tolerance is the ability to recover from failure of individual software entities, with the aim of avoiding reduced functionality. In such cases, the architecture and design of the distributed processing system should allow for failure recovery, to the extent possible. A failure should not ripple throughout the system, but rather should be isolated to enable the rest of the distributed processing system to operate.

▶ **Quality of service:** As with centralized processing, distributed processing is often associated with a specified quality of service (QoS), meaning some timeliness, reliability, or availability need of a business, end user, or software entity. One kind of QoS refers to the ability of a communication system to meet needs such as "a real-time constraint of 10 ms to provide some processing." Another kind of QoS refers to the ability to support the user's needs, such as "within a period of 10 days, a refund check is issued." The processing capabilities of a distributed system must support QoS as specified. Often this requires the provision of a fault-tolerant system, to better ensure that the required QoS be accomplished. The distributed processing system architecture should, to the extent possible, include the ability to meet a QoS requirement.

▶ **Lack of a global state and global clock:** The state of a distributed processing system cannot be precisely determined, nor can time. As such, the distributed processing system needs to address communication and processing activities that are not based on a common global state or single global clock. That is, processing and changes in a distributed system cannot be assumed to take place in a single instant. Instead, the system needs to be architected and designed to coordinate processing and changes, and synchronize activities where necessary.

▶ **Mobility:** Information, software entities, processing, and even hardware may change in location. One reason for such change is to better load-balance some of the processing capabilities for performance reasons. Another reason is the ability to communicate the code to the destination system for execution at that system, such as in the use of Java. Users change location all the time and still require use of the distributed processing system. Separation of software and information leads to the ability to add, change, delete, or remove elements dynamically. The distributed processing system must be aware of any such change. Location is not important to centralized processing. But, location and change of location of software or information need to be known to the distributed processing system. The distributed processing system should accommodate such dynamic changes in physical mobility.

▶ **Security:** Enabling authorized access, detecting unauthorized intrusion, and protecting valuable information are aspects of a secure system. Architecting security capabilities in a distributed processing system is more complex due to the remoteness, heterogeneity, and mobility of parts of the system and end users. The distributed processing system should address how best to architect such security aspects and how the security system interoperates and integrates with the intended distributed processing system. This requires the architecture to address the distribution characteristics of the security solution itself.

▶ **Transparency:** As has been discussed, the distributed processing system should appear as a single virtual system to the end user. It should also appear as a single system to the software entities that comprise the system. Transparency is a property that hides the details, the processing, and the differences in the system from the entity or user using the system. That is, transparency enables the system to appear as a single, cohesive entity. The distribution aspects of the system are hidden. This principle is central to the development of distributed applications. Transparency should hide heterogeneity, mobility, QoS mechanisms, failure and recovery, security, and all other aspects of the distributed system. The alternative is that each distributed application develops its own variation of the knowledge of distribution of the system, which in the end affects cost, performance, and maintainability of the system. Not all aspects of distribution can or should be hidden due to current technologies, cost, or the performance of the added computation for transparency. These are tradeoffs that the architecture should facilitate, but addressing this principle is important to the capabilities of distributed processing.

Thus, physical separation of processing and information complicate the ability to develop a system that supports the business needs, provides interoperability and information sharing, manages the resources, synchronizes the activities, and maintains the consistency of multiple types of change.

Coordination and cooperation across organizations is becoming critical to the success of enterprises. Distributed processing is vital not only for any of these organizations, but also as a bridge between federations of them. Integration of separate functions into a logically single, distributed system increases the effectiveness of the organization and enhances all decision support of that organization and enterprise.

1.2.5   ADVANTAGES

The main advantages of a distributed processing system include the ability to support remote business locations, support remote information, increase the fault tolerance capabilities, improve performance by either providing information that is local or by performing tasks concurrently on different computer systems, sharing of resources, and the ability to adapt to changes in environments and technologies (extensibility). Furthermore, distributed processing systems enable a single system to become part of multiple systems, in support of remote organizations and enterprises. Thus reliability, interoperability, extensibility, scalability, availability, and autonomy are important considerations in constructing distributed processing systems.

1.2.6 Open Distributed Processing

Since a single vendor, or a single set of products from a single vendor, probably will not provide all the capabilities required, it is important that the distributed system architecture be flexible to change and defined in terms of open systems [Nutt-92, Edwards-94, RM-ODP-1]. Because a distributed processing system is composed of multiple autonomous software entities, to be open means that these entities themselves must cooperate in the manner in which they execute, to share the results across the distribution of systems.

Open distributed processing systems provide general connections among software entities because their architecture and design are based on open solutions. An open system enables the distributed processing system principles identified above, in the pursuit of a heterogeneity of system elements that cooperate in the processing and sharing of information.

Advances in technology make it possible to respond to these needs. However, careful architecting of distributed processing systems is needed to mechanize the communication and coordination of the distributed information relevant to the enterprise and to describe how the processing systems are to operate within the enterprise in a coordinated, open manner. The end objective is a distributed processing system that appears to the user as a single virtual system.

1.3   Architecture and Architecting of Software-Intensive Distributed Processing Systems

An architecture is a plan of something to be constructed. It includes the elements that comprise the thing, the relationships among those elements, the constraints that affect those relationships, a focus on the parts of the thing, and a focus on the thing as a whole. It is more than a blueprint for a house, for example. A blueprint coupled with the zoning laws, the building codes, and the placement of the house in its community are all part of the architecture of a house. "The architecture of a software system shows how the system is realized by a collection of components and the interactions among these components." [Shaw-97]

SIDEBAR

ARCHITECTURE SPECIFICATION FOR DISTRIBUTED PROCESSING SYSTEMS

Building distributed processing systems is not easy. Generally, it is a very complex task to reconcile what the customer requires of a system with all the complexities of a distributed processing system. There is no "silver bullet" to solve all the needs of a distributed processing system. After all, a system is the product of unique needs of an enterprise or organizational domain. A single vendor will not solve all the needs. Coupled with this, and despite the introduction of component-based frameworks, system components do not arbitrarily "plug and play."

Without a well-designed architecture, one cannot expect to glue commercial off-the-shelf (COTS) products together and end up with a system that interoperates and provides a shared information environment across a heterogeneity of products, while meeting the business requirements. Well-designed architectures were key to the successful development of systems as diverse as air traffic control systems and telephone systems. The increasing use of digital avionics in modern aircraft has required that careful attention be paid to the processing architectures of these systems as well. Even a house requires a blueprint, in conjunction with building codes, even though parts of the house are analogous to COTS products (e.g., the kitchen cabinet). Although parts can be purchased as COTS products, they must still be selected to work together, provide the functioning required of the system, and be specified by an architecture specification. A *specification* means a precise definition.

RM-ODP provides a flexible, generic, and fully internationally agreed-upon methodology to construct distributed processing systems to accommodate different solutions.

1.3.1 BENEFIT AND CHALLENGES

A major benefit of an architecture is communication among stakeholders[3] and designers[4] of the system. Another major benefit is improved management of the development of a system in support of a business requirement, at lower cost, lower

---

3. Stakeholder is a term used here to represent any customer, user, owner, administrator, acquisition authority, or program manager.

4. Designer is a term used here to represent any architect, system designer, developer, implementer, tester, administrator, or maintainer of the system.

time-to-market, and increased technical performance, taking into consideration all of the tradeoffs involved in doing so, as represented in Figure 1.8. An architecture, then, is a plan for a system at a stage before the realization of the system, that considers the functionality, behavior, and environment in which the system is to operate.

The purpose of an architecture is not just to address interoperability, or how component-based frameworks fit together. It is also to address the support of the business objectives. In terms of an open distributed processing system, an architecture defines some of the properties that the system must be architected to achieve, such as reliability, security, and performance. If the architect in the process of architecting does not address these types of properties (e.g., interoperability, constraints, reliability), it is unlikely they will magically appear in the system solution. Therefore, the architecting process of distributed processing systems should include addressing these considerations in the process of decision-making and optimization.

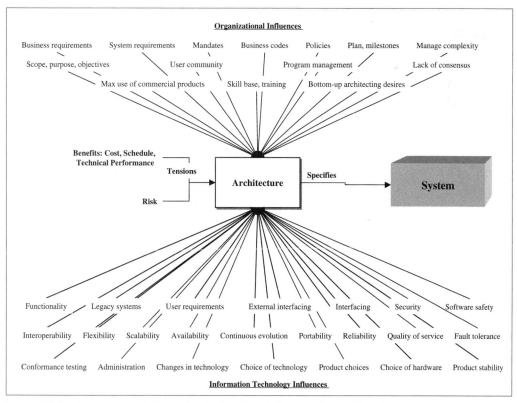

FIGURE 1.8   Business and Information Technology Influences for Architecting

1.3.2 MEANING OF ARCHITECTURE

Today, there are many definitions for the architecture of a system. These definitions focus on a level of granularity. Some define architecture in terms of hardware elements, some define architecture in terms of how software works, and some define architecture in terms of support for an enterprise. However, they all have similar concepts. They all address the configuration of the parts, the interworking relationships of the parts, and the behavior the parts are expected to achieve as a whole. An architecture provides a formal foundation of the informal practice of pictures with boxes and arrows, which leaves a great deal to be (mis)understood. "…diagrams and descriptions are highly ambiguous. At best they rely on common intuitions and past experience to have any meaning at all. Moreover, system designers generally lack adequate concepts, tools, and decision criteria for selecting and describing system structures that fit the problem at hand." [Shaw-96]

A formal foundation is mathematically based, though its use by an architect may not require knowledge of this. A formal foundation is a way of describing the meaning of architectural concepts, such as interface and the rules about interfacing, or something in the architecture. In the use of a software architecture specification for a particular system, a formal architecture specification provides precision, thus enabling analysis of the architecture, simulation of the architecture, and a well-formed architecture of a system.

Some may vehemently disagree with the need for a formal architecture. Some may approach the task of creating an architecture as a development process in which the stakeholders and developers keep critiquing the description of the architecture, generally represented in some tool, until it is adequately understood by all. Some may argue formality can only be approached asymptotically, not ever achieved. To reach a satisfactory level of formality, a collaborative understanding is vital; this is seen with the WinWin [WinWin] approach, more fully described in Chapter 2, "RM-ODP Manager's Primer." It is definitely the case that the degree of formalism in architecture specifications today varies, and none, including RM-ODP, have achieved a fully mathematical formal specification using an appropriate formal description technique (FDT) [FDT]. In achieving consensus through negotiation, making tradeoffs that are founded in analytical methods, and cost/benefit tradeoffs founded on precise models, it is definitely the case that a collaborative environment is crucial and is also part of the WinWin tool. If the informal approach works for a business, and it is coupled with some level of formalism and some collaborative capability, the rest of this book may still provide useful patterns of reasoning for design choices. If, however, the case is it "sort of" works, then this book will strengthen those areas that may need strengthening in the architecture specification, e.g., the semantics of processing. In any case, a tool such as WinWin makes the architect's job much easier.

A *systems approach to architecture* focuses on the system as a whole. It "produces collections of different things which together produce results unachievable by the elements alone." [Rechtin-97] "The *architecture of a software system* defines that system in terms of computational components and interactions among those components." [Shaw-96] Software architecture addresses *software-intensive* systems. A software-intensive system is one in which the software is the central part of the system and its operation. Software intensive systems are the norm today. "A software architecture defines the organizational principle of a system in terms of types of components and possible interconnections between these components. In addition, an architecture prescribes a set of design rules and constraints governing the behavior of components and their interaction." [Boasson] An architecture is a set of structures and components of a program/system, their interrelationships, and principles and guidelines governing their design and evolution over time. (Modified from [Garlan-95]).

In terms of an architecture, a *component* is a software entity that can be small or large. Examples include a database management system, a Web browser, a server, an element of software in a layered system, a software entity that performs some processing, a software entity in a component-based framework, a legacy system, or just about any software of interest. A *connector* includes interfaces and their constraints that support the interworking relationships among the components. They can be simple, such as a socket, or complex, such as the client/server services and connection protocols supporting the communications. They can include multicast asynchronous messaging, isochronous messaging in support of voice, event-based messaging, streams of audio and video for supporting video teleconferencing, database services, and protocols, or just about any mechanism that supports the interworking of services and communication between components.

"Software systems thus comprise two kinds of distinct, identifiable entities: components and connectors.

▶ *Components* are the locus of computation and state. Each component has an interface specification that defines its properties.

▶ *Connectors* are the locus of relations among components. They mediate interactions but are not 'things' to be hooked up (they are, rather, the hookers-up)." [Shaw-94]

An architecture style is a pattern, a set of rules for creating one or more architectures in a consistent fashion. More precisely, "an *architectural style* defines a vocabulary of components and connector types, and a set of constraints on how they can be combined." [Shaw-96]

An architecture, then, encompasses the set of significant decisions about the configuration and relationships of a software system executing in conjunction with its hardware.

1.3.3 DOMAIN-SPECIFIC SOFTWARE ARCHITECTURE (DSSA)

To create an architecture specification, one approach that has achieved great success is DSSA. This approach focuses on engineering and analysis of a domain of interest, and constructing an architecture of the system. DSSA concepts have been applied to the avionics business, as well as others.

A *domain* is defined by a set of common applications. A DSSA domain can apply to large functional areas to reason about them in some way; for example, all of medicine. But to achieve an architecture for a domain, it is important to scope down the domain to a set of achievable goals. For example, all of medicine is a valid domain. It is too large to capture an architecture for, but a hospital system is a domain within medicine that can be specified through the constructs of DSSA into an architecture.

A DSSA is a software architecture for a family of systems that includes behavioral requirements for applications in the domain, a domain model, an infrastructure to support the DSSA, and a process to instantiate and refine the DSSA. This is an architectural framework for a specific class of problems, such as hospital systems within the medical domain, satellite control within the space systems domain, or technical domains such as user interfaces or operating systems.

The DSSA program of the Defense Advanced Research Projects Agency (DARPA), under the program management of Kirstie Bellman, worked on developing new methods and tools for supporting the development of the then-new concepts of "domain-specific" languages and software architectures. It also worked on analyzing, comparing, and evaluating different DSSAs for a given domain. Part of the program also emphasized developing new tools and methods for rapidly developing and specializing domain-specific tools and algorithms that in turn could be used to develop and analyze families of or "product line" software architectures. More information can be found at [Tracz-94, Tracz-94a, Vestal-94, Hayes-Roth-95, Mettala-92]. The concept of DSSA is addressed in Section 5.3, "Using RM-ODP from a Domain-Specific Perspective," on page 173, which discusses RM-ODP's focus on architecting DSSA-like systems.

1.3.4   ARCHITECTING

The role of the architect is to communicate the needs of the customer to the builder of the system, and to track the conformance of the system to the architecture as specified. This role is satisfied by an architecture specification, which is a result of the architecting process.

Architecting is a process of creating an architecture specification. It is both a science and an art. An architect performs the process of architecting, where an architect in this sense may be a single person or a group of people. The process is an evolutionary activity in which the separation of the problem into workable details, and the details of components, connections, and constraints are increasingly included in the architecture and the specification of that architecture. The evolutionary steps of the process move from architecture to design to implementation. The boundaries between architecture, design, and implementation are not precisely defined. In fact, architecting is growing in scope to include more and more design. Hence, the boundaries between these concepts are still "fuzzy."

An *architecture specification* is a definition of the structural elements (software entities) and elements that support their interworking by which a system is composed. A precise definition of the behavior of the interworking relationships among the software entities is also part of the architecture specification.

Behavior is associated and therefore defined for any entity: components, connectors, and their interworkings. Behavior includes class, type, and assertions about the entity. Furthermore, behavior is also composable, meaning that higher levels of behavior specification can result in lower levels of specificity. As an example, a hospital policy is a set of directives for the workings of the hospital systems. The policy is stated at a high level of abstraction: e.g., "all bills must be submitted to the insurance company within 10 days." The policy will eventually be decomposed into system behaviors to support the policy statement. Perhaps some control software agent monitors the issuance of a bill, notifies the hospital administrator if the time has elapsed and the bill has not been sent, or automatically sends the bill to the insurance company. Whatever the final architecture of the system, the point is that the behavior of the system as specified can be a result of a composition of behaviors, each dealt with at a different level of abstraction.

A precise definition of the composition of the software entities, behavioral elements, into a larger (sub)system is a part of an architecture specification.

The process of architecting addresses:

- The rationale for the system being architected
- The scope of the system being architected
- The use of precise terminology focused on distributed processing systems
- Rules of specification
- Rules of structuring of the aspects of distributed systems
- Modeling
- The use of *patterns of reasoning* to describe the architecture or design decisions that communicate the reasons for the decisions, not just the results. Patterns are ways of communicating information, can be used to derive an architecture from its problem statement, can communicate the purpose of the various architectural features, and make choices of how to create an architecture for some aspect of the system.
- Reuse of lessons learned (heuristics, or common sense)
- Satisfaction of not more than two of the organizational influences of affordable cost, lower schedule, and higher technical performance: cheaper, faster, better. An "unprecedented" system (i.e., comparable purposes and architectures have never been done before) need not be either cheaper or faster. Consider Project Apollo 11 to land a man on the moon, where cost and lower schedule were not issues; only meeting the goal by 1970 was. And since it was unprecedented, it wasn't "better" than anything else either, or perhaps it was better than nothing else, in which case it was the best. And it was truly a remarkable end result.

The architect should always maintain a sense of humor throughout this challenging process.

Modeling is a fundamental step in the process of architecting. A *model* represents the system from a set of concerns or foci on the system. A model can be a document, a representation in a visual tool (such as a vendor Unified Modeling Language (UML) tool), or some other artefact.[5] A system, then, is typically represented by a set of models, each addressing some particular area of concern.

Models of a system are important for a number of reasons:

▶ Communication among all persons involved in the development of the system (the stakeholders, architects, designers, developers, maintainers, testers, etc.)

▶ Simulation of some aspect of the system prior to development to determine expected behavior, or some other criteria

▶ Analysis of some aspect of the system for determining a choice of an approach (a particular pattern of reasoning, a particular architecture pattern, a particular design pattern, etc.)

▶ Criteria for selecting system construction decisions (products, technologies, standards, code to implement, etc.)

▶ Performance prediction and possible change of some performing characteristic of the system (network bandwidth, latency in response time, resource utilization, etc.)

▶ Analysis of conformance of the developed system to the architecture

In current practice, models focus on areas of concern. These areas of concern are called *views* of the system. The set of views chosen for a particular model is not fixed; it is dependent on the needs of the architect. Examples of popular view frameworks today include those from the Zachman framework [Zachman], the Department of Defense C4ISR framework [C4ISR], the newest IEEE standard on architectural description [IEEE-1471], and others. In each of these frameworks, a set of views is identified for that framework. [Malveau] Examples of popular views include "data view," where the system is modeled from the concerns of data and data flow in the system; "stakeholder view," where the system is modeled in terms of the operational elements, assigned tasks, and information flows required to accomplish or support the end user needs; and "network view," where the system is modeled in terms of how the network and its topology fulfill the needs of the system. Each view addresses the configuration of the elements, the relationships among the elements, and the behavior. A model, then, is a snapshot in time of how the system is to function and behave, from a particular view.

Each model is a representation of the elements and their relationships. A model needs to include the vocabulary of terms and its rules of use; that is, its ontology. An *ontology* is "a formal and declarative representation which includes

---

5. The *artefact* role is one that is currently being defined in the new enterprise viewpoint specification [ISO-EntVP].

the vocabulary (or names) for referring to the terms in that subject area and the logical statements that describe what the terms are, how they are related to each other, and how they can or cannot be related to each other. Ontologies therefore provide a vocabulary for representing and communicating knowledge about some topic and a set of relationships that hold among the terms in that vocabulary." [KSL] "Ontologies therefore provide a vocabulary for representing and communicating knowledge about some topic and a set of relationships that hold among the terms in that vocabulary." [Gruber] Hence, a model includes the elements, relationships, and behavioral terms and rules associated with the focus of the model.

Each model is mostly independent from other models of the system. However, since the objective is a single system, the models of the system must be consistent. That is, aspects expressed in one model must necessarily be related to aspects expressed in another model. This requires rules of consistency across the modeling mechanisms used for each model. For example, behavior is not incidental to a system; rather, it is fundamental to every model of the system. As a model represents one aspect of the system, the behavior captured in that model must relate to the behavior captured in other models. Part of the architect's job is to determine which views are important to model, and to what extent; to construct the model that represents those views; and to integrate the models into a single architectural specification of the system.

The result of the architecting process is not always unique. That is, there can be several different architectures of the same system. The choices made, the priority of the constraints assumed, and the fact that architecting is still in large measure an art, rather than a science, result in these different architectures. How then can the stakeholder judge which architecture is "best?" This is an art, but supported today by architectural tradeoff analyses to determine which architectural approach costs more, or is less complex, or meets the schedule demands, or some other criteria. ([WinWin] provides more about architectural tradeoffs and a tool to aid in this.) Again, the stakeholder and the architect need to make decisions together about which architecture (if any) to proceed with in constructing the system.

At this point, several concepts have been introduced: architecture, system, architecture specification, model and view, architecting, and architect. Figure 1.9 provides a representation of how these concepts are related.

1.4   ARCHITECTURE SPECIFICATION

Thus far, the word "specification" has been used to reflect the result of architecting. Part of the process of architecting is to determine why, what, how much, and how to create an architectural specification of a system.

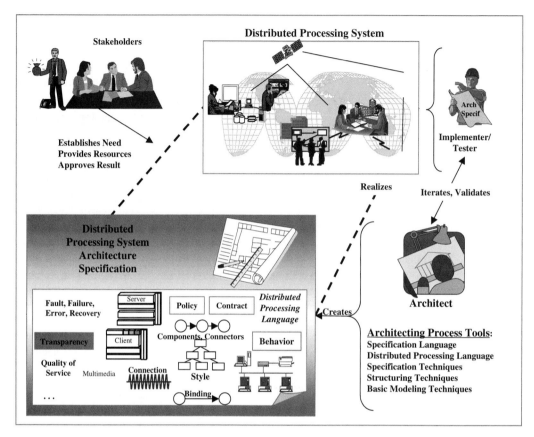

FIGURE 1.9   Relating Architecture Concepts

1.4.1   SPECIFICATION LANGUAGES

A number of current approaches to describing an architecture use informal diagrams (such as PowerPoint® charts) or modeling languages (such as UML) to depict an architecture. These are good techniques to a point; however, they tend to minimize the meaning of the boxes and arrows and constraints associated with an association (in UML, for example). This leads to an architecture description that can be very ambiguous. Furthermore, these techniques of description do not help the architect make fundamental choices of architecture; for example, when should a client/server interface be used? How can a QoS be realized? Can a multicast connection be used for a transaction? How will fault tolerance be accomplished? These and others are very real considerations for architecting a system.

The architect, then, needs tools not only to describe the architecture, but to make choices about the architecture of a system. To do that requires techniques that define the components, their configuration, what and how they are to accomplish, how they behave, what they support, and so forth. The architect must handle large-scale issues from a business and user perspective, as well as small-scale design details. The architect must be able to reuse architecture patterns appropriately, define what can and cannot be realized in current technology, and many more things.

A specification language provides several capabilities for the architect. The purpose of such a language is to aid the architect in describing the architecture, to make choices about the architectural aspects of the system, to define the architectural components and their interworking relationships, and to provide mechanisms to combine these into parts of the system in a consistent manner. Such a specification language needs to provide certain key properties [Shaw-96, RM-ODP-2]:

▶ Composition and decomposition

▶ Abstraction and refinement

▶ Analysis

▶ Configuration of components and connectors

▶ Combined heterogeneous architectural abstractions

▶ Use of architectural patterns of reasoning

▶ Ontology of distributed processing

▶ Tailorable domain-specific terminology

▶ Conformance analysis

The specification language, then, enables the architecting process. A specification language based on mathematical formalisms enables analysis of any such architecture. This does not mean the specification language consists of mathematical symbols, but rather is founded on such precision.

In current practice, there are a few such specification languages of choice. The Architectural Description Languages (ADLs), such as Acme, C2, MetaH, Rapide, Wright, Unicon [Acme, C2, MetaH-93, MetaH-96, Rapide, Wright, Wright-a, UniCon], and others, provide a specification language tailored to specific aspects of a distributed system. Rapide, for example, is used for event-based messaging systems. C2 is used for dynamic assembly of components. MetaH is used for real-time systems. Acme, on the other hand, is used to unify, to the extent possible, all the other ADLs. In addition, formal specification languages such as Z [Spivey] can also be used, though this use is constrained by mathematical symbols. Eiffel is another language of choice [Meyer]. Finally, the languages presented by RM-ODP are specification languages as well.

Once a specification of an architecture is in hand, either partially or fully, that specification can be described informally or semi-formally through popular techniques, knowing that the rigor and precision of the architecture is specified in a specification language.

1.4.2 WHY SPECIFY?

A specification provides precise documentation about important aspects of the system, such as interfaces. To this end, a specification captures the precise definition of interfaces, or of components, or of some infrastructure mechanism derived from a pattern of reasoning. It also provides an abstract definition of the system design. Formal analysis techniques are better accomplished by precise definition than a "warm fuzzy feeling," because the precision is there to substantiate the analysis. A formal specification provides a means of analyzing the correctness of the architecture. It provides a means to explicitly and precisely capture behavior, some functionality, and the explicit relationships among the components. It helps to answer questions such as "what should happen if a failure occurs," or "why did the system fail," in which case the formal specification is an aid to determine this failure. Specification techniques, such as abstraction and composition, help the architect to separate the complex concerns of a system into smaller pieces to address. Appropriate use of specification techniques can aid in all these endeavors.

"You might choose to specify because you want additional documentation of your system's interfaces, you want a more abstract description of your system design, or you want to perform some formal analysis of your system. What you write should be determined by what it is you want to do with your specification." [Wing-95]

1.4.3 WHAT AND HOW MUCH TO SPECIFY?

Some argue that an entire large software system cannot be fully specified, especially formally. This is a judgment call for the architect. As will be shown, RM-ODP does in fact provide this capability. Nevertheless, even with the use of RM-ODP, the architect needs to determine what to specify. Perhaps one high-risk aspect of the system needs to be fully defined. In this case, a specification is appropriate. Perhaps some QoS behavior will affect the function of a mission-critical system. This is another aspect of the system that needs to be specified. If the writing of a specification is about describing some functional capability that can be constructed in a number of ways, it may only require a description, not a full precise definition. If, on the other hand, some behavior must be required in the system, it probably should be specified. If an implementation can be allowed to select among a set of behaviors to implement, but not be required to implement all of them, then the set of permitted behaviors might be described, but not precisely defined in a specification.

1.4.4 HEURISTICS IN CREATING AN ARCHITECTURE SPECIFICATION

Heuristics are useful in determining what to specify. The principal specification mechanisms include abstraction, refinement, composition, and decomposition. These mechanisms, coupled with increments in the specification, are the primary heuristics.

Abstraction is a technique that allows the architect to focus on one level of detail without having to focus on everything at once. It is the primary technique for handling complexity. Other levels of detail, perhaps more or perhaps less, will eventually be addressed. However, these levels of abstraction must be linked together; after all, they deal with aspects of *the single system*. It is easier, for example, to focus on the placement of a house on a piece of property, than the placement of every room in the house on that property. Instead, the level of abstraction is the house. Further detail, the rooms, is addressed in additional levels of abstraction, called refinement. "People sometimes confuse the term abstraction with the common notion of being abstract or obtuse. ...the process of abstraction is anything but obtuse—it is specifically designed to enhance, not frustrate, understanding." [Kilov-99]

Composition is a technique that enables parts to be configured into a whole. The house, for example, is composed of (a composition of) many things, among which are the rooms. Decomposition is useful for focusing on one piece of the whole at a level of abstraction (e.g., one of the rooms in the house). These techniques enable architecture reasoning and specification to result. [Wing-95, RM-ODP-2]

Incremental steps in specifying are needed. If something is not fully known, capture what is known and go on. In dealing with abstraction techniques, the architect is already ignoring unnecessary details, postponing them until later. In order to enable incremental specification work, certain behaviors need to be captured. Preconditions that provide assumptions about how something will work can be specified, and re-addressed later when more is known. Any failures that might result, and any action to be taken on failure, is specified as a postcondition. Any such postconditions that provide assumptions of what is to happen after some action are specified. In each case, these behaviors are initially specified, and re-defined as the specification is elaborated.

In dealing with components, the specification should capture at a gross level what the major components of the system are. In dealing with interworking relationships among the components, the specification should capture at a gross level what the action entails, what component performs the action, and what is acted upon. Details are filled in as part of the refinement process.

1.4.5 REFINEMENT

For those system aspects specified, iterative refinement of the levels of abstraction to more and more detail affects what has already been specified. Updates to the specification are provided. If a particular thing is complicated in its specification, the architect needs to look it over again and try to simplify.

1.4.6 RESULT

The architecture specification is eventually documented in the language of the specification technique, using the syntax and semantics of the specification language. What is captured in the specification is the language of distributed processing. That is, the architecture specification of a system is written in the specification language, but the terms used are those of distributed processing (versus, for example, a "house" with "rooms"). That such a language is based on a formal specification, as in FDT, need not mean the language that is used is mathematically oriented. Indeed, such is the case with RM-ODP, wherein the language of distributed processing is used, but which is founded in Z, SDL, LOTOS, and ESTELLE [Z, SDL, LOTOS, ESTELLE] FDTs. The architect doesn't need to know this.

In essence, writing specifications requires the skills of specifying and abstraction, the language of distributed processing, the language of the specification techniques, and above all else, practice, patience, and common sense. An excellent source dealing with this topic is available from [Wing-95].

1.5　　REFERENCE MODEL OF OPEN DISTRIBUTED PROCESSING

RM-ODP is a standard for modeling object-based distributed processing architectures that separates concerns and simplifies the specification of heterogeneous, open distributed processing systems. RM-ODP enables the process of architecting distributed processing systems, especially ones that are open systems. It provides a way of modeling distributed systems in a language oriented to distributed processing systems, so that there is no ambiguity of intention, and so that the resultant architecture specification is well-formed (both syntactically and semantically). It provides an organization of the issues for distributed systems in terms of a foundation of terminology and rules of use, addressing interoperability and behavior, and addressing not only the functional characteristics of distributed processing systems but also the non-functional distributed processing principles. All of this is provided in a framework of concepts (with precisely defined terms), rules, behavior, and patterns of architecture and design for defining the implementation mechanisms.

The RM-ODP is a standard of international acceptance, importance, and use. It provides a means to capture the business needs, distributed processing system architecture, semantics of processing, and choice of technologies, all in a consistent and complete manner. It focuses on how to capture the components, their interrelationships, and semantics of processing aspects of an open distributed processing system. RM-ODP provides a formal model of:

▶ Distributed processing systems concerns to be addressed in any architecture
▶ Organization of these concerns to provide a foundation for interoperable open distributed systems
▶ Framework of terms and architecture principles (called rules)
▶ Mechanisms to achieve certain aspects of a distributed processing system (such as fault tolerance)

▶ A precise "language" of distributed processing concepts (such as an interface), addressing both functionality of the system as well as non-functional properties of the system (such as reliability)
▶ A process of architecting
▶ Showing how system qualities are achievable through architecture
▶ Specific ways of "architecting a little, prototyping a little, learning a lot"
▶ A set of architecture patterns that can be reused in any system architecture
▶ A process for testing the implementation to the architecture

RM-ODP includes four standards documents. Part 1 of the standard is a non-normative overview and rationale of the concepts and terminology of software-intensive distributed processing systems. Part 2 of the standard is the foundations document, which comprises a glossary of standard terminology for object-oriented distributed systems. Part 3 of the standard is the architecture document. It defines various viewpoints for object-oriented architecture along with their structuring rules and various open distributed processing functions that enable distributed computing. Part 4 provides a formal description of Parts 2 and 3, which the user of the standard can rely upon but does not need to use. That is, it provides the formalisms that are about Parts 2 and 3, to ensure these parts are expressed in mathematical terms, and thereby provides a rigorous well-formed standard. The parts of the standard are shown in Figure 1.10.

Altogether, these four standards documents comprise less than 200 pages of documentation with the normative parts, with Parts 2 and 3 comprising about 100

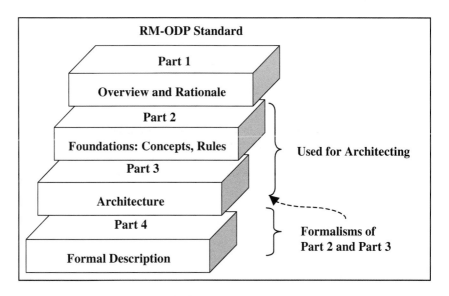

FIGURE 1.10 RM-ODP Standard

pages. Even though this is a relatively short standard, there is a great deal of valuable information. Many ISO standards are relatively inscrutable to the practicing software engineer. This standard is no exception. However, the effort to understand this standard is very worthwhile given the challenges of distributed computing that need to be resolved in business process change.

The standard includes:

- A set of concepts, in a common terminology, that can be applied for the development of systems of open distributed processing
- A standard framework for developing the system or contributing to the standards work under the open distributed processing initiative
- A guide for architects to specify the object-oriented architecture of software systems, which is directly relevant to the day-to-day practices of systems architects

The main concepts in RM-ODP are open systems, distributed processing systems, precise behavior specification, composition, abstraction, refinement, linking multiple levels of abstraction, consistency from specification to implementation, and conformance testing.

The behavior of an object is defined in terms of a set of actions and constraints on those actions, to include QoS and when the constraints occur. RM-ODP also addresses the environment in which the objects and their actions occur. This is important because often the environment will also introduce constraints; e.g., processing resources.

A contract is used in RM-ODP to characterize and control the interworking between objects. Similar to the business, a contract is an agreement among the interworkings of objects, and governs what they can and cannot do. A contract-based approach to software defines what must be done between software entities, not how. The how is determined by the architecture specification. Design by contract is a capability of the Eiffel language. [Meyer-97]

The concept of policy is also used in RM-ODP to further characterize and control behavior and define the purpose of some grouping of objects. A policy is a set of statements that provide permission to do something, an obligation that something must be done, and a prohibition that something must not be done. Policy statements are applicable at all levels of abstraction, and are also composable.

Why a reference model? A reference model provides a general-purpose, formal definition of architecture and design practices. It provides the ability to transform abstract visions into more concrete illustrations. It provides the ability to simplify the discussion of relationships among entities. It provides a durable framework to structure decision-making about an architecture. It guides the choices made in an architecture, which, in turn, guide the choices made in an implementation. In the case of RM-ODP, the reference model is based on a specific RM-ODP object model. The object model provides the ability to define parts of the system architecture, independent of additional details, or of implementation details (called abstraction). The object model provides the ability to hide certain characteristics of the distributed system, when considering some part of the system (called encapsulation). When addressing some functionality of a software entity, for example, characteristics that can be hidden include distribution, heterogeneity, mobility, or failure and recovery of the system in support of the software entity.

RM-ODP can be used to develop a truly object-oriented architecture, in which inheritance and runtime polymorphism play a part. RM-ODP can also be used to develop an object-based architecture for a procedurally based functional system. That the architecture is object-based does not mean the implementation of the system is object-based. So RM-ODP can be used for object-oriented, procedural, real-time, and other based systems.

What is meant by general? RM-ODP is not focused on a particular enterprise, business, or organization, or on a particular choice of technology. Rather, it can capture the architectural concerns of any organizational or technology domain; it is general enough to represent all domain-specific architectures, with all the terminology needed to communicate those architectures across the domain of interest.

RM-ODP separates distributed system complexity (distribution, heterogeneity, current product selection, distributed data, achieving the "ilities" such as interoperability, reliability, security, scalability, portability, evolvability, etc.) into separate specifications on the system. These specifications are reflective of how the customer communicates the requirements of the system, how the designer can distribute software across different locations and computers, how the developer can use current technology to develop the system, and how the tester can validate the system to the architecture (conformance testing). All of these specifications are related to each other by the RM-ODP rules, achieving a consistent set of requirements that reflects the architectural specification of the system of interest. RM-ODP is a key to specifying the functional and non-functional (i.e., behavioral) aspects of the system, and as such is a methodology (abstraction, composition, object-based modeling, etc.) for architecting the system.

RM-ODP [RM-ODP-2] defines a system and architecture as:

System: An entity that is a whole or a configuration of parts or a part. Therefore, a system can be a component, a subsystem, a system of interest, or a system of systems. If a component is a system of a larger system, it is called a subsystem.

Architecture: The concepts and rules that define the structure, relationships, and constraints among the parts.

RM-ODP helps system architects specify complex software-intensive architectures for any domain by describing how to map the requirements and needs of a user to the system specification, and then map from that specification to the current technology and products of the day. The main purpose of the standardization of RM-ODP is to enable consistent and reliable interworking of distributed heterogeneous systems.

RM-ODP is based on object-modeling concepts and an ontology for use. These cover:

- Basic modeling concepts that provide precise definitions of a minimal set of concepts (action, object, interaction, and interface), forming the basis for any ODP system specification

- Specification rules that address concepts such as composition, refinement, abstraction, type, class, and others. These are necessary for reasoning about specifications and the relations between specifications, providing general tools for architecting, and establishing the ontology needed to provide a specification language for use in modeling of a system.

- Structuring rules that build on the basic object model and the specification rules to address distributed processing systems, and concerns pertinent to distributed processing, such as components, objects, interfaces, policy, naming, behavior, reliability, failure, communication, and others

The remainder of this book will address RM-ODP in depth. Two domain-specific cases are used. The primary example used is a medical example, representing a hospital, physician practice, insurance company, state regulation authority, and of course a patient. Another example used is an airline reservation system. The book will build upon these examples as certain aspects of RM-ODP are discussed.

1.6   SUMMARY

Systems today are distributed in reaction to the needs of the customer. Open distributed systems enable interoperability and information sharing across dissimilar systems, software, and hardware. To achieve a well-formed system that behaves as intended requires an architecture. The specification of an architecture is the job of an architect. A specification precisely defines the components, connectors, structure, and behavior of the intended system.

Not all aspects of an architecture need to be specified. Some aspects are permitted alternatives for the implementer. However, a specification enables analysis of an architecture, simulation of the architecture, tradeoff determinations in terms of cost, commercial product choices, technical performance, and time to market. The choice is the architect's, whose job it is to provide a sufficiently well-defined architecture specification that can be used to communicate the needs of the customer to the implementer, and to test the resultant system to the architecture.

Accomplishing the task of creating an architecture is challenging, especially in light of the organizational influences the architect must contend with. Tools are a necessity for any architect. Tools that aid the architect to create an architecture are essential. RM-ODP provides a rich set of specification tools to aid the process of architecting, meeting the demands from the architecture community for well-formed formal model-based specification techniques.

Some lessons learned in the pursuit of architecting, from many who have participated in construction of large-scale architectures, include:

▶ Architecting requires good engineering skills, coupled with specific architecting skills in the language of distributed processing systems.

▶ Architecture is key to achieving interoperability. Standards on the interface are not enough.

▶ An open system is key to interoperability and information sharing.

▶ An open architecture specification is key to heterogeneous interworking software systems at any size.

▶ Architecture is key to achieving a well-performing system. It doesn't just happen.

▶ Architecture is key to achieving evolvability to new technologies, scalability to increased resource requirements, and flexibility to adapt to change. These characteristics need to be constructed into the plan of the system.

▶ Architecture is key to achieving a more fault-tolerant system that knows what to do in case of failure. The alternative, which is to allow a failure to happen and then check out the design to see what went wrong, is unacceptable in the mission-critical systems of today (e.g., a telecommunication system that must "get the call through").

▶ Architecture is key in enabling the complexities of a system to be hidden from the end user and/or application using the services of the system.

▶ Architecture is key in enabling a choice of "better, cheaper, faster" benefits of a system development.

▶ A specification is a precise definition.

▶ Architecting is the construction of an architecture specification of a system, along with appropriate choices of the degree of specificity.

▶ Architecting is both a science and an art. The science aspect is gaining ground, especially with tools of specification such as provided by RM-ODP.

▶ The architect needs to identify the degree of variability to support, to help in evolving architectures.

▶ One size does not fit all; that is, there may be more than one architecture relevant for a system.

Architecture overcomes the problems of varied interpretation. Often at the end of a day of meetings, a person has pictures of boxes and lines representing architectures. Interpretations of what is intended are as varied as the number of people in the meetings.

Specifying an architecture of a system, supported by the RM-ODP, narrows the gap of "architecting and the search for the Holy Grail."

The remainder of this book will detail what RM-ODP is about, discuss how to use it, and provide patterns of reasoning for specifying the architecture of a system.

RM-ODP Manager's Primer

This chapter provides an opportunity for each reader to gain a better understanding of the Reference Model of Open Distributed Processing (RM-ODP) from a management perspective. Future chapters cover RM-ODP in depth.

This chapter discusses:

- Motivation for RM-ODP
- Benefits of using RM-ODP
- How RM-ODP fits into the lifecycle
- How RM-ODP is used
- How RM-ODP facilitates business specifications
- RM-ODP elements for use
- What knowledge is prerequisite
- Investment needed

2.1   Motivation for RM-ODP

Today's complex distributed systems introduce heterogeneity of architectures, designs, and product choices. This results in a challenging program management task. Consider attempting to capture all the possible solutions to achieve an enterprise-wide distributed environment of heterogeneous systems, enabling information sharing across geographically separated user groups with different functions. The management challenge of providing a system solution in the face of all the alternatives is immensely difficult. Program managers often expend resources (time and personnel) in the hopes of solving such a problem, believing using more must be the way to achieve a result. It's not. What is important is to communicate the scope of the problem to be solved, the objective of the solution, the business rules that constrain the solution, expected behavior of the solution, and to capture these explicitly in a form that can be communicated to the architect of the system.

RM-ODP provides a general framework for any enterprise business architecture, and is equally applicable to an enterprise-wide system of systems, a single system, or a software product. It provides a means of specifying the business independent of the system, a means of specifying the system to support the business and solve a business problem, and the means to interrelate the two (i.e., the business and the system supporting it).

This reference model has been broadly used because it is effective for specifying (precisely defining) business required distributed systems. What this means is that the concepts and structuring rules in RM-ODP are general and apply to any architecture endeavor. Some of the business industries that have successfully used RM-ODP include:

▶ Telecommunications industry companies, such as AT&T®, Lucent Technologies®, Nortel Networks®, GTE®, and others
▶ Financial industry companies, such as Merrill Lynch℠, Morgan Stanley℠, and others
▶ Manufacturing industry, such as the work in product data
▶ Health industry, such as specific health care companies, and specific health care services such as patient identification services
▶ Geographical systems
▶ Consortia, such as the Object Management Group (OMG)
▶ Government agencies
  – U.S. Department of Defense health domain
  – United Kingdom logistics
  – United Kingdom C3I interoperability
  – Norway C2
  – Australia C2
  – United Kingdom air traffic control

Represented in Figure 2.1 are some of the domains that have used RM-ODP successfully.

The elements of architecting with RM-ODP are shown in Figure 2.2. The business objectives, business processes, business rules, and business constraints drive the need for a system. The system exists only to support the business. This is the approach taken by RM-ODP. As such, business scope, objectives, and policies are

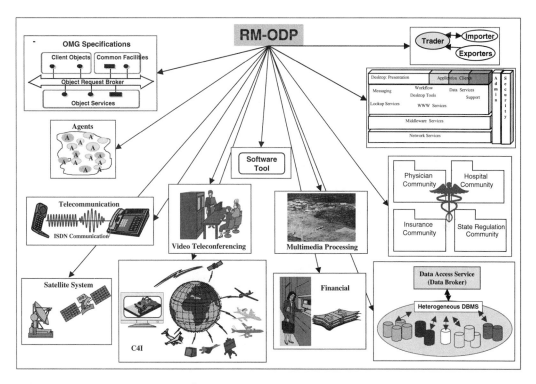

FIGURE 2.1   Representative Use of RM-ODP

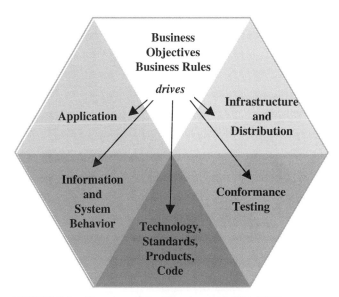

FIGURE 2.2   Elements of Architecting with RM-ODP

defined through RM-ODP and drive the architecture of a system. The architecture of the applications, infrastructure, and behavior of the system are all results of the business specification, first and foremost. RM-ODP facilitates the difficult task of change management. It provides the ability to make a change and know where the ripple effect will occur. Further, part of RM-ODP is the ability to conduct conformance testing (on the whole or part or changed part). This validates the system to the architecture, and the architecture to the business. Because choices of technology may be delayed in the architecting process, not only does RM-ODP provide criteria for selecting products, but it also provides the ability to incorporate "black box" services into the implementation and then test them for conformance.

The process of architecting is iterative. It takes place from the business specification through the deployment of the system. Architecture evolves throughout the lifecycle of the system, to include upgrades. This is depicted in Figure 2.3.

RM-ODP was completed in 1996 and is the result of 10 years of work by the International Organization for Standardization (ISO), as well as the International Telecommunications Union (ITU). It is a joint standard of the international information technology community and is the current formal standard for object-oriented architecture of a software-intensive system. It is fully relevant to today's systems development projects. The significance of an international standard is that all of these software-intensive systems' architecture concepts and approaches have achieved agreement from companies across the world.

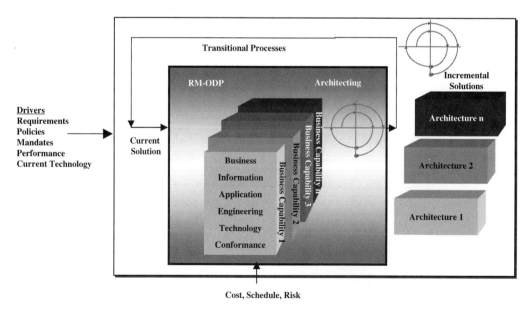

FIGURE 2.3   Evolutionary Architecting

2.2   Benefits Achievable from Using RM-ODP

Benefits can be assessed in terms of cost savings, shorter schedules, and enhanced technical performance. Cost savings are realized through faster time to market, quicker response to the customer, lower maintenance costs, higher return on investment (ROI), and so forth. Schedule savings are realized in reducing the time required to implement a capability or make changes. Technical performance amounts to form, fit, function; in other words, how well the system performs technically, how well the system adheres to the expectations, how well the system compares against competing systems, ease of maintenance, ease of upgrading, and so forth.

A summary of the benefits achieved by using RM-ODP, as addressed in this section, include:

- *Technical performance*
    - Meets the customer expectations
    - Facilitates communication between the customer and architect
    - Scopes the problem to be solved
    - Reuse of architecture patterns and system solutions
    - Enables a more robust, reliable, scalable, and changeable system
    - Defines the system requirements before choices of technologies, facilitating evolutionary growth
    - Facilitates upgrades to the system, knowing the impact
    - Supports incremental development
    - Enables a spiral approach
    - Enables a visionary architecture, with incremental solutions over time
- *Cost savings*
    - Minimizes application development
    - Minimizes cost of rework
    - Accrued costs spread out over the lifecycle
    - Costs of fielding a non-conformant system can be avoided
    - Reusable patterns of architecture minimizes the "how to" costs
    - Smaller architect team groups
    - Minimizes maintenance costs
- *Schedule savings*
    - Lifecycle schedule savings
    - Less time in communicating between the customer and the architect
    - Less time selecting products that don't work
    - Minimizes miscommunication and associated time for rework

Upfront investment in time and cost is needed for any architecture activity. The manager needs to understand the business, and where the system is to play a part. The architect should capture the business specification in RM-ODP terms, which are similar to business terminology. The architect can then proceed to fully specify the software system.

The manager needs to allocate resources to the process of architecting. The manager needs to establish the schedule, the requirements to formulate the system, and so forth. In fact, the manager needs to manage the project.

Section 2.7 and Section 2.8 discuss more in terms of the prerequisite skill base and the investment needed. Tool support to aid the architect to create and describe the architecture is discussed in Chapter 4, "Tools, Relationships, and RM-ODP Standard."

2.2.1   TECHNICAL PERFORMANCE

In order to achieve a well-performing technical solution, the architecture must be communicated clearly to the customer. The concepts and rules of RM-ODP enable this.

RM-ODP facilitates meeting the customer expectations of the system implementation. One of the problems between customers who want and pay for a system, and system implementers is a lack of stakeholder communication. Often, the customer uses words from the business domain that mean something in that domain, and at the same time mean something else in the information technology domain, where the architect comes from. A mapping or relationship between "words" is needed to make sure that what is wanted is not miscommunicated, and that what the architect says will be provided is not miscommunicated.

For example, consider the word *integration*. In the business environment, this term often means to link processes, like supply chain, inventory control, transportation, billing, etc. to include all the parts, personnel, systems, and whatever else comprises those processes. There is no indication that this word means "software systems." On the other hand, in the information technology (IT) vocabulary, *integration* means combining software (only) parts together to act as a single unit. Analogies can be drawn from these two environments, but in normal communication each side needs to be sure what the context of the communication is and what the word means to the other party. Actually, consider the word *communication*. In the business world, this term means conversation or correspondence; in the IT vocabulary this term generally means protocols and networks. RM-ODP describes how to capture the business, how to capture what the customer wants of a system, describes how the system should function in support of the business needs, and how to select current technology and products to meet those needs. This is the nature of an architecture form using RM-ODP.

How well the system performs technically is based, in part, on how well the customer, architect, designer, implementer, and tester communicate. RM-ODP provides a language that communicates the requirements from the customer to the architect, the architect to the designer, the designer to the implementer, and the implementer to the tester. This enables a better-functioning technical solution. More people involved in attempting to specify a distributed system solution, without a common way of communicating among themselves in a language that all understand, generally results in a poor-performing technical solution or a lot of time is spent doing rework.

Defining the scope of the problem to be solved as requirements and relating the requirements to available technical solutions are complex tasks, prone to error. RM-ODP enables a technical solution through its constructs. First, the scope, objectives, and policies of the business are specified. In similar fashion, the scope, objectives, and policies of the system in the context of the business are specified. This latter specification then bounds the system solution within the business boundary. Then, through the process of architecting using the rules of RM-ODP, the business requirements are related to architectural choices, and from there, to technologies and products. RM-ODP defines rules that result in a solution that meets the business requirements.

A common methodology to pull elements of a system together is absolutely essential for an accurate specification. Key personnel who understand the generic concepts, principles, and methods of the RM-ODP will find that these very precise constructs are a sound basis for specifying the architecture of either large or small systems, by one or more persons, either local or geographically distributed. In the end, the program manager can expend fewer resources to achieve a technically sound working solution.

RM-ODP provides patterns for reuse in developing systems that are better performing, minimize application development, minimize maintenance, and maximize distribution. Capabilities realized through these patterns include:

- Minimized interface development by enabling reusable interface elements

- An interface that can reference a recipient by name, instead of by an exact network address

- Reliability achieved through fault-tolerant mechanisms

- Load-balancing achieved through the ability to move any software to a different location (such as from a server to another computer)

- Mobility achieved through the movement of software and its interfaces to any desired location. In RM-ODP, software mobility is separate from load-balancing. Software can be moved to any location within the same computer, or to another computer, for any purpose desired, and this movement is dynamic; that is, it can be done at runtime.

- Better performance of some part of the system achieved through replicating those parts of the system, not just databases

❿ Reuse of communication mechanisms

❿ Policy administration on the software in the system

❿ Hiding complex infrastructure designs from the application developer

❿ Interoperability achieved through well-specified constructs about interfacing, more than just a protocol specification

❿ Scalability achieved through the distributed infrastructure patterns

❿ Portability achieved through the appropriate specification and design of language bindings

These are technical performance savings, applicable in the implementation of the infrastructure mechanisms, which provide a more robust, reliable, migratable, scalable system. These capabilities can make a system more competitive with other systems.

RM-ODP enables not only better technical performance, but also minimized cost of application development across the enterprise. This is achieved by reusable infrastructure services that offload what the developer needs to develop. Furthermore, RM-ODP provides the capabilities to achieve the "ilities," hide the details from the application developer, and allow the infrastructure developer to develop. These are reusable constructs specified by an architecture and design patterns in RM-ODP. For example, the capability of locating an interface, or accessing the distributed software, or use of a connection with a specific protocol, or fault tolerance, are all infrastructure developer mechanisms that the application developer need not implement.

One major benefit of using RM-ODP is the ability to define what the system needs to do, before choices of technology and products. Once the needs are captured in an architecture and all the expectations of how that system will work are specified, then one can look for technologies and products that fit those needs.

RM-ODP also provides mechanisms that enable a more flexible and adaptable system to be developed. This is achieved through the architecture specification techniques that provide criteria for selecting technologies. Then, as technology changes, deciding if and how to use the new technology is a matter of assessing the criteria. If that criteria is met, the new technology can be inserted into the system in the correct place, because the specification indicates exactly where it goes.

Likewise, the specification and the rules of consistency of RM-ODP facilitate upgrading a system due to a change in a requirement from the customer. The architect can determine the impact of the requirement change precisely, by knowing the perturbations in the specification (and therefore in the system), what needs to be changed, and how. Because of the consistency and specification rules of RM-ODP, the change is not a matter of guessing, but a matter of knowing where the change needs to be made, and, as necessary, respecifying a part of the system accurately.

RM-ODP facilitates an incremental approach to a technical solution. Sometimes a manager has a vision of what is wanted, realizing that today's technology cannot yet accomplish that vision. How can the manager proceed?

1. One alternative is to scale back on the requirements, and only specify what can be accomplished today. The cost and schedule of doing this is minimized, but technology advances so rapidly that by the time the solution hits the marketplace, it may be obsolete. So the cost of the solution, in fact, results in a negative return on investment.

2. Another alternative is to bypass the architecture process, and select the best products in the marketplace to put together and realize a solution. This too is cost effective and can be accomplished in a reduced schedule. But what does the manager do when what is delivered is not what was intended, less functional, too cumbersome to be considered "user friendly," or cannot accommodate some functionality or some emerging technology? A Band-Aid™ approach is generally used. However, after a certain number of Band-Aids, the system becomes exceedingly difficult (and hence expensive) to maintain.

3. Another approach is to use a well-formed specification process of architecting that allows the system to be developed to current technology, specify the visionary needs, identify where aspects of the vision are not (yet) implemented, and allows for changes in technologies to be correctly used in the system based on the specification. The upfront costs of an architecture offsets the back-end costs of maintainability and extensibility. Furthermore, if the specification and implementation can be managed across multiple organizations, it provides a great deal of flexibility to the program manager. If the specification provides a means of assessing programmatic risk, and incremental implementation, such as through the use of the Spiral Model shown in Figure 2.4, the up-front costs can be allocated over time. If the specification methodology allows for a full specification of a part of the system, along with a partial specification of a part of the system, the manager can specify a little and build a little, incrementally. This is based on the ability to combine, at some future time, the specifications in a consistent manner. This too enables costs to be spread out over time. All of this, and more, can be achieved through the use of the RM-ODP methodology of architecting.

One of the major benefits for using RM-ODP is the ability to create an architecture for only a part of the system that may be envisioned. If a specific Web browser and Web server are needed or required, RM-ODP allows the architecture of these parts. If they are commercial products, which is generally the case, RM-ODP allows the architecture to define the use of these parts. If later on, a messaging middleware part is required, perhaps for guaranteed delivery of a message, RM-ODP provides the foundation to "plug in" that part to the current architecture, in the correct way so that the system works as expected.

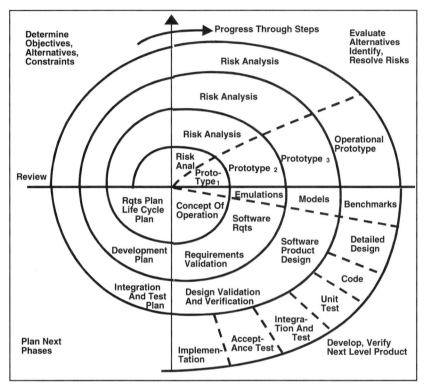

FIGURE 2.4 Original Spiral Model [Boehm-88]. Reprinted by courtesy of Professor Barry Boehm.

2.2.2 COST SAVINGS

Cost savings of the system solution are achieved by meeting the customer requirements, by minimizing application development by specifying the architecture to some requirements and not necessarily all, and by decreased maintenance time and skill level required. These cost savings are achieved because of the rules of architecting, reusable patterns of architecture and design, and the conformance testing process, all part of RM-ODP. Up-front costs (see Section 2.8) are required to support the activity of architecting, but the lifecycle costs are reduced.

Within the context of the overall system design and implementation, RM-ODP is intended to save the cost of rework. RM-ODP provides the ability to "require a little, specify a little, and build a little" of the system (in stages) without expending the costs up front. This is achievable in RM-ODP by requiring parts of the system in stages. Without having to fully define all requirements for all aspects of the system up front, the result is the specification of parts of the system. This is achievable because of the rules of specification and consistency associated with RM-ODP.

Hence, the cost savings may accrue from reduced expenses and fewer resources being used within the overall system in the up-front requirements of the system.

Another cost saving may be achieved by precisely capturing the requirements, tracing them through the specification to the implementation, and communicating with the customer how the system meets these requirements. This is achievable because RM-ODP allows the architect to develop criteria for selecting appropriate products, against which code will be developed to meet the up-front requirements. This validates the selected implementation of the requirements to the customer prior to full implementation and fielding of the system.

One benefit is to avoid the cost of fielding a system that is not conformant with the specification. Another cost saving is achieved by conformance testing. The prototype system, before it is fielded, can be tested for conformance with the architecture. If it is not conformant, it is re-implemented or re-architected depending on the outcome of the test. In any event, the system and architecture will be agreed upon before fielding of the system, saving the cost of rework once fielded.

Another cost saving is achieved by reuse. Most distributed processing requirements are addressed by RM-ODP and hence by any specification using RM-ODP. RM-ODP provides patterns of architecture that are reusable in the implementation. They form the mechanisms to be implemented in any distributed processing system. Not only are these mechanisms reusable, but since they abide by an international standard, they are also interoperable. The program manager does not need to fund multiple developments of the mechanisms identified across all systems in an enterprise. The program manager does not need to fund the discovery of *how to accomplish* such things as interoperability, fault tolerance, policy administration, quality of service specification, or even a business enterprise specification. RM-ODP provides patterns of how to do these things, and these patterns can be reused in any distributed processing system. What the program manager does need to fund is the specific use of these patterns, and the specific implementation choices. All the constructs for defining the architecture of certain capabilities are provided by RM-ODP as patterns for reuse.

Minimizing application development resources, which includes time and people, reduces the amount of coding, analysis, design, etc. This in turn minimizes the cost of development, and therefore actually reduces the time to market. RM-ODP provides patterns of architecture and design for the infrastructure that frees the application developer from having to develop the capabilities.

The application developer can develop reusable interfaces instead of point-to-point interfaces, minimizing the cost of development as well as the cost of maintaining so many interfaces. Reusable interfaces are achievable through the use of the RM-ODP concepts that deal with interfacing across the enterprise, providing most of this in the infrastructure so that individual application developers can make use of the capabilities.

Smaller groups are more efficient than larger groups, and hence less costly. The RM-ODP constructs provide the ability to use distributed organizations to build parts of the system. The system specifications are then integrated, through the rules associated with RM-ODP, resulting in a system that meets the customer requirements. Further, these rules also enable the architect to specify a part of the system at different points in the lifecycle, with the knowledge that through RM-ODP the different parts can be composed into a single specification.

The conformance testing capabilities of RM-ODP provide a way of validating that the system meets the architecture specification. The rules of RM-ODP validate that the architecture meets the customer requirements. Together, these provide a system that is well-functioning, and in turn minimizes the maintenance costs of that system.

The costs of rework are also minimized. In RM-ODP, system behavior is captured explicitly in the architecture specification. An error in the system can be detected, traced back to the architecture specification, and result in minimized time (and cost) to figure out what went wrong, or why something didn't work correctly. The architect, designer, and/or implementer can then fix the problem in a way that minimizes the rework of the system. For example, if a particular interface keeps failing, it's probably a result of an incorrect design or architecture for that interface. That interface can be located by the conformance testing points, the design information can be obtained by the specification, and the interface can be re-architected or redesigned. Because the specification indicates what communicates with the interface, only those software parts need to be looked at for possible change. In fact, the interface may be failing because some quality of service specification was incorrect. This amounts to a change in the value of the quality of service associated with that interface. A well-formed specification allows the troubleshooting required if something goes wrong, without having to "reverse engineer" what the implementer did, and without having to read the code to determine how something was implemented.

2.2.3   SCHEDULE SAVINGS

The use of RM-ODP can lead to lifecycle schedule savings, through the ability to validate the requirements to the specification, and the specification to the implementation.

Less time is required in communicating between the customer who sets the requirements and the architect who creates the architecture. This is achievable because of the well-formed concepts (language) used in RM-ODP. Furthermore, less time is required for the architect to communicate the architecture to the designer and implementer, for the same reasons. In the end, less time is spent clearing up misunderstandings through well-formed concepts.

Less time is spent in selecting products that don't work. RM-ODP provides selection criteria for products, to realize the system from the specification. This is achievable because of the explicit rules and concepts in RM-ODP. The implementer can select products based on these criteria, and using the conformance tests identified in RM-ODP, can make sure those products work "as advertised," prior to fielding. All of this saves time.

Miscommunication nearly always results in extended schedules, so minimizing miscommunication minimizes schedule delays. One of the primary responsibilities of an architect is to clearly communicate to the customer the needs of development for time, staff and functionality. Another is to clearly communicate the scope of the problem and developments needs from the customer to the development organization. RM-ODP facilitates communication among the architect, software developer, and the customer. *How* is achieved by the viewpoint specifications. *When* is achieved throughout the viewpoint specifications and the conformance testing.

2.3 WHERE RM-ODP FITS IN THE LIFECYCLE

RM-ODP is applicable throughout the entire lifecycle of creating a system and evolving that system; from specifying the needs of a system, to its architecture, design, its implementation, testing, and then to its re-engineering to accommodate advances in technology.

The reason it is applicable throughout the lifecycle is that it has a very precise, general distributed processing foundation that can be used for any specific system.

RM-ODP provides the method of capturing the business requirements as the driving force for the system architecture. It also provides a way of relating those requirements into an architecture for parts of a system. It provides a way of relating the parts of the system to the way it will be deployed on computers and across networks. It provides a way of relating choices of technology and products that can provide the functionality and behavior of the parts. And it provides a way to test the implementation to the architecture of the parts, tracing it back to the business requirements.

How RM-ODP architecture fits into the system lifecycle is shown in Figure 2.5. This figure has a notional representation of the steps taken to architect, and how those steps fit into the lifecycle. The RM-ODP–specific steps are shaded gray.

RM-ODP defines a "language" to talk about distributed processing. It says what an "interface" really is; what an "enterprise" consists of; what a "communication protocol" really does; how one can achieve "reliability"; what it takes to provide "mobility"; and so many more distributed processing concerns. All of this is intertwined to make sure that, in the end, it all holds together as an architecture for a single system.

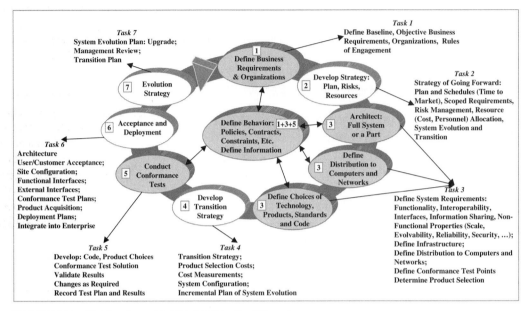

FIGURE 2.5   Architecting with RM-ODP in the Lifecycle

2.4   HOW RM-ODP IS USED

Systems are complex partly because there are many different human beings playing very different roles in the development, maintenance, and use of the system. These different roles and needs result in very different views of the same system. One of the failures of many architectures is not taking into account these different points of view (or viewpoints).

RM-ODP, on the other hand, provides a powerful and useful generic decomposition of a system into five viewpoints: enterprise, information, computation, engineering, and technology. RM-ODP provides concepts and rules to capture information, determine what information to capture, capture the information about the behavior of the system, and the processes for capturing all of this information to a structured and useable form. RM-ODP also provides consistency across the viewpoints in a way that results in a single cohesive system specification, instead of independent "stove-pipe" specifications of the system. This consistency enables a valid conformance testing process.

RM-ODP viewpoints separate a large complex problem (the architecture of a system) into separate achievable parts. Each viewpoint represents a particular focus on the system that can be specified. Generally, each viewpoint represents the views from a set of stakeholders (the business customer, the system engineer, the designer, the implementer, the information analyst, and the tester).

The use of viewpoints can be likened to building a house. It's easy to plan for a normal doghouse, in which case most of the architectural considerations are not necessary. But if a "dream home" or "skyscraper" is intended, an architecture is a requirement. The general contractor plans the house with the architect, the individual subcontractors provide focused solutions to a part of the house (e.g., a plumber, an electrician, and a rough-framer), the lumberyards and hardware stores provide the implementation parts, and the building codes specify the policies and constraints to build the house correctly within its community. It is the architect who focuses on all of the construction, specifying a blueprint in detail to be followed by the subcontractors. The lumberyard provides products for selection, independent of how the house is being constructed. It is like the products for selection in a system. It would not be wise to pick out a bunch of locks and keys and a security system first, and then decide what kind of doors are sufficient for the locks and keys, which in turn means deciding how the doors fit within the hallways, and so forth. This "bottoms-up" approach is unwise. Likewise, a "top-down" approach is unwise also, because the expense of a "dream home" has to take cost into consideration along the way. To ensure that all specifications of the house (or the system) work together, a Spiral Model approach is wise, in which incremental architectures, designs, and implementations, are iterated to a final architecture and implementation, all of which will work together to provide a single cohesive well-functioning house (or system).

It is not necessary to understand and use all the details in RM-ODP, just the basic concepts and rules. Furthermore, it's not necessary to use all the viewpoints, just the ones important to a precise specification. What is important is to put off decisions about implementation, including programming languages to use (e.g., Java™) or certain choices of middleware technology (e.g., a message-oriented middleware product) until criteria for the appropriate choice of technology is in hand. It's more important to expend the resources in making sure the needs of the customer are specified. All of this is enabled through the appropriate use of RM-ODP, providing working solutions. As Professor Boehm said, "Only about 5 percent of the difficulty in software development lies in the code itself, with much more of the difficulty in specification, and design." [Boehm-81]

Consistency and well-defined conformance test points enable the Spiral Model [Boehm-88] approach to software architecting: specify a little (but completely) about some important part of the system, analyze it, and fold it back into

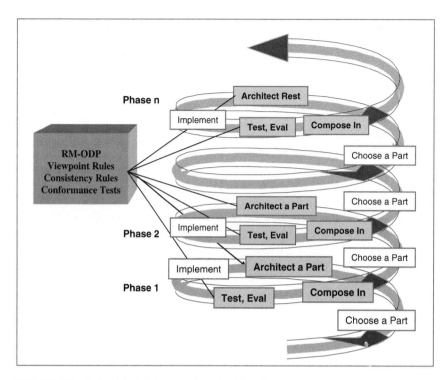

FIGURE 2.6   Spiral Model Approach to Architecting

the architecture. This also is one of the principal reasons why at any point in the viewpoint specification, any or all of the viewpoints can be used to more fully specify a single entity (software, interface, middleware choices, networks, user workstation) in the system, and be assured that it will be consistent in the specification later on. This is depicted in Figure 2.6.

2.5   HOW RM-ODP FACILITATES BUSINESS SPECIFICATION

RM-ODP provides a language (the enterprise language) for use in specifying a business. The language has few terms and rules, and is notionally similar to business terminology. Using the RM-ODP language to structure the business specification provides sufficient detail for the architect to understand and use in architecting a system solution. Furthermore, the use of the RM-ODP way of specification results in a short, precise specification, instead of, perhaps, hundreds of pages of requirements that the architect must digest and understand. Finally, the use of the RM-ODP way also enhances human communication between the business customer and the architect. This section will explain what the RM-ODP way is all about, and, by example, show how the results capture the business specification that the customer, as well as the architect, can understand.

The concepts and constructs of RM-ODP provide a precise foundation for defining the business, the elements of the system to support the business, their operations, and their constraints. The RM-ODP enterprise language provides the capability to specify the business concerns in a precise way, to bring consistency of specification. So words like "constraint," "policy," "relationship," "process," "contract," and "component" are precise, not intuitive. After all, one's interpretation of what is "obvious" is often different from another's interpretation. And all too often, a business "specification" is a set of viewgraphs that are interpreted differently: "a picture is worth a thousand words," and a picture can result in a thousand different interpretations! After all, in the worlds of, for example, finance, insurance, state regulations, and telecommunications, there are often precise, concise, and explicit specifications, not only for certain processing but also for certain operating procedures or codes or legal contracts.

The most important step is to capture the business specification, independent of any technical solution. The reasons for this are

▶ Without understanding the need for a system, the wrong solution may be developed.

▶ Without understanding how the system functions in the context of the business, the wrong solution may be developed.

▶ Specifying a business in terms of technologies results in overspecification, and in premature selection of technologies that may force fit the business processes to accommodate the technological solution!

So how does RM-ODP achieve this? The enterprise language is used, along with the rules of specification. The language consists of a small number of well-defined terms, based on formalisms that the customer need not worry about. The language has no mathematical notation; rather, it can be expressed in English text.

The following sidebar presents an example of business requirements specification. In the discussion of this example, common usage of a business term is shown as well as the RM-ODP terms in brackets ([ ]), to notionally relate to the RM-ODP term without definition of the term. That is, through the following discussion, how to use RM-ODP to specify that business is shown. Chapter 12 provides a more in-depth discussion of an enterprise business specification. Figure 2.7 in the sidebar shows various communities. Healthy Hospital is the case study used throughout the book. It is the [community of interest].

HEALTHY HOSPITAL BUSINESS REQUIREMENTS

The business to be specified is patient care and management at Healthy Hospital [community]. The particular scope of interest in this business includes billing, patient admission, patient treatment, physician support, and state regulation codes [scope]. The objectives of this business are to provide quality patient care, support the needs of the medical community that forms the enterprise with Healthy Hospital, use a system to provide an interoperable information-sharing environment, facilitate a better-performing set of activities across the organizations, adhere to a changeable hospital policy, adhere to insurance billing policy (which may change), adhere to state regulations, be more efficient, encourage patients and physicians to use the facilities, and make a profit [objectives].

A computer system shall be specified to interface to the business user [role of type party], and shall provide the functionality of that business [enterprise objects, actions, and behavior]. All such computer systems shall be integrated into a single working system, from the perspective of any user.

As requirements in the regulations and policies [policy] change, the hospital computer systems shall keep up and change accordingly. As more and more patients [role] are "customers" of the hospital, the business shall be able to scale easily. As new medical domains [domain] become part of the environment [environment] of the hospital, the relationships in terms of interfaces shall be added easily, and information sharing across all such domains shall be provided [federation]. Privacy of information shall always be part of the solution [security]. State regulations shall be specified and shall be part of the solution [policy and contract]. Hospital policy [policy] shall be specified and shall be part of the solution. Periodic changes to policies shall be provided. When this occurs, the solution shall accommodate the change easily, without major impact to the system [dynamic and static schemata].

The hospital administrator [role] shall be able to access any information pertinent to the hospital. The hospital administrator shall determine the functions and interfaces to the other external organizations [environment interactions] (insurance company, state regulation, physicians, patient). The hospital administrator shall ensure all policies [policies] (hospital, state regulation, insurance company) are adhered to. The hospital administrator shall manage the functioning of all systems.

A patient [role of type party] shall be treated at Healthy with all medical treatments [roles] available. Healthy shall bill [action] the patient for any outstanding balance due.

The hospital admitting agent[1] [role] shall perform the actions [actions] of admitting a patient to the hospital, schedule appointments with hospital physicians, and schedule radiology treatments. To this end, the hospital admitting agent shall [all of the following are constraints in terms of policies and invariants] validate patient information, validate or assign a unique hospital identification code, and validate that the patient can pay. In the case of the use of insurance, the admitting agent shall validate the insurance company is a member of Healthy. In the case of an emergency, the admitting agent shall be permitted to bypass the payment validation, in accordance with the hospital policy. The hospital admitting agent shall access and see only appropriate information for these functions: appropriate patient record information [role of type resource], schedule information [role of type resource], and hospital policy information [role of type resource]. The admitting agent shall update the patient record information with schedules. The admitting agent shall prepare [action] a summary schedule [object or resource] for issuance to the patient agent [role].

The hospital treatment center person (radiologist) [role] shall perform equipment safety checks [action and policy]. The radiologist shall record equipment certification from the state regulation authority. The radiologist [role of type party] shall treat the patient in accordance with the physician order [role of type resource]. The radiology software system shall be able to access patient information to perform the treatment. The system shall provide the ability to validate patient information, access the physician order, validate equipment safety, and record the treatment to the patient record. The recorded treatment results shall be accomplished within a 24-hour period [invariant].

All patient records [role of type resource] shall include all information associated with that patient throughout all hospital activities. This information shall include patient name, patient address, patient phone number, hospital unique identification, patient insurance information, patient payment required, patient outstanding balance, authorized physician(s), physician order, physician treatments, radiologist treatment and results, all schedules, in-hospital stays, medications dispensed, all information associated with all hospital activities, and shall authorize access to the patient record [static schema for an information object]. All information associated with a patient record shall be able to be updated with authorized access.

The physician [role] shall perform the scheduled patient evaluations and treatments, bill the patient for services rendered, join Healthy Hospital, and achieve valid accreditation from the state physician board of licensing.

---

1. An agent is a role in the system. It can be performed by a human, or software, or both. At this point, agent is nothing more than "a representative of the hospital organization" providing a particular function, such as admission.

A physician shall be able to obtain all records from the hospital about that patient. The system shall validate that the physician is a designated physician by the patient. The system shall validate the physician credentials, and shall validate the physician has hospital privileges [policies]. The physician shall have the ability to update the patient record [policy].

Patients must have a valid means of payment. If this is medical insurance, the medical insurance company [environment] shall be validated to be a member of the hospital group [precondition as specified by policy]. If this is not an insured patient, the hospital policy of admission shall be followed [postcondition].

The billing agent computer system [object in the Healthy Hospital community, as well as a separate community] shall perform all functions with respect to billing. The billing agent [role] shall receive all bills from the organizations within the hospital. The billing agent shall compute a total cost of all bills [action]. The billing agent shall ensure that the appropriate billing codes are associated with all billable treatments [policy]. The billing agent shall submit all bills to the insurance company in accordance with their billing procedures [policy]. The billing agent shall submit all bills to the insurance company within 10 days [invariant]. All balances due shall be billed to the patient. The insurance company is required to submit the explanation of benefits (EOB) to the patient within 30 days of receiving the bill [policy and invariant]. That same EOB must be submitted to the hospital, along with payment, within 10 days. The billing agent shall notify the hospital administrator if such actions have not occurred within the time designated [action]. All billing information shall be recorded in the patient record.

By state regulation, the hospital shall not overbill for any procedure [policy and invariant]. The hospital is not responsible for the bill from the physicians. The state regulation authority shall provide the appropriate state regulation codes for use by Healthy.

The insurance company shall be a member of Healthy. The insurance company shall provide EOB results to Healthy within 10 days [policy and invariant]. The insurance company shall provide the formats to submit an electronic bill. The insurance company shall provide the appropriate policies for use by Healthy.

The pharmacist [role] shall make sure all pharmaceuticals [role of type resource or artefact] are currently in stock, in accordance with state regulations [policies] that may limit quantities. The pharmacist shall [actions] dispense medications and restock medications. All pharmaceuticals prescribed to the patient by the pharmacy organization while under the care of the hospital shall be available [policy]. The computer system shall provide an accurate inventory of all medications. All medications dispensed shall be recorded in the patient record [postcondition]. The system shall create an order for additional medications, and submit in accordance with hospital policy. The system shall interface with admissions [relation that may be one or more interactions] for when a patient is admitted to the hospital.

When a patient is admitted to the hospital [the following are postcondition actions] a notification shall be sent to the appropriate persons and associated systems involved with admission and their computer systems: nursing staff, physician, cafeteria, hospital room assignment staff, and so forth.

All patient records shall be kept online for ready access. Updates to patient records shall be made within 24 hours for any hospital- or hospital-physician–provided treatment [policy and invariant]. Access to patient records shall be provided on a 24-hour, 7-day-a-week basis [policy and invariant], to anyone authorized to access those records [precondition].

The system shall provide 24-hour access service for records [policy] throughout the hospital. The integrity of the data shall be verified. Authorized access to the system shall be verified.

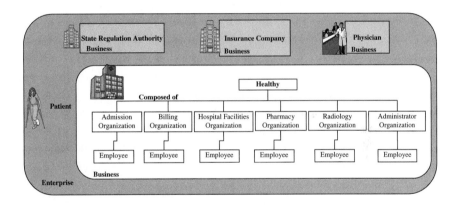

FIGURE 2.7   Healthy Hospital Business Example

The Healthy Hospital business is an enterprise [community] of different organizations, each of which has a software system. These organizations have a number of relationships [interactions] to other businesses (state regulation authority, insurance company, physician practices) and the patient. However, the external business system [environment] is not defined. Only the relation between Healthy's organization system and the external system is defined.

Healthy has a number of organizational objectives [scope and objectives]: the business of billing, the business of patient admission, the business of radiology treatments, the business of scheduling, the business of relating to all the other enterprises, and so forth. Further, Healthy Hospital consists of employees, medical equipment, medications, patients, physicians, as well as a system [roles].

The rules of engagement [contract] among the business organizations within Healthy and external to Healthy [environment] are defined.

Figure 2.8 shows what might be some of the entities of Healthy community, and some of their relationships, based on the sidebar description of this community. This figure does not represent a specification; it represents a visualization of what might be written down in a formal document, or represented in a visualization tool that has related the constructs of RM-ODP to the constructs of the tool.

In terms of the systems, the software performs functions, constrained by the business rules [behavior defined by the policies, preconditions, postconditions, and invariants].

Any policy [policy] or business code [contract or policy] that affects the business is specified. Sometimes a business wants to be sure certain things happen first [precondition], or certain things happen afterwards [postcondition]. These are specified as well.

The way the system is to behave, then, in the context of Healthy, is the set of preconditions, postconditions, policies, contracts, and any other constraints, such as what must always be true [invariant], and constraints on the actions performed.

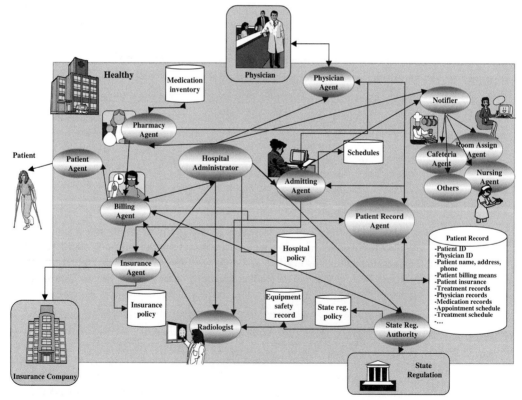

FIGURE 2.8   Configuration of Entities in the Healthy Community

With respect to this example, insufficient detail about the processes among the entities is provided. Insufficient detail is provided as to how the state regulation policy, hospital policy, and insurance policy relate; in other words, what their priorities are in case of a conflict. For example, it is unclear which entity processes and ensures adherence to a policy. There appears to be no relationship with the notifier and any other entity in the business. The format of the insurance bill to submit is not provided. The state regulations to be enforced are not provided. The details of the interface to the physician are not provided. The details of the format to provide a reminder of scheduled treatments to the patient are not provided. Therefore, only a partial specification can be created at this point.

The relations need to be better specified for the Healthy business because they relate the entities within Healthy, as well as the relation between Healthy and the insurance company, physician organization, and state regulation organization.

A business specification will also define information and information processing across the business, independent of actual interfaces or databases or any other implementation mechanism. Hence, the content of the patient record will be specified in detail.

These examples of insufficient enterprise business specification identify holes in the requirements specification. This shows that there is iteration between the requirements specifier and the architect, to obtain sufficient requirements detail to fully specify the architecture of a system.

Some of the RM-ODP business specification rules include:

▶ Each business is formed to meet a set of objectives.

▶ Each business has a scope, which defines the business organizations, configuration of the system software entities, which are coarse-grain, and the set of actions to be performed by the software entities.

▶ An objective of the business may be fulfilled by a software entity, and is identified as such.

▶ Policies and codes govern the behavior of the software entities and are specified.

An RM-ODP business specification can be written in English text, and can be modeled using a visual modeling tool (such as the Unified Model Language (UML) [Quatrani-98, UML-1.3, Fowler-97, OMG-UML-97, Booch-98, Rumbaugh-99]). RM-ODP does not address how the specification is captured, but rather what should be captured.

The business specification consists of:

▶ A scope that must be satisfied and that defines the situation in which the specification can be used (for possible reuse considerations)

▶ Business objectives

▶ Specification of all software entities and business organizations of interest, both internal and external

- ▶ Definition of all software entities of interest in the business, and the actions they perform
- ▶ Definition of all software resources, such as the patient record, and the actions performed on them
- ▶ Specification of all policies, contracts, preconditions, and postconditions
- ▶ A description of the external organizations with which the system being specified will work, along with the system's relationship to them

After the initial business specification is defined, the customer may decide there are more entities, relationships, and behavior aspects that need to be included. Hence, the business specification will probably go through several iterations to get to a full specification. Once accomplished, that specification has sufficient information for the architect, in the language of the RM-ODP, to then proceed to further refine the business specification into a working system architecture specification. And that, after all, is the objective.

2.6   RM-ODP ELEMENTS FOR USE

RM-ODP is an elegant model in the sense that it identifies the top priorities for architectural specifications and provides a minimal set of requirements, which are adequate to assure system integrity.

RM-ODP contains many concept *definitions* which are essential to the concepts for object-oriented architectures. These concepts and rules formulate the language of distributed processing.

Not only are these precise concepts for specifying the architecture, but also herein are terms defined at an international level of agreement (no small task!). They do not need to be redefined; they have been defined and can be reused. This is a major feat that was accomplished in the development of RM-ODP.

RM-ODP contains *specification rules*. These are essential in defining how the system will work in the business enterprise, how the system will support the users and needs of the enterprise, formulating parts of the architecture from subparts, focusing in on some critical aspect of the architecture for understanding how the system should work (temporarily ignoring other aspects), defining the behavior expected and desired out of the system, and providing the means to "plug and play" parts of a system.

Although RM-ODP defines the use of *object-oriented techniques* for specifying an architecture, the resultant system need not be constructed only of object-oriented constructs. For example, part of the architecture specification could include the use of a Web browser as a client to a Web server, using Web-based protocols to communicate Web pages of information. The business objective may be to provide an electronic commerce system to allow for ordering of medical equipment online. The user is presented with Web pages, the server receives requests from the user for orders, which might make use of a security mechanism such as encryption, and the order is placed. The specification of this system, in terms of RM-ODP, takes on an object-oriented flavor, but the implementation does not (necessarily).

RM-ODP defines *five standard viewpoints*. Because it is difficult, if not impossible, to capture all aspects of an architecture in a single description, RM-ODP defines essential constructs for an architecture and an approach for the use of these constructs in terms of viewpoints. They pick up different information about the system. The RM-ODP viewpoints enable the separation of concerns that divide the business and logical functionality of the system from the distributed computing and commercial technology decisions of the architecture. The viewpoints of RM-ODP provide three important capabilities:

1. The independence of the business and architecture specification from technologies allows evolving technologies to be incorporated into the system without impacting the overall architectural constraints.

2. The architecture specification provides the criteria by which the product can be selected.

3. The architecture specification can be created to be visionary, in which case as products evolve and are included in the system, what has yet to be accomplished is known and defined in the architecture specification. Further, as a product is selected, the selection criteria include consideration for the future, which may provide invaluable criteria in a product selection. An example of this very important point is a fault-tolerant capability for some part of the infrastructure.

The viewpoint provides descriptions that address the questions and needs of particular stakeholders in the system. The enterprise viewpoint addresses the business enterprise: the reason for the system. The computational viewpoint addresses the application. The engineering viewpoint addresses how the system is distributed and supported by distribution mechanisms (e.g., middleware). The technology viewpoint addresses the technologies and products that implement the system. And the information viewpoint addresses the information in the system, as well as the manner in which the system is to behave. The viewpoints each have different interests in the system at hand, different requirements from that system and different evaluation criteria; therefore they contain different information and have different specifications for the system. The four viewpoints (enterprise, information, computational, and engineering) are independent of specific implementations. In other words, the majority of the architectural specification is independent of the specific product selections which are used to implement the system. An overview of the viewpoints on the system, as specified by RM-ODP, is shown in Figure 2.9 .

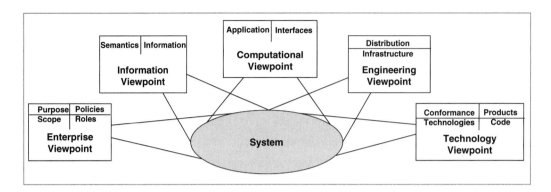

FIGURE 2.9   RM-ODP Viewpoints

Further, the viewpoints can be used in any order and can be nested, and not all of the viewpoints are required—only those that make sense to achieve a precise specification. This latter point is crucial in inserting new requirements, or new designs from a modernized system, or a new technology. For example, Figure 2.10 provides an enterprise lifecycle approach to using RM-ODP. It shows three cases: one is specifying the entire system; one is incorporating a transitional or modernized system, or a new technology; and one is incorporating incremental system parts. The viewpoints are shown in the first case, associated with the process. In each case, it is possible that not all viewpoints are used, or are used in a different order. In all cases, the use of the viewpoints is not ordered (although it appears as such in the figure). It is whatever the architect needs to do to architect.

By standardizing five viewpoints, RM-ODP claims that these five perspectives are sufficient for resolving both business functionality and distributed systems issues in the architecture and design of a distributed processing system.

Only the enterprise viewpoint, by the way, was shown in the Healthy Hospital community example. If any of the organizations, for example, that form a part of the hospital were geographically distant, a technology specification would define this. If any of the entities of the Healthy community were in need of further detail, the computational specification would be used. Although these viewpoints are defined separately, they are intended to be used collectively. The computational viewpoint provides the application view of the system. The engineering and technology viewpoints provide the virtual machine for the system—the application components use of and support by the infrastructure that is specified.

The enterprise and information viewpoints are views of the business. The enterprise, information, and computational viewpoints are not concerned with either distribution or implementation. The computational viewpoint must, however, define aspects of the architecture that enable distribution. The engineering viewpoint defines the designs for the infrastructure, how software is distributed,

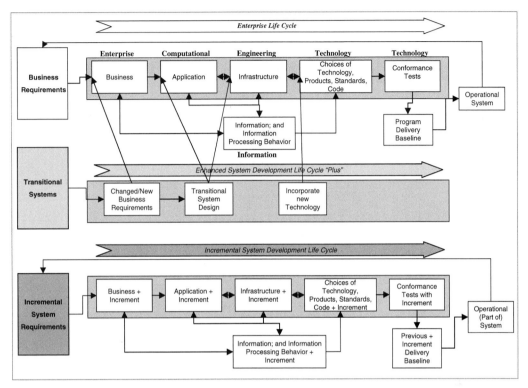

FIGURE 2.10   Enterprise Lifecycle Approach Using RM-ODP Viewpoints

what communication capabilities are provided, the qualities of service that are needed, the external communication, distribution transparencies[2], and so forth.

Many systems today break or are very costly due to the details that need to be coded into their interfaces. When a user or application chooses to interface to another application, the application developer can "hard-code" in the exact network address of the intended receiver. Doing this for every possible receiver results in a very brittle, point-to-point system, that is not only costly to create, but costly to maintain. RM-ODP provides a framework about interfaces that separates an interface into separate parts, each of which provide some aspect of interfacing, but allow much of it to be discovered at runtime. This offloads the development required in the application code, and enables a great deal of interface reuse.

---

2. Distribution transparencies are capabilities in the infrastructure that hide the impact or effects of distribution from the user, application developer, or system developer. An example is a Web server that "transparently" finds the right Web page to present to the user.

Consistency across the viewpoints is important for tracing business requirements generation to system implementation. Further, consistency enables analyses
of an architecture specification. A consistent set of models collectively provide an
architecture specification of *a system*.

RM-ODP is *not just* a set of viewpoints, such as those that many current
architecture methods include today. Rather, it's a set of distributed processing terms and rules for structuring and specifying an architecture. It provides
the ability to architect a system, not merely depict the architecture of a system in a graphical tool. In order to achieve an architecture specification of
a system that works and behaves as expected by the customer, all the rules
of RM-ODP are used throughout the viewpoints. The viewpoints only provide a separation of all the distributed processing concerns to focus on in
order to minimize having to deal with all the complexities of a distributed
system all at once. It is the precise terminology, and the architecture rules
that provide a process of architecting.

Another important point about consistency is that it enables geographically
distant multi-organizations to independently specify different parts of the architecture, and implement different parts of the system separately. This is achievable
because of the rules of consistency across the specifications that will enable them
to compose into a single specification, or be realized into a single system. This is
a powerful capability for current needs in the architecture of systems.

Today's environment addresses large-scale systems of systems, wherein different organizations must build architecture specifications for a part of the overall
system. Bringing those parts together and ensuring they fit together is problematic.
It amounts to a system engineering "mismatch." Using an architecture specification suite of languages, as is provided by the RM-ODP viewpoint languages, coupled with consistency rules across those viewpoints, greatly enhances the ability
to accomplish this goal.

Using RM-ODP, some organizations are successfully specifying systems of
systems. The primary customer organization defines the enterprise specification
for the business, along with the information specification of the processing of the
system. Contractors are engaged to further refine these specifications to a computational and engineering specification, possibly also using the "tools" of the full
viewpoint languages. Another contractor is engaged to implement the specification to a working system. And the customer organization then tests the conformance of the system implemented to the specification. The changes to the semantics
of the processing are managed by the customer organization through the information language. This is depicted in Figure 2.11. The shaded viewpoint behind the
primary viewpoint is suggestive of what other viewpoint may be used, or one from
which the primary viewpoint may need input. In addition, at the far right of the
figure is a possible use in terms of the Healthy Hospital case.

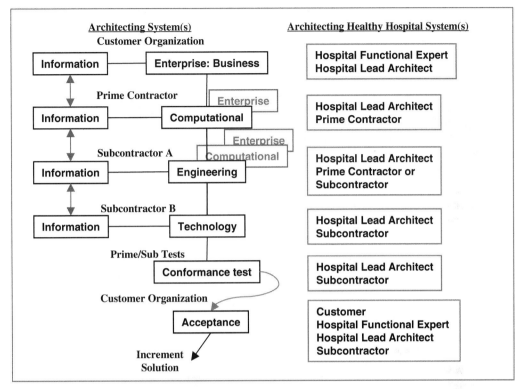

FIGURE 2.11   Cross-Organizational Approach to Architecture Specification

One of the most important features of RM-ODP is its definitions and rules; these enable *conformance* testing of the implemented system to the architecture specification. After all, what is the purpose of architectural specification unless conformance of the implemented system can be assessed to the architecture? RM-ODP defines rules of consistency across the specifications, which in turn support the process of conformance testing, and the analysis of the results, which can then be part of the conformance test plan.

2.7   PREREQUISITE SKILL BASE

The architect skill base needs to include knowledge of how to reason abstractly, how to specify, and knowledge about the current technologies. These are merely listed here, and further expanded in the next chapter. As a manager, however, it is wise to ensure that the architect(s) chosen are, in fact, cognizant of these areas.

The prerequisite knowledge for an architect includes:

▶ Specific business domain knowledge, such as the terminology and meaning from the domain (e.g., *radiologist* in a medical domain), and the ability to relate the domain-specific language to the architecture specification language

▶ Distributed processing

▶ Distributed processing principles, such as enterprise-wide naming, policy administration, system administration, security, distribution, remoteness, and so forth

▶ Architecture specification principles, such as abstraction, refinement, composition, modeling, and so forth

▶ Technologies, such as object modeling, products, standards, and tools like UML

▶ Testing

If these skills are not readily available in the architecture personnel, training will be required. The architect must have a working knowledge of these concepts to architect.

2.8   INVESTMENT NEEDED

The investment required to use RM-ODP includes, first and foremost, management approval. Along with management approval comes the necessary resource allocation in terms of personnel and cost. Establishing the schedule and milestones paves the way for the architect to conduct the architecting process.

Management should recognize that there are up-front costs in the development of an architecture specification. This cannot be overemphasized. "If a project has not achieved a system architecture, including its rationale, the project should not proceed to full-scale system development. Specifying the architecture as a deliverable enables its use throughout the development and maintenance process." [Boehm-95]

The types of reviews required for the RM-ODP approach are lessened. Since the process of architecting is to refine a specification into more and more detail, as the architect completes a specification of a part of the system, a review of the incremental additions to the specification can be conducted. Formal reviews of software requirements, preliminary design, full-scale design, etc., are really not necessary. The reason is that adherence to the rules of RM-ODP ensures a consistency from the business specification all the way through testing. The architect cannot deviate from the business specification without violating the RM-ODP rules.

The architect can detect where a particular business requirement will lead to an unmanageable system, or a costly system. The architect can ascertain that a choice of products for realizing the system is available. In this case, the architect needs to inform the management team that a cost analysis of the product selection may be in order. The process should then be to input such risks into the management process for decision making.

A collaborative tool capability that ties together the management and architecture teams is very useful. One that provides negotiation of requirements, infusing any changed requirements into the specification, requirements costing analysis, commercial product tradeoff analyses, and testing analysis is available through the WinWin Web-based collaboration tool from the University of Southern California, under the management of Professor Barry Boehm. WinWin [WinWin, Boehm-97, Boehm-98, Boehm-99] and its extended Model-Based (System) Architecting and Software Engineering (MBASE) tool is a toolkit that aids in the capture, negotiation, and coordination of requirements for a large system. It executes in a Web environment. It supports stakeholders in identifying, discussing, refining, and resolving conflicts in requirements, architecture, and product choice decisions. WinWin contains tools for:

▶ Capturing the desires (win conditions) of the stakeholders

▶ Organizing the terminology so that stakeholders are using the same terms in the same way

▶ Expressing disagreements or issues needing resolution, offering options as potential solutions

▶ Negotiating agreements that resolve the issues

▶ Using third-party tools to enlighten or resolve issues

▶ Producing a requirements document that summarizes the current state of the proposed system

▶ Tracing requirements decisions

▶ Checking completeness and consistency of requirements

The MBASE tool includes WinWin as well as tools for commercial product analysis, architecture analysis, and much more. Though this tool is free from the university, a commercial product is emerging, that is more robust and features additional capabilities. More information can be found at http://sunset.usc.edu.

The architecture team should comprise a small number of individuals. The team must either have the skills for architecting, as was previously discussed, or be trained accordingly. It is essential to have well-trained engineers to conduct the architecture, implementation, and testing processes, all part of RM-ODP specifications. Investment in the correct skill categories of these persons is critical.

As was discussed previously, the team can be geographically distant, each contributing to a part of the overall architecture specification. This is a management decision. However the team is constructed, there should be a lead architect who can mediate decisions, ensure adherence to RM-ODP rules, and combine the different specifications into one. A view of this for the Healthy Hospital example was shown in Figure 2.11.

Experience in using RM-ODP has shown that the architecting process is about a 3–4 month effort for a medium-sized single business, and longer (up to two years) for an enterprise-wide distributed system of systems. Again, incremental solutions can be strategized, reducing the time to market of some capability, followed by more capability over time. The manager and architect should collectively define this strategy; the manager comes from the business perspective, and the architect offers the IT perspective in terms of risk and appropriate risk mitigation.

When the architecture specification is completed for the full system, or a part of it, the following are also precisely defined:

▶ Business specification
▶ All behavior of the system at all points in the system
▶ Software that forms the operational system
▶ The distribution transparencies that form a part of the operational system
▶ All the interfaces, bindings, protocols, and connections
▶ The information that flows in the system
▶ All quality of service requirements and mechanisms to achieve it
▶ All control objects, and the actions they perform for a well-behaved system
▶ All policies and how they are achieved
▶ Any replication required
▶ Any fault tolerance required
▶ Any migratability or mobile software capabilities
▶ All aspects of the operational system that are dynamically determined
▶ All data schema
▶ All presentations to the end user
▶ All conformance test points, and the information to be tested for
▶ All software-to-computer topologies
▶ All network topologies
▶ All standards, technologies, products, and developed code used and where they reside
▶ All conformance test plans

2.9   SUMMARY

Business needs must drive the need for and specification of the system, which exists to solve a business problem. A business specification should not only account for the system, but also the real-world entities in the business. RM-ODP enables the specification of a business to include real-world entities (humans, machines, equipment, etc.), specification of a system to support the business, and a specification of how the system works within the business.

Software engineering and architecture are still required to build a system. Business experts must work with the architect to realize a precise specification of a solution.

In systems, a vision of what is wanted may not be realized for some time. The manager has a choice to either specify the "visionary" system, or to partially specify the "visionary" system in terms of business requirements, or to partially specify a part of the system incrementally over time. In addition, in most systems, there is a need to constantly enhance to meet changing requirements. Therefore, the architecture must evolve to meet the changes.

The cost of an architecture, which is an up-front cost, minimizes the overall lifecycle cost, enables a rapid schedule to market, and increases the technical performance of the system. However, managers should be sure that the architecture provided is not just a visual depiction with boxes and lines; too many interpretations can result, which in turn results in a poor architecture. Instead, providing a formal, consistent, conformance-tested specification will result in a better product.

An achitecture team skilled in distributed processing is essential for success. A tool will not replace a precise architecture specification; it will aid in developing it.

RM-ODP provides all of this, and more. RM-ODP has broad application and is used in a number of commercial environments because it is effective and beneficial for specifying distributed systems that work.

T H R E E

RM-ODP ARCHITECT'S PRIMER

In this introductory chapter to the Reference Model of Open Distributed Processing (RM-ODP), highlights of RM-ODP are discussed. This chapter introduces the motivation for RM-ODP, and discusses why the architect should consider its use in architecting a system. Following chapters will discuss these topics in more depth.

This chapter discusses:

- ▶ More about RM-ODP for an architect
- ▶ Overview of RM-ODP architecting techniques
- ▶ How to use RM-ODP in creating an architecture specification
- ▶ How RM-ODP relates to a distributed processing system and to an architecture
- ▶ What knowledge is prerequisite

3.1   MORE ABOUT RM-ODP

RM-ODP is an internationally agreed-upon object-based architecture standard for use in architecting distributed systems. The standard provides mechanisms to architect distributed processing software systems and distributed information, and to support the integration and interoperation of applications in a reliable and consistent manner, across a heterogeneity of enterprise rules, software, protocols, programming languages, component-based frameworks, computers, and networks. RM-ODP provides a rich, precisely defined set of distributed processing concepts for architecting systems that depend upon distributed processing, as well as a rich set of techniques to use in specifying the architecture.

RM-ODP provides:

▶ A guide for architects to specify distributed software systems; this is based on object modeling, which is relevant to the practices of systems architects

▶ A set of precise concepts and structuring rules used for development of a system specification

▶ A set of separate interrelated viewpoint specifications used for specification of open distributed systems

▶ A system conformance testing framework

▶ A distribution transparency framework

▶ A set of functions specific to the system infrastructure that supports the capabilities of the distribution transparencies

▶ An overall framework for development of additional standards under the RM-ODP initiative that are related to open distributed processing

A system can be an enterprise-wide system of systems, a large information processing system, or a major component of another system, such as data. Any of the rules of architecting apply to any such "system."

Consider the example in Figure 3.1. With RM-ODP, all rules could apply to the Data Broker component. Once specified, it becomes an object in the Org B architecture specification. Once Org B is specified, it becomes an object in the Enterprise architecture specification. These levels of abstraction and concepts of composition and refinement are exceedingly important in RM-ODP and pervade all aspects of architecting, as will be discussed later.

Capturing the needs of the stakeholders of the information processing system in such a way as to reflect these needs into system requirements has long been a problem in technology transfer of knowledge. That is, the stakeholders[1] state their requirements in a language particular to a functional or organizational domain (e.g., finance). The system designers (system engineers, software engineers, architects, implementers, and testers) discuss system capabilities in terms of information technology language. Often these needs and capabilities are misunderstood, due to differences in the language of discourse. RM-ODP facilitates communication by capturing, in its *enterprise* model, aspects particular to an enterprise. Additionally, RM-ODP provides all of the concepts and rules needed to transform these aspects into other models applicable to the system semantics, information, and processing.

---

1. *Stakeholder* is a term used here to represent any customer, user, owner, administrator, acquisition authority, or program manager.

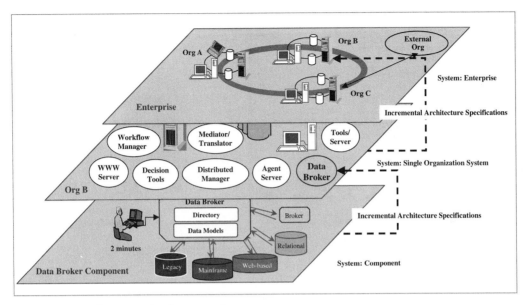

FIGURE 3.1 Different Kinds of "Systems"

RM-ODP describes how to capture the needs of the stakeholders, how to capture the information processing semantics, how to specify the components, interactions, and constraints of the system, and how to select products and technologies to realize the system. These are all different areas of focus on the system. These are all described in RM-ODP in a consistent manner so that decisions made in one area of focus are reflected in other areas.

RM-ODP uses object-based constructs to help system architects specify complex software-intensive architectures. But it goes further. It also provides precise rules to relate what the customer wants of a system, how the system should function in support of the customer needs, and how to relate all of this to the current technology and products of the day, through a set of viewpoints.

Figure 3.2 provides an overview of the concepts of RM-ODP and how they relate. These are further discussed below.

An architecture specification is precise. It clearly defines all aspects (of interest) of the distributed processing system. The specification generally results from abstract concepts, at various levels of detail, which are themselves precisely defined and constructed in accordance with well-defined rules.

RM-ODP provides terminology about distributed processing that has achieved international agreement, consistently defined throughout the development lifecycle. It also specifies the process of how to use the terms in an explicit, precise manner so that the resulting specifications will be precise, understandable, and consistent, not "intuitive."

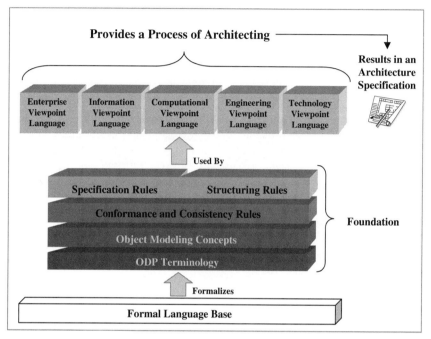

FIGURE 3.2   Overview of RM-ODP Concepts

A warm fuzzy feeling is not a specification. The precise specification that results can be refined into more and more detail, until a well-performed technical solution is realized as derived (refined) from the business specification.

The RM-ODP rules are categorized into basic rules, object modeling rules, structuring rules, specification rules, and conformance rules. The concepts and rules form the foundation of RM-ODP. The use of this foundation provides a process of architecting that comes along with precise terminology and rules that apply throughout the entire architecting process.

The *basic rules* are used throughout all the specifications. They address distributed processing, information, data, and what constitutes an open distributed processing (ODP) system. Further, these rules include abstraction, a very important concept in any architecting endeavor.

The *object model rules* are used to construct the architecture, in terms of objects, interfaces, state, and other elements. Each architecture specification is constructed in terms of an object-based model.

The *structuring rules* are used along with the object model and basic rules. They include how to address distribution, what constitutes a contract, what constitutes a policy, what is a group of objects, how to describe the behavior of a binding between interfaces, and so forth. These are the "hows" of a specification, based in object terminology and extended distributed processing terminology.

The *specification rules* are used to provide a consistent set of viewpoint specifications. The rules discuss how to compose, what a composition and component are, and how they are related. Further, these rules address how to specify behavior, interface signature, binding, and so forth.

Conformance rules discuss the conformance testing process and the points where conformance testing can occur. These apply throughout the viewpoint specifications as well.

In principle, one can create a specification of a system by taking a single view of the system. Often, though, the system is large and complex. The result can be a system description that is too complex to accomplish and too cluttered to understand. One of the key uses of RM-ODP is to address the architecture of a system from separate aspects of concern, called viewpoints. RM-ODP provides the ability to separate business application functionality from distributed system complexity, and distributed system complexity from choices of technology and products. This is accomplished by the use of the RM-ODP viewpoints, in conjunction with the rules discussed above. That is, *viewpoints* separate the areas of concern of the system into manageable parts to specify the architecture. The RM-ODP viewpoints fully capture an architecture specification of a system.

RM-ODP provides this separation of concerns of a system into five *viewpoints*: enterprise, information, computational, engineering, and technology. Each viewpoint captures certain concerns about *the entire system* from that viewpoint. Each of the viewpoints addresses certain aspects of distributed processing: how the user uses the system, how the policies of the organization affect the functioning of the system, how the designer selects current technology, how the tester ensures a correct implementation to the specification, and so forth.

The viewpoints are not layered. No viewpoint is more important than any other. They all provide a view of the same system, but each is focused on a different aspect of the system. These viewpoints are separate, but interrelated and consistent. Each viewpoint is defined in terms of a language, with defined concepts and structuring rules pertinent to that viewpoint language, all founded on an object model. An overview of the viewpoints and their purposes is shown in Figure 3.3.

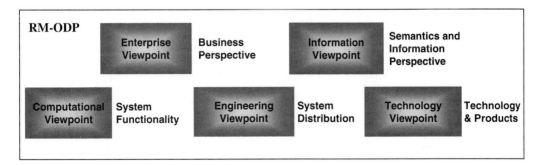

FIGURE 3.3 RM-ODP Viewpoints

RM-ODP facilitates communications with stakeholders and those involved in creating the system. The domain-specific needs are related to the elements of RM-ODP, such as a hospital (domain-specific) is a community (RM-ODP enterprise concept). The architect then uses the concepts of RM-ODP (community) and their relationships to other concepts to create an open specification that uses a well-defined distributed processing language to communicate exactly what is wanted. The problem of "what I meant was…" versus "what you understood was…" goes away. The resultant architecture specification is clear to all stakeholders. Further, because it has been so precisely defined, parts of the architecture specification can be reused as an architecture or design pattern. Parts of the working system can also be reused as plug-in components (or subsystems). All of these are doable because of the use of precisely defined "open" constructs, with well-defined terminology, and rules to explicitly define the system.

RM-ODP is one of the hallmark standards of the International Organization for Standardization (ISO) and the International Telecommunications Union (ITU). It is a foundation for any distributed processing system architecture.

Creating a standard such as RM-ODP is an international accomplishment. Developing shared terminology and ideas for what needs to be specified (such as partitioning the work of architecting into five viewpoints) is a theoretical idea that can be very powerful when used, but that use is not as simple as picking up an editing tool and "doing it." The emphasis here is on what needs to be accomplished in order to build an architecture specification. RM-ODP provides a systematic methodology for gathering knowledge from a variety of stakeholders and information technologists. This is accomplished using the viewpoints. For engineered systems, this can include users, operators, developers, and maintainers. For service industries, this can include not only operators, developers, maintainers, but domain-specific users such as patients, teachers, students, and doctors in the medical domain.

The RM-ODP concepts are not only precisely defined but also general. As such they are also abstract. They need to be understood in terms of the process of architecting and distributed processing. They do "work," but only if a talented software engineering effort (hopefully supported by good tools) is applied. The positive side is that the concepts are already defined for use, the architect does not need to redefine them first, and the concepts allow for higher precision in a specification—which is what architecting is about.

3.2   RM-ODP CONCEPTS AND TECHNIQUES FOR USE

RM-ODP is a precisely defined reference model that can be used for any distributed processing system. Its proper use can help ensure a well-formed, precise specification of an architecture, with consistent architectural concepts. Because of the rules and consistency, incremental additions to the system can be easily inserted into the architecture specification, generating technological solutions that are composable with the existing system. And this is generally a requirement by the customer of the architect: cost savings, reduced time to market, incremental evolution, and evolvability with emerging technology.

The concepts and techniques for specifying an architecture can be thought of in terms of three fundamental parts:

▶ Techniques of specification (that can apply to many things, not just distributed processing)
▶ The language of distributed processing
▶ The techniques of conformance testing

Architecture applies to many things, not just distributed processing systems. The specification techniques defined in terms of a set of rules are general and can actually apply to other things, such as how a heart works, or how a business is to be organized. However, in order to apply the specification techniques, a language of the area of interest is required. For example, the language of aorta valves, hypertension, arteries, veins, and so forth applies to the functioning of a heart; but the specification techniques can apply to whatever domain is of interest.

In RM-ODP, the language of distributed processing is defined. The viewpoints are defined in terms of this language, to enable focusing in on small parts of the topic (distributed processing) to create the specification. Because distributed processing pervades many business domains, relating the terms of distribution to those specific to the domain can aid the understanding of the architecture specification, though this is not required. For example, "Healthy Hospital Business Requirements" on page 58 deals with a "billing system," a "patient agent," and so forth. In RM-ODP, these are "objects that assume a role." Mapping the RM-ODP terms to the hospital terms aids the understanding of the architecture specification.

Keeping this in mind helps one to understand how all these foundational aspects of RM-ODP work together to formulate an architecture specification of a distributed processing system. Figure 3.4 provides a representation of how these aspects are related.

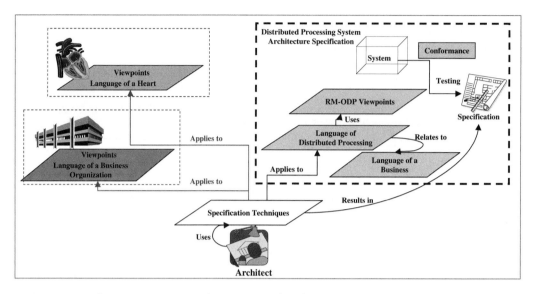

FIGURE 3.4   Relating RM-ODP Use of Concepts and Techniques

Each of the concepts and techniques defined by RM-ODP are covered in this section, at a high level. The remainder of this book covers these topics in more depth.

3.2.1   CONCEPTS

A common ontology (the set of defined concepts and rules of structure) is essential and powerful. It provides the power of clear communication. It provides the power of clear specification for what needs to be captured (such as interfaces). But using such precise terms and associated concepts for structuring are also difficult because of the generality involved, and therefore require skills in software engineering and abstract reasoning.

The terms are structured along the lines shown in Table 3.1 and are defined in the remainder of the book. Hence, this table provides all the terms without the definition, at this point, to show what each category covers and precisely defines.

TABLE 3.1 Concepts

CATEGORY	PURPOSE	CONCEPTS (TERMS)
Basic concepts	Used throughout	Distributed Processing, Open Distributed Processing, ODP System, Information, Data, and Viewpoint
Basic interpretation and linguistic concepts	Provide the concepts of interpretation of the models constructed from the RM-ODP language	Entity, Proposition, Abstraction, Atomicity, System, Architecture, Term, Sentence
Basic object model concepts	Used in building the architecture	Object, Environment, Action, Interface, Activity, Behavior, State, Communication, Location in space, Location in time, Interaction point
Specification concepts	Used across all the viewpoint languages to provide a consistent set of specifications from each viewpoint; Forms a part of the overall architecture specification	Composition, Decomposition, Composite object, Behavioral compatibility, Refinement, Trace, Type, Class, Subtype/supertype, Subclass/superclass, Template, Interface signature, Instantiation, Role, Creation, Introduction, Deletion, Instance, Template type, Template class, Derived class/base class, Invariant, Precondition, Postcondition
Structuring concepts	Used in conjunction with the basic concepts, basic interpretation concepts, object model and specification concepts to provide viewpoint-specific specifications; Used to address distribution	Group, Configuration, Domain, Subdomain, Epoch, Reference point, Conformance point, Transparencies, Contract, Quality of service, Environment contract, Obligation, Permission, Prohibition, Policy, Persistence, Isochronicity, Name, Identifier, Name space, Naming context, Naming action, Naming domain, Naming graph, Name resolution, Activity structure, Chain (of actions), Thread, Joining action, Dividing action, Forking action, Spawn action, Head action, Subactivity, Establishing behavior, Enabled behavior, Contractual context, Liaison, Terminating behavior, Causality, Binding behavior, Binding, Binding precondition, Unbinding behavior, Trading, Failure, Error, Fault, Stability, Application management, Communication management, Management information, Managed role, Managing role, Notification
Conformance	Used for testing of conformance	Conformance to ODP standards, Compliance, Consistency, Correspondence, Testing, Reference points, Programmatic reference point, Perceptual reference point, Interworking reference point, Interchange reference point, Change of configuration, Portability, Migratability, Conformance testing process, Result of testing, Implementer role, Tester role, Relation between reference points

In addition, the five viewpoints include such terms as:

▶ Enterprise—objects, policy, purpose, scope, action, community, process, step, and others

▶ Computational—objects, interaction, binding, signal, client, server, producer, consumer, interface, and others

▶ Engineering—objects, interface, binding, communication, transparencies, functions, channel, node, management, and others

▶ Information—objects, invariant schema, dynamic schema, static schema

▶ Technology—conformance points for testing

The terminology for use includes terms not only from RM-ODP but also additional terms from the General Relationship Model (GRM) [ISO GRM, ITU-GRM], which is another international standard. GRM provides a suite of concepts that enhance and interrelate to those of RM-ODP. An example is a further explanation and expansion of the term "invariant." In addition, the new Enterprise Viewpoint international standard [ISO-EntVP], not yet fully formalized, adds terms for specifying a business, to include such terms as community, process, step, and further expansion of other enterprise viewpoint terms.

3.2.2   SPECIFICATION RULES

The rules of specification include precision, abstraction, and composition. *Precision* means that something is well-defined, unambiguous, and consistent with other definitions. This includes the business rules, the properties of the business, the policies of the business, and the scope and objectives of the business. Precision is about how well something is defined—not how well something is detailed with attributes. At each level of detail, everything should be defined "precisely," whether the thing is the organization of a business, the details of an interface, or the specifications of a billing system used by the business.

Abstraction is a process of simplifiying. It is a key principle of specification. It provides a structure to a set of specifications that enhances understanding at each level. It allows key aspects of something to be addressed at one level, ignoring the details at a different level. Abstraction means that the customer does not need to worry about a bunch of things irrelevant to the specification of the business "language," such as what information technology terms to use.

"One of the key principles of RM-ODP is abstraction. People sometimes confuse the term abstraction with the common notion of being abstract or obtuse. In actuality, the process of abstraction is anything but obtuse—it is specifically designed to enhance, not frustrate, understanding. In RM-ODP, the purpose of abstraction is to provide a logical structure to a set of specifications by dealing first in the key aspects...and progressively pushing the rest to the lower levels of abstraction..." [Kilov-99] That is, the customer can define the business in terms that enhance understanding. Enhanced understanding leads to a better architecture specification and system solution. The business is specified in terms understandable by the customer (such as "the hospital must submit a bill to the insurance company within 10 days"). The architect then takes the specification and further refines it to a system specification (such as a component that performs the calculations of a bill, a constraint on the interface of the component that it must meet the quality of service = 24 hours, or the interface binding to the insurance company to provide the bill).

For example, at one level of abstraction, a hospital admitting procedure is specified with respect to how it works with hospital billing and patient care. At a more detailed level, the interfaces to the database are defined, the interfaces to the patient records are defined, the manner of submitting the bill to the insurance company is defined, and so forth. Abstraction levels are progressively refined through more and more levels of detail, until the system is finally fully specified. Since the terms in RM-ODP are consistently defined, and since the rules of using the terms are consistent, abstraction coupled with further refinements results in consistent specifications.

POINT All levels of abstraction need to be precisely defined. It is important to realize that the higher levels of abstraction need to be more precisely defined than the lower levels. The reason is that once imprecision sets in at a level of abstraction, it then generally affects all lower levels of abstraction. [Kilov-99] In the case of a business specification, it is exceedingly important to precisely define what the business rules are. Imprecision at this point will probably lead to a solution that is neither workable nor wanted by the customer.

A *composition* is a combination of entities that results in a new entity, at a different level of abstraction. That is, a composition is a grouping of entities that can be addressed as a single entity. One example of a composition is the collection of all employees in a department. Another example is the collection of all "database objects" in a "data store object." The "data store object" might be specified as an object at one level of abstraction, whereas each of the component "database objects" are specified at a lower level of abstraction. Composition is important in the business specification. A community can be a composition of other communities. They may be related in different ways, with cross-references between them. One community may be a refinement of another, or perhaps a community may be a specification for a community that is a refinement.

A relationship is "a collection of...objects together with an invariant referring to the properties of the...object." [ISO GRIM] An invariant defines what must be true during some timeframe of the relationship. For example, an invariant may state that the role constraints of a client/server relationship of the data store object are not violated. Hence the behavior of a relationship is defined by its invariants, preconditions, and postconditions.

3.2.3   OBJECT MODEL

RM-ODP defines a specific object model upon which everything else is based. This model is discussed in detail in "Essentials of the RM-ODP Object Model" on page 183. An *object* represents an entity. An *object state* is a condition of the object that determines the actions that object will next perform. This model is somewhat different from some other object models today; it is more capable. For example, in the object model for RM-ODP an object can have multiple interfaces. This model underlies the concepts "composition" and "component." An interface is part of the object model. An *interface* is an abstraction of the behavior of an object along with constraints. It includes a set of interactions.

3.2.4   VIEWPOINTS

Each of the five defined viewpoints is a form of abstraction, as discussed earlier. A viewpoint discusses the concerns of interest in specific concepts, along with structuring rules that apply to those concepts.

The following list provides the rules associated with the use of the RM-ODP viewpoints. These are discussed later in this section.

- Each viewpoint defines a set of concepts and allowable rules of structure
- Viewpoints are not layered
- Viewpoints address independent concerns
- Viewpoints are formal, founded on mathematical formal descriptions of predicate calculus
- Consistency across the viewpoints is defined
- Enterprise, information, and computational viewpoints are independent of distribution concerns
- Enterprise, information, computational, and engineering are independent of technology choices
- Conformance reference points are defined
- Viewpoints are based on the RM-ODP object model
- RM-ODP specification rules apply to the viewpoint
- RM-ODP structuring rules apply
- Viewpoints can be nested
- Viewpoints can use multiple levels of abstraction and refinement
- Viewpoints can use composition and decomposition
- Not all viewpoints are required for a given specification
- Combinations of viewpoints can provide different views of a system
- Additional viewpoints can be added

3.2.4.1 Synopsis

Enterprise Viewpoint. The enterprise viewpoint of RM-ODP takes the perspective of a business model. The enterprise models should be directly understandable by stakeholders (such as managers and end users) in the business environment. The enterprise viewpoint assures that the business needs are satisfied through the architecture and provides a specification that enables validation of these assertions with the end users.

This viewpoint is extremely useful to communicate the customer needs with the architect. It provides far more precise descriptions than, say, a Unified Modeling Language (UML) Use Case view. This viewpoint provides the customer the ability to define a policy such as, for example, "the state regulation policy for medical equipment has to be implemented in the system," or "our airline's policy is to overbook passenger seats to a maximum of 10 seats." These are "precisely" defined in the architecture. In UML, there is no concept of a "policy," though a policy can be represented as a class or a note or some other non-uniform manner.

Further, this viewpoint enables a customer to require a subsystem to be architected and implemented that will plug into an existing system. An example is "I have a legacy system that needs to work in my new system. Architect a means to do this." Or, "Architect something that will allow me to get to all the different databases in my system, and make it a part of my modernized system." Of course, it is the responsibility (and indeed the duty) of the developers to analyze and point out the probable impact of such proposed features on the rest of the architecture (e.g., greater complexity, cost).

This viewpoint can also be used for a subsystem part itself. Software tool vendors, for example, need to determine the scope and objectives of their tools. The parts that comprise a tool, coupled with their interactions (how that tool may interact with another tool), and the policies that apply are all part of an enterprise specification. This viewpoint sets the stage for further refinement of any software subsystem.

The terms used in this viewpoint include community, actor role, artefact role, purpose, scope, objectives, enterprise objects, interaction, process, task, policy, contract, environment, and environment contract.

Information Viewpoint. The information viewpoint defines the universe of discourse of the information system in two ways: the information content of the system, and the information about the processing of the system (its behavior).

The first is from the perspective a database model. The information viewpoint, in this case, is a logical representation of the data in the distributed system.

The second is from the perspective of the rules to be followed in the system, such as policies specified by the stakeholders, and then throughout the system in terms of how different components work together. For example, the information viewpoint provides constructs to define constraints of all aspects of the system (such as behavior), constraints defined by policy, rules of allowable changes in state, things that must always be true (invariants), as well as quality attributes, and information.

Examples of constraints on the system could be the policy of overbooking airline seats, the interpretation of the policy on medical equipment, or the way two components work together in the system. The information viewpoint also captures the valid states of the objects. Finally, it captures the actions that are allowed to change the state of an object.

The information viewpoint is very useful in capturing the semantics of the operational system. It identifies schemata to do this. This viewpoint is an object-based logical model of the information assets in the business and the constraints on how these assets are processed and manipulated.

The terms used in this viewpoint include information objects, static schema, dynamic schema, and invariant schema.

Computational Viewpoint. The computational viewpoint partitions the system into functional modules that perform the capabilities of the system and are capable of being distributed throughout the enterprise. The computational viewpoint takes the perspective of a designer of application components and program interfaces. This viewpoint is similar to many architecture representation models, such as the logical model of UML, or the designer's view from Zachman [Malveau].

The computational viewpoint captures the components and interface details, without regard to distribution (which is addressed in the engineering viewpoint). Therefore, the architect need not be concerned if the application is on a particular server, or if the client must use a particular set of protocols to interact with the server. Rather, it is the viewpoint on the functioning aspects of the system, not on the distribution or implementation aspects.

In particular, this is where the software subsystem boundaries are specified in terms of application program interfaces (APIs), however those subsystems are distributed (as specified in the engineering viewpoint). Generally, these boundaries are the architectural controls that assure that the system structure will embody the qualities of interoperability, portability, scalability, and distribution in management of complexities that are appropriate to meet changing business needs, and adaptability to incorporate evolving technology.

The terms used in this viewpoint include computational objects, interface, interface signature, interaction, interaction signature, environment contract, policy, binding, operation type interface (client/server), stream interface, signal interface, client, server, producer, consumer, initiator, responder, binding object, trader, and others.

Engineering Viewpoint. The engineering viewpoint exposes the distributed nature of the system, and provides standard definitions that enable abstract descriptions of engineering constraints. These engineering objects are capable of defining the characteristics of all forms of distributed infrastructure, including remote procedure calls, video teleconferencing, client/server communication, asynchronous interfaces for signaling, mobility of software and interfaces, multimedia, services providing fault tolerance, and so forth.

One of the engineering objects that RM-ODP defines is a binder, which forms the binding between interfaces. Another is a channel, composed of objects, one of which is the binder, and forms the full communication mechanism to tie together object interfaces. The engineering objects are capable of defining the characteristics of all forms of distributed infrastructure, including remote procedure calls, screening data interfaces, and asynchronous interfaces for signaling.

The perspective of the engineering viewpoint is similar to that of an operating system engineer or a networking engineer who is familiar with "thin clients" or "fat clients," Web servers, communication protocol stacks, and allocation issues that are necessary to define the distributed processing solutions for the distributed system.

The terms used in this viewpoint include engineering objects, interface reference, binding, channel, node, cluster, capsule, stub, binder, protocol, interceptor, relocator, migrator, checkpoint/recovery, failure, storage, node management, replicator, interface, policy, schema, and transparency.

Technology Viewpoint. The technology viewpoint serves two very important missions: to describe where to apply the technologies and products of choice, and to allow the conformance testing of the system implementation against its architectural specification. The technology viewpoint defines the mappings between the architected objects and interfaces to specific standards, technologies, product selections, and required developed code. The architecture specification provides the selection criteria for choices in this viewpoint.

The viewpoint defines four types of reference points that can be used as conformance test points. The reference point is a place where there is a set of interfaces. The four reference points for use as conformance test points are programmatic reference point, perceptual reference point, interworking reference point, and interchange reference point. Each conformance point defines the information to be observed during test, and how that information traces back through the architecture specification.

The perspective of this viewpoint is similar to that of an implementer who is familiar with the Web browser, the Web server, the communication between the two, the use of Enterprise JavaBeans™, network protocol standards, and other products to configure the information system.

3.2.4.2 Viewpoint Rules

The terms are not defined here, nor are the structuring rules that apply. Viewpoints are addressed in more depth in Chapter 6, "Separation of Concerns: Using RM-ODP Viewpoints." For now, let us say that viewpoints focus on a set of issues or concerns about a system, while reserving other concerns for later consideration.

Viewpoints are not layered, address independent concerns, are consistent, and support conformance testing. Each viewpoint is concerned with certain aspects of the system. Viewpoints are *not* layered; no one viewpoint depends directly upon any other, nor is one viewpoint used before another. They are independent in that they address different aspects of distributed processing.

However, they are also coordinated and as such do not stand alone. There are correspondences among the concepts of the different viewpoints that lead to consistency of the viewpoint specifications. An interface in one viewpoint, for example, corresponds to an interface in another viewpoint, but each addresses different considerations.

The information viewpoint, for example, captures the behavior of the system. Behavior affects everything. So the information viewpoint is coordinated with the remaining viewpoints. But it stands alone in the sense that the behavior is defined in that viewpoint alone. How the behavior is implemented, or how the behavior affects an interaction in a computational viewpoint, is where the coordination comes into play. That coordination is specified as part of the consistency rules, and correspondences among the parts of each viewpoint.

Further, all five RM-ODP viewpoints are co-equal in the sense that they each provide a complete model of the distributed system that is object based and corresponds to the other viewpoints. The RM-ODP viewpoints provide separation of concerns that divides the business and logical functionality of the system from the distributed computing and commercial technology decisions of the architecture.

With these viewpoints, a well-formed architectural specification can be created, which can result in a well-formed working system that can be tested for conformance.

Viewpoint Foundations. There are five viewpoint foundations: RM-ODP object model, specification rules, structuring rules, distribution independence, and technology independence. Each of these RM-ODP viewpoints is object based, based on the RM-ODP object model. They provide a complete model of the system from a given perspective of distributed processing (e.g., business perspective, behavioral perspective, engineering perspective).

Each viewpoint language consists of a small number of well-defined terms, based on formalisms whose detailed understanding is unnecessary. The language has no mathematical notion; English text can be used in relation to the viewpoint concepts. However, the RM-ODP concepts have been formally described in a mathematical language, to ensure a well-formed foundation. This has been accomplished, and need not be understood or used by the customer or architect. What this means is that statements of consistency and conformance are assured; they are not merely intuitive. Just knowing there is precision and a mathematical foundation is conducive to doing the analysis, consistency mapping, and conformance testing offered by RM-ODP.

All the viewpoints make use of, and are affected by, the specification and structuring rules. All the viewpoints make use of not only viewpoint-specific ontologies, but also the distributed processing ontology. That is, they are not just terms to use in a specification; they include terms to use in conjunction with all the RM-ODP specification rules. All the viewpoints require engineering skills. Stakeholders work with the architect in using the enterprise and information viewpoints to specify the business. The stakeholder defines business objectives and the architect relates the business terms to RM-ODP concepts. For example, a stakeholder in the hospital business states a business objective "to manage patient admission," and a policy statement that "all emergency patients must be admitted." The architect relates these to RM-ODP concepts and rules of expression: an admission *role*—to manage patient admission; a *policy* statement—the admission role is *obligated* to admit all emergency patients. More on this topic is covered in Chapter 12, "Enterprise Business Specification."

The concerns of the enterprise viewpoint are from a scope and objectives perspective. This concern can apply to a business (such as the Healthy Hospital business of Chapter 2), or to a software-component specification, such as a data broker. The information viewpoint captures the behavior of the system. The computational viewpoint captures the components and their interactions, as affected by the behavior specified in the information viewpoint. Notice that none of these concerns addresses how the software is hosted on computers, how a network is used, or if all the software is co-resident on the same computer. These concerns of distribution come into focus in the engineering viewpoint, where all such considerations are specified. But the engineering viewpoint is not concerned with a choice of technologies, such as which database vendor is used (e.g., Oracle®), which data broker is used (e.g., Enterworks™ Virtual DB® [VDB]), which Web browser is used, which type of network is used, and so forth. These choices come into play in the technology viewpoint. This is represented in Figure 3.5.

The enterprise, information, computational, and engineering viewpoints are independent of specific implementations. In other words, most of the architectural specification is independent of the specific product selections used to implement the system. This characteristic of RM-ODP provides three important capabilities:

1. The independence of the business and architecture specification from technologies allows evolving technologies to be incorporated into the system without impacting the overall architectural constraints.

2. The architecture specification provides the criteria by which the product can be selected.

3. The architecture specification can be created to be visionary, in which case as products evolve and are included in the system, what has yet to be accomplished is known and defined in the architecture specification. This can yield selection criteria for products that include consideration for the future. An example of this very important point is a product that now provides visualization of stock inventory, or a product that has emerged to provide fault tolerance. The architecture specification provides the criteria of how these products must behave, how their interfaces must be used, and other criteria for how and where to compose them into the system.

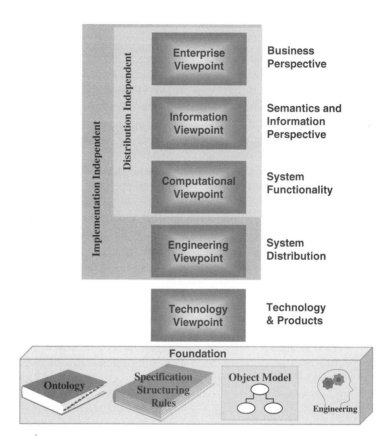

FIGURE 3.5   Viewpoint Foundation

Viewpoints can be nested, can use multiple levels of abstraction, and use composition.   In the process of using the viewpoints, the architect does not need to fully use all concepts of a particular viewpoint before using another viewpoint. In fact, this would not work. For example, the use of a low-bandwidth network (determined in the engineering viewpoint) may require an additional object to manage binding of interfaces (a computational viewpoint consideration). This, in turn, may affect a quality of service statement in a policy (determined in the enterprise viewpoint). What the architect does is begin, capture as much as is known, soften constraints until more is known, and branch off to another viewpoint to perhaps learn more about a particular aspect. The use of the viewpoints is, in this sense, nested or iterative.

At any point in the use of the viewpoint, the architect can use any of the viewpoints *within* that viewpoint, to better specify something. Or the architect can use a subset of the viewpoints only sufficient to specify some part of the system. Hence, the RM-ODP viewpoints are full viewpoints on a system, that can be used recursively within or partially, according to the needs of the architect. Through the consistency rules provided by RM-ODP, it all works together; it enables composition of architecture parts of the system, partial specification of a system, or a full specification of a system.

For example, in the process of architecting a portion of the system, it may become important to digress and define that portion of the system more fully. A synopsis of one way the viewpoints could be nested, for use in specifying a business, is shown in Table 3.2, all for a business specification that requires the use of a common message transaction service (MTS).

TABLE 3.2 Nested Viewpoints Example

VIEWPOINT	BUSINESS SPECIFICATION
Enterprise	A required message transaction service to be used, as an enterprise object, with interactions to other enterprise objects of the business
Information	Processing behavior that relates to the constraints about the MTS
Computational	Functional system configuration of objects and interactions that provide the business function using the MTS. More detail about the message transaction service to be used
Engineering	Distribution designs and distribution transparency mechanisms for the MTS and its use
Technology	Technology (e.g., OMG's Messaging service coupled with the Object Transaction Service), product (e.g., BEA's Object Transaction Server™ product)

An example of nested viewpoints may be seen in using the OMG Trader specification. In the architecting of a system, the architect may discover that a Trader is an appropriate component for use in the system. The architect does not need to fully specify the Trader component since OMG and ISO [ISO-Trading] have accomplished this. The architect need only identify its use within the context of other components, and reference the Trading specification. If there are certain behaviors that need to be addressed by the use of a particular vendor's Trader product, however, the architect needs to determine this technology viewpoint choice, and abstract the behaviors into the remaining system specifications. Again, this is both a nesting and iteration in the use of the viewpoints.

As another example, the Healthy Hospital example identified a hospital policy that affects the actions of the enterprise objects acting in their various roles (e.g., admission agent role, billing agent role). The architect wants to further refine the effect of the hospital policy on these actions. So the architect uses the computational viewpoint to better define the components and interactions, introducing a new policy administrator object. The policy administrator object controls the appropriate use of the data associated with each of the agents. How? Perhaps the architect chooses to use a data broker that provides a single point of entry to all the data sources, and associate the policy administrator with that component. Perhaps the architect then wants to determine the distribution of the data broker and the data sources, and even the technology choice, to better understand the behavior. So the architect has drilled down on a particular aspect of the enterprise specification to better understand the interworking and semantics of the system components, and will then incorporate such knowledge into the information and enterprise viewpoints. This example is shown in Figure 3.6.

As was discussed in Chapter 2, "RM-ODP Manager's Primer," the viewpoints provide an approach for specifying the entire system, a part of the system in an incremental approach, or a visionary target system. In the latter case, the enterprise and information viewpoints will likely be used, and possibly the computational viewpoint as well. Engineering and technology viewpoints provide a

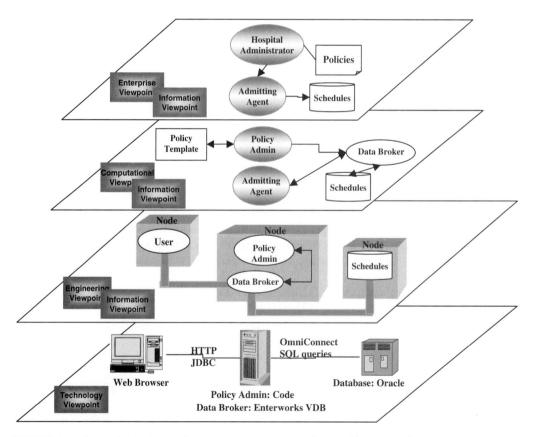

FIGURE 3.6   Example Nesting and Iterating Viewpoint Use for Healthy Hospital

virtual machine, which must be implemented by available technologies. If these are not yet in hand, the architect can still specify the visionary system, and then that portion of the system that is implementable, using the engineering and technology viewpoints. As technology emerges, the architecture is in hand to specify where that technology can be inserted with minimal impact. If the new technology is completely unanticipated, the full architecture specification may need to be revisited to ensure the technology meets the business needs, and does not adversely affect the current architecture specification and system. Cost avoidance, risk management, and schedule impact are all considerations at this point.

Not all viewpoints are required for a given specification. The architect does not need to use all the viewpoints, or even all aspects of a viewpoint. The choice is up to the architect to decide what it will take to provide a specification.

A prime example of this is the need to specify a business, the system, and the placement of the system in the business. The details of the distribution of the system and the technologies to use are perhaps left for some contractor to decide. So the organization's architect uses the enterprise, information, and parts of the computational viewpoints to clearly define what is wanted in the system. This too is a specification of the needs for a system. It is a method actually used in the creation of a service specification, or of a standard that is under the RM-ODP initiative. It is a method that can be used to construct a "reference architecture," which is popular today.

Taking a look at a reference architecture and what it means may help elucidate the use of the enterprise, information, and computational viewpoints. A *reference architecture* can be considered a high-level system specification that defines its overall target structure (components and relationships among them) in a systematic, consistent manner. A reference architecture frames, or bounds, choices, ensuring concepts and rules of structure are incorporated into all intermediate solutions, spiraling towards a target architecture. The essential difference between a reference architecture and an architecture is that an architecture is a more fully specified instance of a reference architecture. A reference architecture defines the envisioned target architecture, without addressing engineering or technology viewpoint concerns. So a reference architecture specifies:

- ▶ Objectives and scope
- ▶ Information
- ▶ Processing
- ▶ Business constraints and policies over the system composition (and components) and interactions
- ▶ Qualities of service (QoS)
- ▶ Distributed system objectives, without details of distribution
- ▶ Business objectives of incorporating previous (legacy) solutions
- ▶ Concepts and rules for business systems

▶ Decomposition into cooperating components and compositions

▶ Component relationships

▶ Delaying:

    – Considerations of technologies and products

    – Considerations of distribution

    – Considerations of data

In essence, a reference architecture provides the structure and rules to be used to define an incremental system solution. It is considered incremental because the current technology choices may not, in fact, achieve all that is specified in the reference architecture, and may need to incrementally evolve to the "target" or visionary solution.

A representation of a reference architecture is shown in Figure 3.7. It shows that the RM-ODP enterprise, information, and computational viewpoints can be used to provide a specification of a reference architecture.

Combinations of viewpoints provide specific views of a system. Each viewpoint either enables a viewpoint specification to be created, or contributes to a specification of multiple viewpoints. That is, sometimes several viewpoints are used to provide a particular specification, such as a business specification that includes the enterprise and information viewpoints.

Table 3.3 provides an overview of the viewpoints and the focus of concern in that viewpoint. When used in accordance with the RM-ODP rules, it becomes a viewpoint specification of the system, singly or in conjunction with another viewpoint, as exemplified in the Specification column. Some combinations of viewpoint uses result in commonplace views, such as a business specification, or a data management specification. Other combinations are possible; it all depends on the objective of the architect.

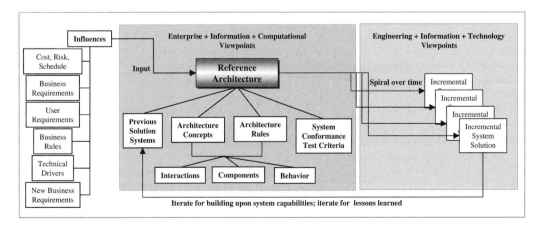

FIGURE 3.7 Reference Architecture and RM-ODP Viewpoint Use

TABLE 3.3   Viewpoint Concerns and Specifications

VIEWPOINT	CONCERN	SPECIFICATION
Enterprise	Purpose, scope, policies	Enterprise Specification
Information	Semantics of processing, and information	Information Specification
Computational	Functional decomposition into objects or components and their interactions, and their behavior and constraints	Computational Specification
Engineering	Distribution and distributed mechanisms, infrastructure, distribution transparencies	Engineering Specification
Technology	Technology, standards, products, and code choices; conformance test points	Technology Specification
SOME COMBINATIONS		
Enterprise + Information	Business requirements along with behavior, and information	Business Specification
Computational + Information	Application "virtual machine": Application, application programming interfaces	Application Specification
Computational + Engineering + Information	Distributed processing "virtual machine": allocation of software to hardware, networks, etc.	Infrastructure and Distribution Specification
Enterprise + Information + Computational	Software component purpose, scope, policies, behavior, functional decomposition	Software Component or Standard Specification
Enterprise + Information + Computational + Engineering	Purpose, scope, policies, data, data flows, data stores allocated to computers	Data Management Specification
Engineering + Information + Technology	Implementation, Evolution to New Technologies, Incremental Implementation	Incremental Specification
All	Conformance testing	Conformance Specification

As was shown in the Healthy Hospital example of Chapter 2, "RM-ODP Manager's Primer," RM-ODP provides the means of specifying a system from a business perspective. That is, RM-ODP provides the mechanisms to capture how to realize the business requirements through a distributed processing system. This is not an easy task for any architectural framework. Using RM-ODP also provides the ability to capture business-related rules of engagement for the system. These concepts are further discussed in Chapter 12, "Enterprise Business Specification." As an example, the computational viewpoint discusses the concept of an interface. The rules associated with interface address different types of interfaces, how interactions are captured in an interface, some of the semantics of the interface, how a contract affects the interfacing (called a binding), and so forth. Perhaps this is all the architect needs to specify for some part of the system. Hence, the architect uses the computational and information viewpoints, and not all of the constructs in them.

Additional viewpoints can be added. Sometimes it's useful to view the entire system from a particular capability, such as security. Some of today's architecture frameworks (such as Zachman [Zachman] and UML [UML-1.3]) contain "views" of the system. However, the RM-ODP viewpoints are different in that they separate the concerns to stakeholder and architecture aspects, not just capability aspects. A capability is discussed in each of the RM-ODP viewpoints. For example, one common view of a system is the "data" view. This view may be depicted in a data flow diagram, representing the inputs and outputs of the data in the system. In RM-ODP, the five viewpoints define the need for the data, the elements of the data (the schema), the elements of the system that manipulate the data, the behavior of these elements (the data business rules), how the data is distributed, and how the data is managed by products or code. Another view of the system may be a security view. In this case, all aspects of an enterprise-wide security capability that exists in the system may be specified in a separate view. The RM-ODP set of viewpoints is not closed so that additional viewpoints can be added as the needs arise.

3.2.5 TRANSPARENCY

Finally, RM-ODP addresses what is called "distribution transparency." There are eight transparencies defined by RM-ODP. These eight transparencies are called access, location, migration, relocation, persistence, transaction, failure, and replication. The reason RM-ODP calls the set of transparencies "distributed" is that these transparencies hide the effects of distribution from the user, application developer, or system developer. The transparency constructs of RM-ODP are "orthogonal" in the sense that there is a separate set of defined constructs and concepts associated with each transparency, and the transparencies can be used somewhat independently.

However, once a transparency is "required," the constructs and concepts are intertwined with the mechanisms of the engineering viewpoint. That is, a transparency imposes constraints on the way the system works, focused on the engineering viewpoint (the infrastructure). These constraints are defined by RM-ODP. For example, if "failure" transparency is required, then the infrastructure needs to control what happens in the infrastructure, detect a failure, and set into motion activities that try to recover from the failure. All of this is done without knowledge of or impact to the application or the rest of the system.

The eight RM-ODP distribution transparencies are described in Table 3.4, from [RM-ODP-3].

TABLE 3.4 Distribution Transparencies

TRANSPARENCY	PURPOSE
Access	Hides the details of accessing another object, within or across heterogeneous systems. This includes hiding how the object is invoked, any data formats between the objects, and the interfaces required.
Failure	Hides the details that something has failed in the system, and the act of recovery. This transparency enables fault tolerance.
Location	Hides the details of a name and physical address used to locate some information and to interface to it.
Migration	Hides the details that an object has moved to some other location. This transparency enables other software objects in the system to continue to interact with the moved object, as though it were still in the same place.
Relocation	Hides the details that an interface has changed location, even if that interface is being used. An example is moving a server to some other location, and hiding that fact from the client. This can be used to support load balancing.
Replication	Hides the existence of copies of the software object in the system. Database replication is an example. This is often used for performance and reliability.
Persistence	Hides that an object continues to exist in the system, even if the object is deactivated and then reactivated in the system. This is used for stability and robustness of the object(s).
Transaction	Hides the coordinated activities of software objects in support of any transaction (e.g., database, messaging). A transaction is classified by the properties of atomicity, consistency, isolation, and durability (ACID). This enables a consistent transaction to occur, and establishes a more reliable system.

"Transparency" is about freeing an application program from having to provide some service or function. One has essentially "hidden" the details of where and how this service or function will be provided, and hence made the application "transparent" in regards to that function or service. The use of the term "transparent" is historical, but think of it as if having to look through an application to see where that function or service is occurring. This detail is hidden from a user. For example, locating a particular Web page is accomplished by merely accessing the local Web server, even if the Web page is geographically distant. An application is unaware of an infrastructure service that supports automatic recovery on a failure. An infrastructure service, such as something providing database services, is unaware of the management of a connection.

One typical use of transparency is to hide the complexity of some service provided by the infrastructure. In this way, for example, a complex service that supports a database replication function is hidden from any application or infrastructure service using that service.

A second use of transparency is to reduce effort of application development by relegating the complexity to the infrastructure developer, which can then be reused by all applications. This means that now the application developer does not need to develop his own version of some service or function, and can instead rely on some generalized version of that service or function in the infrastructure. This concept arises in such familiar situations as a single log-on feature that provides both the user and application the ability to log on the system once, and access anything that log-on privilege allows; mathematical functions that are usually called from libraries; or naming an object without having to know how the system refers to that object. What is different here, and perhaps unfamiliar, is how this same principle of reaching outside the application to libraries or repositories or infrastructure services can now be utilized for many other parts of the software application that may never have been considered.

Using access and location transparencies, the target location (e.g., the receiver of a message) does not need to be known. Instead, the application need only "refer to" the receiver in some way, say by some "name," and the infrastructure provides all the details to locate the target through its "name," ensure access to the receiver is valid, and establish the connection to the receiver. This frees the application developer from having to code target end details into his application (actually, into every application that would need to communicate with the target). It also reduces the number of interfaces to be developed, because the sending application can use the same interface for some data to multiple receivers, by putting in a parameter that indicates the receiver "name." The interface becomes reusable, and that reduces the cost of developing the system and maintaining it.

As another example, imagine that the user is logged on to a Windows® product. Now the user launches two applications, a vendor spreadsheet and a vendor database management system. Each one requires a log on. "Access transparency" allows the infrastructure for the user to log on each of these programs without requiring the user to know the details of the log-on processes; they are filled in automatically. Thus access transparency has "hidden" the complexity of the log-on process and the connection process from the user, and from any other applications the user may have running as well.

A Web browser also provides access transparency. When the user clicks on a "link" on a Web page, the Web server transparently accesses the necessary servers by invoking the communication paths to the possibly heterogeneous servers, and then downloads the information from the distant server to the browser. These details are all hidden from the user by the Web server browser, and by the distributed name server that determines the location. Notice that the application developer does not need to be concerned with these details; the infrastructure services of the Web server are reused. An example of a request for a lung (versus a heart) image is shown in Figure 3.8. The "where" and "how" the lung image was obtained is a response to the user (client).

Load balancing is supported by the migration transparency. This is the ability, for example, to move a server to a new location or a different computer, without impact to the client software. Instead, the infrastructure records and manages the new location, much like a mail forwarding capability. The system keeps the forwarding address for a period of time. In addition, the system can also re-establish the connections of any interfaces being used, without knowledge of the application.

In order to achieve distribution transparency, RM-ODP offers important constructs in several of the viewpoints. The enterprise viewpoint allows the user to specify the transparency as a requirement. The information viewpoint supports this requirement in terms of specified constraints on the software and interfaces. The computational viewpoint specifies the constraint on the interfaces involved. This high-level specification of what talks to what, and the transparencies

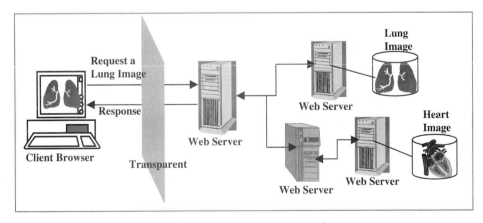

FIGURE 3.8 Web Location and Access Transparency Example

involved, allows one to identify potential services and functions that could be moved from the application level to the infrastructure level. The computational viewpoint supports distribution transparencies by abstracting the object interactions in terms of the constraints associated with the transparency. Lastly, the engineering viewpoint describes the mechanisms in the infrastructure to actually implement the transparency, and allows an application developer to see what mechanisms could be used to off-load some functions and services in the application to the infrastructure (e.g., locating a lung image). RM-ODP describes these mechanisms for any application and, as such, makes these mechanisms automatically reusable by each application. The key is to identify a transparency as a "requirement" from the customer in the enterprise viewpoint—then everything else cascades through the viewpoints.

3.2.6 CONSISTENCY

Viewpoint consistency ties together the constructs of one viewpoint to another. As an example, an interface as specified in the computational viewpoint corresponds to an interface as specified in the engineering viewpoint.

Consistency enables architecture evaluation, a common understanding, and increased completeness and consistency of the full system specification. Consistency across the viewpoints provides the ability to relate the specification of the architecture to a system implementing that specification, provides a consistent set of specifications that reflect what is wanted, and provides the ability to check conformance to the requirements.

There are several key points of correspondence that must be addressed. The computational viewpoint must support any dynamic behaviors that are specified in the information viewpoints. There is an explicit correspondence requirement between the computational and engineering viewpoints, and there is an explicit set of correspondences between the enterprise and computational, engineering, and information viewpoints. An example of a correspondence between an enterprise policy and enterprise role and constructs in the other viewpoints is shown in Figure 3.9.

There are typically more engineering objects than there are computational objects, because the engineering viewpoint exposes all the objects (which may be numerous) in the distributed infrastructure. For every computational interface defined in the computational viewpoint, there must be an explicit correspondence to an engineering interface in the engineering viewpoint. Each computational object corresponds to one or more engineering objects. In other words, the computational objects must map onto distributed engineering objects so that the distribution strategy is clarified by the architecture.

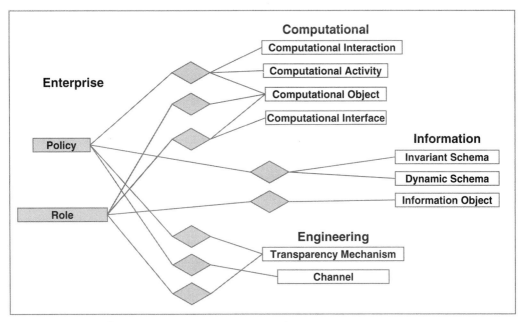

FIGURE 3.9   Sample Enterprise Viewpoint Correspondences

Another important point about consistency is that it enables geographically distant organizations to specify different parts of the architecture independently, and implement different parts of the system independently. This is achievable because of the rules of consistency across the specifications that will enable them to compose into a single specification or be realized into a single system. This is a capability provided by RM-ODP that addresses many programmatic needs in the architecture of systems.

RM-ODP defines the consistency of certain constructs between the various viewpoints. However, there are several areas not yet defined. Some of these are in the enterprise viewpoint and how the constructs of that viewpoint correspond to other viewpoints. The work in [ISO-EntVP] is furthering these consistency definitions.

Consistency checking coupled with conformance testing will increase confidence that the system will operate correctly and reliably. These activities are amenable to syntax and semantics checkers, architecture tradeoff analysis, simulation of the system based on the architecture, and other analytical capabilities.

3.2.7   CONFORMANCE

One of the most important features of RM-ODP is its concepts and rules supporting conformance assessment. Conformance assessment ensures that the implementation of the system corresponds to the architectural specification.

The RM-ODP rules of consistency across the specifications support four types of conformance reference points for testing, available for use by the tester of the system: perceptual, interchange, programmatic, and interworking. RM-ODP then proceeds to specify how conformance is achieved and represented in the architectural specification. The four types are represented in Figure 3.10.

One type of conformance test point is called *programmatic conformance reference point*. This reference point is used in the usual notion of testing the behavior of software interfaces. Many of the programmatic conformance tests address the architecture specification from the computational viewpoint specification.

A second type is *perceptual conformance reference point*. This is used in the testing at user interfaces in communications ports that represent external boundaries to the system. Usability and user interface testing, as expected by the business user, can be defined through perceptual conformance assessment.

A third type is *interworking conformance reference point*. This is used in testing between systems implementations, to make sure they interoperate. It is not sufficient for individual systems to have programmatic conformance (that is, only interface agreements) in order to guarantee interoperability. Interworking conformance includes interoperability testing between working implementations, making sure certain qualities of service are there, making sure that all the connections through all the software components work, and so forth.

The fourth type is *interchange conformance reference point*. This involves testing of the exchange of external media, such as disks and tapes. Interchange conformance assures that information stored on external media can be interpreted and incorporated in other systems that conform to the same standards.

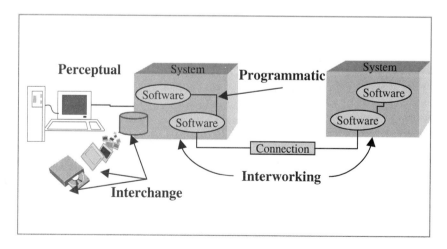

FIGURE 3.10   Conformance Reference Points for Testing

3.3   How RM-ODP Is Used

Thus far, the building blocks from RM-ODP have been discussed. Some use of RM-ODP has also been discussed, primarily with respect to the viewpoints. In this section, the approach to architecting, using RM-ODP, is discussed.

3.3.1   Prerequisite Knowledge

To specify a distributed processing system, certain knowledge is required. First, distributed processing issues need to be addressed. They occur in specifications time and again. Such issues include naming, timing, policies, administration, security, and remoteness. Understanding of the architecture specification principles of abstraction, refinement, composition, modeling, and so forth is necessary as well as knowing the difference between specification and description. This was covered in Chapter 1, "Open, Distributed Processing, Architecture, and Architecting," and more will be discussed in Chapter 7, "Architecture Specification and Representation." If this understanding is missing, training is in order. Knowing is prerequisite.

There is no value in creating a specification model per se—only in what that model allows one to do or subsequently understand. A specification model is not a physical, real, system (yet). It defines what the system is to do, precisely. Designing and building a software architecture is largely a modeling activity. The downside is that a model is abstract and takes effort to create. The upside is the ability to compare and analyze the appropriateness of an individual architecture from choices of architecture and the ability to tailor and specialize an existing architecture rapidly to new environmental circumstances, new technologies, or new functional requirements. A model founded on RM-ODP is also founded in mathematics. This enables analysis of the model, and assertions about consistency to hold true.

A tool is something that aids the architect. All of RM-ODP may be considered a tool for architecting. The architect must still use engineering skills to use the tool appropriately. In addition, graphical tools, commonplace in the market today (e.g., UML tools), are part of the architect's toolkit. Graphical development tools, also commonplace in the market today, are part of the architect's toolkit. Architecture analysis, product tradeoff analysis, testing, and even the use of a natural language are all tools for the architect's toolbox. The problem the architect has is to use the suite of tools in an integrated fashion, to generate a cohesive architecture specification, and to relay that specification to the stakeholders. There are no "silver bullets" that can provide an integrated toolkit for the architect. Hence, the architect not only needs to utilize engineering skills to architect, but must also use engineering skills to combine the use of all tools available to bring together a well-formed architectural specification.

Certain technologies today come into play in the solution. Knowledge of these technologies, what they do, and how they can be integrated in the system, are things that the architect needs to know. Examples include object modeling, abstraction, composition. Products and tools include IDL, UML, CORBA, DSSA[2], infrastructure middleware, Java™, Web, and so forth.

Tools for representing an architecture are always useful. In this book, UML models are used extensively. They provide not only a graphical representation, which is useful for communication with the stakeholders, but also some of the details about the architecture specification. They enable a better understanding of what is intended to be developed. But, as will be discussed in "Tool Support and Limitations" on page 129, UML has limitations that the architect must deal with.

Since RM-ODP and UML are generic, any domain can use them. To use them in a specific domain requires knowledge of the domain, knowledge of the appropriate language from the domain (e.g., *radiologist* in a medical domain), and someone who can relate the domain-specific language to the architecture specification language. The result of the architecture specification is focused on that specific domain and is called a DSSA (discussed in Chapter 1, "Open, Distributed Processing, Architecture, and Architecting").

3.3.2   CONTINUING WITH HEALTHY HOSPITAL EXAMPLE

Let's look at a continuation, as a refinement, of the Healthy Hospital medical example, for use in the remaining sections. The requirements for Healthy Hospital, in part, were identified in Chapter 2. The customer[3] wants the hospital to work smoothly. The customer wants the hospital admitting agent to manage patient administration. This includes admitting a patient for treatment by a radiologist, scheduling an appointment with a physician, and adhering to state regulations.

The customer is interested in a distributed system, but wants it explained in his own terminology. He wants to be sure that the kind of system he envisions will be realized. And he does not want to learn 60 years' worth of (computer) science and (computer) engineering, including 10 years of object-oriented technology, to determine whether the system will or will not work to his expectations.

An architect must also know something about the hospital business. Her understanding of this field may be abstract or minimal. She must also understand software architecture and design, to be able to communicate the architecture of the system to the implementers of the system.

The technology transfer of ideas and communication across functional and information technology domains has always been a critical issue, leading to lots of miscommunication, which often results in a system that was not what was envi-

---

2. IDL is Interface Definition Language; CORBA is Common Object Request Broker Architecture; and DSSA is Domain-Specific Software Architecture.

3. *Customer* here refers to the stakeholder who specifies the requirements of the hospital system.

sioned. This is largely due to a lack of a common language to explain what is wanted. RM-ODP provides the capability, through its well-defined constructs, to discuss hospital enterprise business functions and policies with the architect. This takes the form of describing the enterprise boundaries, the community of users, the system roles, the policies that constrain the system, and a high-level view of the main functional parts of the system and how they interact.

3.3.3 WHERE TO BEGIN

The objective, in the initial steps, is to capture as much as possible at a high level of abstraction. Details will come as further refinement is done. But at this early stage, some things may not yet be known, and therefore cannot be specified. So part of each step is to plan on revisiting what has already been specified. That is, the specification techniques are incremental and evolve. It is important to capture what is known, as soon as it is known, so that it is not forgotten.

Plan to refine the important parts (based on the highest risk, quickest time to market, lowest cost, or some other programmatic reason), capture behavior as known along the way, fill in the spots, and revisit. This is the essence of the initial step.

Begin the process by determining the scope of the system through the enterprise and information viewpoints. As part of the business specification, the scope, objectives, configuration of objects, roles assumed by those objects, the relation among the objects in terms of processes they perform, and activities they perform within each process are all part of the business specification.

The scope of Healthy Hospital is defined as what things are accomplished by humans, machines, or other real-world entities, as well as the system. The objectives of Healthy Hospital are specified. The objectives will define what the system is to accomplish, so they are important. Where the software system(s) is to operate within the business is defined. These are shown in Figure 3.11. There may be one software system or multiple software systems in Healthy Hospital (possibly different enterprise specifications combined into one). The software system is specified in terms of roles and objects and their relationships (interactions and processes), even with the nonsystem entities, and with the external systems.

Certain actions in a business may be assigned to certain users or software to perform, some of which are shown in Table 3.5. Each of these is a role, whether automated or a real-world entity related to a system in the enterprise. A role is a formal parameter providing an identifier for a functioning part of the community behavior. Initially, each role is very coarse-grained. As the refinement process continues, the role defined may result in additional roles in the specification. For example, the admitting agent of Healthy Hospital is a role. It may result in two roles: one that admits patients, and one that schedules appointments. The details of the refinement of the role will come later.

Scope: Healthy Hospital
(Roles):   Functions:
Hospital administrator: Access to all patient records
Hospital admitting agent: Admit patient, access admission records, create new record, update existing record
Radiologist: Access patient record, access physician order, record treatment
Physician: Access patient record, update patient record, place treatment order, place admission order
Patient: Receives admission, receives treatment, pays bill
Patient record: All activities captured
Pharmacy agent: Dispense medications, ensure adequate supply of medications, order medications
State regulation authority: Provides policy, authenticates equipment tests, conducts tests of equipment
Insurance agent: Provides policy, negotiates payment, submits explanation of benefits to patient
. . .

Objectives:
Provide quality patient care
Support the needs of the medical community
Provide an interoperable information sharing environment
Facilitate a better-performing set of activities
Adhere to a changeable hospital policy
Adhere to insurance billing policy, which may change
Adhere to state regulation
Be more efficient
Encourage patients and physicians to use the facilities
Make a profit

FIGURE 3.11   Scope and Objectives for Healthy Hospital

TABLE 3.5   Healthy Hospital Entities and Functions

ENTITY	KIND OF ROLE	FUNCTION
Administrator	Person	• Uses the software system
Administrator	Software system	• Defines the interfaces with the other external organizations • Ensures that the policies are adhered to • Manages the functions of the systems • Is able to access all records
Admitting	Person	• Uses software system
Admitting Agent	Software system	• Schedule appointments with hospital physicians • Schedule appointments with radiology treatments • Schedule admission to the hospital • Validate patient information • Validate that the patient can pay • Admit emergency patients • Update patient record information with schedules
Billing	Person	• Use billing system • Validate total bill

TABLE 3.5　Healthy Hospital Entities and Functions　(Continued)

ENTITY	KIND OF ROLE	FUNCTION
Billing agent	Software system	• Compute a total cost of all bills • Ensure that the appropriate billing codes are associated with all billable treatments • Submit all bills to the insurance company within hospital policy timeframe • Submit bill of all balances due to the patient • Ensure the insurance company has submitted the explanation of benefits (EOB) to the hospital, along with payment, within hospital policy rules • Record all billing information in the patient record
Radiologist	Person	• Perform treatment • Perform equipment safety checks
Radiologist	Software system	• Validate patient information • Access the physician order • Validate equipment safety • Record the treatment to the patient record in accordance with hospital policy
Patient	Person	• Receive Healthy Hospital services
Patient agent	Software system	• Provide schedule of physician and radiologist treatments • Submit bill
Patient record	Software system resource	• Record patient name, address, phone number, place of employment • Record patient insurance information • Record patient outstanding balance • Record authorized physicians • Record physician order • Record radiologist treatment and results • Record all schedules • Record medications dispensed • Manage access control
Physician	Person	• Perform scheduled patient treatments • Access patient records • Achieve valid accreditation
Physician agent	Software system	[This is an external system, so the details are unknown. However, with respect to Healthy the following is provided by Healthy.] • Access patient records • Validate physician credentials • Enable updates to the patient records
Pharmacist	Person	• Manage inventory of medications • Dispense medications

TABLE 3.5   Healthy Hospital Entities and Functions (Continued)

ENTITY	KIND OF ROLE	FUNCTION
Pharmacy agent	Software system	• Provide an accurate inventory of all medications • Record all medications dispensed in the patient record • Submit an order for more medications as inventory decreases
Insurance company	External business	• Provide policies • Provide EOB to patient • Provide EOB and payment to Healthy Hospital
Insurance agent	Software system	• Provide EOB results to Healthy Hospital within amount of time specified in hospital policy • Provide the appropriate policies for use by Healthy Hospital • Ensure EOB and payment received by insurance company
State regulation	External business	• Provide state policy • Certify physicians • Certify Healthy Hospital • Certify equipment safety
State regulation authority	Software system	• Provide state regulation codes • Provide equipment safety certificates • Provide physician certifications
Notifier	Software system	• Interface with admissions for when a patient is admitted to the hospital • Notify all appropriate systems involved with admission (ill-defined in the example): nursing staff, physician, cafeteria, hospital room assignment staff, and so forth

The behavior is part of the information specification. The business and behavior information should be captured at a high level of abstraction. But initially, not everything is known. To the extent possible, the architect needs to capture:

▶ Cooperation—To what degree are the parts of the system to execute tasks jointly, and separately?

▶ Autonomy—What parts of the system are to be autonomous? That is, what parts are to retain their independence, though they may cooperate with other parts?

▶ Policies—What are the policies that drive the business and system needs? These should be expressed in terms of what is permitted, what is obligated, and what is prohibited.

▶ Quality of service (QoS)—In the sense of the enterprise viewpoint, a QoS requirement is an end-to-end user requirement. That is, a QoS may state that a bill must be submitted to the insurance company within 10 days. At this point, the QoS specification is not about real-time needs (necessarily, unless that is the subject of the enterprise specification).

▶ Shared environment—What are the objectives in terms of interoperability and sharing of information?

▶ Other "ilities," such as scalability, reliability, evolvability, flexibility, portability, dependability, availability, and security. A set of objectives about the different ilities should be specified at this point. "Ilities" drive the system specification. They are difficult, if not impossible, to add later. Hence, even if the stakeholder does not address these system properties up front, the architect needs to guide the stakeholder toward specifying what is important.

▶ Functionality—What the system is to accomplish, functionally, is specified. This specification will lead to the identification of enterprise roles, actions accomplished by those roles, and constraints on those actions.

The architect begins the process of refining the functionality into additional roles and relationships. An object is associated with a role, and as the role is further refined, different objects may assume different aspects of the role. That is, an object is identified to perform the functions of the role. For example, object "Guy" may assume the role of the admitting agent in Healthy Hospital. Another object "Linda" may assume that same role, at the same time or at a different time, depending on the constraints associated with that role. In each case, the functioning and behavior of the role is specified once, despite how many objects assume the role. Constraints are associated with a role. They apply to the behavior expected of any enterprise object that is to fulfil the role. For each role-based object, the interworking with another role-based object is captured, in terms of a set of actions or a single action. The architect specifies the set of actions between objects, not yet worrying about the specification of actual interfaces, what information is shared in the actions (which will be part of the information viewpoint specification), and what constraints are associated with the interworking.

The architect, then, captures the states of the objects, types of objects, and parameters about the object, to the extent known. The actions that allow the objects to transition from one state to another are captured in the dynamic schema of the information specification. The states the objects are allowed to transition to are captured in the static schema of the information viewpoint. The type and parameters of the object are captured in the information object specifications. This allows the architect to abstract the objects of the system, how they transition from state to state, and the actions that allow them to transition.

All along the way, the architect must diligently capture whatever behavior is identified. If the behavior is determined by a policy, the architect needs to also determine what the policy statement applies to, and the strength or weakness of the policy statement. This is done in terms of what is permitted, prohibited, obligated, and associated with a role.

The architect must also begin the process of capturing environment contracts. Environment contracts define the interworkings with the external communities of the business. Contracts establish certain behavior and constraints on the business and need to be specified. These elements to be specified were addressed in the Healthy Hospital example, with the insurance company providing a policy that affects the way the hospital submits and processes bills. Some of the policies and environment contracts are shown in Figure 3.12.

The architect should fill in preconditions and postconditions as they are known, and revisit the behavior to update appropriately. (See [Wing-95] for more information about pre- and postconditions.) Preconditions in RM-ODP act as a guard to allow an object to transition, so it is important for the pre- and postconditions to be explicit at some point.

Hospital Policy
Must provide access to patient records 24x7
Must authenticate access to patient records
May only admit patients with no more than $100 outstanding balance
Must admit all emergencies
Must abide by state regulation policy
May adhere to insurance billing policy
Must follow physician orders
Must bill insurance company within 10 days
Must record all treatments to patient record within 24 hours
Must not overbill, subject to state regulation policy
Must not bill for physician
Must dispense medications in accordance with physician order
Must dispense medications in accordance with state regulation
Must assign unique identifier to patient record
Must record patient name, address, billing information in patient record
...

Insurance Company Billing Policy
Must submit bill to insurance company within 10 days

State Regulation Policy
Must authenticate physician credentials
Must establish safety of equipment

Environment Contract: Healthy with State Regulation:
Precondition: current valid hospital credentials
Precondition: current valid physician credentials
Obligated to allow safety checks of equipment

State Regulation Contract (Code)
What constitutes authentication of a physician
What constitutes equipment safety
What constitutes hospital authentication

Environment Contract: Healthy with Insurance:
Must establish billing agreement with hospital
Must submit EOB to patient within 30 days
Must submit EOB and payment to hospital within 10 days
Healthy prohibited from charging <unknown> amount
for procedures

Insurance Contract
What constitutes a billing statement

Environment Contract: Healthy with Physician:
Precondition: Valid physician of the hospital
Precondition: Valid credentials
Permitted to access patient records
Permitted to notify results of tests
Prohibited from billing insurance company for fees
Obligated to fulfill physician order

Physician Contract
What constitutes a physician order

FIGURE 3.12 Initial Healthy Hospital Policies and Environment Contracts

In terms of the business, there may be patterns of business specifications for reuse. A business pattern is a structured set of concepts that reflects a specific business domain, what operations are involved, and how it can accomplish some objective. The patterns discovered for reuse help to fill out some of the specification for the business.

Some existing business patterns are founded on RM-ODP for reuse. Others are not, but can be adapted to the RM-ODP concepts. An example of the former is the general ledger specification from the Object Management Group (OMG) [GenLedger-98], wherein the enterprise, information, and computational viewpoints were used to specify the general ledger transactions, and the associated interfaces were then defined using IDL. An example of the latter is the specification of the Uniform Commercial Code (UCC) [UCC, and Kilov-98], which deals with the sale of goods costing at least $500. In this case, the specification results in a contract specification that is written down explicitly. An excellent discussion of such semantics for a business specification is [Kilov-98]. More information about enterprise business specification is provided in Chapter 11, "Enterprise Business Specification."

Specifying invariants as they become known is an important part of the process. An invariant is a property of one or more objects that remain constant (do not change) as the object goes from state to state. An invariant can be used to constrain the set of actions of an object, and in the case of RM-ODP, often leads to precondition statements. In particular, the invariants are specified in the invariant schema of the information specification, and constrain both the dynamic and static schemata. Therefore, as the architect determines the invariants, the architect needs to revisit the static and dynamic schemata to determine any possible changes. "Hard questioning of system invariants can lead to radically new designs." [Wing-95]

Another potentially critical factor is the handling of system failures. Since most systems fail on occasion, the architect needs to capture conditions of failure, and actions to take on failure. Some conditions of failure result in not adhering to a policy or violating an invariant. If certain critical actions must not result in an error, then a policy statement prohibiting such actions needs to be captured. If the system is to attempt a recovery, then fault tolerance is captured as a contract on the behavior of the system. For example, fault-tolerant systems generally have a rather complex infrastructure to support error detection, analysis, and recovery. (More about this topic is covered in Chapter 16, "RM-ODP Fault Tolerance Framework.") Sometimes error handling is addressed through an exception raised in the interface, and specified as such. This is a computational specification consideration (the specification of an interface and exception handling), which at this point, the architect may or may not choose to capture. But it's important to capture the objective that recovery from error is required in the enterprise viewpoint, to be refined later in the computational and engineering viewpoints, because the results of specifying error conditions generally lead to additional required capability in the system.

In terms of the objectives, certain critical factors may be invariant. These set the stage for how to proceed throughout the specifications, using the different viewpoints. One such factor that occurs often is the desire to use commercial products to the maximum extent possible. If this is required, then stating this up front as a part of the invariants is important. It affects decisions made throughout the entire architecture specification. The role the product plays in the business needs to be defined. The interworking of the product with other parts of the enterprise needs to be specified. Any known behavior, such as preconditions, postconditions, or dependencies, needs to be defined.

If the business requires the use of a product, the architect needs to position that product in the enterprise specification, and determine the effects (behavior) the product has on the business objects, and the effects the enterprise objects have on the product. Therefore, at some point, the architect may decide to find out more about the required product. The architect may then decide to elaborate the specification using the computational and possibly engineering viewpoints to determine the operations made available across the product's or object's interfaces and the behavior. This may require creating a component in the specification that represents the product, specifying the component as part of the environment of the system, and defining the constraints associated with interworking with the product. As these are exposed, the architect captures the specification in the appropriate viewpoint. The product, then, becomes part of the system, as well as part of the environment of parts of the system. The internal operation of a product is usually not made known. Capturing the specification of what is known in all the viewpoints, as applicable, better enables a system that can work together. This is represented in Figure 3.13.

In addition, through the process of architecting, criteria for any such product may be identified as constraints on the product selection. In other words, the constraints of a choice of product at this stage may later prove to be unsatisfactory to the solution. This may lead to a different choice of product or a refinement of the business rules because of the product selected. Whatever happens, the end result is captured in the architecture specification.

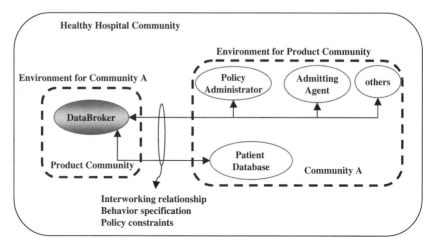

FIGURE 3.13 Specifying the Use of a Product in the Enterprise

Another critical factor that may emerge is the requirement that the solution must be delivered to market within, say, one year. This factor may limit the use of a formal specification to only those things deemed critical. These things are determined by the business specification. Typically, the things to be specified are database information specification, interapplication specifications, and the user interface, all in conjunction with the expected behavior. Functionality considerations that are "nice to have" may be delayed to an incremental release of the product. This will be easy to do with the RM-ODP specification, because where those additional capabilities fit into the solution will be clear, and can therefore expedite the delivery to market.

Another critical factor that may emerge is the need for a consistent user interface. A well-defined information specification and how that information is displayed to the user are derived from the information viewpoint specification. The definition of the information objects (the information displayed to the user), along with the allowable actions that change the state of the object (the actions to display different units of information), come from the information specification. The enterprise specification specifies the actions that take place across the objects to provide the information, and the actions the user can perform.

A point about using the enterprise viewpoint is in order here. The objects of the enterprise specification may include human users or machinery (such as in manufacturing), as discussed earlier. These objects can be modeled in the enterprise, along with their interworkings on the parts of the system, and the constraints applied to those interworkings. The physical entities are specified as a separate community, and the interworking with the system entities are specified in terms of an environment contract.

Another critical factor may be integration of the applications (components, in RM-ODP terminology) to better provide an information sharable environment. All sharable information should be defined in the information specification, as a single consistent model. The information model then drives applications and their interactions, specified in the computational and engineering viewpoints.

The architecture specification rules of composition, abstraction, refinement, precision are used throughout the enterprise specification, to get to a point of an adequately specified business. Once there, the architect can start refining the business specification to more detail towards a system solution.

All of the specifications created are founded on the RM-ODP object model and concepts. However, as was shown in the Healthy Hospital example, these concepts allow a domain-specific language: hospital, insurance, billing, physician, patient, and so forth. These are concepts from the medical domain, but are formulated in terms of the concepts from RM-ODP: objectives, environment contract, roles, policies, etc.

The information specification is the cornerstone for all the other specifications (from each of the viewpoints used). It is generally the most precise specification of the semantics of business and of the system to be developed. The behavior of the system is defined once, not threaded throughout all the remaining viewpoint specifications. The information viewpoint captures the terms of all the other viewpoints into a single set of terms, to describe the behavior of the system. As such, throughout the architecting process the architect needs to pay close attention to the specifications in the information specification. Even though at the initial stage, preconditions, postconditions, and invariants are somewhat defined, the architect needs to constantly revisit this particular specification to ensure its correctness. As an example, date and time should be specified in the information viewpoint. Why is this important? Consider the Y2K (Year 2000) problem, for example. Had the date and time been correctly formulated in one place, it could be changed in one place, instead of the possibly thousands of places in the system.

A business specification will also define information and information processing across the enterprise, independent of actual interfaces or databases or any other implementation mechanism.

At this point, the results for Healthy Hospital might include what is represented in Figures 3.14 and 3.15. The use of UML has limitations, as noted in previous discussions, and as will be discussed in future chapters. But UML is adequate to use for some of the RM-ODP concepts, such as those shown in Figure 3.14. The limitations of UML revolve around the ability to adequately specify semantic behavior and constraints, as shown in Figure 3.15.

Figure 3.14 represents the roles and responsibilities in terms of a Use Case diagram. The "environment" notation is to represent external roles assumed. The

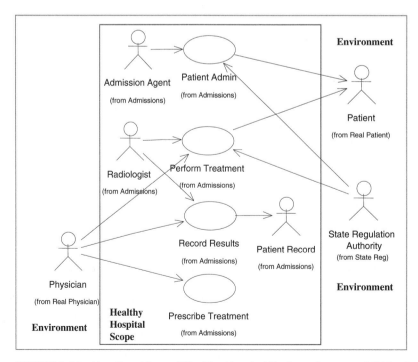

FIGURE 3.14   Use Case View of Healthy Hospital Business Scope and Objectives Example

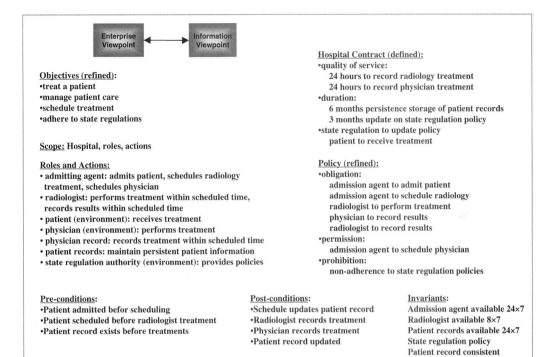

FIGURE 3.15 Some Refined and Defined Specifications of Healthy Hospital Example

scope of the system is shown as the internal set of actors and Use Cases. Figure 3.15 represents the details of the business scope, objectives, roles, policies, and behavior for the architecture specification, represented in English text.

At this point in the specification, the objectives and scope for the distributed processing system become clear. Issues related to distributed processing (discussed in Chapter 1, "Open, Distributed Processing, Architecture, and Architecting") are addressed in the next step.

3.3.4 NEXT STEP: REFINEMENT OF THE ARCHITECTURE SPECIFICATION

Once the business specification is partially defined, to include the behavior, the architect can refine it further using the computational and engineering specifications. The architect, who can relate these constructs to the RM-ODP viewpoint constructs, easily understands the language used to specify the business.

Decomposition into interacting components is captured in the computational viewpoint specification. Further refinement into infrastructure supporting objects, distribution, and communication is captured in the engineering viewpoint specification. These two specifications provide the refinement of the business needs into a distributed processing system, constrained by the semantics captured in the information specification.

The next step is generally to use the computational viewpoint, to refine the business specification to a decomposition into objects and interfaces. Following this, the architect uses the engineering viewpoint to refine the specification into distributed software across different nodes (computers) and different networks (channels). Further, if distribution transparency is required (e.g., single log-on capability, virtual addressing, or replication), the mechanisms are defined in this viewpoint. Eventually the architect and implementer make product, standards, and technology decisions to realize the architecture and create a solution.

One might object that this resembles a waterfall approach to the use of the viewpoints, which in essence will not work! A waterfall approach would address each of the viewpoints in layers. First, the enterprise is fully defined. Next, the information, then the computational, then the engineering, then the technology, then the testing viewpoints are added. But architectures are not created this way. They are created incrementally, as more knowledge is learned about a subject. So the methodology of "specify a little, refine a little, learn a lot, and cycle through" is the approach that works. This approach was successfully used in work for Europe's Air Traffic Management infrastructure [Tyndale-Biscoe].

Again, what does work is using the viewpoints for parts of the specification *incrementally*, and folding back in the determining factors realized. This may require changes to the viewpoint specifications already accomplished. What's an example? Suppose the architecture to this point provides a single component in the system that interacts with the "physician" community, but there are hundreds of such communities associated with the hospital. Furthermore, their procedures differ, and a patient may be a patient of several physicians. Not only is there a single point of failure in the system (the physician component), but there is no concurrent access to the patient records allowed. A change to the business specification might be to allocate a separate physician component to each physician community, provide a control component that monitors the status of these components to ensure good working order and provides multiple accesses to another component in the hospital which, in turn, allows concurrent access to the patient records database. Maybe each of these components has a separate quality of service requirement: one physician wants "immediate" access on demand; one physician wants "results within 3 hours," etc. Each binding from the hospital component to the physician component would be different, based on these qualities of service. Again, this results in a change in the architecture, and these changes permeate throughout the rest of the specifications.

As can be seen, the viewpoints are not layered, nor must they be used in a waterfall approach. They are used, as needed, to provide more detail about a set of concerns in the architecture.

The architect may choose to employ a "spiral model" [Boehm-88] approach, as described in Chapter 2, "RM-ODP Manager's Primer." Perhaps there is a high-risk area determined from the business specification, such as interoperating between the hospital and the insurance company that may have different policies or different architectural approaches. That particular interaction may be refined further throughout all of the viewpoints necessary to achieve a good, precise specification. Maybe the architect and implementer devise a solution to this high-risk area, prototype it, and iterate with the customer on how well it works. Using the conformance tests, the prototype can be validated to follow the architecture specification, so that if the customer doesn't like it, the specification changes.

An important step in this part of the specification process is to capture refined behavior in the information viewpoint. The architect should always look to the information viewpoint as the central important area of capturing the behavior of the entire system. It is not only a place to provide the behavior, but also a place to determine what behavior affects the decomposition of the system. For example, as was shown in the Healthy Hospital example, a QoS (billing must be accomplished within 10 days) affects how the interfaces are constructed, and how the binding of the interfaces works. This type of constraint may also result in additional components to make sure the binding behavior is followed, or produces a failure if it is not, followed by notifying a user of the failure.

Figure 3.16 further refines the medical example of Healthy Hospital, showing a possible distribution to client, server, and database platforms. A component named "State Regulation Procedures" is shown that reflects the state regulation

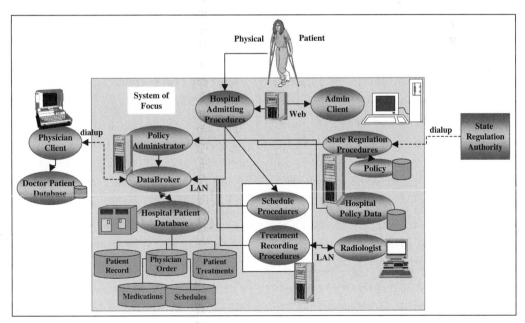

FIGURE 3.16   Example of an Architecture Using Computational, Engineering, and Technology Viewpoints

constraints identified in the previous two figures. The interfaces are shown as arrow lines, though in a true specification the details of the interface and bindings would be defined. The components "Schedule Procedures" and "Treatment Recording Procedures" are shown as residing on the same computer. Each of these components in a real architecture specification would be refined to much smaller components; e.g., the "Schedule Procedures" would define the objects and interfaces involved in its function. Also, not much is shown in the way of infrastructure service support (such as security, administration, management, and the like). The physician and state regulation authority are considered to be outside the scope of the system, but interact with the system as part of the system's environment. For each, a dialup connection is identified, and therefore must be provided. This is an example of how RM-ODP focuses on the specification of the system through the use of three separate RM-ODP models: computational, engineering, and technology. The effect of the information specification would show up as part of the true specification of each interface, binding, and even the object's behavior. This example is only notional.

Although technology today is capable of realizing many user needs through the use of the Internet, with very capable and resource-rich workstations, distributed component frameworks, and the like, the architect should still architect the distributed system. The large number of technologies, some that work alone, some that can work together, coupled with the need for designing the system to be cost effective, reliable, available, and well performing, remains a challenging task!

RM-ODP helps map the architecture onto the technologies and products of choice. The architecture specification captures the functioning and behavior of the system. With this knowledge, a technology is chosen that relates to what the function is to perform, how that function is to behave, what it must interact with, and how it must be distributed. Product selection then becomes easier, because what to look for and what to ask for become part of the criteria for selecting the product.

Part of this process also involves identifying where the specification cannot be met due to some insufficiency of the current technologies. When a new technology emerges, the architect is able to determine if it can perform the needed capabilities, within the constraints of the expected behavior of the system. That is, RM-ODP provides the architect with a set of criteria to evaluate product selection, and determine (through the specification of behavior) what properties the product must have to interact with other parts of the system.

In addition, RM-ODP provides the ability to establish conformance test points to test the system implementation to the specification. In the choice of a technology or product, then, the architect can identify where testing points need to be provided in the product and what information needs to be provided from the product. The tester can then observe the behavior of the system from these test points, and relate the information provided in terms of the architecture specification.

SIDEBAR

UNDERSTANDING SPECIFICATION AND TECHNOLOGY CHOICES

Technology today is both exceedingly capable and complex. Understanding what a given technology can provide requires the architect to understand its architecture, behavior, interfaces, and management. A common approach to the problem is to "buy commercial off-the-shelf (COTS)," to "glue COTS together," and then to convince the customer the end result is what was really wanted.

RM-ODP provides a common, consistent approach to specifying a system that is essential for a full and accurate specification. It is okay to realize the 80% solution, but have you ever wondered how you calculate the 80% when you do not know the 100%? Attempting to define the 100% is not easy. But attempting to find all the alternatives, understand them, and combine all the possible solutions from the technologies and products of today to achieve the system wanted is immensely difficult.

With limited budgets and limited time, the enterprise and information models define what 100% means. Many financial, telecommunications, and European government agencies are doing just that. Use of the rest of RM-ODP for architecting the business solution and design is a choice. The architect could define what 80% means, and proceed to architect the 80% solution. The architect could architect the 100% solution, and select technologies to solve 80%. Whatever is decided, all the business rules, processing semantics, and top-level functional needs of the system should still be specified. Then mapping the specification to the technologies and products becomes a planned decision, not an ad hoc one.

If the system requirements are informal at this stage, the architect needs to further specify them. This occurs by spiraling through the viewpoints and expressing the requirements in RM-ODP terminology. Evaluation of technical choices leads to possible refinement of the enterprise specification to allow for technical feasibility. For example, if a security technology product provides some capability that must interwork with the system administration capability, the enterprise specification needs to address this in terms of enterprise objects and their interactions, coupled with a policy statement that defines this need. Development of information and computational specifications may have security and management implications. This results in similar changes to the enterprise specification, information specification, and possibly the computational specification. The point of this discussion is that the viewpoint specifications are incrementally specified, refined, and even updated, as more information is gathered.

3.3.5   ITERATIVE REFINEMENT

The use of the viewpoints is to a certain level of abstraction. The architect has the tools of not only abstraction but also composition. So the architect may, at some point, have a precisely defined, but high level of detail about the architecture. What happens next?

The architect continues the process of refining the abstractions, refining the compositions into finer-grained objects that make up the composition, and further precisely defining their properties. The architect does this through the use of the viewpoints, always capturing more and more behavior details into the information viewpoint, and always using the information viewpoint to affect decisions on interfaces and bindings.

The architect in essence specifies a little, builds a little, tests a little, and determines if the result is what is needed, iteratively. The use of the viewpoints is represented in Figure 3.17.

When all of the coarse-grained objects (which are compositions of a group of objects) have been refined and defined, and all the abstractions have been defined in terms of implementation capabilities, the architecture specification is completed. Again, only those viewpoints necessary to get to the implementation

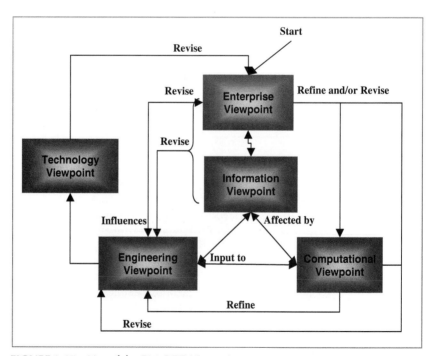

FIGURE 3.17   Use of the RM-ODP Viewpoint

point are necessary, and only concepts from each of the viewpoints that are necessary to precisely define the constructs of the specification are used.

For example, RM-ODP provides the concept of a node. This is in essence a computer and its operating system. The architect may already know, from previous iterations, that a Sun Solaris™ operating system and platform will be used. Therefore, the use of the resource management of this operating system, the threading capabilities, and how a channel is established, are specified by the operating system. The architect needs to translate the vendor-supplied information into RM-ODP terms, and either use the vendor concepts or the RM-ODP concepts. Whatever the architect chooses to do, a relationship between vendor and RM-ODP concepts is necessary to achieve the consistency and conformance checking of the viewpoints.

The process of writing specifications is similar to the processes of writing programs and writing mathematics. You need to worry about the big picture (e.g., the overall structure, organization, and meaning of concepts) as well as the fine details (e.g., syntax and special symbols). You need to learn the rules and concepts. You need to learn what rules must always be followed, and what rules you can break. As with writing programs and mathematics, writing specifications takes learning, practice, engineering, and patience. [Derived in part from Wing-95]

Even if the architecture depends on future technology becoming available, it may still be considered complete as long as the basic functionality of the system is isolated from the dependency of that technology. That is, if that technology is isolated to be part of the environment of the rest of the system, there are mechanisms in RM-ODP to address interaction with an environment. The future technology then has minimal impact on the rest of the specification. This was shown as an example in Figure 3.13. If the use of that future technology is intrinsic to the entire architecture, then the architect needs to re-specify the architecture to isolate the technology for use when it becomes available.

Once again, if the intended system solution does not need all of these, that's okay, as long as what is needed is precisely defined and specified through the architecture specification; a composition of viewpoint specifications.

3.3.6 When Will I Be Done

The process of architecting is iterative. It iterates through the viewpoints (of interest), and then iterates back through them to make changes as more details emerge affecting the overall architecture. The rules of abstraction, composition, and object model foundation are always used in conjunction with each viewpoint.

If current technologies do not accomplish all that is wanted, then the architecting process continues until the emerging technologies and products are in hand to use.

When will you be done? When the system as wanted is in hand. But then the business stakeholder may want changes, added functionality, use of a particular new technology (e.g., voice capabilities, visualization techniques), requiring the architect to determine where and how to include these technologies. The short answer is the specification is completed when an implementation becomes feasible. The long answer is the specification is completed when the customer decides it's completed.

RM-ODP provides some patterns of reasoning for use by the architect in specifying more about the distributed processing system:

▶ Interactions are defined in great depth, and covered in Chapter 13, "Interaction Framework: Interoperability." The rules in RM-ODP define how constraints and behavior are associated with the interactions, how the interactions can be specified independent of distribution, and how the actual mechanisms for communication are specified.

▶ Support for composition is provided throughout the RM-ODP specification. In fact, just about anything in RM-ODP can exist as a composition, including behavior. It's interesting to note that a component in RM-ODP can be as small as a library or as large as a full system. What this means is that the RM-ODP rules and constructs of composition and architecture specification can apply to the full distributed processing system as well as to a fine-grained component that is part of the system.

▶ Heterogeneity, a problem in "plug and play" system composition, is handled by explicit specification of the behavior of the entity, associated with the RM-ODP specification of coupling heterogeneous parts through the interaction specifications. RM-ODP also addresses quality of service constraints, and how they drive the specification. More is discussed about this topic in Chapter 8, "Composition and Semantics: Quality Composition Minimizing Architectural Mismatch."

▶ A failure model and fault-tolerant set of mechanisms are provided. This topic is covered in Chapter 16, "RM-ODP Fault Tolerance Framework."

▶ Specifying QoS, and how it relates to the objects and interactions are specified in a companion RM-ODP standard [ISO-QOS, Sluman-97]. This topic is covered in Chapter 17, "Quality of Service Model."

▶ Federation provides the ability of multiple domains to remain autonomous, and yet share in the distributed processing. Federation is also addressed by RM-ODP, and covered in Chapter 15, "Federation."

▶ As was addressed in the initial step, specifying a policy determines a lot about the behavior of the system. How a policy is specified and how that specification affects the parts of the system is covered in Chapter 14, "Policy Framework."

▶ RM-ODP defines mechanisms for distribution transparencies, as discussed in this chapter. These are discussed in more detail in Chapter 10, "Hiding System Complexities: Distribution Transparencies."

▶ RM-ODP defines mechanisms for consistency and conformance testing. More is discussed in Chapter 11, "Architecture Analysis and System Conformance Evaluation."

▶ Certain infrastructure capabilities are supported by RM-ODP functions. An example is node management, which among other things manages the allocation of threads to objects, resources of the computer, and establishment of a connection. This is discussed further in Chapter 9, "RM-ODP Functions."

3.4 SUMMARY

The RM-ODP constructs and concepts are relevant and most important for any architecture specification. Viewpoints aid in this decision-making by separating concerns for the different stakeholders, omitting unnecessary details, and avoiding the expression of requirements in terms of solutions.

The RM-ODP patterns of reasoning provide the architect with many useful starting points.

RM-ODP is feature rich and will challenge industry to surpass existing capabilities for distributed systems architecture in the areas of behavior specification, delegation, conformance testing, and inter-domain administration: openness (portability and interworking), integration, flexibility, modularity, federation, manageability, QoS, security and transparency. Figure 3.18 provides a final overview of the parts of the viewpoint specifications, and a notional representation of the consistency across the viewpoints. The viewpoint mechanisms, coupled with a precise ontology for distributed processing, are powerful tools for architecting. The rules of specification and structuring are fundamental for any architecture endeavor. RM-ODP defines all of this.

Above all else, use of software engineering and software architecture techniques, as defined in RM-ODP, complement the domain area expertise in specifying an architecture. Rigorous software engineering is essential. Object technology and architecture technology are more than programming or a topology of computers and networks. It is essential to manage the levels of abstraction for an architecture specification of a system, defining the business rules, the interrelationships, and the semantics of the system's processing, and capturing this analysis through a model.

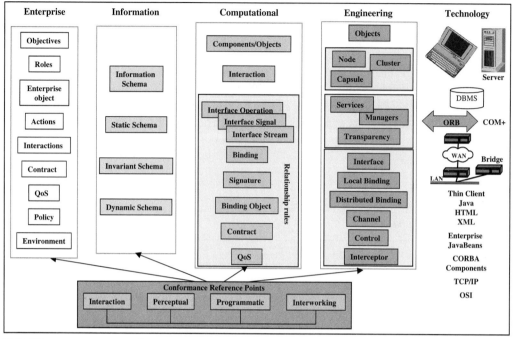

FIGURE 3.18   Overview of Viewpoint Concepts and Relationships

Some other benefits of RM-ODP are cited by [Holmes-94]:

▶ "A Common Language for expressing the behaviour, the problems and the requirements for heterogeneous organisations and systems, based on international standards

▶ A focus on externally observable behaviour rather than internal structure

▶ Support for 'what-if' analyses including effectiveness tradeoffs

▶ Support for evolutionary growth and technology interception"

The products of a standard such as RM-ODP are abstract. RM-ODP attempts to provide a general model for use in specifying any distributed processing system. It does work, but it takes a great deal of work to use the standard accurately.

Architecting is not easy. It is very easy to get it wrong, and very hard to get it right. Some automated tools exist that are claimed to help "architect." But use of a tool is only as good as the engineering and analysis that accompanies it. This chapter has attempted to elucidate the concepts of abstraction and composition as defined in RM-ODP, provide examples of their use, and guide the use of RM-ODP for specific needs in the remainder of the book.

One can be pragmatic about the use of RM-ODP. Not everything is always needed. One only needs to include those things that help plan the business objectives, the architecture, and the system implementation for the purpose at hand. One does need to use the terminology of RM-ODP, and the rules of specification and structure. However, one can elect to use a subset of the viewpoints, and a subset of the concepts and rules that make sense for the purpose at hand. However, use of RM-ODP should be correct. In this way, a cohesive system specification will result through the consistency constructs, from which analysis and conformance testing can be accomplished.

In this chapter some of the concepts and use of RM-ODP have been described. Subsequent chapters in this book provide more detail of these topics.

F O U R

TOOLS, RELATIONSHIPS, AND RM-ODP STANDARD

A discussion of available tools for use in conjunction with the Reference Model of Open Distributed Processing (RM-ODP) is provided in this chapter. The relationship between RM-ODP and the Object Management Group (OMG) and Open Systems Interconnection (OSI), commercial support, and some consortia is discussed. The parts of the standard, coupled with some of the emerging RM-ODP related standards, rounds out this chapter.

4.1   TOOL SUPPORT AND LIMITATIONS

The use of a tool never replaces the needed system engineering, system analysis, software analysis, or architecture engineering of the system. Tools are always limited. They have limitations in capturing semantics, in performance modeling, in forecasting, in assessment of reliability, quality, interoperability, costing, and so forth. The architect's toolkit, then, must include not just the modeling tools of the day, but the software engineering discipline, architecture analysis methods, architecture patterns, design patterns, and a reference model of precise concepts and rules for capturing and managing the consistent analysis of the system (i.e., RM-ODP).

If your only tool is a hammer, then all of your problems appear to be nails. An architecture modeling tool does not replace the required engineering of the problem domain to derive an architecture.

To date, there are no RM-ODP specific tools available commercially. This is a great business opportunity. Nevertheless, organizations using RM-ODP are adapting different vendor tools to capture RM-ODP architecture specifications. The architect can use more generic tools to capture some aspects of RM-ODP. Some of these tools are:

▶ Specification languages, such as Z [Z]
▶ Interface Definition Language (IDL) vendor tools
▶ The Object Constraint Language (OCL)
▶ iContract (a contract definition tool)
▶ SPIN, an analysis tool [Holzmann]
▶ The Architecture Description Language (ADL) tools (discussed in Chapter 1)
▶ The Object Modeling Technique (OMT) [Rumbaugh-91, Rumbaugh-96]
▶ Shlaer-Mellor Method of object-oriented modeling [Shlaer-88]
▶ Semantic Solutions™
▶ WinWin and MBASE tools
▶ The Unified Modeling Language (UML) [UML-1.3] tools
▶ UML augmented by the work ongoing in OMG called Enterprise Distributed Object Computing (EDOC)
▶ XML (Extensible Markup Language) tools
▶ XMI (XML Metadata Interchange) tools
▶ RM-ODP and patterns of reasoning
▶ Any combination of tools from this list

This list of tools is not a suggestion that any one will provide a representation of all of RM-ODP; in fact, no single tool can accomplish that.

So what can be done? First, focus on the business domain of the system: the problem domain. Then select a tool that can be used to represent or specify a part of the system in focus. However, whenever a tool is selected, RM-ODP constructs need to be mapped onto the constructs of the tool. Otherwise, the use of the tool will not represent the use of RM-ODP. Figure 4.1 provides a view of this and a UML example. When an RM-ODP construct has no mapping onto the tool, the architect must be creative in how to use the tool that is accurate with respect to RM-ODP and with the tool itself. If the tool is insufficient, add commentary or other mechanisms to that tool to capture the analysis of the problem domain, or other tools. Be prepared to use a number of vendor tools instead of all the models

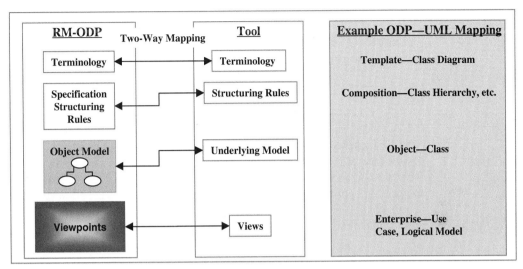

FIGURE 4.1   Mapping RM-ODP and the Use of a Tool

of a single vendor tool. For example, a finance problem domain has found that they needed to improve the use of Use Cases and model the entity interactions using SPIN2. [SPIN]

Be careful in the selection of a modeling tool for RM-ODP concepts. The object modeling concepts of RM-ODP are different from those of most modeling tools. One will need to map the concepts used from RM-ODP to those of the tool selected.

4.1.1 SPECIFICATION LANGUAGES

Part 2 of RM-ODP [RM-ODP-2] states that each viewpoint language must relate the concepts of RM-ODP to the specification language chosen. Different mappings for each of the viewpoints of RM-ODP can be defined. However, the correspondences among the concepts of each viewpoint language must be established so that a consistent model of the system results. From a consistent model, one can perform conformance checks, ensure that a specification in one viewpoint is carried through to other viewpoints, and perform end-to-end analysis on the model of the system.

4.1.2 SPIN

The SPIN tool is a generic verification tool for asynchronous process systems focused on proving the correctness of process interactions. [Holzmann]

4.1.3 IDL

IDL is a tool for the definition of the interfaces [ISO-IDL], provided by OMG and others. It captures the structure and exceptions associated with the interactions of the interface. However, there are some limitations with IDL. It captures the specification for operational type interactions, but not stream or signal interactions (which are other types of interactions defined by RM-ODP). IDL does not allow specification of binding or object behavior. Commentary in the IDL specification can be inserted to define behavior and binding, but the commentary has no semantics.

4.1.4 OCL

Capturing the RM-ODP semantics remains difficult. There are some tools that can capture some aspects of the semantic behavior of RM-ODP. An example is the OMG OCL [OCL1, OCL2].

OCL is part of the OMG's UML specification. But even OCL cannot provide all the semantics of RM-ODP, such as timing constraints. There is ongoing work in OMG and other organizations to define the use of UML and OCL to map the concepts of RM-ODP into them.

It is anticipated from these groups that certain semantics will not be captured, and will require the architect to augment the use of UML/OCL. Nevertheless, a metamodel of RM-ODP in UML should be available at the time of the publication of this book (see "EDOC" on page 135). There is also work in OMG to extend IDL to consider constraints and other semantics in the language.

Most automated tools that claim to support UML usually do not support OCL, and some UML tools do not support the full UML specification either.

4.1.5 iContract

Some of the RM-ODP semantics can be captured by iContract [Kramer]. The iContract tool supports uniform implementation of invariants, preconditions, and postconditions, testability, documentation of these constraints, and a specification of what a class offers. It preprocesses Java™ code that has preconditions, postconditions, and invariants associated with class and interface methods, and then converts them into code. This tool is in support of the Design by Contract concept from [Meyer-97, Meyer-2000, Meyer-2000-2], which refers to interfaces among system components as contracts that are specified as integral parts of the source code. iContract is a freely available Java preprocessor. [iContract]

4.1.6 SEMANTIC SOLUTIONS™

A not-yet-publicized RM-ODP–based tool to provide a business specification using the enterprise and information viewpoints is emerging. The Semantic Solutions [CItech] product line is a family of tools used for enabling the integration of business communities, via the integration of the automated systems used by those communities. It is based on a new concept of what it means for systems to truly communicate with each other: the concept that true communication is what people do, and that systems should communicate in the same rich variety of ways, reflecting the needs of the people who use the systems, and using, as people do, an implicit knowledge of the structure and purposes of their community. By including the intent of the communication with every message, the Semantic Solutions products provide a powerful integration tool for forming federations of very different systems.

    The Semantic Solutions product line consists of an integration framework together with separately packaged Semantic Solutions products tailored for various kinds of communities, including several e-commerce Semantic Solutions software packages, a Semantic Solutions software package for internal use by communities within a single enterprise, and Semantic Solutions software packages for other specialized purposes, such as component integration.

4.1.7 WINWIN AND MBASE TOOLS

"The beginning is the most important part of the work"
[Plato, 428–348 B.C.]

"A bad beginning makes a bad ending"
[Euripides, 485–406 B.C.]

The purpose of the system is established in the beginning. It is derived from the process of negotiated agreements among the stakeholders and architect team. A tool to facilitate a good beginning is WinWin.

    WinWin is a Web-based collaborative tool that supports distributed users, depicted in Figure 4.2. It aids in the capture, negotiation, and coordination of requirements for a system. It executes in a Web environment. It supports stake-

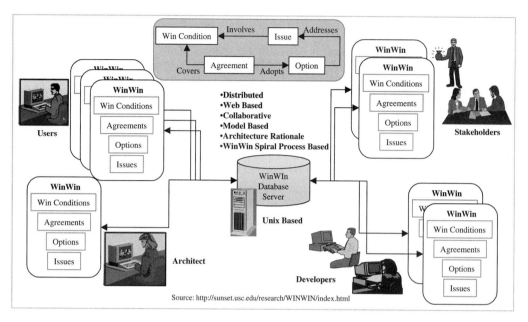

FIGURE 4.2   WinWin Tool Capability Overview (Source: University of Southern California)

holders in identifying, discussing, refining, and resolving conflicts in requirements, architectural, and product-choice decisions.

WinWin is an integrated suite of tools (see [WinWin]). It contains tools to:

▶ Capture the desires or needs (win conditions) of the stakeholders

▶ Establish the terminology for use across the stakeholder community to ensure everyone is using the same terms in the same way

▶ Express differing opinions or disagreements or issues that need to be resolved

▶ Provide differing options as potential solutions

▶ Negotiate agreements that resolve the issues

▶ Use third-party tools to enlighten or resolve issues

▶ Analyze architecture quality properties and tradeoffs

▶ Trace requirements decisions

▶ Check completeness and consistency of requirements

▶ Produce a requirements document that summarizes the current state of the proposed system

The WinWin tool is freely available from *http://sunset.usc.edu/research/WINWIN/index.html*.

The Model-Based Architecting and Software Engineering (MBASE) tool is another freely available tool from the same site. MBASE addresses the incompatibility among the underlying assumptions of models used to architect a system. This tool "focuses on ensuring that a project's product models (architecture, requirements, code, etc.), process models (tasks, activities, milestones), property models (cost, schedule, performance, dependability), and success models (stakeholder win-win, IKIWISI—I'll Know It When I See It, business case) are consistent and mutually enforcing" [http://sunset.usc.edu/research/MBASE/index.html]. The MBASE tool uses the WinWin suite, additional tools, and the new COCOMO II suite of tools (see [Boehm-2000] for more information, or visit the Web site). The additional tools include:

▶ View Integration Model tool that provides a UML analyzer, supported by Rational Rose®

▶ Software Architecture, Analysis, Generation and Evolution (SAAGE) tool for architecture modeling and analysis

▶ Architect's Automated Assistant (AAA) Java tool, founded on Z [Z], that performs architectural style mismatch analysis on architectures of systems that are modeled as compositions of subsystems with the corresponding connectors

COCOMO II tools include:

▶ COCOMO—a constructive cost model tool

▶ COCOTS—a commercial off-the-shelf (COTS) software integration and analysis tool

▶ COQUALMO—a delivered defect analysis tool

▶ CORADMO—a Rapid Development (RAD) cost and schedule tool

▶ COPSEMO—a phase/activity distribution tool

▶ COPROMO—a productivity analysis tool

4.1.8 UML

Many architects will use UML to capture an architecture, and to be sure, there are many concepts from RM-ODP that can be modeled using UML: objects, interactions, roles, type, actions, and so forth. There are examples of success in specifying an architecture using the UML vendor tools, such as Rational Rose (mentioned throughout this book), Rational Rose RealTime™ [UML-Rose-Realtime], SELECT® [SELECT-98], 4Keeps [UML-4Keeps], and many others. Realize that UML can be used only to some extent in an RM-ODP architecture specification. Current limitations in UML will be addressed below and in following chapters.

4.1.9 EDOC

OMG is furthering the work on using UML to represent EDOC architecture [EDOC-UML, EDOC-UMLa]. In this case, the proposal is to use RM-ODP concepts and rules, and associate these to UML notation. In other words, the EDOC proposals provide an architecture foundation from which to use UML, and do not depend upon the object model of UML itself. Using the foundations of EDOC, and using UML to represent these concepts, provides a consistent well-formulated architecture specification that can be represented in UML, and visualized in a vendor UML product.

4.1.10   SOME UML LIMITATIONS AND MITIGATION

There are concepts from RM-ODP that are not found in UML, and there are concepts in UML not directly mappable to RM-ODP concepts.

Capturing RM-ODP semantics is non-trivial, and most tools, including UML [Jackson-96, Jackson-2k] and OCL, are not complete in this regard. A few OCL parsers are available for use. However, vendors have not yet merged OCL with UML to provide a better description of the behavior of a system, nor have they created an integrated suite of tools for representing RM-ODP constructs.

UML seems to have too broad a spectrum, is not focused on architecture (but rather design), and has insufficient ability to capture behavior, as defined by RM-ODP. [Jackson-2k] UML does not support RM-ODP concepts in the following areas [Miller-97]:

▶ Distinction between type and class, as is the case in RM-ODP: UML allows the architect to specify a type as a stereotype of class. But a stereotype is not a modeling construct against which analysis can be performed (e.g., type matching).

▶ Multiple interfaces for an object: An interface in UML cannot be directly instantiated, so the concept of a binding is missing as is a reference to the interface. The architect can specify an interface class, however.

▶ Interface properties: An interface cannot be used as the type of a parameter. Since it cannot be instantiated, UML cannot model such concepts as action failure, interface reference, location, migration of an object's interface, binding, and so forth. Further, an interface in RM-ODP has a set of actions, each with a possibly different direction. This is not part of UML.

▶ Multiple types for an object: In RM-ODP, an object can assume multiple types. In UML, an object has a single type.

▶ Different types of interfaces: An interface in UML has a single type. There is no way to specify the three types of ODP interfaces in UML. Only the interface type that reflects client and server roles can be captured in UML. Two other interface types, signal and stream, are further discussed in Chapter 6, "Separation of Concerns: Using RM-ODP Viewpoints."

Some concepts in UML have no direct counterpart in RM-ODP, such as "association," "generalization," and "aggregation." Therefore, the architect needs to define their usage in line with RM-ODP.

As an example of a limitation in the use of UML, consider the simple Use Case diagram in the left of Figure 4.3. The line between the actor and the Use Case is called an association. What is the meaning (semantics) of that association? Is it independent, one-way, two-way, or something else? What, exactly, is a "request?" Does it include either a "reply" or a "response?" What is a "reply" or a "response?" RM-ODP makes this clear and unambiguous. In UML, the "association" in a Use Case could be augmented with a "Note" construct, containing information about the semantics of the association. This is shown on the right of Figure 4.3. Although RM-ODP provides the terminology to do just that (e.g., policy, interaction type), the UML "Note" construct is not a first-class modeling construct, and as such is not propagated through the other models or able to be used in any analysis of the model. In fact, searching for words in a "Note" construct doesn't work either. The ability to express the semantics of relationships is very important. "An architecture that allows you to express coupling between actors and components in a single language and is independent of any specific tools supports semantic integration (assembly of components that interact in meaningful ways)." [Tyson-97a]

The EDOC architecture [EDOC-UML, EDOC-UMLa, OMG-UML-97, UML-1.3, OMG-UML-ODP, Booch-98, Rumbaugh-99, Jacobson-99] proposals are building bridges between RM-ODP and UML. The architect can make use of this in the use of UML.

For example, Figure 4.4 shows some of the constructs currently being proposed (though modified for this example). The figure shows that an interface is specified as a class, stereotyped as an interface. A service offering by an object consists of one or more interactions. The interactions can in fact be partitioned across one or more interfaces, uniquely. In this example, the object offers one service consisting of three interactions (for example, this could be log on, access, and administer).

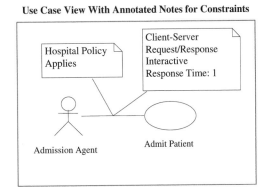

FIGURE 4.3 Limitations of UML Tool Use Case Example

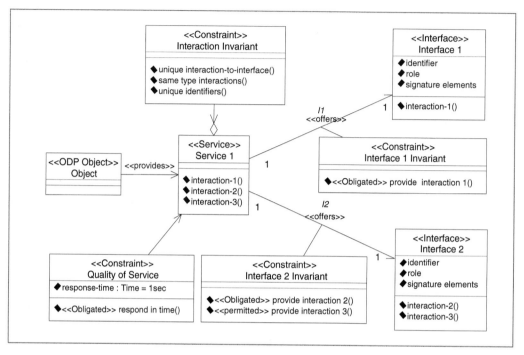

FIGURE 4.4   RM-ODP Proposed Mapping to UML Constructs

In this figure, interface 1 provides the interaction 1 (perhaps administer) associated with service 1, as shown. Interface 2 provides interactions 2 and 3 (perhaps log on and access) also associated with service 1. The first observation is that an interface is a first-class object. The second observation is that an object may offer more than one interface for different parts of the service being offered. The third observation is that of constraints. The current EDOC proposal is to model such constraints as association classes. However, limitations of this proposal include:

▸ Only one association class can be associated with an association.

▸ An association class can only be associated with an association; there is no counterpart for a dependency relation.

▸ An association class cannot be associated with two associations.

The result is that the UML user has to overcome the limitation. One way is to duplicate the representation of constraints into more than one association class, in order to link them into different associations. Alternatively, the architect can group all the constraints into a single association class. Then there is one association class to link to an association. However, the architect must then refine this class to properly relate the constraint to the intended association. And hopefully, the architect will make sure all of the refined constraint (classes) are semantically correct (a constraint on the constraints!). In this example, the QoS constraint has been associated with the service, not with the interface(s), where it properly belongs. More work is needed to use the UML capabilities to reflect the RM-ODP behaviors. Nevertheless, this is progress.

4.1.11 XMI

OMG has recently specified a language called XMI to communicate UML models across vendors. Interest in XMI appears to be high. [OMG-XMI-98] Coupled with RM-ODP–specific UML usage and XMI to interoperate UML models across vendors, sharing of open distributed processing specifications will soon be feasible.

4.1.12 RM-ODP AND PATTERNS OF REASONING

Agreeing to terminology, for example, is one of the major tools useful in any architecture, and RM-ODP provides numerous terms of international agreement. RM-ODP also provides precisely defined terms associated with distributed processing and architecture and viewpoint languages.

Structuring the approach to architecting, and using a well-formed set of consistent concepts and structuring rules is another tool for the architect. And an architecture specification can be captured in English text, using the RM-ODP concepts.

RM-ODP provides patterns of reasoning (architecture patterns and design patterns) that are, themselves, tools for use, provided in detail in Part Three of this book. Patterns of reasoning can be reused by the architect in any architecture specification. And remember, all of this has earned the agreement of organizations at the international level.

4.2   MATURITY OF USE

Support for RM-ODP comes from the formal standards bodies that created RM-ODP:

- International Standards Organization (ISO) standards
- ITU-T/CCITT–Formal Telecommunication standards
- OMG for the specification of the architecture that underpins all of the Common Object Request Broker Architecture (CORBA) services

In addition, RM-ODP has been used by many different organizations to specify business-specific software architectures.

The telecommunications industry supports RM-ODP. Companies such as Lucent Technologies®, AT&T®, Nortel Networks®, and others have used RM-ODP in specifying their systems. The Telecommunications Information Network Architecture (TINA) telecommunications consortium has founded its work on RM-ODP.

Companies in the financial industry, such as Merrill Lynch[SM], Morgan Stanley[SM], United Bank of Switzerland, and others have used RM-ODP to define their business specifications, information semantics, and designs for their distributed financial systems.

The health industry has also used RM-ODP. One software vendor is using RM-ODP for specifying the software for the health care industry. They have currently used RM-ODP for business, engineering, application, and information specifications. They are promoting RM-ODP to the Department of Defense, and within some of the health care standards bodies. [Kilov-99]

A legal organization within a telecommunications organization is using RM-ODP to provide a specification of their business. [Kilov-99]

A large insurance company is using RM-ODP to provide a business specification, including the business rules. [Kilov-99]

RM-ODP has been used by a large consulting firm for business process reengineering. Use of business specification, information specification, and specifying the interfaces has provided solutions to the reengineering of an existing system. [Kilov-99]

Government organizations such as the United Kingdom's Logistics domain, Norwegian's Command, Control, Communications, Computer and Intelligence (C4I) domain, and others, have all used RM-ODP in specifying their software systems architectures. Open-IT Ltd. (UK) Joint Command Process Study, working with the U.S. Department of Defense, created an RM-ODP–based framework to model the overall processes in the conduct of joint operations. Joint Logistics developed process and interaction models, representing an enterprise specification and information model. This resulted in a high-level requirements statement of how a set of federated existing systems could provide the required information services to Joint Logisticians. Many of these industries also use the OMG CORBA products. Nevertheless, the actual specification of business specifications, business object patterns, and business objects is accomplished using the RM-ODP constructs.

The most popular commercially based industry-supported realization of RM-ODP is the OMG CORBA. The use of RM-ODP in OMG is also required by the OMG Request for Proposal (RFP) template, required of all who respond with a proposed addition to the OMG Object Management Architecture suite of capabilities.

Not all organizations, however, have included or used RM-ODP for a variety of reasons. One reason is that there has been small exposure to this standard. It is, after all, a standard, and some believe that standards hinder rather than aid a process.

Another reason is that RM-ODP requires an in-depth understanding of distributed processing. Not all architects are skilled in this. RM-ODP requires an understanding of formal techniques for specification. Again, not all are skilled in this.

Precision and abstraction are not normally used today in architecting, with its desire to pick up a tool to represent the use of products, and the desire to jump to a product for use, without first determining its usefulness. RM-ODP postpones the decision of a product until the reasons for using a product are better defined and the criteria for selecting an appropriate product are better defined. This leads to a system of products (and code) that works in accordance with the business requirements. Many systems and software engineers are skilled today in the current products, but at the same time, are rarely skilled in architecting. To use RM-ODP requires an architecting and engineering skill set to architect the solution *before* the product is selected.

RM-ODP is well-defined and precise. It is also concise, leading to terseness and some ambiguities. The extreme terseness of the RM-ODP standard, the lack of complex system architecture examples for (re)use, the lack of an appropriate skill base about the concepts and structuring rules of RM-ODP, and so forth, lead to minimal use of RM-ODP.

Finally, there are no RM-ODP tools on the market for ODP-specific architecting. But this is all changing. More and more architects are adopting RM-ODP. Tools are emerging, and uses of RM-ODP are being published. More and more industries are finding that their existing architectures are deficient in some way, and that they need a more precise specification of those architectures that represent the lifecycle of the system. All of this provides the management and architecture teams a way ahead. And that is RM-ODP.

4.3 RM-ODP SUPPORT

Besides those identified in Chapter 2, a major supporter of RM-ODP is the Architecture Project Management (APM) Limited company. They introduced the original concepts of RM-ODP, based on their work on Advanced Network Systems Architecture (ANSA). In addition, APM created the following ODP-based products:

▶ ANSAware and ANSAware/Realtime

▶ Quartz, a CORBA/MBone interface product

▶ Distributed Control of ATM Networks, a lightweight ATM Object Request Broker (ORB) product

The APM commercially available ORB is fully RM-ODP based: the Distributed Interactive Multi-Media Architecture (DIMMA) ORB. "It has particular support for those applications that have soft real-time constraints, and those that make use of multimedia." [Dimma-98]

The Distributed Systems Technology Centre (DSTC), a consortium of research, industrial, and end-user organizations in Australia, has been a founding member of the RM-ODP committee, and produced ODP-based products as well.

The telecommunications industry consortium founded their TINA reference model on RM-ODP.

DAIS from PeerLogic [DAIS], which originated in England, is another RM-ODP–based ORB product.

4.4   RELATIONSHIP WITH OMG

Significant portions of RM-ODP overlap some of the OMG specifications. In 1994, the ISO Working Group 7 (WG7) formed a formal working relationship with the OMG to share common work, standardize some of the OMG specifications, and to implement some of the RM-ODP specifications through the OMG process. The nature of the agreement between OMG and ISO included:

▶ Cooperatively adopt each other's specifications in areas where they complement

▶ ODP adopts OMG's IDL

▶ ODP adopts OMG's Object Services

▶ OMG adopts ODP's Trader standard

▶ ODP quickly establishes an international standard for those OMG specifications adopted

▶ OMG sponsors ODP and adoption of the ODP Trader as an official specification by OMG

▶ Adoption by each group would be at its option; neither group is obligated to adopt any technology through the liaison relationship

Over the course of time, the end result is that OMG adopted the ODP Trader and the current work in the Object Management Architecture (OMA) guide is now using RM-ODP as the General Object Model for all of OMA, merging the RM-ODP concepts with those of the CORBA object model and component models.

The RM-ODP committee has proceeded with new work, based on OMG specifications. Principal among these is the new ISO RM-ODP Type Repository standard, which is based on the OMG Meta Object Facility (MOF) specification. ISO also standardized the OMG IDL. ISO based its work of the RM-ODP naming standard on the OMG naming service, and so forth. Hence, there is a tight relationship between OMG and RM-ODP specifications, as represented in Figure 4.5.

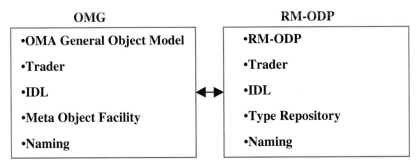

FIGURE 4.5   OMG and RM-ODP Specification Liaisons

In addition, many OMG domain service specifications adhere to the use of RM-ODP, and OMG sponsors the use of ODP in OMG specifications by its request for proposal (RFP) statement:

"Proposals shall be compatible with the architecture for system distribution defined in ISO/IEC 10746, Reference Model of Open Distributed Processing (ODP). Where such compatibility is not achieved, the response to the RFP must include reasons why compatibility is not appropriate and an outline of any plans to achieve such compatibility in the future." [OMG-RFP-97]

RM-ODP is also used to support the standardization of common functions for a particular domain, as defined by a specialized reference model. An example of this is the General Ledger service standard specified by the Financial domain committee in OMG [GenLedger-98]. In this case, the enterprise, information, and computational languages were used to define the General Ledger architecture, the semantics of the transaction processing, and the transactions in terms of interface specifications using the IDL [ISO IDL]. Another example is a standard set of interface specifications for telephone connections, as specified by TINA [TINA-97].

In constructing a distributed processing system, the architect may wish to use some OMG technologies in conjunction with RM-ODP. The specifications from OMG are used in the computational and engineering specifications. The products that OMG vendors produce from the OMG specifications are choices made in the technology specification. This relationship is represented in Figure 4.6.

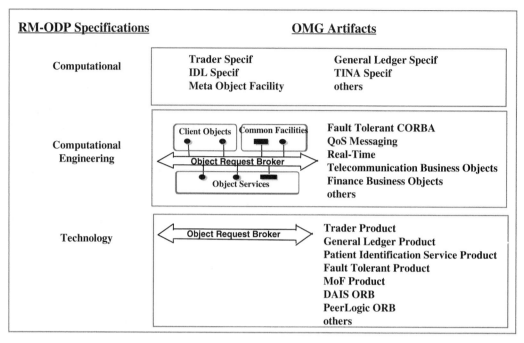

FIGURE 4.6   Using OMG Artifacts

4.5   RM-OSI AND RM-ODP

RM-ODP is a framework for all standards addressing the aspects of distributed processing, much like the Reference Model for Open Systems Interconnection (RM-OSI) [OSI] seven-layer stack is a framework for additional standards addressing aspects of telecommunications. Each model has been developed to meet specific business needs: distributed network communication for OSI; object-based distributed processing systems specification for ODP. The two models are synergistic, as will be shown.

The goal of OSI is to provide a framework for the definition of services and protocols in support of system interconnection. It is focused on the communication aspects between computer systems. ODP is focused on the interaction aspects between components, distributed across computers and contained within a computer.

OSI specifies the framework in terms of seven layers: Application, Presentation, Session, Transport, Network, Data Link, and Physical. Each is a layer in that the protocols and services of one layer support those of the layer above it. The seventh (topmost) layer consists of all OSI-based applications based on communication. This layer is where the standard for electronic messaging (X.400), directory services (X.500), remote procedure call (RPC), file transfer, network management, and others are specified. Figure 4.7 provides an overview of the OSI framework layers, and a description of the functionality at each of the layers.

At the time RM-ODP was formulated, there was no standard way to address the distribution aspects of software, and the interrelationships among those software components. Nor was there a way to provide for system properties and mechanisms (interoperability, scalability, reliability, and the like) in an open way. Several ISO and ITU-T standards did address aspects for distributed processing: the ISO Upper Layer Architecture and the X.500 Directory Services. Nevertheless, these standards did not formulate a framework for describing distributed application processing.

RM-ODP, on the other hand, provides a framework in terms of viewpoints. The five viewpoints are not layered: they represent different aspects of the same system, addressing a subset of concerns about the system. Altogether, they provide a single cohesive model of the system.

The RM-OSI not only aided in defining the different protocols for communication, it also helped position industry communication protocols defined by ISO, the Internet, and the private vendor protocols from AT&T for voice and from

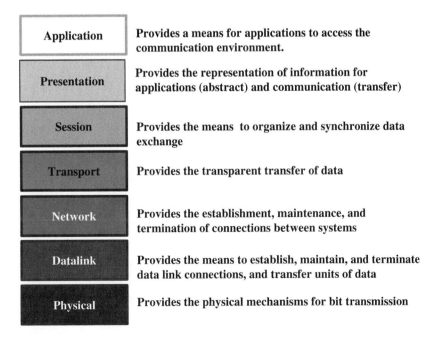

FIGURE 4.7   RM-OSI Framework Layers

IBM for the standard network architecture (SNA) protocol suite. It is hoped that RM-ODP will, in a similar fashion, help position industry distributed processing interactions and behavior of component-based systems.

When one looks at what each of the models actually addresses, one finds that OSI and ODP approach aspects of a system in similar ways. The frameworks have at least one objective in common: to promote syntactic and semantic interoperability between heterogeneous computing components. Although the frameworks differ in their approaches to specifying interoperability and their choices of the representing aspects of interfacing where interoperability is to exist, they are very complementary. In addressing interoperability, both are concerned with agreement on the syntax and semantics of information interchange. The syntax and semantics of the protocols specified is of concern to OSI. ODP, on the other hand, addresses interoperability in terms of component interactions and behavior.

Fundamentally different, but again synergistic, is the manner of addressing interfaces. OSI is concerned with the interfaces (actually, bindings in RM-ODP terminology) between systems, whereas ODP is concerned with the interface bindings between components of systems. These differences result in different styles of interface, but each addresses the need for a set of parameters and behavior to be expressed, along with the openness of the interface. Some of these similarities and differences are shown in Table 4.1, derived from [Rutt-93]:

TABLE 4.1 OSI vs. ODP

ITEM	OSI MODEL	ODP MODEL
Intended use	Distributed network systems, focused on networks	Object-based distribution, focused on software development
Business advantage	Open distribution of heterogeneous network components	Open distribution of heterogeneous system components, with distribution transparency hiding underlying heterogeneous platforms
Interoperability	Protocols and services across interfaces, at the syntactic and semantic level	Semantic specification and interaction definitions, at the syntactic and semantic level
	Focus on communications interoperability	Focus on interaction behavior
Interfaces	Boundary at which a prescribed protocol is supported	The behavior of an object at a subset of the object's interactions constrained by the circumstances for when they occur

TABLE 4.1 OSI vs. ODP (Continued)

ITEM	OSI MODEL	ODP MODEL
Conformance testing points	Protocol interface based on observing the behavior and syntax of the communication	There are four, the first is similar to OSI: 1. Interface binding between protocol objects called the interworking conformance point, similar to OSI 2. Programmatic conformance for testing of software substitutability and language binding 3. Interchange conformance addressing the behavior of some physical storage medium 4. Perceptual conformance for testing of the form of information presented to a human being, such as a graphical user interface
Protocols: 1. Rules for exchanging 2. Semantics of the information 3. Syntax of the information	Explicit protocol specification at each of the 7 layers: 1. Specification of services and exceptions 2. Specification of message content in each protocol: abstract syntax 3. Specification of the transfer bits for the information: transfer syntax	Abstractions of the intent for interaction, with no explicit transfer specification: 1. Interaction, behavior, constraints of interaction 2. Types of interfaces, specification of interface types, typed parameters, exceptions (e.g., through the use of IDL) 3. Left as a choice of technology in the Technology Viewpoint. This is where OSI-specific protocols are identified for use.
Cross-usage	OSI does not reference ODP, but some of the application layer standards, such as Network Management, address concepts similar to ODP	ODP explicitly addresses OSI in part of the specification in the Engineering Viewpoint communicating mechanism (called the channel), and in the Technology Viewpoint for selection of specific OSI protocols

From the beginning, the OSI reference model did not adequately address the structure of the seventh (top) layer, where all the distributed applications were placed. Since OSI focuses on communication, the seventh layer only addressed capabilities that use communication, not how they themselves are structured or composed to provide distributed services. Furthermore, OSI never addressed how all of these standards worked together in an enterprise to meet customer needs and ensure business requirements with enterprise-specific constraints, and enterprise-specific policies, which may affect the capabilities of the telecommunications aspects (such as security). Hence, RM-ODP was perceived by ISO and ITU-T as a needed reference model to pull together all the complex issues associated with distributed processing within an enterprise: specifying system properties, interaction among components, use of communication capabilities, support for enterprise requirements, semantics of information processing, and where communication capabilities fit into the framework of distributed processing. RM-ODP allows the use of OSI communication, as well as any other communications mechanism, which is a choice of the architect.

Figure 4.8 shows the relationship between RM-OSI and RM-ODP by example, where RM-ODP defines the system of focus (that part of the system of concern for the architect), part of which is the use of the OSI communications protocols.

Enterprises such as the finance industry and the medical industry and organizations such as OMG have seen the value of RM-ODP in specifying not only aspects of distributed processing, but also rules of the enterprise. These communities have used RM-ODP to formulate specializations of the standard as applied to that community. That is, they have taken RM-ODP and tailored the requirements to apply to their distributed processing endeavors.

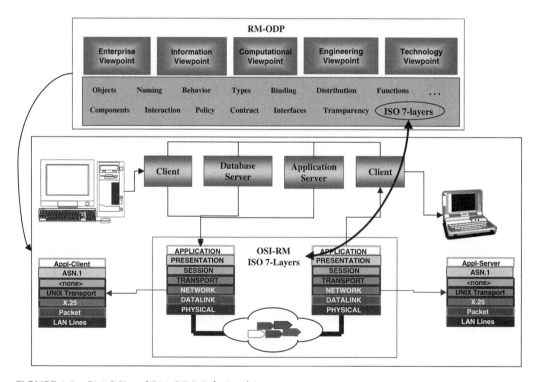

FIGURE 4.8   RM-OSI and RM-ODP Relationship

RM-ODP has also been created to provide a framework for providing the specification of additional standards for distributed processing, much like OSI provided for communication. Several standards have emerged that fill out various parts of the framework. These are discussed in the next section. This flexibility enables the ODP framework to have a reasonable lifetime, incorporating new developments as they mature. That is, a specific standard will specify a particular solution for some ODP requirement, such as naming. Different vendors will implement the standard in different ways, but by adhering to the specifications of the component standard, they will interoperate. Over time, then, as new technologies emerge, these new technologies will be incorporated into different design solutions, leading to a new generation of standards (such as for visualization) and a selection of products that interoperate across an open distributed processing system, all defined within the one RM-ODP framework.

4.6 PARTS OF THE STANDARD

The RM-ODP standard consists of four separate parts. The two main parts of the standard are foundations (Part 2) and architecture (Part 3). These comprise only about 100 pages of text, with very few examples. Part 2 provides the precisely defined concepts and terms, and a framework for describing a distributed processing system and for assessing conformance. Part 3 provides the mechanisms for specifying open distributed processing systems. These parts are the ones most used, most referred to, and form the foundation for specifying a system, or other RM-ODP standards. Part 4 is a formalism of Parts 2 and 3. Finally, Part 1 is an overview of the concepts of RM-ODP provided in a tutorial fashion. The official status of the parts of RM-ODP is captured in Table 4.2.

TABLE 4.2 Official Standard Status of RM-ODP

STANDARD	ITU-T	ISO/IEC	PUBLICATION DATE
Information technology—Open Distributed Processing Reference model: Overview and guide to use	X.901	IS 10746-1	1997
Information technology—Open Distributed Processing Reference model: Foundations	X.902	IS 10746-2	1995
Information technology—Open Distributed Processing Reference model: Architecture	X.903	IS 10746-3	1995
Information technology—Open Distributed Processing Reference model: Architectural Semantics	X.904	IS 10746-4	1997
Computational formalization	X.904 Amd. 1	IS 10746-4/ Amd. 1	Target 6/99

4.6.1 HISTORY OF RM-ODP

Such a standard did not originate over night. The creation of an international standard is a long and arduous task. First, a committee is formed by ISO to formulate the particular standard. Organizations from around the world participate in the formulation of the standard, representing specific organizational interests for the standard.

The ISO/IEC Joint Technical Committee 1 (JTC1), subcommittee 21 (SC21), WG7 was formed in 1988. In the U.S., the Accredited National Standards Committee (ANSI) X3, Information Processing Systems, created a new technical committee (X3T3), to represent the U.S. position in the international WG7. The purpose of WG7 (and X3T3) was to develop a reference model that would structure and organize international standards in the area of distributed processing, and promote a common understanding and agreement of distributed processing.

At its very first meeting in Sydney, Australia, 17 countries (National Bodies) plus 7 international groups (Liaison Organizations) participated. Over the course of the years, the committee members changed somewhat and the international representation grew.

In 1995, after 10 years of work, the ISO committee produced the Reference Model of Open Distributed Processing (RM-ODP). This committee was represented by many countries, with members who understood the elements of distributed systems and architecture, and brought to the table organizational domain-specific issues such as finance, telecommunications, government command-and-control, research, frameworks, and so forth.

Why did it take so many years to produce RM-ODP? The standard explicitly defines an ontology for use, defines in great depth the rules of specification, defines in great depth the separation of concerns into viewpoints, defines in generic terms the capabilities of an infrastructure to realize many of the "ilities," and so forth. RM-ODP terminology is a reflection of consensus by the working group, and affirmation by the international organizations. That is, these terms achieved international agreement from a great many different organizations. It takes time to achieve such work. The terms and rules are explicit, well-formed, and well-defined; achieving this level of precision is a long and arduous task. There is no looseness about these definitions that may occur in other frameworks. In fact, the definition for "architecture" (defined in Chapter 1) itself is difficult to achieve, but was accomplished by consensus in RM-ODP.

As it turns out, the architecture research community is now dealing with many concepts already defined in RM-ODP, such as interfaces being considered first-class citizens [Shaw-94]; the kinds of behavior to specify to enable composition [Abd-Allah-95, Abd-Allah-96, Gacek-97, Gacek-98, Gacek-Boehm, Medvidovic-2000]; and even the very definition of the term "architecture." Furthermore, additional standards are emerging under the RM-ODP initiative to further define distributed processing concepts. Notable among these are the emerging standard on Quality of Service framework [ISO-QOS], and the Enterprise Viewpoint [ISO-EntVP].

4.6.2 RM-ODP PART 1

Part 1 is the Overview [RM-ODP-1]. This part provides an overview of RM-ODP, and an idea of the elements that constitute the ODP reference model. It also contains some of the very few examples in the whole of RM-ODP, to help explain the concepts of RM-ODP. Although this part is at a full International Standard level, there are areas in this part that are inconsistent with Parts 2 and 3. It is a useful document, but be advised to treat it more as a white paper than a required part of the formal standard.

RM-ODP Part 1 should not be taken as completely accurate. It is non-normative, which means the standards bodies did not agree to make this a required or normative part of the RM-ODP standard. It contains some very useful discussion of the scope and motivation for ODP, but there are many places where the details are inconsistent with Parts 2 and 3. It is Parts 2 and 3 that form the requirements for RM-ODP.

4.6.3 RM-ODP PART 2

The "Bible" for RM-ODP is Part 2, Foundations. Part 2 contains the definitions of concepts and a conceptual framework for specification of distributed processing systems. It consists of very precise and general terms along with structuring rules. It is general because it applies to any distributed processing system. The Foundations part is the vocabulary of terms, the specification of the object modeling language used throughout RM-ODP, and a few rules about some of the terms. This part consists of only about 20 pages.

Part 2 forms the foundation concepts for the entire ODP family of standards, as well as the basic concepts to specify the components of an open distributed system. The structuring rules are defined to enable compliance checking of additional standards with the RM-ODP. This part also forms the foundation for modeling of ODP systems, definitions of distributed processing, and principles of conformance of ODP systems to their RM-ODP specifications.

Terminology and "buzz words" are prevalent in the software architecture arena, where each term may have a variety of overlapping meanings. However, in RM-ODP Part 2, every term is explicitly defined in a sentence that is, itself, explicitly stated, with few extraneous words (such as for clarification). There are a number of "Notes," to further explain something, however, which are also very explicit and sometimes terse.

RM-ODP Part 2 is very precise and general. As such it is exceedingly terse, with little in the way of helpful aids in interpretation (such as an example). For example, binding is defined as "a contractual context, resulting from a given establishing behaviour." To understand this definition requires understanding what contractual context means, and what establishing behavior means. Once that is accomplished, the well-defined precision is there. This 20-page part may take several readings over some time to grasp the intent of the standard.

4.6.4   RM-ODP PART 3

Part 3 is the Architecture. It contains an architecture, which establishes a framework for coordinating the development of existing and future standards for ODP systems, for specification of ODP systems, and includes a framework of abstractions and a set of required functions, structured in terms of viewpoints.

It too is terse, but not nearly as much as Part 2. Part 3 defines the concepts, which are terms and their meaning, and the structuring rules of how to put the concepts together for any architecture of an open distributed processing system, using a RM-ODP viewpoint-specific object modeling language.

In addition to the viewpoints, Part 3 also defines the distribution transparencies. Further, Part 3 goes on to define a number of RM-ODP specific functions. These functions provide the infrastructure services that support distributed processing, as well as supporting the eight RM-ODP transparencies. In all, there are 24 ODP functions. These functions are discussed in Chapter 9, "RM-ODP Functions."

One of the main contributions of RM-ODP is a full interworking framework, from the most general concepts to the most concrete specifications—from a recognized need to interwork through a network connection setup. It is this framework that greatly enables interoperability. This framework is discussed in depth in Chapter 13, "Interaction Framework: Interoperability."

Part 3 also defines management of a system, using the defined ODP functions, the interworking framework, and adding in the semantics to process the management functionality correctly.

Part 3 defines the constructs and rules for achieving consistency across all the viewpoints.

In addition to the consistency rules and methods, Part 3 also defines how and where to capture extra information in order to test the system implementation to the ODP specification. These are the rules for conformance testing and analysis. More is discussed concerning these rules in Chapter 11, "Architecture Analysis and System Conformance Evaluation."

4.6.5 RM-ODP Part 4

The last part is Part 4, Architectural semantics [RM-ODP-4]. This part contains the formalisms of the RM-ODP concepts and rules, as defined in Parts 2 and 3. This part actually uses formal description techniques (FDTs) to capture the semantics. The FDTs used include Language of Temporal Ordering Specifications (LOTOS), Specification and Description Language (SDL), and Z. This part is normative, meaning it forms a formal part of the standard. This part is not addressed in this book. It would require a great deal of explanation of the different FDTs, and how RM-ODP is represented.

4.6.6 Emerging RM-ODP Standards

The international community of ISO and ITU is furthering the work of RM-ODP by the specification of additional standards. They each use the Enterprise, Information, and Computational Viewpoints to specify the standard. As such each of these standards provides an example of the use of these RM-ODP viewpoints.

The status of the standards for RM-ODP are shown in Table 4.3, along with some detail as to the purpose of the standard and a reference for the standard. A discussion of these standards is not provided, except to exemplify certain aspects of RM-ODP in the subsequent chapters (e.g., the new Enterprise Viewpoint standard is used Chapter 12, "Enterprise Business Specification").

TABLE 4.3 RM-ODP Component Standards Official Status

Standard	ITU-T	ISO/IEC	Publication Date
Information technology—Open Distributed Processing—Reference model: Quality of service	X.905	TD5200-15935	March 2000
Information technology—Open Distributed Processing—Naming framework	X.910	14771	1998
Information technology—Open Distributed Processing—Enterprise viewpoint	X.911	15414	March 2000
Information technology—Open Distributed Processing—Use of specification techniques	X.912	TR 14466	March 2000
Information technology—Open Distributed Processing—Interface Definition Language	X.920	14750	1997

TABLE 4.3   RM-ODP Component Standards Official Status (Continued)

STANDARD	ITU-T	ISO/IEC	PUBLICATION DATE
Information technology—Open Distributed Processing—Interface references and binding	X.930	14753	1998
Information technology—Open Distributed Processing—Protocol support for computational interactions	X.931	14752	June 1999
Information technology—Open Distributed Processing—Trading function: Specification	X.950	13235-1	1997
Information technology—Open Distributed Processing—Trading function: ICS and test cases	X.951	13235-2	Work terminated
Information technology—Open Distributed Processing—Trading function: Provision of trading function using OSI Directory service	X.952	13235-3	1997
Information technology—Open Distributed Processing—Type repository function	X.960	14769	June 1999

Additional specialized architecture frameworks are needed to fill out the specifications in security, federation, and others.

In addition to these standards, there are two others of importance: the General Relationship Model (GRM) (ISO/IEC 10165) and the Open Distributed Management Architecture (ODMA) (ISO/IEC 13244).

The GRM focuses heavily on components and component composition, and emphasizes behavioral semantics and relationships between objects. General relationships are defined, such as composition, reference, and subtyping. Some of the concepts include:

▶ *Relationship:* "A collection of … objects together with an invariant referring to the properties of the … objects" [ISO GRM, ITU-GRM]
▶ *Invariant:* "A logical predicate that must remain true during some scope; a scope might be the lifetime of a managed relationship or the execution of a relationship management operation" [ISO GRM, ITU-GRM]

The composition operations and relationships defined include terminate, establish, bind, unbind, query, and notify, as well as other rules defined regarding composition. For example, a composite object, which is a composition of objects, has a type that must relate to one or more of the objects in the composition, each of which is an object with a type of component. An instance of a composite object corresponds to zero or more instances of each component type. A property of the composite object depends upon the property of a component. The behavior of the composite depends on the behavior of the components.

The ODMA standard is a suite of standards addressing management architecture. Policy rules, interface behavior, functions such as notification and dispatching are addressed in this standard. This standard then addresses the distributed management of systems and associated management functions that are open and hence interoperable across different vendor realizations of this standard.

The standards committees are open, for a nominal yearly fee. If one or more of these standards are important to a business, this is an opportunity for the business to get involved in the formulation of the standard.

4.7   SUMMARY

 RM-ODP is visionary. The architecture specification concepts are still pertinent today and visionary as well. They may aid the progression of the discipline of software architecture.

A descriptive tool will not provide an architecture specification; it does, however, facilitate communication among stakeholders. RM-ODP, with its extensive precise concepts and rules, provides an analytical tool to create an architecture specification and model of the system, which can then be represented in one of the popular visual tools of the day.

There are a number of tools that can be used to represent a RM-ODP architecture specification, but no single tool can represent all of it (yet). UML is a good aid for *describing* an architecture specification, but because of its limitations, is not adequate for *specifying* an RM-ODP architecture.

Standards writers, such as those in OMG and those formulating additional RM-ODP standards, capture the specification of the standard in terms of the enterprise, information, and computational languages. They leave the engineering and technology languages for use by different vendors, who can elect to implement the standard in different ways, providing value-added services to their product. It all holds together because of the consistency rules in RM-ODP. Trader, a service of OMG's CORBA, is a prime example of this. There are several vendor Trader service products, all of which are founded on the ISO Trading standard, which used the enterprise, information, and computational languages to define the trading service.

So-called vertical business domains use RM-ODP to facilitate either a business specification, or behavioral specification of the semantics of the system, or complete specification of a system. The way in which this is accomplished, in light of the limitations of the tools available, is to use the foundations of RM-ODP, coupled with the viewpoint specifications, and relate the results in a tool of choice. Since the concepts of RM-ODP hold together (are consistent), and since the tool used requires the architect to map the RM-ODP concepts to the tool, the result of the tool will also hold together.

In addition to the vertical domains, RM-ODP is supported by OMG. Some OMG specifications have become RM-ODP standards; some of the RM-ODP standards are mostly the OMG specification.

RM-ODP as a reference model for additional standards is similar to OSI. The reference model of OSI specified the seven layers of a communication protocol suite, and the concepts of each layer. Through the standardization process, additional ISO and ITU-T standards were created that filled out the OSI specification.

There are four parts to the RM-ODP standard. They include a tutorial about RM-ODP, the foundations for RM-ODP, an architecture model, and formal descriptions of RM-ODP. Additional standards are emerging to fill out a variety of architectural issues, such as naming, binding, type repository, and others. Some of these standards are in everyday use, such as the ISO standard for Trading and the ISO standard for IDL.

In summary, RM-ODP addresses not only precise terminology and architecting foundations, but also patterns for reuse in an architecture that focuses on system capabilities (e.g., fault tolerance). RM-ODP is an elegant standard that addresses many of the research and industry concerns of architecting today.

RM-ODP CONCEPTS AND RULES, AND THEIR USES

RM-ODP Architecture Model

In this chapter, the Reference Model of Open Distributed Processing (RM-ODP) architecture model of a system is explored. Topics to be covered are:

▶ Overview of the RM-ODP architecture model

▶ Overview of the five RM-ODP viewpoints

▶ Using the RM-ODP viewpoints

▶ An overview of the prescribed transparencies

▶ An overview of the ODP functions, upon which the infrastructure and transparency mechanisms are constructed

▶ RM-ODP specific object-based model, upon which all viewpoint languages are based

▶ Rules of specification

▶ Rules of structuring

5.1   RM-ODP Architecture Model Overview

The RM-ODP architecture model consists of a set of five viewpoint models, the concepts and rules associated with the language of each model, the distribution transparency constructs, and the ODP functions. All of the RM-ODP model is based on the RM-ODP foundations of an object model, rules for specification, and rules for structuring. In this chapter, each of these will be addressed.

The five viewpoints consist of the:

1. Enterprise viewpoint
2. Information viewpoint
3. Computational viewpoint
4. Engineering viewpoint
5. Technology viewpoint

Along with the foundation constructs, these five viewpoints form the basis upon which an open distributed processing (ODP) system is specified.

Each viewpoint is **on** a system, as depicted in Figure 5.1. A viewpoint-specific language is associated with each viewpoint and is used to specify an ODP system from that viewpoint. The language includes precisely defined concepts and terminology, and rules of how those concepts are related in considering issues associated with distribution and distributed systems. Within each viewpoint language, consistency of that viewpoint with the other viewpoints is provided by explicitly identifying the correspondences of the concepts in one viewpoint with those in other viewpoints. This consistency leads to the ability for each viewpoint to define conformance criteria, and for conformance checking across the view-

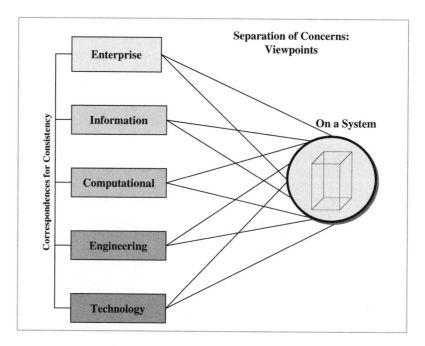

FIGURE 5.1 RM-ODP Viewpoints on a System

points. Each language is founded on the principles of the RM-ODP object model, and makes use of the specification and structuring rules of the foundation.

The ODP functions are those capabilities needed to support ODP systems and the distribution transparencies. There are four main categories of the 24 ODP functions, which are discussed in this chapter. The four categories consist of:

1. Management: This category includes four functions that manage the engineering viewpoint node constructs.
2. Coordination: This category includes eight functions that manage the movement, consistency, and coordination of node constructs, including the objects and interfaces.
3. Repository: This category includes five functions supporting storage, type repositories, and the trading function.
4. Security: This category includes seven security related functions.

RM-ODP forms a framework for additional standardization of capabilities that specify ODP system capabilities. Many of the RM-ODP functions, as identified in Chapter 9, "RM-ODP Functions," are standards to fully specify one or more of these functions, such as the trading standard [ISO Trading]. RM-ODP provides the patterns of reasoning of the functions for the architect to use, but not the actual mechanisms to achieve the processing of the function.

A distribution transparency is a mechanism for hiding the complexities of an infrastructure support mechanism from an end user or application developer. RM-ODP defines eight distribution transparencies: access, failure, location, migration, persistence, relocation, replication, and transaction. These eight distribution transparency constructs are requirements on how to achieve a transparency in such a manner as to be open and interoperable across multiple heterogeneous distributed systems.

The transparencies are selective. This means the architect can select any number of them for use in the specification, ignoring others, as long as the dependencies of one upon the other are adhered to. For example, the architect may choose the access transparency to provide access to some service in the system, without the application needing to know the details of "accessing" that service. This particular transparency needs the location transparency as well, to hide the details of determining the location that the service is to access. In this case the architect would specify both the access and location transparencies. Additional discussion of this important topic occurs in Chapter 10, "Hiding System Complexities: Distribution Transparencies."

An overview of the RM-ODP architecture model is represented in Figure 5.2, showing the parts and relationships among the parts of the architecture model, and the other standards that provide additional distributed processing capabilities. The parts of the architecture model are addressed in the remaining sections of this chapter. For now, the figure provides a representation of how the parts relate in the architecture model.

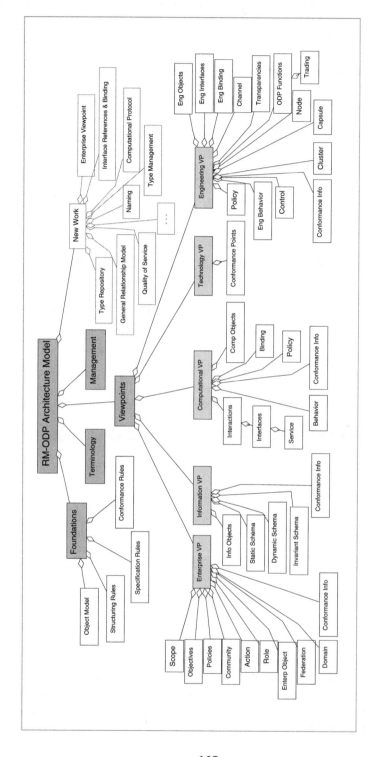

FIGURE 5.2 RM-ODP Architecture Model

162

5.2   RM-ODP VIEWPOINTS OVERVIEW

An RM-ODP viewpoint is a perspective from which one views the system, considering some aspects of a system (e.g., business objectives) and ignoring other aspects (e.g., distribution). It is too difficult to represent everything about a system in a single monolithic specification. The architect may end up missing critical details, not addressing needed additional components in a system, and not adequately communicating the architecture of the system with either the stakeholder or the system implementer. Instead, narrowing the scope of what to consider to a viewpoint helps focus in depth on those specific aspects of the system.

The collection of the set of viewpoints needs to be tied together to provide a consistent and total view of the system. A viewpoint is a "tool" to scope what needs to be specified from a particular aspect of the system. There are many viewpoint approaches available in today's literature. Some address the functionality of the system, some address the lifecycle of the system, some address aspects of the architecture (not the system).

 The five RM-ODP viewpoints provide a necessary and sufficient set to capture the specification of any information distributed processing system that is open.

RM-ODP [RM-ODP-2] defines a *viewpoint* as an abstraction of a set of concerns on a system, derived by using a set of concepts and rules of structure.

 RM-ODP viewpoints are viewpoints **on** a system. Furthermore, they are not layered, but rather different abstractions on the same system focusing in on certain areas of concern.

Figure 5.3 provides an overview of the five viewpoints and their general focus. The elements in each viewpoint are discussed at length in Chapter 6, "Separation of Concerns: Using RM-ODP Viewpoints." An overview of each of the viewpoints follows.

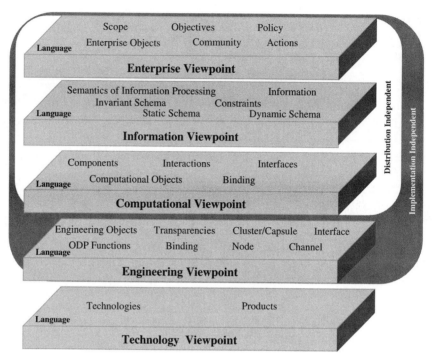

FIGURE 5.3 RM-ODP Viewpoints and Focus of Concern

The viewpoints are always used in conjunction with the foundations of RM-ODP. The viewpoints do not merely define concepts for use; these concepts are always subject to the foundation rules. As an example, an object in the computational viewpoint may in fact be a composite object that equates to a full subsystem, using the foundation rules of abstraction and composition. As another example, a policy is also subject to the rules of abstraction and composition. Hence, at one level of abstraction, a policy may state a high-level obligation. But at another level of abstraction, that obligation may be a composition of several obligations associated with different objects and their interactions.

5.2.1 ENTERPRISE VIEWPOINT

The enterprise viewpoint provides constructs useful to communicate the needs of the stakeholders to the systems architect. If a graphical representation is used, such as many of the emerging modeling and development tools provide, communication becomes even clearer, though care needs to be exercised in the use of such a tool to ensure constraints are represented accurately.

The enterprise viewpoint provides a means of capturing requirements and the intended overall structure and behavior as a community within an environment. This viewpoint deals with the following concepts, discussed further in Chapter 6, "Separation of Concerns: Using RM-ODP Transparencies," Chapter 8, "Composition and Semantics: Quality Composition Minimizing Architectural Mismatch," and Chapter 12, "Enterprise Business Specification."

▶ Purpose and objectives—To capture the reason for the system, and its use in the environment. It defines a set of objects formed to meet an objective, their activities, and the processes in which the system participates. It also defines the reason for the specification, and what the system is to achieve, such as "interoperable system."

▶ Scope—Set of roles and associated behavior

▶ Community—The boundaries to be focused on, such as "Healthy Hospital and its internal organizations."

▶ Policy—Guide and constrain the system design; it may change over time, dynamically. Used to describe what is permitted, prohibited, and obligated by an object in its actions and behavior of an enterprise, such as "it is an obligation on the admitting agent to admit all emergency patients."

▶ Environment—Those entities that are not part of the object, leading to the ability to specify what an object expects of its environment, and what constraints the environment places on the object, such as "the state regulation authority."

▶ Action—Some function being performed, such as "admit a patient."

▶ Role—An identifier, or placeholder, for a set of behavior and activities to be performed, such as "the admitting agent."

▶ Contract—An agreement between parties, such as a quality of service of "availability."

▶ Enterprise object—An object in the enterprise that assumes a role.

▶ Environment contract—A contract between an object and its environment, including quality of service constraints, and usage and management constraints.

Figure 5.4 shows an overview of how these concepts apply in the Healthy Hospital case study.

5.2.2 Information Viewpoint

The information viewpoint focuses on the information processing semantics and the information of the system, through the constructs of information objects; static, invariant, and dynamic schemata; and rules associated with them. These three schemata capture the semantics, structure, and relationships among the processing of the system: the metadata. Metadata is that extra information about the system that relates to the existence of objects, the constraints about the use

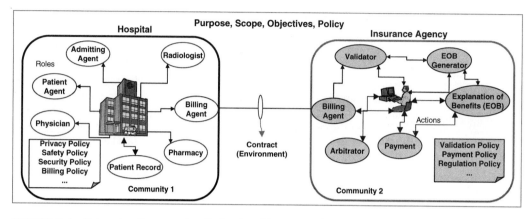

FIGURE 5.4   Enterprise Concepts Applied to Healthy Hospital

of the objects, and the rules for use of the object. It includes type, allowed state changes, allowed object states, and the rules that direct the behavior of the object throughout its existence. For example, the properties that define an interface are explicitly captured in an interface template. Obligations from a policy are captured as constraints in the invariant schema, constraining all behavior of the object for a period of time. Actions that cause an object to change state are captured in the dynamic schema.

Figure 5.5 shows an overview of how these concepts apply in the Healthy Hospital case study.

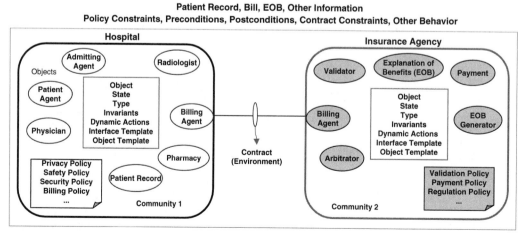

FIGURE 5.5   Information Concepts Applied to Healthy Hospital

5.2.3 COMPUTATIONAL VIEWPOINT

The computational viewpoint focuses on the computational aspects and refinement of the system in terms of components and objects, connectors (in terms of interactions, interfaces, and bindings), and constraints including policy statements, contracts that include quality of service (QoS), and other constraints. The computational viewpoint helps to capture the objects and their interaction details, without regard to distribution (which is addressed in the engineering viewpoint).

Figure 5.6 shows an overview of how these concepts apply in the Healthy Hospital case study. Notice that there are no indications of where the objects are distributed, just the objects and their interactions.

5.2.4 ENGINEERING VIEWPOINT

The engineering viewpoint focuses on distribution, the configuration of the node (such as a computer and its operating system), the services provided by the infrastructure (such as store), and the interfacing and binding mechanisms needed to realize distribution. This viewpoint uses the constructs of engineering objects, ODP function objects, node configurations, channel objects that perform the communication and interception, and distribution transparency objects. It describes an application component's use of and support by the infrastructure that is specified.

Figure 5.7 shows an overview of how these concepts apply in the Healthy Hospital case study.

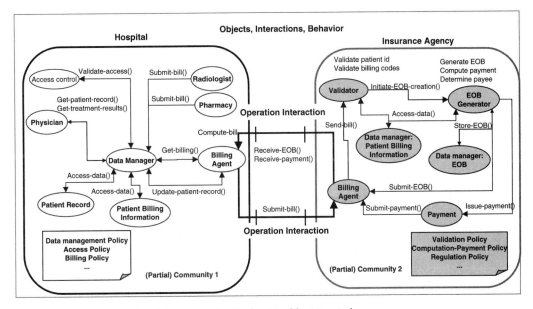

FIGURE 5.6 Computational Concepts Applied to Healthy Hospital

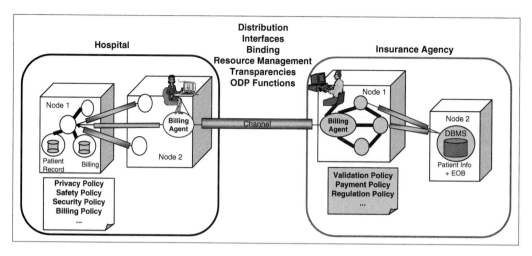

FIGURE 5.7   Engineering Concepts Applied to Healthy Hospital

5.2.5 TECHNOLOGY VIEWPOINT

The technology viewpoint focuses on the technology and products for implementation. RM-ODP does not stop here; it provides four reference points in each of the viewpoints to test the system implementation against the system specification. That is, these reference points are points for conformance testing.

 There are very few examples in the standard to explain the concepts. There is no acceptable standard for an approved interpretation of RM-ODP either.

5.2.6 DIFFERENT VIEWPOINTS

A different viewpoint might be something from a domain perspective, such as a viewpoint on the patients interacting with their doctors. Or the architect may need a security viewpoint that addresses the physical elements (building and computer), network, distributed processing (security policy, access control, transparencies, etc.), guards (humans), etc. RM-ODP does not prescribe against this approach. Rather, in the use of such a viewpoint, chances are that each of the five RM-ODP viewpoints will be used as well. Figure 5.8 represents how a data view of a system will cut across all the RM-ODP viewpoints, narrowing the focus within each viewpoint to that particular capability (issues about data).

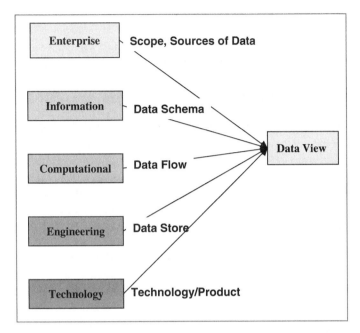

FIGURE 5.8   RM-ODP and Other Viewpoints

5.2.7   INDEPENDENCE OF DISTRIBUTION AND IMPLEMENTATION

In terms of RM-ODP, the enterprise, information, computational, and engineering viewpoints are defined independent of any choice of product or technology. For example, the use of an Oracle® database management system (DBMS) is not part of the architectural specification until the architect addresses the choice of products in the technology viewpoint. However, the need for a data resource is addressed in the enterprise viewpoint; the data schema is addressed in the information viewpoint; the data flow and access to the data are addressed in the computational viewpoint; and the use of a data store is addressed in the engineering viewpoint. The architect selects the appropriate DBMS vendor, version, type (e.g., relational, object-oriented, network) in the technology viewpoint.

Although the engineering viewpoint addresses issues of nodes (computers), groups of software, software allocation to specific nodes, and communication mechanisms, the engineering viewpoint is implementation independent. The details of the implementation technologies and products for which computer fulfills the needs of the node, which software products fulfill the needs of a software function, and which communication product fulfills the needs of the channel are postponed to the technology viewpoint. For example, the engineering viewpoint will provide details of the interfacing mechanisms and associated objects to achieve interworking with another node. It might address certain aspects of the Internet or Common Object Request Broker Architecture (CORBA) services, such as naming services, but not the specific vendor Object Request Broker (ORB) or Web-server products, nor a specific communication protocol.

The enterprise, information, and computational viewpoints are independent of considerations of distribution. For example, the architect focuses on how a client object interacts with a server providing Web-based capabilities, and a server providing application capabilities, without worrying if the client is on a specific computer, or in a specific geographic location, or if the Web server and application server are in one geographic location or distant from each other.

The computational viewpoint does address distribution enablers. The need for a distribution transparency, for example, is addressed in the computational viewpoint. The means of engineering the transparency are addressed in the engineering viewpoint. As another example, the specification for binding two interfaces is part of the computational viewpoint, whereas the actual binding of interfaces, and where those interfaces are located, are part of the engineering viewpoint.

In the computational viewpoint, the architect does not need to address client workstations or server hardware, or even the distribution of software. The focus is on the functioning of the components, their behavior, and the specification of the interfaces to achieve interaction among components. In particular, this is where the software subsystem boundaries are specified in terms of application program interfaces (APIs), however those subsystems may be distributed.

The engineering viewpoint is focused on distribution. Its concepts include nodes (computers and their operating systems), the placement of software on the nodes, the grouping of software on a node, the binding mechanisms, the transparency mechanisms, the ODP function mechanisms, and the communication mechanisms to bind the software together.

5.2.8 EXAMPLE: BUILDING A HOUSE

Let's discuss a real-life example to exemplify the concept of viewpoints: a view of some part of a system.

Shannon is building a house. Shannon first hires Steve to develop (or buy) a structural blueprint for her house. This blueprint provides:

▶ A stated purpose—The house is a single-family dwelling. The number of occupants will be four: Shannon and her three dogs.

▶ The scope—The number of rooms is eight: living room, dining room, kitchen, four bedrooms, and a family room.

▶ Structure and style—The house will be a New England Colonial style house. The position of each room is stated. The flow from one room to another is stated. The number of levels is stated.

▶ Environment—The house will be part of a small town community, situated on property that borders other houses, with an easement for public works access. The details of the house are not yet determined.

Next, Steve commissions the rough-framing architect, Joe, to develop a rough-framing blueprint. Here, Joe captures the placement of the joists, beams, studs, size of each, roofing materials, and so forth. Steve also captures the amount of lumber, nails, bolts, screws, roofing material, and sheetrock that will be needed. The rough framer has a blueprint of how these parts fit together to form the rough framing.

As the framing is developed, Steve needs to have a blueprint of the electrical system of Shannon's house. In this blueprint, the electrician will focus on the electrical conduits, outlets, the master control panel, the number of electrical outlets, and how they are interrelated. Likewise, Steve needs a plumbing blueprint that provides the view of the house from the perspective of water lines, internal and external valves, shut-off valves, water filters, faucets, bathroom fixture plumbing, kitchen plumbing, and how they work together.

The consistency is accomplished by more than directing what needs to be accomplished (e.g., a conduit for an electrical cable). It is accomplished by a set of well-defined concepts and rules for each blueprint: building codes. The language of the rough framer is "stud," "joist," etc. These terms carry meanings for the electrician who directs that a conduit be "hung" between two "joists," or for a plumber who directs that an "electrical outlet" not be placed closer than 10 feet from a "water source."

Each blueprint developer understands the meaning of these terms, and hence communicates consistent relationships using these terms.

In both the electrical and plumbing views, Steve needs to make sure the proper holes and spacing are provided in the rough framing, that the wiring can be placed before the sheetrock walls go up, and so forth. That is, there must be consistency across the framing, electrical, and plumbing blueprints.

Steve must also make sure he does not cross the water system with the electrical system; the "interaction" between the two must be distant.

Shannon is concerned with the "flow of the house": it needs to be open, and accommodate people flowing from one room to another without a lot of walls and doors to go through. This is specified by the functioning of the rooms, the constraints of where the walls are placed, and the actual mechanisms of entering and leaving a room (e.g., through a door not a breezeway).

Shannon wants a truly fabulous kitchen, and so Steve develops a kitchen specification to show how many cabinets she wants, where she wants them, where she wants the kitchen appliances, etc. Of course this blueprint must also be consistent with the plumbing, electrical, and rough-framing blueprints as well.

Notice that, so far, Shannon has not identified specific products or vendors for her kitchen, bathroom, light fixtures, doorknobs, and other items. She will, of course, get to these in the course of implementing her house architecture.

Each of these blueprints is a view of the whole house, addressing certain areas of concern; e.g., electrical while ignoring others such as rough framing. The use of all these blueprints ends in a specified blueprint for the house.

But the house architecture still needs to adhere to building codes, address the strength of certain sized beams, and other constraints, generally implicit in such a blueprint. These constraints come from experience of the home architect (hopefully), and the building codes that direct what can and cannot be done. Further, the house may be placed on some property that might have covenants associated with that property. These are like environment contracts.

Altogether, the blueprint, the building codes, the constraints on the parts of the house, and the external rules and regulations comprise a specification for the house, and in similar manner, for a system.

So does RM-ODP. It defines a language (the enterprise viewpoint language) to capture what the user or customer wants. From this, RM-ODP provides defined capabilities for the architect to fully specify the architecture of the system. It defines:

▶ A language for use in each of the viewpoints, to capture the structure and constraints of a system, at different levels of abstraction

▶ Abstraction techniques for use by the architect to focus on some aspect of the system, delaying addressing other aspects until later

▶ Composition techniques for use by the architect to address coarse-grained objects, delaying the details of the objects in the composition until later

▶ Correspondences across the viewpoints to achieve consistency

▶ Composition techniques for behavior

▶ How to capture behavior and constraints of the system

▶ How to check for conformance

RM-ODP separates the large problem of a system architecture into focused aspects of the system. This is how we address problems in general: divide the problem into smaller parts that can be solved, and roll the parts up into a full solution.

Each of the problem areas addressed represents the concerns of users involved in the creation of the system: stakeholders who are concerned with the business specification; software architects who are concerned with what the system components are and how they function, their interfaces, and the constraints on their behavior; system programmers who are interested in the operating system, the communications mechanisms, the distribution of the software across different computers, and how these are tied together; the product evaluators who know the current technologies and products, and can map the architecture specification to the use of specific products and technologies; and the information analysts who are concerned not only with the information schema but also the semantics of how the system performs.

This is the architecture team. They are all needed for generating a well-formed system architecture specification.

Constructing an architecture is similar to building a home: a house is constructed through a team of future homeowner, planner, electrician, plumber, rough-framer, and so forth. The general contractor is like the domain-specific software architect: the person who knows about all the parts, but focuses on the overall construction of the architecture, ensuring it adequately captures the functionality, performance, and composition of the parts. The building codes, semantics of the parts of a house, and rules of the community form the rest of the specification for a house. (We'll ignore the tax person.)

5.3	**USING RM-ODP FROM A DOMAIN-SPECIFIC PERSPECTIVE**

RM-ODP is a generic standard, applicable to any domain-specific architecture. It provides the general mechanisms for specification and refinement of a system. To accomplish this feat, RM-ODP provides very explicit (and terse) concepts. The concepts and rules defined for each of the languages, along with the RM-ODP object model, result in a standard that is a mature conceptualization of software architecture. Recall that this conceptualization has achieved international agreement.

RM-ODP provides the general foundation for describing any domain-specific reference model, from which are derived domain-specific software architectures, and domain-specific systems. One way of using RM-ODP is to bypass the domain-wide reference architecture, and use RM-ODP for both the reference architecture and the domain-specific software architecture (DSSA), with appropriate mapping of the RM-ODP concepts to the domain concepts.

For example, the Object Management Group's (OMG) Object Management Architecture (OMA) makes use of the RM-ODP architecture model. Parts of OMA address the domains for medical and finance. Within the finance domain reference architecture the general ledger specification was created by using RM-ODP. Within the financial, telecommunications, health, and other business domains, RM-ODP is being used (this was addressed in Chapters 2, 3, and 4). All of these are domain-specific, requiring a domain specialization of RM-ODP to satisfy the needs of that domain.

An overview of the relationship among RM-ODP, a reference model for a specific domain, and a DSSA is depicted in Figure 5.9. Examples are shown in italics.

Some of the domains that have used RM-ODP have specialized that use by providing additional constructs for use. For example, the enterprise viewpoint allows the architect to specify a policy. Some communities have used RM-ODP to provide a specification of a policy, and reused this specification across the domain. So, real usage of RM-ODP has resulted in RM-ODP–based patterns of use. More about policy is covered in Chapter 14, "Policy Framework."

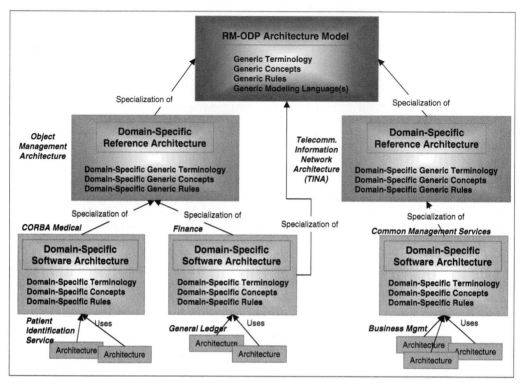

FIGURE 5.9   RM-ODP and DSSA

As an example, Healthy Hospital has a policy that obligates the "privacy of the patient record." This policy is related to the concepts in the information viewpoint (a patient record object, a privacy control object, and constraints), and the computational viewpoint (the patient record object, the privacy control object, perhaps a role-based access control object, and the interface specifications for all interfaces). This policy specification, and the mechanisms to realize the policy statement, can then be applied to all hospitals in the local region where Healthy Hospital exists, for example. What is happening here is that a use of RM-ODP can constitute a pattern of reasoning for reuse by an architect of the domain.

An example of this is the OMG Medical domain specification for Patient Identification Services (PIDS) [OMG-PIDS]. The services specified are interface definitions, constraints associated with those interfaces, and common patterns for reuse, all related to common identification of patient information (e.g., name, address, Social Security number, etc.). The use of PIDS turned out to be so general that it is now specified as a person identification service in OMG, not just patient identification. As such, PIDS was renamed to be Person Identification Services, and is reusable across multiple domains.

Another example for domain-specific use of RM-ODP is the French Tele-communications domain. They used RM-ODP to help decouple specifications of their systems. In particular, RM-ODP helped them to address:

▶ "What is the system supposed to do?"
▶ "What kind of information is managed by the system?"
▶ "How can access to the information be accomplished, independent of specific protocol specifications?"
▶ "How can the communication be mapped onto many different protocols?"

The success of their project led to a creation of an internal tool to aid in the use of RM-ODP. They are now working to drive any use of a Unified Modeling Language (UML) tool to using the concepts of RM-ODP and that of the General Relationship Model. [Cornily-99]

5.4   USE OF RM-ODP VIEWPOINTS

RM-ODP is equally applicable to a system of systems, a system, or a software component. The technical objectives of RM-ODP are to provide:

▶ Business specification of a domain
▶ Semantics of behavior of the system and its parts
▶ Full support for aspects of distributed processing
▶ Interoperability across heterogeneous systems
▶ Portability across heterogeneous systems
▶ Interworking between systems
▶ Hide consequences of distribution to the systems developer

With a common language about distributed processing, and with the ability to relate that language to a domain-specific language (such as medical), RM-ODP enables communication among stakeholders and the architect; the architect and the designer; the architect and the implementer; and the architect and the tester.

Communication between stakeholders and the architect is facilitated by the use of the enterprise viewpoint. The constructs of this viewpoint are easily related to the business, and can thereby facilitate the communication. For example, a *role* in the enterprise language relates to a physician, or a hospital administrator in the language of the domain. A *community* in the enterprise language relates to an organization within the business. Actually, a community is used for more than a business organization. It can also be used to group roles within a business organization. This is part of the architect's job of refinement. But as a vehicle for communication with the stakeholder, a community can, among other things, represent an organization in a domain.

These are common terms, though defined precisely in RM-ODP, for development of an architecture specification. RM-ODP just happens to also define rules for the architect to make sure that an interface has a type, for example, and that the interactions between two objects are part of an interface. Once the architect has specified these constructs, the implementer of the system will understand (exactly) what needs to be implemented, and the architect can determine whether the implementation meets the architect specification through the conformance test points.

How one goes about using the viewpoints has proven through industry experience to be domain-specific, depending on the objectives most interested in. The enterprise and information viewpoints, for example, provide a business specification, or basic requirements, of the system. The information, computational, and engineering viewpoints form the basic architecture viewpoints. The computational and engineering viewpoints form the detail specification of the software architecture of the system, from the concept of components and composition, to that of architecture styles of interaction. The technology viewpoint provides the implementation details of products used and, thus, forms a constraint on the realization of the system specification.

Not unlike object-oriented analysis and design, the architect will probably need to iterate through the viewpoints a few times to make sure the refinement is correct and not overly large or complex. Figure 5.10 provides an overview of how one might iterate through the viewpoints. The discussion follows.

One can start with any of the viewpoints. However, it is important to initially capture the objective for the specification, and the general statements of constraints, through the use of the enterprise viewpoint. The enterprise viewpoint is used for more than a business specification. It is also used to provide the scope and objectives for any major component building block of a system. There are examples of this use in the OMG General Ledger specification and both the OMG Trader and ISO Trading specifications. All of the new RM-ODP standards use the enterprise viewpoint language to capture the scope, objectives, constraints, objects, and actions of the component standard.

Iterating between the computational and engineering viewpoints allows the architect to fully refine some aspect of the architecture. Incrementally approaching the different major components of the computational specification in this manner eventually achieves a fully refined architectural specification.

Top-down, performing all the enterprise and information specifications first, followed by the computational specification, then the engineering specification is generally ill-advised. Behaviors may be determined in the engineering viewpoint that affect the architecture in the computational viewpoint or the policies in the enterprise viewpoint. Hence, iteration among the viewpoints, coupled with incrementally addressing all aspects of a viewpoint, produces the best result.

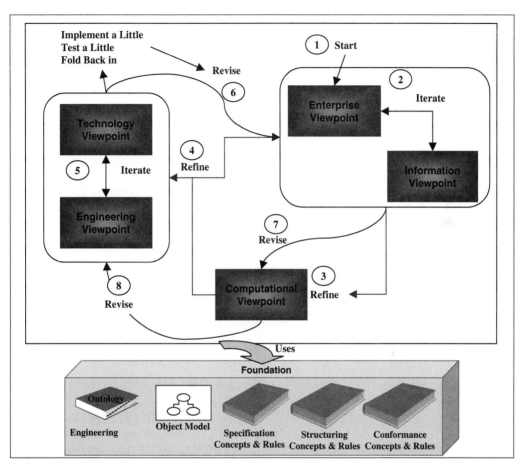

FIGURE 5.10 Using the Viewpoints Iteratively

Initially, begin with the specification (top-level) of the business through the use of the enterprise and information viewpoints. For some major aspect of the resultant partial specification, refine it to more detail using the computational viewpoint. Continue to the engineering viewpoint. At this point, iterate with the technology viewpoint to implement a part, test that part, and learn what to fold back in and revise. Revisit the enterprise and information specifications, updating as needed. Continue to update the computational and engineering specifications. Continue with additional prototyping. Incrementally build upon the lessons learned through this spiral activity. Always use the foundation and engineering skills throughout the process.

The engineering viewpoint is used to refine the specification to more concrete aspects of the actual objects that comprise your system, the concrete specifications of the interface mechanisms, the infrastructure services, bindings,
constraints that apply across the bindings, and so forth. Many of these concepts
are detailed in Chapter 6, "Separation of Concerns: Using RM-ODP Viewpoints."
For example, replication of some object for load-balancing reasons is specified in
terms of a requirement in the computational viewpoint, and refined into the details
of the replication, the details of the objects that make up the computational
objects, and the details of the interfacing in the engineering viewpoint.

What this all means is that as the architect identifies major components and
their relationships, the process of refinement is also initiated. The architect may
discover that fully refining the component to a greater level of detail is needed
before continuing to capture all the components of the software architecture in the
computational viewpoint.

Along the way in the use of the computational, engineering, and even the
enterprise viewpoints, all semantics about the processing of the objects of the system are captured in the information viewpoint. When the architect refines the
architecture in the computational or engineering viewpoints, previously defined
information viewpoint constraints should be revisited. The information viewpoint
is used throughout the specification process.

The results of the viewpoints provide criteria for selecting the choices of
technologies and products. As is so often the case, the products of the day do not
provide full capability. With RM-ODP, the architect has a specification that identifies what is currently implemented, and importantly, what is not yet implemented
due to insufficient available choices of the day.

The technology viewpoint is also the area where the architect specifies
where to place the reference points for conformance testing. The architecture team
can define the test cases for use, what to observe across the reference points, and
establish the test plan for the system.

Through the use of RM-ODP composition, RM-ODP addresses systems of
systems as well as a single system or a system component. The term "system" here
is used very loosely. Each system can be a system in an enterprise (called a community in RM-ODP) or a software component in an enterprise. RM-ODP provides
a means of capturing other domain-specific reference models, from which different domain-specific architectures can be constructed.

Figure 5.11 provides a view of system composition. In this figure, the enterprise consists of the communities shown. Each is an independent community, but
must interact to support the needs of the medical enterprise. Within a particular
community, there is a full system. A particular component in the Hospital Community, for example, is also considered a system, such as "record results."
Through composition, the system composes with the other components in the
Hospital Community, which together compose into a single enterprise system of
systems.

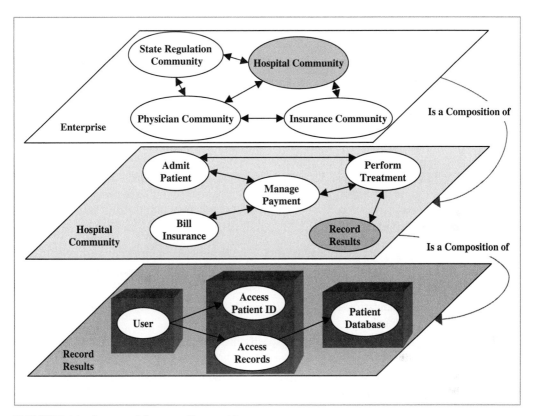

FIGURE 5.11   System of Systems Composition

 POINT The use of the enterprise, information, and computational viewpoints provides a domain-specific reference architecture specification, that guides the development of specific system instances of a DSSA in the domain, realized through the engineering and technology viewpoint usage.

RM-ODP viewpoints do not cover, for example, the process for domain engineering, or the functionality of a set of components that may or may not be reusable artifacts in a domain-specific system. The architect may use or define some other viewpoint to explain the functionality of, for example, billing across the domain. Another viewpoint could be from a business perspective concerning a particular domain, such as a viewpoint on the interaction between patients and doctors. Or one may choose to use a viewpoint on security for a business, that includes the physical security (building and computer), network security (and all the Open Systems Interconnection (OSI) security), distributed processing security (security policy, access control, transparencies, etc.), human security guard, and so forth.

The five viewpoints are recursively used. Reverting back to the house architecture example, a kitchen cabinet also has separate designs: the purpose, scope, and policy as directed by the homeowner; the rough framing of the cabinets; the doors and drawers and their relationships; the details and finishing touches as per a particular vendor. One can construct a kitchen cabinet from a set of blueprints, each representing a particular viewpoint. So it is with RM-ODP. A component identified in the computational viewpoint, for example, may itself be fully specified by one or more RM-ODP viewpoints. If there is a need for a data broker in the system (a component that brokers user requests to multiple database management systems), the specification of that data broker should itself be done through the RM-ODP viewpoints:

▶ Enterprise viewpoint to specify the purpose, scope, and policy of the broker

▶ Information viewpoint to specify the information processing and metadata repositories required

▶ Computational viewpoint to specify the internal broker components and their interactions

▶ Engineering viewpoint to specify the detailed interfacing mechanisms and infrastructure objects

▶ Technology viewpoint (possibly) for identifying products upon which the data broker itself is constructed

The kitchen cabinet, medical enterprise, and data broker examples show how the use of the viewpoints is composable. The Trader specification [ISO-Trading] does just this. It specifies the Trader by using the enterprise, information, and computational viewpoints. It does not go further, because it is a standard specification. The specification is then used by commercial vendors to finish the engineering and technology viewpoint specifications to implement a vendor-specific product.

However, the architect may identify the use of a Trader in a system specification, without the need to construct a full Trader specification; that has already been accomplished, and is reusable. The architect needs only to state the use of the published interfaces and address how the system components interact with the Trader.

Many of the modeling tools today define different viewpoints. Notably are the four viewpoints of UML: Use Case, logical, component, and deployment. The architect can freely use any UML vendor tool to facilitate the process of architecting and communicating with stakeholders. However the architect needs to relate the RM-ODP concepts to those of the tool used. For example, the architect may choose to use the use case model of UML to represent the enterprise concepts, to better communicate with the stakeholder. The architect may, in the process of refinement, choose to use the logical model to provide more details of the architecture, such as class type. But UML, for example, is not RM-ODP; the models are not the same. An association in UML has no counterpart in RM-ODP, for example, nor does a use case. But they can be related to RM-ODP concepts, and that is what the architect needs to accomplish.

POINT

The viewpoint-based approach of RM-ODP satisfies the ultimate goal of an architecture: human communication across different domains and technology specialties, and across time.

A word about the use of RM-ODP: the architect needs to be pragmatic about the use of RM-ODP. Include only what's useful for planning the architecture. Use the RM-ODP terminology as reflected in the viewpoint languages to achieve a best-of-breed architecture specification. The architect can select which viewpoints are important to use and select the amount of detail in a viewpoint language to use to capture a particular specification. Omitting a viewpoint specification altogether works. All of this is a decision of the architect. After all, the system architecture specification and the level of understanding desired in the specification, is the architect's decision.

It quite reasonable to expect to only use RM-ODP for some important subset of a problem or a particularly high-risk area, excluding the rest. A health care industry (discussed in Chapter 2, "RM-ODP Manager's Primer") is using RM-ODP to capture the constraints of the system. Several organizations today, such as some in the financial domain, are currently focusing their efforts on using the enterprise and information viewpoint languages only, in order to specify the business.

RM-ODP is powerful. It enables the specification of some capability in a system; it supports multiple implementations; it provides conformance testing points; and all of this is captured in a common and consistent manner that facilitates "plug and play." It is a strong enabler for semantic interoperability in a system of systems, and presents the foundation to evaluate composability.

5.5   Distribution Transparency

Distribution transparency is one of the parts of the architecture model. A transparency hides from the user or application developer some processing accomplished by the infrastructure. There are eight transparencies:

1. Access: Hiding the details of data formats and mechanisms to interwork with another object
2. Failure: Hiding the details of failure and recovery to enable fault tolerance

3. Location: Hiding the details of resolving a logical address to a physical address for the purposes of binding an interface

4. Migration: Hiding the details of changing the location of an object

5. Persistence: Hiding the details of maintaining the existence of an object

6. Relocation: Hiding the details of changing the location of an interface

7. Replication: Hiding the details of duplicating an object and its interfaces

8. Transaction: Hiding the details of managing consistency among a group of objects

RM-ODP specifies what mechanisms need to exist for achieving a distribution transparency, without going into detail about how an architect might actually design and implement the mechanism. In order to make this an open interoperable capability, the focus is on the mechanism with respect to the interfacing constructs, and the semantics of the information exchanged with respect to transparency, whether these are local to the node or distributed across multiple nodes.

Hiding the underlying services supporting distribution offloads the application developer from both knowing how this is accomplished, and more importantly, implementing the service inside the application. In addition, the distribution transparencies provide several of the distribution properties: reliability, load-balancing, failure management, scalability, mobility, etc. Distribution transparency is addressed in depth in Chapter 10, "Hiding System Complexities: Distribution Transparencies."

5.6   ODP FUNCTIONS

An ODP function is a basic service required to support open distributed processing. The RM-ODP functions identify the requirements for all enabling services, and support the computational language, distribution transparencies, the engineering language, and additional component standards specifications of ODP systems. There are four main categories of functions:

1. Management functions include Node Management, Object Management, Cluster Management, and Capsule Management functions.

2. Coordination functions include Event Notification, Checkpointing and Recovery, Deactivation and Reactivation, Group, Replication, Migration, Engineering Interface Reference Tracking, and Transaction functions.

3. Repository functions include Storage, Information Organization, Relocation, Type Repository, and Trading functions.

4. Security functions include Access Control, Security Audit, Authentication, Integrity, Confidentiality, Nonrepudiation, and Key Management functions.

Only the ODP Trading function is identified for use in the computational viewpoint; all others are for use in the engineering viewpoint specification, since they address engineering-related aspects.

Each function provides a pattern of reasoning for the architect, described in terms of an explanation, required structure, and required behavior. Other ODP functions that depend on it, and that it depends on, are identified. The actual specification of the function is left for further standardization.

The RM-ODP functions are addressed in depth in Chapter 9, "RM-ODP Functions."

5.7   ESSENTIALS OF THE **RM-ODP** OBJECT MODEL

RM-ODP defines and uses an object model on which the foundations of an RM-ODP architecture are specified and developed.

In the context of RM-ODP, the object model is *object-based*. The foci of the object model are *objects* and their interactions.

Object: a model of something. It is not a concrete instance of a class, as is often the case in object-oriented (OO) languages. It is defined by state and behavior. It changes state as a result of some internal or external action. The state of an object is unique. [RM-ODP-2]

Objects interact through well-defined interfaces. An object is characterized by state, behavior, and activity. An object has a unique identity. It is autonomous and able to perform some independent activity. It can assume one or more types and can have one or more interfaces. Multiple types and multiple interfaces of an object are unlike most OO modeling concepts, where an object generally has a single type and a single interface. In RM-ODP, objects are distinct from their interfaces, and can perform functions independent of their interfaces. An object is the unit of distribution in RM-ODP, and the unit of management. Remember that an object may be a composite object: a composition of additional objects.

An object *state* is determined by the previous states, and the allowable actions that can change its state determined by the object's behavior. The behavior identifies possible actions which the object may participate in, given its current state. The allowable actions are either actions internal to the object, or actions with another object, which are then called *interactions*.

State (of an object): The condition of an object that determines its behavior: the set of constrained actions in which it can participate. [RM-ODP-2]

RM-ODP object modeling is not considered to be OO. The distinction reflects the focus of the modeling of RM-ODP: objects and their interactions. In traditional OO methods and languages, *class* is the focus of modeling and an *object* is an instance of a class. In RM-ODP, *object* is the focus of modeling. Object instantiation is through a defined object template, not a class.

RM-ODP does define a *class.* In this case, it is the set of all members that satisfy some type, where the elements of the set are considered members of a class. Hence, one can specify a class of objects of type X, a class of interfaces of type Y, a class of templates of type Z. The normal OO concept of class relates to the RM-ODP construct for a template.

Class: The set (possibly zero) of all members that satisfy a specific type, in which case each entity is a member of that class. [RM-ODP-2]

In traditional object-orientation, the concepts of identity, encapsulation, inheritance, polymorphism, and instantiation are fundamental. The RM-ODP object model also makes provision for these concepts.

Objects have unique *identity,* identified through a naming context. A *naming context* is a relation between names and identities, where the identity is unambiguous.

In RM-ODP, *encapsulation* is part of the object model. The only access to an object is through an invocation of the interfaces offered by the object. Otherwise, the object hides its internal processing. That is, another object cannot determine how an object performs its functionality; it is encapsulated.

RM-ODP is strongly typed. A *type* is a set of conditions and constraints that can classify an object, and are evaluated for an object. A type is a predicate. That is, an object belongs to a collection of objects by some set of characteristics; the predicate is a function yielding a "yes" or "no" answer.

In RM-ODP, an object can assume multiple types, which is not a normal object-oriented modeling concept. This becomes important in many places in RM-ODP. For example:

▶ An object as a single entity may assume a type of "X"
▶ The same object may be part of a composition, in which case it assumes a type of "component"
▶ The same object may be a composite object

▶ The same object may be part of a federation of objects, in which case it assumes a type of "federated"

▶ The same object may be considered a full community of enterprise objects from the perspective of a different community that wishes to interact with it, in which case it assume a type of "community"

Type: A conceptualization of a property of one or more entities. Type applies to at least an object, interface, and action. A specification can associate type with other entities (e.g., a domain). In RM-ODP, the phrase "<X>" designates the collection of entities that has a type. Type is a predicate: a set of conditions and constraints that can classify an object, and are evaluated for an object. [RM-ODP-2]

It is rare that any single object would assume all of these types in different abstractions, but common for an object to be both a single type, a component, and possibly federated. Multiple typing supports multiple levels of abstraction and encapsulation for modeling the complex details of a distributed system.

RM-ODP does not define how to select among the types of an object. This is a lack of a complete specification of RM-ODP.

A *class* is the set of all entities that have the same type. In RM-ODP, a class can be empty; nothing satisfies a given type. A class may have members during a certain period of time, and then go away. Unlike many other object-oriented paradigms, a class is not used to instantiate an entity. A template is used for this purpose. A class only defines the set of entities that satisfy a type.

A *subtype* is where every property that satisfies an entity of that subtype also satisfies an entity of its parent type. A *supertype* is the parent. It may contain properties beyond the subtype.

A *subclass* is the set of all entities that satisfy a subtype relation. A *superclass* is the set of all entities that satisfy a supertype relation. A subclass is a subset of its superclasses. Multiple inheritance is supported by these concepts.

A *template* is an important concept in RM-ODP. It forms the basis for instantiation of an entity. The template specification contains sufficient detail of the entity to instantiate an instance of it. More than one instance can be instantiated from the template. The parameters of a template are typed. The template has a type. An object, interface, binding, and many more things in RM-ODP all have a template to define how to instantiate them. An example of what is contained in an object template is shown in Figure 5.12.

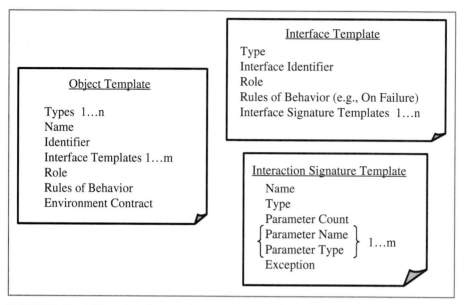

FIGURE 5.12 Object, Interface, and Interaction Templates

Think of a template as a pattern of features, or as a recipe of features that describes the entity (e.g., object, interface, domain, policy, etc.). The parameters of the template define how to instantiate the entity. A parameter of a template may in fact be another template. The concepts of an object, and its interface, type, template, and instantiation are highlighted in Figure 5.13.

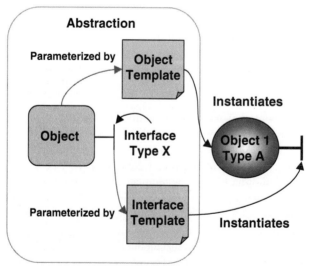

FIGURE 5.13 Object, Type, Interface, and Template Concepts

NOTE

Template: A specification that contains sufficient detail of an entity to instantiate it. More than one instance can be instantiated from the same template. [RM-ODP-2]

The interface template defines the type of the interface, the causality role assumed across the interface, and the interactions. For each interaction, the interface template defines the name and type of interaction, the typed parameters, the directionality, and any exceptions raised. The interface, interaction, and template concepts are shown in Figure 5.14. In this example, the three interactions are "get," "list," and "search" across interface 1. Shown is an additional interface that offers the interaction "update." Constraints on the use of the interface are determined by the binding associated with the interface, which may limit which interactions are available to an interacting object (not shown), as described above. The template that defines the interface shown in this figure is only exemplary. No particular language is used.

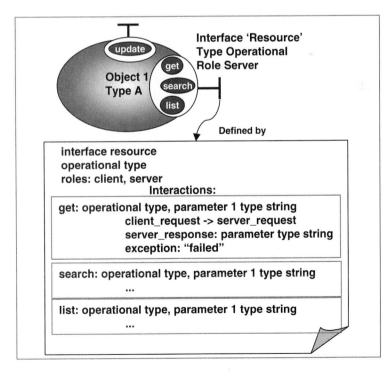

FIGURE 5.14   Interface, Interaction Template Concepts

A *template class* is the set of all things that satisfy the template type. Each template defines only one template class.

A *derived class* is the set of all instances of a template that have resulted from some incremental modification of that template. Perhaps additional properties are added to a template, in which case the template is in the *base class,* and the derived class contains the template that was enhanced by the properties.

RM-ODP also defines *inheritance hierarchy, type hierarchy,* and *class hierarchy.* The derived and base classes form an inheritance hierarchy, where the arcs define the derived class relation. A *type hierarchy* is where the arcs denote the subtype relation. A *class hierarchy* is where the arcs denote the subclass relation. That is, if template Y is derived from template X by incremental modification, then the class of all instances of X (that is, of all instances of the template class of X) is a derived class of all instances of Y, and Y forms a base class for X. Inheritance means that classes can be arranged in an inheritance hierarchy according to derived class relationships. If there are several base classes involved, then this is a *multiple inheritance.* A *type hierarchy* is where one class may be a subclass or subtype of another class. A derived class may or may not be a subclass. These two hierarchies are different in RM-ODP, though they may coincide.

Polymorphism is the ability for one instance of one type to be treated as an instance of another type. Satisfying many types is fundamental to RM-ODP.

In OO, an object has a single type and a single interface. In OMG's Object Management Architecture (OMA), an object is an interface. In traditional OO languages, an object is an instance of a class. In RM-ODP, an object is an abstract entity used for modeling. These are big differences.

Further, in RM-ODP, *action* is a central concept for *behavior,* and *interaction* is an action that involves one or more objects and their environment(s) at an *interface.*

An object interface consists of one or more *interaction specifications,* of the same type as the interface. Some examples of interaction types are listed below. RM-ODP defines the first three:

▶ Operational interaction, such as "client/server" or "remote procedure call (RPC)"
▶ Stream interaction, which is a single-direction sequence of messages of a specific type, such as a data stream
▶ Signal interaction, which is a single-direction atomic shared action
▶ Multicast interaction, which involves a sender and multiple recipients of a message, and associated constraints
▶ Others may be defined

An interface defines the behavior of the object that fulfills some role during the binding of the object. An *interface type* defines the semantics of the object's behavior and state associated with an interaction with another object. The semantics are associated with the interactions in the interface and constraints on those interactions and on the binding.

For example, an object can offer an interface that includes the interactions "get," "list," and "search." During a binding with another object, a constraint may be in place that only allows the other object to use the "get" interaction. So the interface instantiated for the other object would only allow the "get" interaction, and produce an error for any other interaction attempted, even though the "list" and "search" interactions are defined in the interface.

Action: What an entity does. It is an occurrence or a happening. [RM-ODP-2]

Interaction: An action that involves one or more objects and their environment(s) at an interface; set of services that are offered across a single interface, and are linked to another object with a binding. [RM-ODP-2]

Interface: The behavior of an object at a subset of the object's interactions constrained by the circumstances for when they occur. An interaction is associated with a single interface. [RM-ODP-2]

Communication: The way in which information is transferred from one object to another. This transfer of information can include a single transaction, or more interactions. The transfer can be direct between two or more objects, or include one or more intermediate objects.[RM-ODP-2]

Location (time or space): Specifies an interval of arbitrary size in time or space when or where an action can occur. [RM-ODP-2]

In RM-ODP, behavior is defined by actions and their constraints. This includes more than preconditions (meaning what must happen before some action) and postconditions (meaning what happens after some action). RM-ODP behavior is pervasive throughout. It includes things such as the effect of a policy on an interaction, the effect of a required quality of service (QoS) property on an interaction, temporal qualities, location in space, location in time, and so forth.

In RM-ODP, the concept of multiple interfaces is a powerful concept. It enables the architect to define separate types of interactions with an object; for example, an object may provide a "server" interface to a "client," an "administration" interface for management, a "control" interface for session control, and a "client" interface to some server. All of these different interfaces may be associated with a single object. The interactions of an object, for which there are specified interfaces, include those that the object initiates as well as those that the object participates in. For example, an object may participate in a multiparty conference call, in which case it uses the interface signature provided by another object for such an interaction.

In RM-ODP the concept of an *environment* includes all those elements not part of the object. The reason for environment is to be able to specify constraints from the environment that affect the workings of the object, and to define those elements the object needs from the environment (e.g., a certain bandwidth connection) to perform its objective.

An example is where the environment constrains the amount of resources available for use by the object, such as an available network connection. In turn, the object may require the environment to provide at least one such network connection when needed. This example closely approximates the interrelationship between an object in its operating system environment.

In Figure 5.15, object 1 is of type A. It has a single interface, across which it offers two interactions: I1 and I2. The interface is of type X, and its behavior is represented by role Y1 (such as "client role"). Object 2, of type B, has multiple interfaces. Each interface offers a different interaction. If object 2 wants to interact with object 1 (for I1 or I2), it does so by using the interface of type X, and a role (Y2) (such as "server role") that is complementary to that of role Y1. A binding is set up between the two objects to perform the interaction across the interface. In the case of object 1, the environment consists of object 2 and the binding between them. Depending on the viewpoint used, the environment can consist of a different domain (enterprise viewpoint), a different object space (computational viewpoint), or infrastructure objects such as the operating system or name server (engineering viewpoint).

 NOTE *Environment:* All those elements or entities not part of the model of the object, leading to the ability to specify what an object expects of its environment, and what constraints the environment places on the object. [RM-ODP-2]

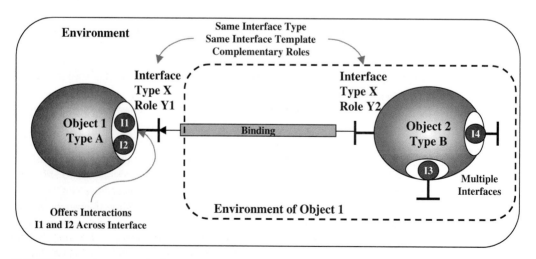

FIGURE 5.15   Concepts of Object, Interface, Interaction, Binding, Role, and Environment

As a more businesslike example, the environment for a set of hospital administration objects includes all external objects that affect the working of the hospital administration objects; e.g., state authority objects that define the state policies of operation. The environment constrains the hospital administration objects to obey certain state-regulated policies. A hospital administration object, then, can require that the environment provide updates to all such policies for use in constraining the interfaces and actions of the hospital administration object.

The basic modeling concepts in RM-ODP are the building blocks for any ODP architecture. Whatever specification language is chosen to model the constructs of an ODP architecture, it needs to be based on the 11 ODP basic modeling concepts.

5.8   SPECIFICATION CONCEPTS AND RULES

Part of the foundation for RM-ODP, used throughout the viewpoints, addresses the rules of specification. The concepts of specification are generic. Further, they are not concerned with issues of distribution or distributed systems. To specify the architecture of a system, the architect uses the concepts and the rules of usage. These specification techniques are composition, decomposition, composite object, behavioral compatibility, refinement, trace, type, class, subtype/supertype, subclass/superclass, template, interface signature, instantiation (template), role, creation, introduction, deletion, instance (of a type), template type, template class, derived class/base class, invariant, precondition, and postcondition. Abstraction is part of the foundation as well. Some of these concepts were addressed as part of the object model in the previous section (e.g., type, class, and template).

Most of these concepts are covered in detail in later chapters. A top-level discussion is provided here.

Abstraction is a process fundamental to architecting. It addresses focusing in on a high-level entity to specify it, suppressing its detail until a later time. An entity is any abstract or concrete thing. For example, the billing agent is an abstraction of the processing that actually takes place. The refinement of this abstraction may yield additional objects or interfaces.

Composition is also a fundamental part of architecting. Composition is a grouping of two or more objects. The result is a *composite object.* The architect uses composition to address a coarser-grained object, not worrying about the details of the objects that make up the composition at that point. Composition and abstraction are closely associated. The composite object is at one level of abstraction, whereas the objects that make up the composition are at another level of abstraction. The object that is part of a composition is called a *component.* In fact, the object assumes an additional type called component, in addition to any other type. An example of a composition is the patient admitting agent that may be several different objects, such as one that admits a patient and one that schedules treatment. A composition is an object. Just like any other object, properties are defined for it: name, identity, one or more types, one or more interfaces, and a behavior specification. An overview of composition, component, and composite object are in terms of RM-ODP is shown in Figure 5.16. More discussion is provided in Chapter 8, "Composition and Semantics: Quality Composition Minimizing Architectural Mismatch."

Behavioral compatibility means that one object can replace another object because the objects behave the same. The criteria for determining this are that if a second object replaces an object, the environment of the object detects no change. For example, if an interface offers the "get" and "search" interactions, it could be replaced by an interface that offers the same interactions plus a "list" interaction. That is, substituting one interface specification for another is behaviorally compatible if the environment of the first could not detect a change. Behavioral compatibility also applies to templates as well.

The concept of *substitutability* (called behavioral compatibility in RM-ODP) is a powerful concept in RM-ODP. It permits one object to be substituted for another and one interface to be substituted for another, as long as the environment cannot detect a difference, a set of criteria are met, and a template type captures the design for substitutability. For example, binding happens when a contract between two (or more) interfaces is agreed upon, and that contract may limit the interactions of the interface that can take place. The result is the interface providing only those allowable interactions is substituted for an interface allowing all the interactions.

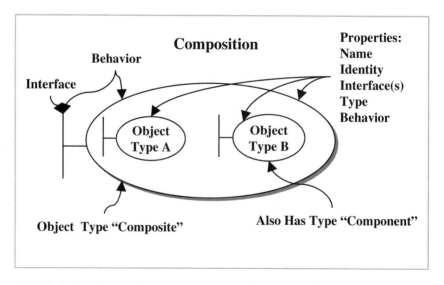

FIGURE 5.16   Composition, Component, and Composite Object

Refinement is the process of taking a specification of something at one level of abstraction and drilling down into a more detailed specification. It is the companion process to abstraction. For example, the hospital billing agent interacts with the insurance billing agent. In a refinement of this interaction, two separate interfaces may result: one to submit a bill, one to receive a payment. Similarly, the billing agent in the hospital performs a number of functions. In a refinement of the billing agent, more detail about accessing the patient records, updating the billing portion of those records, computing the bill from all sources in the hospital will be detailed.

A house example showing the relations among abstraction, refinement, and composition is shown in Figure 5.17. The house is an object, at one level of abstraction. It is composed of (a composition of) a number of other objects, shown in abstraction 2. Each of these components is an object, and can be further refined. The stairs are refined into a set of objects and relations, shown in the refinement.

A *trace* is a history of an object's interactions, generally used by some capability in the system to record a history of the object. The result is a finite sequence of the object's interactions. This is particularly important in security systems.

An *interface signature* is a set of interaction templates for an interface. An object may define many interfaces with the same signature, or many interfaces with different signatures.

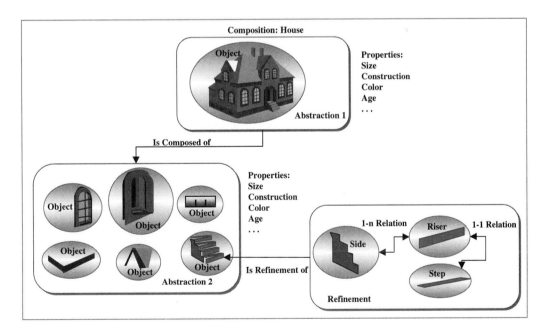

FIGURE 5.17 Composition, Abstraction, and Refinement House Example

Instantiation means to create an instance of a specific template. The parameters of the template may involve instantiating other templates, or even creating a binding. An object is instantiated by an object template to its initial state.

A *role* identifies a behavior. It may be a parameter of a composite object template. When the template is instantiated, the role-parameter instantiates a component that fulfills that role.

Creation is the same thing as instantiating, except that it results from some action. For example, an object's interface may be "created" at a point when that interface is to be used.

Introduction is the same thing as instantiating, except that it is not a result of an action of an object. For example, a policy may be introduced into a part of the system. It is not created by an object.

Deletion is the act of removing or destroying something that was instantiated, such as an object or interface. There are rules associated with what is able to delete an entity. For example, an object can delete its own interface, but another object cannot.

Instance is the <X> that satisfies the type.

A *template type* is a predicate in the template that defines the requirements for instantiations of the template. Examples of a template type are "an interface template type" and "an object template type." So an object template for a billing agent would be, in RM-ODP terminology, "the object template type associated with the template for a billing agent." What this means is that templates are formats for possible reuse, depending on the specification language used. One specifies the format for objects; one specifies the format for interfaces; one specifies the format for policies; etc. A specific object (billing agent), interface (submit bill), and policy also has a template because it has unique parameters associated with it. Template type and type of template are two closely related concepts, that are often confusing, even to the originators of RM-ODP.

Figure 5.18 provides a view of the relationship among a template type, a type of template, instantiation, instance, and subtype. All of these concepts are important in the specification of an architecture.

An *invariant* is a predicate that is required to be true for a set of objects over some time.

A *precondition* is a predicate that must be true prior to an action, and result in success for that action to occur.

A *postcondition* is a predicate that must be true and occur after an action.

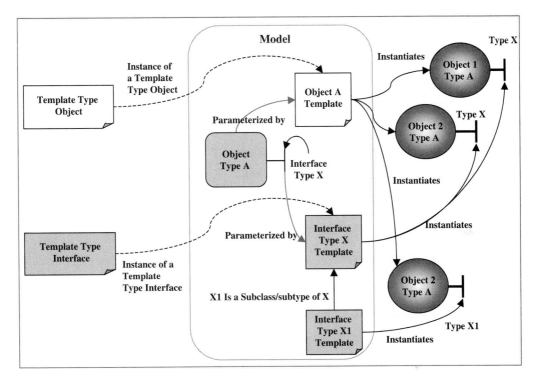

FIGURE 5.18   Relationship of Templates, Instantiations, and Instances

5.9   STRUCTURING CONCEPTS AND RULES

In addition to specification rules, RM-ODP defines structuring rules. These are used to consider issues of distribution. These concepts are classified as organization, properties of a system, naming, behavior, and management.

Most these concepts are covered in detail in later chapters. A top-level discussion is provided here.

5.9.1   ORGANIZATION

The concepts discussed here are those that arrange objects into some structure, for some particular purpose.

A *group* is a set of objects with a specified structural or behavioral relationship (called a characterizing relationship). An address group, a replica group, and a communication group are examples.

A *configuration* of objects is a collection of objects involved in an interaction. A configuration can be static or dynamic, in terms of mechanisms that define the configuration at execution time, such as a binding. A configuration can be subject to a composition, in which the result is a composite object at a different level of abstraction.

A *domain* is a set of objects with a characterizing relationship, and with a control object that may be part of the domain or outside it. The control object determines the membership of the domain, and administers policies across the membership in the domain. An example is a security domain, where the control object administers the security policy, and the members are all objects subject to the security policy. Domains can, and often do, overlap. A naming domain, defining the naming context to be used by all objects in the domain, may overlap with a security domain, where the naming domain has a wider scope, for example. Some examples of such domains include:

▶ Addressing
▶ Naming
▶ Security
▶ Administration
▶ Policy

A *subdomain* is a subset of the membership of a domain.

An *epoch* is a defined period of time. Generally, this is used to define some behavior of an object, such as the epoch during which an invariant holds true. A change in a number of things can be associated with an epoch. For example, a change in a type of an object, supporting type evolution, may be related to a change in epoch. So in essence, epoch is really associated with duration, rather than time.

A *reference point* is a point at an interaction used as a conformance testing point. At a *conformance point,* behavior of the system is observed and related to the architecture specification.

5.9.2 PROPERTIES

Properties that may apply to a system and specified in an architecture include transparencies (covered in Chapter 10, "Hiding System Complexities: Distribution Transparencies"), policy (covered in Chapter 14, "Policy Framework"), and temporal aspects (discussed here).

Persistence and isochronicity are temporal properties. *Persistence* determines that an object continues to exist, despite changes in state, context, or even an epoch. Often a store is associated with persistence, such as a database, where data is stored and persists even though the application may come and go, or change state. *Isochronicity* means a sequence of actions that are equally spaced in time and are unique. This type of activity is associated with voice media.

5.9.3 NAMING

Naming is an important concept. In RM-ODP, a naming context is defined. A *name* is associated with a naming context. An entity is referred to by a name from the naming context. A *naming context* is a relation between a set of unique names in a name space to the entities that are named. A *name space* is just a set of terms used as names. An *identifier* is an unambiguous name in the naming context. So an object may have a name ("admitting agent") and another object may have the same name. To distinguish one object from the other, an object identifier is used.

An entity is given a name from the name space. This is a *naming action*. A *naming domain* is the set of all entities that are named from the same naming context by a name authority object. A naming domain may consist of a subset of the naming context, not the entire naming context. So a naming context may result in more than one naming domain. Figure 5.19 provides an overview of the naming context concepts just discussed.

A *naming graph* is a directed graph associating a naming context and an association between a source naming context and a target naming context. A *name resolution* is a process that can discover a named entity given an initial name and naming context.

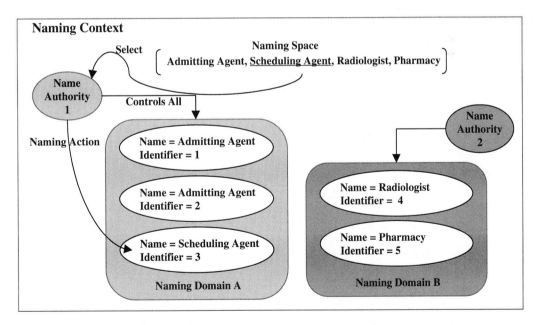

FIGURE 5.19 Naming Context

5.9.4   BEHAVIOR

Behavior: A set of actions and indications of epoch for these actions (which are constraints). Constraints define the dependencies that exist between actions. The actions are also constrained by the object's environment. [RM-ODP-2]

Behavior is addressed in terms of activity context, contractual behavior, causality, and dependability. All but the last are discussed below. Dependability is covered in Chapter 16, "RM-ODP Fault Tolerance Framework."

5.9.4.1   Activity

The next set of concepts addresses behavior with respect to an activity structure.

Activity: An ordered set of actions, where each action is determined by the preceding actions. An activity is a directed graph of these actions that has a single starting point and does not cycle back. It is a sequence of actions, one or more. [RM-ODP-2]

An *activity* is a sequence of actions, one or more. A *chain of actions* is an ordered sequence of actions. A *thread* is a chain of actions that has at least one object participating in all the actions. If an action is shared between chains (two or more), this is called a *joining action,* and results in a single chain. A *dividing action* is the reverse of a joining action. It is an action that separates a chain into two or more chains. If the dividing action enables the chains to rejoin later, this is called a *forking action.* The separate chains cannot either join other chains or terminate separately. If the dividing action does not enable a forking action, it is called a *spawn action.* In this case, each divided chain is a separate chain, and can interact independently. Another concept is a *head activity,* which is the initial action in an activity. A *subactivity* is a proper subset of the activity, and if it includes one action that eventually will fork-join, the subactivity must include these fork-join actions of the parent as well.

5.9.4.2   Contractual

Another set of concepts also address behavior, from a contract perspective. A contract is an agreement to some behavior. It is put in place between objects to constrain their behavior. The behavior results from the interaction of the objects, or from a third-party object. A contract template is instantiated to *establish this behavior* between objects. The behavior that characterizes a particular set of objects is *enabled* by the establishment of the contract, which may apply differently to the different objects. The knowledge that a contract is in place among a set of objects is called the *contractual context*. It defines the behavior of those objects. An object can participate in more than one contractual context. A *liaison* is a relationship that results from enabling a behavior in accordance with the contract established that defines the behavior of the liaison. Examples of a liaison include a binding, a distributed transaction, a publish/subscribe transaction, and others. A *terminating behavior* ends a liaison, as identified in the contract. Figure 5.20 provides an overview of the relationships among establishing behavior, enabling behavior, and terminating behavior, over some time.

5.9.4.3 Causality

Behavior is also addressed by causality. *Causality* is a categorization of roles of interacting objects that is associated with the type of interaction. As such, causality constrains the behavior of the objects while they are interacting. An example one of kind of causality is a "client" object, in an operation interaction. Its dual is a "server" object. While an object is acting in the role of a "client," it requests a service. It can also act in the role of a "server," but across a different interaction. Hence, an interaction of a particular type has a client side and a server side, and each of these is called causality. The different kinds of causality are:

◗ Initiating object—starts a communication

◗ Responding object—an object participating in the communication, but not the initiating object

◗ Producer object—source object of some information exchanged

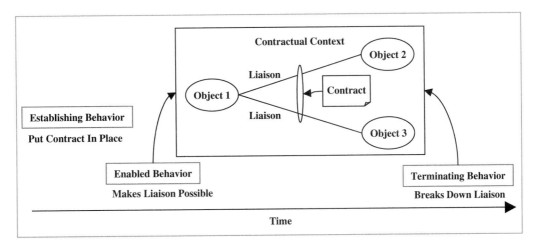

FIGURE 5.20 Contractual Behavior

- ▶ Consumer object—target object of the exchanged information
- ▶ Client object—an object that requests a service be performed by another object
- ▶ Server object—an object that performs a requested service

5.9.4.4   Establishing Behaviors

Another set of concepts also address establishing interaction behaviors between objects. One such behavior is a *binding behavior.* This is a behavior established between two or more interfaces. A *binding* is a contractual context; a contract establishes the behavior of the binding. This behavior can be the same for all objects (the same role), or different (e.g., one role is client and the other is server).

Binding: A contract between two or more object interfaces that is the result of agreed-upon behavior. [RM-ODP-2]

The binding behavior can establish a binding between two or more interfaces. In order to bind two or more interfaces, the identifiers of all interfaces must be known by the object performing the binding. This is a *binding precondition.* If a binding is terminated, this is called an *unbinding behavior.*

5.9.5   MANAGEMENT

The final set of concepts are the systems management concepts. *Application management* includes the management actions of applications. *Communication management* includes the management actions of the objects that support communication. The information relevant to the management of the objects is called the *management information.* The *managed role* is the object role being managed. The *managing role* is an object role that performs the management actions. *Notification* is an interaction initiated by a managed role based object.

The remaining structuring concepts are fully covered in the following chapters: transparencies, contract, quality of service, environment contract, obligation, permission, prohibition, policy, binding, binding precondition, trading, failure (violation of a contract), error, fault, and stability.

5.10   CONFORMANCE CONCEPTS AND RULES

Conformance concepts and rules focus on the required correspondences across the concepts of the viewpoints to achieve consistency. From a consistent model, reference points are associated with the concepts of a particular viewpoint. Within each viewpoint specification, the architect defines the information to be observed at a reference point, related to a viewpoint concept. This extra information, coupled with the reference point in a consistent model, becomes a conformance testing point.

RM-ODP defines the conformance testing process to test the implementation of an architectural specification to that specification.

Compliance testing is also addressed. Compliance testing is associated with testing an ODP standard with RM-ODP, which generally occurs during the standardization process.

Chapter 11, "Architecture Analysis and System Conformance Evaluation," covers this topic in detail.

5.11   SUMMARY

The RM-ODP architecture model consists of five viewpoints of the system, eight distribution transparencies, and 24 ODP functions. The viewpoints provide a view of a system in terms of modeling languages for each viewpoint. The viewpoint languages are all founded on precise terminology of approximately 122 defined terms and the RM-ODP foundation.

The RM-ODP foundation for using the viewpoints includes the object model, specification concepts, structuring concepts and rules, and conformance concepts and rules. This set provides unique capabilities to architect a system: abstraction, refinement, composition, behavior specification, structuring specification, and much more. The object model provides the powerful concepts of multiple types that an object can assume, and multiple interfaces that an object can offer. These particular concepts support composition and an interoperable interaction framework, both of which we will discuss in future chapters.

The viewpoints are not layered. They each represent a view of the entire system, addressing certain aspects of distributed processing.

The viewpoints are composable. The templates that describe an entity are composable. The objects in each viewpoint are composable. The templates that describe an entity are composable. The result of such a powerful concept is the ability to use RM-ODP as a model of a system of systems, a single system, a subsystem, or a major component in a system. In RM-ODP these are all designated as a "system."

The distribution transparencies hide the effects of distribution from the application developer and end user, and provide some of the "ilities" a system should be architected for. What RM-ODP defines are the requirements, some of the interactions, and some aspects of the constraints associated with each transparency. As a result, RM-ODP does not direct how a transparency is to be implemented, but rather focuses on the interactions so that distribution transparency is interoperable across heterogeneous ODP systems. This important topic is further explored in Chatper 10, "Hiding System Complexities: Distribution Transparencies."

The ODP functions support the needs of the infrastructure and the distribution transparencies. Most of these functions are specified in additional RM-ODP–based standards. This important topic is further explored in Chapter 9, "RM-ODP Functions."

As depicted in Figure 5.21 on the following page, the RM-ODP architecture model is a precisely defined set of concepts and rules from which the architect can construct an architectural specification of a system that will be precisely defined, specify the behavior, and enable some of the "ilities" (such as interoperability, reliability, fault tolerance, portability, etc.).

RM-ODP viewpoints are interrelated through the concepts and rules defined in each of the languages. This interrelationship establishes consistency across the viewpoints, unlike many architecture frameworks today. What this results in is that coordination across viewpoints and assertions about some aspect of the viewpoint models can be made with assurance that they are founded in precision and have a mathematical underpinning.

Consistency also enables the architect to perform architecture analysis of the specification. Consistency also supports the conformance criteria established in each viewpoint so that the architect or tester can test the system implementation to the architectural specification. Consistency and conformance enable, therefore, analysis and evaluation of a well-formed architecture and well-constructed distributed processing system that is open.

The foundation and viewpoints provide an explicit manner of using levels of abstraction to specify the architecture, addressing system behavior, software distribution, interoperability, reusability, portability, and composibility. RM-ODP also supports the specification of seamless integration of disparate applications or components over multiple, dissimilar systems, achieving interoperability and even federation. Through the use of the distribution transparency mechanisms, transparent sharing of resources and services can be specified. To round it all out, conformance testing of an architecture specification to a system implementation is defined. The architecture that results from this process consists of the rules for construction of the system.

RM-ODP provides, therefore, a full system construction lifecycle focus, or any subset, as desired.

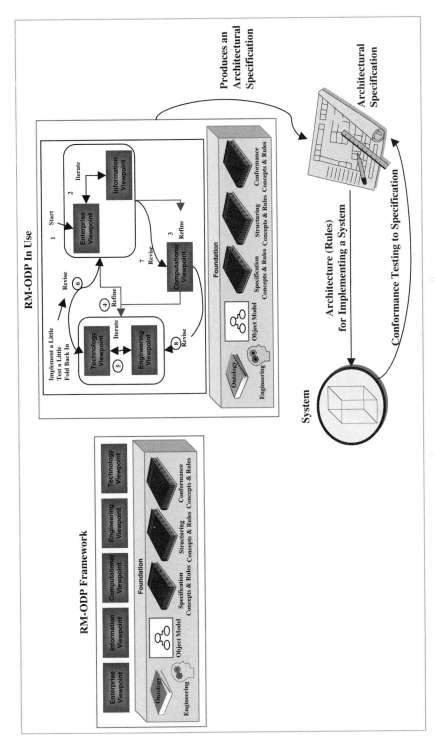

FIGURE 5.21   RM-ODP, Architectural Specification, Architecture, and System Relationships

S I X

SEPARATION OF CONCERNS: USING RM-ODP VIEWPOINTS

This chapter provides a detailed description of the concepts and rules of each of the five viewpoint languages of RM-ODP, both as expressed by the standard and as described by the author.[1] What is covered includes:

- Each of the five RM-ODP viewpoints, which are the building blocks for the specification of an ODP system
- Some of the concepts and structuring rules associated with each of the viewpoint languages, and used for specifying an ODP system
- Examples of the use of each of these viewpoint languages to create an architecture specification from that viewpoint

References are made to the foundation aspects of RM-ODP, covered in Chapter 4, "Tools, Relationships, and RM-ODP Standard." These include the object model, the specification concepts and rules, and the structuring concepts and rules. The medical case study of Healthy Hospital is further refined in this chapter, and used for examples of key concepts.

---

1. Errors of interpretation of the standard are the author's, and do not necessarily reflect the actual wording of the standard.

6.1   OVERVIEW OF SEPARATION OF CONCERNS

Systems are complex partly because there are many different human beings play-ing very different roles in the development, maintenance, and use of the system. These different roles and needs result in very different views of the same system. One of the failures of many architectures is not taking into account these different viewpoints. RM-ODP, on the other hand, provides a powerful and useful generic decomposition of a system into five viewpoints, as discussed in Chapter 5, "RM-ODP Architecture Model." And an architecture specification of a system is com-posed of one or more viewpoint specifications written in the viewpoint language of that viewpoint.

The viewpoints each have different interests of the system at hand, different requirements from that system, different evaluation criteria and therefore contain different information and have different specifications for the system. A recap of the different viewipoints and their concerns are shown in Figure 6.1.

Each member of the architecture team can capture those things pertinent to that viewpoint in the language of that viewpoint. What this means is that the infor-mation analyst can focus on the information and semantics of the system using the information viewpoint, whereas the system programmer can focus on how to con-

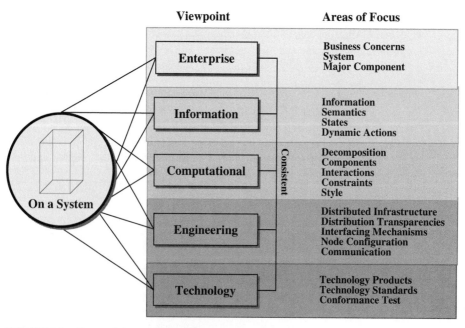

FIGURE 6.1   Focused Areas of Concern

struct the infrastructure and mechanisms for distribution using the engineering viewpoint, while the implementer is analyzing and selecting products of choice to match up with the specification using the technology viewpoint.

In RM-ODP, this works because each of the viewpoints includes a set of concepts, rules, and structures that formulate a viewpoint-specific language, and these languages use concepts that are consistent across the viewpoints due to the rules of consistency. This is important because the rules of consistency gives assurance that what one team member specifies in one viewpoint has a correspondence in other viewpoints. It's a means of coordinating across the team using the constructs of the viewpoint languages.

At times, the subject matter may appear too difficult. So, a word about the use of RM-ODP: The architect does not need to use all of the RM-ODP concepts and constructs identified for an architectural specification, but must choose some. For example, the architect ~~~~~~~~~~~~~~~~~~~~~~~~~~~~~~~arency, and ignore the others. O   se and information viewpoint lan   aining viewpoints. These are cho   sed in accordance with the rules

One of the   the viewpoints through the c

697-2594

703693-9789

As stated   M-ODP is very general. It can   tion processing systems, a singl   cific domain of objects, or a coll_____ or objects that comprise a major component in the system. The recursive property of RM-ODP enables a full specification of an object, which is an entity of one viewpoint specification, as depicted in Figure 6.2. An object in one viewpoint specification may be a major component of the system, a subsystem, or a system of systems in another viewpoint suite of specifications. All of this becomes part of the same architectural specification. What this means is that the architect can use the viewpoint languages to specify a full distributed processing system, or a major component of that system. This is an important aspect of RM-ODP and affects the use of the viewpoint languages. Figures 6.6 and 6.7 provide additional examples of this property.

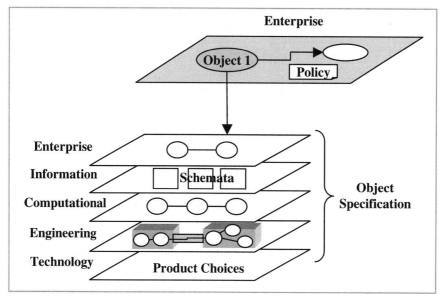

FIGURE 6.2   Example of RM-ODP Recursiveness

The use of the viewpoints is captured in Table 6.1, for use in the following discussion of the viewpoints. It provides an overview of the focus of the viewpoints, singly and collectively. This table supports the discussion of what's contained in each viewpoint and how the architect might use them for a fully specified architecture, or a partially specified architecture for a system, or a fully specified architecture for a part of a system.

TABLE 6.1   Use of RM-ODP Viewpoints

VIEWPOINTS	USE
Enterprise	Scope, objectives, and policies
Information	Information and information processing semantics
Computational	Components, interactions, and constraints
Engineering	Distribution, transparencies, connectors, explicit interfacing constructs, and decomposition to a node level
Technology	Technologies and products, and conformance reference points for testing
Enterprise + Information	Business specifications, rules of engagement, business rules, policies, and information flows, scoped to a specific domain with respect to other domains

TABLE 6.1 Use of RM-ODP Viewpoints (Continued)

VIEWPOINTS	USE
	System-wide architecture requirements
	Requirements for federating across domains
Information + Computational	Software architecture
Engineering + Technology	Solution for a (sub)system specification
	Infrastructure virtual machine
Enterprise + Information + Computational	System component or a related RM-ODP standard specification
	Specification of some major component of a system
	Composability requirements
	Distribution transparency requirements, use, and constraints on the system design
Information + Computational + Engineering	Application and infrastructure specification
	System management of the objects
	Fault tolerance mechanisms
	Interfacing specification, including constraints
Enterprise + Information + Computational + Engineering	Capture technology, independent specification of a system, and incrementally assessing technological solutions as they exist and as they emerge in solving system objectives
All	Domain-Specific Software Architecture (DSSA)and instantiations of that
All	Complete specification for a system
All	Management of the processing of cross-organization specification and implementation of a system of systems

6.2 USING THE ENTERPRISE VIEWPOINT

The enterprise viewpoint focuses on the purpose, scope, and policies of a system. The enterprise language includes the concepts, rules, and structures for specifying an ODP system from the enterprise viewpoint. The concepts are independent of distribution details and of implementation details.

The enterprise viewpoint is used to organize the requirements, structure, and constraints of a business specification or of a subsystem. That is, the use of the enterprise language is more than for a business; it is also used to capture the requirements of a main component of a system.

An enterprise specification uses the enterprise language to describe the system and its behavior within the enterprise, and the behavior of the system with those elements of the enterprise that are outside of the system (the environment of the system), including other information technology systems, humans, enterprises, components, etc.

One can think of the enterprise viewpoint as a human dialogue bridge between a stakeholder requirement and the system architect who needs to understand the capabilities of the system. The problem of technology transfer is so pervasive today that systems can succeed or fail based on this one problem. The languages used by stakeholder and an information technologist are not the same. Each tries to understand the language of the other, but all too often without success. A stakeholder does not have the many years of information technology (IT) experience needed to architect a distributed processing system across heterogeneous elements. An IT person does not have the 30 years of experience it would take to understand what is needed and desired for a system to fulfill some enterprise objective. The problem is not in the specification, but in the understanding of that specification. The enterprise language bridges the necessary dialogue between the domain-specific stakeholders and the domain-specific software architects.

An enterprise specification contains:

▶ Community definition of the objects to satisfy some purpose of the enterprise

▶ Objective statement for an enterprise community; why the system is required and what it will do

▶ Identification of enterprise objects that comprise the enterprise community, including both actor roles that perform some action and artefact roles[2] that are resources for use; i.e., the abstract view of what is required for the system to perform its function

▶ Roles fulfilled by one of the enterprise objects within the community, constrained by the policies of the community

▶ Policies (rules) for the objects, which either constrain or enable actions:
  – Obligations—what must be done
  – Permissions—what can be done
  – Prohibitions—what must not be done

▶ Activities performed by the enterprise objects

▶ Configuration of the objects

▶ Environmental contracts for defining the constraints on the community by the environment, and on the environment by the community

▶ Contracts that define the constraints, to include the policies

---

2. The *artefact* role is one that is currently being defined in the new enterprise viewpoint specification [ISO-EntVP]. This term is used where appropriate, instead of "artifact."

Each community is formed to meet an objective. It is composed of one or more enterprise objects, each of which may also be a member of a different community. Within a community, the enterprise object fulfills a role, which describes its behavior in the community and its support in the objective of the community. The objective of the community, then, is fulfilled by the collection of enterprise objects fulfilling their roles.

An actor role is an identifier for a behavior, realized by the set of interactions it participates in with other object roles. Policies are statements that constrain or enable behavior of the roles. That is, policies govern the behavior of the roles. The artefact roles are those roles that act as resources to the actor role objects. The policies may also impact the artefact roles.

Figures 6.3 through 6.5 provide refined examples of Figure 3.14 in Chapter 3, and of Figure 5.11 in Chapter 5. The figures show four communities that make

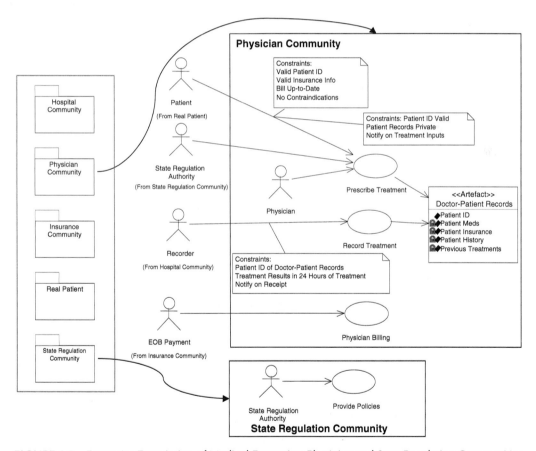

FIGURE 6.3 Enterprise Description of Medical Enterprise: Physician and State Regulation Communities

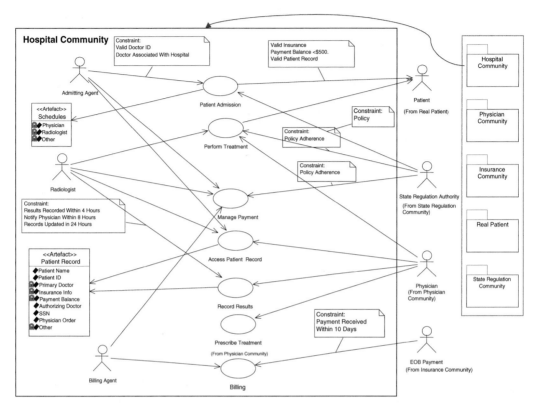

FIGURE 6.4   Enterprise Description of Medical Enterprise: Hospital Community

up part of the enterprise specification of the medical business case example. In these figures, a Unified Modeling Language (UML) vendor tool is used to show the configuration of enterprise objects that assume the actor roles and artefact roles, as well as the constraints applied to the actions of those roles as determined by policies. The artefact roles shown in these figures are doctor-patient records, hospital patient records, hospital schedules, and the Explanation of Benefits (EOB). The distinction between the types of roles, as well as having to identify constraints as an annotated box (box with the rounded corner) show some of the limitations of the modeling constructs of any such tool. Nevertheless, the tool provides a visualization of this enterprise. The enterprise scope, purpose, objectives, roles, and policies are captured in Figure 6.6, in English text, as is generally the case.

A Use Case, as shown in Figures 6.3 through 6.5, enables requirements to be captured in terms of the roles the different actors assume in the processing system: the patient, physician, hospital admitting agent, billing agent, radiologist, and state regulator. The Use Case depicts the processing and the interactions among the roles. For example, a radiologist cannot simply perform a medical treatment

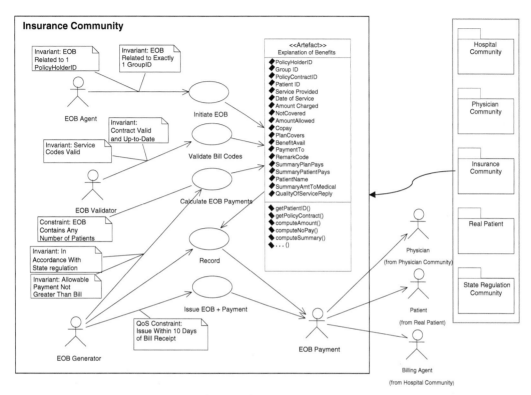

FIGURE 6.5 Enterprise Description of Medical Enterprise: Insurance Community

without having the state-regulated qualified credentials. Of course, the hospital itself is regulated by the state, and so checks and balances are conducted to make sure the accreditation for both the hospital and radiologist is valid. Likewise, the physician must be appropriately licensed, and associated with the hospital, for which the order (in accordance with a hospital order form) is provided. However, the Use Case does not include policy statements, unless they are attached as a "Note." Hence, the Use Case of Figure 6.3 is represented as English text in Figure 6.6.

Refining the enterprise specification may result in the need for additional enterprise objects and interactions, to fulfill additional roles. For example, the impact of state regulation policies on the Hospital Community have not been analyzed. It may be that there is a quality of service policy requirement whereby the Regulation Authority must inform the hospital of new policy, allow the hospital a certain time to adhere to the policy, and resolve conflicts. Further, the hospital may require information about a state policy before it can proceed with a treatment, but remains bounded by the quality of service (QoS) requirement of the physician. In this case, a conflict resolution object may be required to fulfill this role. Hence, in analyzing the system, the architect may find that behavior of another community

---

Hospital Community Scope:
The set of enterprise objects include Admitting Agent, Radiologist, Billing Agent
Behavior defined by Hospital Roles: Admitting Agent, Radiologist, Billing Agent, Patient Record, Schedules
Behavior includes Environment Roles: Physician, Recorder, State Regulation Authority, Insurance, Patient, EOB Payment

Hospital Objective:
To perform an authorized treatment on a patient, in a prescribed amount of time for the treatment, through the valid authorization of
a physician associated with the hospital, qualified radiologist, and to ensure the appropriate payment for the treatment

Hospital Policies:
Obligation to follow State regulation policy on treatment facility
Obligation to ensure State regulation policy on physician credentials
Obligation to follow State regulation on hospital capabilities
Obligation to follow quality of service time for treatment to be scheduled and performed
Obligation to follow quality of service time for bill to be submitted
Obligation to follow quality of service time for treatment results to be recorded
Obligation to follow policy of privacy of patient record information
Prohibition to allow radiologists to perform the treatment that are not qualified
Obligation to follow policy on retaining patient records
Obligation to follow policy on submitting bill to insurance companies
Prohibition to bill more than cost associated with treatment
Permission to make patient records available to technician
Obligation to follow policy of reduced bill according to contract with insurance company
etc.

Role Responsibilities:
•<u>Admitting Agent</u>: to use Patient Identification, Records, Physician Authorization, Insurance, and Physician Order to admit patient,
schedule treatment, setup billing, to the required quality of service dictated by the time of treatment authorized by the physician, and
the availability of the treatment facilities, and the state regulations on billing
•<u>Radiologist</u>: to perform a treatment service in accordance with a physician order, as per schedule, an to ensure proper working of
treatment facility in accordance with state regulations for regular inspections and maintenance
•<u>Billing Agent</u>: to authorize treatment in accordance with insurance regulations, to setup billing, to manage billing iterations with
insurance, to enforce pre-payment requirements on the patient, and to ensure proper billing codes and amounts are issued to the
insurance company. To ensure full payment is received, with any agreement of lower costs associated with insurance company policy
•<u>Patient Records</u>: to accept report of treatment results, record in patient records, and to transmit results as required by physician and
hospital policies
•<u>Schedules</u>: to accept schedules of treatment and physicians, associate with patient records

•<u>Physician (environment)</u>: to provide proper physician order form, with the required time of service for the treatment, to provide
pertinent patient information (not necessarily physician patient record), and to record the results to the patient's records
•<u>EOB (environment)</u>: to accept bill of treatment results, compute payment, and to transmit results to hospital and patient
•<u>State Regulation (environment)</u>: to ensure proper authorizations are followed in accordance with state regulations; to ensure
treatment facilities are maintained and inspected in accordance with state policy; to ensure billing is issued within the bounds
according to state policy; to ensure proper authorized hospital; to ensure proper physician credentials

FIGURE 6.6   Enterprise Description of Hospital Community, Sample: Scope, Objective, Policies, Responsibilities

is essential to the achievement of the objectives of the community of interest, resulting in introducing new roles (and associated enterprise objects) into that community. This is not shown in the previous figures.

Refining the enterprise specification may also include specifications for an object to capture decisions made about what medicine to use for the treatment, based on the disease as well as any problems the patient may have with other medications that would prohibit the use of a specific medicine. Further, an organization may want to capture the use of certain medicines for laboratory analysis and disease control factors, especially if the patient travels internationally. These are examples of "using" the system for a variety of reasons.

The enterprise modeling language is based on the RM-ODP foundations, with enterprise-specific concepts and rules. The small set of concepts and rules are presented next. Originally, the enterprise language consisted of more. The concepts of an actor and artefact (which defines a resource) roles were originally in the standard, for example. But primarily due to a lack of a clear specification at that time, these concepts were eliminated from the final standard. Some of these additional language concepts are now re-emerging in the new standard for the enterprise language, along with other constructs. [ISO-EntVP]

To recap, the medical examples showed certain things about the enterprise model: community, role, actions, artefact, policies, constraints, objectives, scope, and environment.

6.2.1   CONCEPTS

The enterprise language provides the concepts and rules for the enterprise viewpoint. The foundation support for the enterprise language includes the following main concepts:

▶ Role, activity, policy, environment, contract, and behavior (discussed in Chapter 5, "RM-ODP Architecture Model")

▶ Environment contract: A contract between an enterprise object and the enterprise environment. The contract addresses a number of constrains, such as quality of service constraints, usage, and management constraints. Management constraints would include distribution transparency constraints. The environment constraints describe the requirements of the environment to support the behavior of the object, and the behavior required of the object to be a member of the environment. [RM-ODP-2] Actions are constrained by the environment.

Two additional concepts of the enterprise language are:

▶ Community: A configuration of objects, as defined by a community contract. The objects fulfill the objective of the community. [RM-ODP-3]

▶ Federation: A community of domains with the same properties as the federation, <X>. [RM-ODP-3]

Community is a central concept. It consists of those elements that the architect focuses on in specifying the enterprise. Environment is important, because the objects in the environment may interact with or affect the behavior of the community. A community can be thought of as a set of roles that defines behavior, a set of objects that assume those roles, and the interactions among the objects in the community and the environment. What the objects can and cannot do is defined in the policy statements. What the community can and cannot do is captured in the community contract and the environment contract. The enterprise model specifies the structure of the community as the configuration of enterprise objects that fulfill the objectives of the community.

An enterprise consists of one or more communities, each of which will achieve some enterprise objective, such as shown in Figure 6.4. Here, the enterprise consists of the Physician, Hospital, Insurance, and State Regulation communities. The Hospital community is the target of the Healthy Hospital enterprise specification, and the other communities are only identified with respect to the roles, their interactions, and the objects that assume those roles.

As the Hospital community is further refined, other roles will be defined, and other objects defined. For example, the Hospital community identifies a single role called "Billing Agent," but a billing system tends to be a complex system. The architect can choose to fully describe "Billing" as a separate community, and then refer to it as an object in the Hospital Community. Herein is an example of the levels of abstraction and composition promoted by RM-ODP: an object in one level of abstraction is a composition of objects in another level of abstraction; and a community can consist of compositions, any of which may also be a community. The Billing Agent role in the Hospital Community could be a separate community of role-based objects with specified behavior, as part of the Billing Community. This aspect of the use of the enterprise language is shown in Figure 6.7.

A commercial version of this same example is the use of a Trading Community, as shown in Figure 6.8. Trader is one of the Common Object Request Broker Architecture (CORBA) services, which some Object Request Broker (ORB) vendors have implemented. A Trader is an object of a community, for example, that is also a community defining the Trading Community. An enterprise viewpoint for the Trading Community has been specified in [ISO-Trading]. A sample of this is shown from the enterprise viewpoint through a UML model, as derived from [ISO-Trading]. In identifying the use of a Trader in an architecture specification,

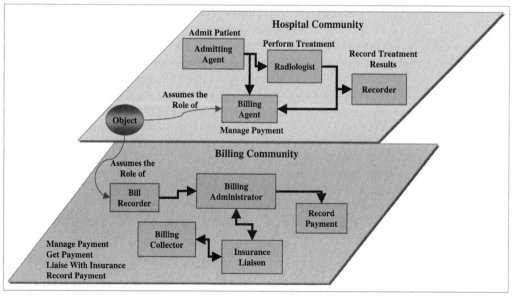

FIGURE 6.7 Community Composition

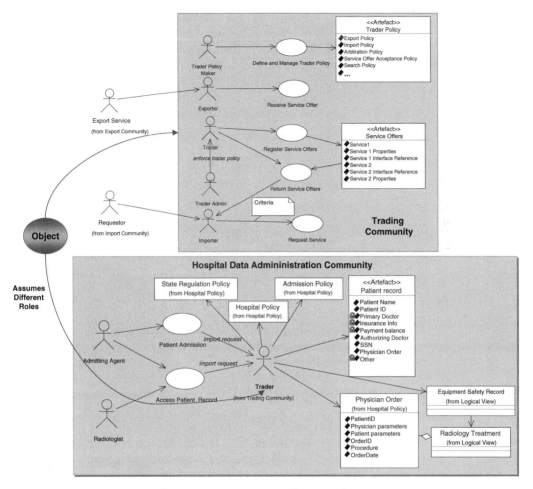

FIGURE 6.8   Recursiveness of Enterprise Viewpoint Trader Example

at some level of abstraction, the architect need only identify Trader as an object, since Trader is already fully specified.

With respect to a federation, RM-ODP minimally addresses this important concept in the enterprise viewpoint. Nevertheless, a federation is a collection of domains, each of which are constrained by the policies of that domain, such as a naming policy, a security policy, an administrative policy, and a resource usage policy. These policies, then, become important in a federation because of the need to negotiate the differences across the domains in the process of establishing a federation. The negotiation process becomes important in the interaction among the objects of the federation in order for the objects to enter into a federation. Sharing of resources the domain offers to other domains also becomes important. The ability to enter and leave a federation or change the nature of the sharing are part of the autonomy specification for each domain, captured in a domain-specific contract with the federation. These behaviors and actions are then captured in terms of a community (the federation), and associated environment contracts, one for each domain. As such, the federation itself is defined by a contract and constrained by federation policies. Federation is discussed in depth in Chapter 15, "Federation."

6.2.2 STRUCTURING RULES

The rules guide the specifier as to how to express the purpose, scope, and policies of an ODP system. Roles identify some of the behavior of the system. A role can be an entity of the system or a real-world entity, such as a person that interacts with the system in some way. An enterprise object assumes a role, perhaps more than one. Therefore, the distinguishing entity is role, not object.

The system performs some activities in pursuit of satisfying the objectives of the community. The things that can and cannot be done are directed by policy statements about the system, as well as policy statements about the environment. Recall that a community, for which the enterprise specification is created, is the system in its environment, as defined by a contract.

The *purpose* of the system is defined in terms of the community and environment. The scope is defined in terms of the roles and their actions in the community. The constraints on the behavior of the system are captured in terms of the policy statements. The objectives and scope of the system are specified in terms of the roles it fulfills within the community and policy statements regarding those roles.

A *community contract* forms the agreement of the behavior of the community within and with its environment. The behavior is specified by the roles, the objects that assume those roles, the configuration of the objects, and the constraints specified by the policies and environment contract.

An enterprise specification for a community includes:

▶ The contract of the community of focus:
  - Purpose
  - Scope
  - Roles
  - Objects
  - Activities performed by the objects
  - Policy statement(s) about the configuration of which objects assume which roles
  - Policy statement(s) about the interactions of the objects
  - Policy statement(s) about the creation, use, and deletion of resources
  - Policy statement(s) about the interactions of the community objects and the environment

      – Policy statement(s) about the QoS attributes expected of the environment, duration, and behavior that violates the agreement with the environment

▶ Other communities with which the community interacts and the associated environment contract

When an object assumes a role, it will perform one or more actions constrained by policy statements regarding obligation, permission, and prohibition. That is, an object can fulfill an obligation, can incur an obligation, can assume a permission from another object, or must not perform some prohibitive action. Hence, the specification of a role includes the policy statements that affect any object that assumes that role. Again, an enterprise object can assume one or more roles in the community of focus, and can also assume a role in a different community.

Although this seems confusing, it's quite powerful. What it means is that the enterprise specification focuses on particular areas of concern with respect to the full enterprise or a part of it. When it is about a part, it may well be the case that an object assumes multiple roles in different communities, which are exposed when the architect focuses on those communities. For example, the Billing Agent role in Figure 6.7 is defined in terms of what it can and cannot do, according to the policies; it is obligated to bill for the treatment for a patient and it is permitted to access the patient identification information. Now, the object that assumes the Billing Agent role is defined with respect to the Hospital Community. But that object can also assume the role of a Billing Recorder, with respect to the Billing Community, where the actions are different: obligated to record a bill, obligated to ensure the proper billing codes, obligated to update the patient records.

The environment contract is an agreement between a community and its environment. It states two-way expectations and constraints by one on the other. It may well include expectations of the community from its environment, such as quality of service statements, availability of resources, support for certain response times, and so forth. Since a contract is an agreement, it forms the agreement between the community and its environment in order to ensure the proper behavior of the community within its environment. The environment contract can also place constraints on the behavior of the community, such as allocation of a certain quantity of resources, or state regulation policies that must be enforced. So the environment contract is the mechanism to describe and constrain how the community of the enterprise specification performs and behaves within the enterprise.

The enterprise language doesn't address interaction as such, except in a general way. Clearly, objects interact. But the refinement of an interaction is provided in the other viewpoint languages. The focus of the enterprise viewpoint, then, is the relationships among the enterprise objects, whose behavior may be constrained by policies. The focus of the computational viewpoint is interaction and enabling distribution. The result is that the enterprise language focuses on the actions of the objects and how they are constrained within the community.

The enterprise viewpoint starts setting up what the system does, who does what, how the system exists within the business, and what talks with what. And all of this is associated with explicit semantics of the behavior of how these things must occur. Tightly coupled with all viewpoints, but especially the enterprise viewpoint, is the information viewpoint. The information viewpoint is concerned with the constraints on what the parts can and cannot do (semantics), how the parts are organized, and the information pertinent to the processing in the system.

6.3   USING THE INFORMATION VIEWPOINT

The information specification is a model that specifies the semantics of an ODP system, and the information structures. From this, for example, the architect can better understand the business specification, and better communicate the intended system semantics to the remaining architecture team. The information language helps answer the questions "What kind of information is managed by the system?" and "What constraints and criteria need be applied to access the information?" and "What constraints are applied to the interfaces?".

As the architecture specification is further defined, the information specification captures the semantics of processing and the schema of the data from each of the viewpoint specifications. It is not only updated by additional semantics from the viewpoint specifications, but also used by the viewpoint specifications to determine constraints affecting that specification from that viewpoint. Hence, one can think of the information specification as the hub in a wheel, where the spokes of the wheel are the other viewpoint specifications. That is, the information specification is central to all other viewpoint specifications.

The information language consists of concepts, rules and structures for the specification of an ODP system from the information viewpoint. The concepts are independent of distribution details and of implementation details.

An information specification contains:

▶ Identification of the set of information objects
▶ The static attributes of the information objects
▶ The associations among the information objects
▶ A specification of the behaviors of the information objects
▶ The relationships among the behaviors of the information objects
▶ Environmental contracts for information objects

The information specification is captured through the use of the three schemata discussed below. The schemata define the information processing aspects of an ODP system, as constrained by the conditions that must always be true (captured in the invariant schema). Schemata also describe the relationships among the information objects. Information flow and data flow are not captured in the information viewpoint. Flow is a subject of the computational viewpoint. But the schema of the data or information is captured in the information specification.

The information language helps define the semantics of the enterprise policies, the object templates, the community contract, and the environment contract through the invariant and static schemata. The allowable enterprise actions are specified in both the dynamic and static schemata, as well as any pre- or post-actions. The behavior and constraints on an object and its interactions will be further refined in the computational viewpoint, along with additional template definitions related to the computational viewpoint, such as interface and binding templates, and possibly additional policies. These constraints, template definitions, and policies are also part of the information specification. As the computational interface specification is further refined in the engineering specification, additional policies, template definitions, and other constraints most likely will emerge. These too become part of the information specification.

In line with the composition rules of RM-ODP, even the schema can be composed from other schemata. This aids the specification of composite objects, such as the Hospital Community objects shown in Figure 6.4.

It is left up to the architect to decide how best to format the information specification. UML class diagrams, with annotations of invariants; entity-relationships models, with annotations of invariants; or English text are possible tools for use. However, know that an information specification is not the same as the UML class diagrams. UML might be a partial way of representing, for example, invariant schemas. But to do so, concepts like "aggregation," "generalization," and the very loosely defined "association" need to have precisely defined semantics with respect to RM-ODP. They currently do not, unlike the concepts of RM-ODP and the General Relationship Model [ISO GRM]. A mixture of the use of UML, graphics, and English text is used to show some examples of these schemata. Text is used to specify invariants as "Notes" in the UML diagrams.

In Figure 6.9, another medical example is shown for use in this section. This example might further refine the aspects of Billing to reflect the manner of payment from an insurance company. Although Use Case and Class Diagram methods are indicated, these are notional diagrams, used only to represent the aspects of the information language. From the health example of Figure 6.5, how an insurance carrier's EOB may be created and provided to a patient is shown.

When a patient visits a doctor, a bill is generated. If the patient has insurance, the insurance company is provided with the bill. If the doctor also prescribes a treatment for the patient, the treatment center also bills the insurance company. In both cases, a treatment code is used to identify the treatment being billed. This code is used by the insurance company to process the insurance claim, to determine what amount of money to provide to the provider, and what amount of money the patient owes, through the processing of an EOB. (Notice, not included is the case where the insurance company provides the patient with payment, which, in the author's experience, is rare.)

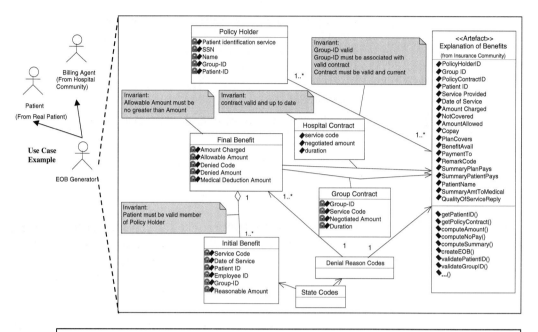

FIGURE 6.9   Information Viewpoint Medical Example

The EOB is the mechanism the insurance company uses to explain what is covered, how much, and what is not covered, and to explain the payment issued. The contents of the EOB (a schema) can include:

▶ The treatment code

▶ The date of service

▶ The service provider (that is, the doctor or the treatment center)

▶ What is covered financially

▶ What are "customary and reasonable" expenses in the area

▶ What is not covered

▶ What the patient must pay

The EOB is a template in the information model. The cardinality is shown in Figure 6.5 to indicate an EOB is associated with only one Group Contract. Patient identification may be a service provided to the hospital, physician, treatment center, and insurance provider. This service may be used by all to link together all the parts that finally result in the EOB. Again, note this is only an example.

The information viewpoint for a distributed system may be further refined to many more class objects, related schema, and additional processing. In the discussion of the concepts and rules for the information language, reference will be made back to Figure 6.5. An actual EOB is represented in Figure 6.9, for reference as to what is generally included in an EOB.

The invariants and quality of service semantics shown in Figure 6.9 are examples of where the modeling language constructs should be consistent in capturing semantics. That is, a perception of what one model says needs to be the same as another model, independent of the modeling constructs. There are few tools that capture and consistently model the constraints, and are consistent in the use of constraints across all the models provided. There are two issues here. One is that vendor UML products don't provide modeling of constraints as specified in the UML standard, which addresses the use of the Object Constraint Language (OCL) standard. The second is OCL captures some aspects of constraints, but they are not complete for RM-ODP. Hence, the architect needs to figure out a way of using a vendor tool for representing the architecture. It is clearly advantageous to capture the necessary semantics in each model. Classes basically capture structure, not semantics. But RM-ODP extends this notion in its definition of the schema used to capture not only structure, but also semantics, and the actions that dynamically are allowed to change the state of an object. More detail is provided below about these very important schemata and how they accomplish what today's models are not able to capture.

6.3.1   CONCEPTS

Prescription in the information viewpoint is restricted to a small basic set of concepts and rules addressing the scope and nature of information specifications. The concepts include three schemata: invariant schema, static schema, and dynamic schema. In many cases, invariant, static, and dynamic schemata can refer to several objects, not to a single object, provided that the information viewpoint does not describe some aspect of the implementation.

6.3.1.1   Invariant Schema

The *invariant schema* is a set of predicates that must always be true for one or more information objects for some specified period of time or interval. They constrain the possible states and state changes of the object(s). A single architecture specification can include one or more invariant schemata. These schemata define the properties of a stable state, not the stable state itself (there may be different "stable states" all of which satisfy the invariant). RM-ODP types are defined by invariants (predicates) and, as such, capture semantics. The invariant schema, therefore, constrains the dynamic and static schemata. The invariant schema is exceedingly important. It, in essence, captures the constraints on a system, and certain properties such as quality of service. It contains the unvarying rules for the object, despite state changes.

An invariant schema for Figure 6.9 might include:

▶ The insured must be a valid subscriber.

▶ The Patient_ID must be valid.

▶ The Patient_ID must be a valid member of the policy holder.

▶ An EOB can be associated with multiple valid patient identifications.

▶ The Group_ID, which specifies a valid agreement with an organization, must be valid and up-to-date.

▶ Payment must be less than or equal to the total amount billed.

▶ The contract with the Hospital Community must be valid.

▶ The contract with the Hospital Community must indicate the percentage deductible from the total bill.

▶ The payment must be issued within 30 calendar days from receipt of the bill.

▶ State regulation must be used to determine payment.

▶ Each EOB must be associated with a single group policy identification.

▶ Each service code must be recognized by state regulation.

▶ The types associated with each role must be defined.

There is ongoing discussion among those actively involved in RM-ODP as to whether a contract is an invariant. Most agree that statements in a contract can be invariant. However, as was described in Chapter 5, "RM-ODP Architecture

Model," a contractual context is associated with a contract in place. That context exists and is invariant until it is terminated. In this sense, the contract itself is an invariant for the duration between enabled contractual context and termination of that context. The end result is the specifier (the architect) decides what is and is not invariant, and specifies it accordingly.

6.3.1.2 Static Schema

The *static schema* defines the state and structure of one or more information objects at some point in time. A static schema may be used for observations "of interest." The static schema is constrained by the invariant schema. The importance of the static schema is that it captures the effect on the object of some action that results in a change of state or structure of the object, such as one of the actions of the dynamic schema, object creation, object destruction, or some property of interest.

The static schema for the example in Figure 6.9 might be the states of the objects in the Billing payment object that calculates the fields of the EOB. Other objects may be created to validate a bill, generate an EOB, fill in an EOB, and post the EOB. Each state change of each object is then captured in the static schema.

6.3.1.3 Dynamic Schema

The *dynamic schema* defines all the actions that allow a state or structure change of one or more information objects. The dynamic schema is constrained by the invariant schema. The dynamic schema is a focus on the allowable actions of the system that dynamically affect a change, and helps define the computational aspects of the system, further refined in the computational viewpoint.

Referring to the example of Figure 6.9, the dynamic schema could include the actions:

```
validate-hospital-contract()
validate-patient-id()
validate-group-id()
calculate-percentage-off()
validate-service-codes()
compute-EOB()
report-EOB()
make-payment()
```

The actions that cause the information object to change state are all captured in the dynamic schema for that object, and help define the "rules" as to if payment is due a medical service provider, a patient, or if the patient must pay the medical service provider. Precondition and postcondition actions are captured in the dynamic schema as well. The actions occur as a result of identifying the amounts payable for services that are associated with a valid patient identification (an invariant), a single valid group identification (an invariant), a hospital contract (possibly an invariant), a group contract (possibly an invariant), and so forth.

6.3.2   STRUCTURING RULES

The semantics in the information language are defined by the configuration of the information objects, the behavior of those objects, and the environment contract. Once again the environment contract is visible in this viewpoint, as it was in the enterprise viewpoint, and will be in the computational viewpoint.

The dynamic schema defines the possible dynamic changes of state of an object. This includes how an object is created and destroyed. Parameters may change, new values may be assigned, and a subset of the dynamic schema actions becomes available in this state to affect the next change. The states and structures of the objects are captured in the static schema for the actions captured in the dynamic schema. Further, time constraints may affect a state change as well (such as a quality of service constraint not met).

An information object can be a composition of other information objects, or a single atomic object. When it is a composite information object, the schemas are composed as well. Each component schema describes one of the component information objects in the composition.

The configuration of information objects is independent of distribution; that is, there is no sense or focus on distribution in this viewpoint.

The syntax for a policy is not specified in RM-ODP. For an excellent treatment of the subject of semantics and the information viewpoint, see the work of Haim Kilov [Kilov-94 and Kilov-98], the Workshops on Behavioral Semantics [ECOOP-97a, ECOOP-97b, ECOOP-98a, ECOOP-98b], and the standard on the General Relationship Model [ITU-GRM].

6.4   USING THE COMPUTATIONAL VIEWPOINT

The computational viewpoint is focused on the decomposition of a system into objects that interact at interfaces, and on the constraints on the actions of the objects and the interactions. A computational specification will address the system in terms of configurations of computational objects and interactions necessary to achieve the complete functionality of the system and enable distribution.

The primary framework of the computational viewpoint is an interaction framework. Interaction is the reason for interfaces: one object interacts with another for some purpose, and the "how" is the interface and binding capabilities.

A computational specification will contain a configuration of computational objects, specification of internal object actions, specification of interactions between objects, interface specifications to support interactions, binding specification to support interfaces, policy constraints that apply to the interaction between computational objects, and environment contracts to ensure proper constraints are established between objects in the computational specification and its environment.

The objects in the computational viewpoint can be application objects, service support objects, or even infrastructure objects. For example, the Admitting Agent object from the enterprise example of Figure 6.4 could be a computational object, which is probably a composition of objects. A data store of patient records, which is not shown in Figure 6.4, could be a computational object (only the specification for a patient record is shown, not the storage mechanism). A printing object, also not shown in Figure 6.4, could be a computational object needed. Most objects depicted in the computational viewpoint involve internal actions (actions that happen inside an object) or interactions (actions that involve at least two objects).

The computational language uses the RM-ODP foundations, and makes great use of the object model. What this means is that a computational object offers an *interface* across which an interaction with another object can happen. Objects can offer multiple interfaces; each may be a different type, or may be of the same type but offer different interactions. An *interaction* is a set of services that are offered across a single interface, and are linked to another object with a *binding*. Objects encapsulate behavior. Objects include activities internal to the object, which may be provided to another object using an interaction.

The computational specification is concerned with the structuring of applications, independent of either how the computational objects are distributed or on which type of computers and networks. The computational specification, then, is a logical model, not a physical model of a topology of networked computers and modules. This latter focus is that of the engineering viewpoint. The computational specification enables a focus on the processing of application components, how they interact with other components (in parallel or in sequence), how the dynamic bindings among components are accomplished, and how constraints on those bindings are achieved.

If an object is visible in the enterprise language, it is visible in the computational language. That is, there is a 1-to-1 mapping between the two. Recall that in the enterprise language, a community is defined in terms of roles, not objects. Roles can be assumed by humans, machines, or objects. When a role is assumed by an object, that object has a counterpart object in the computational language. As an example, the Billing Community Bill-Recorder enterprise object can be refined to a Bill-Recorder computational object, which can then be decomposed into more atomic computational objects and their interactions and behavior in the computational specification.

There is a difference between an interface and a binding. Many will confuse the two, but they are different, producing different end results. The software architecture community is now trying to separate the meanings of interface, binding, connector, and other related concepts. What RM-ODP did was to separate the concepts into different areas of focus: the computational that deals with the abstract constructs of interaction, interfacing, and binding; and the engineering that deals with the connector-like mechanisms to realize an interconnection. Mixing the areas of concern often confuses what is really important to focus on, mixes what can and cannot be accomplished, and often misses some important semantics. Some of the work of the software architecture community in both architecture styles, focused on the constraints and behavior of connectors, and of connectors that may be better progressed by separating out the areas of concern in alignment with the concepts of RM-ODP.

Figure 6.10 presents two objects, each with a single interface that is associated with one interaction. The interfaces are identified by a name, A1 and B1 in this figure. The first step is to request an interaction from object A with object B using the interface B1 of object B. The binding is a result of some processing that determines if the two object interfaces can be joined together, or bound. The second step checks a number of things to ensure the two object interfaces can be bound. The determination is based on type matching (making sure that the interface type for object 1 is the same type as the interface type for object 2), the constraints are agreed to (making sure if a quality of service constraint is identified,

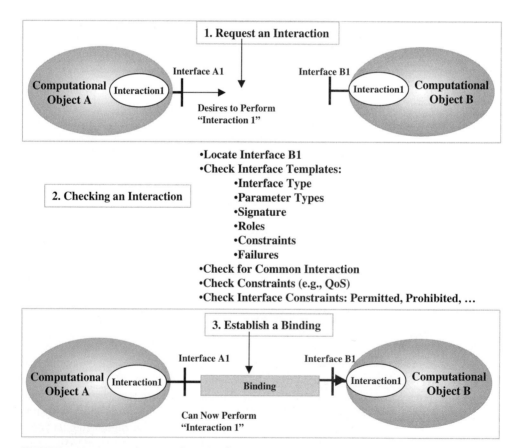

FIGURE 6.10   Interaction, Interface, Binding

and both objects agree to adhere to it), and so forth. Once all these checks are accomplished, then the third step is to establish a binding to join the interfaces and proceed with the interaction. Although this appears to be simple, it's actually much more involved. The interaction model is discussed further in Chapter 13, "Interaction Framework: Interoperability."

An interface can be complex. It can include multiple interactions providing some service, each with its own name, type, a set of typed parameters, constraints, and failures. The ability to specify the behavior of the interface (constrained actions, as captured in the information language and reflected in the computational language) makes RM-ODP very valuable, as well as the RM-ODP object model that allows an object to have multiple interfaces. The actual mechanisms to achieve an interaction are specified in the interconnection model, which is part of the engineering language. The interaction specification, therefore, encompasses the information, computational, and engineering languages.

Figure 6.11 provides an overview of a computational object and the elements discussed so far. The objects shown in Figure 6.11 are possible objects in the computational specification that perform some of the actions of Figure 6.5. In this example, the FinalEOB object is responsible for creating a final EOB. It interacts with the Validate object to validate the Patient and Group Policy ID. It interacts with the EOB Init object to create an initial EOB, with associated constraints. And it interacts with the Patient Record Database object to affect an update. The interaction is specified as an action that occurs between two objects. The interface is identified, and the interface template for the interface is shown. Constraints on the interaction, which includes the interface, binding, and objects involved, are shown (e.g., QoS, other conditions). The computational bindings are shown between the interfaces offered by each object in the interaction.

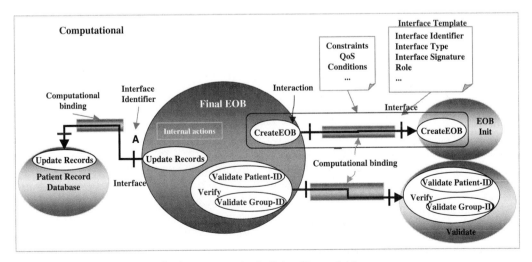

FIGURE 6.11 Computational Object Example, Refining Figure 6.10

Interaction among objects can be simple or complex. It all depends on the semantics of the interactions: how many objects are involved in the interaction; how the objects will behave; what constraints are applicable to the objects and to the interface to be bound between them; and how can dynamic binding occur. Although the example above shows only two objects, any number of objects can be involved in a binding. This is the nature of multimedia and multiparty bindings, such as support for a video teleconferencing or collaborative workflow session.

A special computational object, the *binding object*, is an object that is used to describe complex interactions. A binding object joins two or more objects to an interaction of an object. A binding object is addressed in more detail below, and in Chapter 13, "Interaction Framework: Interoperability."

The computational language sets up the computational constraints in order to achieve the distribution transparencies necessary for distributed processing. The mechanisms to achieve the transparencies are provided by the engineering language, through further refinement and decomposition.

The concepts and rules for the computational language are very precise and extensive. They address naming, types, templates, interactions, interfaces, bindings, failure, and portability. They address the concerns of when and why objects interact.

The computational language constructs for the interaction model are related to the engineering language constructs for the interconnection model by means of the consistencies between the two languages. A computational interface becomes, for example, an engineering interface associated with a binding mechanism called a channel. The channel is discussed in the engineering language section.

SIDEBAR

COMPUTATIONAL INTERACTION IMPORTANCE

In today's distributed systems, interfaces tend to make or break a system. Poorly defined and constructed interfaces result in either an inoperable system or in excessive sustainment costs. Poorly defined semantic behavior of an interaction (or interface) usually results in the inability to interoperate, or compose a system from parts. The beauty of the computational specification is that it precisely defines the very important interfacing aspects of the parts of a system, taking into account the semantic behaviors to be realized across the interfaces, and independent of how those parts are distributed across the networks and computers and of the technologies used. That is, in the computational specification the architect can specify the actions of objects and their interactions knowing that these do not have to change due to distribution changes, that these will be interoperable with other ODP systems, and that the application details are protected from perturbations in the infrastructure. The infrastructure (and distribution) are the focus of the engineering viewpoint, and assume the mechanisms of these changes so that the computational specification does not.

6.4.1 CONCEPTS

The computational language concepts are principally about interaction and identification of metadata about the objects and interfaces. Each computational object
is specified through a computational object template. Each interface is specified
through an interface template. Each interaction is specified through an interaction
template.

    The computational object template includes all of its interface templates.
Each interface template includes all interaction templates associated with the interface. The interfaces are associated with a causality role that captures the behavior
of the interface, as defined by the actions and constraints associated with those
actions. The environment contract constraints the objects and their interfaces.

A *computational interface template* is an interface template. It specifies a
signal, stream, or operation interface (which consists of one or more signal,
flow, or operation interactions, respectively). The computational interface
template is specified in terms of an appropriate interface signature, along
with its behavior and an associated environment contract. [RM-ODP-3]

    The concepts for the computational language relate to interaction. They
include:

- Three interaction types: *signal, operation,* and *flow*
- Three interface types: *signal , operation,* and *stream interfaces*
- Two kinds of operation interaction: *announcement* and *interrogation*
- Three types of interface signatures: *signal interface signature, operation interface signature*, and *stream interface signature*
- Computational object template
- Computational interface template
- Binding object

    The relationships among an interaction, interface, and interface template are
shown in Figure 6.12, along with the kinds of information contained in a computational object template, a computational interface template, and an environment
contract. A discussion about the interface, interaction types, and roles follows.

    An interaction is an action between two objects. The mechanisms of inter-
acting are the interface and its binding. An interface consists of one or more interactions, which are all of the same type and all defined by the interface template.
RM-ODP distinguishes between a type of interaction and a type of interface. Each
of operational, signal, and stream are types of interactions. That is, each interaction template defines the nature of the relationship between two objects, without
going into the interface structure details. So, for example, an operation is defined

in part as an interaction between one object called a client, and another object called a server, and the actions that happen between the two can result in one-way or two-way communication.

 NOTE

The definitions for interaction types, as paraphrased from RM-ODP Part 3 [RM-ODP-3], are:

▶ *Signal:* A one-way interaction between an initiating object and a responding object.

▶ *Operation:* An interaction between a client object and a server object, which is either an interrogation or an announcement. An *interrogation* is an operation interaction that consists of two one-way interactions: one to request, one to respond. An *announcement* is a one-way operation interaction that the client object uses to request something of a server object. The client expects no response, and the server does not respond.

▶ *Flow:* An ordered set of one or more interactions that are communicated one-way, from a producer object to a consumer object.

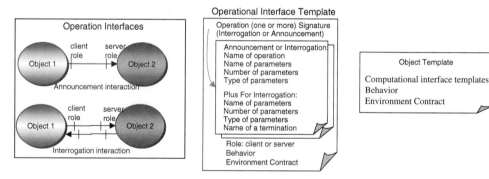

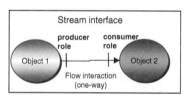

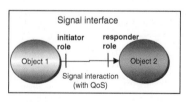

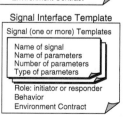

FIGURE 6.12 Interfaces, Templates, and Environment Contract

A *type of interface*, then, is an interface that consists only of a set of specific typed interactions. That is, an interface of type "operational" consists of only "operation" type interactions, but may consist of more than one. So an interface is a means of structuring a number of interactions between objects: one may be to request something; one may be to respond to that request; one may be to check out if the QoS specified will be honored by the receiving end; one may be to provide an indication about failure; and so forth. All of these interactions could be grouped together into one interface specification.

Figure 6.13 shows these relationships just discussed: interface (of a particular type), interactions within the interface (all of the same interface type), and binding (which will be addressed shortly). The causality roles identified must be complementary and specific to the type of interface, and one role is assumed on each end of the interface, as shown.

Next, RM-ODP defines related interface types: *operation interface, stream interface*, and *signal interface* type. In each case, the type of interface defines the type of interaction(s) that comprise the interface.

So, for example, a single operation interface can include the operation interactions between a client and a server such as:

```
Client to Server: Initiate a request
Server to Client: OK
Client to Server: An SQL query
Server to Client: Response as appropriate to the query
Client to Server: Provide a search on some metadata
Server to Client: I don't do that: failure
Client to Server: End
```

All of these are interactions of type *operation*. All of these could comprise a single operation interface. The individual actions of the interface are then invoked as appropriate.

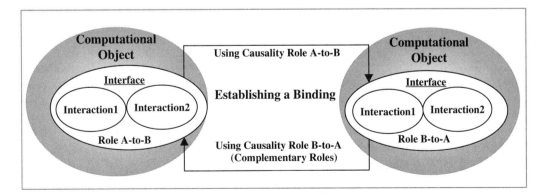

FIGURE 6.13   Relationships of Interaction Constructs

An interaction must be of the same type as the interface. Further, an interaction can only be associated with one interface, though an interface can consist of any number of interactions.

This separation of interaction type from interface type provides many capabilities. In multiparty video teleconferencing (VTC), for example, the communication flows can be all part of the same stream interface, and individually correspond to a dynamic interaction as one user comes on board or leaves the VTC. Furthermore, one can specify a separate interaction in an interface to check out a needed quality of service, before the process of communicating begins. Or the streams can correspond to different types of flows (e.g., video, televised), but are all typed *stream* for the purposes of the interface.

6.4.1.1 Causality Roles

For each type of interface, RM-ODP identifies the name of each end of the interface for the object participating in the interactions of that interface, which corresponds to the causality assumed by the object. These names are different for the different interface types. The names for an operation interface are *client* and *server*. The names for a signal interface are *initiator* and *responder*. The names for a stream interface are *consumer* and *producer*. These are names of causality roles, not names of the interface, nor names of roles assumed by an object. Each end of the interface assumes a complementary causality role. The behavior of the interface is that defined by the causality role of the interface.

Now that the stage is set to the difference between an interaction and interface type, let's look closer at the interface types specifically. (See Chapter 13, "Interaction Framework: Interoperability," for more details.)

6.4.1.2 Operation Interface

An *operation interface* type is an interface in which all the interactions are operations. An operation interaction can be an *interrogation* or an *announcement*. An announcement is a one-way interaction that a client object uses to request something of a server object. The client expects no response and the server does not respond. An interrogation consists of two one-way interactions: the client object uses the *invocation* to request something, and the server object uses the *termination* to respond.

Figure 6.14 shows a metamodel of an operation interface template, using UML, and how it relates to an operation interaction, operation interface signature, and so forth. Notice that the causality role is associated with the interface, not with each interaction. A similar metamodel could be created for both the signal and stream interface template.

An *interface signature* structures the information about a specific type of interface, for use by other objects. It identifies the type of interface, the type of interactions, and for each interaction, the interaction templates as shown in Figure 6.12. It is very common to use the ISO's Interface Definition Language

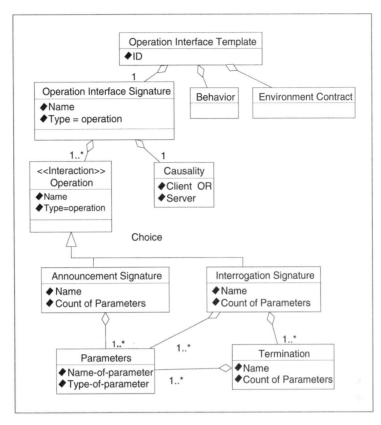

FIGURE 6.14 Metamodel of Operation Interface Template

(IDL) [ISO IDL] to capture a computational interface signature. However, IDL cannot capture constraints. English text around an IDL specification, coupled with associated IDL constructs, is the manner in which IDL can be used to describe constraints.

Let's take a look at an example. This is an IDL example of the "verify" operation interface of Figure 6.11. This is only a representative sample. The "verify" interface provides the operation interactions validate-patient-id and validate-group-id. What these mean are captured in the operation interface signature. There are constraints associated with these operations, as exemplified in Figure 6.9. In this example, "constraint" is identified. This is a placeholder to capture the constraints associated with the interaction. In the patient-criteria example, this is used to contain the criteria for the constraint "Patient must be a valid member of a subscriber," as was identified in the information specification of Figure 6.9. The details of the types are not included here; they are represented only as "sometype." Only the elements that constitute the operations for the operation interface, the direction of the operation parameters, the matching criteria, and the errors are exemplified in part. The IDL statements shown represent an operation type interaction and the operation interface type. Comments are in italics. The operation interface consists of the operation type interactions offer, export, withdraw, and modify.

```
// This is an example of an operation interface type
   signature for "verify" of Figure 6.10
   typedef string Constraint;
   exception InvalidConstraint {
        Constraint constr;
        };
```

The constraint `constr` is the means to convey constraints. The processing of the interaction guarantees that the constraint is satisfied. If the `constr` does not agree to the syntax rules (which the architect defines) for a legal constraint expression, then `InvalidConstraint` exception is raised.

```
interface verify {

// This is an example of an operation interrogation type
// interaction
   void validate-patient-id (
// This is an example of an invocation operation
// interaction
        in unsigned long Patient-ID,
        in unsigned long Patient-EOB-ID,
        in string Patient-Name,
        in unsigned long Patient-SSN
        in Constraint Patient-Criteria,
// This is an example of a termination operation
// interaction
        out boolean Success
) raises (InvalidConstraint, Bad-Patient-ID,
    Bad-Patient-Name, Cannot-Locate, Multiple-Results,
    Invalid-Argument, Remote-Error, System-Error);

// This is an example of an operation some-type
// interaction
   void validate-group-id (
// This is an example of an invocation operation
   interaction
        in unsigned long Group-ID,
        in unsigned long Patient-ID,
        in string Group-Subscriber,
```

```
      in Constraint Group-Criteria,
      in Constraint Contract,
      // This is an example of a termination operation
      // interaction
      out boolean Success
  ) raises (InvalidConstraint, Bad-Group-ID, Undefined-
      Patient-ID, InvalidContract, ExpiredContract,
      Argument-Syntax, System-Error);

}; // end of verify interface
```

6.4.1.3 Signal Interface

Another interface type is *signal interface,* in which the originator knows the destination of the interface. Each end of the interface has a specific causality role: the initiating object to initiate the interface, and the responding object to receive the interface. A signal is an action, such as "invoke" or "respond" or "terminate." A signal interface, then, is a one-way interaction between two objects that includes one or more signals in the interface signature. There is one important rule: a signal interface can correspond to the specification of one side of an operation interface. That is, signal interfaces can be used to specify all of the client/server interfaces, if this modeling construct is important. This capability supports, for example, publish/subscribe messaging. Signals are used to offer services to a Trader, as another example.

Signal interface is a type of interface from an object assuming the role of producer to an object assuming the role of consumer. It consists of only flow type interactions. [RM-ODP-3]

6.4.1.4 Stream Interface

The third type of interface is a stream interface. This interface supports information flows from an object assuming the role of producer to an object assuming the role of consumer. Each stream (flow of information) can be included in a single stream interface. This type of interface is used in support of multimedia, in which one stream may be audio and another stream may be video.

Stream interface is a type of interface consisting of only flow type interactions. [RM-ODP-3]

6.4.1.5 Binding Object

The final concept is that of a binding object. The *binding object* is an intermediate object between two or more object interfaces that manages a binding between them. There can be more than two objects bound by the binding object, and this is generally the case. A binding object can be used, for example, to manage a VTC session, to manage multiparty conferencing, to manage multimedia, to act as an interface broker, to act as a data broker to a myriad of different data stores, or any manner of interaction where the interaction is complex. More of this important concept is addressed in Chapter 13, "Interaction Framework: Interoperability."

6.4.2 STRUCTURING RULES

A computational specification describes the functional decomposition of an ODP system, in distribution transparent terms, as:

▶ A configuration of computational objects (including binding objects)
▶ The internal actions of those objects
▶ The interactions that occur among those objects
▶ The environment contracts for those objects and their interfaces

A computational specification is constrained by the rules of the computational language. These comprise interaction rules, binding rules, and type rules that provide distribution-transparent interworking; template rules that apply to all computational objects; and failure rules that apply to all computational objects and identify the potential points of failure in computational activities. The major rules for the computational interaction and binding are highlighted here. A more in-depth look at these topics is provided in Chapter 13, "Interactive Framework: Interoperability."

6.4.2.1 Computational Objects

A computational object can perform a number of actions. These include:

▶ Instantiate and delete an interface template with an identifier to the interface
▶ Instantiate and delete an object template, to include deletion of itself
▶ Perform a binding action
▶ Invoke or respond to an operation of an operational interface
▶ Produce or consume a flow of a stream interface
▶ Initiate or respond to a signal of a signal interface
▶ Read and modify its state
▶ Obtain an interface identifier for a Trader object

▶ Test for substitutability of a computational interface signature

▶ Spawn, fork, and join

Refinement applies to computational objects and their interfaces. That is, the architect further refines a computational object into additional specifications of objects and interfaces, defining the interrelationships among them.

For example, privacy is important in patient records of the medical examples. In order to ensure privacy of patient records, a security computational object that manages access control may be needed. In order to ensure privacy between the insurance community and the hospital community, as another example, a secure network and encryption may be required. Instead of addressing this area of concern at this point, which would require specification of the details of any such network or encryption scheme, an environment contract can be used to identify this needed quality of service, by stating "secure binding" or some such. The engineering viewpoint can then further refine this QoS specification.

Likewise, the Insurance Community is contractually bound (through the environment contract) to provide payment in a certain amount of time (say, two weeks). This is a quality of service that is specified. Therefore, computational objects and their refinements into additional computational objects and interfaces might require the specification of additional environment contracts or additional environment contract statements to capture the additional computational behavior. This is an example of where a computational specification may affect a portion of the information specification: addition or update of an environment contract. It should be pointed out that QoS specifications for binding are just now emerging. Nevertheless, the architect can specify this need in the computational specification so that when technology becomes available, it can be incorporated to support the QoS constraints.

6.4.2.2 Computational Interaction

The computational language defines three types of interactions between objects: operational, stream, and signal, as discussed above. The rules are different for each.

Operational interfaces provide a client/server-based model of distributed interaction. Client objects invoke operations using the interface provided by the server objects. The operational interface is strongly typed, along with strong typing for the parameters of the interface signature. Operation interfaces can be either one-way or two-way. A one-way operational interface is called "announcement" because it does not return a termination; a two-way operational interaction is called "interrogation" because it does return a termination.

In an interrogation, the server must respond, although there is no particular time associated with the response. That would be a QoS attribute defined. In addition, the client can invoke an operation interaction in the operation interface in any order it chooses; there is no order defined.

The server can limit the operation interactions available to clients through a constraint in the interface template relating to the policy associated with the interface. That is, the operational interface signature may be specified to contain a number of different operation interactions, but the client-side use of that interface is constrained as specified in policy of the interaction, and captured in the interface template.

A stream interface provides a flow of information, single or continuous, between a producer object and a consumer object. A consumer object connects to the stream interface of a producer object, to receive the flow. A stream interface enables multimedia continuous flow of information, useful for establishing a VTC session, or a collaborative workflow session. That is, the stream interface can consist of flows such as audio flows, video flows, and televised flows.

A signal interface connects an initiator and a responder object. This is the most elementary of the interaction types. For a signal interaction, the initiator object of the signal initiates the signal interaction. The responder object of the signal responds to the signal. A signal can be used as a point of reference to measure a QoS characteristic. A parameter in a signal can be an interface signature, an interface reference, or both. This is what Trader uses to receive exported service offerings, and associate an interface signature, an interface reference, to respond to a service request from an importer. In essence, a signal is an observable event at some location.

6.4.2.3   Binding

What enables two objects to communicate is a *binding*, with an associated behavior. Behavior is that captured by the contract related to the interface, the role the interface supports, and the parameters of the signature as well as of the type of interactions. In other words, the binding is the dynamic link between two objects that enables all the capabilities of interactions captured in the interface signature, subject to the constraints specified about those interactions. So in terms of "establishing a binding," or the phrase "interfacing," these phrases mean a binding is established.

In the computational language, there are two kinds of bindings: one is implicit and one is explicit. Further, an explicit binding can be either primitive or compound.

The *implicit binding* is used for an operational interface between a client and a server. It is the case where a client uses a specific interface to a server, without any constraints associated with the binding. Of course, there are mechanisms to be set up to establish an actual binding, but these mechanisms are the concern of the engineering language. The computational language merely allows the specification for an implicit binding.

The *explicit primitive binding* is used to define explicit binding constraints and actions (behavior) associated with the binding of an interface, of any type. The architect would specify the interface identifier for both objects in the interface, establish that the interface type of each interface of the binding be the same, and establish that the causality roles and interface signatures are complementary (that is, the initiating object uses the appropriate role of the interface, and the receiving object uses the complementary role of that same interface). These constraints form the establishing behavior for the binding. Deletion of the interface results in deletion of the binding as well.

The *explicit compound binding* makes use of the computational binding object as an intermediate object between pairs of interacting objects. Two or more objects can be bound using the binding object. If a binding is complex, the binding object is used to manage the complexity and control of the interfaces and the bindings. The binding object may manage different interface types as well. Figure 6.15 provides an example of these types of bindings.

The binding object must interact with the source object to intercept the request, map it to the target object interface, and interact with the target object to provide the request. Likewise, the binding object must interact with the target object to receive a response, map it to the appropriate response for the source object, and then interact with the source object to deliver the response.

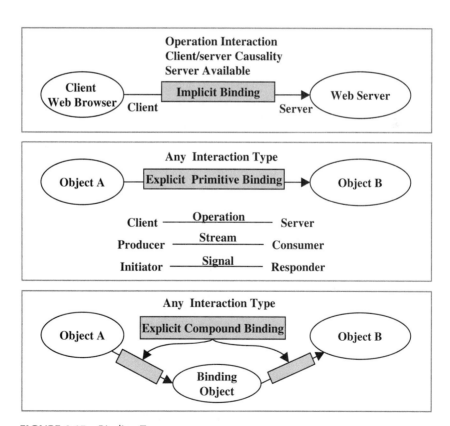

FIGURE 6.15 Binding Types

The binding object includes all the interface signatures of both the source and target objects it manages. That is, the binding object is like an interface broker: it translates requests and responses, brokers the interactions from one object to one or more objects across a number of different bindings, and establishes the appropriate bindings, as per the establishing behavior specification(s). When the binding object brokers an interaction to more than one target object, it must track the relationships among the interactions as well. The Trader is similar to a binding object, except that the Trader does not actually transfer the interactions between its trading objects. It only provides the interface reference to the source object, which then establishes its own binding to the target object for further interaction.

The binding object is an important computational object. It allows management and control over the bindings of the other computational objects. Auditing of interfaces, perhaps security, can be accomplished with a binding object. A certain QoS can be stated and must be met before the establishment of a certain binding, which would be evaluated in the binding object. The binding object facilitates cross-domain management, federation of domains, and further refinement of the specifications of interactions in the federation and across the domains of the federation (which is discussed in Chapter 15, "Federation").

Although the binding object is very important for complex bindings, it is also one of the ambiguities of RM-ODP. How a binding object maps onto objects in the engineering viewpoint is not clear. How two binding objects interact is not defined. In one place, RM-ODP equates the binding object to the binder in the engineering language; in other places, the binding object equates to a full channel (which, by the way, is not an object); in other places, it is left open to interpretation. Multiplexing (the interleaving of multiple communications) is most likely an action of the binding object, but not addressed in RM-ODP. Multiplexing different interface types is not addressed. These turn out to be architecture refinement decisions. The architect should, therefore, be sure to specify the mapping and use of the binding object to whatever engineering constructs are used.

A binding object is represented in Figure 6.16. This particular computational binding object is a general data manager, or data broker, that locates the correct store of information, binds the requesting object interface to the receiving object interface, for the appropriate interface signature. Notice that, in this example, interfaces labeled 1 and 2 are operation type interfaces, whereas interface 3 is a stream interface. Sometimes medical treatments result in video images of the procedure (such as a heart catherization). In this example, a computational object, called Get Treatment Results, obtains the video stream from the store computational object. And the computational binding object, General Data Manager, manages the appropriate bindings (shown as gray rectangles inside the binding object). Of course, this is only an example of any such binding object. Not shown, for example, is the use of a directory, a data schema object, a control object that might manage the length of time of response, any QoS control object that ensures appropriate response time, and so forth. These are objects the architect could specify in the computational specification.

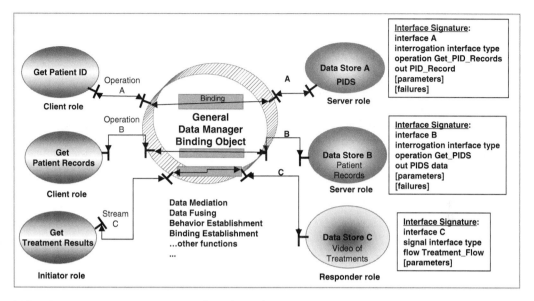

FIGURE 6.16 Using a Computational Binding Object

6.4.2.4 Naming and Typing

Names of objects, interfaces, interactions, and parameters are unique identifiers in the computational language. The name is associated with a naming context, as discussed in Chapter 5, "RM-ODP Architecture Model." This context will probably be associated with a specific management domain, because management domains manage, among other things, the naming of objects within their domain. The Internet Domain Name Server is an example of an object (a large coarse-grained object for the purposes of this discussion) that manages the naming within its domain, and federates that naming context across domains.

Everything in RM-ODP is strongly typed. An interaction has a type, which is directly associated with an interface of that same type, and an interface signature of that same type. Inheritance of an interface type may create a subtype relationship, which is then substitutable for the parent type. This is the concept of substitutability that is addressed in Chapter 5, "RM-ODP Architecture Model."

Type matching, therefore, becomes very important. Just matching names of entities is not enough; types must also match. Rules are needed to determine type equality in order to check for matching types and subtypes. RM-ODP provides notations and rules for typing to determine how to match types of the first order [RM-ODP-3], but does not expand this to lower levels of subtyping. This is not covered here. Further information is provided in the Annex of [RM-ODP-3]. In addition, type management and type matching are the subject of further standardization. Also, capabilities such as the Trader provide type matching according to their methods, as defined by the trading specific policies.

6.4.2.5   Portability

Portability rules are provided to give guidance to developers of future ODP portability standards. These standards will address ordering and delivery of announcements, instantiation of computational objects and interfaces, subtyping test rules, composition and associated rules, and others. As such, RM-ODP itself has not really supported the original objective to provide portability; instead, it has established a framework to be filled in by additional standards that will realize portability.

6.5   USING THE ENGINEERING VIEWPOINT

The engineering viewpoint is focused on the mechanisms and functions that support interactions between distributed objects, and the distribution transparency objects that hide the complexities of the interactions. The engineering language defines the concepts and rules for the mechanisms of distribution and the infrastructure services from the engineering viewpoint. The concepts address distribution details but are independent of implementation details.

The primary parts of the engineering viewpoint are the channel model, the distribution transparencies, the ODP functions, and the node model. The channel model is a generic model of the distributed infrastructure. The distribution transparencies guarantee abstractions of the distributed infrastructure. The ODP functions provide basic services that enable distribution. The node model is a configuration of the objects that form the infrastructure of a single node (a computer). The node and channel models are addressed at a high level in this section. The channel model in addressed in more depth in Chapter 13, "Interaction Framework: Interoperability"; the distribution transparencies in Chapter 10, "Hiding System Complexities: Distribution Transparencies"; and the ODP functions in Chapter 9, "RM-ODP Functions."

The engineering language provides the concepts and rules for specifying the mechanisms to achieve physical distribution to support the logical processing of application objects specified in the computational language. It deals with the "how" of object interaction: how the infrastructure and communication mechanisms support distributed transparent object interaction.

An engineering specification defines the infrastructure required to support functional distribution of an ODP system and is expressed in terms of:

▶ Basic engineering objects that correspond to computational objects

▶ Engineering interfaces that correspond to computational interfaces

▶ The ODP functions required to manage physical distribution, communication, processing, and storage

▶ The roles of different engineering objects supporting the ODP functions (e.g., the nucleus)

▶ The distribution transparencies required to hide the details of distribution from the application developer and end user

▶ A configuration of engineering objects, structured as clusters, capsule and nodes

▶ The activities that occur within those engineering objects

▶ The interconnection mechanisms of distributed or local bindings to support computational interactions

An engineering specification is constrained by the rules of the engineering language. These comprise channel rules, interface reference rules, distributed binding rules, and transparency rules for the provision of distribution transparent interaction among engineering objects. They also comprise cluster rules, capsule rules, and node rules governing the configuration of engineering objects, and failure rules.

The engineering specification is particularly important to the system designer. A specification using this viewpoint is closely aligned with many architecture endeavors today. It focuses on the processing capabilities of each node, and the distributed interconnections among them. This viewpoint is similar in content to some of the lower-level software architectures, the System Architecture of the C4ISR framework [C4ISR], and the Physical Model of the Zachman framework [Zachman].

6.5.1   CONCEPTS AND RULES: NODE MODEL

The engineering language concepts focus on the configuration of basic engineering objects and (support) engineering objects of the node, and the interconnection mechanisms to support distributed computational interaction. The engineering language does a great deal. It should; it's addressing the concerns of the infrastructure and interaction mechanisms. An overview of the configuration of the node is shown in Figure 6.17. Each of these concepts is addressed in the following paragraphs of this section.

The concepts of the node model include:

▶ Basic engineering object: corresponds to objects from the computational specification, which are the application specific components

▶ Engineering object: corresponds to objects only in the engineering language, used for infrastructure specific functionality

▶ Cluster: a grouping of objects from the computational specification, to be treated as a single unit

- Cluster manager: manages a specific cluster
- Capsule: a grouping of clusters, which form a single unit of processing (such as a software module)
- Capsule manager: manages a single capsule
- Nucleus: similar to the operating system
- Node: the computer and operating system

Basic engineering objects are directly related to the computational objects. A computational object is refined into one or more basic engineering objects (BEOs) coupled with engineering objects (EOs) that are not visible in the computational language, but are visible in the engineering language to support such things as distribution transparency mechanisms, ODP functions, binding capabilities, and so forth.

 NOTE   *Basic engineering object* is an object in the engineering viewpoint that needs the services of the distributed or local infrastructure to perform its function. [RM-ODP-3]

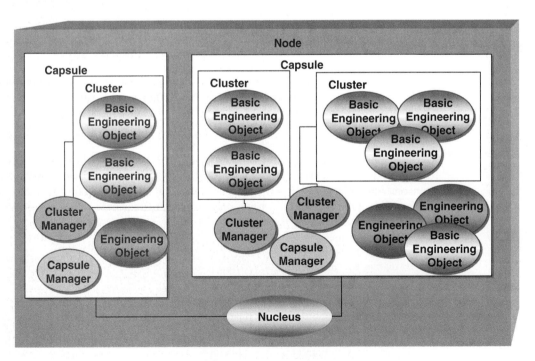

FIGURE 6.17   Engineering Node Model

Each computational object maps to one or more basic engineering object(s). This is an important rule. It says that there are no holes in the mapping between computational objects and the basic engineering objects. This is one of the rules that provides the consistency across these two viewpoints, as discussed in Chapter 11, "Architecture Analysis and System Conformance Evaluation."

As important as this rule is, RM-ODP is also ambiguous. Part 1 of the standard [RM-ODP-1] says that the mapping between a computational object and a basic engineering object is 1-to-1. That is, there exists exactly one basic engineering object that reflects exactly one computational object. Part 3 of the standard [RM-ODP-3] states that the mapping can be 1-to-n. That is, a computational object may map to one or more basic engineering object(s). What a difference! However, Part 1 is not prescriptive, but both Parts 2 [RM-ODP-2] and 3 are prescriptive. That is, Part 1 describes RM-ODP, but does not require anything. Parts 2 and 3 define the requirements. In all cases, the prescriptive parts of the standard supercede the descriptions in Part 1.

6.5.1.1 Engineering Objects

The BEOs correspond to the objects that provide application services, as specified in the computational language. These objects have a counterpart computational object. What this means is that the architect must have defined the basic engineering objects in a computational specification. These are the specific objects that RM-ODP does not address in terms of functionality. Rather, RM-ODP addresses the *support* for these objects through EOs to interact, across the distributed system.

As defined by the engineering language the *engineering objects* support the distribution mechanisms, the infrastructure, the binding, ODP functions, and transparency functionality. This does not mean the architect cannot define additional objects to achieve some capability. What RM-ODP has done is define the engineering objects that are in support of distributed processing in an open manner, but not the objects that constitute some additional functioning of a specific system infrastructure. In fact, many of the emerging RM-ODP standards are doing just that. They are defining additional engineering objects to accomplish some task. The factory object service of the Object Mangement Group (OMG) is an example of such an engineering object. It is an infrastructure object that creates and destroys objects for use. A session manager, which manages activities across multiple objects, may be one of the EOs defined in an infrastructure to accomplish some task. Mediators or agents may be others.

6.5.1.2   Node and Nucleus

The *node* is the computer. It has a *nucleus* (like an operating system) that manages the resources, processing, creation, deletion, and communication for objects of the node. The ODP Node Management function defines some of the functions, such as establishing a channel, for a node manager object in the nucleus.

The node itself is configured into collections of BEOs and EOs, called clusters and capsules. Each of the clusters and capsules include a management object, to aid in the creation, deletion, and general management of the grouping of objects. A node consists of one or more capsules, and a capsule can consist of one or more clusters. A more detailed representation of the node, nucleus, capsule, capsule manager, cluster, and cluster manager is shown in Figure 6.18. The arrow lines represent a binding, though the details of the interfaces and binding are not shown.

6.5.1.3   Capsule and Capsule Manager

Engineering objects of the node are configured into capsules. A *capsule* is a unit of processing and storage and can contain either BEOs or EOs. A capsule is like a software process or component of an application, encapsulating the processing and storage needs. The nucleus instantiates the capsule and all objects associated with the capsule, including the clusters.

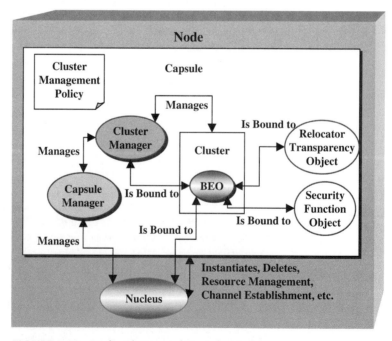

FIGURE 6.18   Node, Cluster, and Capsule Model

Each capsule has a capsule manager engineering object that manages the capsule and interacts with the cluster managers of the clusters in the capsule, in accordance with a management policy the architect defines. The role of the capsule manager is overall management, to include instantiating and deleting objects and interfaces, providing a name space for engineering interface identifiers, and binding to a specific interface of the nucleus node manager. In other words, the capsule manager provides administration functionality of the capsule and everything in it.

6.5.1.4 Cluster and Cluster Manager

A *cluster,* contained in a single capsule, is a configuration of basic engineering objects that can be considered a single unit for the purposes of activation, reactivation, deactivation, checkpointing, migration, and recovery. [RM-ODP-3] Each basic engineering object is bound to the nucleus and to the cluster manager engineering object associated specifically with the cluster. In this manner, object management is supported: instantiation, deletion, movement, binding, naming, and so forth. The functionality of the cluster manager object is that defined by the ODP Cluster Management function (see Chapter 9, "RM-ODP Functions").

A cluster is like a portion of virtual memory that consists of a tight grouping of basic engineering objects. These objects are considered a single unit, or an encapsulation of objects. As such, they appear to be one entity. Interfacing among the objects in the cluster is handled differently than across a cluster boundary. A cluster cannot determine the internal objects or services of another cluster. A cluster is always treated as a single entity, but objects in a cluster can use the services of the infrastructure.

Further, a cluster, as a unit of encapsulation, is subject to mobility, or movement. A cluster is subject to security checks as a whole, management as a whole, fault tolerance as a whole, and other services.

The objects in a cluster have an engineering interface reference identifier (EIR) for each interface. The EIR defines the needs of the binding, which is addressed below. The objects in a cluster can bind with an object corresponding to an ODP function, or a transparency object, depending on the specification. So a security engineering object, for example, supporting the ODP Security functions can be bound to the objects in the cluster.

The treatment of a cluster as a single entity provides a degree of autonomy for the cluster. The separation of a cluster into a single encapsulated entity also means that if one cluster fails, it is isolated from other clusters and potentially the affects of failure. A Java™ applet is like a cluster.

6.5.1.5 Failure

Failure is addressed by the policies of the manager objects, and of the channel template for channel failures. What this means is that there is a place to define what should be done on failure. The architect specifies the actual actions to take on failure, which make use of some of the ODP functions to help recover from failure.

6.5.1.6 Management

Management is accomplished through the manager objects and the policies associated with them. If a failure occurs, the manager objects receive a failure notification. The policies, defined by the architect, should address creation, deletion, movement, recovery, checkpoint, deactivation, reactivation, and other functionality, most of which is defined by the ODP functions. In addition, the policies will also capture and be constrained by whatever distribution transparencies are selected. Whatever is desired to happen is specified in a policy. (See Chapter 9, "RM-ODP Functions," for more information about the ODP functions; see Chapter 10, "Hiding System Complexities: Distribution Transparencies," for information about the distribution transparencies.)

Careful reading is required of this standard. Sometimes a very important point will be missed because a term is missing that is not caught at the first reading. For example, a cluster consists of basic engineering objects only. A capsule consists of engineering objects, or basic engineering objects, or clusters of basic engineering objects. But what is stated in the standard for a capsule is only that a capsule consists of engineering objects, which is missing the "basic" type. [RM-ODP-3] What isn't stated here is as important as what is stated.

The concepts of cluster and capsule for a node are not clear. In fact, several of the standards originators do not understand these concepts, as they apply to a system specification. The architect can choose to use these concepts, or not. Care should be exercised, however because a number of the ODP functions are defined in terms of these concepts.

6.5.2 CONCEPTS AND RULES: INTERCONNECTION MODEL

The interconnection model consists of the channel model, binding, and interception.[3] The channel model supports static and dynamic object interaction, the specifications for the use of the ODP functions, and the specifications for the selected distribution transparencies, by establishing the communication mechanisms. The binding model manages the dynamic analysis of interface specifications to ensure the proper channel establishment. The interception model provides the capabilities

---

3. Interconnection model is a term used here. This is not a RM-ODP term.

of cross-domain interaction and federation. Together, these models provide the mechanisms for realizing computational interactions.

The mechanism to achieve interconnection between objects, in support of an interaction, is the channel and all the engineering objects that make up the channel. These models:

▶ Set up the appropriate configuration of objects, based on the type of interaction required and based on the behavior of the binding required

▶ Marshall and unmarshall parameters

▶ Maintain the binding

▶ Provide any necessary policy enforcement

▶ Provide transformations required (of formats, policies, etc.)

▶ Create the physical communication mechanisms to achieve an end-to-end interconnection

Each of the objects in the channel includes a control interface, to manage the workings of the channel, change QoS as needed, manage cross-domain communication, and other actions. Figure 6.19 provides an overview of the channel model between two nodes. The concepts of this figure are discussed in the following paragraphs.

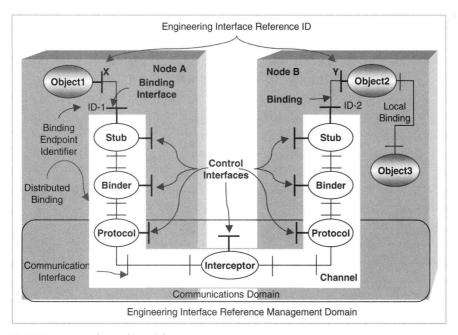

FIGURE 6.19 Channel Model

The concepts of the interconnection model, as paraphrased from [RM-ODP-3], include:

▶ *Interface:* The same as in the computational language—there is no engineering viewpoint distinction.

▶ *Interaction:* The same as in the computational language—there is no engineering viewpoint distinction.

▶ *Channel:* A configuration of four engineering objects (stub, binder, protocol, and interceptor objects) that provides a binding in support of interaction between basic engineering objects.

– *Stub:* An engineering object in a channel that provides interpretation and support of the interactions in the channel to the basic engineering object, such as marshalling and unmarshalling of parameters.

– *Binder:* An engineering object in a channel that manages the binding in the channel.

– *Protocol* object: An engineering object in a channel that provides the communication mechanism to achieve interaction.

– *Interceptor* (of a specific type): An engineering object in a channel that manages any policy enforcement and transformation required across a specific type of domain.

▶ *Distributed binding:* A binding that makes use of a channel.

▶ *Local binding:* A binding that does not require a channel.

▶ *Communications domain:* Interworking protocol objects.

▶ *Communication interface:* A protocol object interface, which is bound to either another protocol object in the channel, or an interceptor in the channel, at a point called the *interworking reference point.*

▶ *Binding endpoint identifier:* The identifier of a binding of the basic engineering object, which may be involved in more than one binding.

▶ *Engineering interface reference:* The identifier of an engineering object interface, used for purposes of binding and management.

▶ *Engineering interface reference management domain:* A naming domain for engineering interface reference identifiers (names).

▶ *Engineering interface reference management policy:* A policy (permissions, prohibitions, and obligations) that applies to a federation of engineering interface reference management domains.

6.5.2.1 Binding

Binding is one of the RM-ODP foundation concepts (in Part 2 of RM-ODP), and applies throughout all of the viewpoints. A binding requires a context establishing the behavior of the binding. This is accomplished by defining the interface templates (associated with the binding), a binding template, and the management objects that ensure the binding established adheres to the required behavior. The mechanisms to achieve binding are those of the engineering language.

A *local binding* is a simple binding between two engineering objects, which does not require a channel. This may be used for intracapsule or intranode interaction between objects.

The *distributed binding* is much more involved. It always involves a channel, and the objects that make up the channel. A distributed binding is most often associated with interconnection between nodes. However, a distributed binding can also be established within a node, perhaps across different clusters or capsules.

A basic engineering object in a cluster binds to another basic engineering object within the same cluster using a local binding. It may also bind to another basic engineering object in another cluster on the same or different node, using a distributed binding. The engineering interface reference identifier is used for either binding. This identifier provides a distribution transparency object to act on the object or its interface, such as transparently migrating the object to a different cluster, or relocating a bound interface to a different location.

The interconnection model is discussed in depth in Chapter 13, "Interaction Framework: Interoperability," in terms of the interface framework, binding framework, and the interception framework. Here, highlights of the constructs and rules of the parts of the interconnection model are provided.

6.5.2.2 Engineering Interface Reference

In order to establish a channel between two basic engineering objects, an *engineering interface reference* identifier for each interface of the objects is used. This is a reference to an interface, not a physical address. That is, it points to the interface, which can then be used to say, for example, "bind to interface identified by A."

The engineering interface reference contains important information about the expected behavior of the binding. This information includes, either directly or by reference:

◗ Interface type
◗ Channel descriptive information (a channel template)
◗ The communication interface where the binding is to take place
◗ Relocation information: what to do if a bound interface moves to a different location, such as re-establish the channel or terminate the binding
◗ Failure information: what to do if a failure is detected in the channel, such as re-establish the channel or terminate the binding
◗ Protocol information, including the appropriate transfer syntax for use

Alternative channel configurations can be specified in an EIR, and then selected for a particular channel establishment. For example, the architect may want a secure connection in one case, but in another doesn't care. Hence, the architect may specify the use of a secure encrypted transport protocol in the first case and an unencrypted transport protocol in the second.

6.5.2.3 Channel Configuration

An engineering specification defines the mechanisms and functions required to support distributed interaction between objects in an ODP system. Each of the channel objects (stub, binder, and protocol object) is associated with its counterpart at the remote end. That is, a stub at a one end of the channel associates the interaction with its counterpart stub at the other end of the channel.

However, in order for an object to use a channel, the channel must match the properties associated with the interface, which are type and behavior. The object's engineering interface reference template defines the needs of the object interface initiating the interaction. A channel template is used to define the configuration needed for the interaction. These two templates define the behavior and type of channel to use. Once a channel is created, and because an object can have multiple interfaces each using a channel, a specific binding endpoint identifier is associated with the channel and provided to the object using the channel. The object can then reference a particular channel binding, if needed.

6.5.2.4 Stub Object

The stub is the engineering object that interacts between the basic engineering object using the channel and the rest of the channel objects. It is responsible for the formatting and unformatting of the message associated with the interaction across the channel. The stub can also have separate interfaces to different basic engineering objects. This is useful if the interaction is to be multicast to several objects or if several objects want to use the same channel setup. The stub can also be used for a number of other functions, such as:

- Access control evaluation, or interface with a security object to perform access control
- Audit logging, or interface with an audit log object to perform this function
- Support for replicated object interfaces, where an object is replicated for load-balancing or performance reasons
- Interact with an ODP function to provide some capability, such as storage, trading, relocation, replication, migration, etc.

Once the stub and the engineering object have interacted and performed these functions, the stub must then initiate the communication by interacting with the binder object.

6.5.2.5 Binder Object

The binder object establishes a binding with a protocol object and manages the binding integrity in the channel. If the channel has a failure, the binder is informed. The engineering interface reference template and the channel template correspond to what the binder does.

If failure transparency is used, the binder will notify the specified object of the failure. The binder is also capable of re-establishing a binding, or of re-establishing a new channel.

The binder interfaces with the protocol object to establish the communication. To do so, the binder must format (and unformat on the receiving end) the message into a protocol-specific format. If encryption is required, as stated in the channel template, the binder will also encrypt the message.

In addition to these interfaces, the binder also interfaces with some of the ODP function objects. It can interface with the Relocator object (in support of the ODP Relocation function), a Trader object, a federation object, and so forth.

6.5.2.6 Protocol Object

The protocol object is the object that sets up the communication path. The protocol object is bound to the interface of another protocol object, or an interceptor object that exists in-between two protocol objects. The protocol object deals with the transfer syntax of the protocol.

6.5.2.7 Interceptor Object

The interceptor object is used to provide translations across domains. In RM-ODP, a domain may include a technology boundary. Hence, if the endpoints of the channel have different protocols, for example, the interceptor would provide the mediation of the protocols. If the end points have different naming conventions, the interceptor can interact with each naming domain object to mediate names, or provide the capability (although this is more complex than it seems). The interceptor also can perform actions such as:

▶ Map the engineering interface references in each domain, making sure that these references are valid

▶ Determine compatible endpoint behavior in order to establish or deny a communication, to include:
  - Interface types
  - Interface signatures
  - Compatible roles
  - Protocol object types
  - QoS capabilities

▶ Negotiate or change a QoS capability

▶ Mediate transfer syntaxes

▶ Mediate data formats

▶ Mediate naming

▶ Audit the channel usage

▶ Perform some security authorization

▶ Mediate policy

▶ Negotiate policy

Issues of name resolution, type matching, and policies are all part of the negotiation process required to bind across domains (as well as much more, typically). The interceptor plays this role in the communication: mediating, negotiating, and binding.

Sometimes to provide the appropriate mediation, the interceptor may, itself, set up a completely different channel. This is particularly true to manage a federation of domains (see Chapter 15, "Federation"). But the basic structuring rule for the interceptor is to mediate. The concept of interception is covered in greater detail in Chapter 13, "Interaction Framework: Interoperability," because interception along with the constructs of interaction, interconnection, and semantic behavior enable interoperability.

6.5.3   EXAMPLE

Figure 6.20 depicts the computational data manager example from Figure 6.16, and how it could be visible in the engineering viewpoint. In this example, each of the computational objects is visible as basic engineering objects, associated with a particular node. Establishing the binding is accomplished by channels: one provides interconnection for operational interactions; one provides interconnection for stream interactions. The data manager binding object is depicted as a data manager basic engineering object. Also the data store objects may each be associated with the ODP Storage function object, to manage schema and data for the data store.

Focusing on the channels, Node A has an instance where two basic engineering objects bind to the same stub: Get Patient ID and Get Patient Records objects. In Node C, a stub binds with both the PIDS data store and Patient Records data store objects. Node B consists of the Data Manager basic engineering object, which in this example is a computational binding object. In this node, the protocol object of the stream channel binds to two separate protocol objects on behalf of the Data Manager object: one for the Get Treatment Results object and one for the Video Treatment Store object. The thread of binding in the data manager is shown by a gray line. The node model, which is the configuration of objects in clusters and capsules, is not included here. The focus in this figure is the use of the channel for multiple interfaces, and a computational binding object for complex multicasting and multimedia support.

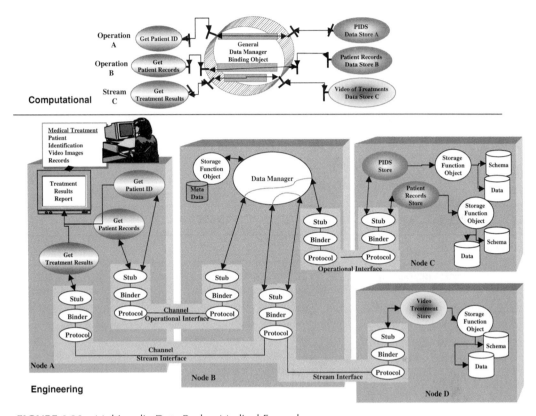

FIGURE 6.20   Multimedia Data Broker Medical Example

6.5.4   AMBIGUITIES AND INCONSISTENCIES

One of the ambiguities or inconsistencies in RM-ODP deals with identifying the type of object involved in a distributed binding. The difference between BEOs and EOs is clear with respect to the computational objects: a computational object is visible as a basic engineering object. But the distinction between BEOs and EOs is very unclear in the standard with respect to the infrastructure.

The channel definition defines that a channel connects basic engineering objects. In fact, in places, the standard is ambiguous: sometimes it states only a basic engineering object interacts with a channel; sometimes it states any engineering object interacts with the channel, basic or not. Similarly, the definition for the engineering interface reference identifies an engineering object interface for distributed binding, versus a basic engineering object.

It should not matter which engineering object uses a channel. But, the primary purpose of the channel is to provide the mechanisms in support of the basic engineering object interactions, as defined by the computational viewpoint.

Another ambiguity in the standard deals with the computational binding object and how it maps onto the constructs of the engineering language. It seems that a computational binding is visible in the engineering viewpoint as a channel, or as a binder in the channel, or as a basic engineering object that the architect specifies more details about. Although RM-ODP addresses distributed binding in the computational viewpoint, it never addresses the mapping of the binding object to an engineering viewpoint construct.

6.6   USING THE TECHNOLOGY VIEWPOINT

A technology specification defines the implementation of the ODP system, using the technologies and products of the day. The technology specification defines:

▶ Choices of technologies

▶ Choices of products

▶ Choices of standards

▶ Configurations of technology objects

▶ Specifications of all interfaces for use between technology objects

▶ How the ODP specifications are implemented

▶ Relevant technologies and mapping to relevant standards and specificationsd

▶ Conformance testing support information

The technology specification could include the use of specific Open Systems Interconnection (OSI) protocols, specific ORB vendor products, a specific database management system, specific networks, a specific transaction message manager, some proprietary interfaces, other specific vendor products, and so forth. It shows how the software, hardware, networks, operating systems, storage devices, database systems, security certificates, communication protocols, and so forth, are configured to support the mechanisms defined in the engineering specification. The technology viewpoint does not go into detail about how to map to technologies and products, but rather indicates that the correspondence of a technology choice must map to the specifications of the other viewpoints. These specifications amount to the criteria for selecting technologies.

The technology language provides a link between the other viewpoint specifications and implementation details, through the use of extra information needed for implementation and conformance testing, called *Implementation eXtra Information for Testing (IXIT)*.

The architect must still analyze the marketplace and determine the most viable technologies of choice. The technology specification must identify a technology of choice, and capture the configurations in terms of objects and interfaces. The technology specification must also include a definition of how the ODP specifications are mapped onto the technology choices, identify the technologies appropriate to the implementation of the system, identify the appropriate ODP function for use, explicitly state if a technology object is an instance of a specific standard, and specify the IXIT needed by identifying the set of templates and all associated reference points required to support testing.

It is recognized that the testing process itself could equal the entire implementation process, in terms of effort and cost. Therefore, the technology viewpoint allows the architect to choose what to test, and the level of detail. The activities of conformance assessment include checking the mapping between the viewpoint specifications, checking the validity of a single specification, consistency checking across specifications, and testing the implementation to a specification. More information is provided in Chapter 11, "Architecture Analysis and System Conformance Evaluation."

As an example of a technology choice, if the architecture specification makes use of multiple object interfaces in determining the componentization of an application, the choice may be the CORBA Component Model, since it is the only component-based model that supports multiple interfaces. If the use of multiple interfaces is not in the specification, however, there are several component models that can be chosen; e.g., Enterprise JavaBeans™ (EJB).

RM-ODP has very few rules applicable to technology specifications. The architect needs to determine the functionality, the system performance characteristics, and the technology constraints for each choice of technology. The architect needs to then analyze the technologies and their constraints with respect to the architecture specification. Then the architect will know which of the system's functionality and performance requirements will be realized in today's technologies, which can be projected for tomorrow, and which need a breakthrough in research in order to achieve. So the architect will recognize what is achievable, as well as what has not *yet* been achieved.

What cannot yet be achieved does not impact the architecture specification, but does impact the choice of technologies. This is the main reason that RM-ODP did not include technology choices in the other viewpoints. The technology choices always change, and the architecture specification (as the set of enterprise, information, computational, and engineering specifications) should be immutable to technology changes. That is, choices in technology should be separate from the other viewpoint specifications, to be able to plan for and evolve the system as newer technologies become available, without re-architecting the system from those viewpoints.

When the architect specifies what is needed to support the business specification, independent of implementation, the architect establishes what the system is to do, why, and what mechanisms achieve the "how." The technology language, coupled with analysis, takes all of that and links it to the concrete "how," while identifying what cannot yet be implemented. The architect is therefore making an informed decision of the 80% solution, but knowing the 20% that cannot be realized today and must be planned for tomorrow, and not requiring a re-specification to accomplish it. Further, the 20% also indicates the direction of the technology needed, so that the choices made today will also address the strategic vision of tomorrow.

An example case and technology uncertainty forecast in the Australian Defence Force Command, Control, Communication, Computers and Intelligence (C4I) domain that supports this claim can be found in [Herring-97].

POINT

The strength of the technology viewpoint is that it consolidates the conformance reference points for use in testing conformance of a system specification to the RM-ODP rules, and for conformance testing of an implementation to the system specification.

6.6.1 CONCEPTS

A technology object is a template of an implementable standard or specification. Implementation is the process of realizing a system from the specification, subject to conformance testing the validity of the implementation to the specification. Each technology used for implementation must offer conformance test points. *IXIT* information is the extra information associated with the conformance test point to use in testing, and to define what observable behavior is expected. The IXIT information is defined in each of the viewpoint specifications, and includes the reference points of interest, the templates of interest, the mapping of the concepts of the viewpoint language to the implementation, etc.

A *reference point* is an interaction point that the architect identifies for use where one can observer some behavior (as identified by the IXIT information). A *conformance point* is a reference point that can be used to test conformance of an observable behavior of an implementation. If what is observed conforms to the architecture specification, the system is conformant with that architecture specification.

There are four different conformance points defined:

1. Programmatic: a reference point where behavioral testing of software interfaces can be performed, through the use of a programmatic interface that is a programming language binding.
2. Perceptual: a reference point where testing of an interaction between the system and the physical world can be performed, such as a user interface or communications port.
3. Interworking: a reference point where interoperability (exchange of information between two or more systems) testing between systems can be performed.

4. Interchange: a reference point where the behavior of a physical media can be tested, such as testing of the recording or exchange via external physical storage (i.e., disk or tape files).

More detail is provided about conformance testing in Chapter 11, "Architecture Analysis and System Conformance Evaluation."

6.6.2 RULES

A technology specification defines the choice of technology in terms of:

▶ Technology choices
▶ Technology objects and their configurations
▶ Interface specifications and resultant bindings between technology objects
▶ Interfaces for use in testing
▶ Specification of how the ODP system is implemented using ODP specifications
▶ IXIT to define the observable behavior at a reference point for use in testing
▶ Any specifications related to the technologies selected
▶ Any information that an implementer needs to support the testing process

The few rules about the technology language address two things:

1. The use of any technology specification must include a mapping of that technology's constructs to those of the RM-ODP viewpoint constructs.
2. Any technology or product chosen must offer interfaces for conformance testing, through the use of the IXIT information.

In other words, if the architect selects an EJB product, the architect needs to relate the constructs of the product to the RM-ODP viewpoint constructs, in order to test for conformance. Any language can be used, including English, to accomplish this. If a UML vendor tool is chosen, for example, the architect needs to relate the constructs of the UML product to the RM-ODP constructs, and then relate those to the EJB constructs. This is a three-way mapping. Then the architect can test the implementation using EJB to the architecture specification using RM-ODP, representing it through a UML product.

6.6.3 EXAMPLE

Because technology and commercially available products may lag behind what is wanted based on the architecture specification, an implementation of the system is therefore constrained by the choices made. That is, the technology specification is merely a reflection of the capabilities of the products and technologies that can be chosen, augmented by the value added software capabilities that developers provide.

Figure 6.21 shows a technology medical example, refined from the previous example. In this figure, the previous computational specification (from Figure

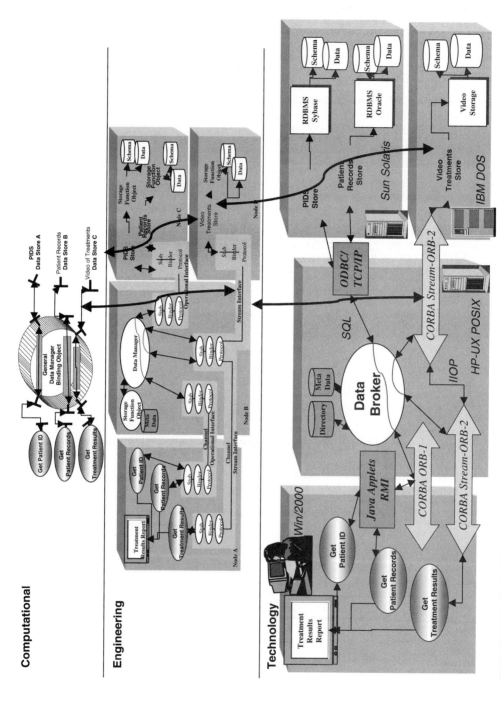

FIGURE 6.21 Technology Viewpoint Example

6.16) is shown, the engineering specification (from Figure 6.20) is shown, and the technology specification of the same example is shown. The choice of technologies and products is shown in italics. Many other technologies could realize this example; the ones shown here are only representative.

Notice that the computational objects (e.g., Video of Treatments, Data Store C) are visible as basic engineering objects (i.e., Video Treatments Store) along with the supporting engineering objects of the infrastructure. These engineering viewpoint objects are then realized in the technology viewpoint (i.e., Video Treatment Store, Video Storage), along with the technologies to support the channels (e.g., a particular ORB, Stream-ORB-2). The identification of the node technologies is also specified (e.g., Sun Solaris™). The details of the constraints or actions are not shown, but these too would be part of the technology specification.

6.7 SUMMARY

Many of the RM-ODP architecture principles were discussed in this chapter in terms of viewpoint language concepts and rules. Several examples of usage of these languages were provided. Some of the inconsistencies and ambiguities in the RM-ODP standard were identified.

The five RM-ODP viewpoint languages are structured well-defined concepts and rules to specify a system, focusing on certain areas of concern for that viewpoint, hiding other areas of concern to be focused on in another viewpoint. The five viewpoints are not layered; they are abstractions of the same complete system. That is, each of the viewpoint languages is an architecture specification language that:

▶ Provides a language to address the rules and concepts of the area of concern, to ensure a well-formed specification

▶ Provides rules of consistency across the other viewpoint languages, enhancing completeness and understanding, and enabling analysis of the specification

▶ Provides rules of conformance testing to ensure a well-formed implementation of the specification

▶ Refines and specifies some aspects of software architecture components, connectors, and constraints

▶ Is generic enough to capture any Domain-Specific Software Architecture(DSSA) or Reference Model for a DSSA

▶ Founded on the principles of an object model

▶ Founded on the concepts and rules of specification

▶ Founded on the concepts and rules of structuring

▶ Founded on precise terms of distributed processing

Using the RM-ODP viewpoints provides a complete and consistent specification for an architecture of a system, addressing the provisions for interoperability, portability, distribution, transparency, behavior, refinements, and so much more. Unlike some other architecture methods and frameworks, RM-ODP defines what is meant by a viewpoint in explicitly defined well-formed terminology, concepts, and rules.

Not all of the elements of these viewpoints may make sense to use, depending on the objectives of the architecture. The architecture team selects which to use. But dividing the areas of concern about distributed processing into well-defined viewpoints provides a method of architecting the complexities of a distributed processing system.

The computational and engineering viewpoints provide a powerful interaction framework, to capture not only the functionality of all interfaces and bindings, but also their behavior. The information viewpoint provides the explicit semantics of the behavior and constraints across all interactions. It enables or constrains the specifications of the computational and engineering viewpoints.

The technology viewpoint serves two very important missions: to tell the architect where to apply the technologies and products of choice, and to allow the architect to test the system implementation to the architectural specification for conformance.

Due to the precision of the viewpoints, and the extensive language constructs, there are several uses of RM-ODP. Among them:

▶ The architect can use it to completely specify the system.

▶ The architect can use it to completely specify a component in the system.

▶ The architect can use it to completely specify an enterprise system of systems.

▶ The architect can use the consistency rules of RM-ODP to distribute the organizational responsibilities in specifying the system. For example:

  – The system requirements team specifies the business requirements, using the enterprise and information viewpoints.

  – The architecture team specifies the computational aspects of the system, using the computational viewpoint, and iterates with the system requirements team, using the enterprise and information viewpoints.

  – The system designer team specifies the implementation aspects of the system. This can be a team in the organization, or perhaps a result of a contractual agreement with another organization, which is provided by the enterprise and information (and possibly the computational) specifications. In fact, this is exactly how component standards of RM-ODP are specified. They make use of the enterprise, information, and computational viewpoints to specify the reasons, needs, behavior, functionality, and interactions of some aspect of the system. The rest (engineering and technology) are then left for a vendor to use to implement the standard, adding in some value-added capabilities.

▶ The architect can use only the enterprise and information viewpoints to capture a business specification.

▶ The architect can use only the information viewpoint to try to capture why a system has failed; often this is because of some implicit, undocumented behavior, which is well suited for the information viewpoint.

▶ The architect can use the enterprise, information, computational, and engineering viewpoints to specify a target (strategic vision) system, and the technology viewpoint to provide incremental evolution of a target system.

▶ The architect can use the viewpoints to provide a portion of the target system specification, incrementally evolving the architecture itself. This is enabled by the consistency rules across the viewpoints and the concepts and rules within each viewpoint.

The ability to leverage the use of the viewpoints in a distributed organization is a powerful acquisition strategy. It enables a distributed organization and teams to separately architect the system. The cohesion of the system is enabled by the precision of the viewpoint languages, the consistency rules across them, and the conformance testing capabilities defined for them. The result is a well-formed architected system, a flexible architecture acquisition and system implementation in a business.

However, RM-ODP has some inconsistencies and ambiguities. Some of the more important ones include:

▶ Part 2 of the standard says there can be many viewpoints, but Part 3 says there are exactly five viewpoints that are necessary and sufficient to specify a system. This is not an inconsistency. What it means is that a viewpoint is about a "viewpoint on something," so the five RM-ODP viewpoints are viewpoints *on a distributed system.*

The architect might want to define a domain-specific viewpoint, from a business perspective, such as a viewpoint of the management of Patient Identification in the system. Or another viewpoint might be the security of physician-patient confidentiality and access control to patient records. This is fine within a specific domain. But what needs to be remembered is that this is a specific domain, not necessarily the same domain as in another enterprise with which it needs to interoperate. As such, the open property of the distributed systems may be limited due to decisions made in domain-specific viewpoints. As such, the architect needs to specifically relate (define correspondences) across the domain-specific viewpoints and the five RM-ODP viewpoints. This apparent contradiction is in fact not a contradiction, but an ambiguity, because RM-ODP did not expend a few more paragraphs to explain it.

▶ An object has a type. It may acquire one or more additional types. How one type is selected among the types of the object is not defined in RM-ODP. As an example, a physician and a patient can be defined as separate roles. But an object may assume more than one role; for example, a doctor is sometimes a patient. How to identify the role of an object and "selection" among the types is not addressed. It is just done. This is an incompleteness of RM-ODP, as well as an ambiguity.

▶ A computational object is refined to a basic engineering object. Part 1 of RM-ODP says that this mapping is 1-to-1. That is, for every computational object, there exists exactly one basic engineering object, and vice versa. Part 3 of RM-ODP says that one computational object can map to one or more basic engineering objects. What an inconsistency!

▶ One of the computational objects in RM-ODP is the binding object. It is an object. Nowhere in RM-ODP does it say what this unique computational object maps to in the engineering viewpoint. Many believe that the computational binding object maps to the engineering language channel, which is not an object, but rather a configuration of objects. Some believe the computational binding object maps to the stub object (or the binder object) in the channel. The emerging standard for Interface References and Binding seems to map the computational binding object to an engineering object called the binding factory object. In the end, this is up to the architect to define, but it is nevertheless an ambiguity in RM-ODP.

The emerging standards for RM-ODP will help resolve some of these ambiguities. The architect is encouraged to become aware of these standards as they emerge, and to always keep in touch with implementations of RM-ODP that are emerging in the telecommunications, C4I, finance, and medical industries.

POINT Overall, for such a precise standard with so many concepts defined, it is extraordinarily consistent and well-formed, despite the few apparent ambiguities.

There are currently no tools specific for RM-ODP that enable the architect to capture a specification in accordance with the viewpoint languages. IDL is a tool that has been used to capture the specification of the interface signature for an operational interface type. However, it does not capture the behavior of the interface. Likewise, UML can represent certain aspects of the viewpoint languages, and the behavior can be partially represented by OCL. However, because the UML tools do not capture all of UML and because most of the tools do not capture OCL, the architect must be careful in how to represent a RM-ODP architecture specification through these tools. To this end, the use of UML in this book is not a definitive use for RM-ODP. These should be considered as UML examples only, to depict some concept of RM-ODP, not as a way to represent RM-ODP. OMG and others are working to provide a preferred usage of UML, with extensions, to represent RM-ODP languages. Tools that aim to addess these limitations are emerging into the marketplace. Or perhaps a business may construct such a tool as a business venture, for the rest of the RM-ODP users.

SEVEN

ARCHITECTURE SPECIFICATION AND REPRESENTATION

Current practice in the specification of an architecture is to use models, which provide a language for use. Model languages range from very generalized to very specific, and from prescriptive of architecture concerns to descriptive of the architecture created. This chapter will provide examples to show the distinction between a specification of an architecture, using a model and associated language, that addresses the concerns of a system architecture, as well as a representation of an architecture, using a model and associated language to describe what has been specified. Most of these examples come from the use of the Unified Modeling Language (UML) and the Reference Model of Open Distributed Processing (RM-ODP) concepts.

 RM-ODP provides a set of rules for how to specify an architecture of a distributed processing system. The process of architecting is the use of specification rules as adapted to a particular subject (e.g., distributed processing system). The architecture specification itself provides a defined set of rules (consisting of terminology, constraints, structure of components, interrelationships among components, etc.) for how to implement a distributed processing system. The architecture can define more than one system because of the variability allowed in the rules, such as implementation choices, details of quality of service, etc.

This chapter will provide an overview of the techniques used for specification and discuss the difference between an architectural specification and a representation of an architecture. These are two very different concepts, often mixed in current practice. It is important to understand the differences, and to know about the concepts and rules of specification for use in defining the architecture of a system.

7.1	OVERVIEW

Specifying is the process of writing things down in a well-defined, precise manner using the language of the subject matter (e.g., for a system, using the language of distributed processing).

Specifying is a process in which the specification is a product of that process. An architectural specification is a definition of everything (important to specify), including types, interrelationships, constraints, and so forth. *Architecting* is a process of specifying an architecture of a system. RM-ODP defines an architecture as *a set of rules* *to define* structure, behavior, and relationships among the parts of a system. That is, an architecture defines the rules to construct a system, allowing for some variability, as long as the set of rules are used. As such, an architecture can apply to more than one system, depending on choices of such things as implementation or constraint values. An architecture is the result of using the specification rules to create an architecture specification for a system, which in turn defines the rules to construct the system.

A description, even English text, can be precise and complete as long as the rules of specification in the process of specifying are adhered to. A precise, complete, well-defined description can be a specification. But, generally, a *description* only provides rules about describing or presenting, not about specifying or defining. That's the difference. One can use descriptive techniques to present some aspect of the architecture, to be sure. However, this is a representation of an architecture that is already the result of specifying.

A well-formed *architectural specification* is a model. A set of specification rules consists of the things to do using well-defined concepts. This set of rules in use (a process) results in a specification (assuming the rules are followed in conjunction with the concepts associated with the rules). Writing down the rules results in a specification of how to specify an architecture. Because description does not come along with what to define, how to define it, and how to perform the process of architecting (such as how to use abstraction; how to use composition; how to specify relationships; how to specify behavior; etc.), the description technique is generally useful for presentation, not definition. For example, Microsoft[®] PowerPoint[®] charts are generally charts with boxes and lines, defining neither fully. What's the semantic behavior? Do the lines represent an interaction or an interface? Is the interface two-way or one-way? Is the interface an operational interface or a stream interface? What are the rules to attach (i.e., bind) the line to each box? Are there rules of order? Some Architecture Description Languages (ADLs) use the concept of connector and port, where the port is defined by the type of connector associated with the ADL. This definition is generally captured in the ADL manual. If the PowerPoint chart defines the "line" as a "pipe" connector, for example, and then references the full definition of "pipe," then that line is defined and is a specification, as long as there are no other constraints associated with that line, such as quality of service. Again, specification is about well-defined precise rules to construct a system, in whatever language captures such rules. Description is about representing or presenting something for discussion, and hopefully not for interpretation.

The main benefit in specifing is to provide a deeper understanding of the system to be developed. It is through this specification process that architects determine inconsistent customer requirements, inconsistencies, ambiguities, and incompletenesses. A byproduct of this process is an artifact, which itself can be formally analyzed (e.g., analyzed to be internally consistent), used to derive other properties of the specified system, or analyzed for conformance. The specification is a useful communication device between customer and architect, between architect and designer, between designer and implementer, and between implementer and tester. It serves as a companion to the system's source code, at a higher level of description. [Clarke-96]

"A general-purpose approach embraces a family of design notations with a much broader, systemwide focus (e.g., the Unified Modeling Language). Thus, for instance, UML emphasizes modeling practicality and breadth..." [Egyed] UML has strengths of a standard notion that represents a general set of concerns from different levels (business concerns through a Use Case model, to development concerns using a Deployment model). This is addressed as a representation. RM-ODP emphasizes architecturally relevant distributed processing concepts (interactions, policy, composition, objects, semantic behavior, constraints, binding, rules of structure, modeling, linguistics, patterns of reasoning) in a rigorous, precise, and expressive manner to result in a well-formed architecture. This is addressed as a specification.

Why is this so important? Because the purpose of an architecture specification is to clearly and completely define the architecture of a system (or a part of the system, clearly defining what is not included), and to leave little or nothing to interpretation by either the stakeholders approving the architecture, or the implementers developing the system from the architecture.

What is not defined is often as important as what is defined, and may be more important. The necessary but undefined elements lead to systems not wanted, ill-performing systems, or failures, sometimes at the risk of life.

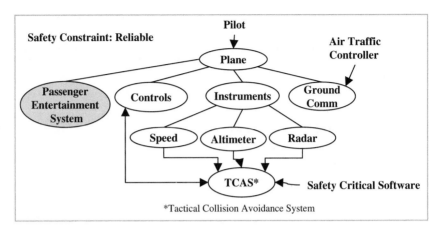

FIGURE 7.1   Example of Safety-Critical Software

Consider Figure 7.1 in which a safety constraint is defined: reliable. The Tactical Collision Avoidance System (TCAS) is software on board an aircraft that monitors and measures any potential collision with another aircraft and takes appropriate action to avoid such collision. To ensure that TCAS is safe, each component and its interaction with TCAS must also be safety-critical. It would seem that the passenger entertainment system need not be safety-critical. Subsequently, Swissair flight 111 crashed September 2, 1998, due to faulty wiring and arcing damage from wires of the passenger entertainment system. Herein is an example of a subsystem that needed to be reliable as well. [http://aviation-safety.net/specials/sr111/report.htm] Further, safety-critical components may also affect the development environment. One TCAS failure was a result of loading a simulation component in place of the developed component. Safety constraints, then, are important to specify where such a constraint applies. An incomplete specification of this kind can lead to disastrous results. See [Leveson-95] for additional software safety issues.

Both of these reflections of architecture (specification and representation) are needed to communicate architectural choices to stakeholders who pay the bills, and to designers who implement the architecture specification. To accomplish this, the modeling languages of choice require a mapping from the constructs of a specification model to a representation model.

POINT The objective of an architecture specification for a system is to communicate what is wanted, precisely, in the language of distributed processing systems.

"The right question to ask isn't 'How comfortable is it to write specifications,' but 'how comfortable is it to read and (re)use them.' Good specifications are hard to write but easy to read, bad specifications are easy to write but just about impossible to understand. This is partly due to the inherent difficulty of expressing exactly what you want, no more and no less, instead of expressing something that does sort of what you had in mind, more or less." [Kilov-93]

7.2   ARCHITECTURE MODEL

A model is a representation of something. A model includes the elements, relationships, and semantic behavioral terms and rules associated with the focus of the model. To be useful, there must be a way to relate things in the model to the things being modeled. The things being modeled, in the case of an architecture for a system, are related to a system. As a model exists at one level of abstraction (the architecture) and the thing itself (or solution) at another (the system), relating the model to the thing itself requires crossing levels of abstraction using concepts from the domain of the solution.

What is an architectural model? An *architectural model of a system* is a specification of an architecture that relates the system concepts and behaviors to the users of the system in the domain in which it participates, and to the designers that will implement the model into a system that serves the purpose of the domain. It consists of precise, well-defined rules and concepts that address all aspects of the system, from functionality to nonfunctionality to semantic behavior. It defines the rules to construct the system, in the language of distributed processing. Whatever is specified is precise. Not everything needs to be specified for a system, but when it is specified, it must be precisely well-defined. Specification languages are formal-based languages that can be used to specify an architecture.

A software architecture should be defined in terms of the software system it will specify. To this end, the software architecture needs to address the functionality and performance attributes of the solution system. In addition, a software architecture must address the nonfunctional characteristics of the system. These include transparencies, modification, interoperability, portability, and the like. It should address semantic behavior. In order to accomplish this, the language of a specification must be rich enough to allow an architect to use concepts and rules to formulate an architecture model in the language of the distributed system.

How that architecture model is represented requires the use of another model for description. In choosing a representation model, the architect needs to observe the concepts, rules, and constraints of the architecture model in whatever form the architect chooses to represent it: English, graphical visualization tool, or a formal specification. Hence, there are two types of models to be addressed in this chapter: one for specification of the architecture of a system, and one for representing that architecture in a manner to communicate the requirements of the architecture to the appropriate user community (stakeholders, other architects, designers, implementers, maintainers, etc.).

Why are these models different? They are not always different. However, in current practice, generalized representation modeling languages, such as UML, are so generalized as to allow the architect to use them in any way desired, for anything wanted. A programming language, such as C++, is also a modeling language for code. C++ can be used to represent an algorithm of choice in a system. But to do so, the concepts and constructs of the architecture have to be mapped onto the programming language, and also onto the representation language. Clearly, the resultant C++ code is a specification; a very detailed specification, but not necessarily complete or well-defined.

RM-ODP provides a suite of languages for specifying an architecture, in terms of viewpoint models. RM-ODP tools for visualization have not yet emerged in the public domain for use. Hence, this chapter will address some of the ways of using UML to represent the architecture concepts of RM-ODP, mapping the concepts of architecture from RM-ODP onto the capabilities of representing those concepts in UML.

7.3　SPECIFICATION, REPRESENTATION, AND DIFFERENCES

7.3.1　SPECIFICATION

Webster's dictionary [Webster's] defines a *specification* as:

> *"1 : the act or process of specifying*
> *2 a : a detailed precise presentation of something or of a plan or proposal for something—usually used in plural b : a statement of legal particulars (as of charges or of contract terms); also : a single item of such statement"*

Specifying is defined to be:

> *"1 : to name or state explicitly or in detail*
> *2 : to include as an item in a specification"*

A specification is rigorous in defining the thing it specifies in the language of the thing. For example, a car is specified as a model in the language of car-concepts, not in the language of house-concepts. Furthermore, the rules of the car-concepts are specialized for a car, and generally do not apply to a house. It uses concepts and rules in the world of the thing to specify the thing.

In terms of an architecture, the structure and relationships of the elements in an architecture need to be precisely specified. This is a tall task for any system of any size. Techniques for specification, coupled with reuse of patterns of reasoning, is what RM-ODP provides for use.

In research today are architectural description languages (ADLs). These are model languages that provide specification techniques for specific architecture needs. For example, Rapide [Rapide] is an ADL that provides a specification for an event-based architecture. Examples of ADLs include Aesop, Adage, Meta-H, C2, Rapide, SADL, UniCon, and Wright [Aesop, Adage, MetaH-93, MetaH-96, C2, Rapide, SADL, UniCon, Wright, Wright-a]. These languages address architectural design issues, but with different capabilities. For example, MetaH supports architectural designs for real-time avionics control; Rapide supports architectural designs for events that can be simulated and analyzed; Wright supports specification of interactions. These different ADLs present a set of challenges. Each uses different architectural design specification concepts. Each stands alone. Several overlap in features and design support, such as graphical visualization tools.

Acme [Acme] is a research attempt to unify all of the ADLs, or a subset of them, into one cohesive architectural specification. Acme was developed by the Carnegie Mellon University [Acme]. It is used as the basis or foundation for Architectural Description Markup Language (ADML). ADML is in research, but being promoted by The Open Group© through its work in The Open Group Architectural Framework (TOGAF) as a tool to help define an architecture. Acme and other ADLs qualify as specification models. [TOGAF]

Acme has been sponsored by the Defense Advanced Research Projects Agence (DARPA). The purpose of Acme is to unify the myriad of research architecture description languages, such as Rapide, C2, Wright, MetaH, and others. Each of these ADLs provides a language/tool (in some cases) for describing an architecture that is based on a certain set of modeling constraints (called styles), and connectors that support that style. It is recognized that in large-scale systems, a single architecture description of a system involves more than one style. To interoperate the different ADLs, and to provide a unifying model, Acme is being created. The Acme group is defining the underlying foundations of what is meant by connector, style, event, behavior, etc. However, Acme still has far to go. Behavior, for example, is defined in some ADLs as "data + control"; in others as "functionality + data"; etc. The unification of foundational architecture specification concepts has yet to be accomplished through Acme. However, Acme has indeed gone a long way towards this unification.

"Architecture description languages (ADLs) have been proposed as modeling notations to support architecture-based development. There is, however, little consensus in the research community on what is an ADL, what aspects of an architecture should be modeled in an ADL, and which of several possible ADLs is best suited for a particular problem. Furthermore, the distinction is rarely made between ADLs on one hand and formal specification, module interconnection, simulation, and programming languages on the other." [Medvidovic-2000]

7.3.2 REPRESENTATION

Webster's dictionary [Webster's] defines a *representation* as:

"1 : one that represents: as a : an artistic likeness or image b (1) : a statement or account made to influence opinion or action ...
2 : the act or action of representing"

Representing is defined as:

"1 : to bring clearly before the mind
2 : to serve as a sign or symbol of
3 : to portray or exhibit in art
4 : to serve as the counterpart or image of
7 : to describe as having a specified character or quality
9 : to serve as a specimen, example, or instance of
11 : to correspond to in essence"

In current practice, many modeling languages are used to represent an architecture. Principal among these is the UML in current practice, and the Architectural Description Markup Language (ADML) [ADML], which is a software architectural model using Acme coupled with the eXtensible Markup Language (XML).

Representation is about describing software architecture. All ADLs can represent an architecture, through the use of a well defined set of concepts and symbols, to describe some of the complex aspects of connectors, components, and constraints. ADML addresses a representation as a means of creating hierarchical specifications, and a system as a specification of the structure. A mechanism provides a map between properties associated with an element and the system. It is, in essence, a mapping from the concepts inherent in the representation model and the system representing the structure of the solution. [ADML]

In addition, several ADLs are being mapped onto UML constructs in an attempt to provide rigor to UML for architecture analysis of mismatch, primarily. One such ADL is C2.

UML has its limitations. However, it's the de facto model language for use in architecture descriptions. It does not yet adequately provide modeling capabilities to capture semantic behavior as defined in the RM-ODP concepts: constraints, invariants, pre- and postconditions, "ilities," policy, contract, n-ary relations, and so forth.

Unique to each modeling language is an underpinning model, from which the language derives its concepts and rules of structure. In the case of UML, there is a defined object model to represent various models for use in UML: Use Cases, logical model, component model, and deployment model.

UML is used to represent something. Examples throughout this book use UML to represent certain concepts from RM-ODP. But one's use of UML for a particular architecture concept may differ from someone else's use of UML for the same concept. That is the nature of using a modeling language to describe, or represent, something.

7.3.3 DIFFERENCES

When it comes to an architecture specification, rigorously well-defined concepts and rules are required to exactly specify the architecture of a system. These rules and concepts can be mapped onto the modeling language of choice (e.g., UML), creating what is termed a metamodel. In this way, the architect clearly defines how to represent an architecture specification by identifying the use of the modeling language concepts to represent the exact architecture concepts, while using the concepts and rules of the architecture specification mechanisms to specify an architecture.

Mapping RM-ODP with UML is a nontrivial task. One challenge is the difference in the object model underpinning of each, the constructs of the language used to describe the model, and the semantics associated with those constructs. Another challenge is the use of the same term to represent very different models; e.g., UML uses class, object, component, as does RM-ODP. But the meanings of these terms are quite different, as exemplified in Table 7.1.

Another challenge is to identify the consistent use of UML models to represent an architectural concern from RM-ODP, or from any other reference model for that matter. For example, one user may use a class diagram to represent a policy, whereas another user may use a collaboration diagram with notes to represent that same policy, or a state chart with a particular design to represent the effect of a policy on the system. These are very different uses of UML for a common RM-ODP construct. Another challenge is that UML does not provide constructs for some of the RM-ODP concepts, thus requiring enhancements to UML. Often, constraints are represented in UML as notes associated with the model. These are not part of the modeling aspects of UML; the notes are not carried throughout the models of UML. And yet, RM-ODP makes use of constructs for specifying constraints in the architecture. Another challenge deals with consistency in the UML models. This is not addressed by the UML designers very well and, as such, cannot be addressed by a simple mapping of RM-ODP onto UML. By using RM-ODP for specifying the architecture, consistency across the architecture is provided. By mapping RM-ODP onto the constructs of UML, that model consistency migrates to UML by use of the mapping. The two techniques of specification and representation provide a rigorous, consistently defined architecture represented in a common de facto language with associated tools for visualization. The challenge is to provide a precise mapping of RM-ODP onto the use of UML concepts, ensuring changes in one model are reflected in the other.

TABLE 7.1   Comparison of Some RM-ODP and UML Concepts

ITEM	RM-ODP	UML [UML-1.3]
Object	A model of an entity, defined by behavior, state, and encapsulation	An instance of a class, with a well-defined boundary and identity that encapsulates state and behavior
Class	The set of all entities satisfying a type. A type is a predicate that defines a collection of entities.	A description of a set of objects with common attributes, operations, methods, relationships, and semantics
Component	An object in a composition	Components in class diagrams are classes and packages. Packages are collections of classes. There are other components, such as instantiated classes.
Behavior	A set of actions and associated constraints on when they may occur	The observable effects of an operation or event, including its results [UML-1.3]
Specification	Concepts related to the requirements of the languages used in RM-ODP	A declarative description of what something is or does [UML-1.3]

Once the mapping of architectural constructs to a representation model has been accomplished, the representation model can be used for system design and implementation. UML is well-suited as a design language.

Work is currently emerging from the Object Management Group (OMG) that maps RM-ODP onto the use of UML [EDOC, EDOCa]. The UML designers have issued a request for proposal to specify a method of enterprise distributed object computing modeling concerns, and map those onto UML identifying extensions where needed. The word *profile* is being used to represent a UML adaptation for a particular domain, such as representation of a real-time architecture specification or an enterprise distributed object computing (EDOC) architecture specification. What is important to this discussion is that a profile is a use of UML to describe the model of something, and in the case of EDOC, it is used to describe the architecture specified by a different model—RM-ODP, for example. Hence, a Profile is what is termed a metamodel.

UML profiles are being defined for a number of different models: EDOC, Real Time, Enterprise JavaBeans™ (EJB), the Common Object Request Broker

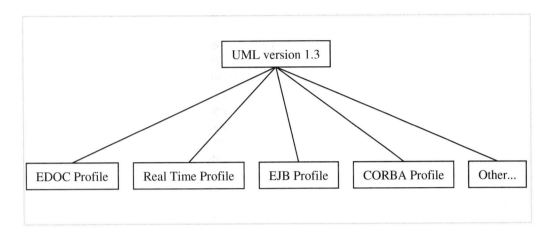

FIGURE 7.2   UML Emerging Profiles for Representing a Specification

Architecture (CORBA), and others. In some cases, extensions to UML are being identified in order to support the profile, such as the need to represent events, and the need to represent semantic behavior in terms of expressing their rules. In some cases, a profile does not make use of all of UML. CORBA, for example, does not make use of the UML Use Case model. In all cases, each profile defines its own model (such as what is needed to specify a real time system), and identifies or maps those profile model constructs onto the UML model constructs for use. Figure 7.2 shows the profiles emerging for UML.

Figure 7.3 shows an example of how an architect makes use of a profile, which is a metamodel for UML. Each of these are models. That is, UML is a model, a profile is a model, and an architecture is a model. The issue is ensuring the correct representation of the specification elements that form an architecture (model).

What are some of the possible extensions? In RM-ODP, an invariant is something that holds true for some duration, across one or a set of objects. An invariant may apply to a relationship. That relationship may address properties of a composite object in a composition relationship, and is determined by the properties of its component objects. The composite object is a simple object at some level of abstraction, and is able to be represented in UML as a class or class-instance object. What may happen is that the invariant relationship properties may include:

▶ Cardinalities (which are representable in UML)

▶ An invariant that requires some specification to ensure the composite object can include the addition or deletion of components, changes in properties, and so forth

▶ Different roles (for each of the components) that are exposed in the composite object

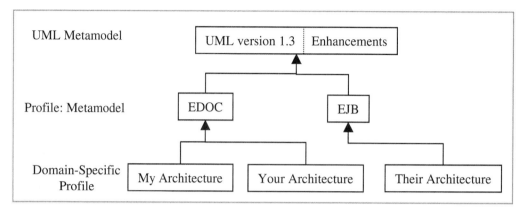

FIGURE 7.3   Use of Profile for Architecture

Hence, a relationship invariant may include some or all of these properties. It is not clear how this can be represented in UML. This example relationship is an n-ary relationship, specified as a composite of binary relationships, to adhere to the relationship invariant. How this can be described in UML is still under debate. [Kilov-email] What is being discussed is shown in Figure 7.4. The "some component" interacts with the composite object in one of two ways: assuming Role B or Role D, with associated cardinalities. How is this n-ary relationship described in UML? UML describes binary relationships. Herein is an example of how a semantic constraint, a relationship invariant, is a valid architecture specification but is not (currently) describable in UML.

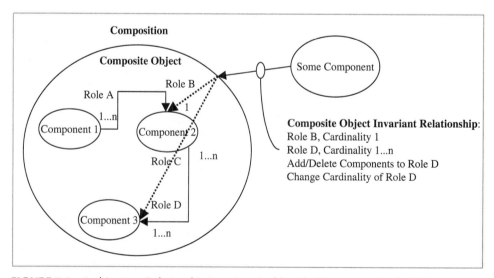

FIGURE 7.4   Architecture Relationship Invariant Problem for Representation in UML

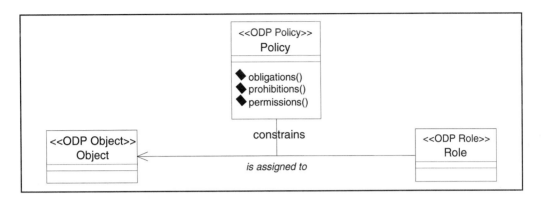

FIGURE 7.5 RM-ODP Policy Represented as UML Model

The relationship between specification and representation, using UML as an example, is shown in Figure 7.5. In this figure, RM-ODP policy is specified, in accordance with the specification rules of RM-ODP. UML has no construct called "policy." And as already discussed (and further expanded in Chapter 8, "Composition and Semantics: Quality Composition Minimizing Architectural Mismatch"), policy is one of the behavior elements in RM-ODP. The representation in UML is as an association class. An association class is a class that has attribute(s) and/or operation(s) between other classes. UML allows policy features to be captured inside an association class. The differences in Figure 7.5 show that UML can represent a policy in a certain way (there are other possible ways), but that a policy is an architecture specification on the correct behavior of an object when it assumes a particular role. Policy is not a concept in UML.

As an example, the policies for a hospital were shown in Figures 6.4 and 6.6. Figure 7.6 shows a technician role that is assigned to a technician object, constrained by the hospital technician policy. The policy statements at this level of abstraction are reflected in an association class, associated with an ODP object assuming an ODP role. Through further refinement of this model, additional ODP objects, interfaces, and possibly other policies will be specified. These too will follow the same representation in UML as in Figure 7.5.

Let's look at another example. In RM-ODP, an object can provide or offer multiple interfaces, each of which may offer multiple interactions. In UML, a class has a single interface, and a single role. To get around this problem, one method of using UML to represent multiple object interfaces is shown in Figure 7.7. In this example, a class defines the service offered and associates this class to classes that define the different interfaces offered. In this example, a service offering provides two different interfaces, I1 and I2. I1 offers an interface that provides for a single interaction. I2 offers an interface that provides two interactions. Perhaps one interface provides administrative capabilities, while another provides search and

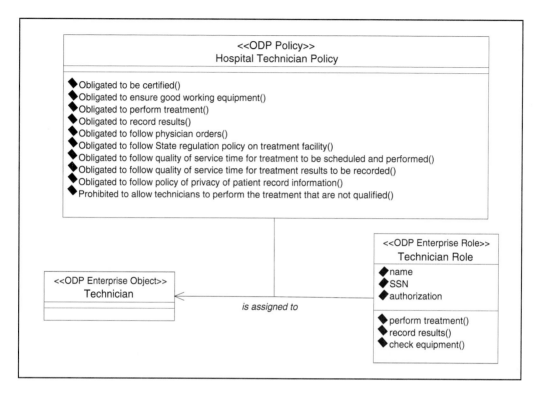

FIGURE 7.6   Example of Hospital Technician Policy Specification Represented in UML

access capabilities. The specification rules in RM-ODP for an interface include what is shown as a constraint on the service offering. An example is the rule that interactions are unique to an interface. This example is drawn from [EDOC-UML], though it uses UML somewhat differently.

Now that multiple interfaces are represented, the architect needs to be able to represent the use of the interface. Figure 7.8 shows a use of Interface 1 by a Service 2 entity. The service provider, Service 1 (the same as in Figure 7.7), must implement the interface offered and required by another entity. This is a constraint, represented as an association class in UML.

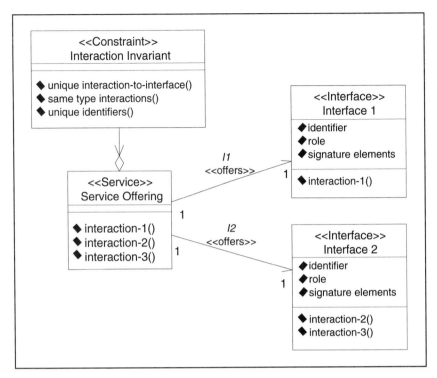

FIGURE 7.7   Multiple Interfaces Represented in UML

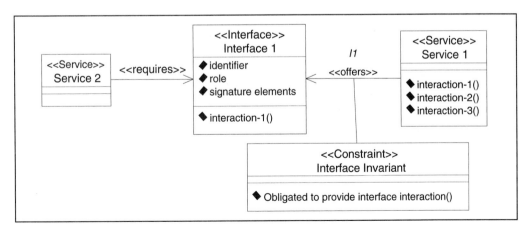

FIGURE 7.8   Using an Interface UML Representation with Constraint

7.4   RM-ODP ARCHITECTURE SPECIFICATION CONCEPTS

The RM-ODP modeling concepts are defined in Part 2 of the standard. They are powerful modeling concepts, aimed at a specification for an architecture. The specification concepts are categorized into four fundamental approaches:

1. An object model approach to an architecture specification
2. A viewpoint approach to an architecture to specify the system in terms appropriate for the viewpoint abstractions
3. A defined set of concepts and rules from the domain of system architecture
4. A testing approach to analyze and test an architecture for compliance to RM-ODP

The RM-ODP viewpoints are each associated with a specific RM-ODP modeling language. The architect can choose to use the languages specified in Part 3 of the standard for each of the viewpoints, or provide one. However, the language must follow certain modeling rules and concepts as defined in Part 2 of RM-ODP.

The *basic concepts* are used to specify and interpret the modeling constructs of any RM-ODP modeling language. They address entity, proposition, abstraction, atomicity, system, and architecture.

The *basic linguistic concepts* are used to address concepts in the language. The language must specify its grammar in accordance with these concepts. Then an ODP architecture is specified in terms of these concepts. The concepts defined are term and sentence.

The *basic modeling concepts* are the constructs to use to specify an ODP architecture. The modeling constructs of any modeling language used must adhere to these concepts. The concepts defined are object, environment, action, interface, activity, behavior, state, communication, location in space, location in time, and interaction point.

The object modeling approach provides a formalism for abstraction and refinement, as well as encapsulation. The concepts provide a general object-based model for use in the architecture models. Abstraction enables the specification of a system, separate from the solution of the system, in terms of technologies and product implementation. Encapsulation allows the hiding of a myriad of complex details, such as transparencies, distribution, failure, security, communication mechanisms, and the like. The basic modeling concepts provide a focus on a set of precisely defined concepts that form the object model underpinning for an ODP specification.

The *specification concepts* are requirements on the language chosen, and are to be considered in the specification languages used for an ODP architecture. These concepts include composition, decomposition, composite object, behavioral compatibility, refinement, trace, type, class, subtype/supertype, subclass/superclass, template, interface signature, instantiation (template), role, creation, introduction, deletion, instance, template type, template class, derived class/base class, invariant, precondition, and postcondition.

The specification concepts address those concepts used to reason about an architecture specification. The specification concepts are reflected in a specification language. The relationships among the specification languages, and requirements on any specification language chosen, are provisioned by the concepts in this category. The concepts in this category are language-independent; that is, they can apply to any specification language.

The *structuring concepts* provide ways of viewing distribution and distributed systems. The specification language must be able to specify objects and functions that require the structuring concepts in an ODP architecture. These concepts include group, configuration, domain, subdomain, epoch, reference point, conformance point, transparencies, contract, quality of service, environment contract, obligation, permission, prohibition, policy, persistence, isochronicity, name, identifier, name space, naming context, naming action, naming domain, naming graph, name resolution, activity structure, chain (of actions), thread, joining action, dividing action, forking action, spawn action, head action, subactivity, establishing behavior, enabled behavior, contractual context, liaison, terminating behavior, causality, binding behavior, binding, binding precondition, unbinding behavior, trading, failure, error, fault, stability, application management, communication management, management information, managed role, managing role, and notification.

The structuring concepts are the basic building blocks for defining the structures and relationships of distributed systems. The structures in RM-ODP are patterns of reasoning for reuse in any architecture specification.

The final set of concepts is categorized as *conformance concepts*. These are concepts used to define conformance testing of an ODP architecture to both the RM-ODP standard, and to a system implementation of the architecture. These concepts include testing and reference points, classes of reference points (programmatic, perceptual, interworking, interchange), change of configuration, portability, migratability, conformance testing process, result of testing, and relation between reference points.

The conformance concepts provide a framework to assess the conformance issues, expressed in terms of the object model. The conformance framework identifies conformance points for use within the viewpoint specifications, where conformance observations can be made and analyzed. It specifies what conformance criteria should be asserted in each viewpoint, and the relationships among these criteria. It defines the different classes of reference points to specify where certain conformance criteria are to be observed.

These categories of concepts are used by the RM-ODP viewpoint languages. They partition the specification and structuring concepts, using the basic concepts and linguistic concepts, to specify an architecture.

The language for the Enterprise Viewpoint provides the specification of the objectives, policy constraints, and purpose on the system.

The language for the Information Viewpoint provides the specification of the information and information processing aspects of the system. The language captures the objects and their behavior in the system. The concepts defined in the information language, therefore, include concepts for the specification of the meaning of information and information processing, independent of the system implementation of the processing functions. The information language must therefore ensure that the interpretation of its concepts is consistent.

The language for the Computational Viewpoint provides the specification for the decomposition of the system into objects and interactions at well-defined interfaces. It uses the object modeling concepts to define the object, interfaces, interactions, and binding. It uses the specification and structuring concepts to specify the actions that can be performed, the behavioral aspects of those actions, the form of objects and interfaces, and the constraints on distribution aspects of the system, without specifying the actual distribution. It can use the composition concepts as a means of encapsulating an application as it exists in the larger system context, without regard to its distribution.

The language for the Engineering Viewpoint provides the specification for the distribution characteristics of the system. It specifies the "how" of objects and their interactions. The engineering language is also based on the object model concepts, and uses the specification and structure concepts to specify how a node is structured and managed in terms of its resources and infrastructure services, and how interaction is achieved, along with the behavior expected.

The language for the Technology Viewpoint specifies the implementation of the system: the solution. The language is the least well-formed in RM-ODP. It is primarily a discussion of what results in the implementation, in terms of standards, products, hardware, and software components. The language would take into account the nonfunctional aspects of the system: return on investment, the maturity of products, the cost to implement a solution, and so forth.

Of importance, however, is the specification of conformance, the specification of testing information needed, and where that information is associated in the other viewpoint languages. It relates the concepts in the viewpoint languages to observations of behavior that can be understood by the tester. The concepts of conformance are used throughout the enterprise, information, computational, and engineering viewpoint languages.

The technology specification may affect additional constraints on the architecture specification from the other viewpoints. If a technology is not available to provide some specified behavior, that behavior is further constrained by the technology specification. An example is fault tolerance. The technology of choice may not offer a complete fault tolerant solution, as specified in the other modeling languages. Additional constraints on the fault-tolerant–associated policies may be required to reflect the choice of a fault-tolerant technology. Thus, the technology specification provides the relationship between a set of viewpoint models and a solution.

7.5   SUMMARY

Architecture specification is about well-defined rigorous concepts and rules in the domain of discourse of elements of a system. A specification includes patterns of reasoning, architecture patterns for reuse, well-formed concepts, well-formed structures, consistency, and analysis of the architecture models, which cannot happen until there is a means of providing a consistent specification capable reference model for use.

The use of the RM-ODP specification concepts provides the ability to specify the characteristics for an architecture. These concepts are structured in RM-ODP into the set of viewpoint languages associated with each viewpoint. The notations used in the language are specific to the language, as long as they adhere to the different categorizations of concepts for specification: basic concepts, basic linguistics concepts, basic modeling concepts, specification, structuring, and conformance.

It is also recognized by RM-ODP that the notations used can be in any form: English text, graphical representation, or formal language. Whatever choices of languages are used, they must be consistent with respect to each. That is, the collection of languages chosen to specify an architecture must work together to provide the overall architecture specification.

EIGHT

COMPOSITION AND SEMANTICS: QUALITY COMPOSITION MINIMIZING ARCHITECTURAL MISMATCH

This chapter discusses the RM-ODP concepts of abstraction, composition, and components, which are more powerful concepts than the component-based frameworks (CBF) or component-based development (CBD) of today. Important concepts of semantic behavior are discussed in terms of type, templates, invariants, contracts, policies, and quality of service (QoS). This chapter provides an opportunity for each reader to gain a better understanding of the semantic behavior constructs in RM-ODP for use in an architecture specification.

8.1   OVERVIEW

Specifying an architecture requires the specification of semantic behavior. All too often, behavior is implicit, never captured, and rarely communicated. The result of this tends to be a broken system, one that doesn't quite meet the intended needs, one that has a number of failures, one that has mismatches, or some combination of these. For example, what does an interface "name" mean? Is it an "identifier?" Is it a pointer "name" to something? Is it an "address?" Is the "address" current? The answer is in the defined semantics that are associated with the interface signature.

The architect's toolbox should include a set of tools to address the semantic behaviors, to deal with identifying and eliminating inconsistencies in an architecture specification, and, in general, expose a better understanding of the problems to be solved. Part of this set of tools is abstraction. The need for abstraction is essential for clear understanding and for simplifying a set of issues to address. To understand a large complicated system, the architect and user should be able to separate concerns from intricate details: from the high-level business concerns about the customer needs for a system to the low-level implementation concerns about the developer needs for using a particular product in the system.

POINT

"To understand anything, you should not try to understand everything."
[Aristotle]

Current practice tends to require use of commercial off-the-shelf products (COTS) as components to create a system. The concept is that components provide reusable software elements that have already been developed and can merely be used in a system. The concept of component software originated from the principles of megaprogramming [Boehm-92]. The concept is a good one. But current practice has not yet found a way to ensure composability without mismatch [Garlan-95a].

COTS vendors provide application programming interfaces (APIs) for using their product. Some vendors state that the use of one or more standards allows composability. However, system architects and developers have learned, often the hard way, that composition problems are immense, that components are not simply pluggable because they are reusable, and trying to plug components together often results in side effects. These side effects, or the inability to compose reusable components despite well-defined *functional* behavior, are a direct result of the lack of *semantic* behavior specification and choices made based on the exposed semantic behavior.

Consider trying to install a suite of products, such as Microsoft® Office, that share a dynamic link library (DLL). How many times is there some sort of discrepancy in the installation process? This is an example of mismatch. Consider a product that uses multiple threads (say, for event notification). There is the potential for mismatch if the product is used on a system that offers only single threading.

At a higher level of abstraction, a security policy may allow only a few select users to gain access to an application. Assume only the user Joe has access to the application "budget." But Mary has access to the application "planner," that in turn needs access to "budget." Is it acceptable for Mary to use "budget" this way, or is it a mismatch? The architect needs to at least determine this potential mismatch, and decide if there is some mitigation needed.

In specifying the meaning of something, a "warm and fuzzy feeling" is insufficient. A "meaningful name" is not a definition, and an example is not a definition. [Kilov-99]

There is a great deal of discussion in the literature about the urgent need for a semantic framework in support of CBF, CBD, composability in terms of mitigating mismatch, and reuse. Such a framework is provided by RM-ODP as patterns of reasoning of what should be included in a semantic specification. However, RM-ODP does not explicitly provide the syntax to do so. This is left to the architect to specify, or to one of the RM-ODP standards.

The "language" for modeling the semantics of RM-ODP consists of the viewpoint languages, each adhering to the structuring and specification rules addressed in this chapter. The result is a formal foundation for a semantic framework that provides the means to express semantic behavior properties:

▶ Openness, by the very nature of RM-ODP

▶ Distribution, through the choices made in the viewpoint specifications and interaction (addressed in Chapter 13, "Interaction Framework: Interoperability")

▶ Composition, as addressed by the rules of RM-ODP

▶ QoS (addressed in Chapter 17, "Quality of Service Model")

▶ Design by contract, as addressed by structuring and specification concepts of this chapter

▶ Consistency, as addressed by the conformance framework of RM-ODP (addressed in Chapter 11, "Architecture Analysis and System Conformance Evaluation")

▶ Object-based model as addressed by the object model of RM-ODP

RM-ODP addresses the need for semantics, where semantics plays a key role, and how those semantic elements are consistent across the viewpoints. This in turn enables quality composition of the components of the system, specification of the semantic behavior of the system components, minimizing architectural mismatch.

8.2   SEMANTIC BEHAVIOR

The term "semantics" really means "meaning." Behavior means "constrained action." *Semantic behavior*, then, is the specification of allowable actions with a set of constraints (such as invariants) on what is to be accomplished and when those constraints may occur.

Some principles to consider in specifying the semantics of a system include:

▶ Abstraction levels to simplify what is addressed in a specification at one level, and further refined at other levels

▶ Separation of concerns to focus on what is important to specify

▶ Composition to address a single entity, even though it is composed of parts

▶ Invariants and other semantic behavior concepts such as contract, policy, pre-conditions, postconditions, and failure conditions

▶ Use of the same concepts and rules throughout, enabling consistency across the levels of abstraction and composition

> The emphasis in RM-ODP is semantic behavior. Indeed one of the hallmarks of RM-ODP is the provision for semantic behavior patterns of reasoning for the architect to use to specify throughout an architectural specification.

To create such a specification, the architect needs to account for the objects, their allowable states and state changes, those things that must always be true for the life of the object (invariants), and the environment in which the object exists and acts. An object, recall, is defined by its state and behavior.

The concepts dealing with semantic behavior are precisely defined. Precision is important in an architecture specification because by understanding the most basic concepts, the architect can create more-complex structures from the basic concepts. For example, understanding the meaning of an "action" leads to a full interaction framework (see Chapter 13, "Interactive Framework: Interoperability").

The specification methods of composition and abstraction provide the ability to combine precise concepts correctly, resulting in concepts of greater complexity. This is actually the nature of the real world. For example, abstracting the details of the precise meanings of subatomic elements and how they can be composed eventually results in the specification of a complex system, such as a medication.

Semantic behavior must be defined at the relationship between or among objects and at the system level; it cannot be defined at the object level. All important semantic behavior is in the relationships between objects and should be explicitly defined in order for two objects to properly interact, match up, or plug and play. "It is impossible to understand behavior of the system by looking only at the behavior of its parts." [Hall-97]

8.3   ABSTRACTION AND REFINEMENT

Abstraction is a fundamental technique used to specify different aspects of a system and is used throughout RM-ODP. Suppressing irrelevant detail really means to simplify what is being addressed by focusing on only the important aspects of something. The rest will come in other abstractions, or as refinements to the abstraction.

Abstraction enables the separation of concerns into different "levels." For example, consider a house as a single level of abstraction (a single object). A different level of abstraction of the house is considered in terms of its constituent parts: rooms, a roof, a foundation, and other components. It's a matter of what is important to focus on at the point of trying to determine aspects of the architecture. Whether or not hierarchical levels of abstraction are used as part of the architectural specification is an architect's choice. Hierarchical levels of abstraction are not an inherent part of the abstraction.

"A significant engineering project begins with a specification describing as directly as possible the observable properties and behaviour of the desired product. The design documents, formulated at various stages of the project, are indirect descriptions of the same behaviour. They are expressed in some restricted notation, at a level of abstraction appropriate to guide the physical implementation. This implementation is correct if its detailed description logically implies its specification; for then any observation of the product will be among those described and therefore permitted by the specification. The success of the whole project depends not only on correct reasoning at each level of design, but also on the soundness of the transition between levels of abstraction." [Hoare]

This method of creating an architecture specification enhances better understanding of the problem and results in a simplified model. It also facilitates communication among the stakeholders and architect because the model is simplified, which simplifies the discussion about salient parts of the architecture.

Abstraction is the process of rendering something into a more general model. Abstraction is either a verb or a noun (the result of abstracting). A general model simplifies wht is to be addressed by hiding or encapsulating details not to be addressed.

Refinement is the dual of abstraction. It is a process that addresses the detail abstracted away, providing a more granular detailed specification. [RM-ODP-2]

A specification is a model of the thing being specified. The model is a level of abstraction from the physical thing it models. The process of abstraction is to remove irrelevant details from consideration. The process of refinement is to bring more and more of those details into focus. To work, that is to relate the model of the thing to the actual thing, requires abstractions at different levels of granularity, and relationships among them. To do this requires a relationship that defines the way in which what is being specified corresponds to one or more specifications at another level of abstraction. These relationships are the specification and structuring rules in RM-ODP that the architect applies to create an architecture specification.

Separating concerns into abstractions is the heart of object-oriented software. Numerous benefits can be realized in applying the methods of abstraction and refinement to an architecture specification, including:

▶ Improved understanding by reducing the complexity of details to other levels of abstraction

▶ Additive change by adding in further refinements

▶ Reuse of the abstraction, such as a pattern for architecture, pattern for design, or component in a CBD environment

▶ Customizability of the refinement keeping the higher-level abstraction (the common aspects) stable

▶ Adaptability: (a) in terms of reuse of the abstraction in the specification, and (b) adapting decisions in the refinement (details) of the thing abstracted

▶ Simplified integration of the abstractions

▶ Others

To benefit from using abstraction and refinement, the architect needs to correctly modularize the concerns being separated, at the right time in the specification. A house is one abstraction. But to abstract the front door, kitchen sink, and bathroom sink probably wouldn't be the right modularization. On the other hand, abstracting the front door, the kitchen door, and the bathroom door might be the right modularization if, for example, the focus of concern was "same properties of doors." This is similar to classes of objects, and classes are an example of a kind of abstraction. Class hierarchy, then, is an example of abstractions and refinements of classes. The same principle applies with modularization of architecture areas of concern.

There is no cookbook to tell the architect how to abstract areas of concern with respect to an architecture of a system. Different architects must contend with different stakeholders; a developer may need one level of abstraction, a customer may need another. At one abstraction, an enterprise community is specified and communicated to a business area customer, for example. At a refinement of a community, the data representation of a set of (information) objects may be provided to the database developer. At a different refinement of the community, a set of computers and associated software is specified for the system implementer, which identifies a specific vendor database management system (DBMS). These are all levels of abstraction on different aspects of "community," related through the rules of RM-ODP and the different viewpoints (which are part of the rule set).

Abstraction, refinement, and modularization are key methods for the architecture specification of a system. Object modularization and encapsulation are major assets to these methods: modularization in breaking up the areas of concern into parts; encapsulation to hide the details of the parts (until later). Rules for accomplishing these are provided by RM-ODP. However, it remains the task of the architect to determine how to apply these methods in the system model. Sometimes abstraction will be by class, feature set (database), property (such as a policy), view (such as "data view"), or viewpoints. The choice is the architect's how best to specify the architecture.

For example, a house can be described in terms of certain aspects, such as size, age, condition, and so forth, without having to go into the same discussion for every external element of the house, such as the roof, front door, windows, etc. The communication to the stakeholder is enhanced by suppressing irrelevant details and by simplifying the item of focus (the house; not all the external parts). Clearly, however, a house is composed of these parts. Figure 8.1 shows two levels of abstraction using the house example.

The five viewpoints of RM-ODP are a form of abstraction. The viewpoints are not layered, but there can be levels of abstractions within each. How do these relate? Each viewpoint, recall, addresses the entire system from a specific set of concerns, abstracting away concepts that are not of concern at that point of view.

For example, a "binding" is specified in the computational language, and can be further refined into a binding object. Addressing the binding within the computational specification addresses the form of the binding, the interfaces being bound, and the objects that interact across the binding. Any of this can be represented as iterations of abstraction and refinement, all within the computational specification. But the computational viewpoint only addresses objects, interactions, interfaces, binding, and so forth. It does not address, for example, issues of distribution across nodes, or channels that provide the bindings to the binding object; these are engineering viewpoint concerns.

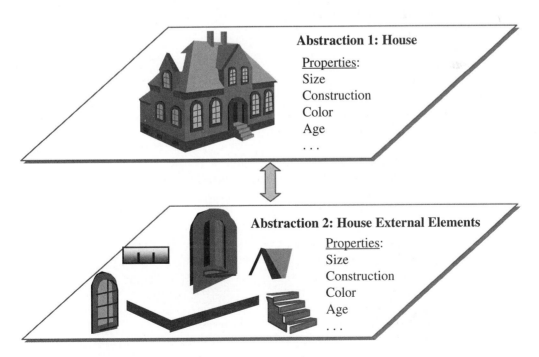

FIGURE 8.1   Abstraction Example

The engineering viewpoint provides the means of addressing these concerns. Whether the engineering viewpoint model of a binding object with two interfaces is at the same level of abstraction, or a refinement of the computational viewpoint model of the binding object, is not of concern; the only concern is the language of concepts that apply to one viewpoint or another. Within each viewpoint, there are most likely levels of abstraction to refine into more detail those things about the specification pertinent to the viewpoint language.

Figure 8.2 provides an example of this discussion. The figure shows both a computational and an engineering model of a binding of objects. In the computational model, there are three levels of abstraction, because they all address computational viewpoint concepts. The engineering specification shows what might be the distributed nature of the binding. It deals with different concepts, but not necessarily at a different level of abstraction. There is great similarity between the level of abstraction of the most refined computational specification and the engineering specification—only the concepts differ.

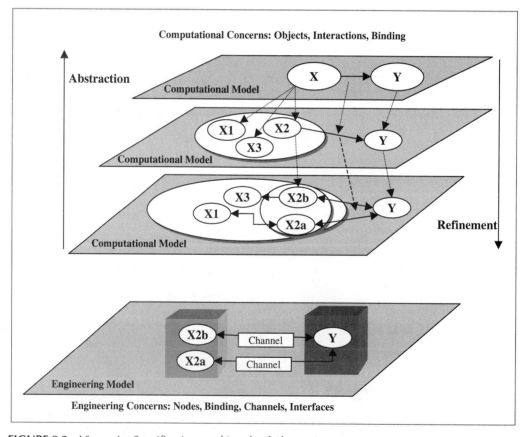

FIGURE 8.2   Viewpoint Specifications and Levels of Abstraction

The purpose of abstraction and refinement is to focus on *any* concern at various levels of granularity. The methods of abstraction and refinement are fully usable within any of the viewpoints as well as across the viewpoints. So a house, for example, can be considered an enterprise object, that is further refined in the enterprise model to address how that house may relate to the community of other homes, or how the relationship of the building codes constrain the development of the house. In the computational model, the house may be further refined to computational objects (e.g., roof, door, window) and how they interact. The building code for the house may be refined into building codes for how a door is placed on the frame, how a window must be insulated, etc. The "part-building codes" are refinements from the overall house development building code. But the focus of concern in the computational model (part-building codes) is different from that of the enterprise model (house building code). As can be seen, abstraction and refinement are techniques across the viewpoints.

Moving to a focus on a system, an architecture specification is hard enough. The key objective in an architecture is communicating the system and its behavior to the business stakeholders as well as to the system designers and implementers in such a way as to be consistent and complete and leave little or nothing to interpretation. Levels of abstraction facilitate this. In addition, consistent handling of each level of abstraction to ensure consistency across the levels is paramount and accomplished in RM-ODP. Some good patterns of thought along these lines, derived from [Kilov-97], include:

▶ Separate business and system concerns in such a way as to enable different specifications while communicating among the stakeholders.

▶ Specify aspects of the system concern declaratively; that is, use invariants and contracts.

▶ Be explicit and precise in order to be able to defend your specification when challenged, and to capture your thoughts in a manner that can be properly interpreted—a warm fuzzy feeling is not enough!

▶ Be simple and elegant, so that the main ideas are not lost in lots of fragmentary elements and so that the main points are very clear to all stakeholders (business user through implementer) who need to understand the system specification.

▶ Use the same concepts throughout to facilitate communication across the stakeholder community.

Levels of abstraction play a key role in the definition of components and composition in RM-ODP, which are addressed next. Remember, something defined at one level of abstraction is done so to facilitate explicit and precise semantic definitions, which are based on the concepts defined in RM-ODP. Levels do not mean hierarchical layers; rather, they mean "abstract away irrelevant details" to discuss some part of the system. The viewpoints of RM-ODP are all based on these concepts.

8.4 COMPONENTS, COMPOSITION, AND DECOMPOSITION

There are three primary uses of components and composition. One is to be able to abstract away certain details in focusing on a particular architectural concern. Another is to enable the implementation of reusable software in different ways by different developers. The last is to enable a well-specified component to be plugged into a system, without incurring mismatch, or with the ability to mitigate any exceptions raised. This latter use of components requires that a number of criteria be met, independent of the internal details of the component, but dependent on the context in which the component exists: its behavior in its environment, its behavior in a composition, and its internal behavior. With these criteria, components can be added, deleted, or replaced in a system, while minimizing the mismatch potential of "plug and play."

Much is in the literature about components and composition. Szyperski [Szyperski-98] speaks about components being important for reuse and evolvability. Composability is important, and applied to binary elements such as Enterprise JavaBeans™ or Common Object Request Broker Architecture (CORBA) objects. A wider definition is offered by RM-ODP. It addresses not the form of the component as a binary unit, but the process of specifying a component, whether that form is a binary unit in the end, or an abstraction for use in an architectural specification. Clearly, a component will result in some software, but it may result in several software units, dependent upon specific hardware, and other software. That is, RM-ODP addresses components and composition as a generalization of expressing fine-grained or coarse-grained software (systems).

Nevertheless, composability is the important topic at hand. And it's important to address both static and dynamic composability. Static composability follows from a specification. Dynamic composability is much more difficult. Not only must the architect specify the functional and nonfunctional properties of the component, but also provide mechanisms to dynamically add and delete components in a composition during execution of a system. Herein lies much in the area of mismatch; the behavior of one component may not match the behavior of another, resulting in the inability to compose, or an ability to compose resulting in errors.

Szyperski also says that a component is a unit of deployment. "Object technology has brought to light and tried to free us from the limitations of the traditional view of a program as an executable that does one thing. Beyond this simple view, object technology introduces the notion of class, providing a number of well-specified operations (commands and queries) on a certain data abstraction. We can take a program and make it into a component… If we move forward and design new components, there seems to be little doubt that classes will provide a convenient and effective means of encapsulation." [Meyer-2000]

The argument from Meyer is that classes provide the right form of components, though a class is not a component. One might componentize a legacy system, for example, which is not the same thing as a class. The point being made is that the form of a component is likened to that of a class, but may not be a class.

The criteria that are important for componentization include:

▶ The component is identifiable

▶ The component encapsulates elements and behavior

▶ The component is (re)usable by other objects or components

▶ The form of the component contains sufficient specification to be usable as a black box: defined by someone else

This means that it is difficult to use *software modules* as components, unless the same developer has developed the components as the one to reuse those components. This is one of the major reasons why software reuse endeavors of the past have not been very successful. However, in RM-ODP composition, rules adhere to all of these items in the definition of components, including the ability to compose behavior. Hence, RM-ODP components include a specification of functional and semantic behavior that enables them to be composable.

Much is in the literature about the distinction between a component and an object. In RM-ODP, a component is an object, and a composition of such components is also an object. Hence, RM-ODP rules allow a component to be a system, a subsystem, a group of interacting objects, or an object. This is a powerful concept of component and composition.

8.4.1 RM-ODP RULES OF COMPOSITION

RM-ODP's concept of composition provides a path to solving the needs identified in the literature. A key aspect of RM-ODP composition is information hiding; a composition hides the objects, interactions, and their behavior from the focus at hand. An overview of a composition of objects that forms a composite object is shown in Figure 8.3.

Composition is closely aligned with the rules of abstraction. What is composed are a group of common elements yielding a single composed element to focus on. The group of elements is addressed (focused on) at a different level of abstraction than the composition.

A *component* is a part of a *composition*. A composition is a result of composing like-type entities into a single entity of the same type. Its members are component objects, along with their interfaces. An object that participates in a composition is both a component object and an object as well. When that object assumes the role only as an object, independent of the composition, it is only considered an object in that role, not a component. Only when the object participates in the composition is that object assuming the role of component.

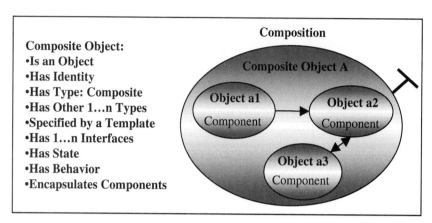

FIGURE 8.3   Composition and Composite Object

The composition is itself considered an object (if its members are objects). It is termed a *composite object*.

Levels of abstraction play a part here. The composite object is at one level of abstraction. It is a single object. The component objects that participate in the composition are at another level of abstraction. They are component objects. And the component object, when it is only considered as an object, not part of the composition, is at another level of abstraction.

The rules for composition are considered invariant over all members of the composition (i.e., all components) and the composite object itself.

Composition is a configuration of related entities (e.g., objects) that results in a new entity (e.g., object) at a different level of abstraction. [RM-ODP-2] *Decomposition* is the dual to composition. It is the specification of the composed entity (e.g., object), which means a specification of all of its constituent entities (e.g., all of the objects that form the composition. [RM-ODP-2] A *composite object* is a composition considered as an object. [RM-ODP-2]

The rules of composition are extremely powerful in RM-ODP, providing a wonderful tool for the architect to modularize areas of concern in the specification, to treat those as single objects in the specification, and to know that the consistency rules of a composition and its components are well-formed.

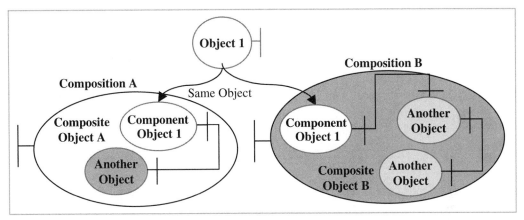

FIGURE 8.4 Component in Multiple Compositions

An object can participate in more than one composition, at different levels of abstraction, at the same time or at different times. Figure 8.4 shows this case. At one level of abstraction, object 1 is only an object. At the same time (or at a different time in the specification) and at another level of abstraction, object 1 is a component object that participates in composition A. At another level of abstraction (over some time) object 1 is a component object that participates in composition B. Object 1 is the same object throughout: a single object with a specified type, an object of type component in composition A, and an object of type component in composition B.

Since the composite object is an object, it can also participate as a component object in a different composition, at a different level of abstraction, at the same time or at a different time. Figure 8.5 provides a view of this case, where

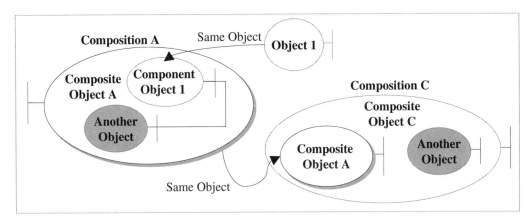

FIGURE 8.5 Composition of a Composite Object

object 1 and composite object A are the same as in the previous figure, and composite object A is a component in composition C.

Hence, composition of objects in RM-ODP is recursive. There is no hierarchy implied. What is seen as representations of this concept in the preceding figures can all co-exist in the same specification.

The *behavior* of the *composite object* is determined by the way in which the objects are composed, and the way in which they participate in the composition. In the case of the composite object, this is the composite object template.

Since the composite object is an object, its behavior can be specified as properties of the individual component objects. That is, the behavior specified in a composite object template relates to the behavior of one or more of the component objects. To do this, the behavior can be parameterized in the composite object template, identified, and related to the component objects.

For example, behavior associated with object 1 in the preceding figure can be specified, as shown in Figure 8.6. The composite object A template defines the behavior of object 1 as it participates in the composition (in this case, part of a fault tolerant control object). Part of the composite object template includes the object templates themselves. As a single object, object 1 may be defined to be available for use as a fault tolerant object (in the composition) but being persistent and a part of a replica, adhering to the naming conventions within the domain. The point is that the composite object template not only defines the behavior of the component objects as they participate in the composition, but also includes the object templates of those component objects. The behavior of the composite is also affected by the constraints placed on the behavior of the individual components.

The way in which objects are combined can include such methods as sequential, concurrent, choice, or interleaving. That is, to create a composition, the architect may "choose" the objects, or sequentially include objects, dynamically or statically. The behavior of the component is defined. The behavior can be evaluated either statically or dynamically, to determine if a mismatch in composition will arise.

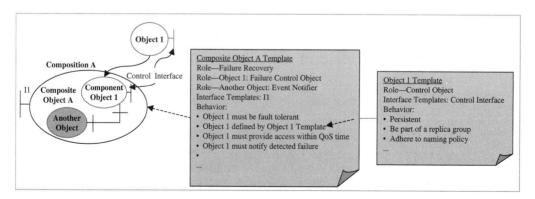

FIGURE 8.6   Composition Behavior

In Figure 8.6, the templates are also composed. In this case, the composite object template is a composition of roles. Object 1 assumes the type of "component" in composition A. As such, in the instantiation process, object 1 is associated with the role of "failure control object" within the composition. This is compatible with the role of object 1 "control object," so no inconsistency arises.

Care should be exercised in composing objects so that conflicts do not arise for an object in different compositions. If, for example, object 1 participates in another composition that requires it to behave with a different QoS, a conflict can occur. This is an example of where a decomposition of object 1 in one composition may conflict with the decomposition of object 1 in a different composition.

RM-ODP allows for compositions of anything that have some relationship, whether or not it is an object. This includes templates of some type, communities, policies, contracts, and so forth. If the entity being composed is an action, the composition is a composite action and the members are component actions. If the entity is a contract, the composition is a composite contract and the members are component contracts.

To generalize Figure 8.6, then, a composition can be as shown in Figure 8.7. The Hospital Policy is of type "policy." It is a composition of the component policies "Hospital Treatment," "Billing," and "Admission." Also shown in this figure is that "Hospital Treatment" is an abstraction of the "Billing" and "Admission" policies, which further refines the policies of Hospital Treatment. This will be an important point when contracts, templates, and policies are discussed.

This powerful modeling construct enables the architect to discuss the same system concept from multiple perspectives, and also allows the architect to abstract away certain details, while focusing on other areas of concern. A composition can be as fine-grained as two objects, or as coarse-grained as a full domain of objects. When the architect specifies a system, a coarse-grained object may be identified as a simple object in the specification. For purposes of minimizing the details to address, it is best not to worry about the individual objects in the composition. For example, in specifying a hospital information processing system, the architect could identify "admitting patient" and "billing" as a single composite objects. Then, in some other part of the specification, each is refined into its constituent component objects and interfaces, such as shown in Figure 8.8. When the components of a composition are specified to include any further recursive composition, this is called decomposition, as shown by the objects in the gray background. There is no rule that an object is particular to a composition. Indeed, an object may be reusable across compositions, as is shown in this figure. And an object, such as the Patient Identification Service (PIDS) object may be reusable across a federation of domains. Each object, whether a composite object or a single object, and its interfaces are fully specified. The relationship between abstraction/refinement and composition/decomposition is also shown Figure 8.8. Note that all of the objects shown in this figure could be part of a single viewpoint, or span viewpoints. In this case, they would be more appropriately part of the computational viewpoint, or possibly the enterprise viewpoint, depending on the focus of what is being specified.

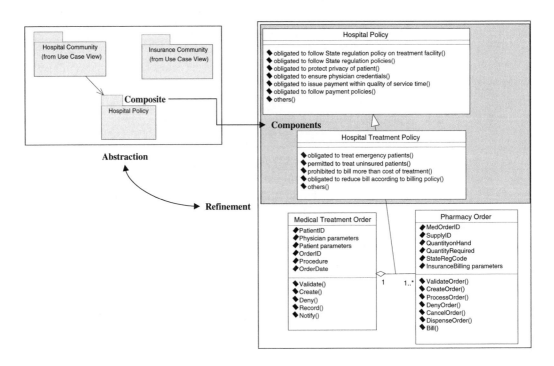

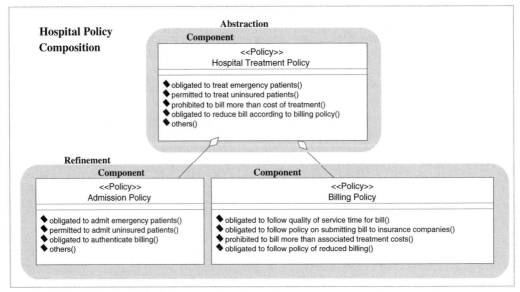

FIGURE 8.7   Composition and Refinement of a Policy

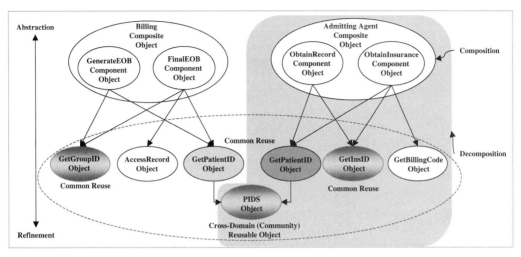

FIGURE 8.8   Composition, Decomposition, Abstraction, Refinement, and Reuse

The properties of a composite object depend upon the properties of the components, but at least one property of a composite object is independent of the collection of properties of the component objects. For example, the *objective* of a hospital community is a property that is independent of the properties of the hospital community components.

A composite object can be established, has an identity, can have one or more interfaces, can be constrained by preconditions and postconditions, can be constrained by policies or contracts, and in essence is treated as an object. A composite of a typed entity follows the rules of the entity. That is, the rules for establishing a policy, for managing a policy (including its enforcement), apply to the composition of policies as well as to the individual component policies. Therefore composition is a method of aggregating components into a whole, and assumes the rules as appropriate to the type of composite entity.

A difference between a composition and an abstraction is that a composition results in a single entity of some type, dealt with as that type of entity. An abstraction is a collection of one or more entities with something in common, as deemed appropriate by the architect. It does not (necessarily) have a specific type, and is not (necessarily) acted upon by certain rules. The only rule is refinement, and to do so, requires the ability to substitute a part for the whole (addressed as behavior compatibility in RM-ODP, which is discussed in "Substitutability" on page 308).

Consistency of the objects that form a composition is very important. In the preceding discussion, the discussion has alluded to "time." In RM-ODP, time for a composition is referred to as an epoch. An *epoch* is the span of time that an object behaves in a certain manner. Since an object can be in multiple compositions, or as a single object, different epochs are associated with its behavior. These epochs (or timeframes, loosely speaking) can be concurrent, sequential, or overlapping.

This concept is also a powerful argument in support of extensibility. An object may assume a different type in a different epoch, thereby supporting type evolution. An object may assume a different role in different compositions, over different epochs, thereby supporting usage evolution and even technology evolution.

> **POINT** For a distributed system to behave correctly, its component objects must behave consistently, over all epochs.

Going back to the way in which behavior is specified, it becomes clear that behavior of a composite object must also include its epoch: how epoch relates to time (local and global), how the composite object's epoch relates to the epochs of the component objects, how the epochs are combined, if an epoch is part of the state of an object, and so forth.

The concept of epoch associated with the behavior of an object has a direct relationship to dynamic composability. Over the course of execution, an object changes state and assumes behavior associated with the state. That object is therefore composable only if the behavior at that point in time (epoch) matches the expected behavior of the composition into which the object may be composed. If the behavior of the object in a particular state cannot be combined with the behavior of the composition, then the object cannot be dynamically composed. Therefore, dynamic composition can be facilitated by:

▶ Labeling epochs and capturing them as part of the behavior of the object
▶ Associating epoch with an object's state and identity
▶ Making epoch a parameter, observable to the runtime system
▶ Relating epoch to time
▶ Defining the rules for combining epochs in a composition

Unfortunately, RM-ODP does not provide the specification tools for this; it merely identifies how these concepts should be expressed in a specification. Nevertheless, the importance of specifying epochs, or compositions of epochs, and the rules of combining epochs is a pattern of reasoning for the architect to focus on.

> **WARNING** The definitions and rules about what a component is and does, and what composition means, are exceedingly terse in RM-ODP. Though RM-ODP allows for the composition of anything, this capability is not explicitly stated (in a precise standard!). For example, the following is from Part 2 of the standard: "Specification of a template as a composition of roles enables the instantiation process to be explained as the association of a specific component of the resultant composite object with each role."

8.4.2 CRITERIA FOR WELL-FORMED COMPONENTS

A component in RM-ODP, then, is considered a generalized or specific object, specified as part of an overall architecture, or implemented as a single unit of computation in the context of the system. Well-formed components, then, need to exhibit the following criteria.

8.4.2.1 Encapsulation

Encapsulation is a property of hiding the details. Its importance to composition is to abstract away details that are not important to the external behavior of the component, and what that component offers in terms of services. Furthermore, encapsulation is important in hiding the details of how the component functions, how it provides its services, and how many objects and interactions are required to do so. Encapsulation also allows different implementations of the same component (such as the Trader).

8.4.2.2 Identification

Identification is a name. The name for a component must be a distinguished name, ensuring that the component is unique among components for selection. An architect must be able to identify a component and distinguish it from another component. A component that is of possible use by a system must offer a means of selecting it from among other components. If a user wants to use a component, the user must be able to discover and choose the component for use. In each case, a common naming context must be available and defined, otherwise discovery of the component cannot be accomplished.

8.4.2.3 Functional Specification

Precisely specified services define the functional capabilities the component will provide. The names of the interfaces, their interactions, and their parameters are a part of the needed specification. However, the behavior of the interface must also be specified as part of the next item.

8.4.2.4 Behavior Specification

Precisely specified expected behavior addresses how the component behaves, what it requires of the environment in which it will be placed, and what it provides to the environment.

Behavior specification requires a specification of type, class, constraints on actions, QoS, policy, duration, configuration of components fulfilling some role, and behavior of an environment contract. An example of an environment is the business enterprise in which the system exists.

With respect to interaction, a structured specification is insufficient. What needs to be specified is how the interface is used, what services are provided through what interactions, what role will be used, what preconditions are expected, what postconditions are expected, what invariants apply, and any constraints on the interaction, such as quality of service expectations.

A component has state. This is another aspect of behavior. A state defines the possible actions on a component that are valid to move to one of a allowable set of additional states. So, for example, a component that receives an event as input, processes that input, and as a result moves to a new state, perhaps, that records the event.

The dynamic behavior of a component's state may result in different behaviors, depending on the input to the component. This is the importance of environment behavior: the environment in which the component exists and operates may change the constraints on the component behavior seen through its interactions.

Behavior of a component in its environment is arguably the most important property to specify, especially to mitigate mismatch.

8.4.2.5   Usability

A component must be usable by other objects, independent of how the component was implemented or by whom. This criterion says that the component is well-specified so that anyone can use the component, understand its functionality and behavior, and understand the constraints on its use.

8.4.2.6   Substitutability

A component must be able to be added to and deleted from an architecture specification. This criteria deals with specification in terms of layers of abstraction. To be able to incorporate a component into an architecture specification, that component must itself be fully specified. It is up to the architect to determine if the full specificity of the component is included in the architecture specification, or referred to. Such is the case with the Trader specification. An architect need only identify the use of Trader, reference the specification for a Trader, and ensure the proper use of the Trader component in the architecture specification.

A component (in its implementation state) should also be able to be substituted by another component, added to, and deleted from a system. This is the property often referred to as "plug and play." To accomplish this task, a component must be assessed to execute in a well-understood environment, behaving in a manner that is acceptable to the environment. To substitute one component for another, the rules of behavior compatibility need to be followed.

Two objects must be behaviorally compatible for mismatch to be minimized. In particular, "behavioral compatibility" determines the relationship criteria to substitute one object for another. With respect to a set of criteria, an object is behaviorally compatible with a second object if the first object can replace the second object without the environment being able to notice the difference in the objects' behavior. This means that behavior must address existence, compatibility, availability, failure modes, and invariants. Invariants, pre- and postactions, rules of behavior with the environment, rules of behavior of object interactions are the different kinds of constraints related to interacting objects, which can be represented as a "contract" (discussed in "Contracts" on page 326). The contract provides a specification of the rules which must be agreed to among a set of interacting objects, so that those objects are allowed to interact.

A dependability policy, for example, abstracts and can substitute for a checkpoint/recovery policy if it is possible to replace the instantiated dependability policy with the instantiated checkpoint/recovery policy, maintaining the environment behavior in either case.

All component dependencies should be specified. If, for example, version 10 of a component is replaced by version 12, this may require replacing other components on which it depends. Consider a browser that depends on certain plug-ins. When that browser is upgraded, the plug-in components most probably also need to be replaced.

8.4.2.7   Composable

A component must itself be composable. When a component enters into a composition with another component, that composition must define the rules of structure, the functional capabilities, the behavior, and in essence everything in the criteria list. Hence, composability is recursive, resulting in layers of abstraction.

8.4.2.8   Reliable

Part of the semantic behavior of a component is reliability. What if the component were developed to a two-digit year? Is this an important behavior to be specified? How does one use a component with a two-digit year in a Y2K-compliant system? From a real-world perspective, what must be specified for a power cord rated for 110V to be reused in a country using 220V? The form of the plug is one. The behavior of U.S. 110V current versus 220V is another, despite the case where the plugs themselves are composable.

Issues of reliability and recovery come into play when a component misbehaves. Then the system must be able to detect such behavior, assess the failure modes, and determine (through the architect's specification) if that component is deleted or recovered. In this case, the primary importance to a system is stability. The pattern of reasoning for fault tolerance is the subject of Chapter 16, "RM-ODP Fault Tolerance Framework."

The problem in composition today is that not all expected behaviors can be specified. We do not yet know all the behaviors to capture, let alone how to specify them. So, we must mitigate these possible mismatches by specifying common failure modes, and either give up or attempt some recovery.

8.4.2.9   Type Specification

One of the behaviors that needs to be specified is type. Everything in RM-ODP is strongly typed; e.g., object, parameter, interface, and even a template. The Interface Definition Language (IDL) provides a means of capturing type in interface signatures, thereby capturing the type of the component's interface and parameters and interactions. In addition to the specification of type, the binding of two interfaces requires the types to match. The substitutability of one object for another object requires the same type of objects. Type matching is necessary (e.g., U.S. 110V current), but not sufficient (e.g., plug differences) for composability.

8.4.3   RECURSIVENESS OF RM-ODP

As discussed, the concepts of composition and abstraction are recursive, giving the architect powerful tools of specification. Depending on the epoch, an object can be specified as an object in an interaction, as a component object interacting in the composition, or as a component object in a different composition, all at the same epoch, sequential epochs, or overlapping epochs.

The behavior specification techniques make clear how an object will behave in any of these cases. If the architect exposes, or makes observable, the behavior specification of an object, dynamic composability is enhanced. If the behavior can be analyzed during execution time (because it is visible to the system), whether or not certain behaviors are composable can be determined. This, in turn, facilitates determining if the object can be composed into the system.

The exact behaviors to be specified for a component remain the task of the architect. It may be important, for example, to specify if an object requires a single thread, or is multithreaded. Several mismatches have been identified that address this problem. It may be important to expose quality of service requirements on bandwidth expectations. The system can determine if the composition of the objects each expecting certain bandwidth capabilities can be met. These are techniques in a toolkit of other techniques available to the architect to specify, to better facilitate dynamic composition.

Interaction behavior (addressed in Chapter 13, "Interaction Framework: Interoperability") is complex, and is defined in terms of layers of abstractions and compositions. Figure 8.9 is an example of a set of objects interacting at different levels of abstraction, in different compositions. The objective is to highlight the behavior specification of an object, in whatever role it assumes; this is critical to the proper-functioning of the distributed system.

In Figure 8.9, object 1 is defined by a template to provide three interfaces. At abstraction level 1, object 1 has a type A and offers two (of the three) interfaces. One of these interfaces (interface 1) is used for an interaction with object 2, with a certain constrained behavior (say, a QoS of 10ms). At abstraction 2, object 1 is

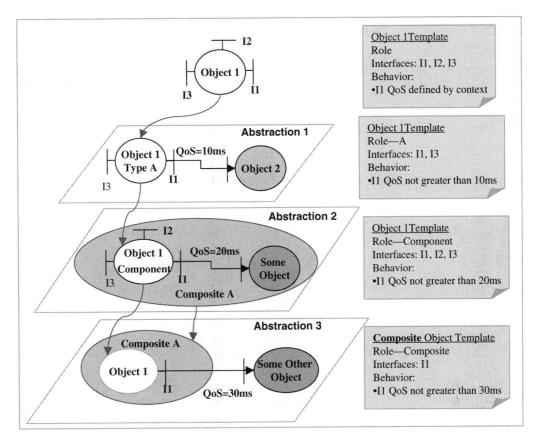

FIGURE 8.9 Concepts of Composition, Abstraction, Behavior, and Interaction

now a member of a composition, and as such assumes the type component. In this epoch, object 1 offers all three interfaces. But the behavior in this epoch for interface 1 is now QoS of 20ms. The composite object offers an interface, which happens in this case to be the same interface 1. In the case of the composite object's offering of the interface, its QoS may be defined as 30ms. All of this is compatible, if the behavior rules of composition and abstraction define the states (epochs) when interface 1 behaves with different QoS properties. If the rules do not do this, or if the epochs are concurrent with the same object, a mismatch occurs. So, though the rules of composition and abstraction are powerful tools, care must be exercised that the behaviors of the object be composable within the epochs defined.

8.4.4   TOOL SUPPORT

A problem today is that there is no graphical tool for use in representing component behavior of an architecture specification, as defined in this chapter. Some tools provide some capability in this regard, such as the Object Constraint Language and iContract (see Chapter 4, "Tools, Relationships, and RM-ODP Standard," for more discussion).

RM-ODP provides the modeling languages to specify component behavior. This takes the form of a contract, policies, template definition, environment contract, and rules of behavioral compatibility.

Szyperski talks of designing by using a contract for composition. The Eiffel language [Meyer-97] provides a language to express some aspects of a contract, including exception handling. The language is not complete.

Work is progressing in OMG to map the RM-ODP model concepts and rules onto UML model artifacts [EDOC-UML, EDOC-UMLb]. These mapping rules will result in exactly what UML models and associated artifacts to use to capture the RM-ODP constructs of behavior. Buy using UML in this precisely defined way, the consistency across the models will be realized by the underlying consistency across the viewpoints of RM-ODP, thereby minimizing mismatch of model integration.

Hopefully, these UML constructs will find their way into the marketplace as part of one or more vendor UML products.

8.5   ARCHITECTURAL MISMATCH

Systems today are often constructed by gluing COTS products together. However, COTS products are typically very difficult to plug together, even when they originate from the same vendor. The system developer then has to create "glue" to enable COTS products to plug together. This "glue" becomes complex, large, and in the end may still result in a system that does not perform according to expectations, or may not work at all. It is not an easy or simple task to plug together various products (COTS or custom developed) even though the functionality seems to indicate compatibility is achievable. It's the side effects that result in incompatible products.

Architectural mismatch has become a subject of great importance in determining the composability of systems and of architectural models. The term "architecture mismatch" was originally coined by Professor Garlan of Carnegie Mellon University [Garlan-95a]. It deals with the inability to combine or compose components of an architecture based on adverse behavior. In essence, mismatch deals with semantic conflicts or conflicts in engineering mechanisms, as a result of incompatibilities, inconsistencies, and incompleteness of behavior that adversely affect or prevent composability.

Mismatches occur when the semantic behavior of a component is insufficiently defined to enable the architect or system implementer to detect a conflict in composition, resulting in clashes between components. These mismatches happen during both composing system components and composing system model views. [Egyed] For example, each of two components of the system may expect absolute guaranteed usage of a single control object. When composing these components into a single system, unexpected behavior (a clash) may arise if the single control object is not multithreaded or cannot handle simultaneous interactions with two different components. A mismatch has occurred.

To deal with the complexity of a system, the architect will use models of specific views of the system, as is the case with the Unified Modeling Language (UML) models. The views of the UML models address different stakeholder concerns. The Use Case model, for example, helps communicate the role of the system to the business stakeholder. The Deployment model helps communicate the system topology, hardware, and software allocation to the system implementer. In model methodologies such as UML, composing the models into a consistent, complete, compatible model often results in side effects that result in mismatches affecting the resultant system implementation. [Egyed-99] For example, when a new class is added to the Logical model in UML, the architect may also have to deal with adding that class or instance in many different views. If the architect identifies a constraint in a UML model using a stereotype or note, that artifact will not carry forth to other models. Hence, the architect must manually insert that artifact in every model affected, hoping the consistency is manually achieved. Mismatches in models, therefore, generally are about incomplete, inconsistent, and incorrect information.

In software architecture today, a great deal of current emphasis is placed on dynamic architecture, in which components are dynamically defined and composed into the system. Of course, for this to happen, the components must adhere to a particular architectural style (e.g., C2 [C2]) and be compatible with the specified behavior of the surrounding components, also specified in the same language. What is important here is to understand that behavior plays a key role in the composability of a system, whether that component is statically or dynamically defined. Functional or structural specification for a component is insufficient for components to "plug and play" in a runtime environment.

In the case of system components, a lack of behavior specificity can result in mismatch. In the case of view composition, the lack of consistency of concepts, rules, and often an overabundance of extraneous information increases the complexity of the model, which in turn leads to a poorly defined, unreadable, and non-understandable system model. And this can result in model mismatch.

RM-ODP helps alleviate the mismatch problem at both levels:

1. Component-based integration minimizing component interaction mismatches through the specification of semantic behavior and the rules of composition

2. Model integration through the precise specification of concepts and rules for use in modeling the system at various levels of abstraction, within various epochs

Let us look at an example of an airline reservation system, which actually has a lot of similarity to hospital admissions. Figure 8.10 shows an initial abstraction of the components that could be part of such a system, and their interactions.

A Use Case provides a representation of the overall objective. The Logical view provides more detail, such as the specification of a policy that applies across all parts of this system. A composition is represented as a UML package. However, note that a UML package is not a first-class entity in UML, and as such does not really represent the full composition rules of RM-ODP. But, for purposes of this example, it will suffice.

Much is unknown at the Use Case view about the details of the components and their interactions. However, potential mismatches can still be identified. For example, presumably, multiple clients will simultaneously interact with the Reservation Service (RS) component, and yet each Client must assume a full independent session with the RS component. To mitigate such a mismatch, a session monitor may be introduced to manage the multithreading to the RS component. In addition, to maintain the state of the reservation (which would be an invariant con-

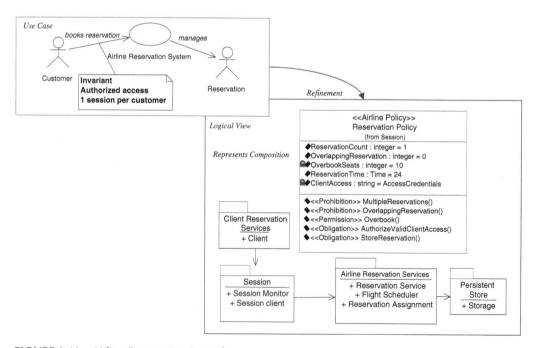

FIGURE 8.10   Airline Reservation Example

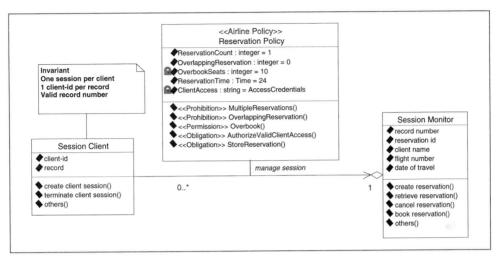

FIGURE 8.11   Adding a Session Monitor Constrained by a Reservation Policy

straint), each RS component session monitor may need to be replicated in case of failure. A reservation policy may be defined to apply to the session monitor. The relationship of the policy to these added components (session monitor) could be as shown in Figure 8.11.

Then, each Client may require an additional interface to its own Client Session component to maintain the state of the session. Multithreading, persistent state, session management, and session control are all part of the specified behaviors for such a system. Given these behaviors, a possible resultant system may be represented in UML as shown in Figure 8.12.

If any of these components share data, such as the Client ID or the Reservation ID, backtracking of the component could lead to a serious mismatch. Here, backtracking describes the path selected to solve a problem where the solution for one subproblem affects a later subproblem, the path is backtracked to a different subpath to attempt to recursively solve a subproblem, and so on. Solving a subproblem and then backtracking without rollback of previous solutions can lead to a serious mismatch. Database technology typically allows for rollback of a transaction if some subproblem is not solved, returning the database to its former state. Rollback restores any subproblem solutions; backtracking does not necessarily. [Gacek-98a]

The Storage component must, then, be able to distinguish different input sources, provide concurrency control, transaction management, and fault tolerance. As can be seen, each detected mismatch appears to result in additional components and interactions in the system and model of the system.

Of note is the importance of the current work on mismatch, and its limitations. Mismatch is important to identify risk in the system, and to attempt to mit-

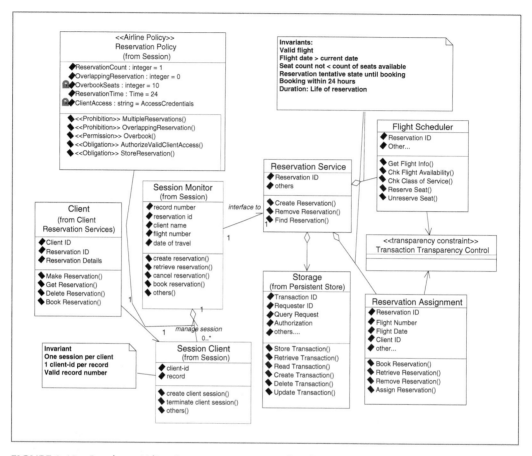

FIGURE 8.12   Resultant Airline Reservation System with Behavior

igate it before the system is implemented. To date, however, most mismatch work deals with the system at a detailed level of component interaction. That is, components are already allocated to nodes; interactions are already identified in terms of interface and binding characteristics; QoS details of interface response times are known; etc. But mismatch can be detected in all levels of abstraction, and within all compositions. It remains the task of the architect to "keep a heads up" on possible mismatches, and try to mitigate them before they result in design or implementation mismatches, which will cost more to mitigate. The following list identifies some areas of mismatch to watch out for.

▶ Policy constraints
▶ QoS constraints
▶ Multithreading versus single-threading

▶ Types of interfaces

▶ Types of interactions

▶ Composition rule violation

▶ Composition of object templates resulting in mismatch behavior

▶ Failure and recoverability

▶ Mismatches in environment contracts

▶ Mismatches in sharing of resources

▶ Nondeterministic set of composition actions

▶ Changes in data through backtracking

▶ Epoch time specification differences (different granularities, for example)

In addition, more design-related mismatches have been identified as a result of some research in identifying a set of architectural mismatches based on component interactions. [Gacek-98a]

8.6   MINIMIZING MISMATCH THROUGH BEHAVIOR SPECIFICATION

Sometimes mitigating mismatch is simple; just provide a bridge between the components. Sometimes this work is extremely difficult, if possible at all, because the underlying mechanisms in support of the component, and the behavior of the component, make it difficult or impossible.

The use of RM-ODP roles, types, contracts, environment contract, interface templates, object templates, binding contracts, policies, and invariants define behavior and can offset the unexpected mismatch situations that may occur. Many of the incompatibilities between components can be determined before runtime environment composition.

For example, one of the mismatches identified in [Gacek-98a] is "Incorrect assumption of which instantiation of an object is either sending or receiving a data transfer." With the use of RM-ODP interface template specification, which addresses not only the interface signature but also the behavior and roles assumed when using the interface, this mismatch is minimized or eliminated altogether.

Hence, before the details are known, the architect can use the semantic behavior concepts of RM-ODP to determine what areas are possible mismatch risks, what constraints must be employed in the specification to mitigate system mismatch, and what behavior must be observed in the system to detect mismatch and how to detect it. All of this minimizes architectural mismatch of the system, thereby reducing the risk elements.

In large federated systems, such as finance, health, and telecommunications, mismatch among feature interactions causes adverse effects on the system. If a complete and consistent specification of the features (and their service offerings)

is provided, feature mismatch and interaction problems can be better detected and repaired.

Let's look at some of the behavioral specification techniques defined by RM-ODP.

8.6.1 ROLE

A *role* in RM-ODP is an identifier for a behavior. So, for example, a "client" is a role that identifies the behavior of the object for some client interaction in an interface. Another example previously used is that of "billing," which is a role assumed by an object. A role is of a type; it's a set of statements.

There is a big difference between a client/server system and a system constructed of objects assuming the role of client or server. In the former case, there is a physical division of services that define a client (or server), that are traditionally placed on certain types of platforms (a client is associated with a workstation; and a server is associated with a mid-tier computer). The server is never the client, and the client is never the server. In RM-ODP, no such distinction is made. An object, in fact, can be both a client and a server. The placement of the object on a workstation or mid-tier platform is not discussed during the specification; only at the point of the technology viewpoint is it defined. This is the difference between a physical separation of services (client services versus server services) and role-based services. Figure 8.13 exemplifies these differences.

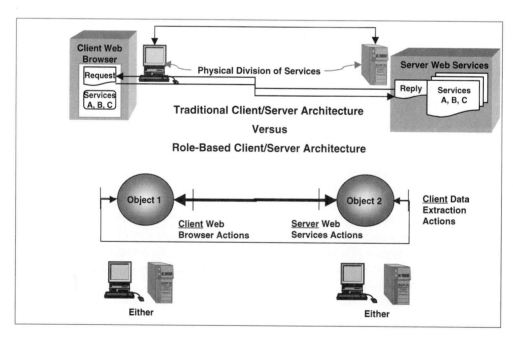

FIGURE 8.13 Client/Server vs. Role-Based Client/Server Concepts

The definition of role is not as specific as other concepts in RM-ODP. A *role* is a placeholder for a portion of a specification that allows a behavior to be instantiated in some way. Each role stands as a placeholder for an enterprise instance. Roles are defined by the architect. They can be such things as a *user, administrator, security officer, database broker*, or whatever behavior is expected of that object.

8.6.2 TYPES AND CLASSES

Type is an important semantic construct. An object has a type; an interface has a type; a parameter in the interface signature has a type; a binding has a type; a relation has a type; and so forth. A *type* is a tool for the architect to specify a characteristic of an entity. A type is an invariant. As such it can determine what must hold true for all things of that type.

In RM-ODP, a type is a predicate. That is, something has a type "X" if you can apply "X" to that thing. The answer will be a Boolean response: yes or no. If it is yes, then that thing has type "X." For example, an Anjou pear has the type "green," a green car has the type "green," but an orange does not have the type "green." Hence, Anjou pear, car, and Granny Smith apple are all of the same type "green," shown in Figure 8.14.

A thing is of a particular type if its properties satisfy (the predicate of) that type. A thing may have several types, which is important to the concept of composition. A thing can assume new types (such as a "component"), or lose a type in a different epoch.

A thing can assume a subtype if the thing satisfies the properties of the type, and the properties of the subtype. Hence, an Anjou pear has the type "green" and may assume the subtype "green fruit," whereas green car has the type "green" but does not have the subtype "green fruit."

Types must match before some action can occur. Therefore, type-matching is almost always a precondition for some action to occur.

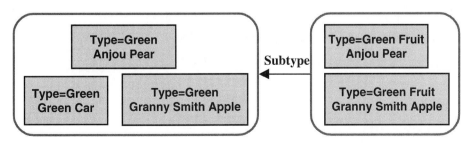

FIGURE 8.14 Type: Things That Are Green

In a common type management domain, where types are allocated in the same manner to things, and are defined in the same language, then it is fairly straightforward to match the type of one thing to another. On the other hand, in different type management domains, it is very difficult. Crossing type management domains involves a pre-precondition to be fulfilled: namely, negotiation across the domains must be accomplished to resolve the manner in which types are defined (the first precondition), and then the types of the things must be determined to match or not (the second precondition).

A class then consists of all those things that satisfy a particular type. In Figure 8.14, all entities form a class of "green" things.

Though these are simple constructs, they are also orthogonal and can result in rather complex relationships. An object can assume multiple types, and therefore participate in multiple classes. Figure 8.15 shows a set of classes, each based on a common type. There are three classes: green, red, and car. The object "green car" assumes the types *green* and *car*. Similarly, the "red car" object assumes the types *red* and *car*. These concepts facilitate well-formed compositions at multiple levels of abstraction.

To recap, a "type" is a predicate (e.g., "it-is-green"). A class consists of all things that satisfy a type (e.g., "All things that are green"). An object can have multiple types and be a member of multiple classes that satisfy that type.

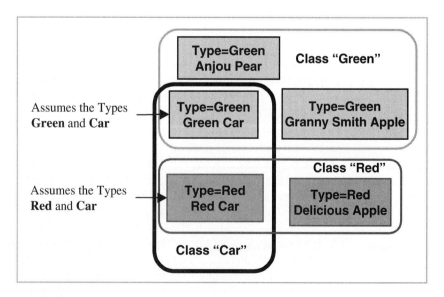

FIGURE 8.15   Multiple Types and Classes

8.6.3   <X> RELATIONSHIP

<X> is a relationship. It refers to or describes either a behavior or a structure among objects. [RM-ODP-2]

<X> is just like the *x* in algebra. In RM-ODP, <X> stands for different things, depending on the concept where it appears. In the case of <X> domain, it stands for a relationship, the "characterizing" relationship. In the case of a type, <X> stands for a type of relationship.

Examples of the kinds of <X> relationships include addressing relationship, where a set of objects are addressed in the same way; naming relationship, where a set of objects are named in the same way; fault tolerant replication group, where a group of objects provides a level of fault tolerance.

Examples of the kinds of <X> type include patient, admitting agent, physician, green, and hospital. In other words, one can ask the question "Is this object an admitting agent?" and get back a yes or no answer. If "yes," the object is of <X=admitting agent> type. If the predicate holds for <admitting agent>, the entity is of type <admitting agent>.

<X> is associated with many things in RM-ODP. Examples are:

▶ <X> domain

▶ <X> template

▶ Type of an <X>

▶ Class of <X>s

8.6.4   TEMPLATE

A *template* is the specification (e.g., of an object or interface) in sufficient detail to be able to instantiate one or more instances from it, as discussed in Chapter 5, "RM-ODP Architecture Model." It is the metadata used to specify the parameters of the item, which includes statements of behavior in terms of constraints and rules associated with actions. A template is a tool used to specify a model of an entity. An instance of a template is instantiated. When an instance of the template is used, the template may be tailored to less capability than the template specification. An interface template, for example, defines the interaction for both roles (e.g., both the "client" and the "server"). When an instance of the template is selected, it may be constrained to only contain the "client" portion of the interaction. When that template instance is instantiated, an interface with the role of "client" is created.

RM-ODP discusses everything in terms of the template. It always includes the behavior to be expected. Figure 8.16 provides an example view of the instantiation from a set of templates. An object template defines its purpose and behavior. The instance results in an object that behaves according to the template. For example, one object template instance is an airline passenger, another object template instance is a server, and two object template instances are selected for the databases in use, defining some part of the airline reservation needs.

The template approach to defining the behavior (functional and well as behavioral) is based in providing a language for specifying RM-ODP concepts. It offers structuring of those concepts so that one can construct RM-ODP–compliant specifications. However, templates are very static and very prescriptive, unless the architect designates that such templates are made dynamically observable and stored in some persistent repository for use in the runtime system.

An object template details the interface templates, the behavioral specification, and a contract with the environment in which the object interacts. The interface template consists of an identifier and one or more interface-type–specific signature templates, each of which in turn consists of the relevant parameter count, names, and types associated with the operations in the interface. Both the interface and object template contain rules (behavior) of what to do on failure, such as an inability to fulfill some quality of service. In Figure 8.16, the interface templates associated with the objects were also instantiated.

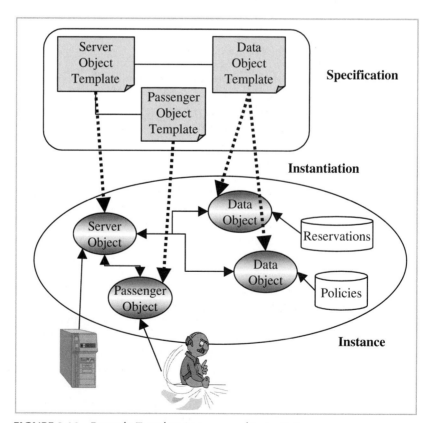

FIGURE 8.16   Example Template Instance and Instantiation

The RM-ODP engineering viewpoint mechanisms to support realizing the distribution transparencies use the engineering interface reference template, which specifies the information required to create an appropriate binding, manage that binding, create an appropriate channel for communication, and reference to the interface to be bound. This template also consists of the transparencies required, location information, relocation information, security information, channel requirements, migration information, quality of service, protocol options, and the behavior expected on a binding.

In addition to object and interface templates, a channel also has a template associated with it. This template specifies the type of channel, the configuration of the objects in the channel, control interface templates, role-interface template pairs, and rules of behavior for the group of objects, as defined by a policy.

The *types of templates* in RM-ODP include an object template, an interface template, a policy template, a composite object template (which was discussed earlier), an engineering interface reference template (which is discussed in detail in Chapter 10, "Hiding System Complexities: Distribution Transparencies"), a channel template, and a binding template; anything that is instantiated and has a type.

RM-ODP does not provide an explicit syntactic specification of either the full content or form for a template. Rather, it provides patterns of reasoning to identify those elements that should form a part of a template specification. Each type of template provides a set of properties for a particular type of entity. Figure 8.17 provides an overview of what properties comprise an object template, an interface template, an engineering interface reference template, a binding object template, and a channel template. In fact, notice that a binding object is an object, and its template is an extension of the "object template." This is done to specify those extra properties important to instantiate a binding object. In the case of the binding object, it must instantiate pairs of interfaces, each associated with a role. Again, these are patterns of reasoning of what should be included in types of templates; these are not explicit specifications of a metamodel for a template. That remains the work of the architect to define, and use consistently across the architecture specification.

There is an important subtle relationship in RM-ODP: the relationships among interface template, interface signature, and an instantiated interface. An interface template specifies an interface signature. A template for an interface signature instantiates the interface signature, not the interface. The interface signature defines the form and behavior of the interface during runtime. It can also be specified in IDL, stored in an Interface Repository for dynamic access and reuse, or merely complied into the objects of the system. It is the interface template, coupled with the behavior specified by the environment contract, that defines how the interface itself is instantiated in the runtime environment and subject to a binding. Hence, Figure 8.18 provides an overview of points in the lifecycle when an interface template is used, when an interface signature is used, and when an interface is created for use.

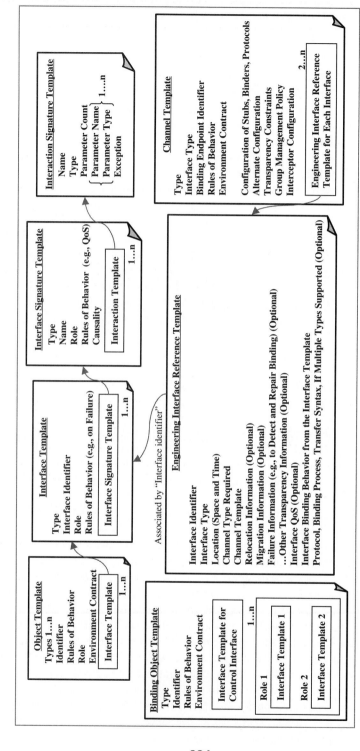

FIGURE 8.17 Templates: Object, Interface, Engineering Interface Reference, Binding Object, and Channel

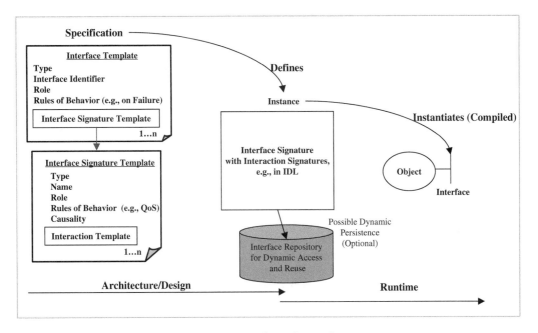

FIGURE 8.18   Template, Interface Signature, and Interface Relations

 WARNING

There are two similar and confusing relationships in RM-ODP: type of template and template type.

A template can have a type, referred to as a *template type*. A template type is the type of the thing (e.g., object template passenger) for which a template is used. A *type of template* is a pattern of templates, such as object templates, interface templates, interaction templates, binding templates, channel templates, and so forth, which are instantiated from its template. This is useful to define a pattern for each type of template, which is then used to specify a specific instance. As an example, consider a signal interface template. The type of template is "interface template." The template type is "signal," referred to as "signal interface template."

```
template type = choice {object, action, interface, policy, contract, …}
type of template = type associated with the thing to be instantiated, such
as {stream interface, signal interface, composite object, object type A,
reservation-policy, failure-policy, …}
```

There is some question in the RM-ODP community if it is possible to define templates for all concepts: policy, contract, community, role, etc. Ongoing work in the further specification of the Enterprise Viewpoint language [ISO-EntVP] includes templates for enterprise communities, for example. The debate rages on, but an architect can choose to define such templates for a specification. The architecture specification only needs to specify the functioning and behavior captured in such a template in order for that entity to be instantiated from the template.

RM-ODP does not consider the case where a template is constructed dynamically, and instantiated at some time. RM-ODP does not prohibit this case either. It is simply not addressed.

8.6.5   CONTRACTS

A contract specifies behavior common to a configuration of objects, and thus tells the environment the behavior to expect. A contract is an agreement among objects that governs what can, should, and should not be done, and governs the behavior of the interaction among the objects. It is a general concept in RM-ODP and defines the behavior not only of interacting objects, but also objects and the environment in which they exist. A general contract is applicable to objects, interfaces, environments, at certain reference points, etc.; in other words, wherever behavior must be agreed to.

QoS here is application end-to-end. It includes not just real-time considerations but also deadlines (temporal), throughput, availability, reliability, maintainability, security, and safety. A QoS standard for a framework to specify QoS is now emerging, and will be discussed in Chapter 17, "Quality of Service Model."

The contract embodies the rules that constrain the interactions, within a specified timeframe. Generally a contract is explicitly defined. It includes such things as:

▶ Configuration of objects

▶ The roles an object may assume, and the expected behavior of the object in each role

▶ Interfaces associated with each role

▶ The quality of service properties that govern an interaction, such as characteristics of probability of a communication error, probability of a system failure, latency, dependability, correctness, safety, security, and others

▶ The behavior that invalidates a contract, such as some action that is not allowed

▶ Duration or length of time for which the contract is valid

▶ Policies of permission, obligation, and prohibition that govern actions

An object template is a form of a contract. The object template defines the behavior of all objects instantiated from that template, and what the environment may assume about the objects and their behavior.

Instantiation of a contract results in a composite object representing a community of interacting objects, assuming certain roles, possibly constrained by one or more policies defined in the contract. This is shown in Figure 8.19. The concept of a contract can be used to specify a community for instantiation. This use of a template is being explored further in [ISO-EntVP]. To do so, the contract should cover the agreed upon:

▶ Objective of the community

▶ Type of community, including the processes performed by members of the community to fulfill the objective

▶ Configuration of components (or objects) and types

▶ Roles assumed by the components

▶ Relationship among the roles assumed, and how they relate to the processes

▶ Behavior of the components assuming the role

▶ Policies that apply to the components, and which applies to what component action

The community of objects satisfies some objective, defined by the contract and constrained by the contract. That is, a contract establishes the agreed upon behavior of interacting objects. What the architect might use as a metamodel for a contract, including an environment contract discussed in the next section, is shown in Figure 8.20.

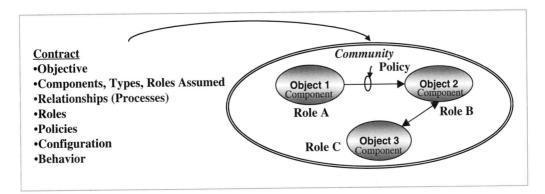

FIGURE 8.19   Contract Instantiating a Community

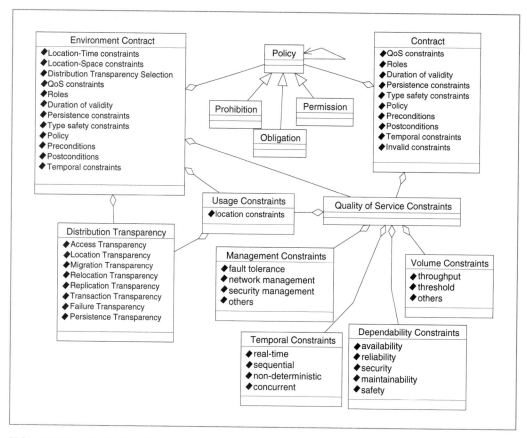

FIGURE 8.20   UML Model for a Contract and Environment Contract

8.6.6   ENVIRONMENT CONTRACT

An *environment contract* is a contract between an object (which can also be a composite object) and its environment. The environment contract constrains the behavior of an object and the environment in which the object acts.

Environment contract: is a contract formulated between an object and its environment which contstrains the environment as well as the object within that environment. This particular contract addresses such things as QoS, resource usage, and other constraints. [RM-ODP-2]

The environment contract defines the rules placed by the object on its environment, and the rules the environment places on the object. Considerations of quality of service constraints, requirements for the environment to support the correct behavior of the object, constraints on the actions of the object in a correct environment, resource usage, and management constraints are all examples of what might be included.

An environment contract includes specifications of:

- QoS
  - End-to-end
  - Deadlines (temporal)
  - Throughput
  - Availability
  - Reliability
  - Maintainability
  - Security
  - Safety
- Constraints on use and management
  - Location in time and space
  - Distribution transparency

Usage constraints consist of location constraints in time and space, as well as selection of one or more of the eight distribution transparencies, which is addressed in Chapter 10, "Hiding System Complexities: Distribution Transparencies."

An example of an object behavior constraint is that it only use a certain amount of resources (such as threads, or memory, or bandwidth). An example of an environment behavior is that it provides sufficient on-demand resources required by the object when it engages in a binding. As another example, if the object is constrained to perform within a certain latency (say, 10ms), then the environment must provide sufficient resources to enable the object to react within 10ms. If the environment cannot, this is considered a violation of the contract, and a failure can occur. Hence, environment constraints are two-way: constraints on the object in the environment, and constraints on the environment to support the object.

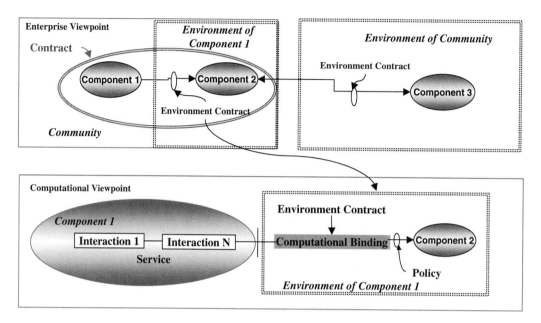

FIGURE 8.21   Application of Environment Contract

The all-important environment contract leads directly to analysis and possible mitigation of mismatch and composability. Figure 8.21 provides a view of where an environment contract is applied. It is not only applicable to cross-community interaction, but also constrains (or enables) the behavior of an object and its interaction with another object. This latter point is very important in the behavior specification of an architecture. What it says is that there is a specification technique to define the behavior of interactions between objects. The architect can choose to expose this in the runtime system, thereby enabling better mismatch detection and mitigation. The architect should at least capture environment contract details on the interactions within the architecture specification, to more explicitly define that behavior.

The impact of this figure should be clear: semantics defines not only the behavior of interaction, but also the behavior of the environment in which an interaction takes place. The environment contract in the enterprise specification is also part of the computational viewpoint. In this figure, a particular policy applies to the computational binding of component 2 with component 1.

A binding contract is an example of an environment contract. It establishes the behavior to be agreed upon across a binding. The binding contract includes such things as:

▶ Engineering interface references and roles assumed
▶ Binding type (related to the interface type)

▶ QoS to be realized across the binding
▶ Any of the distributed transparency specifications to be honored
▶ Actions to perform:
  – Instantiate/delete interfaces
  – Start/stop flows
  – Change QoS
  – Change interface location
  – Monitor events
  – Others
▶ Binding policies, such as naming, type-matching, and others

8.6.7   POLICY

RM-ODP uses the concept of *policy* to capture the rules on the interactions between objects, and to define actions. The rules define what is obligated, permitted, and prohibited from happening.

To achieve valid access control could be stated in a security policy, for example. A fault tolerant policy, for example, could identify the objects to be addressed, the constraints on the actions, an indication of validity for which the policy holds, and possibly other properties. The architect determines the form of a policy. The pattern for a policy could be as the metamodel represented in Figure 8.22. A possible usage of such a metamodel is also shown, for an airline policy that, among other things, keeps private the count of seats it is permitted to overbook. Each action identified as part of the policy must be further refined into a set of actions, and then into a set of interface signatures. This shows how a policy might be specified, using stereotypes on the policy and on the actions of the policy.

Policy is addressed in Chapter 14, "Policy Framework." A small description of the parts of a policy is repeated here:

▶ An *obligation* defines the behavior that is required.
▶ A *permission* defines the behavior that is allowed to occur.
▶ A *prohibition* defines the behavior that must not occur.

Figure 8.23 shows a UML representation of some airline policies, how the architect might relate the policies, and specify them. The policy constraints are represented as attributes. The policy actions are represented as operations. Each of these policies could then be associated with the part of the airline reservation system, where appropriate, as also shown in Figure 8.12.

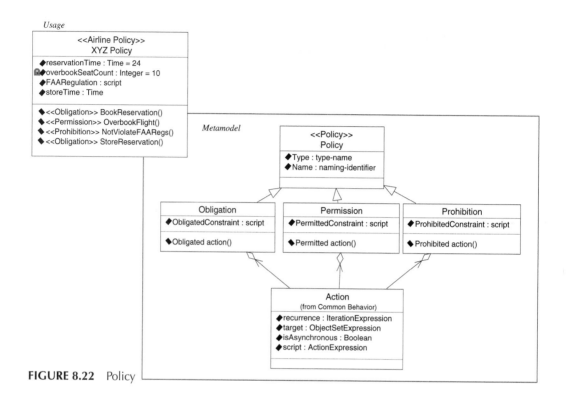

FIGURE 8.22   Policy

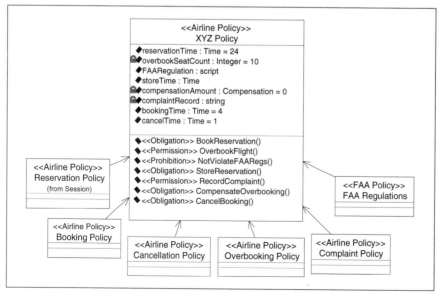

FIGURE 8.23   Example Airline Policy Relationships in UML

A policy can stand-alone, or form part of a contract specification. A contract consists of a number of behavior properties, including one or more policies. Figure 8.24 shows the relationships between a contract specification and a policy in UML. The use of a policy was shown in previous figures.

The architect determines what makes sense to specify for a policy. The architect can choose to use the template construct to capture the policy statements and instantiate the policy from the template. The architect can determine the level of detail to specify in a policy. Furthermore, it makes sense to type and subtype policies. A policy could be typed "fault tolerant," and all refined policies from that type form a class of "fault tolerant dependable" policies. This is a very useful construct for specifying the behavior of a system, as constrained by the policies of the system.

Furthermore, as policies are captured explicitly, the potential of mismatch across policies can be minimized. If explicit, someone or some tool can analyze the obligations, prohibitions, and permissions to determine if an inconsistency (mismatch) occurs in the composition of policies. This is a very useful concept for specifying a more robust architecture. The more that is specified, the better the explicit behavior of the system that is captured.

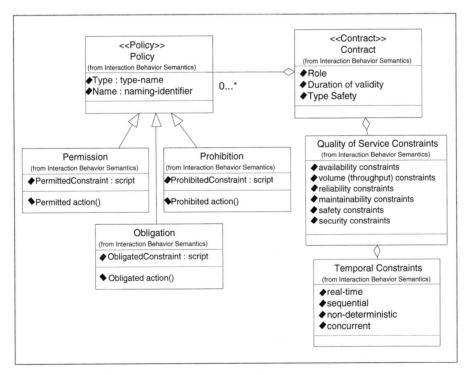

FIGURE 8.24 Policy Related to Contract in UML

In emerging work today, there is a great deal of focus on policy managers, and infrastructure components that controls and manages policies within a distributed system. Work in federation is addressing cross-domain policy negotiation, in terms of the policies of naming, type-matching, security, fault tolerance, and so forth.

8.6.8 INVARIANTS

 POINT

One of the hallmarks of RM-ODP is the capability of specifying those semantics of the system that do not change, over some timeframe. These types of behavior semantics are captured as invariants.

Invariants define what must remain unchangeable across two or more objects, over some specified time. Invariants can enable or constrain a relationship between objects. Invariants also generally involve existence dependencies or property derivations. The Information Viewpoint invariant schema is used to capture invariants in the specification.

In addition to RM-ODP, another international standard has emerged that describes relationships between objects in a precise and consistent manner. This is the ISO General Relationship Model [ISO-GRM]. It describes much in the way of behavioral semantics, invariants, and relationships. It is based on RM-ODP.

 NOTE

An *invariant* is "a logical predicate that must remain true during some scope. A scope may be the lifetime of a managed relationship or the execution of a relationship management operation." [ISO-GRM]

A *relationship* is "a collection of objects together with an invariant referring to the properties of the objects." [ISO-GRM]

Examples of relationships include the preconditions and postconditions of an operation such as "establishing a bind" operation. An example of a generic relationship is "composition," which was addressed earlier. QoS is another one of the behaviors the architect can specify. It is an important one because it provides the ability to define how the system is expected and contracted to perform, under specified circumstances, according to the rules of the contract. A QoS may be specified as an invariant over the lifetime of a binding, for example, constraining the allowable latency in the binding.

Invariants vary widely, and are completely up to the architect to define for the system. They can be very simple or quite complex.

An example of an invariant is the Chief Financial Officer (CFO) Act of 1990. CFO compliance states that all organizations whose systems contain financial data must abide by the Act. This means that any external application desiring to interact with a financial application must adhere to the federal financial management laws before acceptance of an interaction. This clearly constrains the way the interaction with an external object takes place; a policy describing the rules of the Act must be associated with each such interaction, and failure modes associated with each violation.

Let's look at an example use of invariants (and policy). A system is defined for reservations of airline XYZ. A client makes a reservation on airline XYZ with the following details:

- Passenger name
- Originating departure date
- Originating departure time
- Originating departure city
- Originating destination city
- Originating flight number
- Return date
- Return departure time
- Return departure city
- Return destination city
- Return flight number

A system specification that supports airline reservations needs to ensure that the departure date precedes the return date. The system needs to also make sure that the airline has an aircraft that flies between the departure city and destination city, for both the originating and returning portions. The system needs to make sure the reservation is successfully put into the system, and that the available seats on the aircraft is reduced by the number of passengers (in this case, one) for the reservation. The system must also make sure that the passenger holds no other reservation on either the originating or return dates for the same destination. The system must also determine a great many other details such as cost, time when the reservation will be ticketed, payment, and so forth.

A UML package diagram might be represented as in Figure 8.25. Note that a "reservation policy" is depicted. This should be represented as an association class; however, UML does not allow an association class to be associated with a dependency between packages. Nevertheless, the reservation policy would apply throughout.

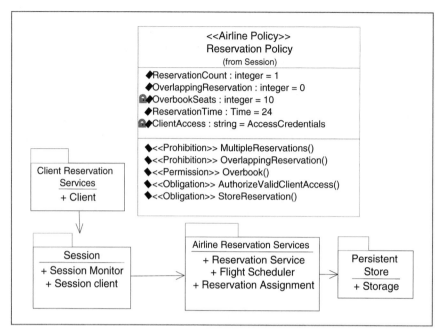

FIGURE 8.25   UML Airline Reservation System Package Diagram

An expansion of each of these packages results in Figure 8.26. Here, invariants are represented as notes. These are not UML modeling constructs, and as such, do not carry from one model to another. Therefore, invariants must be manually re-entered in the various UML diagrams.

In this example, the invariants could be as follows, some of which are depicted in the figure:

▶ The flight number must be valid.

▶ The flight date must be greater than the current date.

▶ The seat count available must be less than the total count of seats.

▶ The reservation must be associated with a "tentative" state until booked.

▶ The reservation must be booked within 24 hours.

▶ There is a 1-to-1 mapping between each client and reservation for a particular travel date and time.

▶ The reservation must persist.

▶ The reservation must be associated with a unique reservation number.

▶ A client can only be associated with at most one reservation session.

▶ The origination reservation must reduce the available seats on the flight by one.

> The return reservation must reduce the available seats on the flight by one.

> The available seats on any flight must be no less than zero (although some airlines overbook reservations, so this number may be negative. (Notice that the policy indicates overbooking is allowed. To mitigate this conflict, the invariant takes precedence.)

> The reservation departure date must precede or equal the return date.

> The duration is the life of the availability of all schedulable reservations.

In order to support these invariants, however, the architect probably needs to specify additional components and interfaces for the reservation capabilities shown (although this is not always the case). A session manager is shown to maintain client state, within the constraints of the invariants. A repository is shown to make the reservation persistent. The architect may also specify a repository of flight, passenger count, and passenger list elements for each available flight and that is accessible only through proper access controls, which is not shown. The architect may specify to have a seat allocation system that allocates a passenger to a flight, and reduces the available seats by one, which is not shown. The architect

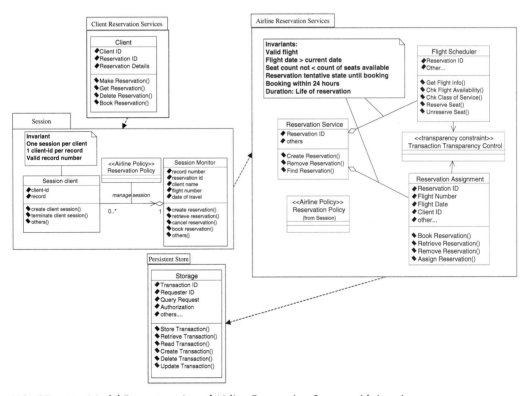

FIGURE 8.26   Model Representation of Airline Reservation System with Invariants

may specify a system that can check for duplicate reservations across all flights that day to the destination city, which is not shown. But the architect does need to specify the management and coordination of these actions in the system.

The architect can specify such a system in terms of the compositions shown, as represented by the packages, or as represented by the classes in each package. This is totally dependent on the architectural design. The invariants specify a portion of the behavior of such composite objects. The use of the Object Constraint Language (OCL) also provides a means of formalizing the invariants. One can attach an OCL statement as a note in a UML diagram to better represent such a constraint. However, once again, the note is not a UML model construct so that analysis of the model does not take the content of a note into account.

The invariants are handled by the objects offering the associated interface. If an invariant is violated, an appropriate exception is raised, and appropriate action taken by the object or some other object in the system (such as terminating the session). It is important to notice that specifying the invariants of a system drives the behavior of the objects and the interfaces provided by those objects. Explicitly specifying the invariants communicates from the architect to the implementer exactly the behavior to be designed and implemented. Otherwise, the behavior may be designed by the designer without ever explicitly defining it. And if the designer leaves, the system will behave in a manner for which there is no record. The stakeholders certainly do not want that to happen!

[Kilov-94, Kilov-97] provide a wonderful treatment on invariants, and a great deal of detail on the use of invariants, and specification techniques.

8.6.9 REPRESENTING BEHAVIOR IN IDL SPECIFICATION

An example IDL specification for the airline reservation system is provided, to show how invariants could be specified and realized in an interface specification using IDL. Of importance is to note that, though IDL is a structure definition, English text is also used to specify expected behavior of the objects using the interfaces. Through the use of IDL constructs, and English text for specification of the meanings of various constructs, the architect can fairly successfully specify an interface structure and behavior using IDL.

```
IDL Sample for Airline Reservation System
module ReservationServices {

    interface CreateReservation;
    interface CancelReservation;
    interface RetrieveReservation;
    interface AssignReservation;
    interface BookReservation;
    interface RemoveReservation;
    interface GetFlightInfo;
```

```
interface CheckFlightAvailability;
interface CreateSession;
interface TerminateSession;

typedef string ReservationId;             //Record number for a reservation
typedef string ReservationLocatorID;      //Locator identification for
                                                //reservation template
typedef string FlightID;                  //Flight Number
typedef string Aircraft;                   //Aircraft type and number
typedef integer Seats                     //Count of seats available for booking

struct Reservation {
    ReservationId   resv-orig_id;     //Unique Origination Reservation Identifier
    ReservationId   resv-ret_id;      //Unique Return Reservation Identifier
    string          passenger_name;   //Name of Passenger
    string          notes_ref;        //Conversation Notes
    Date            start_date;       //Origination date of travel
    FlightInfo      orig_flight;      //Origination flight number
    Date            end_date;         //Return date of travel
    FlightInfo      return_flight;    //Return flight number
    };
typedef sequence<Reservation> Passenger_List;

struct FlightInfo {
    FlightID        flight_id;        //Unique Flight Number
    Seats           seat_count;       //Total count of seats available
    Time            departure_time;   //Time of departure
    string          crew_ref;         //Crew Information Reference
    Aircraft        aircraft_type;    //Type of aircraft
    };

struct SeatAvail {
    FlightInfo flightinfo;        //Can verify flight id and obtain seat_count
    Seats      available_seats;  //Dynamically changing count of available seats
    };

struct FlightInfo {
    FlightID        flight_id;        //Flight Number
    Passenger_List  passenger_list;   //List of passengers
    };

// The invariants when violated will minimally raise exceptions across
// the interface.
// Some of these exceptions are captured below:

exception InvalidDate {//The return date precedes the origination date
    string error_msg;
    Date start_date;
    Date end_date;
      };

exception NoReservation {//There is no reservation for that person with the
                    //flight details given
```

```
            string error_msg; };

    exception UnknownResvID { //Invalid reservation ID passed
            string error_msg; };

    exception InvalidFlightID { //Invalid flight number passed
            string error_msg; };

    exception NoSeats {//There are no more seats available for the designated
                       //flight details given.
            string error_msg; };

    exception PermissionDenied {//The reservationist does not have the permissions
                                //to create a reservation.
            string error_msg; };

    exception SeatReservationDenied {//The change in seat count detected an error.
                                     //Hence, the reservation cannot be made.
            string error_msg;
            Seats avail_seats; };

    exception MultiplePassengerReservations { //The invariant is that the passenger
                                              //cannot book multiple reservations to or
                                              //from the same city for the same time, or
                                              //within the same timeframe: This invariant
                                              //prohibits overlapping reservations
            string error_msg; };
    exception MultiplePassengerSession { //The invariant is that the client id session
                                         //can only occur at one time
            string error_msg; };

    // Note - Invariants: There must be an available seat to assign;
    // the client_id must have permissions to assign a seat;
    // there must be a valid reservation identifier

    typedef IR string; //Interface Reference ID to a Session Client
                       //(which should be a full struct to an interface
                       //template, but will not be shown here

    interface CreateSession {
       IR open_session {
            in string client_id,
            in string accessperms,
            in string passenger_name,
            out IR interface_ref_id)
            raises (PermissionDenied, MultiplePassengerSession);
    };

    interface CreateReservation {
       unsigned long get_reservation_template () //Retrieve blank reservation form
       ReservationLocatorID create_reservation (
            in string passenger_name,
            in ReservationID resv_orig_id,
```

```
            in ReservationID resv_ret_id,
            in string notes_ref,
            in Date start_date,
            in Date end_date,
            in FlightInfo orig_flight,
            in FlightInfo return_flight,
            out ReservationLocatorID)
            raises (InvalidDate, NoSeats, PermissionDenied, SeatReservationDenied);
//Create reservation object
CancelReservation cancel_reserv();
};

interface BookReservation {
    void book_flight (
        in ReservationLocatorID resv_id )//A number of invariants are tested for
                                //in the component that handles this interface
        raises (MultiplePassengerReservations, PermissionDenied, UnknownResvID);
};

interface GetFlightInfo {
    FlightInfo get_info (
        in FlightID flightnumber,
        out FlightInfo flightinfo) //gets the flight information
                                //for the reservation
        raises (InvalidFlightID, PermissionDenied)
};

interface RetrieveReservation {
// not expanded here: retrieves a previously booked or assigned reservation
    raises (NoReservation, PermissionDenied);
};

interface AssignReservation {
    void assign_reservation (
        in ReservationID resv_orig_id,
        in ReservationID resv_ret_id)
        raises (SeatReservationDenied,NoSeats,NoReservation,PermissionDenied);
        //Post the persistent list of reservations associated with this flight
    void post_reservation(in Passenger_List passenger_name)
        raises (BadReservationList, PermissionDenied);
};

interface CancelReservation {
    RemoveReservation remove_res(
        in ReservationLocatorID res_id)
        raises (UnknownResvID, PermissionDenied);
};

interface RemoveReservation {
    void remove_reservation (
        in ReservationLocatorID res_id)
        raises (UnknownResvID, PermissionDenied);
    void remove_reservation(in Passenger_List passenger_name)
        raises (BadReservationList, PermissionDenied);
```

```
   };

   interface CheckFlightAvailability {
      Seat get_avail_seats (
            in FlightInfo flight,
            in Date date,
            out Seats seat)
            raises (NoSeats, PermissionDenied, SeatReservationDenied);
   };

   interface TerminateSession { //Close the session, destroy Session Client
      void close_session( in IR interface_ref_id);
   };

};   //end of Reservation Services
```

8.6.10   QUALITY OF SERVICE

QoS is a property that defines how the behavior of one or more objects will provide a certain desired level of quality. Quality is concerned with such things as bandwidth, latency, probability of failure, probability of resource consumption, and so forth. Quality is also concerned with timeliness to achieve some processing, timeliness to receive some data, quality of presentation of information, quality of the results of a mediation, etc. That is, wherever quality of processing is important, a QoS requirement is placed on the behavior of the objects involved.

QoS also addresses issues of some of the "ilities." Availability is an example. It can be provided through the use of one or more distribution transparencies (see Chapter 10, "Hiding System Complexities: Distribution Transparencies"). It need not be associated only with reliability metrics associated with the interaction. Other examples of a QoS are correctness of type-matching across typing domains, or naming across naming domains. In essence, quality applies to many things in an architecture, from a user's need to see a Web page within a few seconds to a real-time constraint on an embedded system. The architect decides what is important to specify.

QoS can apply to relations associated with Enterprise Viewpoint communities, to real-time latency issues across a communication portal. It is up to the architect to determine where rules of QoS apply, how those rules are refined into lower levels of QoS parameters, additional components in the system, and additional interaction among components. This topic is discussed in Chapter 17, "Quality of Service Model."

8.7   SUMMARY

Semantic behavior is crucial to a working system that meets on the one hand the objectives of the customer, and on the other hand the needs of the user. Semantics means "meaning." Behavior means "a set of actions and their constraints."

Architecting a large-scale "system of systems" requires that mismatch be addressed with respect to semantic behavior (as well as functional behavior).

Behavior is addressed by the structuring rules of abstraction and refinement, composition and decomposition, as well as by the semantic rules of type, class, template, policy, contract, quality of service, and role. Multiple levels of abstraction help to focus on the areas of concern, postponing other detail issues to a later point in the architecture specification. These methods enable a well-formed architecture specification to be created.

Composition addresses combining common entities into a single entity in order to discuss their attributes. Rules of composition address how behavior is composed, what can be composed, and how a composite object is addressed. RM-ODP allows all sorts of things to be composed: objects, interfaces, interactions, behavior, templates, policies, and even communities. This is a terrific tool for the architect to drill down into the important properties of something, without worrying about the internal details (yet).

One of the principal mismatches is behavior. Representing behavior in a precise manner can minimize architectural mismatch, since mismatch typically involves undefined incompatibilities and inconsistencies of component behavior. The appropriate level of architectural specification will define what can and cannot be composed. The architect can then architect in additional constraints, additional exception handling, mediation of the inconsistencies, additional components in the infrastructure (such as a control monitor), or some other mitigating technique.

The result of attempting to compose architectural styles is mitigating "mismatch": addressing some functional or behavioral incompatibility between the composition elements. The architecture foci on a large system must address semantic behavior to offset the potential for mismatch, no matter if that mismatch is at the design level or higher levels of abstractions. COTS products come with whatever specification they choose. Selecting COTS products, therefore, results in not architecting the COTS system, but architecting the bridgeware to minimize some functional and behavioral incompatibility between them. This often leads to conflicts in system properties, such as the "ilities," QoS, performance, etc. When these properties are not clearly specified in an architecture, ambiguous component relationships result, which in turn makes the job of bridging the disparities in the relationships very difficult. Then, of course, design choices, technology choices, and product choices compound all of this.

In the dynamic binding and dynamic architecture environments, runtime assessment of the specification metadata will enable determination if two components can be composed and retain the integrity of the system, or if an exception should be generated instead. The ability to parameterize behavior and represent it in the dynamic system as additional system processing metadata enhances "plug and play" and support for dynamic architecture.

The need to recognize behavior as part of all interactions, components, and systems, results in a need for behavior modeling expression through levels of abstraction, and a more focused effort on composition of all things. Behavior specification includes a specification of constraints on the behavior of the environment.

Two components must be behaviorally compatible for mismatch to be minimized. This means that behavior must address existence, compatibility, availability, failure modes, and invariants. Invariants, pre- and postactions, rules of behavior with the environment, and rules of behavior of component interactions are the different kinds of constraints related to interacting components.

To mitigate some of the behavioral mismatches, this book uses a model represented in the UML, though some of the semantic behaviors to be architected into the system can not be explicitly captured in UML. Hence, the UML models presented have attempted to consistently represent how a particular behavior can be described in UML. Clearly, the need to specify semantic behavior in models is necessary. To parameterize such behavior so that it can be dynamically analyzed and managed results in better composition evaluation. However, dynamic semantic behavior parameterization is still state-of-the-art, and in need of much more work from the software architecture and UML vendor communities.

A solid set of precisely defined concepts, as provided by RM-ODP, with specification methods at varying levels of abstraction and composition, will lead to a better architecture specification and understanding of potential architecture mismatch.

The mitigation techniques that can provide a reasonable software architecture today still fall short of the techniques that are generally needed to support all of the user community's needs. Tools are needed to aid the architect in architecting and to provide adequate analysis and architectural tradeoffs. The architecture community needs to solidify on concepts and rules across the spectrum of architecting.

The process of architecting still remains ad hoc; however, the process should fold in how the system (or system of systems) functions, as well as how it behaves in its automated environment, within disparate organizational enterprises or disparate domains of the enterprise. The software architecture research community is just beginning to address this. And RM-ODP already provides the foundation for use.

For an excellent discussion on semantic behavior, especially invariants, see [Kilov-94, Kilov-97, ECOOP-97a, ECOOP-97b, ECOOP-98a, ECOOP-98b]. For an excellent discussion of composability characteristics, see the work by Professor Barry Boehm, Professor Christina Gacek, and Professor Abd Allah [Gacek-Boehm, Boehm-92, Abd-Allah-95, Abd-Allah-96, Gacek-98, Gacek-97]. For excellent discussions on formal approaches to behavior and specification see [Clarke-96], [Jackson-96], [Liskov-94], [Liskov-99], [Moormann-97], [Wing-95], [Wing-98a], [Wing-98b], [Wing-98c], [Wing-99]. Recent work in addressing different ways of abstracting areas of concern can be found in aspect-oriented programming [Kiczales], adaptive programming [Mezini], and role modeling [Andersen]. For an excellent discussion of abstraction, see [Shaw-95]. Additional work about multidimensional separation of concerns is to be presented at OOPSLA 2000. Considerable work is ongoing to define approaches to using abstraction and refinement in an architecture specification that best provides the focus of distributed processing systems.

NINE

RM-ODP FUNCTIONS

In this chapter, the Reference Model of Open Distributed Processing (RM-ODP) functions are addressed in some depth. Addressed are:

▶ The purpose of the RM-ODP functions

▶ Open specification

▶ Interrelationships of functions, and supported distribution transparencies

▶ Patterns of reasoning for ODP functions

9.1   PURPOSE OF THE RM-ODP FUNCTIONS

RM-ODP defines a set of functions necessary to support distributed processing that is open and interoperable across different systems. That is, these are functions that describe the behavior of a set of services in support of distribution and processing in such a way that any system is able to interoperate with any other system as long as the rules and concepts defined by the function are adhered to.

The ODP functions are generic functions, enabling heterogeneous solutions of distributed processing systems and providing interoperable distributed processing capabilities (not just communication). These generic functions allow the architect to choose cost-effective technologies for these functions, at once solving a particular business requirement and allowing the system to interoperate with other ODP-compliant systems.

The RM-ODP functions are basic services necessary to support an ODP system. These functions identify the requirements for the infrastructure services. The functions support the distribution transparencies, management of the node, management of communications, and so forth. In addition, these functions enable a number of system properties, such as accessibility, load balancing, transaction management, persistence, and security.

Each function in RM-ODP is defined in terms of required concepts and processing rules and the required behavior to be specified. However, none of the functions are defined in terms of an actual design; rather, they provide patterns of reasoning for the architect to use about what must happen and how. The specification of the function is left for further standardization through an ODP component-based standard, such as the Trading standard [ISO-Trading].

Nevertheless, because RM-ODP is a reference model, for each function it defines the concepts and rules, the behavior, the structure, and the interdependencies on other functions. This is similar, for example, to the way the Object Management Group's (OMG) Object Management Architecture (OMA) defines what is meant by the "object services," what is accomplished in that layer, and how that layer interacts with the common services in other layers.

9.2   OPEN SPECIFICATION: RM-ODP COMPONENT STANDARDS

The actual specification for each ODP function results in what is termed a *component* or *component composition standard*, each of which forms the specification of the interrelationships and use of a set of components to achieve some distributed processing capability. In no case is an actual design or implementation provided. Instead, the use of the enterprise, information, and computational languages are used. Sometimes the engineering language will also be used to formulate some important engineering construct. Each of these standards therefore enables different implementation approaches as new technologies mature. Over time, as new technologies mature, additional RM-ODP standards can emerge to achieve some additional provision of an ODP requirement.

For example, in Chapter 6, "Separation of Concerns: Using RM-ODP Viewpoints," a representation of "record patient record" was shown as part of the engineering specification. In fact, RM-ODP functions are needed to support that capability, but the architect does not need to specify the details of the functions; this is accomplished by the standard for that function. The architect merely needs to identify its use in the architecture engineering specification, as is shown in Figure 9.1. Here, two ODP functions are used: engineering interface reference tracking (EIRT) function to locate and track interfaces in the system; and storage function to manage persistent storage, such as through a database management

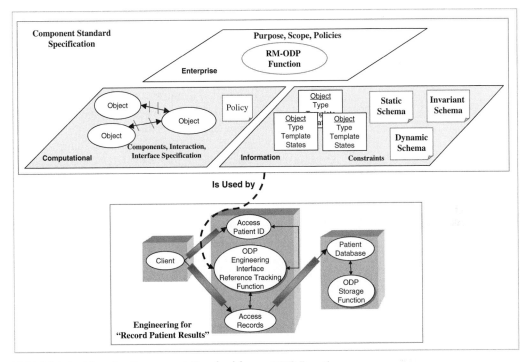

FIGURE 9.1   Use of a Component Standard for an ODP Function

system (DBMS). Both are a result of a component standard specification using the engineering, information, and computational specifications. This is shown for the function "engineering interface reference tracking function," which is discussed later in this chapter. The bottom portion of the figure represents how the architect takes a component standard for a function and uses it by referring to the function and, typically, the actual standard reference.

Because of the nature of the International Organization for Standardization (ISO), each of these RM-ODP standards results in an open specification of some provision for distributed processing, with open interface specifications and specified behavior specifications. This results in a suite of standards that enable distributed processing to be open, composed, and to minimize mismatch. They will result in "plug and play" distributed processing components.

For example, RM-ODP includes a component standard for Trading. [ISO-Trading] The OMG Trader specification is a specialization of the RM-ODP ISO Trading standard. "The concept of a component composition standard corresponds closely to the concept of a specification of an object framework as introduced in the recent revision of the OMA Reference Model." [Wood-97]

Different domains can specialize the use of this suite of standards since neither design nor technology are addressed in the specification. This is an important capability. A business domain, such as medical, can use the standards to formulate a design across the domain that will be open and interoperable across the systems in that domain. The telecommunications domain has done just that with their Telecommunications Information Network Architecture (TINA)-C specification.

OMG's Common Object Request Broker Architecture (CORBA) specification (and suite of object services) is another example of a specialization of RM-ODP. There are certain functions defined as services in OMG for use with CORBA. Some of these services are specializations of the RM-ODP functions. Some of the RM-ODP functions are being developed through the standards committees, using a service of the OMG. One example is the ODP Type Repository function, which is founded on the OMG Meta Object Facility (MOF) service [OMG MOF]. Hence, there is a liaison between some of the OMG specifications and the ISO work on ODP standards.

Domain-specific distributed systems can be specified using the RM-ODP framework; the RM-ODP functions; the concepts of federation, transparency, system management; and reference points to support the composition of the ODP functions from different implementations. The result will greatly enhance the interoperability of systems.

Each ODP function standard provides an example of using the viewpoint languages for an architectural specification that an architect may wish to investigate for reuse. Some of these RM-ODP functions are shown in Table 9.1.

TABLE 9.1   RM-ODP Functions Standards

ODP FUNCTION	STANDARD	ITU-REC	ISO/IEC	PUBLICATION DATE
Engineering Interface Reference Tracking	Information technology—Open Distributed Processing—Interface references and binding [ISO-IRB]	X.930	14753	1998
Trading	Information technology—Open Distributed Processing—Trading function: Specification [ISO-Trading]	X.950	13235-1	1997
Type Repository	Information technology—Open Distributed Processing—Type repository function [ISO-TR]	X.960	14769	June 1999

Over time, the RM-ODP suite of component standards will include all of the ODP functions, as well as other standards important for distributed processing, such as the current work on a full enterprise viewpoint standard to augment what RM-ODP itself specifies. [ISO-EntVP] The result will be a full reference model (RM-ODP) and a framework of standards to achieve open distributed systems.

9.3   RM-ODP FUNCTION CATEGORIES AND FUNCTION DEPENDENCIES

Each function in RM-ODP provides a pattern of reasoning. Each consists of a set of subfunctions along with an explanation of use, rules about its structure and behavior, and other functions on which it depends. The complete set of ODP functions are grouped into four major categories:

1. Management functions include the RM-ODP functions Node Management, Object Management, Cluster Management, and Capsule Management functions.
2. Coordination functions include Event Notification, Checkpoint/Recovery, Deactivation/Reactivation, Group, Replication, Migration, EIRT, and Transaction functions.
3. Repository functions include Storage, Information Organization, Relocation, Type Repository, and Trading functions.
4. Security functions include Access Control, Security Audit, Authentication, Integrity, Confidentiality, Nonrepudiation, and Key Management functions.

The architect specifies the use of an ODP function in the engineering specification, to provide distribution, transparencies, resource management, node management, communication, and processing. Recall that an engineering specification is expressed in terms of a configuration of engineering objects in terms of clusters, capsules, and nodes; interaction among these engineering objects; activities that each engineering object performs; and semantic behavior of what is expected of these engineering objects. In addition, the ODP functions include a definition of the roles assumed by the different engineering objects in support of the function capabilities. A function-specific policy defines the function constraints.

The exception to this is the Trading function. The use of this function is specified in the computational specification. It provides many of the capabilities of the computational binding object, for example. Similarly, the *use of* the distribution transparencies (covered in Chapter 10, "Hiding System Complexities: Distribution Transparencies") is specified in the computational language. But the way in which they are used, and the way in which the ODP function supports the transparency, is an engineering specification concern. The way in which distribution itself is provided, supported by the ODP functions, is also part of the engineering specification.

RM-ODP does not clearly delineate the interdependencies of the ODP functions. One reason is to allow the architect to specify the use of the ODP functions to achieve some distributed capability. An example of this is Fault Tolerance (see Chapter 16, "RM-ODP Fault Tolerance Framework"). Another reason is an insufficient specification of the use of the RM-ODP functions. However, Table 9.2 provides these interdependencies and shows all the RM-ODP functions, the other functions that may be required to support the functionality, and the distribution transparencies that are enabled by the function. A full discussion of each of the distribution transparencies can be found in Chapter 10, "Hiding System Complexities: Distribution Transparencies."

TABLE 9.2   Dependencies of ODP Functions and Support for Transparencies

ODP FUNCTION	USES	TRANSPARENCY SUPPORTED
Management Functions:		
Node	None	All
Object	Node	All
Cluster	Node, Object, EIRT, Storage	All
Capsule	Node, Cluster	All
Coordination Functions:		
Event Notification	Node, Group, Replication, Transaction	Failure
Checkpoint/Recovery	Node, Object, Cluster, Capsule, Storage	Failure
Deactivation/Reactivation	Node, Object, Cluster, Capsule, Storage	Failure, Migration
Group	Node	Failure
Replication	Node	Replication, Failure
Migration	Node, Cluster, Capsule, Replication, Deactivation/ Reactivation	Migration, Failure
Engineering Interface Reference Tracking (EIRT)	Node, Event Notification	Location, Access, Failure, Migration, Replication, Relocation
Transaction	Node, Object	Transaction

TABLE 9.2 Dependencies of ODP Functions and Support for Transparencies (Continued)

ODP FUNCTION	USES	TRANSPARENCY SUPPORTED
Repository Functions:		
Storage	Node	Failure, Persistence
Information Organization	Node	
Relocation	Node, EIRT	Relocation
Type Repository	Node	
Trading	Node, Type Repository	
Security Functions:		
Access Control	Node	Access
Security Audit	Node	
Authentication	Node, Key Management	
Integrity	Node, Authentication	
Confidentiality	Node, Authentication	
Nonrepudiation	Node, Integrity, Authentication	
Key Management	Node	

An ODP function may also depend on another ODP function. The relationship among the 24 ODP functions is depicted in Figure 9.2, and further discussed in the remainder of this chapter. The direction of the arrow is to be interpreted as "depends on." So, for example, Trading depends on Type Repository, as shown in the line between them. The discussion of the RM-ODP functions is derived from [RM-ODP-3].

WARNING Part 3 of RM-ODP does not fully address the ODP function interdependencies. Sometimes a dependency is noted in one function description, and not noted in the dependent function description. Unfortunately, an analysis of the ODP function descriptions in RM-ODP is required to build an interdependency graph,.

A discussion of the ODP functions and the patterns of reasoning provided by each is presented next. As a guide, Figure 9.3 provides a generic overview of how the ODP function is configured in a node. A policy is specific to a function,

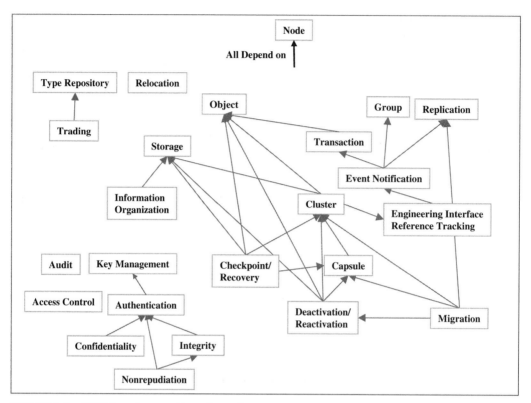

FIGURE 9.2   ODP Functions and Interdependencies

and constrains (or enables) certain capabilities of that function. Engineering objects subject to the function must usually provide an interface to a distinguished control object in the infrastructure. This object, in turn, manages many of the interactions among the ODP functions, as well as interaction with the basic management functions of the node.

The architect specifies the use of the function, as well as how the function is activated. The architect can elect to specify that the function acts dynamically, such as "migrate a filed cluster to a more stable state for fault tolerance reasons." Perhaps some functions are invoked through a system administrator interface specified by the architect. An example of this is to "migrate and relocate server software to another node," which would invoke both the Migration and Relocation functions. The architect can also choose to specify that the function continually performs its actions, such as "continually checkpoint certain mission-critical software every 10 minutes." How the function is used is an architectural decision. The architect also specifies the policies that constrain the actions of the function. The property values of the policy, however, may be administrated in some cases, such as which checkpoint to use. These are all architectural decisions.

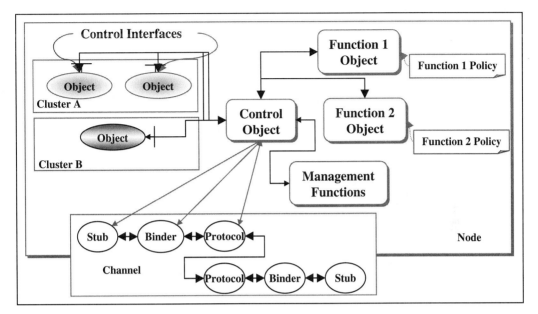

FIGURE 9.3 Generic ODP Function Configuration

9.4 MANAGEMENT FUNCTIONS

The Management functions include Node Management, Object Management, Cluster Management, and Capsule Management functions. These functions manage the engineering elements of the node. They describe the structure and functionality of the node, nucleus, capsule, and clusters, capsule manager, and cluster manager.

9.4.1 NODE MANAGEMENT

The ODP Node Management function is similar to the operating system functions in support of the node, in that it manages the processing, storage, and communications of the node. It discusses what fundamental properties are required, how to instantiate a binding or an object, and how to allocate resources.

The Node Management function provides the fundamental organization of the node: the computer, in terms of hardware and software, resource management, time and scheduling, and instantiation of objects, interfaces, bindings, functions, and so forth. An engineering object interface is used to bind it to its node.

The nucleus of the node provides the management functionality. Among the resources it manages are the clusters, capsules, and channels. Management here means it creates, deletes, and performs consistency management for these node elements. In addition, the Node Management function also manages threads, interfaces, clocks, and timers. Threads are created, synchronized, joined, and delayed through the functionality of the Node Management function.

Figure 9.4 provides an overview of the interface structure that enables the node management function to manage the resources in the system.

To create a capsule, the Node Manager also creates a capsule manager object, along with an interface to it. The Node Manager provides a unique interface reference for the capsule manager to use to allocate resources, create and delete objects, create and delete channels, create and delete bindings, timer functions (such as access to the current time; start, deactivate, and monitor timers), and clock functions, all in support of the elements of the capsule. The Node Manager also allocates processing, storage, and communication resources for the capsule.

When the Node Manager creates (or deletes) an interface and binding, it establishes the channel of the correct type required for the interfaces, creates the binding engineering interface reference for binding objects to the channel, establishes (or manages the establishment of) the binding, and provides the ability to access a Trading function object. The Node Manager is also responsible for establishing the correct configuration of objects in the channel (through the use of the interface template of the objects that wish to communicate), to include providing

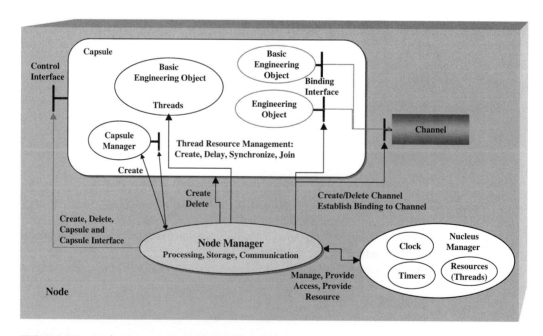

FIGURE 9.4   Node Management Interface Structure

access to one or more interceptor objects. All of these actions support the needs of the capsule, and the engineering objects in the capsule.

The capsule itself provides the Node Manager with an interface to use to delete the capsule and all engineering objects within it, which can occur for failure or migration reasons.

All other ODP functions depend on the Node Management function.

9.4.2 OBJECT MANAGEMENT

The ODP Object Management function is used to delete basic engineering objects, all associated channel objects, and all associated bindings of the object, in a cluster. Any channel in use by one of these engineering objects is deleted as well. This function also provides the management interface of the engineering objects in order to checkpoint the object and its interface(s) to a stable state, which is used by a number of other ODP functions. This interface is also used to delete the object.

The ODP functions that use the Object Management function are Cluster Management, Transaction, Deactivation/Reactivation, and Checkpoint/Recovery.

Object Management depends on the Node Management function.

9.4.3 CLUSTER MANAGEMENT

The ODP Cluster Management function is provided by a cluster manager object using a cluster management interface. The cluster manager provides checkpoint, recovery, deactivation, replacement, deletion, and migration of its cluster. The ODP Cluster Management function also provides for deleting its cluster, all objects, bindings, and channels associated with the cluster and the cluster manager itself.

Cluster management functions are enabled through a cluster management policy. This policy directs, for example, that each engineering object in the cluster provides an object manager interface, which allows the checkpoint function to act on the engineering object in the cluster.

To checkpoint a cluster, the cluster manager provides information about the configuration of the engineering objects and their interfaces, and makes this information available to the Checkpoint/Recovery function object. To migrate a cluster to another cluster, the cluster manager must interact with the Migration function to provide information about the cluster used for migration, and must interact with the capsule manager object to allow the cluster to be migrated and activated. Once accomplished, the original or source cluster is deactivated. Deleting a cluster means that all objects, interfaces, bindings, channel stubs, and binders are deleted, as is the cluster manager object itself.

As another example, the policy may direct the cluster manager to allow the capsule manager to reactivate the cluster from one of its checkpoints, or recover the cluster, on error. Actually, the cluster manager can recover the cluster as well. The cluster manager can also deactivate its cluster. In this case, it can provide a checkpoint of the cluster and all of the objects and interfaces in the cluster, delete all the objects, interfaces, and channels, then delete the cluster itself.

The ODP Storage function is used by this function for storage of checkpoints. Several of the other ODP functions depend on the Cluster Management function. These include the Capsule Management, Deactivation and Reactivation, Checkpoint and Recovery, and Migration functions. The Cluster Management function depends on the Node Management, Object Management, Storage, and Engineering Interface Reference Tracking functions.

9.4.4   CAPSULE MANAGEMENT

The ODP Capsule Management function is used to instantiate, checkpoint, deactivate, delete, and reactivate clusters within a capsule. It also provides the functions to recover a capsule. Like the Cluster Management function, the Capsule Management function identifies a capsule manager, and associated management interface, to accomplish the functions of this ODP function. The capsule manager is able to perform these functions, such as deactivate, on all clusters in the capsule. The capsule manager is also able to delete the capsule (and all clusters in it) and the capsule manager itself.

Associated with this ODP function is a capsule management policy, to direct what can and cannot be done to the clusters.

Capsule Management depends on the Node Management and Cluster Management functions, and is used by the Migration, Deactivation and Reactivation, and Checkpoint and Recovery functions.

9.5   COORDINATION FUNCTIONS

Coordination functions include Event Notification, Checkpoint and Recovery, Deactivation and Reactivation, Group, Replication, Migration, Engineering Interface Reference Tracking, and Transaction functions. These functions are used to manage and coordinate the actions of objects, clusters, and capsules to maintain a consistent state of the node, and to manage interfaces and transactions. This includes management and movement of elements in the engineering structure. For example, migration addresses the movement of an object.

To accomplish the Coordination function, RM-ODP identifies the need for a distinguished engineering object in the infrastructure to manage the steps involved in the coordination of the functions. This engineering object may in fact be a composite object, which is an architectural decision. This object is identified as the "Control object" here, though RM-ODP gives it no name. The pattern of reasoning for this object is as follows.

Control Object

To provide for several properties in the infrastructure, such as stability, availability, and load balancing, an engineering object must provide a control interface for binding to a Control object. The Control object specifies the interactions supported across this interface. In the case of fault tolerance, for example, the Control object may initiate the checkpoint and actions to checkpoint the internal state of the object. It may also be a principal in detecting a failure, or checking for some security capability. It may be used by the binder to inform the system of a binding failure, and the recovery action. As discussed further in Chapter 15, "Federation," multiple domains can be federated through interaction of these Control objects, one in each domain. These Control objects can address the federation policies, the scope of the domains, the rules of interaction, and uses of the channel for mediation and negotiation across the domains. The Control object also interacts with most of the ODP function objects, as well as the transparency objects.

The Control object can consist of one or more objects, as defined by a specific architecture, can be replicated across multiple nodes, or exist only within a single node. RM-ODP does not dictate a particular structure; rather, it defines what needs to be done, how to specify choices of actions, and what interactions need to occur to restore the system to a stable state. In other words, RM-ODP provides a pattern of reasoning for specifying a Control object, its interfaces, and its actions. The important points are that there is an engineering object (or composite object of a set of engineering objects) that manages the coordination of the ODP functions, and that every engineering object must provide a special Control object interface to bind to it.

9.5.1 EVENT NOTIFICATION

The ODP Event Notification function manages events and event histories. It supports access to and update of this information by other objects. When an event occurs, an object that acts in the role of an event producer records the event in an event history. An object that acts in the role of an event consumer is notified of the event, and is allowed to access the event history.

An event notification policy drives the allowable capabilities of this ODP function, and addresses:

▶ Event history types
▶ The object that can create an event history
▶ The object or objects that are notified of an event
▶ When the object is notified of an event
▶ The action(s) that causes notification

- The storage for the event history to make it persistent
- Stability requirements for event histories
- The length of time events are retained

In the case of fault tolerance, the Control object can be informed of failure events. The Control object can in turn interact with the Event Notification function object to notify other objects or cluster and capsule managers of an event, such as a failure or recovery event.

Event Notification depends on the Node Management, Replication, Transaction, and Group ODP functions. The Transaction and Replication functions support the persistence of the event histories. The Group function provides for ordering of event notifications. The Event Notification function may support the EIRT function to notify objects about changes in the location of an interface.

9.5.2   CHECKPOINT AND RECOVERY

The ODP Checkpoint and Recovery function is important to maintain a valid stable state of the objects, clusters, and capsules in the node. The Checkpoint/Recovery function provides sufficient detail of the object or group of objects so that the infrastructure can restore the state of the objects and recover them to a stable environment. The Checkpoint and Recovery function provides the functionality to checkpoint an object (or a cluster of objects) to a stable state, and then recover that object (or cluster of objects) to a previously checkpointed state, defined by the checkpoint/recovery policy.

This function may be used for movement of a cluster and objects. This includes checkpoint to a state, migrate the cluster, and recover the cluster and objects to the checkpointed state. A checkpoint/recovery policy directs what is to be performed. It should also state where the checkpoints are stored, and under what circumstances a cluster (and objects) should be checkpointed or recovered.

This function depends on the Node, Storage (for the checkpoints), Capsule Management, and Cluster Management functions. It is not used by any other ODP function directly, though in the use of this function, other ODP functions may be associated with it. Such is the case for Fault Tolerance, where the Checkpoint/Recovery function may be used in conjunction with the Migration, Relocation, and other functions (see Chapter 16, "RM-ODP Fault Tolerance Framework").

As always, behavior is defined through a checkpoint/recovery policy. The policy includes:

- When an object or cluster should be checkpointed
- When that object or cluster should be recovered
- What should be checkpointed

- Where the recovery should occur
- Where the checkpoints are stored
- Which checkpoint is used for recovery, and which others to use if that fails
- Duration of validity of the checkpoints
- What security policy, if any, affects the Checkpoint/Recovery function (such as applicable to the storage of the checkpoints)

In other words, the policy (or set of policies) defines what actions, under what conditions, will be performed to checkpoint and recover.

The action of checkpointing is the capability of the Control object in the infrastructure that manages these actions for each object or cluster. To checkpoint an object or a group of objects requires that each such object instantiate an interface for use by this Control object in the node. This object coordinates the actions of checkpoint and the actions of recovery. The steps defined in RM-ODP include the following:

Setup:

- Define the objects of interest to the object that performs the Checkpoint/Recovery functions.
- Each object must define a specific control interface for use by a control object in the infrastructure.
- Instantiate a binding to the control interface of the object(s).

Repeated Steps:

- Obtain a checkpoint for each object of interest.
- Construct a group checkpoint for all objects of the group, and make this group checkpoint persistent by storing it.
- Repeat these steps for all groups of objects (clusters) that participate in coordinated activities with the group, depending on the rules of the policy statements and the following consistency rules:
  - The group of objects must be in a stable state before it is checkpointed.
  - The other groups of objects must be consistent with respect to the initial checkpointed group before they are checkpointed (that is, all of the checkpoints of all of the groups reflect the same set of stable interactions having occurred).
- When the group of objects is checkpointed, all other groups having checkpoint constraints with the group must be checkpointed as well, recursively, to result in a closed set of groups that can be consistently checkpointed (and later recovered).

To recover a group of objects, RM-ODP defines the following steps: The group can be recovered to the same environment in which it was checkpointed or to another perhaps more stable environment. That is, if the recovery to the same environment repeatedly fails, the policy may state to select another environment in which to recover the group (or object). To recover an object group, the previous group must have been removed or deactivated (perhaps as a result of a failure recovery set of actions), and the new object group reactivated to a specified checkpoint.

9.5.3 DEACTIVATION AND REACTIVATION

The ODP Deactivation/Reactivation function focuses on a cluster of objects. Its function is to support movement of a cluster from one capsule to another. When a cluster is moved, it is reactivated. Reactivating a cluster involves recovering the state of all the objects to a previously checkpointed state, and instantiating a cluster manager object for the reactivated cluster.

The Deactivation function is used to delete a cluster or it can be used to simply delete a cluster or it may be used to delete a failed cluster, once that cluster is migrated to a new environment and reactivated to a specific checkpoint. The environment of the reactivated cluster and deactivated cluster can be the same or they can be different. Sometimes the system administrator may want to reactivate and deactivate a cluster to a new environment, or even a new node, for load-balancing reasons.

The Deactivation/Reactivation function is governed by a deactivation/reactivation policy. It defines:

- When clusters can be deactivated
- Where the checkpoint is to be stored
- When clusters can be reactivated
- What functions are performed on the reactivated cluster
- What functions are performed on the deactivated cluster
- What object is notified of reactivation
- What object is notified of deactivation
- Which checkpoint must be used
- Where clusters are to be reactivated
- Security policy affecting this policy

The Deactivation/Reactivation function depends on the Node Management, Object Management, Cluster Management, and Storage functions. It is used by the Migration function (to migrate or move a cluster and its objects).

9.5.4 GROUP

The ODP Group function provides the management and coordination of a group of interacting objects. This function is useful for multimedia and multipoint bindings.

A number of policies direct the capabilities of this function:

▶ An interaction policy identifies the objects that can participate in the group interaction as well as the order of the interactions.

▶ A membership policy controls what objects form the group and the management of those objects.

▶ A collation policy manages the consistency of the interactions in the case of a failure.

The Group function depends on the Node Management function and is used by the Event Notification function.

9.5.5 REPLICATION

The ODP Replication function clones an object or object group, and all of its interfaces, for purposes of enhanced performance: faster access, load balancing, reliability, etc.

The Replication function acts on replicas, where each object of the group is behaviorally compatible and is instantiated from the same object template. That is, it replicates an object or object group, and the resultant group (of replicated objects) is called a *replica group*. This function ensures that the replica group acts as though it were a single object. It does this by making sure that all interactions and the order in which the interactions occur are the same for each object in the replica. When the Replication function acts on a cluster of objects, the cluster as a whole is replicated into identical clusters. The objects in each replicated cluster form the replica group. That is, a replicated cluster of objects is a coordinated set of replica groups.

A replica policy defines how the function is to behave. It includes:

▶ Replica group membership
▶ Authority for membership
▶ Which object has the authority to define membership of the replica group
▶ Rules of placement of the replica objects
▶ Rules of adding to the replica group
▶ Rules of leaving the replica group
▶ Actions on a cluster of objects

The ODP Replication function is important to replication transparency.

The Replication function depends on the Node Management function and is used by the Event Notification and Migration functions.

9.5.6   MIGRATION

The ODP Migration function provides the ability to move (or migrate) an object and its interfaces, or a group of objects and their interfaces. If a cluster is migrated to a new capsule, all objects of the cluster are also moved to the new capsule. All interfaces of the objects are also moved, though to move bound interfaces is not the function. That is the action of the Relocation function. Once migrated, any active channel involved is terminated. A new channel, with the same properties, can be reactivated in the new environment.

The Migration function is very useful for changing the configuration of software on nodes. If a number of applications are co-hosted on a single node, for example, and after awhile the resources cannot support the functioning of the node, the application can "migrate" to a different node. Or, perhaps the application is mobile. That is, it moves from one node to another in support of some capability. The Migration function supports this action.

The Migration function supports the management of all the linkages that need to be moved, and re-establishes the existence of the application on the target node. The distribution transparencies can be coupled with this function to hide the movement details from any clients that are using the application, or to hide the movement details of a new location for the interfaces, and so forth.

The Migration function is governed by a migration policy. The policy defines:

▶ When to migrate an object or group of objects

▶ Termination policy of any active channel involved

▶ Instantiation of any new channel, with the same properties

▶ What environment

The Migration function depends on the Node Management, Replication, Cluster Management, Capsule Management, and Deactivation/Reactivation functions.

The Migration function is important to migration transparency.

9.5.7   ENGINEERING INTERFACE REFERENCE TRACKING

The ODP EIRT function maintains the information about the logical and physical interfaces of an object, and manages information about their use. Recall that an engineering interface reference is a logical reference to an interface. It does not resolve the physical address; other infrastructure services provide this action.

When an interface is bound, a physical address is associated with the logical address. It is the EIRT function object that provides and maintains this logical-to-physical interface address mapping, and maintains information about the use of all object interfaces. When an interface is relocated, for example, the EIRT function manages the information about the new location for the interface, relating it to the old location for some period of time. This is similar to the postal mail forwarding information capability when someone changes their residence.

This function also maintains information about the interfaces of an object and manages the information about the use of all object interfaces, including properties of the interface, the type of interactions of the interface, quality of service properties to be adhered to, type of channel for use in binding, and other elements.

In managing the use of an interface, the EIRT function can track when the binding is not available or has failed, and can notify the cluster manager of this in order for it to act (e.g., cleanup).

The policy for the EIRT function defines the actions that take place. It includes:

▶ Which object interfaces to maintain
▶ Information about object interfaces—the engineering interface reference template, including such things as properties of the interface, type of the interactions of the interface, quality of service properties to be adhered to, interface type, required channel properties, and other information
▶ New interface location information
▶ Duration of association of old-to-new interface location
▶ Notification actions on a binding failure

The EIRT depends on the Node Management and Event Notification functions, and is used by the Cluster Management function.

This function is important for the distribution transparencies as well as for the management of the interface references of an object and the cluster of objects. This topic is fully discussed in Chapter 10, "Hiding System Complexities: Distribution Transparencies."

9.5.8 TRANSACTION

The ODP Transaction function manages the consistent behavior, such as concurrent access, of objects whose state may be distributed.

Transaction is an ordered set of actions that causes a set of object state changes. These state changes are in accordance with the dynamic and invariant schemata of the information viewpoint. [RM-ODP-3]

In other words, a transaction is a single basic unit of work. It may require one or more actions to accomplish. A transaction can be reversed if an error occurs in one of the actions. A single transaction could be defined as a set of actions executed in a specified order; e.g., an action to establish a connection, an action to establish access, an action to request some processing, or an action to retrieve the result. The set of actions, an activity, all need to be successful for the transaction to be considered successful. Typically, a transaction uses one or more shared system resources, such as a database management system or a message-oriented middleware (MOM) product, that results in some change to a system property or state. A general ledger is a transaction of services that must be performed in a certain order, for example.

The objective of the ODP Transaction function is to provide to other objects:

▶ Permanence, so that any state changes are stable

▶ Recoverability, so that the transaction be atomic and that on failure, the state of an object is recovered and the details of any inconsistency of the object are identified

▶ Visibility, so that the transaction is isolated from other transactions

▶ Consistency, so that the transaction will be correct and in conformance with the dynamic and invariant schemata of the transaction

These are properties of being atomic, consistent, isolated, and durable (ACID). This is a popular database transaction model. It is also a subset of the capabilities identified for the Transaction function, which is a more generically applicable capability, such as in messaging capabilities provided by a MOM capability.

The ACID properties characterize a transaction in a number of ways.

▶ *Atomicity* means that all actions of the transaction are considered as a single atomic action. If a transaction fails in any way, all preceding actions that comprised the transaction are undone (*rollback*).

▶ *Consistency* means that the transaction will always produce the same result, preserving invariance.

▶ *Isolation* means that a transaction's internal states are separate from other transactions and invisible to them. A transaction may be composed of a complex set of states, and a transaction may execute in series or concurrently. All of this is hidden from other transactions and other parts of the system.

▶ *Durability* means that a transaction is stable, in that the effects of the transaction are reversible and persistent.

The Transaction function is governed by a transaction policy that captures the actions to be started, canceled, committed, aborted, and so on.

Transaction management is a capability that is part of CORBA version 3 [Corba-OTS and Corba3-messaging], and Java™ Transaction Service [JTS]. Other transaction services are provided through MOM products, such as BEA Transaction Processing [BEA-TP] and IBM MQSeries [MQS].

The Transaction function depends on the Node Management and Object Management functions. It may be used by the Event Notification function.

9.6 REPOSITORY FUNCTIONS

ODP Repository functions include Storage, Information Organization, Relocation, Type Repository, and Trading functions. These functions provide repositories of different information: types, persistent store, and service offers (trading). They also manage the movement (through the Relocation function) and the management of interfaces.

9.6.1 STORAGE

The ODP Storage function supports the persistent storage of data and access to that data for purposes of retrieval, modification, and deletion. This function is used by other functions to provide a persistent store of some information. For example, Checkpoint/Recovery may use this function to provide a persistent store of the checkpoints. Event Notification may use this function to provide a persistent store of event histories. Or the architect may specify the use of this function to provide a persistent store of some information about a system (e.g., a store of patient records).

The Storage function depends on the Node Management function, and is used by the Cluster Management, Deactivation/Reactivation, Checkpoint/Recovery, and Information Organization functions.

9.6.2 INFORMATION ORGANIZATION

The ODP Information Organization function deals with the schema of the data. It ensures the data is consistent with the schema, and allows no modifications to the repository or schema that result in inconsistency. It also provides functions to modify, query, and access to the schema and its repository. The query language is not specified in ODP.

The Information Organization function depends on the Node Management and Storage functions. No other function depends on this ODP function, though other functions may make use of it. For example, Checkpoint/Recovery may use this function to manage the checkpoint information; Reactivation may use this function to manage the interface used to reactivate a cluster; Recovery may use this function to manage the interface to recover a cluster.

9.6.3 RELOCATION

The ODP Relocation function provides the ability to move or relocate an interface, primarily focused on a bound interface. The Relocation function maintains a repository of interfaces, and associates locations and changes of locations to those interfaces. An example of such a function is to repair a broken Web browser binding to its server.

The function also maintains the location (and relocation) of groups of objects, not only on a particular node, but also across a set of nodes (perhaps within the same domain). The Relocation function is a key function in the support of mobile systems. Further, this function manages the change of address for not only interfaces but also for clusters, within a node or across a domain.

A Relocator object performs the Relocation function, and manages the location of interfaces, changes in location, and failures in bindings. As such, the binder object may interact with the Relocator object, and by policy, instantiate a new stub or binder to handle recovery of a binding, or it may instantiate a new channel altogether. The binder must interact with the Relocator and other objects to obtain the engineering interface references for use in repairing the binding.

A single Relocator object can interact with one or more interfaces within a single node, or across different nodes or domains. This is a decision made by the architect. If this function is used across domains, however, the interface references must include domain information as well, which is not specified in RM-ODP.

A relocation policy defines:

▶ Communication monitoring rules
▶ Channel rules for repairing a failed binding:
　– Instantiate a new stub
　– Instantiate a new channel
▶ Obtain the engineering interface references

To accomplish the services of this function, the Relocator object is involved in several interactions: It must validate an interface location, it must record a change in location, and it must establish the policy of interaction for use with other ODP functions.

The Relocation function depends on the Node Management function and is important for the relocation transparency.

9.6.4 TYPE REPOSITORY

The ODP Type Repository function is important to maintain persistent type information for use in type checking and trading. Type checking supports all of the interfacing mechanisms, verifying that the types of interfaces are correct, the binding is correct, the channel is correct, and so forth.

Type information is made available through ODP systems to ensure correctness, type safety, and openness. The type of each interface needs to be known, for example, in order to establish a binding between two interfaces; they must be of the same type. For example, Trader must make sure that the service offer matches the type of request from the service requester, and that the interfaces can bind together.

To accomplish type management, this function associates an identifier to each type. This identifier can then be communicated across systems, and across federated domains, to ensure the correctness of distribution.

Type management is not the only function provided. Query for type information, subtyping relationships, and ensuring substitutability are other functions. That is, this ODP function ensures the persistent store of types, and manages type relationships for dynamic checking and eventual binding, and in support of federating systems.

The Type Repository function is currently being formulated as a standard [ISO-TR], based on the OMG Meta Object Facility [OMG-MOF]. This function depends on the Node Management and is used by the Trading function.

9.6.5 TRADING

The ODP Trading function provides a matchmaking "yellow pages" service capability for object service requests, and like a "yellow pages" service, an object must establish a binding to the object offering the service.

The Trading function mediates advertisement and discovery of interfaces. It supports dynamic binding to services. It provides the capability to store service offers, manage the attributes of the service offers, accept service requests, search its service offers to select a service, retrieve a service offer interface reference for use, and reply with a service offer interface reference. A service offer is information about a service, including the service identifier, its interface signatures, and additional information for service discrimination.

An Importer (which is actually a client of a service request, but not in the sense of a client/server architecture) is an object that requests a service, based on specifying a type and certain attributes about the service requested. An Exporter (which is actually a server of a service request, but not in the sense of a client/server architecture) is an object that offers a service for use. And the Trader is an object that matches a service request with a service offered.

The Importer object must then establish a dynamic binding to the Exporter of the service chosen; the Trader is not involved with the actual interaction between the Importer and Exporter objects. It only acts as a matchmaker, to match the request for a service with a service provider. The Trader then provides the service requester (the Importer) with the interface reference to the service provider (the Exporter). This capability is prominent in most vendor ORB products. An overview of the ODP Trading function, provided by the Trader object, is shown in Figure 9.5.

Trading is subject to a trading policy of the domain. A Trader is generally associated with a single administrative domain, although the trading policy can establish a different relationship. The trading policy defines how the import requests are selected from the export offers, how many responses of matched service offers can be provided to the Importer, and so forth. The trading function depends on the Node Management and Type Repository functions.

The first RM-ODP component standard was the Trading standard [ISO-Trading], which is a specification for an object (Trader) to perform the ODP Trading function. The OMG Trader specification is a specialization of this standard, and is specified in terms of the enterprise, information, and computational languages.

The Trading standard also provides a specification for federating traders that is a specialized specification of federation that is provided by RM-ODP.

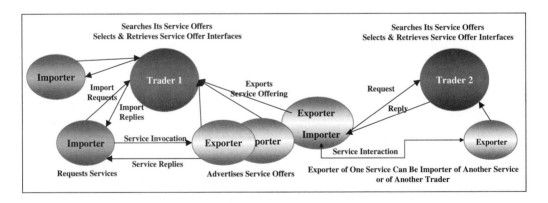

FIGURE 9.5   Trading Service Overview

9.7 SECURITY FUNCTIONS

ODP Security functions manage security and include Access Control, Security Audit, Authentication, Integrity, Confidentiality, Nonrepudiation, and Key Management functions. These functions are based on the OSI Security Frameworks in Open Systems. [Sec-Frmwk and Sec-Arch]

In order to support security in a distributed environment, the security model of RM-ODP extends the normal intranode security mechanisms to interdomain or "enterprise-wide" security. The RM-ODP Security function provides support for delegation of privileges and credentials and for a distributed trusted computing base.

Across all the functions, there are two policies:

1. A security policy that defines the rules for the services, and
2. A security interaction policy that defines the rules for the functions to interact across different security domains. It includes rules to deal with the aspects of different security policies, to allow cross-domain interaction. This may include passing of information to authenticate an object in one domain to another domain, or allowing or prohibiting delegation across domains.

A security authority is a Control object of the domain acting in the role of a security administrator. It is responsible for applying the security policies within a domain. A security domain defines the objects that are subject to the security policy, as administered by the security authority. This is shown in Figure 9.6.

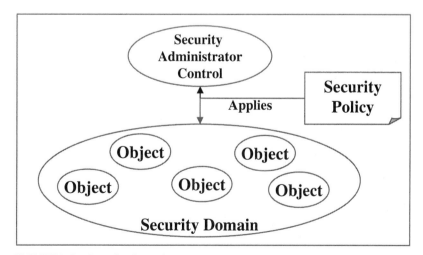

FIGURE 9.6 Security Domain

RM-ODP has specified a minimal Security function capability. Further, the required use of Key Management by all subfunctions is incorrect. Security functions require the use of other security subfunctions, but not Key Management. Where this has been corrected in the discussion below, it is italicized. Furthermore, what is not discussed is how the audit function gets access to all data pertaining to the events involving nonrepudiation. For example, the notary function verifies events, but where that information is stored and how it is accessed are not addressed. How does the adjudicator get that information?

9.7.1   ACCESS CONTROL

Access control ensures authorized interaction with an object, and prohibits unauthorized interaction. An object assumes the role of initiator when it requests an interaction with an object assuming the role of a target. The ODP Access Control function needs the access control privileges of the initiator, target, and the interaction to perform its task.

Delegation is allowed or prohibited, by policy, as part of this function. Delegation is about passing on to another object the ability for that object to perform some task. An object can permit an intermediate object to assume all of its access privileges, to perform a task and for further delegation decisions. By using the composition capabilities of RM-ODP, composite access control allows an intermediate object to assume privileges of a source object. If the privileges are prohibited from being passed, then the delegation cannot be accomplished.

With delegation, the target object receives the privileges allowed from the originating object, as well as the privileges of the intermediate object. This allows the target object to check both sets of privileges and either grant or deny access. Denial of access is enforced as part of the Access Control function as well.

The Access Control function ensures that access control information matches the initiator and target object requests, and will ensure that denied access control is enforced. That is, the target object will only be accessed if the source object has the privileges to do so, independent of any intermediate objects are in the interaction path. More information is provided in [Sec-AC].

9.7.2   SECURITY AUDIT

The ODP Security Audit function collects, monitors, and maintains information pertaining to security-related actions and objects, as defined within a security policy. This function also records, archives, and analyzes audit trails and other security-related information, such as security event notification. Confidentiality, data integrity, accountability, availability, and violations are supported by this function. More information is provided in [Sec-Au].

9.7.3 Authentication

The ODP Authentication function provides verification of the identity of an object. This is accomplished by exchanging and evaluating authentication information.

The roles assumed by an object are:

▶ Principal—the object to be authenticated

▶ Claimant—the object requesting authentication

▶ Trusted third party—the object performing the authentication

There can be one-way, two-way, or multiple exchanges of authentication information between the object initiating the authentication, and the object receiving the request for authentication. This function is defined by the authentication mechanisms in [Sec-A]. All information exchange and the outcome of the authentication request are passed to the Security Audit function.

The ODP Authentication function may use the Key Management function.

9.7.4 Integrity

The ODP Integrity function ensures proper actions (create, change, or delete) on data in order to maintain the reliability of the data. As such, this function monitors the actions on the data, detects any unauthorized actions, and prohibits unauthorized actions. The Integrity function protects data in an interaction between a data originator object and a data recipient object. The data originator object provides an interface to the Integrity function to shield the protected data. The data recipient object provides an interface to the Integrity function to permit it to validate or unshield protected data. The Integrity function ensures that a shield function is provided on any interaction between a data originator object and a data recipient object that includes the protected data. All record of activity performed by this function is passed to the Security Audit function. More information is provided in [Sec-I].

The ODP Integrity function may use the Authentication function.

9.7.5 Confidentiality

The ODP Confidentiality function protects against unauthorized disclosure of information. Confidentiality provides a hide function across the interface to the originator requesting access. It hides the information from the originator to the recipient, and reveals the information at the recipient end. All record of activity performed by this function is passed to the Security Audit function. More information is provided in [Sec-C].

The ODP Confidentiality function may use the Authentication function.

9.7.6   NONREPUDIATION

The ODP Nonrepudiation function makes sure the object involved in an interaction does not deny its involvement. Permanent storage for nonrepudiation evidence, such as audit data, is often required.

There are several roles fulfilled by one or more engineering objects, in support of nonrepudiation. These roles are:

▶ (Nonrepudiable data) originator

▶ (Nonrepudiable data) recipient

▶ Evidence generator—this is the originator of a request as well as the recipient of a request across an interaction. The originator initiates the interaction. The recipient receives the interaction. In both cases, an evidence verifier is used to determine adequacy of the nonrepudiation data received and includes this evidence in an acknowledgement in the interaction.

▶ Evidence user—a recipient role that uses the services of the evidence verifier

▶ Evidence verifier—provides confidence in the nonrepudiation evidence

▶ Nonrepudiation service requester—this is the originator of a request with proof of origin

▶ Notary—this role provides services requested by either the originator or recipient. These services include notarizing, time stamping, certificate monitoring, certification, certificate generation, signature generation, signature verification, and delivery.

▶ Adjudicator—this role resolves any disputes, using the evidence from the originator and recipient, and possibly the notary

The evidence data can be used to prove that a specific originator object initiated a specific action. The recipient uses an object in the role of evidence verifier to ensure the adequacy of the evidence. These subfunctions are defined in [Sec-NR].

The ODP Non-Repudiation function must use both the Integrity and Authentication functions.

9.7.7   KEY MANAGEMENT

The ODP Key Management function manages authentication, identification, and encryption keys. It provides several key-related functions: generation, certification, storage, distribution, deletion, registration, archiving, and de-registration.

There are three roles associated with this function:

1. Certification authority

2. Key distributor

3. Key translator

A key is distributed securely to objects authorized to obtain it, by the key distributor role. Key management information is provided to objects in different security domains, by the key translator role. The actions to create and assign a certification are performed by a trusted third party, the certification authority role, as defined by [Sec-K].

The Key Management function in RM-ODP is incomplete and inaccurate. It only addresses cryptographic keys, and does not identify either identification or encryption keys, important in key management. Further, the Key Management function discusses the use of a certification authority, which actually manages more than just cryptographic keys. The discussion of this function above has augmented that in RM-ODP.

9.8   SUMMARY

RM-ODP specifies a set of 24 ODP functions necessary to support the architecture of an ODP system. These functions are basic services that enable distribution, support distribution transparencies, enable management of the node and resources, provide for a security framework, enable storage management, and so forth.

The architect can choose to specify that the function acts dynamically, such as "deactivate a failed cluster." The architect can choose to specify that the function acts when invoked through a system administrator request, such as "migrate a software system (capsule of objects and clusters) to another node." The architect can also choose to specify the function continually performs its actions, such as "checkpoint a set of mission-critical software objects." However the function is activated, the policies constrain the actions of the function. The architect specifies these policies. The property values of the policy may be administrated in some cases, such as which checkpoint to use.

Each ODP function provides a pattern of reasoning for use by the architect that consists of a description of actions as defined by a policy, along with an explanation of use, rules about its structure and behavior, and other functions upon which it depends. The complete set of ODP functions are grouped into four major categories:

1. Management—includes the ODP functions Node Management, Object Management, Cluster Management, and Capsule Management.
2. Coordination—includes Event Notification, Checkpoint and Recovery, Deactivation and Reactivation, Group, Replication, Migration, Engineering Interface Reference Tracking, and Transaction.

3. Repository—includes Storage, Information Organization, Relocation, Type Repository, and Trading.

4. Security—includes Access Control, Security Audit, Authentication, Integrity, Confidentiality, Nonrepudiation, and Key Management.

All of these functions are subject to further standardization, under the framework of RM-ODP. Many organizations are involved in defining the component standards:

▶ ISO standards committees

▶ Specifications of the OMG

▶ TINA

▶ Others

Each ODP function component standard will use the RM-ODP reference model concepts and rules to specify that standard, and the RM-ODP enterprise, information, and computational languages.

The ODP function standards are open across different technology solutions of the function. These generic functions enable disparate distributed system technologies to be integrated into cost-effective technical system solutions to business requirements, while providing open interaction. RM-ODP adds value by addressing policy, distribution transparency, cross-domain interaction, security, type management, repository management, and the interrelationships among the ODP functions, all in support of the engineering specification of a system.

TEN

HIDING SYSTEM COMPLEXITIES: DISTRIBUTION TRANSPARENCIES

Previous chapters have discussed the very important topic of distribution transparencies at a high level. This chapter will discuss the Reference Model of Open Distributed Processing (RM-ODP) distribution transparencies in depth. Topics addressed include:

▶ Purpose

▶ Several examples of where transparency is used (not necessarily using RM-ODP)

▶ The RM-ODP constructs and structuring rules to realize each of the distribution transparencies, in terms of a pattern of reasoning. Additional information beyond that of RM-ODP is also included

▶ How each of the viewpoints are involved

10.1   PURPOSE

Distribution transparency is a very important topic of RM-ODP because it is a capability that minimizes application development, provides and hides infrastructure services supporting the application, and supports many of the system property requirements beyond the functional requirements (e.g., the "ilities" of interoperability, security, reliability, evolvability, migratability, flexibility, and others).

POINT   One of the hallmarks of RM-ODP is the definition of and patterns of reasoning for distribution transparency.

One purpose of infrastructure is to allow a user or application programmer a great deal of freedom in the formation of the application while at the same time providing as many infrastructure services as possible. When that infrastructure also hides the cumbersome and inevitable distribution details and handling of properties such as location of the objects or movement of an object, the property is termed "distribution transparency." That is, a property of a system is transparent if the user and application programmer do not need to address or be concerned with that property.

The service, in fact, could result in a complex set of infrastructure services physically distributed across a number of heterogeneous systems. But the user does not "see" this; the user sees only the simple use of an interface to the service. The service detail can be hidden from a user, who may simply "invoke" an application from a graphical user interface, or "get access to" a service in the infrastructure, or "access the server to retrieve information," wherever that server is located. From the perspective of the end user, the mechanisms to achieve one of the transparency services are "hidden." So in some sense, the user may see this service as being "transparently" provided; that is, "it just happens."

A second use of transparency is to hide the intricate and often complex details of the infrastructure, its distribution characteristics, and its behavior from the application software. This is the major use for transparency. The application developer does not need to develop a custom version of managing all the distribution aspects of the system to locate and access some service or function. Instead, some generalized reusable version of that service or function, as is provided by the infrastructure, may be relied upon. Further, the application (and hence the application developer) need not be concerned about how something is accomplished. The required components, interactions, and behavior are hidden to make the use of the service simpler.

Transparency, depicted in Figure 10.1, is about freeing an end user or an application developer from having to develop some service or function, while at the same time enabling that service in the infrastructure for reuse by the application. Transparency also frees the end user from the need to invoke a number of individual actions to achieve some service. For example, a single log-on can transparently provide all necessary log-on capabilities to all services in the infrastructure, hiding this from the end user.

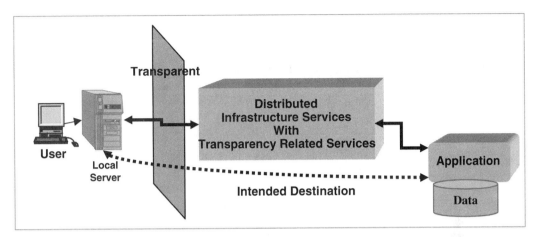

FIGURE 10.1 Distribution Transparency Perspective

RM-ODP defines and specifies eight distribution transparencies. Each of these transparencies is selectable for a system; that is, the architect can choose any number of them for use in a system by specifying them through the constructs of RM-ODP. Which ones to choose is an architectural decision. For example, replication is a transparency that may not be needed in the system, in which case the architect does not need to specify it for a system. On the other hand, transparently locating a service and then accessing that service are two transparencies that will probably be selected and specified in the architecture. The constructs of the transparencies are mostly "orthogonal" in the sense that there is a separate set of defined constructs and concepts associated with each transparency, to the extent that one does not depend on another.

Distribution transparency is a capability that masks (or hides) the consequences of distribution and associated behavior from a user, application developer, or system developer. [RM-ODP-2]

The eight transparencies are:

1. Access: Hides the differences in representation and mechanisms of invocation of a requested application or service. The purpose of this transparency is to support interactions between objects. This transparency is often coupled with security of access control.
2. Failure: Hides the recovery mechanisms for objects on failure from the subject object or other objects, which enables fault tolerance and reliability.

3. Location: Hides the physical location of an object for binding purposes. This transparency enables locating interfaces for the purpose of binding to them. Location transparency is often coupled with access transparency.

4. Migration: Hides the movement of an object from one location to another from that object and from other objects in the infrastructure. This transparency enables changes in location of an object, and is used for reasons including mobility, reducing latency and load balancing.

5. Persistence: Hides the mechanisms (deactivation and reactivation) needed for an object to continue to exist across changes or some time duration. It enables continued object existence, object stability, and robustness.

6. Relocation: Hides the changes in location of an interface from other objects and even any object that has an active binding to that interface. This transparency enables load balancing, reliability, and helps support binding failures when a bound interface needs to be relocated to a more robust channel.

7. Replication: Hides the redundancy of an object or interface, which enables performance and dependability.

8. Transaction: Hides the mechanisms in order to achieve consistent coordination among a set of activities. This transparency enables reliability and consistency.

In the early days of creating RM-ODP, three additional transparencies were defined but were not carried forward into the final standard:

1. Concurrency: Hides overlapped executions that occur simultaneously.

2. Resource: Hides changes in the representation of a service and the resources used to support it.

3. Federation: Hides the details of administrative and technology boundaries.

The reasons for not including these other transparencies in RM-ODP are varied. Sometimes work is not included because there are insufficient member body contributions to fully define and expand a concept. In order to move the standard forward, often the work is removed "for a later day." Sometimes work is not included because of member body differences, which cannot be resolved. Sometimes work is incorporated under another concept. Some or all of these reasons played a part in why these particular transparencies were not included.

However, what this does point out is that RM-ODP defines an initial set of transparencies. RM-ODP does not say that there are only eight transparencies, but rather that an architect can define others for specific use. For example, to hide the complexities of a security infrastructure of objects and their interactions, the architect could define "security transparency." However, the architect is then required to specify the mechanisms to achieve it. As will be discussed, the mechanisms to achieve a given transparency often require interactions that span nodes, objects, and systems, and are interoperable. So the architect must also specify which nodes need to include these mechanisms, and how they will interoperate in a distributed system. Such an additional transparency should be consistently specified, for example, across all the nodes in an enterprise. RM-ODP defines these open and interoperable mechanisms for its eight transparencies. These can be used as a pattern of reasoning for defining any additional transparencies, in terms of a set of concepts and rules, interdependencies, and a structure of services to be used. That is, RM-ODP describes what the transparencies must accomplish and some blueprint for accomplishing that transparency, but it does not explicitly define the infrastructure details to accomplish it. This is left to the architect to specify.

Distribution transparencies help a system achieve reliability (continuity of service), availability (how often the service is ready for use), fault tolerance (recoverability from failure), integrity (correctness), enhanced performance, decreased latency, and other system properties. Management of change includes change in location of infrastructure services. So, transparency enables the mobility of system services as well. It is very difficult for every application to develop all the details required to achieve these "ilities" across a distributed system. In fact, applications alone cannot provide these properties because the "ilities" are properties of the whole system, which is composed of applications including the infrastructure across all nodes of the system.

The RM-ODP transparency mechanisms enable the "ilities" by localizing to the infrastructure explicit capabilities to provide management of the system under failure, replicating components of the system for more assured availability, ensuring the integrity of a binding across a channel, and controlled management of movement of a software component or an an interface.

The principle of reaching out of an application to a service, extending the functionality of the application to additional capabilities, all transparently, can now be used for parts of a system that may never have been realized before. The impact to changes of the location of a server, for example, or the access mechanisms, or that a critical component of software is now replicated with a different interface, are all "hidden" with distribution transparencies. These changes do not affect the software application. These are dynamic changes managed by the distribution transparencies of the infrastructure.

Figure 10.2 provides an overview of the general distribution transparency pattern. The objects in the transparency parallelogram represent those objects that provide and support a transparency. As can be seen, the computational viewpoint has no direct relationship to the mechanisms to realize a transparency; only the engineering viewpoint is considered. Transparency not only hides its actions from the application, but also from objects in the engineering viewpoint.

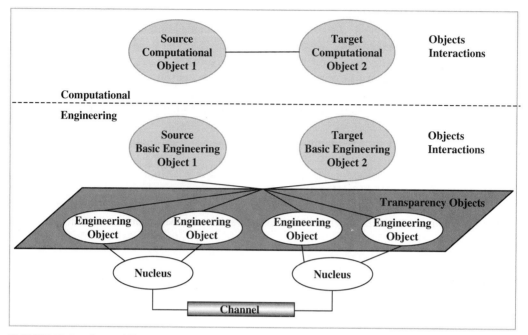

FIGURE 10.2   General Transparency Pattern

10.2   EXAMPLES

Some examples may help elucidate the distribution transparency capabilities.

10.2.1   E-MAIL EXAMPLE

A system includes an electronic mail application to provide Heidi the ability to communicate with Steve. Her personal address book includes Steve's name and e-mail address. That address is really the location of the system that can locate Steve's e-mail inbox. Figure 10.3 shows this example in RM-ODP concepts. A discussion of this figure follows.

Heidi creates an electronic message and initiates the sending of the e-mail through the local e-mail server. The e-mail server interacts with a directory name service object to locate the engineering interface reference of the distant e-mail server: "abc.com." The directory service uses the ODP engineering interface reference tracking function to resolve the logical address to a physical address in order to establish the Engineering Interface Reference (EIR) of the destination and

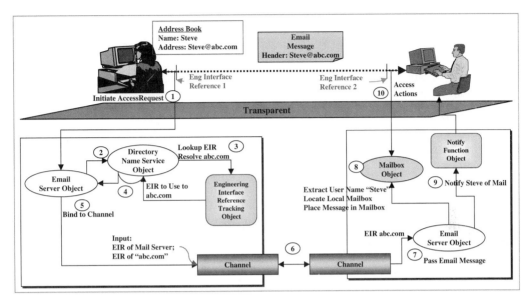

FIGURE 10.3 Transparent E-Mail Example

to establish a binding across a channel. Once resolved, the EIR of the local e-mail server object and the target e-mail server object are provided as input to the channel. The channel uses the physical address to establish a connection to the target location, possibly using more than one channel to accomplish this. The channel completes the binding, and the e-mail message is sent to the destination e-mail server. Once at the destination, the destination e-mail server receives the message, extracts the user name, and locates the e-mail inbox to store the e-mail for Steve. The e-mail server then uses the ODP Notify function to notify Steve of incoming mail. Steve is then able to access the e-mail from his e-mail inbox. All of these infrastructure services are transparent to both Heidi and Steve. Address resolution is also transparent to the e-mail server objects.

Notice that Heidi did not know the physical address of Steve. It was resolved through the EIR object, providing location transparency. Heidi does not need to know the address her local system uses to connect to the target system (which is location transparent to her), or where the inbox for the person is located (which is also location transparent to her). If Steve has moved to a different e-mail address or server, the infrastructure handles forwarding of Heidi's message to Steve (which is relocation transparent to her). Notice, however, in order for her to be unaware of all these e-mail actions, the infrastructure for the e-mail system must perform a number of actions, based on how the system developer developed the system. The e-mail server itself does not need to resolve the addresses or notify Steve of incoming e-mail. These are transparent services as well. These transparent capabilities are made possible by specifying these transparencies in the architecture.

10.2.2 CELL PHONE EXAMPLE

Let's look at what can be accomplished by transparent access provided by tele-communication[1], depicted in Figure 10.4. Jane is in Illinois and wants to call Guy, who lives in Boston. Jane doesn't know where Guy is, but he has a cell phone, registered for the Boston area. Jane dials his cell phone number: 617-555-1111. The infrastructure supports finding Guy's cell phone through the distributed telephony network. Eventually, Guy's cell phone rings, and he answers it in Los Angeles, through the roaming switch 310-555-1234. The cell phone number is a logical reference. Jane's phone is a fixed reference, which means it does not change or move around. Jane did not need to specify the exact physical location of Guy's cell phone or which area of the country his cell phone is located; that is, the interaction between Jane and Guy, and the location of Guy and his cell phone are location transparent to Jane. This location transparency is provided by the telephone switches and the cellular phone infrastructure.

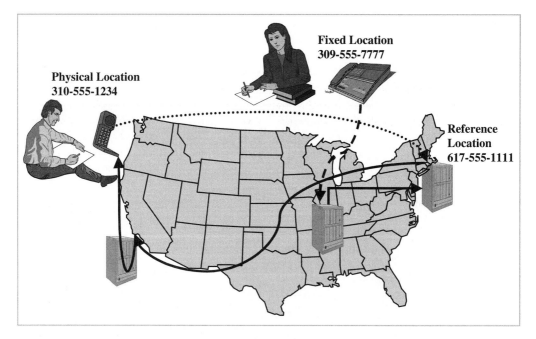

FIGURE 10.4   Location-Transparent Cell Phone Example

---

1. The method of doing this is not that specified in RM-ODP. This example merely shows what transparent access can provide.

10.2.3 Single Log-On Example

As another example, systems requirements today often require a single log-on capability, so that the end user need not log-on to every service and intermediate service to accomplish some processing. Further, this requirement generally extends to the application, which need not worry about checking the access rights of a user. The single log-on capability requires infrastructure mechanisms to:

▶ Log-on initially (to a Windows® client, for example)

▶ Check for proper identification and authorization

▶ Assign and manage access lists to all other services (the database management server, for example)

▶ Associate those access rights to the end user

▶ Communicate or distribute the user access rights for use in checking access rights

▶ Provide for all the communication details to communicate the access control metadata across the distributed system of services provided to the user

▶ Ensure the integrity and protection of the access control list

▶ And so forth

These underlying mechanisms are hidden in the infrastructure of the distributed system. They are hidden from the end user and applications developers; that is, the property of secure access is "transparent," as specified by the architect and as implemented by the infrastructure developer.

10.2.4 Static versus Dynamic Location and Access Resolution

Let's look at an example of location and access transparency. The application uses a service-specific application program interface (API). The API may provide location and access transparency. Preferably, the access to the services will disassociate physical location and access mechanisms, enabling the transparencies to dynamically provide these capabilities. The alternative is that the application developer would either hard-code the location of an interface and method of access, or define its location statically along with the method of access, with a dedicated connection to the target.

Figure 10.5 provides a view of the difference between a statically defined interface location and access method and one that is dynamically and transparently provided. The gray items are those infrastructure services that support the location and access transparencies. Perhaps a directory that provides a resolution of a logical address to a physical address is on a different node (as shown). The transparency objects, such as the engineering interface reference (EIR) ODP function object, make use of this directory. The physical address is resolved, and the

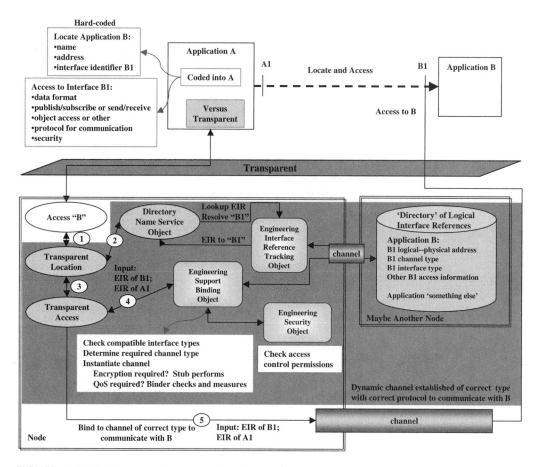

FIGURE 10.5 Static versus Transparent Location and Access

properties of communicating to the target are determined. Once this is accomplished, the infrastructure establishes a channel of the correct type for the interface (B1) and for the protocol. Then the access to B using the channel to access the interface B1 is established transparently for A. More about these infrastructure elements will be discussed later in this chapter. For now, they provide a view of how RM-ODP provides a pattern for some of the distribution transparencies.

10.2.5 WEB ACCESS EXAMPLE

A prime example of the provision for some of the distribution transparencies is the Web (though this example is not RM-ODP specific). To access a particular Web site, a specific URL is provided to the Web browser. There can be a number of handshaking connections that go on between different servers and different sites in order to get to some of these URLs. The manner of access to the desired Web site is generally transparent to the user; it just happens. When the desired Web page is shown, the user may wish to access additional detail from a "highlighted" area. This highlighted area is actually a link to another location for the information. Once the user clicks on it, the Web system infrastructure manages all the access and location mechanisms to retrieve the requested information, download it to the user's system, and display it to the user. To the user, it is transparent how this is accomplished. The average Web browser, then, coupled with the reusable Web infrastructure services, provides access transparency, location transparency, relocation transparency (the information may relocate to some other server), replication transparency (there may be more than one server, for load-balancing reasons), and so forth.

SIDEBAR

INTERFACE COMPLEXITY CONCERNS

The transparency mechanisms are reusable by applications. Let's look at access and location transparencies in more detail to see what mechanisms are hidden and what benefits are achievable by using these transparencies. To access a service somewhere, an application is often developed with some or all of the following details:

- Name of the service to access
- Identification of the service, which is the metadata most often used in computational systems
- If there is more than one instance of the service, select the one wanted based on some criteria (e.g., "closest one")
- Address of the interface to the selected service instance
- Use of a specific application protocol interface (API) that relates to the service being accessed
- Use of a specific interaction with its parameters in the API
- Details for each service offering accessed across the interface
- Error handling
- Details of the protocol to use to get to the remote site, and the messaging capability
- Details of the specific interface protocol (abstract syntax, transfer syntax)
- Details of the specific data to be transmitted across the interface to create a binding to the interface
- Access mechanisms to the service to actually invoke it. That is, if it is a secure service, encryption is either coded into the application or requested of the infrastructure, or perhaps an additional log-in and password is provided to access the service (which is often the case in accessing database management systems)
- Specific administration details

There are possibly more details that may need to be coded into an application to provide the same capabilities as the transparencies.

Remember that all of these details are for *every* service and associated interface an application accesses, and for *every* application in the enterprise. So in addition, developers need to code the details about every service interface to access, and the details of accessing that service providing the interface. Figure 10.6 shows an example of the complexity hidden by location and access transparency. The discussion follows.

The top figure represents the overhead complexity required to develop into every application that wants access to services A and B without the use of these transparencies. The bottom figure represents what application development is reduced when the location and access transparency are accomplished by the infrastructure.

Often the code in each application is designed specifically for that application, minimizing the reusability of that code and increasing the maintainability of that code. In the case of code pertinent to interfaces, this can cause very brittle systems.

Figure 10.7 represents the count of interfaces to develop and maintain, depending on the architecture of the system. As the number of applications increases in the system or enterprise, the count of interfaces to maintain can become unmanageable. For example, a change of some parameter by the service affects unique changes to each application that must be updated to accommodate the change.

The top left figure depicts the point-to-point interfaces from 5 communicating systems to 5 different services. Assume A is the count of applications and S is the count of services accessed. In this point-to-point case, there are:

```
A × S × 2 = 50 interfaces to develop separately and maintain
```

When the code to access each service is localized to the infrastructure, it is more cost effective to update and maintain. As the number of applications increases in the system or enterprise, the complexity of the system is localized to the infrastructure, not to every application. This, in turn, minimizes the cost of maintenance of the system and still allows manageability of the system.

There are two ways to use the transparencies. One is to develop into the application separate accesses to the infrastructure for each service requested, and allow the infrastructure to interface to the service only once. This case is represented in the top middle of Figure 10.7. In this case, there are:

```
A × S + S = 30 interfaces
```

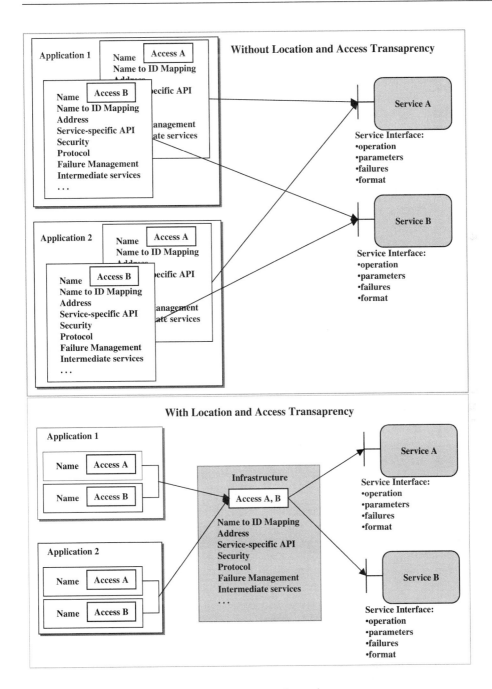

FIGURE 10.6 Access and Location Transparency Example

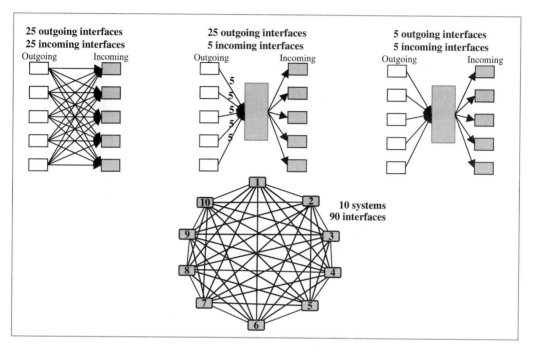

FIGURE 10.7 Interface Explosion

Another use of the transparencies is to allow the infrastructure to manage all accesses to the services from the application through a common API that the application uses, as represented in the top right of Figure 10.7. In this case, there are:

```
A + S interfaces = 10 interfaces
```

However, if all the applications and services represented in the figure were communicating systems, and each communicates with each other, as shown in the bottom of the figure, the number of interfaces increases as the *square* of the number of communicating systems:

```
(A + S)² = 90 interfaces
```

An approach that may be practical between a few systems becomes completely infeasible when many systems must interoperate. Here is where the transparencies are of utmost importance.

Interfacing is an area of focus in any architecture that determines to a great extent whether a system is brittle or robust. Minimizing the details of interface processing, along with reusing the software components to accomplish this across the enterprise, will provide a far more robust system of systems that is more easily tested, changeable to accommodate advanced technologies, and, most importantly, manageable and cost effective to maintain. A large number of developed systems require large sustainment costs in managing, troubleshooting, and fixing interface development software. If an application develops the details for every interface, then every change in that interface requires a change in the application, which includes recompilation, reloading, and extensive retesting—a software sustainment nightmare.

10.2.6   MOBILITY EXAMPLE

Suppose the system administrator wants to *migrate* an application from one server to another, perhaps to achieve better access latency time. *Access, location, migration,* and *relocation transparencies* enable a transparent method of application mobility. All of the services an application accesses, all of the interfaces it uses, and the data it accesses might have to be changed in the application, unless *transparency* is implemented in the system.

One method of moving an application, or a part of an application, is to take the application offline, along with all parts of the system that require change and notification of this migration. The administrator can then move the application, bring it back online, and somehow inform all using applications of the change of location. If some of these using applications have hard-coded the application location that has now moved, these applications will need to be changed.

Alternatively, the infrastructure can support the movement of the application, dynamically and transparently, using the migration transparency. The application need not be aware that it has moved or that some infrastructure service has moved. Relocation transparency moves interfaces that are bound. For example, a client of the server application is unaware that the server has moved. To accomplish this mobility, both access and location transparencies are also needed. Together these transparencies form a basis for transparent mobile applications.

The result is that the application does not need to come offline for a change of location, a client communicating with the application does not need to terminate that binding, the effects of migration are hidden from whatever software is moved, and the effects of migration are hidden from using applications. All of this works through the use of explicit RM-ODP migration and relocation transparency mechanisms in each node. An overview of this capability provided by RM-ODP migration and relocation transparencies, as supported by some of the ODP functions, is shown in Figure 10.8. Access and location transparency support is not shown. For an example of the use of these transparencies in support of mobile agents, see [Bursell-98]. The numbers in the circles indicate logical steps in the process of migration.

For example, a relational Database Management System (DBMS) client may need to access its DBMS server, perhaps to retrieve some desired data using a specific client SQL-based API. If the client only knows a "reference" to a server, and knows that the server implements an interface that uses that reference, then

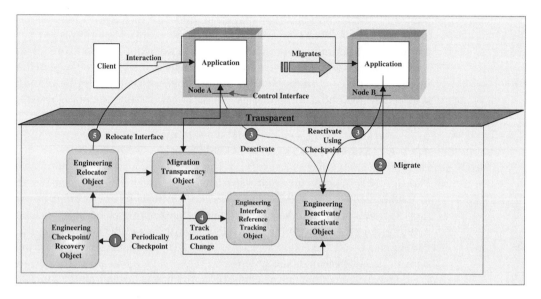

FIGURE 10.8   Application Mobility Example

the client is protected from server location changes at runtime. What this means is that the server can move or the database can move and these actions are all hidden from the application software.

RM-ODP provides explicit prescriptive rules to achieve distribution, which extend to prescriptive rules to achieve distribution transparency. The end result is that distribution transparency can be achieved across all RM-ODP compliant systems, whether or not they are part of a specific domain or some other domain. And because RM-ODP is a general reference model, the details of how to develop a specific transparency do not need to be the same across all systems. That is, the systems can be developed to different technologies and products as long as the rules for distribution transparency are used and as long as the implementation of the system is conformant with RM-ODP rules.

First, a discussion of how the mechanisms required to provide each of the distribution transparencies is provided, from a perspective that can be used in an architecture specification. Following this, a discussion of how the viewpoints work together to provide the distribution transparencies is provided.

10.3   DISTRIBUTION TRANSPARENCIES

The distribution transparencies provide the functionality of basic services in support of distribution, and add in additional guarantees. Extra management objects may be used to control the transparency actions and structures, appropriate channels for use in distributed communication, establishment of a new channel, relocating all the interfaces in case of a channel failure, and so forth.

Many of the transparencies require the channel for distributed binding. Many of the transparencies require the ODP function Engineering Interface Reference Tracking (EIRT), which is manifested as an engineering object; the engineering interface reference template; and possibly the computational binding object. The EIRT object is used to resolve a logical engineering interface reference to a physical address. The engineering interface reference template contains the details about the interface to establish a binding. Some of the details for these engineering mechanisms are captured in a later section, and reference of their use made in the appropriate transparency sections.

The transparencies generally require a number of preconditions to be satisfied, such as ensuring the type of the interface matches the type of the channel. They also require interworking with the ODP functions to perform some action. An example is the use of the ODP security function object. This object ensures that the access control checks are performed successfully before an object access takes place. In order to achieve transparency across a distributed system, however, the transparency rules and distributed communication mechanisms are important to follow. By doing so, interoperable distribution transparency is enabled.

The architect may choose to create a separate engineering transparency object to manage the infrastructure details for that transparency. In some of the more complex transparencies, such as transaction transparency, this can provide a reusable component across the systems. It can also localize the objects and their actions required to achieve a transparency.

Note that a transparency applies to a user, an application, or another infrastructure service. Table 10.1 summarizes the distribution transparencies, providing the purpose and possible benefits of each. A full discussion of each transparency follows the table.

TABLE 10.1 Transparency Purpose and Possible Benefits

TRANSPARENCY	PURPOSE	BENEFIT
Access	Access transparency is used to hide how something works from its users, how to get to a service to use it, and any differences in data representations and invocation mechanisms to use the service.	• Minimize development details of interfacing, access, and security access control to distributed services • Less error-prone applications • Enhanced system robustness • Minimized application change
Failure	Failure transparency is used to get an object to a consistent stable state if some failure occurs.	• Fault tolerance • Partial failure • Reliability

TABLE 10.1   Transparency Purpose and Possible Benefits (Continued)

TRANSPARENCY	PURPOSE	BENEFIT
Location	Location transparency is used to find an object.	• Decouple physical location from requested invocation • Enhanced system robustness • Minimized application change
Migration	Migration transparency provides mobility of an object and its interfaces.	• Load balancing • Enhanced performance • Reduced latency • Enhanced security • Mobile agents
Persistence	Persistence transparency provides persistent objects and resources.	• Robustness • Resource sharing • Recoverability of system services • Enhanced performance
Relocation	Relocation transparency provides movement of a bound interface.	• Moving a component ensuring the integrity of the interactions • Moving a server, without impact to the client • Load balancing • Error recovery of failed channel
Replication	Replication transparency permists an object to be cloned.	• Availability • Enhanced performance • Scalability • Reliability
Transaction	Transaction transparency hides the effects of overlapped or concurrent execution, maintaining consistency among the objects involved.	• Consistency among objects • Reliability

10.3.1   ACCESS TRANSPARENCY

Access transparency provides a mechanism for the application or user to access some service without knowledge of the intricacies to achieve that access.

INTEROPERABLE ACCESS TRANSPARENCY

Access transparency is becoming commonplace across the technologies and product choices today. What is not commonplace is the design pattern used to achieve access transparency. Hence, access transparency may not be interoperable across an enterprise without careful selection of products and technologies, or by developing the mechanisms identified in RM-ODP for open systems across the enterprise.

In Figure 10.9, the admitting agent needs to access the patient record and admission policy, but is unaware of where they are physically located or how to access them. The engineering mechanism is shown as a reusable composite object of component objects that performs location and access transparency functions.

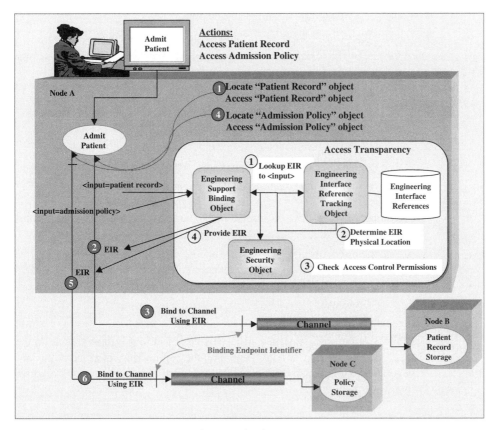

FIGURE 10.9 Access Transparency for a Medical Treatment Service

The logical steps that the "admit patient" object performs are numbered in gray circles. Steps 1 through 3 provide access to the patient record; steps 3 through 6 provide access to the admission policy.

The logical steps performed by the access transparency mechanisms are shown in white circles. To achieve access transparency, the engineering interface reference must be located (step 1) and resolved to a physical address (step 2). Also shown is the use of a security object to validate access (step 3), though this need not be part of the access mechanisms. The EIR to the destination is resolved (step 4) and used to continue the binding to the two channels: one to access the patient record (step 3) and one to access the policy (step 6). The client has then accessed the patient record and the admission policy transparently.

Essentially, access transparency acts between a request for access and the resolution of the distributed binding to that service. The infrastructure manages this interaction. Access transparency requires a number of actions, which are not all represented in Figure 10.9. Some of these actions require the semantics of the information viewpoint. The access transparency actions include the following, not necessarily in this order:

▶ Lookup the EIR template for the source object.

▶ Lookup the EIR template for the target object, which details the access mechanisms, the type of channel, protocol requirements, and so forth.

▶ Check for compatible interface types (operational, stream, binding).

▶ Check the access control permissions (optional).

▶ Resolve the engineering interface reference physical location for the target object.

▶ Determine the requirements for the channel type and configuration.

   – Is encryption required? The stub object in the channel performs this action.

   – Is a certain Quality of Service (QoS) required? The binder object in the channel ensures that the QoS required of the initiating object is at least compatible with the QoS offered by the target object. Binder will also measure the QoS across the channel, if the architect specifies this.

   – Are the protocols compatible? Use a protocol object that is compatible with the receiving protocol of the target object. If this is not possible, or if the access is across domain boundaries, use an interceptor object to manage protocol transformations.

▶ Instantiate the channel.

▶ Bind the engineering interface of the source object (e.g., admit patient) to the local channel binding interface, and bind the engineering interface of the target object (e.g., the patient record storage object) to its local channel binding interface.

▶ Using the information viewpoint dynamic schema for the stub objects in the channel, perform any data representation translations needed. That is, the data formats for the request object may differ from those of the responding object, and vice versa. Hence, necessary data mediation may be required between the two objects.

▶ Using the information viewpoint dynamic schema for the protocol objects in the channel, perform any protocol translations needed to bridge between the protocols of the source object and the target object. Instead of the protocol objects, an interceptor object may be instantiated in the channel to perform this action.

▶ Perform all appropriate security access control checks. The information viewpoint specifies the access control in the invariant schema and dynamic schema in terms of a security policy. The access control constrains the interaction. The stub objects in the channel or a separate engineering security object for the initiator and target objects could accomplish this. If encryption is required, as indicated above, the stub objects in the channel perform this action.

▶ Once the interaction between the objects is completed, the channel can be destroyed or deactivated. Alternatively, the channel may be kept active for other actions between the two objects. The information viewpoint dynamic schema will indicate what to do.

If the location of the engineering interface reference for the target object is local to the node, a channel need not be used. In this case, there is a simple binding required. How that binding is accomplished is a local system matter and the architect must specify it. A computational binding may require the use of the above-mentioned engineering support binding object. This object would manage the access control mechanisms, the interactions across multiple interfaces, the channel establishment, the channel type matching the interface template specifications, the channel establishment, and so forth. This particular object may exist for the life of the node, managing all manner of different channels and transparencies, or only exist for a particular binding. This is a decision made by the architect.

The ODP functions involved in access transparency are the EIRT function, used to maintain a repository of engineering interface references and associated engineering interface reference templates, and optionally the Security functions for access authorization checks. One such implementation of access transparency that makes use of the RM-ODP capabilities is FlexiNet from the Advanced Networked Systems Architecture group. [Flexinet]

Figure 10.10 provides an overview of mechanisms needed for access transparency, including the actions of the objects in the channel. The logical steps are numbered to indicate some order of actions that occur. The dashed connector between the source and target engineering objects indicates the desired access. The actual access is accomplished by the channel that binds the source engineering object 1 to the target engineering object 2 in the figure. This figure represents the choice of using the binding engineering object to support the binding actions,

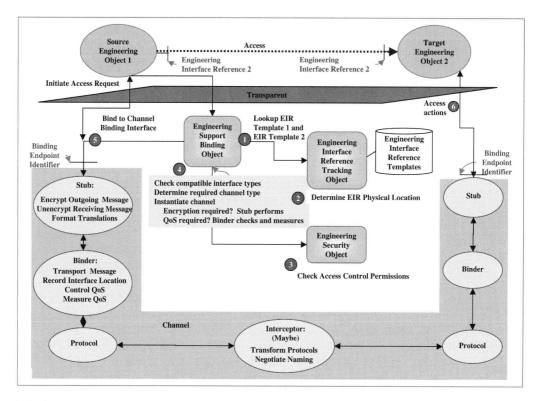

FIGURE 10.10   Access Transparency Engineering Mechanisms

though RM-ODP does not define its use. Otherwise, the actions needed to resolve engineering interface references, to check for authorization, to check interface parameters and types, to instantiate a channel, to bind to the channel, and to use the channel to perform the access actions are part of the RM-ODP definition and are shown.

10.3.2   FAILURE TRANSPARENCY

Failure transparency is used to achieve a consistent stable state if some failure occurs. Clearly, this transparency is used to enable fault tolerance, as well as a more reliable infrastructure. Chapter 16, "RM-ODP Fault Tolerance Framework," covers this topic in more detail.

     Failure transparency operates on objects, hiding the object recovery mechanisms from other objects and from the object itself. In order to accomplish this, certain actions must be accomplished and certain metadata made available:

▶ The object and its state must be visible to a failure transparency object.

▶ The interfaces of the object must be visible.

▶ The actions of checkpoint and recovery must be applied to the object, as defined by the ODP function Checkpoint and Recovery.

▶ The failure modes are visible to the object. That is, the failure modes that can be observed and will be reported are specified. These are typically specified in the object template or contract specification.

▶ A stability schema is specified in the information viewpoint and contains a specification of the failure modes.

▶ A checkpoint/recovery policy is specified in the information viewpoint and contains a specification of the checkpoint/recovery actions on a cluster.

▶ A replication policy is specified in the information viewpoint and contains a specification of the replication actions on a cluster.

The configuration of the engineering objects in support of failure transparency is shown in Figure 10.11. Discussion of these mechanisms follows. Since the channel is not directly involved, nor is the target engineering object, the details are not shown.

The policy of stability for an object is specified in the information viewpoint. It defines those failures that the object must *not* exhibit. Examples of such failures include a violation of authorized access, a failure to perform an operation

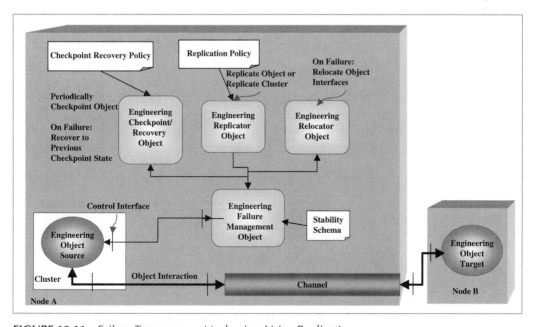

FIGURE 10.11   Failure Transparency Mechanism Using Replication

defined in the interface signature, a failure to honor a QoS offered across the interface, a failure to bind to a valid engineering interface, and so forth. The types of failure modes that may be visible to the object include violation of security, violation of a QoS, violation of an interface operation, and so forth. So the object can be both notified of certain failures (as a broken connection) or the failures that the object cannot exhibit.

The architect specifies which objects require failure transparency, as opposed to all objects. The objects that are critical to the success of a transaction, or are application critical, are examples of objects that should be stable.

To support failure transparency, the infrastructure can place the object in a node that prohibits the failures. Alternatively, the checkpoint action can periodically checkpoint the object to a state that can be recovered if there is a failure. Or the object can be replicated, or cloned, to serve as a backup and to take over should one of the replicas fail.

To accomplish these actions, the object must define an engineering management interface. It is through this interface that the object is checkpointed, or deleted. To accomplish the checkpoint action, the engineering infrastructure must include a Checkpoint/Recover object that performs the actions of the ODP Checkpoint/Recovery function. If a failure occurs, the object is restored to a previous checkpoint state.

To accomplish replicating the object, the engineering infrastructure must include a Replicator object that performs the actions of the ODP Replication function. Those actions may either replicate the object or the object's entire cluster.

The failure transparency may require all the infrastructure mechanisms for relocation transparency. A Relocator object must be included in the infrastructure to support relocating the object's interfaces. Notice that the channel mechanism does not necessarily play a role here.

The discussion about relocation transparency described later in this chapter will highlight the actions and mechanisms required to relocate the interfaces. Chapter 16, "RM-ODP Fault Tolerance Framework," provides a discussion of a fault tolerant framework that uses failure transparency.

10.3.3   LOCATION TRANSPARENCY

Location transparency enables locating an object's interface without the need to know where the object is physically located. RM-ODP is silent as to the exact mechanisms to use in support of this transparency. However, the mechanisms for engineering binding and interface references are involved. So a configuration of objects that are involved, along with some discussion of the actions these objects must perform to support location transparency, is provided.

As indicated above, the engineering interface reference template includes a "location" parameter. This is an indication of the physical address used in a binding. In location transparency, the physical address may not be available, and actually need not be available. To this end, the interface reference is resolved through the EIRT function object. To accomplish this across nodes in a system, or across systems, a federation of the EIR management objects is probably needed. This is discussed later in the chapter.

In order to locate an EIR, the separate EIR management domain objects must interact. Once the physical address is located, it is returned to the source EIRT and binding proceeds as usual. If the binding is local, the ODP Node Management function will establish and manage the binding. If the binding is distributed, a channel is established and used. That is, a channel of the correct type is established, parameters are marshalled and unmarshalled by the stub, failures in the channel are managed by the binder, failure of a resolved engineering interface reference is managed, and a connection is made to the target object.

The physical address can be a network address, a node location, a cluster memory address, a specific DBMS table in a specific DBMS database coupled with a network address to the server, and so on. In other words, the physical address can be as simple as a memory location, or as complex as a full network path plus the metadata to locate data from a distributed DBMS server database.

Resolving an engineering interface reference to a physical location is shown in Figure 10.12. The details of the channel objects are not shown, as they do not play a role in resolving the location. Also not shown is the federation of cross-

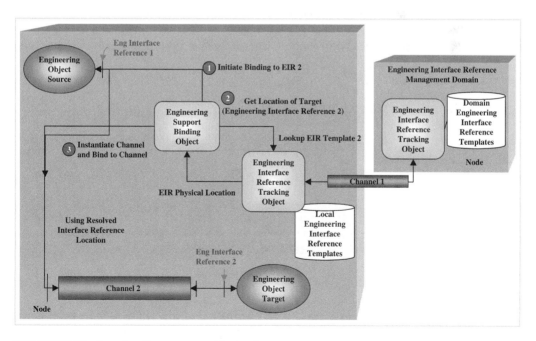

FIGURE 10.12 Location Transparency Mechanisms

domain EIRT objects. In this representation, the EIRT object can be local. The figure shows that a separate channel is used to interact with an EIR management domain to resolve the physical location. Once resolved, the source object and target objects can be bound and make use of a channel.

If the binding is to a local node, or to a single EIR management domain, then the resolution to a physical address is accomplished through a local interaction with the EIR management object. Once again, binding then proceeds as usual.

If an interface has been relocated, the location transparency must interact with the Relocator function at the original destination to locate the new physical address to use. This requires the EIRT object at the destination to maintain a mapping between the original physical address and the new physical address.

What all of this says is that there may be separate channels created, used, and deleted in support of locating an object. Once the target engineering interface reference is located, the channel required to communicate to it may be different from the one originally specified in the channel template. For example, an interceptor object may be required in the channel to mediate differences in protocols, names, interface references, and the like, depending on where the target engineering interface reference is located. This is part of the binding establishment process.

Once the architect has determined the specification for location transparency, that specification and associated design of the mechanisms can be reusable (as a pattern or as an actual implementation) across the systems. Further, the engineering mechanisms, realized in technology products, may also be reusable components. The architect needs to be sure the interface specifications for the components and the engineering objects remain open for reuse.

10.3.4 MIGRATION TRANSPARENCY

Migration transparency enables an object to be moved to a new location. This transparency provides the ability, for example, to migrate a DBMS server, a middleware component, an end-user client object, and so forth. It enables dynamic mobility of an object, and all of its interfaces.

Migration transparency could be selected for load-balancing reasons, for performance reasons, for reduced latency reasons, or for more security. The infrastructure supports this transparency, masking the details from the object and bound interfaces. Well, almost. Actually, migrating a bound interface will probably affect the performance of the communication, and any latency or other QoS attributes in play.

Figure 10.13 shows the steps for migrating an object and relocating a bound interface.

Certain constraints apply when this transparency is used: latency, which may be changed due to a location change; threads, which may perform differently because of a change in location; and security, which may be more or less constrained because of the new location. The policy of migration, called a "mobility

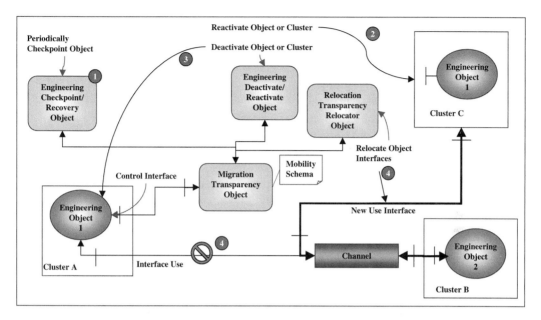

FIGURE 10.13 Migration Transparency Mechanisms

schema," is required. It defines the permitted latency, security, and performance constraints associated with the migrated object.

Checkpoint is needed for migration transparency in order to checkpoint the object to a stable state. It will be reactivated in that state. To accomplish checkpoint, the object must provide a management control interface for use by the migration transparency control object. When the object is to be migrated, the migration transparency object will deactivate the old object (through the control interface of the object). Once the object is migrated, the old object instance will be deleted through the control interface.

The name of the object should remain the same. If a new name is given to the object, a Naming object may be involved to manage the naming and retain the mapping of the old name to the new name. The Naming object here may be a domain-wide component used to manage the domain-specific naming.

In addition, all of the object's interfaces must be made visible and tracked, using the EIRT object. RM-ODP distinguishes the movement of an object and its unbound interfaces, and the movement of bound interfaces. Migration transparency is used for the former; relocation transparency is used for the latter. When an object migrates, it may have bound interfaces. The architect needs to specify in the mobility policy the actions to be performed on bound interfaces that are subject to object migration. These actions can be to terminate any such bound interfaces, to resolve to completion all bound interfaces, or to relocate the bound interfaces.

A Relocator object is required in the infrastructure if a bound interface is to be relocated. When the interfaces are relocated, a mapping must be maintained to the new location of the interfaces for some specified duration. The binder objects in the channel play a role. They must detect a relocation of bound interfaces, suspend the channel operation, and either re-establish a new binder-protocol set of objects to manage the new connection, or re-establish an entirely new channel for the communication.

RM-ODP is incomplete and ambiguous with respect to migration transparency. The transparency is about the movement of an object. The related RM-ODP Migration function is about the movement of a cluster of one or more objects. To realize migration transparency requires the use of the Migrator and Relocator objects. The Relocator object relocates the entire channel-bound interfaces of all interfaces of all objects in the cluster, rather than a single interface of an object. Further, the mobility schema is associated with an object and the migration policy is associated with a cluster, but RM-ODP does not reflect the relationship between the two.

To migrate an object, as opposed to re-instantiating a new object, the object is checkpointed to a stable state. When the object is migrated, it is "restored" to that checkpointed state. The ODP Migration function, manifested as a Migrator object, coordinates the migration of the object in conjunction with the mobility schema constraints.

10.3.5 PERSISTENCE TRANSPARENCY

Persistence transparency says that node resources needed by an object will be made available when the object requires them. If an object is interacting with another object, one or the other may be "suspended" through deactivation, and later "resumed" or reactivated to continue the interaction. Often this happens for scheduling reasons, or for reasons of failure that require recovery actions.

Persistence is a characteristic that an object continues to exist despite changes in time, location, or context in which the object was established. [RM-ODP-2]

Persistence transparency is about maintaining the existence and stability of the object. To accomplish this transparency, the state of the object must always be maintained. In addition, the cluster of the object must also be persistent. Figure 10.14 provides an overview of these mechanisms.

A persistence schema is specified in the information viewpoint in support of persistence transparency. Although RM-ODP does not define the details of this schema, it should include a specification on the use of the system's resources (processing, storage, channel, etc.) for an object that is made persistent. In addition, a reactivation/deactivation policy is required for clusters, to capture what should happen.

The ODP Reactivation/Deactivation function plays a role in this transparency. It is used to re-establish the object, its interface references, its bindings, and its cluster to some stable state, if either failure occurs or the node cannot provide the resources required at that point in time. In order to provide for the necessary system resources to an object, the system may deactivate an object or a cluster for

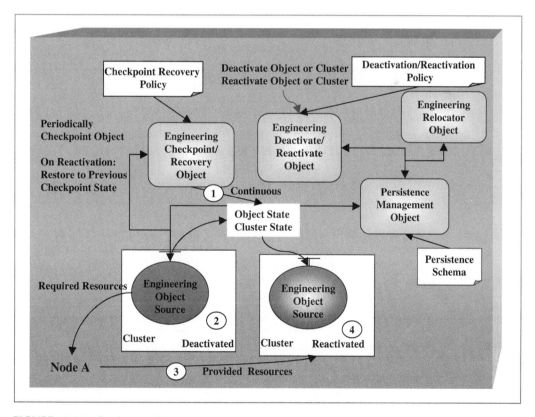

FIGURE 10.14 Persistence Transparency

some duration, and later reactivate it, subject to the constraints set forth in the reactivation/deactivation policy.

The object must provide a control interface for use in checkpointing the object to some stable state and for use in deactivation/reactivation. That is, once the node can provide the resources required, the object is reactivated to the state that it was checkpointed.

If the object to be deactivated has bound interfaces, the Relocator object plays a role in the reactivation of those interfaces. As such, the relocation transparency mechanisms are required for the persistence transparency property.

An object management interface may be used to provide actions in support of the persistence schema constraints. Such actions would include steps to take if the performance is not accomplished, or timing constraints that require additional monitoring and management. RM-ODP is silent on this, however.

10.3.6   RELOCATION TRANSPARENCY

Relocation transparency moves a bound interface. This is useful to move a server to some other location while not disrupting the client interfaces. It's also useful to move a portion of some directory services, for load-balancing reasons, and automatically move the interfaces to it. Perhaps the channel has encountered some error. In this case, relocation transparency can relocate the active interface to a different channel. There are so many reasons to relocate an interface, and this transparency simplifies the developer implementation from having to know about and handle the relocation of an interface, bound or not. Wouldn't it be wonderful if some of the Web browsers would implement this transparency for those linked pages that have moved (relocated) to some other server? Then the Web browser would always link to the most up-to-date Web page.

Relocation transparency enables the change of location of an interface, hiding the results of this change from not only other bound interfaces, but also from the object itself. That is, the object's interface is relocated, and the object is unaware of this relocation. It is transparent to the object. What this enables is that the interaction between objects does not concern itself with the location or address of the object, or any change in it. The object need only be concerned about the interaction associated with the interface.

A view of a relocated interface is shown in Figure 10.15. This is shown in terms of a client and server. The server bound interface is to be relocated from node A to node C (migration of the object is not shown). The Relocator object relocates the bound interface and interacts with the binder to indicate a new location. The binder then creates a new channel (or a new binder in the existing channel), re-establishes the binding, and forwards the binding from the client to the relocated interface of the server. At some point in this process, the EIRT object is informed of the old and new interface locations, which are recorded.

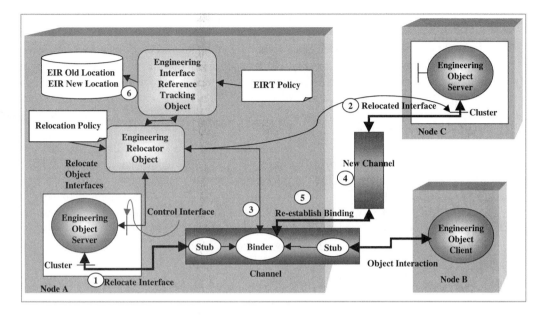

FIGURE 10.15   Relocation Transparency

To realize this transparency, the Relocator object (as defined by the ODP Relocation function) is needed. The Relocator object knows about all the interfaces of a cluster, and about the objects in the cluster. When an object migrates, the object's interfaces need to be relocated. The Relocator performs this action as well.

When an interface moves, the change in location requires knowing where it was located and where it will be located. This requires interaction among the binder object (which knows the old physical address, as well as all the interfaces bound to it in the channel), the Relocator object (which knows about the new location, and must maintain a mapping from the old location to the new location for a period of time), and the EIRT object (which manages old and new EIRs, and their associations).

This transparency must also support finding the location of a relocated interface, typically through the EIRT function object. If a channel binding is in use, due to relocating of bound interfaces, the binder object must ensure the integrity of the channel by communicating the EIRs being re-bound, ensuring the validation of these interface references with the Relocator object, and re-establishing the channel if necessary.

For some period of time, the Relocator must provide notification of the change in every interface relocated, and provide an indication of a "forwarding address" location. The binder object is where any attempt to bind to the old interface will be detected. It will communicate this attempt to the Relocator, which will perform the necessary notification and possible forwarding actions.

When an interface is relocated, a naming inconsistency may arise. If the EIR "name" is different (perhaps because of a different naming domain), a naming support object can be used to provide the transformation of names. In addition, the Relocator object must know about all the interfaces in each cluster, and their names. To the extent possible, though, the Relocator object will try to maintain the same EIR name.

As can be seen, the Relocator is the primary support object for this transparency. It is the object that manages the interfaces, channel, bindings, location references, and naming contexts for the interfaces. It works closely with the channel binder object, which knows about the locations of the interfaces bound to the relocated interface. It also knows about the integrity of the channel, the correctness of the binding to the interface, and if the interface has been relocated.

If a cluster is relocated, the Relocator function object also keeps track of the cluster, all of its objects, and all of the object interfaces. Once again, the Relocator manages the change (relocation), notification of the change, and information about the change.

Resolving engineering interface references to a new physical location is accomplished as indicated in "Engineering Interface Reference Tracking" on page 418, and any re-establishment of a binding is accomplished as indicated in "Channel" on page 421.

10.3.7 REPLICATION TRANSPARENCY

Replication transparency holds that an object can be cloned, with a cloned object performing the same functions as the original object. This may be used for availability, enhanced performance, scalability, and reliability reasons.

Replication is an important topic in today's distributed processing environment. It enables the QoS properties of scalability and reliability, and improves service availability.

A replicated object is an object that has one or more cloned objects, to include its interfaces. Replication transparency then hides that fact from another object (and from the replicated object itself). This important capability is depicted in Figure 10.16, in terms of client/server (though it applies to any type of object and interface).

In this figure, a replication transparency object is shown that enables hiding from the client the replication of the server object across different nodes. This example depicts the typical use of replication today: replicating servers. However, RM-ODP does not limit the use of replication to servers. Rather, it generalizes the approach to replication, so that any engineering object may be replicated. The replication can be hidden from another interacting object through the use of replication transparency.

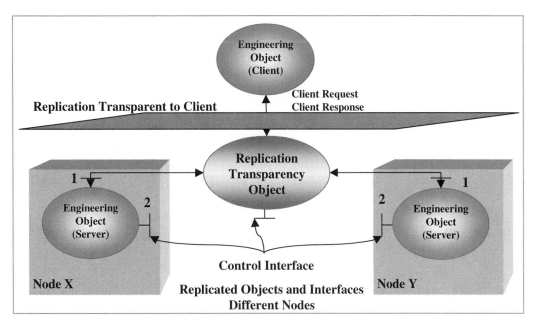

FIGURE 10.16 Transparent Replicated Server Example

The replicated object and interfaces require additional management capabilities in the infrastructure. Each object in the replica performs the same actions; each interface in the replica, therefore, is used in the same way. If an interface is bound in a channel to another object, the same interface of the replica object also needs to be bound. That is, the replica interfaces use a channel that supports multipoint interfaces, meaning binding to more than one interface.

Notice that a replication may result in more than one replica object, and hence each replica object's corresponding interfaces must be bound to the target object. This is more complex if the target object itself is replicated.

The engineering binding object must be able to bind multiple interfaces to the channel, one from each of the replica objects. The stub in the channel is made aware of the replication, and must manage one or more binders to accomplish replicating the messages. The binders in the channel manage multipoint bindings.

Replication transparency requires a replication schema associated with the cluster of the object. This schema, defined in the information viewpoint, identifies any constraints associated with the replication of an object. These constraints have to do with availability of the replicated object, availability of the replicated object interfaces, performance constraints, checkpoint actions, delete actions, and the like. Any of the bound interfaces can fail. Although RM-ODP does not define what the failure policy should be, the architect should define this in the replication policy. That is, if one of the interfaces from one of the replica objects fails, the choices could be to terminate the binding altogether, suspend the binding until the failed interface is re-bound, or some other action.

To achieve replication transparency, a Replicator object that performs the ODP Replication function is needed. It will clone the object, all of the object's interfaces, all of the metadata about the object (such as the object template, the interface template, the interface signatures), and provide a known association between the object and its replica. Checkpoint and deletion are actions performed on the object to be replicated. Thus, the object must provide a control interface through which these actions can be performed. In addition, the relocation transparency mechanisms are required. As such, The Relocator object is associated with the object's interfaces. The EIRT function must be used to associate the different "same" interfaces with each other.

Figure 10.17 provides an example of a replicated object and its interfaces. In this example, each replica object has four interfaces, as labeled. In each case, interface 2 is the control interface to the replication transparency object. Interface 4, in each object replica, is bound to the same channel, resulting in a multipoint binding. The Relocator object has knowledge of all four interfaces of both replica objects, in case an interface needs to be relocated. Object 2 is the target object that is unaware of the replication.

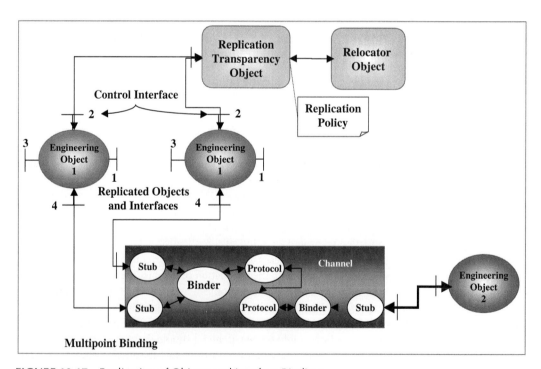

FIGURE 10.17   Replication of Objects and Interface Bindings

The preceding discussion addresses what RM-ODP has to say about replication transparency. However, subsequent work in this area further refines what infrastructure engineering objects and components may be used to enable better reliability, scalability, and availability of replicated services. Some of this is discussed here to provide more detail as to how the architect might realize replication and replication transparency.

The architecture and management of replicas are driven by the statements in the replication policy and invariant schema, all of which are captured in the information viewpoint. The following identifies the elements to specify:

▶ Identity of the replicas

▶ Required ordered delivery of messages in the group

▶ Required reliable delivery of messages

▶ Number of the replica objects to respond to a client request; typically, this is one. However, for reliability, the architect may request more than one response, and manage the actual response to the client through an additional infrastructure object (e.g., a synchronization object).

▶ Failure management on each node to detect and report failed messages, which may require an additional object

▶ Replicated server policy of receiving a client request and forwarding onto the replica objects; this introduces the need for an additional object in the system, which acts as a control object to receive a client request and forward that request on to the replicated objects providing the service

▶ Replica state consistency constraints

▶ Statements that require server replication transparency for the clients (in the case of an operational interface type interaction)

▶ Statements that separate clients from servers, for support of open group replication

▶ Required synchronized request delivery and responses from replicas, such as by blocking (one alternative), or time-stamped messages (which requires a global timing capability), or through an additional control component that provides replica synchronization

▶ Persistent and consistent state of servers

If an object binds to a replicated object interface, then in fact that object may bind to all replica objects. The determination of whether a client binds to one or all replicas is defined in the replication policy. For example, if a client request is determined to be an access request, then the policy may designate that only one of the replicas is involved in the transaction. Further, the policy would also designate how to select among the replicas, such as the "closest" one, the one that is most reliable, the one that is least active, or some other designation. In addition, the replication policy and invariants must establish the management of concurrency and failure. Failure management is complex under the request for replica change. The architect needs to decide what is to happen and the invariant specification of what causes these actions.

Support of dynamic client interactions with replicated servers, for example, requires that each client request be propagated to all replica servers. If one of the servers fails, if one of the messages does not reach a replica server, if some other failure type happens, what happens to the original client request will be determined by the replication policy. The architect could designate that all client requests be rolled back, reporting an error to the client. The architect could designate that a particular replica object must be suspended if an error occurs, for the purposes of refresh at a later time. In this case, the other replica servers would proceed with the client request. The architect may designate that the client request is such that another replica can fulfill the request, and establish the binding between the client and that replica server.

Clearly, there are other replication policy actions that the architect can specify. Those discussed here are only examples. To realize replication transparency, the architect may need to introduce additional objects in the infrastructure. Examples of these objects include a *synchronization object*, which receives the client requests associated with this component, manages the synchronization across all such synchronization components of requests, delivery, and responses, and provides the result to the client. In essence, it acts as a broker of client requests to a replicated set of servers. In a replicated case, this object must interact with its replicated synchronization objects to establish which server object is to handle the request and response, according to the replication policy. This agreement is reached prior to the actual transmission of a client request and a server response.

Another object that may be specified is an *availability object*. This object may perform such services as dynamic reconfiguration of the replicated objects. It also may aid in detection of failure of the replicated object (server), or some other failure. It can report this to a *replication control object* that exists somewhere in the system.

Another object may be *replica multicaster manager object* that communicates among all synchronization objects. It can perform such actions as ensuring the proper order of messages, timestamping of the messages, relating the responses to the requests, and other actions relating to the replica group. It can provide knowledge of failure of a client or of delivery of a client request, ensure correct order of delivery of requests (in the case of asynchronous client requests), and so forth. It can include or interact with the availability object (an architecture decision).

This discussion has introduced the possibility of four additional objects in support of replication in a transparent fashion: synchronization object, availability object, multicaster manager object, and replication control object. These objects provide replication transparency not only for the client(s) requesting services, but also for the replicated servers responding to requests.

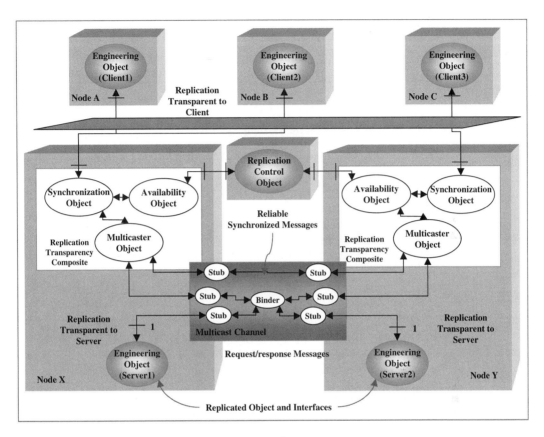

FIGURE 10.18 Replica Group Management Example

Figure 10.18 provides an overview of how these objects might be configured across a distributed system of two replicated object servers on different nodes, serving three clients on different nodes. The synchronization object, multicaster object, and availability object are shown as part of a replication transparency composition, which could equate to the replication transparency (composite) object of Figure 10.17.

In this example, the synchronization objects in each of the replication transparent composite interact through their own multicaster object to determine the replica server object to handle the client request. Once determined, the multicaster object on the node receiving the client request manages the interaction to the designated replica server, through a multicast channel. In this example, not all of the interface crossbar designators are shown, nor are the protocol or interceptor objects in the multicast channel. Further, only a single channel is shown, while the architect may designate a separate channel to communicate among all the multicaster objects for synchronization purposes. For an excellent treatment of the infrastructure objects in support of an open transparent replication capability, see [Karamanolis-97]. Note that the example in Figure 10.18, and the preceding discussion of these additional objects, are not part of what is said in RM-ODP. Rather, this example has extended what RM-ODP says, and provides the architect a view of how to use and realize replication transparency.

10.3.8 TRANSACTION TRANSPARENCY

Transaction transparency hides the effects of overlapped or concurrent execution, maintaining the consistency among the objects involved.

Transaction transparency is used to manage transaction processing, such as database transaction, EDI transactions, banking transactions, etc. Today we see this transparency most used for atomic, consistent, isolated, and durable (ACID) transactions, primarily with respect to database transactions, thus enhancing the reliability of the system.

▶ *Atomic* means that the transaction is fully completed, or not completed at all.
▶ *Consistent* means that the distributed state is consistent before and after the transaction.
▶ *Isolated* means that inconsistencies occurring during the processing of the transaction are hidden.
▶ *Durable* means that once the transaction is committed, the change of state is permanent.

To achieve this transparency, the infrastructure must include the ODP Transaction function. This object will manage the adherence of objects to a specified transaction schema, included in the information viewpoint schemas. The transaction schema captures the transactions in the dynamic schema, and the dependencies and transaction policies in the invariant schema. The dynamic schema defines the transaction actions of interest, the notification action to report the actions of interest, and so forth. The invariant schema defines the properties of the object that remain constant when certain actions should take place (e.g., commit, undo, rollback). Recovery actions need to be specified as part of the object's behavior, in the dynamic and invariant schemas. Actually, RM-ODP does not define the content of these schemas, but the architect should.

The bindings of the object are replaced by a transaction function. That is, the channel is not involved. The objects involved in the transaction must offer a control interface, used to checkpoint the object to a specific state, just before some action of interest. This is a precondition for the object to perform the action.

Transaction is an activity that maintains a consistent set of object states, in accordance with its dynamic and invariant schemata. [RM-ODP-3]

To accomplish transaction transparency, the objects involved must expose their actions, and notify the transaction function of certain actions (such as reading or writing of data). This enables the transaction function to provide control over the actions of interest, and to coordinate these actions. Coordination requires additional actions as well. The transactions must be scheduled, recovered as appropriate, and monitored for correctness and consistency. To achieve these additional actions, the objects of interest must provide additional interfaces to the transaction function.

The RM-ODP functions used for this transparency include:

▶ Checkpoint/Recovery to checkpoint the object, and recover it to some stable state

▶ Transaction to coordinate the actions and behavior of the objects with respect to the actions they perform and schema constraints defined

The Transaction function is notified if an action of interest takes place, and according to the schema defined, the Transaction function will act upon that notification. This action may be to commit a transaction, to rollback a transaction, to recover, or some other action specified in the information viewpoint schemas.

10.4   VIEWPOINT MECHANISMS

Thus far, the description and purposes for distribution transparency have been discussed with examples provided, as have the patterns of reasoning to achieve a transparency. The RM-ODP–defined mechanisms, which in some cases depend heavily on an ODP function, are the RM-ODP rules. The rules are both explicit and are general. They explicitly identify the behavior of the objects involved, and what they must do, and are also general so that the architect can choose whatever product or technology of the day to implement the solution.

The viewpoints that play a part in the specification of the distribution transparency mechanisms are shown in Figure 10.19. The principal viewpoints involved are the information, computational, and engineering viewpoints.

The enterprise viewpoint abstractly provides community policies and environment constraints that may affect the realization of a transparency. Otherwise, there is no direct involvement. The technology viewpoint provides the products for use in realizing the transparency mechanisms. The focus of the following sections will be on the three main viewpoints that provide the architectural pattern for each of the transparencies.

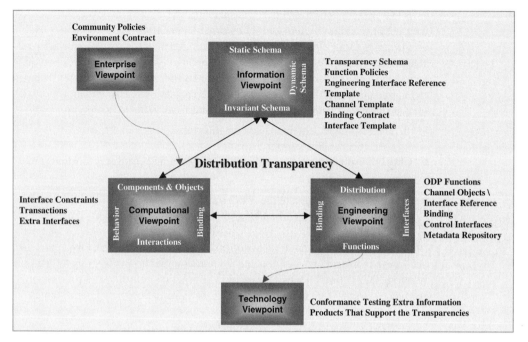

FIGURE 10.19 Viewpoint Mechanisms for Achieving Distribution Transparencies

10.4.1 Engineering Viewpoint Mechanisms

The main viewpoint involved is the engineering viewpoint. It provides the mechanisms to achieve the transparencies, subject to the semantics of the information viewpoint, and any additional details captured in the computational viewpoint. It is at the engineering viewpoint where distribution is exposed, and all properties about distribution are handled.

The primary mechanisms include:

- EIR, which is an identifier for the interface that is referenced
- Channel
- Channel stub object
- Channel binder object
- Channel interceptor object
- Support engineering objects, such as a binding object for complex distributed binding, channel management, and binding management
- Relocator object

▶ EIRT object
▶ An emerging RM-ODP standard such as Interface References and Binding [ISO-IRB]
▶ Some combination

This section will only include those engineering elements of particular interest to distribution transparency. The remaining engineering elements have been discussed in Chapters 6 and 9.

The engineering interface reference and associated ODP EIRT function are the principal supporting capabilities for the transparencies. For reference in the following discussion, Figure 10.20 provides a UML metamodel of the information pertaining to engineering interface references, binding, and interface templates.

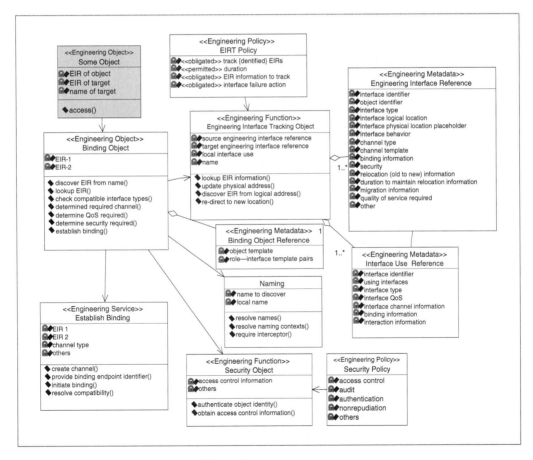

FIGURE 10.20 UML Metamodel of EIR and Related Information

10.4.1.1   Engineering Interface Reference Tracking

The EIRT function manages the repository of EIR templates for the system. This function exists as an infrastructure component or object in the system.

Figure 10.21 provides an overview of the following discussion. The architect may choose to use a domain-specific EIRT object, or a set of such objects that resolve logical interfaces to specific addresses. There may be a hierarchy of these objects across the systems in a domain. The architect may, for example, retain one EIRT object in each node to manage the engineering interface reference templates for that node, as well as references to the location of other engineering interface reference templates. That is, the engineering interface reference may include some logical information to identify the target system.

Actually, the EIRT object tracks all the engineering interface references across all the systems for its management domain. The mechanisms for a distributed EIRT function are yet to be defined, but will probably include constructs similar to those of the Trader. That is, within a management domain, there may be only one EIRT object. All distributed systems within that domain could include a request to access the EIRT object through a separate local EIRT object, resolve the

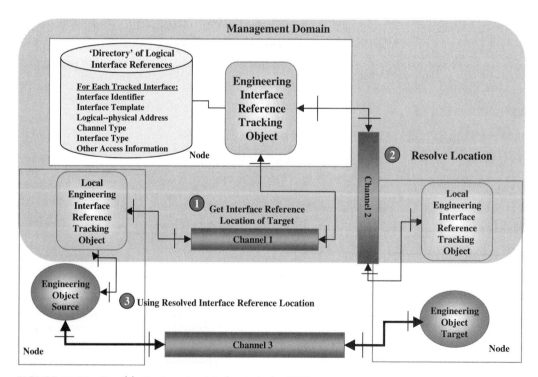

FIGURE 10.21   Possible Engineering Mechanisms for EIRT

interface references to specific locations, and use those results in establishing a binding to the target object interface. This is a separate distributed communication, meaning one from the EIRT object to the local object requesting the interface reference.

This example of two (at least) separate communication channels used to support a single transparency is shown in Figure 10.21, and is a common solution for several of the transparencies. The gray box highlights the local EIRT object use of a channel to establish a distributed binding to the EIRT management domain object. Once the location is resolved, the actual binding between the source and target object interfaces can be accomplished; this is shown by the dark connectors through "channel 2."

This is not unusual. In fact, the URL used for a Web address provides a similar capability. The URL is a logical address that includes the domain-specific logical address. For example, http://www.jtc1.org/ indicates that "org" is a domain of all such addresses, and "jtc1" is the specific address wanted. The Web domain name server will resolve the request to lookup the address "jtc1" in the "org" repository.

A telephone number, as another example, includes an area code, a local area code, and the final 4 digits used to locate the trunk and line to establish the call. So, the fictitious phone number "777-333-1234" means that in the area of the country designated by the area code "777," use the repository to locate the exchange "333." Within that exchange, use the repository to locate the destination address (trunk and line) for "1234."

Therefore the architect should specify that either

▶ All the engineering interface references are retained and managed in one local repository, which may cause a resource problem for the system, or

▶ All the engineering interface references are retained and managed in a hierarchy of interface reference repositories that interact to resolve the logical addresses to physical ones

If the architect chooses to cross domains to resolve addresses, the specification may need to address issues of separate policies as well. Policy management and cross-domain administration management would be services needed.

10.4.1.2 Engineering Interface Reference

To bind, the object that wants to interact with another object(s) must specify the engineering interface reference of the target object. The EIR contains a logical address. It must be resolved to a physical address, such as an IP address. An example is a telephone number. In the white pages, a telephone "interface" is "referenced" by a name, and the actual telephone number reflects the "interface" location to use, which includes the details of country(1)-region(area code)-local(exchange) address.

An EIR contains a name associated with an engineering interface to be bound. As such, an interface reference management domain manages the name. This can be part of a node, or can be associated with a number of nodes, within a domain.

The interface reference management domain manages the EIRs through a policy that is defined in the information invariant and dynamic schemas. This policy includes the information to assign an interface reference, to define the context of the interface reference, to define the format, to track the interface reference, and other actions.

An object obtains an EIR through initialization of the object, by instantiating an interface, or by interaction with another object, such as a Trader or an engineering support binding object.

The EIR template, specific for every engineering interface, is specified in the information schema. It contains such things as:

▶ Identifier for the interface reference, which is used to "reference" the interface wanted

▶ Type of the interface, such as operational, stream, or signal

▶ Computational interface template, which contains such things as:

   – An interface signature compatible with the interface type

   – A behavior specification for the interface, as specified in the information viewpoint schemas

   – An environment contract specification, as specified in the information viewpoint schemas

▶ Interface location, which is a physical address for initiating the binding actions

▶ Channel type information, where the type of channel used must match the type of interface

▶ Relocation information, which indicates where the interface was relocated to as appropriate

▶ QoS, which defines the parameters for the QoS required

▶ Interface behavior, which defines the preconditions that must be met, the QoS offered, and other constraints

The EIR, then, parameterizes all the information needed for the infrastructure to enable access transparency.

When two engineering interfaces are bound, the interface types must match; the causality role of the initiating interface must be opposite that of the target interface; the interaction requested of the initiating interface must match that provided by the target interface; and the count, names, and the types of the parameters for the interaction must match. Type Management rules and actions can be complex. An emerging standard on Type Repository [ISO-T] will provide further details on how this is accomplished, especially across domains, and [DSTC-TM] provides some excellent work in the area.

10.4.1.3 Channel

The channel is discussed at length in Chapter 6, "Separation of Concerns: Using RM-ODP Viewpoints," and Chapter 13, "Interaction Framework: Interoperability." The metadata for a channel includes a channel template and a binding template, both of which need to be specified in information invariant schema. The channel template is used to make sure that the EIRs, which describe the interfaces to be bound and the channel types required, are type compatible with the channel itself.

RM-ODP does not describe these in detail. Much is left for the architect to define: what the descriptive information is for the configuration of the channel, how it operates, under what circumstances an additional channel might be created, and so forth. Rather, the new standard for interface references and binding is expected to further define both the channel template and the binding template [ISO-IRB].

In the meantime, RM-ODP identifies that the channel template contains the following information:

- Configuration, which includes the specific stub objects, binder objects, protocol objects, and interceptor objects for selection, as well as the control interface references for each of these objects, and a binding interface reference for binding to the channel
- Alternate configuration for selection
- Channel type
- Group management policy

The binding contract is currently specified in RM-ODP to contain a set of {role—interface template} pairs. These pairs define the behavior expected of the binding. Emerging RM-ODP standards will expand the specification of the binding contract. For now, it is the architect's decision how to capture the behavior of the binding. However, it must include the {role—interface template} pairs, plus any additional information needed.

The channel passes certain information in support of the binding process. It communicates the computational signature name, the operation names, the termination names, and the computational interface identifier and signature. These are the parameters that define the desired actions between a source engineering object and a target engineering object.

The channel objects can have either local or distributed bindings to support some of the distribution transparency actions. An example is a binding from the binder object to the Relocator object (as defined by the ODP Relocation function) for the purposes of tracking interface references, and determining where the new location of the engineering interface is. More complex bindings can also be defined, such as support for cross-node EIR resolution.

In support of distribution transparency, the channel objects provide the actions indicated below.

A stub marshalls interfaces into and from interface references. The stub may interact with the nucleus of the node, or the engineering support binding object, to identify a need for a specific protocol, or the use of a specific engineering interface reference. The stub can also send the interface reference to the destination stub for use in resolving the addressing. Once the interface reference is received, the target stub requests the engineering support binding object, or nucleus, to bind the target engineering interface to the channel, indicating any binding constraints such as QoS.

The stub can also be aware of any replication policy for an object's interface. In this case, the stub must "multicast" the binding and all messages to each of the designated replicas.

The stub can provide message encryption, if needed by an application, in support of some of the transparencies (e.g., access). The stub may measure the mobility schema properties. The stub, in essence, performs some administration capabilities as required by the channel template, information schema, and the object.

If the application must be shielded from any failure of the binding, both the stub and binder objects provide failure management (to the degree possible), in support of failure transparency. If the application is to be shielded from any movement of a bound interface to another channel, the stub and binder objects manage this through the Relocator ODP function, other functions, and establishment of a new protocol object. Once the new configuration is instantiated, a new binding is created, without affecting the binding from the application to the stub, and hence without affecting the binding of the application to the target object. That is, the stub (and binder and protocol) hide the effects of relocation transparency so that the application is unaware of a new binding.

The binder object maintains the binding across the channel. It also detects any problems with the integrity of the channel by exchanging pertinent information with its counterpart binder object in the channel. The binder is responsible for coordinating communication. It is also capable of attempting to repair a failed binding.

The binder may interact with the EIRT object to resolve EIRs, to record these references, or other actions. The binder may also interact with the Relocator object to manage the relocation of bound interfaces. In this case, the binder may attempt to re-establish the binding with a new protocol object, new protocol and binder objects, or an entirely new channel. All of this depends on the needs of the new channel required for the relocated or failed interface, as specified in the policy associated with failure transparency.

The binder is also responsible for managing a multipoint channel, in support of replication transparency. If an object interface dies or is relocated, the binder is responsible for ensuring other bound interfaces are unaffected while repairing or re-initiating a bound interface. Of course, if the object itself dies, the other bound interfaces are informed of the failure, and the binding is terminated. Note that the channel itself may not be terminated. If there is a multipoint channel, and if the failure policy states that all existing points in the multipoint connection must remain active, the channel itself will remain active.

The protocol object provides no additional support for the transparencies.

The interceptor object is used for cross-domain transformations. In several of the transparencies, interface references and object names may be different. The interceptor transforms these to domain-specific valid names. In addition, the interceptor manages the transformation of protocols. If the communication channel were binding an Object Request Broker (ORB) interface to a COM+ interface, for example, the interceptor would manage the differences in the protocols. It should be noted that the Object Management Group's (OMG) Common Object Request Broker Architecture (CORBA) specification includes an interceptor object to perform many of these actions. The CORBA 3.0 specification includes a number of interoperable interceptors, to bridge among CORBA's IIOP and COM+, RMI, and possibly message-oriented middleware (MOM) as well.

Many of the transparencies that move an object or an interface are accomplished by the control interfaces to the channel objects. It is through these interfaces that the ODP function objects communicate, that the management objects in the infrastructure communicate, etc. These interfaces provide the management of the objects in the channel, some of the transparencies, and some of the QoS aspects of the channel.

10.4.1.4   Binding Object

Access to a target object may involve a computational binding object, as specified in the computational specification. If this is the case, the actions to access a target object are somewhat more complex. First, the source object must bind to the binding object. The procedure to accomplish this is similar to the actions above. Second, the binding object must bind to the target object. Again, the procedures above are used. Once the intermediate binding object includes the binding to both the source and the target, it then manages the communication between the objects. This may require special transformations, or it may require multiplexing other interfaces, or it may require other actions. These actions are what the architect specifies in the computational specification for the binding action between objects.

The architect should capture the dynamic actions in the dynamic schema of the information specification. Here, the architect defines what the actions are inside the binding object that logically bind engineering interfaces, as well as any invariant schemas to constrain the interaction between object interfaces.

The computational binding object may define a control interface. In the engineering viewpoint, the channel objects must each instantiate a control interface that is bound to the control interface of the engineering support binding object. The purpose of the control interface is to manage the consistency of the channel, to enable a reconfiguration of the channel objects, to manage the binding, and other actions the architect may define.

The correspondence of a computational binding object in the engineering specification is one of the ambiguities in RM-ODP. There is no clear mapping between the computational viewpoint and engineering viewpoint for the computational binding object. Further, the emerging work in Interface References and Binding [ISO-IRB] and Computational Protocols [ISO-CP] are not aligned with respect to the computational binding object.

In this chapter, the binding object is depicted as an engineering support binding object (an architecture decision). From this perspective, the engineering support binding object works with the EIRT function object to resolve interface references, the Naming function object to resolve cross-domain naming, and the channel configurations to establish needed auxiliary channels in support of resolving interface details.

10.4.2   INFORMATION VIEWPOINT MECHANISMS

The information viewpoint provides the transparency policies of what to do. Sometimes a particular QoS should be changed. This viewpoint also specifies the interface, channel, binding, and EIR templates that capture the transparency details for these mechanisms. And this viewpoint specifies the transparency schema needed.

The policies of the supporting ODP functions constrain the binding and the channel by defining the channel template and type of channel that must be used for achieving a transparency. They also constrain the actions of the channel objects in binding, such as resolving an EIR to a physical location at binding time (dynamically) instead of at compile time (statically). The schemata are specific to the transparency and augment the ODP functions.

For example, relocation transparency provides the ability to relocate an interface. These actions are specified in the dynamic schema; the relocation schema is specified in either the invariant or static schema; and the policy associated with relocation is specified in the invariant schema. Perhaps the invariant schema specifies a particular QoS latency for a particular interface binding. Now that interface is to be relocated. Relocating the interface may affect the QoS for the interaction. The original QoS can be "overriden" by associating a new QoS in the relocation schema to the interface. The QoS invariant schema will need to include a qualification (state) of when the QoS can or cannot be extended for the purposes of relocation.

The binding template is also specified in the information viewpoint. The binding template identifies the type of channel required to support the binding, the transparencies that affect the binding and any additional actions required, and details related to the actual binding. If location transparency is involved, for example, the binding template can specify a precondition that "all engineering interface references are resolved prior to instantiating a channel for binding." That is, the infrastructure must "find" all the interfaces by using the information in the engineering interface reference template, resolve each of the interface locations to a physical address, and use those physical addresses for binding. Whether or not the actual location of the interface is local or distributed does not matter; the same procedure is followed. The manner of doing this is defined in RM-ODP in a general way. The architect can resolve each location, bind to that location's address, and then resolve the next location. Or the architect can wait to resolve all locations, and bind to all addresses simultaneously once the locations are resolved. This is a decision the architect makes.

The dynamic schema identifies the engineering objects' actions to be carried out in each distribution transparency. An example of such an action for a binder object (in a channel) is to "track the interface if the object moves" in support of migration transparency. Other dynamic schema binder actions are "record the interface location" and "find the location of the EIR using Relocator," in support of location and relocation transparency.

The dynamic schema will also identify the actions for the interceptor object to mediate across domains. Some of the actions here would include "transform engineering interface references," "transform naming contexts," "transform protocols," all in support of all transparencies across domains.

Some of the dynamic schema actions in support of the distribution transparencies include:

▶ Access control actions for access transparency

▶ Transactions of the object for transaction transparency

▶ Binding actions (rules) for all binding objects (stub, binder, protocol, interceptor, and any special support binding objects) for failure, location, relocation, and other transparencies

▶ Deactivation/reactivation of an object for migration transparency

Recall that the dynamic schema is subject to the invariant schema. The invariant schema captures the invariant behavior of all the distribution transparencies used. The same interface (or object) can be associated with more than one transparency. As such, care must be exercised that one invariant for a transparency is not inconsistent with a different invariant for a different transparency. The items below are particular to individual distribution transparencies.

▶ Access control schema for access and migration transparencies

▶ Stability schema for failure transparency, to include prohibited failure modes

▶ EIR template may include the transparency required for that interface for a specified binding duration, an interface identifier, location information, relocation information, security information, as shown in the UML model of Figure 10.20

▶ Channel template may include the configuration of the objects in the channel (stub, binder, protocol, interceptor) and an optional alternate configuration for special purpose, such as for encryption (by the stub)

▶ Binding behavior over the timeframe of the binding, that includes the type of channel required to support the binding, transparencies that affect the binding, binding details, preconditions that are appropriate (such as resolving the engineering interface reference to a location before instantiating a binding channel)

▶ Policy for the EIR management domain to define those permissions, obligations, and prohibitions affecting any federation of EIR management domains

▶ Stability policy for an object that defines the prohibited failures of the object

▶ Policy for checkpoint/recovery

▶ Policy for deactivation/reactivation

▶ Policy for migration, to include performance, QoS latency, and so forth

▶ Policy for replication, defining availability and performance of the object

▶ Persistence schema defining processing, storage, communication constraints

▶ Transaction constraints of the object for transaction transparency

▶ Changes in QoS under certain transparencies, such as relocation, replication, and migration. That is, the invariant schema for relocation must identify the rule to relax a QoS latency. Otherwise, the relocation transparency may fail.

10.4.3 COMPUTATIONAL VIEWPOINT MECHANISMS

The computational viewpoint plays a minor role, since distribution is not addressed in this viewpoint. The computational specification is where the architect specifies the requirements for transparency, and the need for replication or transaction transparency. In addition, the architect may want to specify object management interfaces for use in the engineering viewpoint, or additional actions may be required in support of rollback or recovery actions, or management of timing constraints associated with migration, and so forth. RM-ODP itself does not identify the needed computational viewpoint mechanisms. Those identified here are suggestions only.

"Computational specifications are intended to be distribution-transparent; i.e., written without regard to the very real difficulties of implementation within a physically distributed, heterogeneous, multi-organisational environment. The aim of transparencies is to shift the complexities of distributed systems from the applications developers to the supporting infrastructure." [Raymond-95, pg. 11]

The effect of some of the policies is addressed in the computational viewpoint, as is the binding object. As discussed in Chapter 6, "Separation of Concerns: Using RM-ODP Viewpoints," a binding object is the object for compound binding between source and target objects. As such, it plays a role in the binding of many computational objects, which then become engineering objects and interfaces. Thus, the binding object could play a (major) role in a distribution transparency. The policies and schema associated with the transparencies result in constraints on the computational interactions. If location transparency is required, for example, the computational interface should be specified to dynamically resolve the location, which is accomplished in the engineering specification.

With respect to policy handling, a replication policy specifies a particular object must be cloned, along with its interfaces. This is specified in the information and computational specifications and is accomplished in the engineering specification.

The computational viewpoint also provides support for the transaction transparency property. In this case, the computational specification should include extended interfaces of the computational objects. These interfaces will provide the services to notify if a transaction action happens, and recover the state of the object if the transaction is cancelled.

RM-ODP is silent at times as to which object performs a transparency related action, meaning which object actually resolves an interface reference to an actual physical interface location. That it must be accomplished "locally" is identified in RM-ODP, and that it may require additional communications mechanisms to achieve location resolution is explained in RM-ODP, but which object performs these actions is not necessarily explicitly identified. The architect may decide that the binding object is refined to a channel, or to the binder in the channel, or to a separate engineering object that manages all channels. The architect may further decide that the binding object actions include resolving location addresses. However, if the architect chooses to specify the architecture in this regard, it will still be compliant with RM-ODP.

10.5   SUMMARY

To realize distributed systems that are composable and provide interworking across a heterogeneity of systems, a number of problems need to be solved. One of the major problems to overcome is to provide distributed services for the application developer to exploit. Do to so, the intricacies of these services must be hidden from the application developer.

There are eight RM-ODP distribution transparencies. The separation into eight enables the architect to be selective of the transparencies of interest, and to increase the modularity of the distributed system.

Each of the mechanisms to achieve a transparency is reusable across the business applications, as part of the distributed service infrastructure. The engineering model for the transparency is a reusable architecture pattern. The mechanisms to achieve transparency are product and technology independent. As products are selected for a transparency, they may become part of the reusable distributed services in support of the applications. This is depicted in Figure 10.22. Distribution transparencies result in many of the benefits to the stakeholders, as discussed in Chapter 2. These include technical performance, cost savings (less application development), and schedule savings due to reuse.

The information and engineering models are the key models for enabling the distribution transparencies. The computational model does not explicitly address distribution, but does address major distribution system properties. Transparency requirements are generally captured as environment constraints in the interface specifications. The information dynamic and invariant schemas capture the actions and policies that control the transparency actions, the schema that defines the data and actions for a transparency, and the templates used to instantiate a channel, binding, object, interface, and so forth. The engineering specification provides the model for achieving each of the eight distribution transparencies. Most of the distribution transparencies involve the communication path between objects.

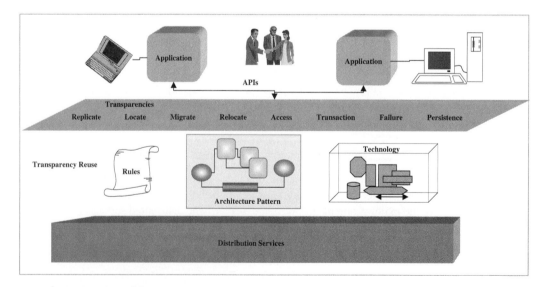

FIGURE 10.22   Reusable Transparency Assets

Some of the distribution properties that are enabled by the distribution transparencies, as well as hidden from the application, were shown to be:

▶ Reliability
▶ Load balancing
▶ Fault tolerance
▶ Availability
▶ Consistency
▶ Reduced latency
▶ Enhanced performance

The details for realizing a distribution transparency exist within RM-ODP (for the most part), but are scattered. These include ODP functions, specifications for the EIRs, all the templates that define the information schemas, detailed information about distributed binding and the binding related objects, and so forth. This chapter has pulled it all together, added some new information, and referenced some additional work in the area.

OMG is providing more and more distribution transparent mechanisms. OMG has initiated this by providing the CORBA Naming Service, which allows objects to be identified by name rather than by location, and the CORBA Trader Service, which matches requestors of services with providers of services through the use of interface references instead of physical location addresses. The Persistent State Service will provide persistence transparency. The Fault Tolerant CORBA provides replication and failure transparency.

Finally, the distribution transparencies hide the complexities of a system while enabling many of the distributed system "ilities." Because RM-ODP is both an international standard and a general reference model, many of the explicit local transparency mechanisms are not specified by RM-ODP. That is, RM-ODP is so powerful that the architect can specify the mechanisms as desired for the local system, defining what objects accomplish what actions, as long as the transparency rules are followed. The rules are defined to enable differences in solutions and ensure that no matter how a transparency is implemented, the distributed processing ensures cross-system and cross-domain interoperability for the purposes of distribution transparency.

ELEVEN

ARCHITECTURE ANALYSIS AND SYSTEM CONFORMANCE EVALUATION

The purpose of this chapter is to introduce the Reference Model of Open Distributed Processing (RM-ODP) constructs and rules for consistency across the viewpoints, and conformance testing capabilities. These are two interrelated topics: consistency and conformance. This chapter discusses:

▶ Purpose of consistency
▶ What is meant by consistency
▶ Why consistency is important
▶ How consistency enables analysis of an architecture specification
▶ How RM-ODP enables viewpoint consistency
▶ What is meant by conformance
▶ How RM-ODP enables conformance testing

11.1   PURPOSE OF CONSISTENCY

The purpose of consistency across the viewpoints is to achieve a well-performing system that solves a business problem and integrates into the business, as specified by the stakeholders. To accomplish this requires achieving consistency across the viewpoints. This, in turn, enables benefits of analysis of the architecture specification, based on the viewpoint languages, perhaps in terms of alternative architec-

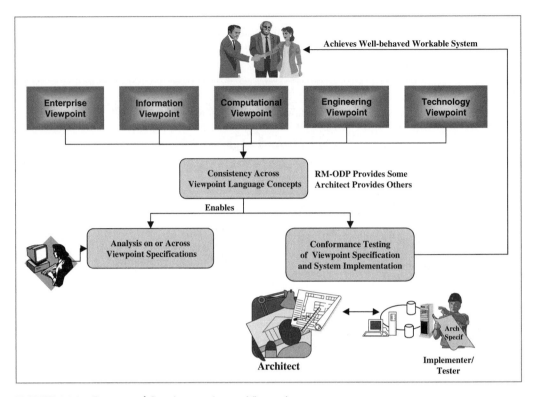

FIGURE 11.1   Purpose of Consistency Across Viewpoints

tures; product trade analyses, selection of the best product at the best price; simulation to see how the system will behave before it is implemented; and many other benefits. Chief among the purposes for consistency is the ability to test the implemented system to the architecture specification, in order to ensure that the system will perform in accordance with that specification. In relating the system implementation to the enterprise viewpoint, for example, the system can be assured to provide a working solution that achieves the business objectives. The relationship of consistency to analysis and conformance testing is the subject of this chapter, and depicted in Figure 11.1.

11.2   WHAT IS MEANT BY CONSISTENCY

Consistency is a relation across the models of a specification that produces no conflicts among the properties across the models. In terms of an architecture specification, consistency means that the relations among key concepts in each model are linked together to provide a cohesive specification. The principal rule for consistency is that there are correspondences among the concepts in the different viewpoint language specifications. That is, a specification statement in the computational specification, for example, corresponds to a statement in the engineering specification.

Some of the concepts of the enterprise and computational languages are mapped in Figure 11.2. In this figure, the enterprise policy and environment contract affect the behavior of the policies and environment contracts specified in the computational specification. They further affect all the interactions defined in the computational viewpoint (though this is not shown). An enterprise object that assumes a role and performs some action corresponds to one or more computational objects, their interactions, and their interface definitions. There are more correspondences, but this shows some of the mappings.

Conformance assessment is the determination of consistency either by testing (conformance) or by model checking (compliance).

For a distributed system to be architected correctly, and to then function correctly, the concepts in the architecture specification must be consistent.

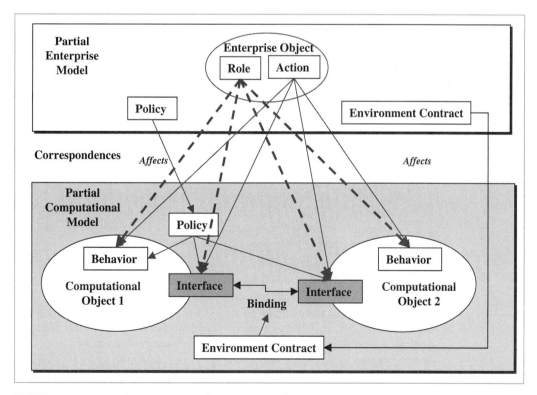

FIGURE 11.2 Example Enterprise and Computational Consistency

RM-ODP specifies some of the correspondences across the viewpoint languages. It is expected that the architect creating a full or partial specification will also specify the correspondences associated with that specification. So if the system specification, for example, defines a specific behavior in the enterprise viewpoint, it may correspond to the computational specification in terms of one or more computational objects and one or more interfaces. These statements of correspondence are considered part of the full specification. However, a full specification does not necessarily need to include specifications from all viewpoints, nor complete specification within a viewpoint. What is meant here is where an architect chooses to use a particular set of viewpoints, and a particular set of concepts from those viewpoints, that statements of correspondences across the viewpoints are also part of the specification.

11.3   WHY CONSISTENCY IS IMPORTANT

Consistency across the viewpoints results in a cohesive set of viewpoints that make them specify a single system, instead of specifying completely independent and possibly incomplete parts.

If specifications from different viewpoints are not related, the result may be an inconsistent specification for a system. It is important that the needs specified in one model of a specification do not contradict the needs specified by another model of the same specification for the same system.

Many architecture frameworks in use today identify views or viewpoints for use in the specification of an architecture, but they generally do not indicate that the views are consistent, how they are consistent, or that they are complete. If, for example, a framework allows the architect to specify a "data" view and a "distribution" view, this may result in two independent views of the same system that are not linked together. How, for example, can the architect be certain that the "distribution" view accounts for all data flows that are distributed, that all aspects of the distributed data transactions are accounted for in the distribution view, and that distribution transparencies do not affect data access?

Unless the framework identifies and specifies rules of consistency, the architect is additionally burdened with aligning the concepts (in the specification) and ensuring the result is an architecture of a consistent and complete system. This in turn complicates the architecture specification, minimizes the ability to execute analysis checkers, and just makes things harder for the architect. And if the architect doesn't get it right, chances are the system implemented from the architecture specification won't be right either.

The important point is that there need to be clear mappings across the viewpoints to ensure the architecture models resulting from the use of the viewpoint languages are consistent and reflect a single consistent system. The architect shouldn't need to do this; the viewpoints should provide consistent concepts and rules.

Once a consistent set of models is enabled, the architect can apply analysis tools on one or more of the models, and determine the completeness, consistency, or the lack of it about the architecture specified. Furthermore, consistency across the models also enables the architect to specify a subset of the system to be architected, implemented, tested, and composed back into the overall system architecture without having to specify everything up front.

11.4   RM-ODP CONSISTENCY RULES

RM-ODP provides some consistency across the viewpoint language concepts in order to achieve a consistent set of viewpoint models, and defines rules for achieving greater consistency. The architect doesn't need to redefine the consistency; but the architect may need to augment what has been defined. The architect then uses RM-ODP viewpoint languages, abiding by the concepts and rules of the viewpoint language, and the consistency is a side effect.

Some of the consistencies are defined in terms of the concepts used across one or more viewpoint models; some are defined as constraints on the use of the viewpoint language to ensure consistency across the viewpoints; some are defined in terms of the relations among the concepts; and some are statements the architect makes. The languages, then, address areas of concern of the distributed processing concepts (e.g., binding in the computational language), which are already linked to each other (e.g., binding in the engineering language). An architect may use a binding object in the computational specification and specify it as a channel in the engineering specification. The statement that the computational binding object corresponds to an engineering channel is one such consistency statement needed. Consistency statements of concept relationships are called *correspondences* between specifications.

The purpose of consistency across the viewpoint specifications is to ensure that what is defined in one viewpoint specification is consistent, noncontradictory, with what is defined in another viewpoint specification. After all, each viewpoint specification is a specification on the entire system. These need to be consistent.

Many of the consistencies across the viewpoint languages occur across the mappings of the computational, engineering, and information languages that capture the semantic behaviors and affect consistency mappings. Consistency results from correspondences that define the mappings of objects, interfaces, and bindings. For example, shown in Figure 11.3 is a computational interface that has a one-to-one mapping to an engineering interface (except for replication). A computational interface is represented unambiguously by an engineering interface reference identifier. The distribution transparencies are specified in the computational language and correspond to the engineering transparency mechanisms, including

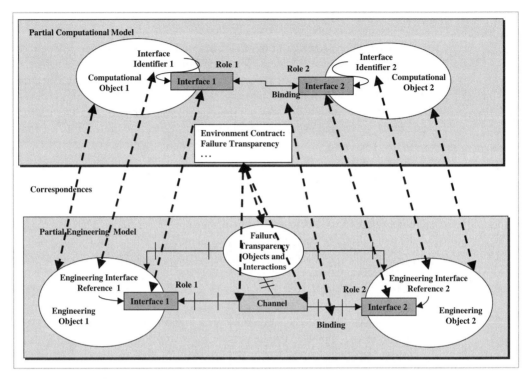

FIGURE 11.3   Example of Computational and Engineering Correspondences

the channel. With these mappings, the engineering specification supports the computational specification, both in terms of functional and semantic behaviors.

The next two sections detail the consistency rules from RM-ODP, and the emerging standard for the Enterprise Viewpoint [RM-ODP-2, RM-ODP-3, ISO-EntVP]. These are rather dry statements, but following these rules are figures to show the correspondences across the viewpoint languages.

11.4.1   GENERAL CONSISTENCY RULES

The language of the viewpoint consists of rules for using each of the viewpoint concepts. It is assumed in the consistency rules that the viewpoint rules are followed within the viewpoint specification.

The object model of RM-ODP provides a common basis for all the viewpoint languages. The use of this model in each language provides the capability of defining relationships across the languages.

Abstraction and refinement rules provide a relationship between two specifications. Consistency is achieved if the more abstract specification can be substituted for the more refined specification, and conformance is valid for either. This ensures that all the constraints specified are reflected in both specifications.

The set of viewpoint specifications of a system should not make mutually contradictory statements.

A complete specification of a system (or part of a system) should include statements relating the terms and language constructs of one viewpoint specification with another viewpoint specification. Though this is a general rule, what it says is that where RM-ODP does not provide this relationship, the architect should include such statements in the specification.

The enterprise objective (specified in terms of roles, actions, purpose, scope, policy, and contract) is captured in all viewpoint specifications.

The contract defined in the enterprise, computational, or engineering specification is specified as an invariant schema in the information specification. This includes the binding contract.

If the architect doesn't care about the configuration of the node in terms of clusters and capsules (and so many specialized uses of RM-ODP do not care!), then all the rules associated with these constructs will not apply in the architecture specification.

The mapping from a business specification to the set of possible system specifications is a partial relation. Further, there can be more than one correct system specification for any one business specification. The architect will need to define the mapping from a partial business specification to its corresponding partial specification of the system, and back. That is, the architect will need to provide correspondence statements between a (partial) business specification and the system specification.

The business specification may include parts that are not automated; they are human related. There are parts of the technology specification that may not map to the business specification. These too will be specified by the architect.

The behavior of stubs, binders, protocol, and interceptor objects are constrained by the transparencies selected.

The enterprise scope of the system (behavior named by the roles the system will fulfill) will specify in sufficient detail the behavior of the system that enables the information, computational, engineering, and technology specifications.

The engineering viewpoint exposes the object in the distributed infrastructure and refines it into infrastructure objects, which may be numerous. Because there are more engineering objects than there are computational objects, every computational interface must correspond to an engineering interface in the engineering specification. In other words, the computational boundaries must map onto distributed engineering objects so that the distribution strategy is clarified by the architecture.

11.4.2   SPECIFIC CONSISTENCY RULES

In addition to the general rules just provided, RM-ODP provides specific viewpoint language consistency rules. These are itemized here. Each section provides a figure that depicts these correspondences. Where there are no correspondence lines (to and from the triangle shapes), there is no correspondence identified in RM-ODP. These are areas where the architect should provide additional correspondence statements in the architecture specification.

11.4.2.1   Enterprise Correspondences to Other Viewpoints

Figure 11.4 provides an overview of some of the correspondences related to the enterprise concepts addressed in this section. Notice that there are some correspondences not addressed. An example is how enterprise scope corresponds to the other viewpoint languages.

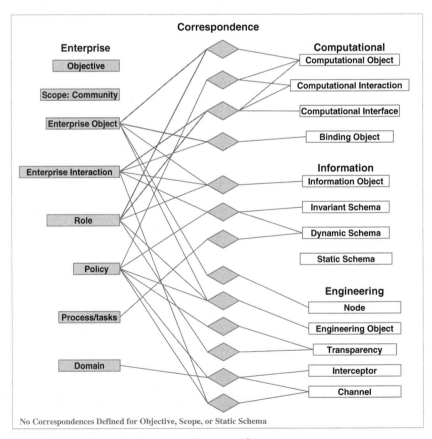

FIGURE 11.4   Enterprise Language Correspondences

Enterprise and Information Concept Correspondences

The enterprise object and the role it assumes correspond to one or more information objects.

The enterprise policies are invariants in the information specification. These invariants govern the allowable states of the information objects representing the enterprise objects, and allowable state transitions represented in the dynamic schema.

The enterprise community policies correspond to the policies and constraints on each information object.

The enterprise task corresponds to an action in the dynamic schema.

The enterprise interaction corresponds to an action in the dynamic schema.

Enterprise and Computational Concept Correspondences

The enterprise role corresponds to one or more computational objects that assume the role.

An enterprise object and the role it assumes correspond to a computational object, or a configuration of computational objects.

An enterprise role's behavior corresponds to one or more computational objects and interfaces.

An enterprise role interaction corresponds to one or more computational interactions and related computational interfaces.

An enterprise task corresponds to one or more computational object interactions.

An enterprise interaction corresponds to one or more computational object interactions.

The type of an enterprise interaction corresponds to the type of the computational interface and the type of the computational interaction.

An enterprise policy associated with a role restricts the actions of the computational objects and interfaces.

The composite behaviors of enterprise objects that identify interactions involving at least two objects corresponds to a computational binding object.

Enterprise and Engineering Concept Correspondences

The enterprise role may include a transparency requirement, as specified in the environment contract in the enterprise language. This corresponds to the associated transparency mechanism in the engineering language.

The location of an enterprise object corresponds to the location of an engineering node.

The enterprise policy corresponds to and determines the engineering transparency mechanisms and supporting engineering objects.

An enterprise policy corresponds to any interceptor required in the engineering channel, within or across a domain boundary.

An enterprise object corresponds to one or more engineering objects at one or more nodes.

An enterprise domain boundary may require and correspond to one or more engineering interceptors to implement the crossing of the domain boundary.

An enterprise policy on an interaction corresponds to constraints on the engineering channel objects.

11.4.2.2   Information Correspondences

Figure 11.5 provides an overview of some of the correspondences related to the information, computational, and engineering concepts.

Information and Computational Concept Correspondences

The mapping between an information object and a computational object is not defined. It may be one-to-one, one-to-many, many-to-one, or many-to-many. The correspondences between the information and computational specifications are specified by the architect, as appropriate for the specification.

If an information object corresponds to a computational object, then the static and invariant schemata of the information object correspond to states of the computational object.

The dynamic schema that represents a change of state for the information object corresponds to one or more interactions of the computational object, or some internal action of the computational object.

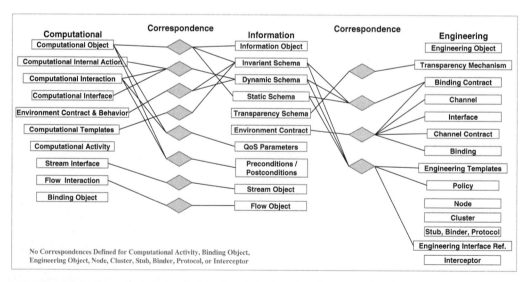

FIGURE 11.5   Information, Computational, and Engineering Correspondences

The invariant and dynamic schemata correspond to the behavior and environment contract of the computational object.

A computational stream interface relates to an information specification interface stream object. Each flow in a stream interface relates to a flow information object. A flow information object specifies the direction and Quality of Service (QoS) parameters of the flow interaction.

QoS parameters in the information specification map to computational objects and interactions, as determined by the architect.

The architect also establishes rules of consistency, applicable to the system being specified. Specific constraints, such as preconditions and postconditions, are stated in the information specification, and related to computational objects and interactions in the computational specification, as deemed appropriate by the architect.

Information and Engineering Concept Correspondences

A binding contract corresponds to statements in the static and dynamic schemata in the information specification, as constrained by an appropriate (optional) invariant schema.

The environment contract, that specifies such things as QoS, are constraints associated with the engineering interfaces and the binding of those interfaces, as defined by the binding contract and the channel contract.

The information specification defines the schema associated with the distribution transparency in the engineering specification.

The information specification defines the schema associated with the engineering templates.

The information specification defines the schema associated with the engineering policy.

11.4.2.3   Computational Correspondences to Engineering Viewpoint

Figure 11.6 provides an overview of some of the correspondences related to the computational and engineering concepts.

Computational and Engineering Concept Correspondences

The engineering specification is constrained by the configuration of the computational objects, their interfaces, and associated policies and contracts of the computational specification. Basic engineering objects are grouped into clusters, which in turn are grouped into capsules.

A computational object template is refined into an engineering language object template in terms of clusters and capsules. In some cases, additional behavior statements may be included in the engineering template to account for certain behaviors, such as synchronization, transparency, or failure transparency. That is,

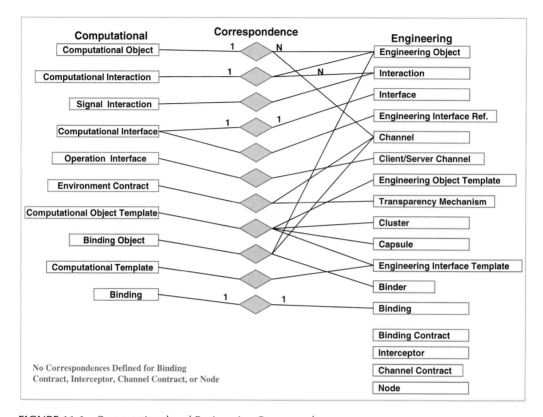

FIGURE 11.6   Computational and Engineering Correspondences

the behavior associated with the computational specification may result in additional engineering objects and interfaces to fulfill that behavior.

A computational object corresponds to one or more basic engineering objects in the engineering language and the channels that connect them.

A computational interface corresponds to one engineering interface.

Each computational interaction corresponds to one or more engineering interactions, originating and terminating with a basic engineering object.

A computational operation interface corresponds to an engineering client/server channel.

If a response on all interface bindings is required (synchronous communication) then the computational specification will only specify operational type interfaces. This will relate to engineering bindings that support only operational interfaces. If a multimedia or multiparty binding is required, the computational binding will be compound and relate to one or more engineering channels to support the binding.

The environment contract is evaluated in establishing an appropriate channel between computational objects.

Cluster templates can represent abstract data types, associated with interface parameters. An engineering object subject to migration includes passing the computational interface parameters as cluster templates.

The engineering interface reference identifier specifically identifies the interface in the computational language.

A computational binding corresponds uniquely to an engineering binding. It doesn't matter if the computational binding is primitive or compound, or if the engineering binding is local or involves a channel. There is a unique one-to-one correspondence between the computational binding (of whatever type) and the engineering binding (of whatever type).

The binding object in the computational language corresponds to a channel configuration, a binder in the channel, or a special engineering object. This is one area where consistency is ambiguous. Hence, the architect will need to establish this consistency rule.

The binding object control interface in the computational specification corresponds to an engineering interface with the rules that the binding control interface links to all binders, stubs, protocol, and interceptor objects required to be controlled. This may require a set of engineering interactions to accomplish.

If a computational interface type is an operation in the computational specification, the engineering binding must provide the exchange of the computational interface signature parameters: name, type, operation interaction names, termination names, invocation parameters, termination parameters, and computational interface identifiers.

Computational interface parameters correspond to engineering interface references when they are passed by reference.

If replication is specified as needed in the computational specification, each computational object and its set of interfaces correspond to the set of basic engineering objects and interfaces representing the number of replicas. Each computational interface, in this case, corresponds to a set of engineering interfaces that represent the replication.

Each computational signal interaction corresponds to a signal interaction at a local binding, or to a set of engineering interactions to support the computational signal interaction.

An engineering cluster can contain basic engineering objects that correspond to different computational objects.

The computational specification that defines the need for a distribution transparency corresponds to an engineering specification that uses ODP functions and engineering structures to support the transparency.

11.5	CONFORMANCE AND COMPLIANCE TESTING

Correspondences are critical and necessary, but not sufficient for a compliant RM-ODP specification that conforms with the system implementation. Testing is required to ensure the correspondences were in fact followed in the language specifications.

Sometimes the architect will use only portions of RM-ODP, such as a subset of one or more viewpoint languages sufficient to specify some part of the system. Sometimes the architect will specify only a portion of the system, but use all the viewpoint languages to do so. So this means the use of RM-ODP may be partial. Then, composing a system will require composition of separately constructed specifications. How can the architect be sure this composition will work? One way is to ensure the specifications created followed the RM-ODP language and consistency rules. Another way is to ensure the implemented system adheres to the specification. Both of these are called conformance testing and compliance testing, and are critical pieces to the architecture specification.

Figure 11.7 provides an example. Assume the architect is further architecting Healthy Hospital and needs to address the items shown in the list. Part of the architecture requires a Patient Directory Services (PDS) capability. The PDS has been fully specified somewhere else, perhaps through a standards or consortia organization. The architect can, therefore, reuse this architecture specification instead of fully specifying it, assuming it has already been fully specified in accordance with the RM-ODP rules. Hence, because of the consistency correspondences and the specificity resulting from an RM-ODP specification, the architect is able to "plug in" the component specification into the Healthy Hospital specification.

11.5.1 WHAT IS MEANT BY CONFORMANCE AND COMPLIANCE

The architect has provided an architecture specification. The implementer has implemented to specification. So, everything is in order and works well. Or does it?

Conformance testing is used to ensure the developed system (or subsystem) agrees with the architecture specification. RM-ODP enables this through conformance testing points and observed behavior at those points. These points are associated with the interfaces to determine if the developed system conforms to the architectural specification. QoS should be observable across the interface, for example, so conformance testing points are identified for validating that the quality of service is met. Furthermore, these tests can be performed not only on the developed system, but also on commercial products that may be included in the system implementation.

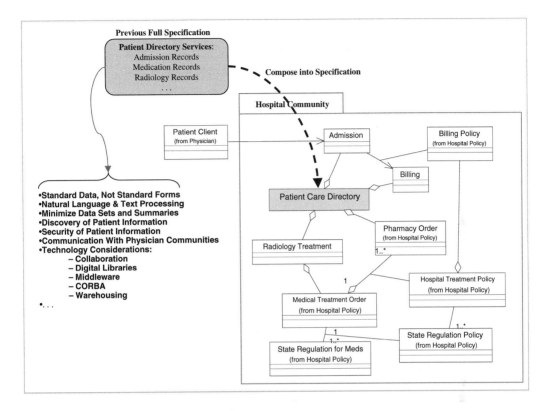

FIGURE 11.7 Example Reuse of a Specification

In order to achieve a well-formed specification to RM-ODP, a set of tests are needed to test the specification to the rules of RM-ODP. This is called *compliance testing*. For example, is the distribution transparency specified as part of the environment contract, and are the infrastructure objects in the engineering specification adhering to the rules of that transparency?

So, then, there are two types of testing: one is conformance and one is compliance.

Conformance is where the implementation corresponds to the specification. In this case, conformance testing will test that the system as implemented corresponds with the architecture specification. This is likened to validation.

Compliance is where the specification corresponds to another specification. In this case, compliance testing will test that the architecture specification corresponds with RM-ODP rules. This is likened to verification.

The reference points identified by RM-ODP enable the conformance testing of the system to the architecture specification. This works because the reference points are not only places where tests are performed, but they also relate to the constructs of the viewpoint languages and the rules of consistency, to bring it all together.

Conformance is not enforceable until there is a test or certification process. RM-ODP provides "principles" of conformance testing and provides points where conformance testing occurs. It does not provide the actual tests to be performed—that is the job of the architect. The principles for conformance testing enable:

▶ Testing the structure of the distributed system to determine its compliance with RM-ODP

▶ Testing the implemented system to the architecture specification, using the viewpoint languages and adhering to the rules of consistency

The points at which testing occurs are identified throughout the viewpoint specifications. A testing point may, for example, occur in the runtime system, associated with a particular interface, but relates to the behavior specified in an enterprise contract. This is achievable because of the consistency rules.

Part of the specification of the system must, therefore, include:

▶ The reference points for conformance testing

▶ The behavior to be observed at those points

▶ The specification concepts to be tested (such as a distribution transparency, or a QoS, or the binding of specific interfaces) at each point

▶ The domain-specific language (such as the "medical language" of patient, physician, billing, patient care services) to relate to the specification concept being tested. This is primarily so that the tester can understand what the test results show, instead of needing to map the concepts of RM-ODP to the test results. Its easier for the tester to see "billing service is correctly bound to patient care directory" than "computational interface xyz is bound to computational interface abc."

The relationship of reference points, conformance points, and consistency among the viewpoints is shown in Figure 11.8. Each viewpoint specification identifies "reference points" for use to observe some testing criteria. Conformance points are those reference points in the implementation at which conformance can be tested. So, part of the specification includes statements that a particular reference point is used as a conformance testing point and that, at that point, certain information is to be observed.

11.5.2   COMPLIANCE TESTING

A compliance test is done to test that the architecture specification adheres to the RM-ODP rules. If the architect chooses to use a language other than that specified in RM-ODP, then the architect must map the constructs of the language used to those of RM-ODP. This generally requires a formal language analysis, which is not addressed here. Standards being created from RM-ODP, such as the Interface Reference and Binding standard [ISO-IRB], will provide their own formal lan-

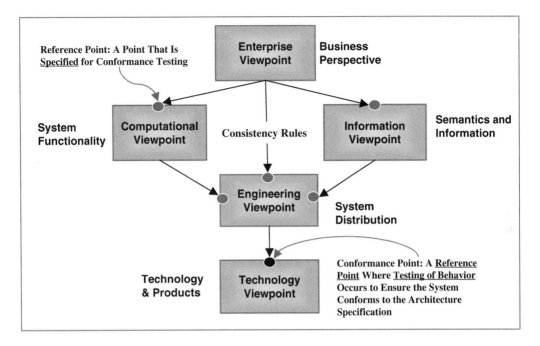

FIGURE 11.8 Reference Points, Conformance Points, and Consistency Rules Across the Viewpoints

guage mapping to ensure compliance with RM-ODP. The architect who uses one of these standards is implicitly assured of compliance. Formal analysis techniques generally make use of formal description languages such as Z [Z], Lotos [LOTOS], SDL [SDL], or some other formal description technique.

11.5.3 CONFORMANCE TESTING

A conformance test is an assertion that what is being tested correctly adheres to the architecture specification. A *reference point* is a place in the architecture specification where some behavior can be observed. A *conformance test point* is a reference point used for conformance testing.

Conformance test points are points used to test observed behavior. The behavior is related to the specification itself. To pass a conformance test, the specified behavior must be the same as that observed at the conformance test point in the runtime system.

RM-ODP specifies types of conformance testing points to be identified in the architecture specification. The architect chooses which of these to use, and makes statements in the specification of the behavior to be observed. When the system is implemented, including the use of commercial products, the reference test points need to be implemented and made accessible for testing.

The process of testing for conformance may relate several test points to the specification. The more abstract the specification, the harder it will be to relate the test results to it. The relation between several conformance points may need to be addressed by the architect. This is one reason why the architect is the one who needs to specify the relationship from the abstract specification to the more concrete implementable results expected. For example, it's rather straightforward to test whether a particular graphic standard is used in the presentation of information to the user's workstation. It's more difficult to test that correct data has been obtained within a certain integrity quality, combined, and laid out correctly in the screen image to the end user.

For example, a specification that is tested to be sure an interface template has been correctly instantiated would need to address one or more tests at a programming language binding (of the interface). One test could be that the language used to represent the template (such as the Interface Definition Language (IDL) [ISO IDL]) and the language used to bind that language to a programming language (such as Java™ or C++) must both be compliant with the use of the languages. Then, the test at the conformance test point that the interface operates as expected is interpreted based on the compliance of the interface template to the programming language. So, an interface template is represented in a language (IDL) that is compiled into a programming language (C++) and is bound in the runtime system. All of these must pass separate compliance and conformance tests to know that the interface behaved as specified.

In this way, conformance testing relates the implemented system to the specification. Tools do not yet exist that can automate these types of testing, based on a given architecture specification. Hence, testing remains a manual procedure.

To help this along, the architect needs to specify the terms used in the specification that are associated with the behavior expected at the conformance test points, and what information the implementer of the system must provide for the testing at those points. The implementer hopefully implements the system to the specification. To be more comfortable that this has occurred, the implementer provides statements that show how the terms specified by the architect map to the implementation, and where the reference points (interfaces) are implemented in the system for use in conformance testing. The tester can then perform the tests at the designated test points, observe and record the behavior, and correlate what is expected (terms) with the results (observations of the test). When a test occurs across an interface, that interface is already bound. The tester who observes certain behavior across the binding, interprets the statements from the implementer that certain behavior will exist across the binding, and then relates that information back to the specification.

An example is shown in Figure 11.9. The architect defines the reference points in the computational specification, along with the behavior to be observed. Notice that the behavior is in terms of Healthy Hospital: patient record, patient

Architect Defines Reference Points and Observable Behavior

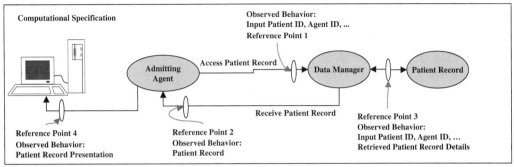

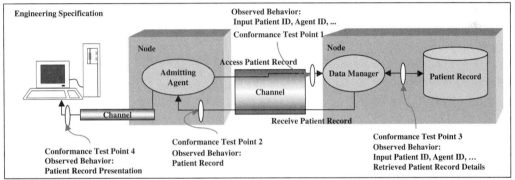

Consistency Rules Relate Computational Reference Points to Engineering Reference Points and Observable Behavior

FIGURE 11.9 Example of Using Reference Points as Conformance Test Points in Healthy Hospital

identification, and admitting agent identification. The reference points are related to the engineering specification (through the rules of consistency). In this specification, they are used as conformance test points that test that the request interaction is correct across the channel, the response (patient record) is correct, that the access to the database retrieves the correct information, and that the presentation to the end user is correct. The tester observes the behavior of the implemented system in Healthy Hospital terms, but can relate these to the expected behavior. All of these tests should pass to ensure the end-to-end correctness of retrieving the patient record.

If the conformance test tests an abstract specification, the implementer would need to map that abstract specification to the implemented system. If, for example, the abstract specification requires a failure transparency, the implementer provides a detailed description of how failure transparency is implemented, where the implementation parts are, and correlates these to the conformance test points identified by the architect.

If the specification needs to test the migration ability of an object, in support of migration transparency for example, then the testing of conformance may be more involved. The implementer identifies the conformance test points of the object and its interfaces. The tester needs to change the configuration of the objects, and observe the behavior when the object is migrated. The migration may be a result of an introduced failure to the system by the tester, which causes a failure recovery to be attempted, which in turn causes the migration to occur. Conformance test points for all these actions are used to observe the behavior of the system. And these points are related to the implementation of the migration capability, which are related to the reference points in the architecture specification. Yes, it's complicated. Yes, it's involved. And yes, it takes coordinated specifications among the architect, implementer, and tester to ensure conformance.

The implementation conforms to the specification if all the tests succeed. If there is a failure, it can be because the specification is inconsistent, the architect did not provide an appropriate mapping of terms to expected behavior, the implementer did not provide an appropriate mapping to the implementation, or the observed behavior cannot be interpreted (doesn't make sense) based on the mappings. In these cases, the conformance test fails. Clearly, then, it is important that the mappings provided by the architect, implementer, and tester are consistent and complete. RM-ODP provides no guidance on how this can be accomplished, other than through the use of the viewpoint language rules and rules of consistency.

Table 11.1 provides an overview of what the architect, implementer, and tester need to specify for conformance tests.

TABLE 11.1   Conformance Test Actions

USER ROLE	ACTIONS
Architect	• Specifies reference points • Specifies type of reference point • Specifies viewpoint language terms at that point • Specifies mapping of terms to domain-specific language (e.g., Healthy Hospital) • Specifies expected behavior defined by extra information to be observed • Specifies any multiple reference point relationships for some observed behavior • Specifies any additional consistencies required
Implementer	• Specifies conformance test point (interface) in the system to test, relating to the reference point • Specifies mapping of abstract specification to a set of implemented constructs, and associated conformance test points for required observed behavior • Specifies information to be observed in testing • Defines mapping of observed behavior back to the specification
Tester	• Observes and records the behavior • Correlates terms with the results seen • Maps observed behavior to the statements from the implementer

11.5.4 CONFORMANCE TESTING REFERENCE POINTS

Conformance testing amounts to testing at interfaces. A test is a series of events that are observed and related to the specification. What is being tested is considered a "black box." Its behavior is only observable at the interfaces. Relating the observed behavior to the architecture specification, then, means that the architect needs to make statements of what to observe, how it relates to the architecture specification, and what is being tested.

There are four categories of reference points for conformance testing. One is the *programmatic reference point*. These are points in the computational specification to test for software interfaces. Another point is called the *perceptual reference point*. These are points at the user interfaces used for usability and user interface testing. In Figure 11.9, this was represented as reference point 4. Another point is called the *interworking reference point*. These are points that test the interoperability between implementations of systems. In Figure 11.9, these were reference points 1 and 2. Interworking reference points include additional requirements beyond programmatic reference points. The final point is called the *interchange reference point*. These are points that test the exchange of external media, such as tapes and disks. This point assures that information stored on external media can be reused by other systems that conform to the same standards. This was shown as reference point 3.

The tester does not need to test each viewpoint specification independently. The points are defined in different viewpoint specifications. Based on the correspondence rules across the viewpoint languages, objects do not have to be explicitly tested. Instead, the reference points identify certain places to test, with the criterion that those places have correspondences to other parts of the specification, through the rules of consistency. So, each viewpoint specification provides an independent specification of the system that is related to other viewpoint specifications, which in turn provides various levels of granularity of specification and constraints. For example, testing a channel in the engineering specification relates to the testing of the behavior from the computational specification, through the rules of consistency.

If the computational specification provides dynamic behaviors, these are specified in the information specification as well. The information language does not itself support the processing that occurs for information (typically called "information flow"); this is accomplished by the computational specification. Therefore, to test that information flows in accordance with the architecture specification means that the interaction of a computational interface needs to be tested. In other words, an invocation of a software interface that causes the processing of information is what is tested.

These four kinds of reference points enable conformance testing as follows [RM-ODP-2]:

▶ *Programmatic*—behavioral testing of software interfaces. This is a point where the behavior of a function can be observed (tested). A programmatic reference point is associated with an interface, realized through a programming language binding. A "programmatic conformance requirement" may state that the object's behavior is compatible with another object that can replace it. This supports the ability of source-code or execution portability.

▶ *Perceptual*—user and usability testing at user interfaces or a communication port. This is a point where the system interacts with the physical world, such as a human/computer interface. A "perceptual conformance requirement" may state that the information presented to the user adheres to a specific form (such as a specific Web page), or it may state what information must be presented to the user.

▶ *Interworking*—interoperability testing between systems. This is a point that allows the testing of communication with another system. An "interworking conformance requirement" may state that certain information is successfully exchanged between systems.

▶ *Interchange*—exchange of external physical storage testing. This is a point that allows the testing of successful off-line storage of information. An "interchange conformance requirement" may state that the access to the information is achievable, in a specified format, within a specified latency. This conformance point enables testing that a physical device can be used by another system.

In addition to the reference points used for conformance testing, conformance testers may require additional information when testing an implementation of the ODP specification. This information is called *Implementation eXtra Information for Testing* (IXIT). It provides details to relate conformance statements to the implementation. For example, at an interworking conformance point, statements are made for the tester to observe, such as:

▶ Observe latency of 20ms

▶ Relate to the computational environment contract for QoS = 20ms

In other words, the behavior of the system, as specified throughout the viewpoint specifications, provides statements of testing criteria, and can formulate the test procedures plan that organizations generally create. In the case of RM-ODP, these test procedures are not "guesses": they are specifications that relate to the architecture specifications, which themselves are consistent across the viewpoints. It all hangs together.

The conformance statements applicable to each viewpoint are described next.

11.5.4.1   Enterprise

The enterprise specification conformance is tested by reference points in the engineering specification that relate to the behavior of the policies and objectives of the enterprise language. To accomplish this, the implementer identifies the points that provide testing of the system, and a specification of how those points map to the information, computational, and engineering specifications. The architect specifies the mapping of the enterprise specification to the information, computational, and engineering specifications, using the already provided RM-ODP correspondences. The observed behavior at the conformance test points are then interpreted in enterprise language terms to check that the enterprise specification is correctly implemented, as defined by the architect. These reference points are then enterprise specification conformance testing points. A view of this process is shown in Figure 11.10.

Any of the four types of reference points can be used by the architect to specify conformance testing capabilities.

As an example, if the enterprise specification defines a 24-hour policy to record a patient treatment result, this must result in an engineering rule, and one or more engineering objects and interfaces that accomplish this constraint. A conformance point is then the point where the action is accomplished in the engineering specification. In short, the concepts and structures are mapped from one viewpoint specification to the other, in order to relate the results of conformance checking.

Because a model is specific to the language of the domain (e.g., patient record for the medical domain), conformance testers may require additional information when testing (IXIT). This information will detail the observations at the conformance test point, and relate it to the language of the domain. The results of the test can then be expressed in terms of the enterprise language (the viewpoints are consistent) and the language of the domain (e.g., Healthy Hospital).

11.5.4.2   Information

The conformance tests for the information specification require that the behavior specified in the static, dynamic, and invariant schemata is conformant. To accomplish this, the implementer identifies reference points in the engineering specifi-

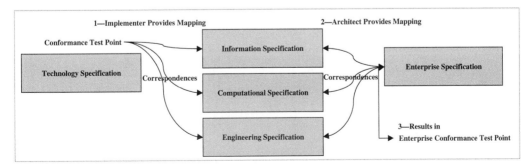

FIGURE 11.10   Achieving Enterprise Conformance Testing

cation where testing can be accomplished. The implementer further provides statements of the computational and engineering specification terms that apply at these conformance points. The architect must map the information schemata to the computational and engineering specifications as well. Then the reference points used in the engineering specification for conformance testing can be interpreted in information language terms to check for conformance to the schemata. A view of this is shown in Figure 11.11.

Any of the four types of reference points can be used by the architect to specify conformance testing capabilities.

11.5.4.3   Computational

Conformance testing for the computational specification addresses conformance of the object and its interfaces, as specified by their templates. A reference point can be specified by the architect for any of the object interfaces. Any of the four types of reference points can be associated to the interface.

The implementer identifies the engineering reference points that can be used for testing and relates the behavior at these points to the object and interface template specifications. In particular, any distribution transparency required in the object specification (which includes its interface specifications) must be mapped to the engineering mechanisms that provide the transparency, and the reference points that can be used to test for conformance to the transparency.

Then, the reference points used in the engineering specification for conformance testing can be interpreted in the computational language to check for conformance to the object and its interactions across the interfaces.

Conformance testing of an object at a programmatic point uses a standard interface specification language, such as IDL [ISO IDL], and a language binding, such as C++. This provides for testing of the portability rules specified in the computational language.

Conformance of an object at an interworking point can be tested in terms of the interactions specified in the object template, and associated interaction template. These interactions are observed in the communications protocols. A view of this is shown in Figure 11.12.

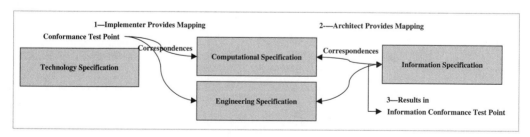

FIGURE 11.11   Achieving Information Conformance Testing

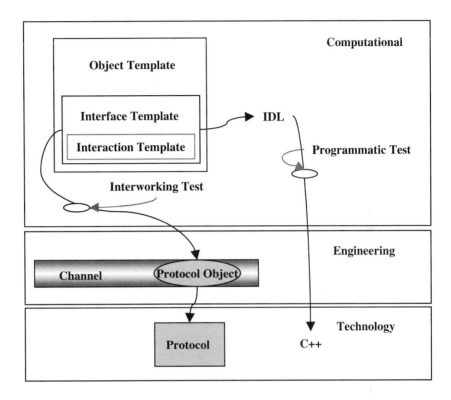

FIGURE 11.12 Achieving Computational Conformance Testing

11.5.4.4 Engineering

The engineering specification provides both the requirements on the correct behavior to be observed in support of the other viewpoint specifications, as well as a specification of where the different reference points are to be associated. RM-ODP does not provide conformance rules for **non-basic** engineering objects and portability to other systems, nor that the engineering object will interwork with other systems. The focus of the engineering specification conformance, then, is the **basic** engineering objects, their interfaces, and the channel objects. The architect needs to augment RM-ODP with conformance rules about any non-basic engineering objects of importance.

The four reference points are associated with specific engineering concepts as follows.

A programmatic reference point can be associated with:

▶ Each interaction between basic engineering objects

▶ Each interaction between a cluster manager and a basic engineering object

▶ Between an engineering object and the nucleus

A perceptual reference point can be associated with:

▶ An interface of a basic engineering object that provides a human/computer interface

A programmatic reference point can be associated with the interaction points:

▶ Between each object interface to a stub in the channel
▶ Between stubs
▶ Between a stub and binder object
▶ Between a binder and a protocol object
▶ Between a protocol object and an interceptor
▶ Between stubs, by abstracting the binders, protocol, and interceptor objects in the channel
▶ Between binders, by abstracting the protocol objects, and any interceptors used in the channel
▶ Between protocol objects in the same node, by abstracting the interceptors used in the channel
▶ At the control interface of a stub
▶ At the control interface of a binder
▶ At the control interface of a protocol object
▶ At the control interface of an interceptor

There is a small inconsistency here. RM-ODP explicitly states that only basic engineering object conformance testing is achieved, but the objects in a channel are not basic engineering objects, generally.

An interworking reference point can be associated with an interaction point:

▶ Between protocol objects in different nodes
▶ Between protocol objects and interceptors in different nodes

11.5.4.5 Technology

The technology specification includes a specification from the implementer that supports the conformance testing of the other viewpoint specifications. It provides a descriptive name for all reference points, the IXIT information required, and how that information relates to the domain-specific language of each specification. In other words, the technology specification captures all the information required of the implementer and tester to use to assert and test for conformance of all the other viewpoint specifications. RM-ODP does not provide any template specification for this information. Hence, this is left to the architect, implementer, and tester to define.

11.6   Summary

Consistency across viewpoints attempts to resolve the "multiple viewpoint problem," and provides a cohesive set of viewpoints that in the end specify an architecture for a system and enable conformance testing at each viewpoint. That is, consistency is important to achieve a unified system specification, not individual specifications that do not hang together. With rules of consistency, all sorts of analysis on the architecture specification as a whole can be conducted: syntactic, dynamic, alternative architecture specifications, simulation, conformance testing, etc. *Consistency* is a relation across the models of a specification that produces no conflicts among the properties across the models.

Consistency is very important to the ability to test an implementation of a system to the specification for that system. How does the architect know the system as delivered by the implementer performs in the manner specified by the architecture? The way to be "more sure" is to conduct conformance tests. *Conformance assessment* is the determination of consistency either by testing (conformance) or by model checking (compliance).

To accomplish the task of testing requires three roles (although in some organizations, this can require one, three, or more individuals). One role is the architect. The architect not only provides the specification of the architecture for the system, but also specifies key criteria for conformance testing. Part of this task is to associate different types of reference points to parts of the specification. These reference points are places to observe the behavior of the implemented system. The kinds of conformance include:

▶ Programmatic reference points where testing of software interfaces can be accomplished

▶ Perceptual reference points where testing of user interfaces or communications ports can be accomplished

▶ Interworking reference points where interoperability between or among systems can be tested

▶ Interchange reference points where testing of the use of external media can be tested

To accomplish conformance testing, the architect must provide, as part of the system specification, the following additional information:

▶ Specification of the reference points to be used in conformance testing

▶ Specification of the type of reference points to be used

▶ Specification of terms to be observed at each point

▶ Specification mapping of RM-ODP terms to domain-specific language terms for better understanding of behavior test observations

▶ Specification of the expected behavior defined by information to be observed

▶ Specification of any multiple reference point relationships for some expected behavior

Another role is the implementer. The implementer implements the system, using technologies, products, standards, and custom code. The implementer needs to assert and show that the implementation is conformant with the architecture specification. To accomplish this, the implementer is required to specify how the implementation reflects the architecture specification, and where the reference points become conformance testing points in the implementation. The implementer must provide the following:

▶ Specification of the conformance test points (interfaces) used to test the system

▶ Specification of the mapping of the abstract specification to a set of implemented constructs, and associated conformance test points for required observed behavior

▶ Specification of the information to be observed in testing

▶ Definition of the mapping of observed behavior back to the abstract specification

The tester conducts the conformance testing procedures. These procedures observe the behavior of the system at designated points in the system. At these points, information is provided to the tester about the functioning and behavior observed. This information is directly related back to the architecture specification terminology in the following way:

▶ The observed behavior is related to the tester through a domain-specific language (e.g., the hospital domain).

▶ The domain-specific language is a result of mapping between the implementation and the architecture specification, provided by the implementer.

▶ The domain-specific language is mapped to the RM-ODP concepts in each viewpoint language by the architect, to relay them to the RM-ODP concepts.

▶ The individual viewpoint specifications are then determined to be conformant by the concepts observed and related to the viewpoint specifications.

This interrelationship among the consistency rules, the conformance test points, and the roles of the architect, implementer, and tester are shown in Figure 11.13.

In RM-ODP, all of the viewpoint languages play a role in the conformance testing process, but RM-ODP only specifies the concept, or principal rules, for conformance testing. It does not provide an explicit cookbook on how to accomplish conformance tests. Finally, RM-ODP consistency rules do not account for consistency across all of the concepts. So, the end result is that the architect has a

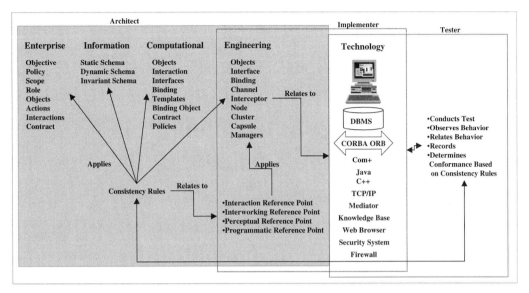

FIGURE 11.13 Consistency Rules, Conformance Testing, and Roles

fair amount of work; she must provide both additional consistency rule specifications and conformance testing specifications. This burden is eased by RM-ODP's set of correspondences and relationships, and the process of how to achieve conformance testing using these correspondences.

PART THREE

PATTERNS FOR DISTRIBUTED PROCESSING CONCERNS

TWELVE

ENTERPRISE BUSINESS SPECIFICATION

$\mathbf{T}$his chapter discusses an approach to enterprise business specification, using the concepts and rules of [ISO-EntVP] coupled with the existing Reference Model of Open Distributed Processing (RM-ODP). These concepts enable real-world entities, such as humans, machines, equipment, as well as distributed processing systems, to be specified. Further, these concepts position the automated system in the context of the business, specifying the interactions of real-world entities, as well as those entities that comprise the system.

Covered in this chapter are:

▶ The importance of a business specification, including how a system solves a business problem

▶ The use of RM-ODP and the emerging Enterprise Viewpoint concepts toward the specification of an enterprise and the businesses that comprise it

▶ An extension to the Healthy Hospital case study

Recall that the enterprise language also applies to a part of the system or a single software component in the system. However, the focus of this chapter will be only on the use of the new enterprise viewpoint concepts [ISO-EntVP] to create an enterprise business specification.

Excellent discussions about business specifications can be found in [Kilov-98, Kilov-99, EDOC-97, EDOC-98, EDOC-99, and Milosevic].

12.1　IMPORTANCE

The functional needs of the business drive the system solution, and the system solution exists solely to provide support to the business. Business specifications are not merely about the functions the system is to perform. Businesses operate according to a set of rules and constraints. Often these rules are implicit to the business stakeholders. One of the major problems in architecting a system is that it's often forgotten that the system is there to support the business. People form a part of the business. Machines can form a part of the business, especially in manufacturing. Thus, a business consists not only of the information technology (IT) system solution, but also those aspects that are not part of the system but still may interact with it. All of these elements must work together to achieve a well-functioning business enterprise.

What needs to be accomplished is the ability to communicate between the stakeholders of the enterprise and the distributed system architect, to define the use of a distributed processing system that supports the business, how it is positioned within the enterprise, and what real-world entities interact with the system. The stakeholders and architecture team need to understand how that system is to function, what rules must be adhered to, what external constraints are important for the processing, and some ability to test that the resultant system indeed satisfies the business specifications. This process of iterating toward a business specification is represented in Figure 12.1.

An enterprise business specification is a specification of the scope of the business within the enterprise, the objectives of the business, business processes,

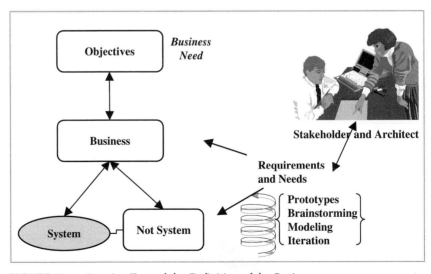

FIGURE 12.1　Iterating Toward the Definition of the Business

business objects, policies, and a delineation of those objects representing real-world entities and those assumed by information technology objects.

As an example, the Healthy Hospital is a business. Along with the physician practices, the insurance company, the state regulation authority, and the hospital pharmacy, this medical business can be considered an enterprise. Healthy Hospital can also be considered an enterprise (there is no rule that states an enterprise is large or small). Each organization in Healthy Hospital can be considered a separate business organization (or domain). Defining the business means to define the boundaries (the scope) of the business, and possibly iteratively define all parts of the enterprise. Figure 12.2 provides an overview of what the hospital enterprise business might include, as an enhancement to Figure 2.7 in Chapter 2. Not only is the hospital composed of separate organizations, but the medical enterprise also consists of the external agencies that interact with the hospital. Altogether, this is an example of an enterprise business.

To accomplish the objective of defining a system solution that solves a problem and supports the business, there needs to be a set of concepts and rules that associate the system being architected and the environment of the enterprise (business) that it operates in. In addition, the enterprise specification needs to include a model of the business and a model of the system, along with their inter-relationships. A set of business objectives, business processing, business policies and constraints, and business rules that define each business round out the information needed to create an enterprise business specification.

An example of the Healthy Hospital objective is to treat patients. Typically this is in conjunction with some timeframe, (e.g., "as soon as the first available appointment"). Business rules are formulated by the needs of the business and the

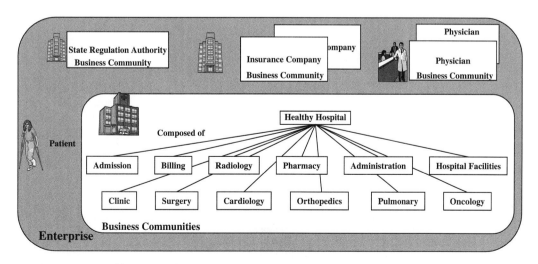

FIGURE 12.2 Healthy Hospital Business

external constraints on the business. For example, Healthy Hospital has rules of procedure to be followed such as "admit a patient," and "perform a medical treatment," "bill the patient," generally in this order. It has business rules to be followed. Healthy Hospital is constrained by the state regulation policies that affect much of what is done in the hospital. Businesses today involve a blend of human roles and distributed processing roles.

From the business perspective, there needs to be a plan defined for a specification of the business. The plan needs to address the purpose of the business. It needs to address the focus or scope of the business in the enterprise. It needs to address the configurations of things in relation to one another in support of the business needs. It needs to state the driving forces, business rules, standards, and policies that constrain the business, to include any information technology business policy. It needs to define the problem being solved by the system supporting the business. It needs to include a set of roles or elements that comprise the business.

A role is a part played in support of some business capability. Roles are important. They define what is to be done, the behavior realized by the role, what can be initiated, cease, or go away unfilled. The focus is on the tasks performed by each role and the associated behavior. In addition, the responsibilities and obligations of each role need to be stated. From this definition, an architecture specification can commence. Clearly, not everything will be known up front. So the process of defining the business and how the system is used to support the business will be an iterative one.

POINT | The challenge is to integrate business objectives with a well-performing system that supports the enterprise business and solves a business need.

A business specification is stated in terminology that is understandable by both the stakeholder and the architect. The plan for the business specification blends into the rules for the system architecture specification. The architecture specification of the system is the basis for defining how an IT solution fits within the business. The specification includes all applications in terms of components, their interactions, data, processes and steps associated with a business task, and processing rules associated with the business rules. It is a specification of the "what," not the "how," which can be further specified.

All semantics that affect certain components and interactions are specified in the architecture:

▶ The rules that always hold true affect the functioning of the appropriate system components and their interfaces.

▶ The rules that require certain checks and balances before some action is performed affect the functioning of the appropriate system components and their interfaces.

▶ The performance of the system is explicitly specified and affects the functioning of the appropriate system components and their interfaces.

▶ The appropriate functions the system is to perform are constrained or enabled by the explicit behavior.

Enterprise business specification is what RM-ODP can provide through the enterprise and information interrelated specifications, and consistent use of terms in the enterprise language.

12.2 USING RM-ODP

The focus in the enterprise viewpoint is on the purpose (the "why"), the scope (the "what"), and the policies (the "when, where, and how affected"). The focus in the information language is the consistent use of and interpretation of the information and semantics of the business.

A business is formed to meet an objective. A business has a scope.

An enterprise specification is defined as a model of a system and its environment. The enterprise specification defines the purpose, scope, and policies using the concepts of:

▶ Roles, especially those played by the system

▶ Activities and processes

▶ Policy statements

▶ A description of the community in which the system exists

The concepts of objective, scope, community, and role are used throughout the RM-ODP enterprise viewpoint. They represent key concepts in specifying an enterprise business.

12.2.1 ENTERPRISE METAMODEL

Figure 12.3 provides a possible metamodel for the enterprise viewpoint concepts and their relationships, as discussed in the remainder of this chapter. This is only one possible metamodel. The group forming the enterprise viewpoint standard has not solidified on the exact metamodel. Further, the following metamodel is not the same as currently being discussed in the standard, so consider this metamodel only as an aid.

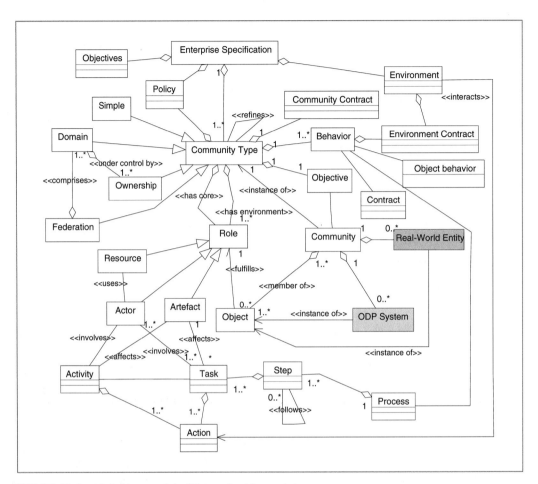

FIGURE 12.3 UML Metamodel of Enterprise Viewpoint

12.2.2 OVERVIEW OF KEY CONCEPTS TO SPECIFY A BUSINESS

The *objective* of a business is a statement that defines the expected outcome. A *community* is a configuration of roles that represent the enterprise business and the system in the context of the business. A *role* is a placeholder for some behavior. It is subject to the constraints of a community contract and policy. An *actor role* is a role that participates in some action in the enterprise. An *artefact role* is a role that is referenced by an action, or that an action makes use of, such as a patient record. A *resource role* is a role that is consumable, needs to be allocated, and is essential

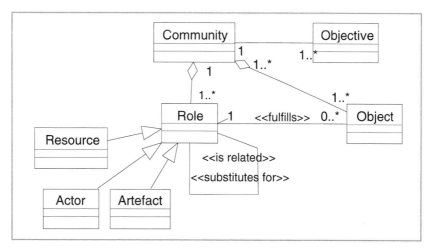

FIGURE 12.4   UML Model of Community, Roles, and Objects

for some behavior of an action, such as a processing resource. A Unified Modeling Language (UML) model of this relationship is shown in Figure 12.4.

As an example, Figure 12.5 shows a sample of perhaps the initial Healthy Hospital business community and actor roles required, similar to Figure 3.14 in Chapter 3. It shows that the state regulation authorities affect the system, although external to the environment of the system. The Use Case figures represent the actor roles in the business, and the Use Case icons represent the business processing. The policies are shown as artefact roles, though they may be represented as annotated notes, depending on the desires of the architect. A resource role is shown as some medical supply that is used up in the treatment. Not shown are the business rules and contracts, and neither are the scope and objectives, except as annotated notes. RM-ODP not only enables one to depict constructs that a Use Case would allow, but also enables one to define the scope, objectives, all the policies, actors, and actions associated with the business (enterprise).

The architect takes this information and further refines it to the semantics of the processing and decomposition of the Use Cases. During these steps, the system specification becomes one that the system designers and implementers can understand. Recall that RM-ODP also provides testing criteria to make sure that the system supports the business as expected. Also recall that RM-ODP facilitates defining the technologies and products to realize the system, all in a consistent, cohesive manner.

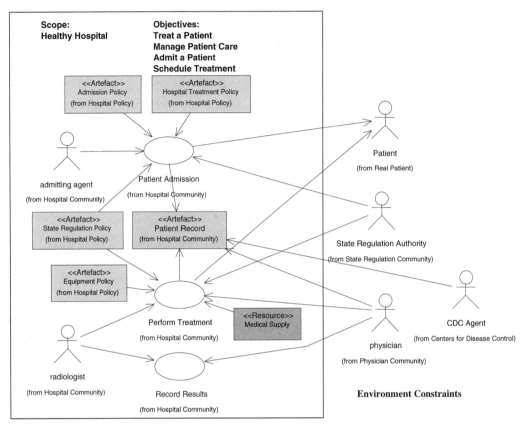

FIGURE 12.5   Healthy Hospital Business Example

12.2.3   CORRELATION BETWEEN BUSINESS AND ENTERPRISE CONCEPTS

The enterprise specification provides the correlation between the business domain and the system from the enterprise viewpoint. The use of the enterprise viewpoint concepts and rules provide this correlation. The language of the enterprise specification and its relationship to the business is shown in Table 12.1.

There is a caveat to this. A business contract or policy is generally associated with some legal consequences. Contract and policy in RM-ODP do not have the enforcement of law, yet. Through the use of authorization and obligation, coupled with an enforcement role, the enterprise language begins to support the concept of legally valid contracts.

TABLE 12.1 Correlation Between Business Concepts and RM-ODP Enterprise Concepts

ENTERPRISE BUSINESS	RM-ODP ENTERPRISE CONCEPTS
Enterprise	Objectives and scope
Boundaries of the enterprise	Scope
Organization within the enterprise	Community and scope
Objectives	Objectives
Business processes	Process, steps, relationships
Business rules	Policies and contracts
Business roles	Roles assumed by enterprise objects
Business policy	Contract, policy
Resources	Artefacts and resources
External enterprise concerns	Environment

12.2.4 Community Concepts

Recall that a community is a configuration of enterprise objects that is established to meet a business objective. A community has a type and a template. A contract defines the behavior of the community with respect to the business enterprise. A community can specify a real-world entity or a system. The system is a community object, at one level of abstraction. It is this method of specification that facilitates conversation between the architect and stakeholders to define the business and what problem the system is to solve in the business. A community, then, is a model of the objects of a business (e.g., patients, physicians, radiology equipment, surgical equipment, and the systems in support of these) and their associated expected behavior. This is represented in Figure 12.6.

Notice in Figure 12.6, every entity in the business has a role associated with it, as well as one or more objects that can fulfill that role. How these objects are partitioned into real-world entities, and those that participate in the system, is a further refinement. So in the case of Healthy Hospital, for example, there are nurse and patient objects in the system, but not a heart or a monitor. The latter two remain real-world objects.

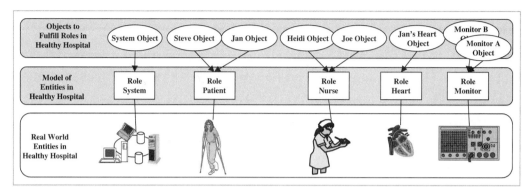

FIGURE 12.6   Roles and Objects in a Business Example

A community is defined by a contract, which includes the configuration of objects, the roles they assume, behavior, and the all important contract with the external environment. The environment consists of all those things that are not part of the community. This includes other communities that may form part of the overall enterprise.

The architect can develop an enterprise specification, where each business domain is specified as a community, and may be an object in a higher-level community. That is, at one level of abstraction, the entire enterprise is a single community, where the roles defined are in fact other communities. At another level of abstraction, the enterprise community consists of additional communities. These were the roles defined in the higher-level community. This process of composition and refinement continues until the roles defined in each community reflect either real-world entities or some business process to achieve.

Figure 12.7 provides a sample overview of these very important concepts, relative to Healthy Hospital. At the top level of abstraction, Hospital is an object in a medical community. The medical community is refined into the Healthy Hospital community and the Insurance Community. Within each community, an ODP system is an object. The Healthy Hospital Community contains Hospital System as an object. This object is also the Healthy Hospital System Commmunity, as shown in the figure, where the objects in that community are those being used throughout this book as part of the system. Not shown are the relationships among the objects in each community, nor the policies. This figure is focused on the composition and refinement of communities, and how an ODP system is specified as part of the business specification.

The importance of this concept coupled with abstraction and refinement includes:

▶ The ability to position a system within the context of a business

▶ The ability to define the boundaries of the separate business parts and of the system or systems that support the business

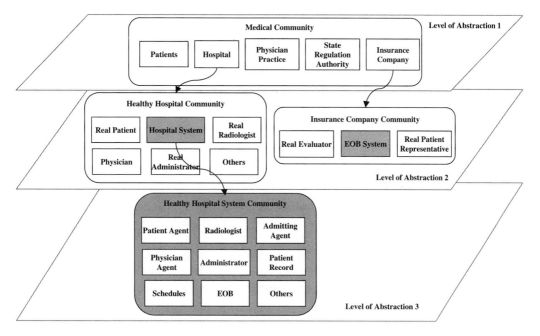

FIGURE 12.7 Community Composition and Refinement

▶ The ability to define the interactions among the different parts of the business

▶ The ability to simplify what is in focus at a particular level of abstraction

▶ The ability to focus on the system specification within the context of solving a business problem

▶ The ability to relate the concepts of real-world entities with those of a system such that they are consistently specified

Further refinement of the Healthy Hospital System may result in additional communities, perhaps one for each major subsystem being specified. It is the architect that decides how to modularize the enterprise, but it is RM-ODP coupled with the new work in the enterprise viewpoint that aids the architect to a business specification of real-world and system entities that "hang together."

A community is instantiated from a template, which is the usual process in RM-ODP. A community template consists of the role-based objects in the community, the constraints on the role and its interactions, the types of enterprise objects that are allowed to fulfill the role, and any additional constraints on the object. A role is instantiated from a template as well. Actually, the community template consists of role templates, which are instantiated by some specified constraint. That is, a role can be instantiated when the community is instantiated, can be instantiated multiple times, or may not be instantiated unless called upon dynamically. So a community template may define roles that are not filled at some point in time.

12.2.5   ROLES IN A COMMUNITY

A role is a formal parameter providing an identifier for a part of the community behavior. Constraints are associated with a role. They apply to the behavior expected of any enterprise object that is to fulfill the role.

A role is a part of the specification. A role is distinct from an object that fills the role. As such, a role defines some behavior of the community, that is then assumed by an object. That is, the definition of the behavior is associated with the definition of the role, not the object. When an object assumes the role (any number of objects can assume the same role), additional constraints may be associated with the object, depending on the identity of the object.

Consider what a patient and a physician are in a hospital. A patient is a role assumed by a human. A physician is a role assumed by a human. The same human (entity) may assume both the patient and the physician role. Alternatively, multiple entities may assume the patient or the physician roles. This is analogous to the role-object relationships in a system. When an entity (Greg) assumes the physician role, the behavior is defined (i.e., physician-Greg). If that same entity assumes the patient role, different behavior is defined (i.e., patient-Greg). But the same entity assumes the different roles in different contexts. The specification and relationship of the roles remain specified, independent of the entity assuming the role.

As an entity may be part of different communities in different roles, the separate contexts in which the object participates becomes clearer. For example, in Figure 12.7, the Healthy Hospital System is a community in one context (abstraction level 3), an object within a community visible in another context (abstraction level 2), and an entity encapsulated in another context (abstraction level 1).

The ability to define the behavior of the entities separate from the objects that assume the roles facilitates the scalability of the business and the system. That is, as the system becomes larger, the participation of the object is defined by the role in the context of the system and the system in the enterprise. As systems scale or as an enterprise incorporates more systems, it is important that real-world and system entities be consistently addressed. If the same entity is specified differently for different systems within an enterprise, for example, the result may be unnecessary duplication and inconsistent definition leading to problems of integration, scale, and maintainability.

In business-to-business (B2B) enterprises, it is important to define the role of the business in the collaboration context and the processes that are shared. As businesses enter (or leave) the enterprise, their roles are specified. Indeed, their behavior while in the enterprise is defined to include the manner in which they interact with other businesses, and the B2B processes are specified that form the interactions in support of B2B. The behavior and the means of collaboration are defined by role, assumed by any business in the enterprise. Part of the role specification will include the role of participant in the process. The role may be user-based or system-entity based. The actions taken by the entity assuming the role, then, determine the next allowable action in the process. These are commonplace concepts in RM-ODP, simply applied to the B2B enterprise, held together by the consistency of role specification.

Further, this separation enables the architect to select appropriate objects to fill roles, rather than the programmer, who may not understand all of the business aspects of the roles.

There are types of roles. *Actor roles* initiate and respond to actions, such as performing a task of the business process. *Artefact roles* are used by actor roles, and do not perform any action themselves, such as the Patient Records. *Resource roles* are similar to artefact roles (in fact, the distinction is not agreed upon yet in the standard). A resource role can be considered as something that is constrained, provided by the system, and can be used up. An example is a medication that is allocated and used up.

There are also other types of objects for the enterprise. A *party* is an object that models a real person, like a real patient. An *owner* is an object that models a real person with authority to control something, such as a stakeholder who is paying for the architecture specification. An owner can also be a business contract owner who enforces the legal aspects of the contract on the enterprise. A *contracting party* is an object that agrees to a contract. Actually, this is not fully explained in [ISO-EntVP], and will not be used here.

An enterprise object may fulfill many roles, in any number of communities, subject to the composed constraints allowing this. Each role has a type, and is fulfilled by an object of the same type. Changes in role-object bindings may occur by substitution or cardinality, according to community policy.

Within a community, roles can be created or destroyed. The life of a role does not exceed that of the community, but may be far less. A role is deleted only if no enterprise object is bound to (fulfilling that) role.

In a given community instance, not all roles need to be filled. For example, in Figure 12.8 a UML model shows that a role is defined for the patient agent, a software component that is acted upon by the system, an emergency patient agent, and a real patient. At some point in time, there may be no emergency patients and, as such, that role is not filled (at that point in time). When an emergency patient arrives, an object in the system assumes the role of emergency patient agent and the processing begins. Also shown is the human that fills the patient role.

A role represents some behavior of a process or a real thing. In the case of this example, the emergency patient and patient roles represent a real patient. An enterprise object is a representation of some parameterized role that behaves in terms of the role. If a role is filled by an object, it is filled by exactly one object at any one point in time. During a time interval, however, several objects may fill one role. But the processing of the system addresses one object at a time, though time may be very small in this case. For example, Jan is a real patient. There are unique

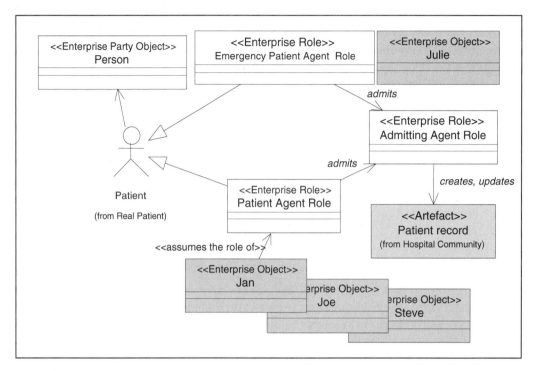

FIGURE 12.8 Sample Roles in Healthy Hospital

properties about Jan. The enterprise model relates the real Jan to a model entity of Jan with the properties associated with Jan. Hence, Jan is an enterprise object. What Jan can and cannot do is associated with the defined enterprise role. Since Jan is a patient, the object-Jan assumes the role of a patient, not a physician. The admitting agent role admits one role-based patient object at a time (Jan in the figure) though the admitting agent may in fact process several role-based patient objects over some time (Steve and Joe). Meanwhile, an emergency patient role is defined in the community, but is not filled. When Julie comes in as an emergency patient, the enterprise object Julie fills the role of the emergency patient agent. This is one of the rules of the enterprise language.

12.2.6 SCOPE AND OBJECTIVES

The set of roles defines the *scope* of the business, and in particular the scope of the system within the business.

Objectives define the purpose of the business. In a community, the objectives are defined as roles, policies, and relationships among the roles. The objective is fulfilled when objects assume the roles, act in accordance with the policies, and produce a successful result of their processes or interactions. An objective can be broken down into subobjectives, and allocated to different subsets of roles in the community. This is an architect's decision.

12.2.7 BUSINESS CONCEPTS FOR USE

The objective of the enterprise viewpoint is to support the specification of a business specification, as well as an enterprise specification of an ODP system within the enterprise. To do this, certain additional concepts are defined.

The business concepts revolve around the ability to specify the contract aspects of a business. A business contract is a set of rules that apply to a set of parties (a binding agreement). A business contract generally has legal consequences associated with it. A business contract can be enforced on all parties. Alternatively, consequential action can be applied to those parties that violate the contract. A contract can be negotiated among parties of different domains, to establish a level of agreement of interworking. A business contract associates an authority to determine adherence to or enforcement of the contract. It also has considerations of value associated to the parties; and it has considerations of (legal) consequences of violation.

The new concepts for business specifications then are the following:

▶ Delegate—entrust to a party the authority to enforce a contract, policy, or to perform some function

▶ Agent—the enterprise object that is subject of a delegation. The agent can be a human or an ODP system or a part of an ODP system.

▶ Principal—the party who delegates

In addition to these concepts, there are concepts of how business specifications are used. In essence, an *act* is a verb that results in something done by a party or agent. An act of *commitment* is establishing a contract with a party (any party, the agent, or the principal) who agrees to abide by the rules of the contract. A *declaration* is the establishment of the contract. A *delegation* is the act of delegating. The act of assigning a value to something is called an *evaluation*. An *instruction* is the act of causing someone to do something. And a *prescription* establishes a rule.

12.2.8 RELATIONSHIPS

The relationships among the objects in an enterprise specification are specified in terms of a process or an activity. A process consists of steps that are actions that perform some business task. An activity consists of actions that formulate interactions between objects.

A *process* is much like a workflow process. It is a collection of steps that together form a task of the business. Objects can participate in the process at specified intervals, not necessarily only from the beginning. So, one object may perform a step in the middle of the process and then interact with another object for it to perform another step in the process. On completion of all steps of the process, the process is completed. The manner in which the process is executed can be determined by a process template, and a type.

An activity has a beginning. It is a sequence of actions. An interaction, in terms of the enterprise, is an action between two or more enterprise objects, or communities.

The difference between a process and an interaction, then, is whether there is a single point of entry, or multiple points of entry. A workflow, or process, can be composed of interactions. But an interaction is not composed of a process. For example, to create a schedule of appointments for a patient, a process of checking if a record exists, creating one if it doesn't, validating payment, ensuring the admission policy is followed, scheduling the appointments, and updating all records constitutes a process of tasks. These actions can happen somewhat in parallel. But within each step, one or more interactions occur: access the patient identification, access the patient record, update the patient record and update the schedule for the patient, all in this order.

12.2.9   POLICIES

Recall that a policy is a set of rules expressed as an obligation, permission, and prohibition. Added to this are the concepts of authorization and violation. This gives more force to the otherwise weak notion of policy in RM-ODP. *Authorization* says that a certain behavior cannot be prevented. *Violation* is the action of breaking a rule. More discussion about policy is provided in Chapter 14, "Policy Framework."

12.2.10   SEMANTICS

RM-ODP provides the capability to capture the semantics of the processing in the system, as per the specification of the behavior, contracts, policies, and quality of service, and ensures the consistency of these semantics are captured for the appropriate components and their interactions. "Behavior must be described at the system level, not the object level. All interesting behavior is in the relationships between objects. It is impossible to understand behavior of the system by looking only at the behavior of its parts." [Kilov-97]

The business rules result in the policies in the enterprise specification, and possibly invariants which are relationships that never change. Many times, the semantic behaviors result in the need for additional components in the interfaces.

Sometimes, the semantic behaviors result in constraints on what can and cannot be accomplished on an interface.

The behavior of a community, then, is specified in terms of the policies that govern the actions of the community, the processes and the interactions defined by the roles, constraints on the roles, the community contract, and all environment contracts. A community contract establishes the contractual behavior of all members of the community.

The structure of the community is defined by the community contract. It determines the objects that fulfill the roles, the policies that apply to a given role, and any behavior that might change the structure of the community. The structure of the community can change by objects filling roles, or being deleted; by objects or communities forming a federation, and then leaving it; etc.

12.2.11 COMMUNITY TYPES

There are two primary additional types of communities that are very useful for specifying a business. These are domain and federation. Recall that a domain is a set of objects with a relationship to a control object. In terms of a community, then, a *domain* is a community. It has a *controlling object* that manages the behavior of the community of objects, with respect to the relationship of the domain. What this means is that a hospital is a community. If there is an object that manages the behavior of the hospital objects in accordance with one or more policies, then the hospital is a domain. A hospital administrator could be considered the controlling object that ensures the policies of the hospital are followed. A community is a weaker construct; it does not necessarily define a controlling object. A community, therefore, is merely a collection of objects formed to meet some objective of the business.

Building on the concept of domain is the concept of federation. A *federation* is a community of domains, of a particular relationship, that manages the federation policy across the domains. For example, several naming domains can form a federation that has the relationship "naming context." The federation enables an object from one domain to interact with an object of another domain. The manner in which this occurs is not defined in RM-ODP or the enterprise viewpoint. The approach is that the controlling objects of each of the domains interact through the federation, which acts much like a binding object. Whether a federation has a controlled object is not clear. How the policies are managed across the federation is not clear. In fact, a great deal is not made clear. Nevertheless, this topic is expanded and enhanced in Chapter 15, "Federation." Figure 12.9 provides a model of these types of communities. The Ownership community consists of the objects subject to the controlling object. The cardinality between an object that is controlled and the controller is not clear. Whether an object can be part of two ownership domains is not clear. Hence, the ownership type is shown in the figure, but is not addressed further.

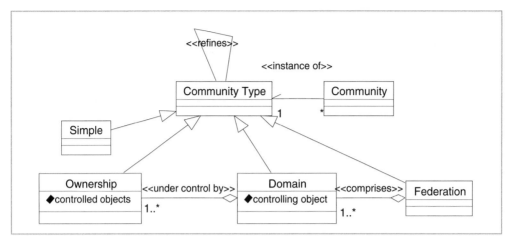

FIGURE 12.9   Community Types

Figure 12.10 provides an overview of community, domain, and federation of domains. The administrator of Healthy Hospital fulfills the role of controller. It manages the hospital policy across its domain, and assumes the responsibility for managing the federation policy across its domain as well. A federation can be formed if the constituent parts are domains: that is, if they have a controller role-based object that will enforce the federation policy. The Patient Community is a set of patients, all independent, but that perhaps form a community because they are the main patients of the hospital. But since there is no controller object, that community cannot participate in the federation.

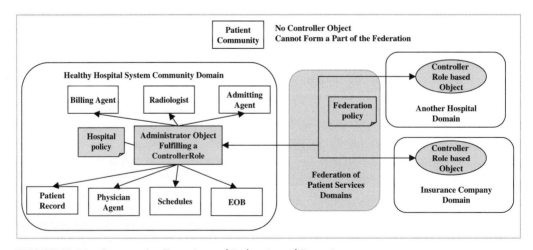

FIGURE 12.10   Community, Domain, and Federation of Domains

12.3 PROCESS OF SPECIFYING A BUSINESS

The levels of abstraction lead to an initial high-level view of the hospital business, and further refinement to the roles that support the business processes, business rules and policies that represent constraints. It also leads to refinement of the business contract that establishes the scope, objectives, and rules of the business and constrains the roles and actions in the business. Not all roles specified are related to a system. Some are human roles, some are system roles, and they need to interact in support of the business.

The specification technique of composition enables a role and its behavior to be a composite, and the architect to further refine what that role performs as defined by its refined behavior. In this manner, the architect can converse with the business stakeholder at one level of abstraction and refine that level of abstraction further. However the architect creates the specification, whether it is top-down, bottom-up, or sideways, the architect needs to always include the constraints, as they become known, into the information specification.

Even within the business specification, all viewpoints may be used. From the hospital point of view, for example, there may be parts of the hospital that can be considered a technology viewpoint. Some parts of the system may be outsourced, to develop a billing system, for example. In this case, an engineering and technology specification may be provided. The use of this product is specified as an object in the business community specification.

Maybe there is some important business activity, such as physician credential processing. This business process is a precondition to a number of other business processes in the Healthy Hospital example. In order to define the business processes, the impact of processing the physician credential may affect how the business process functions. Therefore, to further specify the business process itself, the architect may refine "physician credential processing" in the computational viewpoint to determine what is involved.

A community or domain can apply to a large functional area, which is to be focused on. However, scoping is important, in order to provide a meaningful specification. For example, an enterprise consisting of all of the different organizations that comprise the medical community is too large to specify. It would be difficult, if not impossible, to define a common set of achievable objectives. But a hospital domain, or a patient identification domain, are achievable and have the right "scope." The key here is appropriate modularization in order to simplify what is being specified.

The hospital domain can be specified into an architecture through the concepts of RM-ODP. The Patient Identification system may be generalized enough to also satisfy User Identification across a myriad of other functional domains, which is exactly what has happened in OMG. Thus, a domain may be functionally and enterprise-oriented (hospital), or functionally and technically oriented

(Patient Identification). Further, a domain may consist of subdomains, which are domains. A set of domains may consist of a domain that crosses all of them, which amounts to a federation. This concept leads to the ability to have a system of systems spanning multiple business enterprises.

Hence, the business specification process is probably constructed from a spiral approach to define a little, specify more of a little, and fold back into the business specification.

12.4   HEALTHY HOSPITAL ENTERPRISE BUSINESS EXAMPLE EXTENDED

The Healthy Hospital example of Chapter 2, "RM-ODP Manager's Primer," was specified as a single business of separate organizations. Terms such as patient, physician, and business were used. They are related to the RM-ODP concepts of role. Healthy Hospital used the term "policy," such as the Hospital Policy. RM-ODP defines the meaning of a policy in terms of certain actions that constrain the relationships among the entities in the business, such as "the hospital is obligated to submit a bill within 10 days." The architect knows the form of specification; the business customer need not. But policy is a common term between a business and an enterprise specification. This is one way of conversing between the architect and functional domain expert in terms of a business, while the architect knows how to capture the policy as a specification. The result will be a specific set of specification models for the domain that address the enterprise, rules, concepts, common properties, interactions, and additional functional detail of the domain.

In the following discussion, the actual terms for the enterprise language from RM-ODP and [ISO-EntVP] are used to extend the Healthy Hospital example. These terms are underlined.

The Healthy Hospital business is a <u>community</u> with an administrator <u>controlling</u> the policies of the <u>domain</u> within an <u>enterprise</u> of multiple domains. The Healthy Hospital community is a configuration of entities (humans, software, systems, and resources) that are defined by a set of business rules, and by the scope of the community. The <u>scope</u> is the set of roles in the system. The <u>objective</u> is a set of statements that identifies what is intended. These statements are not necessarily fulfilled by the system being specified, but establish a "vision" of what is wanted so that decisions made about the system take the objectives into account. The business rules define the <u>roles</u> played by the system (being specified), the <u>processes</u> and <u>activities</u> they participate in, and <u>policy</u> statements. A <u>role</u> defines the behavior of the entity, assuming those activities in the community. In the Healthy Hospital <u>environment</u>, roles are the Insurance community, the

State Regulation Authority community, the Physician Practice community, and the patient. <u>Relationships</u> exist among all these communities and the patient, and are constrained by business rules.

What is a business rule? A business rule defines the entities, their relationships, and the actions applied to them. Some relationships never change. These are called <u>invariants</u>. Sometimes these relationships are true for a period of time, such as a state regulation policy statement. In terms of Healthy Hospital, the state regulation policy, the billing policy, the hospital policy, etc., form a part of the invariants of the system.

Sometimes a business wants to be sure certain things happen first, or certain things happen afterwards. In RM-ODP, these are specified as <u>preconditions</u> and <u>postconditions</u>. They can be specified without explicitly defining them to a particular interface. That is, they are defined in a business manner, on business objects and on business object relationships. How these things eventually end up as interfaces is a refinement the architect and designer provide. The business specifier need not worry about it at this point in the specification, though the architect should capture these as initial specifications in the information specification. For example, the physician must have been certified by the state before treating a patient at Healthy Hospital. This is a <u>precondition</u> of any hospital activity regarding that physician.

The statements of invariants, preconditions, postconditions, policies, and even roles are part of the <u>behavior</u> specified for the Healthy Hospital business, and form <u>constraints</u> on the <u>actions</u> of the <u>roles</u> in Healthy Hospital.

Different humans can assume the different roles in Healthy Hospital. For example, an admitting agent is a role in Healthy Hospital. Heidi, Jack, and Danielle all perform patient admission. When they interact with the system, each becomes an object in the system that assumes the role of admitting agent. Each person is assigned a unique identity, maintained by the log-in procedures to the system, to uniquely identify the role-based object for admitting agent. Certain policies constrain what each can and cannot do. For example, Jack is new. He therefore cannot determine "admit emergency patients even if they have no insurance." He can perform all other admitting-agent actions. Danielle, on the other hand, is very informed. She can admit anyone, and decide if an uninsured patient is allowed admission.

Certain activities in Healthy Hospital may be assigned to certain users as well as software objects to perform. A <u>party</u> represents a human that performs some business process that may or may not interact with the system. Even a domain can assume a "role" with respect to another domain. In this case, certain actions, or constraints, are specified as part of the role specification. Notice that all these things can reuse the "role" construct of RM-ODP to specify a variety of business concerns.

SIDEBAR

IMPORTANCE OF THE ENVIRONMENT

The environment is actually a very important concept that often receives little attention in the business environment. The <u>environment</u> consists of all communities that may interact with the community of interest. Consider the all-too-often approach of large-scale systems architecture, by example. The customer and architect define a system to work within a hospital. They don't consider that the Centers for Disease Control (CDC) may want to access certain patient records. So, the architect and designer of the hospital develop a system with the following open standards-based products:

- Communicates through business object messages, defined by an open standards or consortia organization
- Develops to a component-based environment
- Only data steward components can access the database using appropriate open standards
- Uses a message-oriented middleware (MOM) product with an open interface
- Uses a publish and subscribe communication mechanism with an open interface
- Uses a Web browser and Web server to provide the business information to the end user

Assume that all of this satisfies the specification criteria for the hospital (not including the environment).

CDC is data centric, meaning it provides access to data through structured query language (SQL) commands. That is, CDC has an architecture that provides queries to any of the databases by any authorized user. Now CDC wants access to the patient records of the hospital. The only way they can do so is to emulate a component that communicates in terms of a business object, using a publish/subscribe communication mechanism, and queuing of messages. It does not have business objects or a MOM capability, or publish/subscribe in its architecture. This is an architecture mismatch of great proportions that may be difficult to solve.

Had the architect for the hospital considered the environment up front, then an objective would have been stated to define the need to interact with the CDC community. Maybe it would not have changed the architecture for Healthy Hospital, for other valid reasons. Or maybe it would.

But an architecture is not merely a set of standards; it defines how a system operates and behaves. If that system is developed without considering the case where and how an external system (environment) may interact with it, the result can be disastrous to the entire solution. Addressing the environment needs to be captured up front in the business specification, and appropriately tasked for consideration in the architecture workplan.

The state regulation policy of Healthy Hospital defines procedures that must be followed, constraining the Healthy Hospital business. The radiology equipment must be checked periodically for safety reasons, the medications dispensed must be under tight control with explicit record-keeping, the hospital must not over-bill a patient, etc. For example, a state regulation for medical equipment may state that the equipment must be inspected every three months before it is used. This results in a constraint on any processing of a medical procedure, to ensure that the regulation policy has been enforced and currently valid. Policy statements such as these form a part of the business specification.

A contract states things that are relevant, the configuration of the objects in the business, what they are to do, when things are to be done, behavior, quality of service constraints, all as applied to the operations of the business. How a contract is implemented is part of the refinement process of the system specification. That something needs to be accomplished in accordance with some code, rule, or legal contract needs to be specified in its own right, generally as a contract.

In RM-ODP, one form of a contract is an environment contract. It contains the same things as a contract, but adds in certain qualities of service and statements of when the contract is to be in force, where it is enforced, and so forth, associated with elements in the environment. The environment contract is used to specify the contractual relation between one community and another, for example. It is also used in the relation between entities and how they operate. The constructs for an environment contract can be used in the system specification to address some contractual quality of service associated with an interaction. In terms of the enterprise, a quality of service is any value related to the outcome of an action. The quality of service required of physicians to report their patient consultation is eight hours, as an example.

What does a contract specification look like? Figure 12.11 provides a view of a contract.

Part of the business specification is to address the relations among the entities. In RM-ODP, these are process, task, activities, actions, and interactions. The admitting agent initiates the process of admitting a patient. Involved are the interactions to the patient record, to access and update the record. Part of the process is the task to determine the schedules for the patient. This may require a scheduling agent to perform the task. Part of the process is to interact with the billing agent, to determine the amount of the bill to be paid. Upon completion of the process, the patient is either admitted or denied admission.

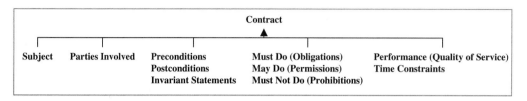

FIGURE 12.11   Contract

In order to share the patient identification and services related to the patient, a <u>federation</u> may be formed across the hospital, insurance company, and physician practice. This capability allows a group of separate domains to work together, to share patient related information, and to maintain a consistency of patient and billing information across the federation.

Each community is specified by the entities that form the community, processes of the business, the roles and relationships among the roles, the policies that govern the behavior associated with the roles, preconditions, postconditions, and relationships across all. Also included in the specification are the objective for which the community exists and the scope of the community.

The process of achieving an enterprise specification is iterative, using the techniques of composition and abstraction. An example of an approach to specifying Healthy Hospital is shown in Figure 12.12. A more enhanced view of the business enterprise specification, in terms of the activities and roles, for Healthy Hospital is shown in Figure 12.13. The policies, also part of the specification, are represented in Chapter 14, Figure 14.7.

A real specification would fully define each of these roles, to include the parameters, operations, and types.

Figure 12.14 shows some of what RM-ODP would include in defining the semantics of Healthy Hospital. The constraints are defined that affect the ability for the system to perform its functions. The information is defined, and the relationships among that information are also defined. The actions that change the state of some object of the system architecture are also captured. Altogether, the semantics of the processing and the information schemas are captured in the information viewpoint model.

In fact, the Figure 12.14 is not a sufficient model. For example, what do the arrows mean? Where do the actions apply? This is the sort of thing, however, that the architect may initially capture as part of the information specification. Through refinement of the enterprise specification, and the information specification, additional details are discovered and folded into the information specification.

More in line with what an enterprise business specification is to contain, are the following examples of invariant, dynamic, and static models in the information specification. Even these, however, are not fully defined.

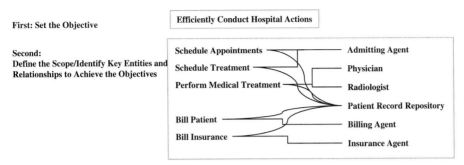

First: Set the Objective

Second:
Define the Scope/Identify Key Entities and
Relationships to Achieve the Objectives

Third: Refine Each Step into Smaller Steps; Each Entity into Additional Entities

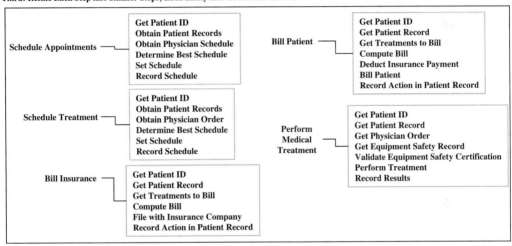

Fourth: Define the Interactions and Processes Between the Requirements

FIGURE 12.12 Process for Specifying Healthy Hospital Business

The information captured in the information specification includes:

◗ A set of information objects, specifying their configuration, attributes, and relations with other information objects

◗ The invariant schema, specifying invariants and the target of the invariant

◗ The dynamic schema, specifying actions and the allowed state transitions of the objects

◗ A specification of preconditions and postconditions, and the relations they apply to

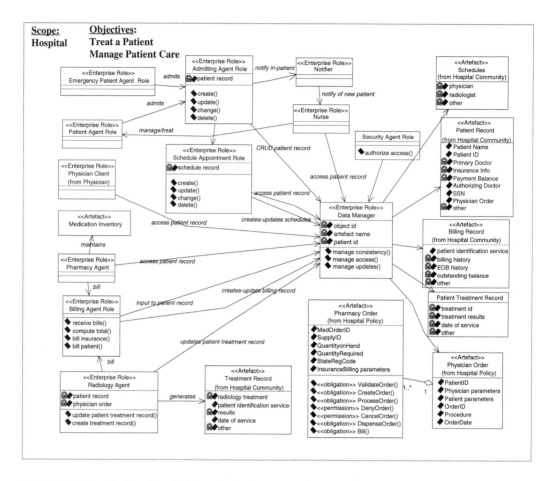

FIGURE 12.13   Healthy Hospital Sample Business Specification

The invariant schema can be represented with the following:

◗ Purpose

◗ Representation of the information content of the system

◗ An object diagram showing the configuration of the objects, and their interactions

◗ A class diagram showing the hierarchy and relationships, in terms of class and type, to each other

◗ Representation of the details of the object interactions

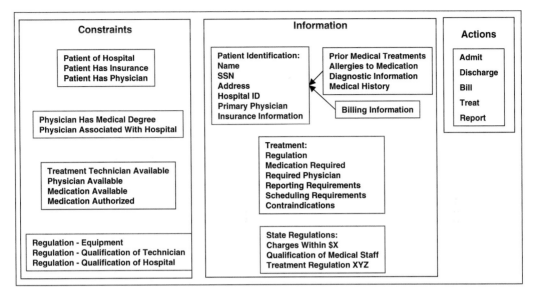

FIGURE 12.14 Medical Behavior Example

A partial example of the invariant schema is shown in Figure 12.15. This representation is shown as a class diagram in UML, though some may desire to use an interaction diagram. The invariants that constrain the artefacts and roles are shown. Policy is also an invariant. But due to a limitation in UML, the stereotype "Invariant" is not shown, so that the "Policy" stereotype can be shown. That is, UML does not allow multiple stereotypes. The details of the roles are not shown. The relationship (partial) among the information objects, and the roles, are shown.

The dynamic schema can be represented with the following:

▶ Purpose
▶ Representation of the dynamic actions that affect the state changes of an object
▶ State transition diagram
▶ Activity model

A partial example of the dynamic schema and associated static schema states is shown in Figure 12.16. This representation is shown as an activity diagram in UML, though some may desire to use an interaction diagram. The dynamic actions that cause state changes are shown. The states are shown in gray boxes. The use of the admission policy, only as a sample, is shown in one of the activity boxes that constrains the activity.

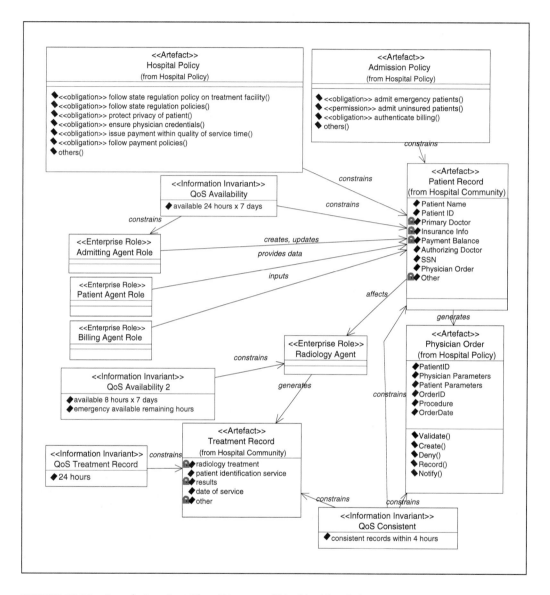

FIGURE 12.15   Sample Invariant Class Diagram of Healthy Hospital

The information viewpoint includes objects that, at this stage, represent concepts from the business that the software system must deal with. In the Healthy Hospital example, information objects might be Patient Record, Bill, Physician Order, etc. The invariant definitions that constrain the business are also part of the information specification. The static relationships among the objects of the business are also contained in the information viewpoint. Finally, the actions that allow

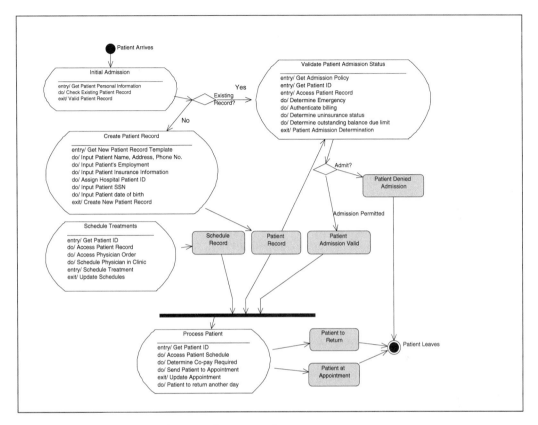

FIGURE 12.16 Dynamic and Static Schema Sample

state changes of an object are part of the information specification. To capture the data in the business, the information viewpoint object contains attributes and structure. These can be used to formulate tables in a relational database schema. So, information objects can represent data as well as objects that play a role in the system.

As the system specification gets further refined through the use of the viewpoints, the information specification is refined as well.

12.5   SUMMARY

An enterprise business specification consists of an enterprise specification using the concepts of the enterprise viewpoint and an information specification using the concepts of the information viewpoint. The enterprise specification consists of a specification of the scope of the business within the enterprise, the objectives of the business, business processes, business objects, policies, and a delineation of those objects representing real-world entities and those assumed by information technology objects. The information specification consists of a specification of the static, dynamic, and invariant schemata from the information viewpoint. The challenge is to integrate business objectives with a well-performing system that supports the enterprise business, and solves a problem in the business.

An enterprise business specification consists of real-world entities and distributed processing system(s) that support the objectives of the business. With a language close to that of real-world business, the enterprise language of RM-ODP and the emerging enterprise viewpoint provide the ability to communicate among the stakeholders and architect teams in specifying the business.

The enterprise language not only captures the business processing, but the business rules, the policies that constrain the business, and the entities that participate in the business. The semantics of processing, as represented by the business rules and policies of the enterprise, are related to the constructs of the enterprise and information languages. Thus, the architect has the means and the tools to create an enterprise business specification that works. This chapter provided numerous examples of the use of the enterprise viewpoint constructs to formulate the Healthy Hospital enterprise business specification.

In this manner, the architect can effectively communicate with the stakeholders to ensure the system is solving a business problem, to understand how the system interacts within the business and with the business entities, to understand how the environment affects the business, to understand how the business rules constrain the system to be architected, and to then refine all of this into an architecture specification of the system.

THIRTEEN

INTERACTION FRAMEWORK: INTEROPERABILITY

T his chapter discusses the Interaction Framework, which is described in and further enabled by the Reference Model of Open Distributed Processing (RM-ODP). Topics addressed include:

- Interaction Framework motivation and overview
- What is interoperability
- Software architecture connectors
- Interaction Framework
- Relationships that define interaction
- Interfacing constructs that provide the conduit for interactions
- Binding that provides the conduit for interfaces to communicate interaction
- Interception across domains
- Semantics of interaction

13.1   MOTIVATION FOR THE INTERACTION FRAMEWORK

Interaction is the reason why two objects exchange information in an agreed-upon manner, as constrained by one or more policies and subject to an environment contract. What this means is that successful interaction between two objects results in distribution and interoperability, and minimizes mismatch.

Interaction is an action between two or more objects, as shown in Figure 13.1 for the interaction "store." It results, through composition and refinement, in a specification of interfaces, additional objects, bindings, use of channels, communication, and the technologies supporting these elements. Some people view an interaction as simply an interface. This is not the case. An interaction, in this sense, consists of the interaction in a specific interface, bound to another interface, which is supported by a particular protocol. That is, an interaction is the reason for interoperating and is a profile of capabilities that support and enable the communication. This is shown in the bottom of Figure 13.1.

In RM-ODP, an interface signature is a means of specifying how an interaction can be communicated between objects. Of course, such an interface signature is particular to the objectives of an interaction, such as interaction type. But an interaction is much more than an interface. Interacting includes binding, and binding addresses the protocol.

The purpose of this chapter is to provide the pattern of reasoning for interaction, and provide a framework capturing the elements to achieve inter-object-action.

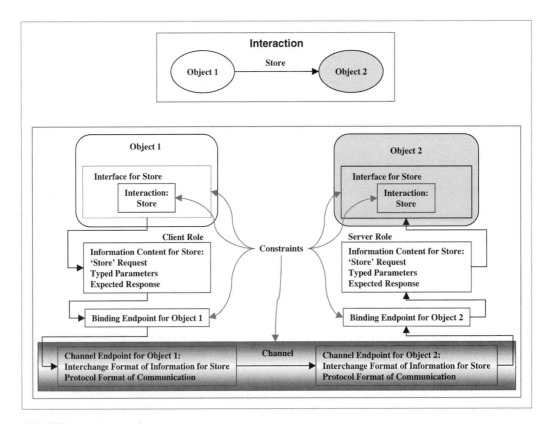

FIGURE 13.1 Interaction

The RM-ODP constructs that define an Interaction Framework enable interoperability. *Interoperability* is the ability of two or more systems, or system objects, to exchange information in such a way as to mutually understand and use the information that has been exchanged. Interoperability is a subject of much importance in building systems today. What RM-ODP brings to bear on this subject is a set of frameworks that collectively provide interoperability. The framework describes the models to support interaction in open distributed systems, independent of implementation details such as specific communication protocols and middleware systems.

Furthermore, the current work in software architecture is focused on a concept called "connector." As will be discussed, RM-ODP Interaction Framework relates to various aspects of the connector concepts, but the RM-ODP concepts are far more encompassing, precise, and consistent. It is the RM-ODP concepts that enable connector concepts to be better defined and analyzed, and to minimize mismatch.

Composition and abstraction of interaction constructs and behavior aspects are addressed. These specification techniques are important in the separation of concerns, composition of concerns, and effective specification of asynchrony, concurrency, multicasting, and complex interactions of different information in open distributed systems.

The Interaction Framework defines high-level concepts reflecting the relationships among objects, as typically defined in requirements. Using abstraction and composition techniques, these relationships are further refined into aspects of interaction that address interfaces, binding, connection, and the behavioral semantics associated with all of this. Such a framework allows the architect to specify different aspects of interaction, that through the use of RM-ODP concepts are consistently specified throughout all levels of abstraction. The result is a well-formed architectural specification of interaction, the expected behavior of interaction, and composable distributed systems.

In reality, the interface signature for a particular product, such as a database management system (DBMS), is simply provided as a client application programming interface (API). The detail contained in typical commercial APIs is far short of the detail specified by RM-ODP. When attempting to glue together different products, an architect typically finds the products have (generally unspecified) behavior that limits their composition, or prohibits it altogether. This mismatch of gluing products together is largely a direct result of a lack of explicit behavior specification, and of a lack of an Interaction Framework that separates the interaction elements to allow independent specificity. That is, the API is often bundled with not only the parameters of the interface, but also the binding characteristics, the protocol required, and the networking required.

One cannot choose his own method of binding or his own method of communication; the entire interaction + interface + binding + networking profile must be used as provided by the vendor. And one product's profile is most probably not the same as the product the architect is trying to glue together. No wonder "plug and play" is difficult to achieve!

RM-ODP separates the interaction concerns into different models to enable a system architect to make choices or to enable the system to make choices dynamically. These choices are related to binding, the need for interceptors, and networking, as well as the dynamic assessment of behavior characteristics to determine the appropriate choices that best suit the system needs.

13.2	INTERACTION FRAMEWORK OVERVIEW

Interaction deals with the exchange of information and services between or among objects. The means of communicating an interaction is through an interface. An interface glues together the different objects in a system, and provides the ability to exchange information. A binding glues together the different interfaces to enable interacting of distributed systems.

The RM-ODP pattern of reasoning that formulates the Interaction Framework is powerful enough to model both current and future technologies, the behavior of objects, the behavior of interfaces, the behavior of bindings, complex interactions, and different abstraction and composition mechanisms. Furthermore, semantic behavior of the interaction concepts is provided.

The ontology provided by RM-ODP provides a precise definition of interaction that includes:

▶ Clear definitions

▶ Specification of behavior

▶ Specification of environmental constraints

▶ Specification of role-based interfaces and constraints

▶ Specification of interfaces

▶ Specification of binding

▶ Specification of cross-domain mediation elements

▶ Specification of distributed system properties such as quality of service (QoS), transparency, reliability, security, flexibility, and scalability

▶ Consistency across the specifications

▶ Rules associated with all

The Interaction Framework structures an interaction, types of interfaces, and types of bindings into a necessary and sufficient set of concerns. Viewpoints contain one or more levels of abstraction with a focus on certain areas of concern. The semantic behavior associated with an interaction can also be represented as a composition at different levels of abstraction. Hence, composition and abstraction play very important parts of the Interaction Framework. (See Chapter 8, "Composition and Semantics: Quality Composition Minimizing Architectural Mismatch.") Furthermore, each of the RM-ODP viewpoints participate in this framework. (See Chapter 5, "RM-ODP Architecture Model.")

An interface represents the object's behavior related to one or more interactions. An interaction occurs at runtime, across a bound interface between objects. This dynamic interaction requires constructs to actually tie together the two objects across the interface. It is the interaction defining the reason for communicating, and the interface and its binding mechanisms that enable a system to be distributed, to share resources of other (reusable) objects, to interwork with other objects, and thereby achieve a greater level of functionality. In fact, it is the Interaction Framework that enables a number of system properties to be realized. These are listed below.

Interaction enables distribution and interoperability, which in turn enables combining different objects into one whole (integration), or sharing of resources across objects, or separating a system into objects for better maintainability (modularity), or enabling a system to change to new technologies (extensibility), or adapt to a different environment (flexibility), etc. Remember that an object can be an entire system, individual subsystems, components, modules, processes, databases, or other entities, represented as an object. Some of the properties enabled by the Interaction Framework include:

- *Distribution:* The ability to place objects in different spaces and to locate them.

- *Interoperability:* The ability to exchange and use information in an agreed manner between objects.

- *Integration:* The ability to join two or more objects resulting in a new object that acts as an addition to or a replacement for the combined objects (i.e., the new object acts as a single object, though composed of multiple objects).

- *Sharing:* The ability to share resources, such as data repositories, metadata stores, or data.

- *Cross-domain interaction:* The ability for two or more different domains to interact across their domains.

- *Data or resource sharing:* The ability to communicate and share data or processing resources (hardware, software, and data).

- *Modularity:* The ability to componentized a system or application into subelements that can be considered individually.

- *Flexibility:* The ability for a system, application, component, or object to adapt to different situations.

- *Extensibility:* The ability for a system, application, component, or object to migrate or change with newer technology, or new requirements.

- *Transparency:* The ability to hide some aspects of the processing of the system.

Interaction is addressed in terms of composition at different levels of abstraction. Composition enables the combining of two or more elements (e.g., objects, interfaces, templates, and behavior). The result is a single element (the composition) that can be addressed without focusing on the constituent elements of the composition. In other words, the single element is at a different level of abstraction from the elements that make up the composition. It is important to recognize that behavior can be composed as well.

Contracts, policies, environment contracts, and templates capture the behavior of an interaction. These elements either constrain or enable an interaction, and are composable.

RM-ODP concepts of interface, binding, and interception round out the remaining parts of the Interaction Framework. These concepts will be expanded in this chapter, and related back to the basic concepts presented in Chapter 6, "Separation of Concerns: Using RM-ODP Viewpoints."

However, what also must be remembered is that the interaction, and even the interface, may be compositions. So an interaction defined at one level of abstraction may say, for example, "store," as shown in Figure 13.2. But in decomposing both the interaction and interface, the result may be a number of decomposed

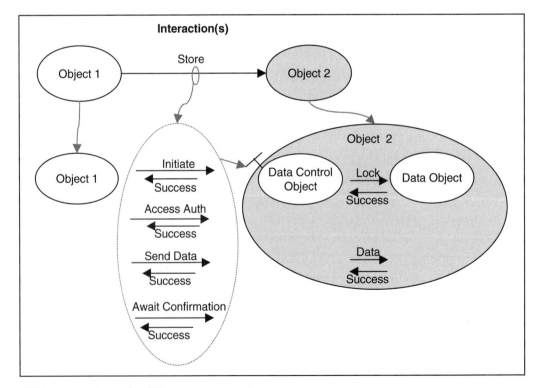

FIGURE 13.2   Example of Composite Interaction

interactions, and even a decomposed object, as shown in the figure. In Figure 13.2, object 2 is a composite of two objects, which themselves have a set of interactions. The interaction "store" is a composite of a number of interactions, shown. The process repeats until the actual engineering details are defined: interfaces, bindings, channel, protocol, behavior, etc.

Once the relationship is defined, that relationship is then refined into more and more detail. The relationship may be defined at one level of composition, which is realized in more detail in lower levels of decomposition. The resulting relationships are then refined into interfaces and bindings to realize the interaction. Recall that an interaction is associated with, at most, one interface and an interface may support one or more interactions (see Chapter 6, "Separation of Concerns: Using RM-ODP Viewpoints").

Each interface represents the communication potential of one or more interactions. Each interface is realized through an interface template. Each binding is realized through a binding template. Interfaces and binding are both computational and engineering viewpoint subjects, though their specifications differ in the different viewpoints (levels of abstraction).

Each interface is then refined into more detail associated with enabling communication, as is each binding. In this level of abstraction, an interface reference template defines the nature of the interface, and a binding template defines the nature of the binding.

Policies associated with the ODP functions enable distribution and supports bound interfaces. Transparency affects the constraints on the binding as well. Hence, policies, templates, and an environment contract affect the semantics of the interfaces and binding.

Part of the channel is the interceptor. This object provides the ability to establish additional channels to facilitate cross-domain federation. This object also provides protocol mediation across systems or domains.

The channel plus interceptor objects thus establish the communication mechanism to support the interaction between two objects, possibly on the same node, or distributed to different nodes, or federated across different domains.

POINT

Anywhere in any level of abstraction it is possible that one or more of interaction, interface, binding, template, contract, policy, and environment contract are composites and subject to composition and decomposition. This is the power of RM-ODP. It all depends on the focus of what the architect is addressing (level of abstraction)—whether it is a portion of the interaction or all of it. And composition of the parts of an interaction coupled with levels of abstraction for addressing each part allows the architect the power of specifying interaction to achieve interoperability, integration, and "plug and play."

Hence, the Interaction Framework is predicated not only on the viewpoint concepts of RM-ODP, but also the specification techniques of composition and different levels of abstraction. Recall that each viewpoint specification might include a fully specified element which itself is a result of the use of all the viewpoints.

An overview of what the Interaction Framework addresses is shown in Figure 13.3. The purpose of an interaction is to provide the means of interrelating two objects (or components). Every architecture specification addresses the functionality of objects, and their interrelationships. The specification defines, at some level of abstraction (e.g., within a viewpoint, or across viewpoints), the relationship to be realized between objects. Each element may be a composite, decomposed to address more and more properties of the element. A composition may be decomposed into a different level of abstraction, where more refinement takes place. The object relationship is constrained by a contract and an environment contract, also composable. The relationship establishes a reasoning for interaction at a level of abstraction. The communication establishes the support for the inter-

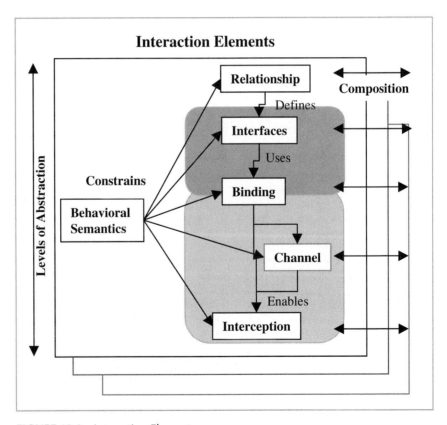

FIGURE 13.3   Interaction Elements

action at a different level of abstraction, making use of a channel and the composite parts of the channel required. For example, a channel can be a composite that includes components such as an ODP function object; a transparency object; the trinity of channel objects stub, binder, and protocol; and possibly even additional channels.

An example of this is shown in Figure 13.4. In this example, the relationship is identified to exist between a "Medical Tests" object and a "Physician" object. There are two relationships: provide and schedule. This set of simple objects may be composite objects, decomposed as shown. This set of objects with their interactions are considered a refinement of the composite "Medical Tests" and "Physician" objects. The architect might refine these decomposed relationships into more objects and associated relationships, shown in the second level of abstraction. As can be seen, more interactions are discovered in this process.

As this process continues, the interfaces and binding nature of the original relationship are more detailed. In this example, a need for a binding object is spec-

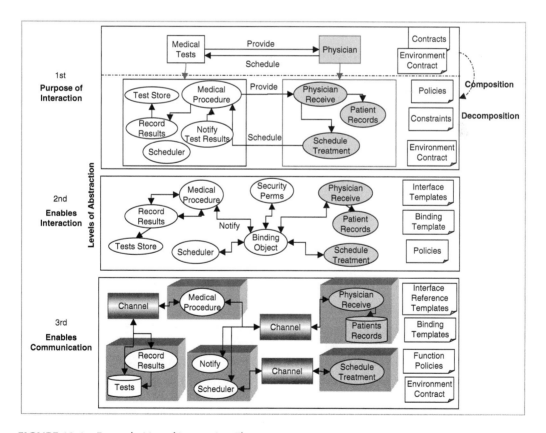

FIGURE 13.4 Example Use of Interaction Elements

ified. It provides the interfaces between objects that represent the Medical Tests composite and objects that represent the Physician object, as exemplified. Eventually, each of these interfaces and the binding object itself are further defined in terms of channels that support one or more interface bindings between objects, objects associated with specific nodes, and objects that are supported by intranode communication, shown in the third level of abstraction. Eventually, the architect will define the technologies in support of the objects, interfaces, and binding, to achieve the interaction between the objects.

All along the way, behavioral semantics are captured in terms of contracts, policies, and templates. These define and constrain what can, must, and may be done.

It takes the full spectrum of each of these specifications to define the interaction between two objects. The concepts of RM-ODP enable this to be accomplished.

13.3   ABOUT INTEROPERABILITY

Interoperability is the capability for two or more applications (or objects) to exchange information in an agreed-upon manner, and to be able to process that information because of the understanding of what it means. Interoperability is about the relationships among components in a system, and the behavior of those components in the process of interacting, related to the information and its semantics in the interchange.

As businesses become more international and, thus, geographically dispersed, their needs require a distribution of services through interoperable distributed systems. But achieving interoperability across systems that are autonomously defined, owned, and managed by a myriad of different organizations is a tall task.

There are levels of abstraction to be addressed in order to achieve interoperability. The recognition of this is one of the hallmarks of RM-ODP; interoperability is enabled through separation of concerns of interaction, interfacing, binding, and interception, all related through the consistent rules and semantics of behavior.

Interoperability is achieved as a result of well-formed, well-specified interaction syntax and semantics; using one or more interfaces; executed through well-formed, well-behaved bindings; across one or more communication channels; managing differences in cross-domain interaction of policies and data representations; and managing failures. That is, in the informal sense, interoperability is all about interfaces and the data message in the interface, how the interfaces behave, and the semantics of the processing of the data. RM-ODP provides a roadmap through a set of different frameworks, discussed in this chapter.

One common approach to achieve interoperability is to define common services and common commercial solutions for use across all systems within an enterprise. This is problematic because:

▶ One commercial solution typically does not execute on all platforms of choice.

▶ A commercial solution will emerge with different versions; these are not generally backwards compatible, resulting in different (not common) solutions.

▶ A commercial solution will typically not meet all the functional requirements of a system.

▶ A commercial solution will typically not meet all the performance requirements of a system.

▶ A commercial solution typically does not explicitly specify its behavior, resulting in unmanageable side effects.

▶ Unmanageable side effects result in mismatch. [Garlan-95]

▶ A commercial solution that is tailorable and tailored for a specific system is no longer "common."

▶ Commercial solutions are difficult to "plug and play" because of a lack of specificity of the semantics of the components and interfaces.

▶ Commercial solutions often are bundled with dependencies of other solutions for exclusive use by the product that often require the system to duplicate the same service (e.g., exclusive use of a DBMS).

In the end, specifying common solutions will enable short-term benefits of cost reduction, but long term problems in composition and interoperability across a heterogeneous environment, not to mention the ever-increasing sustainment costs. So the phrase "the difference between a solution and a working solution is great cost" can be interpreted to mean that high up-front costs are necessary to achieve a working solution for interoperability. However, a non-working solution ends up costing more in the end because of additional costs in testing, fielding, general sustainment, and constant BandAid™ fixes.

Today, many organizations look to one or more commercial products to provide needed interoperability. Indeed, many of these products do so, especially if the family of products chosen come from the same vendor. However, all too often products are chosen primarily for their functionality, overlooking the very important aspects of interoperability, and many of the other "ilities." It's easier to choose a product that provides the functions or capabilities desired. It's even easier to choose such a product when it offers more than is required. But from an enterprise system perspective, it is more important to choose products that provide the required system properties, or "ilities" required.

Many believe that interoperability is achieved by agreeing to the protocols between two applications. Interoperability is more than just a protocol agreement; it must also deal with the semantics of the message, the semantics of the processing (such as side effects of processing), and agreed-upon support services (such as security of handling the data in the message). One component that selects an *optional* protocol service may not interoperate with another component that does not recognize the *optional* service, even though the *protocol* is the same. This is one of the major reasons why components that use the same protocol do not interoperate.

Many believe that interoperability is achieved by agreeing to the standard representation of data, and enabling all applications (within the bounds of security access control) to access that data. Once again, however, agreement on the data representation is important and necessary, but not sufficient. Two components can interchange data in an agreed-upon manner, but must also agree to the policies for use of that data, the management of that data, the meaning of that data when aggregated (or fused) with other data, the presentation of that data, the naming context of the data, the type of the data elements, etc. The exchange of data must also address the agreement to the semantics of the data, i.e., the data format, the data structure, and the metadata (or meaning of the data).

Mandating that data interoperability is achieved through a "common format" is one way to do so. But it has achieved little success in most enterprises. Attempting to get an entire enterprise to agree on the schema used to store the data (for access) is a very difficult organizational and political problem to solve. Instead, defining the data format in a "common interface" is more achievable, leaving to each end system any transformations required to store the data in whatever format chosen. However, this is insufficient for end-to-end interoperability because it does not address the semantics of the processing of the data, nor the environmental support (contract) for that data, such as security or quality.

Many system implementations fail not because of a missing functional capability, but because of an unsupported system property. Lack of interoperation, which relies upon end-to-end correct interfacing, among the components in a system is often one of the biggest reasons for failure. "The problems in building complex systems today often arise in the interfaces between the components—where the components may be hardware, software, or human." [Leveson-96]

Not only must the architect be concerned about the interfaces in the system to achieve interoperability, but must also be concerned with the semantics of the behavior of the objects involved in the interfacing, and of the appropriate interface types among those objects. The interfaces the architect defines, the behavior specified, and the semantics of the environment to achieve the interaction needed (whether the interaction is local, geographically distributed, across different domains) will either enable interoperability or prevent it. Interoperability is also of concern with the ability to extend a system to newer technologies, to achieve composability, and to minimize mismatch. These are the main reasons as to why an Interaction Framework is so very important in the architecture of a system.

In the desire for end-to-end correctness in interoperability, there needs to be a focus on different types of interfaces. Interfacing is complex; it deals with the purpose of the interface (the interaction), what is in an interface (the signature), how one interface is associated with another interface (the binding), how that interface is communicated (the protocol) how that interface is to be processed (the semantics), and the services supporting the interface in the environment (the environment contract).

For example, look at all the interfaces shown in Figure 13.5. In this example, a commonly called three-tier architecture is shown, consisting of a client workstation, an application processing server, and a server that manages the data. Each of these interfaces is often called an API, and yet they are behaviorally quite different, with very different needs from the environment. There is a graphics interface, to present the visualization of the data to the end user. There are potentially four different communications interfaces, depending on the service level agreement of communication protocols, rules, and behavior associated with each end. There are likewise up to three different network interfaces. Perhaps one encrypts the message, perhaps one is asynchronous, etc. And of course there are the interfaces associated with the processing and request for a service from a "server." Each of these interfaces is potentially quite different, requiring different needs from its support environment, behaving differently depending on the environment, structured differently, using different protocols, and so forth. Yet, to achieve this interoperability, there must be end-to-end correctness and interoperation of all these interfaces, both syntactically and semantically.

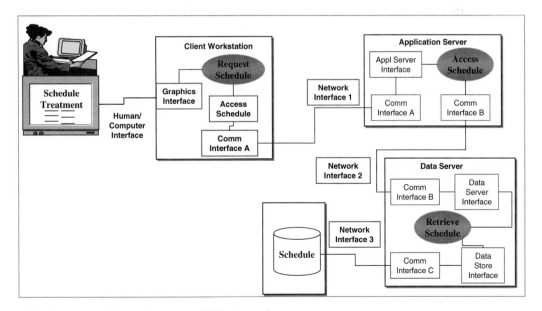

FIGURE 13.5 End-to-End Interoperability Example

13.4   ABOUT SOFTWARE ARCHITECTURE CONNECTORS

Software architecture addresses components, connectors, and styles or constraints.

13.4.1   ABOUT CONNECTORS

An *architectural style* defines a set of constraints on the structure of an architecture and on the connectors between components. *Connector* is defined to be the locus of relations among components. Connectors mediate interactions among components. Each connector has a protocol specification that defines its properties, which include rules about the types of interfaces it is able to mediate for, assurances about properties of the interaction, rules about the order in which things happen, and commitments about the interaction. Each is of some type or subtype (e.g., remote procedure call, broadcast, event, and pipes). [Shaw-96, Mehta-99]

Architectural styles are based on connectors. These connectors include pipe and filter, real-time flows, event-based, message-based, and data flow. (See [Shaw-96, Shaw-97, and Medvidovic-2000] for more detail about architectural styles.) Architecture Description Languages (ADLs) provide a representation of a particular style, with connectors exhibiting certain properties. Care must be exercised in selecting a particular ADL. Only recently is there work in attempting to unify different ADLs into a powerful unification, called Acme [Acme]. It provides abstraction and composition, in addition to mediation. Behavior is deemed to be data and associated control. However, many behavioral concepts are missing, such as a specification of common property types across all connectors. Precise behavioral semantics of the connector and architectural style concepts remains a goal. Until this goal is reached, results will be ADLs that cannot capture the full architectural concepts of the RM-ODP Interaction Framework.

A *connector* is an architectural element that addresses interactions among components, and constraints that apply to those interactions. Some simple connectors include procedure calls, shared data access, and shared memory access. More complex connectors include client/server interaction, database interaction, and asynchronous events. Software connectors deal with the transfer of data and control among its components, and provide certain special services such as transactions, event handling, persistence, and messaging. As such, connectors are separated from the functionality of components.

Software architecture deems connectors important in large distributed systems to determine system properties such as performance, resource utilization, global rates of flow, scalability, reliability, security, and evolvability. [Mehta-99]

An *event* is an observable invocation on a component that coordinates the flow of control among components. The properties of time and ordering are important. An object relationship that results in one or more interactions addresses ordering of the events that make up the interactions. The interface signatures define the content of the events, to include the relationships and specification of their parameters, and any QoS timing constraints. The flow of information in support of the event relationship is specified using the interface and binding aspects similar to the Interaction Framework.

Some work has emerged that associates semantic relationships among the parameters of an event in terms of RM-ODP [Rakotonirainy], to provide further support in event relationships across distributed systems. It does this by composition and levels of abstraction, and defined operators to support composition. This work has shown that the Interaction Framework concepts are not only able to capture the existing definition of connectors, but also provide semantic behavior in a more precise manner, thus enhancing the capabilities of connectors.

13.4.2   THE CHALLENGE

"Many of the problems with current techniques for architectural definition revolve around inadequacies of the mechanisms for defining component interconnection." [Shaw-94] The Interaction Framework provides a rich set of mechanisms for defining object or composite object interconnection.

"With some exceptions…the architecture community has thus far maintained a studied silence on the exact nature of connectors. This has resulted in their inconsistent treatment and sometimes contradictory assumptions. For example, connectors are often considered to be explicit at the level of architecture, but intangible in a system's implementation. This belief has at least partly contributed to the existing lack of understanding of the relationship between high-level and implementation-level connectors. None of these approaches furthers our understanding of what the fundamental building blocks of software interaction are and how they can be composed into more complex interactions. Such level of understanding is necessary in order to fully meet the challenge posed to software architecture researchers of giving connectors 'a first-class.'" [Mehta-99]

"Two levels of structure and abstraction are missing:

▶ Abstractions for connections: aggregation of primitive import/exports to show the intended abstract function of the connection.

▶ Segmentation of interfaces: decomposition of an interface into more-or-less conventional segments corresponding to different groups of users or different classes of functionality. Each of these may involve several abstract connections." [Shaw-94]

Multiple levels of abstraction along with well-defined concepts and consistency rules are needed to adequately specify connectors and semantic behavior, and these are specified in RM-ODP. From these abstractions, definition of high-level abstract connectors as well as low-level connectors, composition of connectors, analyses of behavior, and specification of connector properties at the appropriate level of abstraction, can be accomplished.

13.4.3   THE NEED FOR AN INTERACTION FRAMEWORK

The pattern of reasoning for connectors requires multiple levels of abstraction to reason about interaction among components and the interworking elements that support the interaction between/among components. As such, an Interaction Framework that provides structure and semantics of interworking with multiple levels of abstraction is necessary to represent the different types of connectors, and associate properties with them. Current work in connectors, however, has not accomplished a well-formed specification of *common* concepts and connector properties addressing the different architecture styles.

Current work on connectors has focused mostly on the structure of interfaces and functionality achieved across a communication mechanism. Software connector research is attempting to define connectors more precisely, and attach semantic behavior somehow to connectors. However, the approach to rigorously specifying connector technology is inconsistent and suffers from a lack of specification of the foundations for software interaction, how connectors can be composed to represent more complex connector based interaction, and how mismatch among connectors can be identified and mitigated.

Properties of connectors are important. The work in connectors is attempting to find some means of specifying connector properties consistently, and specifying complex connector relationships to achieve some of the system "ilities": reliability, scalability, and so forth. However, capturing the semantics of those properties, identifying a categorization of concepts to be associated with each level of abstraction, and associating invariants with those properties has not yet been formalized.

The Interaction Framework presented in this chapter supports the missing elements in connector technology and associated architectural styles today: levels of abstraction, common interaction concepts, common behavioral semantics concepts, patterns of reasoning, and even composition of everything to construct more complex connectors from basic connector types. The use of the Interaction Framework furthers the concepts of connectors, giving connectors a "first-class" status.

13.5   INTERACTION FRAMEWORK

The Interaction Framework is a pattern of reasoning that describes how objects interact to fulfill a relationship, not how they are implemented.

The aspects of interaction, in essence, cover the need for a relationship between objects, agreed interface for interacting, rules for establishing a proper binding to include appropriate channel configuration, transport of the message (e.g., protocols), common service-level agreements, and agreed-upon semantic behavior for all aspects of the interaction, all making up the communication between two objects.

These are depicted in Figure 13.6. Here, object A and object B are involved in an interaction. The interaction consists of both the content of the message to exchange for the interaction, and the interaction interface, defined by an interface signature. The nature of the binding is defined, and established through the use of a channel. If the interaction is across domain boundaries, an interceptor is used to mediate differences in protocol, format, policies, and all manner of cross-domain negotiation. The rules of contracts and policies define what is expected at every aspect of the interaction. These aspects of interaction are discussed in four major topics: interface framework, binding framework, interception framework, and semantic framework.

The Interaction Framework addresses roles and their relationships, an interface framework to address concepts of interfacing, and a binding framework to address the connection aspects of interfaces such as message composition, binding

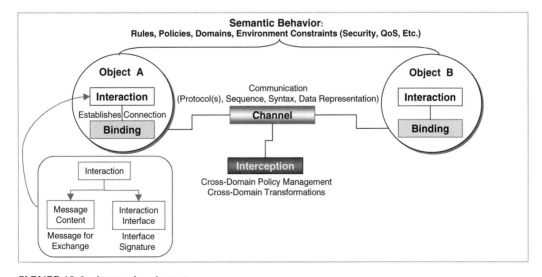

FIGURE 13.6   Interaction Aspects

establishment, communication protocols, and mediation. Further, the Interaction Framework addresses composition of key concepts in the different frameworks and decomposition into possibly additional objects and interactions.

Interoperability in RM-ODP deals with the structure and semantics of the entire relationship, interface, binding, and interception frameworks that enable cross-domain interoperability. All of these frameworks are addressed in this chapter and how they collectively specify an Interaction Framework and provide the interoperability desired of systems today. The Interaction Framework to be discussed is shown in Figure 13.7.

RM-ODP defines what needs to be specified and adhered to, and what can be done to provide value added services and independent designs. It provides a means of specifying solutions that result in interoperability, while enabling different solution designs and choices of technology. It does not, however, prescribe the manner in which semantics are to be designed; this is a specification decision made by the architect.

The use of standard interfaces allows one to mix and match different implementations and hopefully enable interoperability with other types of applications. Focusing on interaction (coupled with the semantics of the behavior) ends up not having to demand all systems in an enterprise adhere to a common environment or a common software solution in order to interoperate. Instead, they are free to choose, as long as the interactions and behavior as defined by the Interaction Framework are agreed to, and the resultant interfacing and interception mechanisms are fully agreed upon for communication and mediation.

The concepts of interoperability are tersely defined throughout RM-ODP. In this chapter, all these concepts are brought together and related, to provide the pattern of reasoning for specifying interoperability in a system. All of the RM-ODP

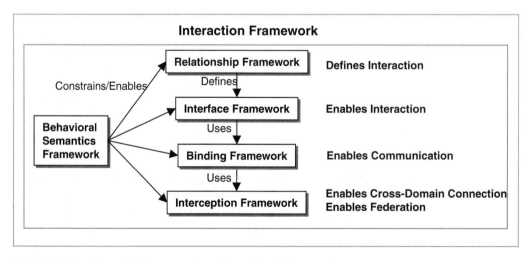

FIGURE 13.7   Interaction Framework and Associated Frameworks

viewpoints come into play. An airline reservation system is used as an example for this chapter, to use a possibly more common real-life example in discussing the complexities associated with interoperability.

13.6   RM-ODP Definitions

RM-ODP does not explicitly define interoperability. It does, however, define the following terms, pertinent to interoperability, some of which have already been covered in previous chapters:

Communication is the way in which information is transferred from one object to another. This transfer of information can include one or more interactions. The transfer can be direct between two or more objects, or include one or more intermediate objects. [RM-ODP-2]

Internetworking is the communication and exchange of information between two or more systems. [RM-ODP-2]

Interaction, Interface, Binding, Communication, Interceptor, Behavior, and *Establishing behavior* have been previously defined.

13.7   Relationship Framework

The Interaction Framework starts with two basic concepts: a role assumed by one or more object(s) and an interaction defined between the objects. The enterprise viewpoint provides the concepts to specify a relationship: a specification of roles, their behavior, objects (that may be components), actions, and activities (sequential sets of actions). Behavior is specified in terms of policies, roles, and contracts, including both the contract of the community in which the objects participate, as well as the environment contract. Community is used to define the scope of the configuration of components and relationships that relate to one or more interactions.

Interaction begins the process of interoperability. It captures the reason for interoperating at the highest level of abstraction. Two or more components interact to perform some message exchange or provide some processing. In the most fundamental case, a single object can interact with itself. This is shown in Figure 13.8. The normal case consists of two interacting objects, shown in the bottom of this figure.

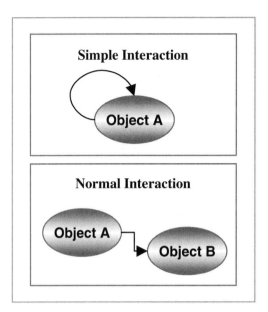

FIGURE 13.8   Simple Interaction

In the more complex case, a relationship is defined between two objects that results in an interaction between the two objects. Some examples of simple dual object interaction are listed below and shown in Figure 13.9 for each case:

▶ Example 1: One object provides a service to the other. For example, object A sends a message to object B. Object B may be active at the time, and receives the message. If object B is inactive, it is unable to receive the message until it becomes active. Only when object B receives the message is the interaction completed.

▶ Example 2: One object provides data to the other. For example, object A generates an event that passes data to some receiving object B, considered the environment of object A. There is no expectation of a return message. This is similar to the communication concept of publish and subscribe.

▶ Example 3: As another example, object A (a multimedia server) sends an audiovisual flow of data to object B. In both cases, the receipt of the message (or data) completes the interaction.

▶ Example 4: One object provides a service to the other object and waits for a return message. For example, object A makes a request, passing a message to object B, which is a server. The server receives the message (or data), performs some action based on the message, and returns some result to object A (the client). Once object A receives the returned message, the interaction is complete.

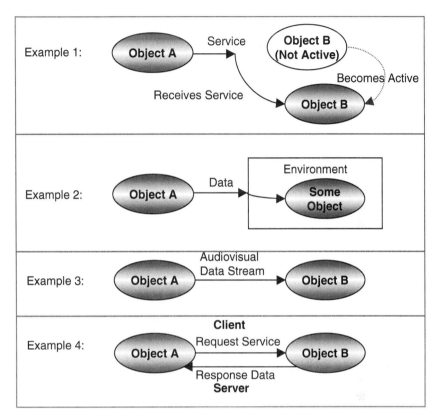

FIGURE 13.9 Examples of Completed Interactions Between Two Objects

A more complex case of a dual object interaction (example 5) is shown in Figure 13.10. Here, both objects are peers. That is, they both assume both roles of an interaction. For example, each object is both a client and a server to the other object, depending on the exchange of messaging.

Examples of more complex object interactions address when multiple objects are involved in the interaction. Some examples, shown in Figure 13.11, include:

▶ Example 6: Two peer objects are shown with a security authority, which establishes an authenticated and secure association between the two peers. In this case, the interaction between object A and object B has a precondition interaction that authenticates the interaction. Once this precondition interaction is completed, the interaction between object A and object B is completed on receipt of the request message and/or response.

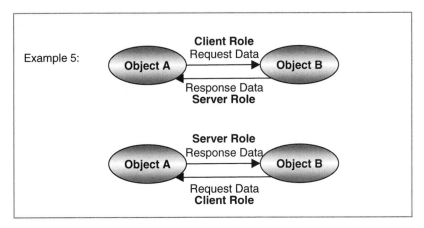

FIGURE 13.10　Interaction Between Peer Objects

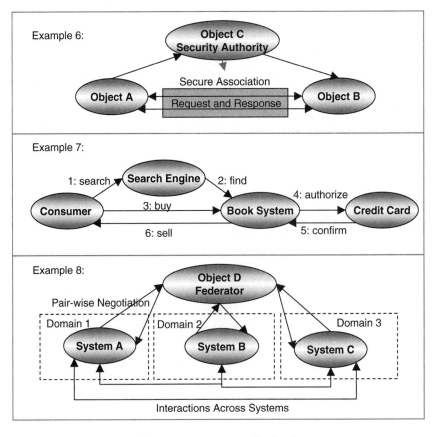

FIGURE 13.11　Complex Interaction Among Multiple Objects

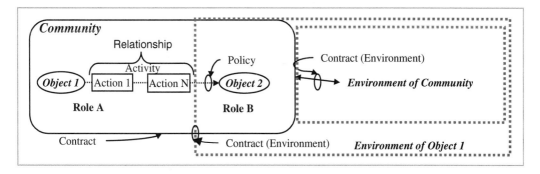

FIGURE 13.12 Relationship Specification in the Enterprise Viewpoint

▶ Example 7: Four objects (a consumer, a search engine, a book system, and a credit card system) interact to buy, sell, and pay for books. Each pair forms an interaction, but the end-to-end interaction is the transaction of discovery, buying, and selling.

▶ Example 8: A set of distributed systems negotiate policies with a federator object to allow future interactions across the different domains. The interaction with the federator and the negotiation interaction with the federator, constitute precondition interactions before any two domain objects (or systems) are able to interact.

The objects in any of the above examples may be composite objects. What that means is that the object may be decomposed and refined into one or more objects and interactions. For example, consider "System A" of example 8. It may in fact be decomposed into any of the previous examples, or a combination of the previous examples. Eventually, the enterprise specification will define all the objects and their interactions in the community of interest.

Shown in Figure 13.12 is the general model for specifying the interaction among objects, from the enterprise viewpoint. It includes:

▶ The community of objects and their configuration

▶ Every object relationship defined in terms of activities and associated actions, which are interactions here

▶ The contracts associated with the community

▶ The policies associated with each relationship

▶ The environment contract associated with an object's relationship with another object

▶ The environment contract associated with the community and the external communities

This sets the stage to further refine each relationship into one or more interfaces and bindings.

13.8   INTERFACING FRAMEWORK

An interface structures the communication of information and service offers. An interface enables distribution of objects to different locations in space. An interface provides the mechanism to access an object independent of its distribution characteristics, whether it be across a network or merely within the same node. The interface is the mechanism that allows distribution, such as the separation between a Web server and its client, for example.

An interface template is an abstraction of an object that specifies a unique subset of the interactions of that object with its environment, coupled with expected behavior. An interface provides the means for objects to interact to share data or services, whether the objects are local to the same node, or distributed across nodes or domains. If an object wishes to offer a service or share data, it must specify an interface that can be used by another object. An interface brings together a set of defined interactions that can be communicated between objects.

An interface is part of an object. An interface may offer a one-way signal interaction, a one-way flow interaction, a one-way client interaction expecting no response, or even a peer-to-peer interaction between two or more objects. As stated above, peer-to-peer interaction means the interface will support service offers and client requests from the same object.

Multiple interfaces allow the separation of different functional accesses to the object. For example, an object may access another object using a client role interface, and access the same or a different object using an administrator role interface. Multiple interfaces allow for an object to interact with multiple objects, and allow multiple objects to separately interact with a single object using a different interface.

The interfacing framework consists of the interface concerns represented from both the computational and engineering viewpoints. The computational language provides the patterns of reasoning to refine a system into interfaces that support the interaction among objects. The computational object template includes the specification of the object interaction and associated interface templates. An interface template addresses the constraints applicable to the object or environment contract, QoS parameters that must be honored, and behavior that defines any pre- or postcondition or operation. Each interface is associated with a causality role that represents the behavior of the interface.

Figure 13.13 provides an overview of the interface framework concepts. A control component is shown that reflects infrastructure support in managing the interface behavior. An object may well be a composite of multiple component objects, allowing for composition of the object and its interface(s). A discussion of these concepts follows.

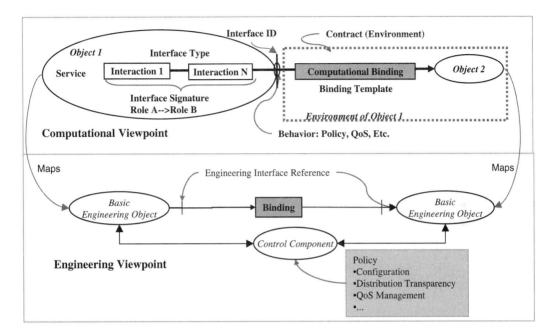

FIGURE 13.13   Simple Interface Concepts

Each interaction occurs at a computational interface, constrained by the policies of the interface and the environment contract. More than one interaction may be included in a computational interface, but an interaction can be included in only one interface. The interactions of an object may affect each other, in different interfaces of the object.

A computational interface maps onto an engineering interface. The engineering interface captures the specification of the computational interface in an engineering interface reference, along with a logical address for that interface. It is the engineering interface reference that must be discovered for a binding to take place. The type of interface, both at the originating source and the terminating source, must be of the same type, as must the parameters of the interface. A contract establishes the agreed upon properties of the binding, such as a quality of service. All of this is predetermined before a binding takes place.

Therefore, each interface is associated with a number of constructs, listed below. Further detail of each of these is captured in this chapter.

▶ Interface type

▶ Interface signature

▶ One or more interaction signatures

▶ Interface template to define the properties of an interface in sufficient detail to instantiate it

▶ Interface identifier

▶ Causality roles associated with the interface

▶ Engineering interface reference

▶ Quality of service characteristics of the interface

▶ Policies associated with the behavior of the interface

▶ Contract associated with the dual behavior with the environment and across the binding

Recall that a computational binding object may be used to address complex binding of multiple object interfaces. In this case, the computational binding object itself has a number of interfaces, one to service each of the objects using the binding object, and one to complete the interaction with the target object(s). All interfaces of the binding object are complete interface specifications, and adhere to the interfacing framework concepts and rules. Again, the objects and interfaces of the computational viewpoint map onto objects and engineering interfaces in the engineering viewpoint. Figure 13.14 provides an overview of these interface framework concepts, including the control component to manage the behavior of the interfaces.

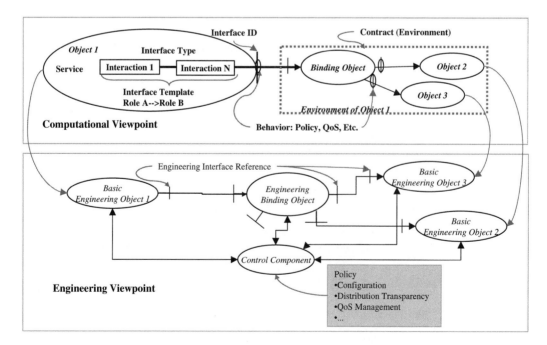

FIGURE 13.14   Compound Interface Concepts

13.8.1 INTERACTION AND INTERFACE TYPES

There are three types of interactions: *stream, signal,* and *operation.* Each of these has their own rules associated with initiating and terminating the interface. Each of these has a different type of causality role associated with the interface. A typed interaction is associated with a single interface of the same type, and that interface can only support interactions of a single type. So, an operation interaction, much like a client and server interaction, can only be associated with an operation interface type. And an operation interface type can only include operational interactions. (See Chapter 6, "Separation of Concerns: Using RM-ODP Viewpoints," for additional details.)[1]

The client initiates the operation interaction, through the operation interface. The server permits any of the operations in the interface to be requested. In the case of an interrogation type of interaction, the server must respond. The timing for this interaction is not specified, but the architect can specify it as part of the QoS parameters or part of the environment contract associated with the interaction.

A *stream interface* consists of a continuous flow of data, from a producer object to one or more consumer objects. A *flow type interaction* provides a continuous flow of data. This is useful for telecommunications applications, where voice and data are provided in a single interface. The rule is that the stream interface must contain one or more interactions that are flows. A flow is a sequence of interactions conveying data from a producer, which initiates the flows, to a consumer which receives the flows.

A *signal interface* consists of one or more signal interactions between an initiating object (initiating the interaction) and a responding object (receiving the interaction). A *signal type interaction* provides a signal between an initiating object and a responding object. In the case of a signal, the responding object is known. A signal is the most basic, atomic, action. Different signal interactions can be initiated from the same initiating object across the same signal interface.

A signal occurs at a specified point in time. As such, it offers the capability to observe an event, and thus to dynamically measure some QoS characteristic. The signal interface can be used for such interactions as "confirm" the receipt of a message, or "commit" a transaction. If a signal fails, then both ends of the interaction fail, no matter where the failure occurs.

The signal parameters include an identifier for a computational interface. It is this identifier, and associated computational interface signature, that enables the Trader to import and export interface references.

A conformance reference point can be associated with a signal interaction to observe and measure some QoS (such as the time to complete a transaction, or latency of the communication).

---

1. Some repetition is included here for completeness.

13.8.2 INTERFACE TEMPLATE, INTERFACE SIGNATURE, AND INTERACTION SIGNATURE

The interface signature contains one or more interaction signatures. The relationship between a set of interaction signatures and an interface signature is shown in Figure 13.15.

The interaction signature details the parameters (number, name, type, value), roles, and behavior in the interface. The relationship between an interaction and an interface is decided by the architect. That is, a single interface signature can include three interactions (shown in Figure 13.15), or each interaction can be part of a separate interface signature. How they are partitioned across the different interfaces is not defined by RM-ODP. The choice is generally based on the configuration of the services offered at the interface. For example, one interface may offer the interactions `search()`, `list()`, `query()`, `change()`, `delete()`, and `create()` across the same interface. But the selection of which interactions are available may be one of the constraints on the interface, identified by the definition of the causality role of the interface. That is, one client may be allowed to invoke only `search()`, `list()`, and `query()` on a database, whereas another client may use the `query()`, `change()`, `delete()`, `create()` interactions. All these interactions may be provided in the same interface, but their use constrained by the object invoking the interface, or by a separation of interactions into separate role-based invocations.

An interface template defines the full interface specification, and is used to instantiate one or more interfaces. What this means is that a template defines the full functionality of an interface, but the instantiation of an interface may subset some of the capabilities. For example, one operational interface defines a query, management, and update set of operation interactions. Yet one interface may be instantiated to offer only the query, and another to offer the update, and another to offer the management. All of these are separate interactions and the interfaces instantiated to support these interactions are slightly different, but the interface template is the same. This is just another example of the flexibility of RM-ODP.

When an interface is to be used, the object may or may not create an instantiation of that interface. So the interfaces are not necessarily instantiated with the object. If the object does not instantiate the interface, a third-party object assumes this action, or the object instantiates an interface dynamically. This capability is particularly useful for object mobility, and dynamic binding. Mobility is about

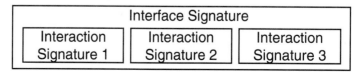

FIGURE 13.15   Interface Signature Consisting of Interactions

moving an object and its interfaces to a different location, using the template of the object. If an object has an active interface, mobility is more difficult. Dynamic binding is about establishing an agreement on the inter-working of the interfaces before they are committed to a communication. This capability allows for negotiated QoS behavior, for a restricted interaction capability based on security considerations, and a number of dynamic decisions. If the interface is active, altering its behavior dynamically is more difficult.

The interface template contains the signature specifications, interface causality role, interface identifier, specifications about the expected behavior, and the specification of a contract. The contract not only includes what is expected of the interface in terms of behavior, but also a specification of what the environment must provide for the proper functioning of the interface. So, for example, a resource required for the interface is a contractual element with the environment that must supply that resource, such as perhaps a node management thread or a channel that provides a certain level of throughput. Figure 13.16 provides an overview of how an interface template relates to an interface signature specification.

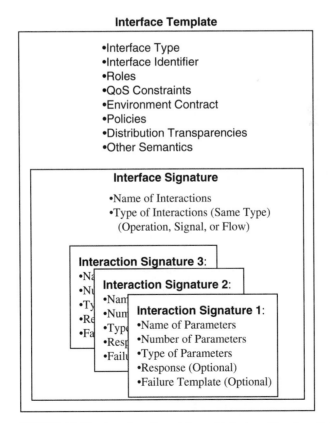

FIGURE 13.16 Interface Template and Interface Signature Relation

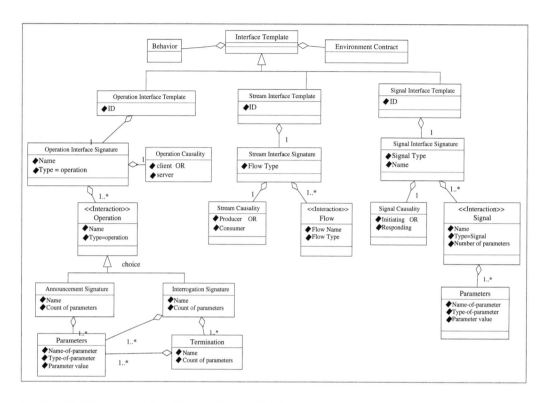

FIGURE 13.17   Computational Interactions UML Diagram

A mix of interactions within a single interface signature is not allowed. But since an object can have multiple interfaces, different types of interfaces can be instantiated from that object. For example, an object might include an operational interface for a query, a signal interface to indicate a status, and a stream interface to flow the information to another object. These would be three separate interaction types with three separate interface signatures, all co-existent in the same object. Of course, an object can include multiple interfaces of the same type as well.

Figure 13.17 provides a Unified Modeling Language (UML) diagram overview of the operation, signal, and stream interactions discussed here and in Chapter 6, "Separation of Concerns: Using RM-ODP Viewpoints."

13.8.3 CAUSALITY ROLES

A set of causality roles is defined along with an interface. An object that initiates an interface assumes a particular role, and the target object assumes the opposite role. Each end of the interface has a unique role associated with it. A *causality role* identifies the behavior assumed by the object at one end of the interface and the set of interactions available to it.

A causality role associated with an interface should not be confused with a role that an object assumes. The former defines the expected functional behavior in the use of the interface, not the overall behavior of the object. The latter defines the behavior of the object, no matter what interfaces are offered or used. For example, an object uses an operational interface as a client. The client is the causality role that defines the behavior the object assumes in using the interface. But that object may be an admitting agent from Healthy Hospital where one part of the admitting agent role includes executing the client side of the interface to access the patient record database. The client end of the interface certainly does not define the behavior of the admitting agent.

The interface signature defines the causality roles assumable by the objects—all of them. When an interaction is used, a binding must link together the interface between objects for communicating the interaction. When an interface is bound between objects, the object assumes one of the roles defined in the interface signature. The rules of RM-ODP state that the object at the other end of the interface must, therefore, assume the complementary causality role.

An example is shown in Figure 13.18. The application object assumes the role of a client, and as such may invoke the interaction to initiate a query to a database server object assuming the role of a server. But the application object may not simultaneously assume both the client and server roles of the interface. The client role is limited to those interactions that are associated with a client, exemplified in

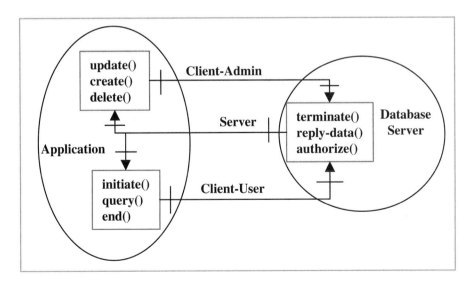

FIGURE 13.18 Causality Roles Example

the figure. At some other point in time, or some other composition, the application object may assume the causality role of "server," and some other object assume the causality role "client." This is an example of a peer-to-peer relationship.

The architect can associate specific causality roles to each end, and add in additional meaning to the roles. So, for example, an operational interface that supports the operations for both access to a database and administration of the database could be designated to different roles to this interface: user and administrator. Then, in the operational interface specification, one role would be defined as the "client-user," and another role as the "client-administrator," for the same interface. The receiving end might be "server-database" that supports the server of the database functionality.

The architect can partition the interactions into a single interface, or more than one. If the interactions are associated with a single interface, constraints must restrict the use of the interaction to the designated role. For example, a policy associated with the interface designates the user identified as an administrator is permitted to use any of the operation interactions in the interface, and a user identified as a non-administrator is prohibited from invoking the administration operation in the interface. A reason for partitioning the interactions into a single interface is to minimize the maintenance overhead of additional interfaces in the system. Using the Interface Definition Language (IDL) [ISO-IDL], the operation interface may be defined as shown below.

The policy rule might be "Obligated: User is designated as an administrator to execute administer-database." Shown are the IDL statements that might form a part of such an interface specification, where comments about other things that might be specified appear in *italics*.

```
struct PermittedRole { string user-role;
                 boolean is_ok; };
struct ProhibitedRole { string user-role;
                 boolean is_ok; };
struct User { string user-role };

//  Define Policy to be pertinent policy conditions
    struct Policy {
            PolicyId          policy_id;
//  Define Permitted Role to identify valid user roles for administrator
        PermittedRole         user_permitted_role;
        ProhibitedRole        user_denied_role;
        //other policy parameters
        };

exception PermissionDenied { string error; };

interface database_access {
```

```
// The operation interaction for user access
void access-database (
        in parameters (something defined)
        out boolean Success
) raises (errors defined);

// The operation interaction for user query
void query-database (
        in parameters (defined)
        out boolean Success
) raises (errors define)d;

// The operation interaction for administrator
void administer-database (
        in parameters (define)d
        in User user-role,   //input the user-role to be evaluated
       in Policy policy,   //input the policy against which to evaluate
                the user role
        out boolean Success
) raises (PermissionDenied, System-Error, other exceptions defined);
}; // end of database_access interface
```

In line with this discussion, and as addressed in Chapter 8, "Composition and Semantics: Quality Composition Minimizing Architectural Mismatch," a client/server architecture differs from a client/server role-based interface. A client/server architecture separates the interactions into different objects: a client can only perform the client service interactions of the client, and the server can only perform the server-related services.

In the role-based situation, the object can be a client when it executes the interactions of the client, or a server when it executes the interactions of the server. This is a separation not of services but of time. In order for this to occur, however, each object must be able to respond to the interactions associated with either the client or server. That is, the entire processing for client-based interactions and server-based interactions can exist within the object, and the object selects which set of interactions to act upon.

In cases such as a DBMS, it is sometimes reasonable to architect client interactions separate from server interactions, physically. This better enables the concept of "thin client," where the majority of the interaction processing is maintained in the "server." However, there are limitations. The client can never act as a server, and the server can never act as a client.

In cases such as remote access communication, it is desirable for each end to be able to act as either a client or a server. How many times has a user wished her PC could either act as a server retaining certain files for access by another PC, or as a client by remotely accessing the files of another PC? To accomplish this requires that the full set of interactions (both remote client access and remote server support) be available for use on the same PC. This exemplifies a difference between a client/server architecture and role-based client/server interactions.

Though these examples have focused on client and server roles (of an operation interface), they apply equally well to the other types of interactions (stream and signal).

13.8.4   INTERFACE IDENTIFIER

An *interface identifier* identifies an interface so that it can be selected for use. The identifier is a unique name for the interface, within the naming context of its domain. The interface identifier distinguishes not only that interface from all other objects, but from different interfaces to the same object. It allows another object to interact with it.

What this means is that a contract is established to define a naming context and a set of objects are introduced in the infrastructure to manage the naming in the domain: allocate a name, update a name, and manage the use of the names. When interaction occurs across naming domains, an interceptor is required to negotiate the names, and to translate from one naming context to another. Federation of domains addresses mediation of naming contexts.

Of course the architect can also use the concepts of global naming and addressing across multiple domains. This is the nature of the Internet Domain Name Server (DNS), which was established before the different Internet domains were established. So, for example, a URL that ends in *.com* represents a commercial address and domain, whereas a URL that ends in *.edu* represents an educational institution. The parts of the URL preceding these suffixes are resolved in that domain. In other words, the URL addresses are composites of different domain addresses, each of which is resolved as the message is passed to that domain. The URL is, in essence, a tree structure of naming contexts.

13.8.5   INTERACTION POINT

An *interaction point* is a location where an object interacts with its environment. It is a location where there may be one or more interfaces. And more than one interaction point may exist at the same location. It is also a point where another object can link to a selected interface, for perhaps observing the nature of the interface, or for managing the behavior of the interface. An interaction point is important as a reference point for observing the interaction.

An interaction point is also important for evaluating compliance of the specification to its architecture, or with the system to its architecture. *Location* is not necessarily a physical location, but rather a logical location. It allows the architect, designer, and tester to specify the details of the testing information to assess the compliance of the system specification. (See Chapter 11, "Architecture Analysis and System Conformance Evaluation.")

13.8.6 ENGINEERING INTERFACE REFERENCE

The engineering interface reference (EIR) contains information essential to the discovery of interfaces subject to binding. These interfaces can span different nodes, use different protocols, and even span different domains. A computational interface corresponds to an engineering interface. Hence, the computational interface identifier corresponds, unambiguously, to an EIR of an engineering interface. The information required to establish bindings is therefore contained in the EIRs of each interface to be bound.

The information content of the EIR enables a flexible, dynamic binding of interfaces. The interface reference can contain different groupings of information for selection. The appropriate selection is then made (possibly by the nucleus) based on the binding behavior desired for the particular object interaction.

In the case where alternative channel configurations are available for use, the EIR information determines the choice of channel objects (i.e., stub, binder, protocol, and interceptor) to best support the communication needs. For example, one binding may require extra security in the form of encryption, whereas another binding may not, based on the networking link available. In the former case, the channel might include a stub that performs encryption, whereas in the latter case, a simple stub can be used. Perhaps one object communicates events and requires a distinct address. This information is part of the EIR. Perhaps one object interacts with multiple object interfaces at a single node. The EIR may then associate a single address to all such object interfaces. But all of this could be specified in the single EIR template. Recall that a template is a pattern to instantiate something. And a template can be instantiated multiple times, with some of the parameters or all of the parameters, as defined by a policy.

The EIR information includes an interface identifier defined relative to a naming context of an interface reference management domain. This domain consists of the nodes from that domain that support the management naming policies of the domain. Policy determines the content of the EIR, how an identifier is allocated, how an address is tracked, how long a previous address is retained, and how to interact across domains in support of federation.

Other information in the EIR for an interface supports a binding between the interfaces in conjunction with one or more selected distribution transparencies. The EIR is fundamental to migration, location, replication, and relocation transparencies (see Chapter 10, "Hiding System Complexities: Distribution Transparencies," for use of the EIR in support of distribution transparency). The different transparencies require different needs of the EIR.

The information contained in an EIR includes an identifier, the interface type of the interface, the template for the channel to use in the binding, and the

```
┌─────────────────────────────────────────────┐
│ Engineering Interface Reference               │
│ Interface Identifier                          │
│ Interface Type                                │
│ Interface Location (Logical)                  │
│ Interface Behavior From Interface Template    │
│ Channel Type Required                         │
│ Channel Template                              │
│ Binding Information                           │
│ Protocol (Optional)                           │
│ Security Required                             │
│ Location                                      │
│ Relocation Information                        │
│ Migration Information                         │
│ Interface QoS                                 │
│ Transparency Information                      │
│         •Failure                              │
│         •Relocation                           │
│         •...                                  │
│ ...                                           │
└─────────────────────────────────────────────┘
```

FIGURE 13.19   Engineering Interface Reference

details of the stubs, binders, protocol objects, and interceptors to be used, or a selection criteria to choose from a set of these objects, an address of the interfaces for use in binding, and information to repair broken bindings. This is represented in Figure 13.19, as well as in the UML model in Figure 10.20 on page 417.

If an object is migrated from one node to another, the address of the interface changes. The EIR information maintains the current address, and previous address, to allow a bound interface to be re-established with the new interface address and to allow interactions designated to the old address to correctly use the new address. However, RM-ODP does not prescribe the information or its form. An emerging RM-ODP component standard, Computational Interface References and Binding [ISO-IRB], is accomplishing this.

13.9   BINDING FRAMEWORK

A *binding* is the mechanism to tie together two or more interfaces so that an interaction can take place. A binding provides an environment where the interactions can be executed. A binding is dynamic. That is, it is created and terminated at runtime. The interfaces to be bound are determined dynamically as well.

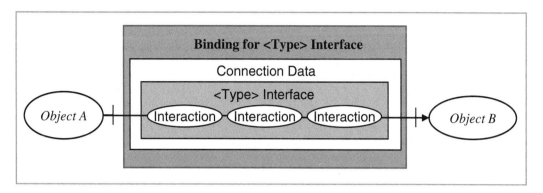

FIGURE 13.20 Binding

The interface framework provided the specification details for an interface, independent of its binding between objects. The binding framework focuses on the nature of the binding: the specification of a binding, the behavior of the binding and how it is specified, and the runtime aspects of a binding.

What may be statically defined are the interface specifications and the behavioral aspects of the binding, which depend on the behavioral aspects of the interfaces and the environment in which the binding takes place. A binding establishes the connection between object interfaces. The ability to connect is supported by connection data, such as a protocol, which encapsulates the interactions of the interface. The actual interaction(s) is not important to the binding, nor is the connection data important to the interface. But the process of establishing a binding must make sure the type of interface matches the type of binding. This is shown in Figure 13.20, though "connection" is expanded in further sections. The connection data is that data to establish a connection between or among object interfaces.

SIDEBAR

SYSTEM INTERACTIONS: THE WHOLE IS GREATER THAN THE SUM OF THE PARTS

A system is composed of parts, which interact through interfaces that are glued together by bindings. The system as a whole, when all the parts are glued together correctly, results in capabilities that are unachievable by the parts alone. For example, a house is composed of a roof, foundation, electrical system, plumbing system, rooms, and so forth. Individually, they do not constitute a house, but together, assuming the parts are "interfaced and bound" correctly, the result is a house.

A good interaction specification provides the ability to establish a binding to the right objects so that the composition of the objects, their interfaces, and the binding achieve the desired capability of interaction, and the parts now act as a single unit. A bad interaction specification results in unstable outcomes (produces side effects that are not desirable), or the inability to be flexible, or the inability to complete.

In the house example, the electrical system must "interface" with the lighting system, which in turn must "interface" with the correct appliance. The appliance interface is the electrical outlet with the right voltage (semantics) that interacts (interfaces and binds) with the electrical panel of the house. Together, these parts (objects) create a function (power) that separately could not be achieved. This function performs as expected when the parts provide a good interface, are specified correctly, and are bound in accordance with that specification. However, if the appliance is faulty, or made from inferior material, or the mice have eaten away at the insulation at the connection point with the outlet, either the appliance or the circuit panel will fail sooner than later. This is a bad interface; it enables connection (binding) with the electrical system in the house, but has an unexpected side effect of poor fault tolerance strength.

"Critical details aside, the architect's greatest concerns and leverage are still, and should be, with the systems' connections and interfaces: first, because they distinguish a system from its components; second, because their addition produces unique system-level functions..." [Rectin-97]

A binding is determined by a contract. In some systems, a contract is specified and coded into the system. The contract parameters do not change, in this case. This results in a static (early) binding, which may be desirable. Static bindings lock in predetermined specifications. To change them, such as to change a contract to get a better quality of service, the system must change the actual interface specifications, and may need to change the objects that offer those interfaces and the ones that use them.

In many systems today, the specifications of the interface signatures and behavior are predetermined statically, and coded into the object. There is no changing of the specification. And the interface specification determines exactly which other object to bind to. That is, the interface and binding specification result in point-to-point specific, statically defined, unchangeable interface bindings. This is often termed "brittle interfaces," and has been the cause of enormous system sustainment costs.

In contrast, the binding framework supports the ability to specify interfaces and bindings separately, using the dynamic schema, bounded by an invariant schema of what must be constant. This results in a system that can accommodate interaction changes across heterogeneous and even proprietary systems. In this case, a binding is created dynamically, based on the parameters specified in several templates as well as policies among the objects involved in the interaction. The binding rules establish that the policies of all objects are consistent before a binding is established. This is the concept of late binding, sometimes called dynamic binding.

Dynamic binding is desirable to better achieve greater flexibility of the system. Objects that wish to interact can be determined at runtime. This is the type of service offered by a federation: domains can enter or leave the federation environment. Binding occurs only when a request for a service is matched with a service offered by an existing object. A binding contract directs what is possible. As another example of flexibility, contracts can be changed and renegotiated. All of this is enabled by dynamic binding. The elements of a binding contract are shown in Figure 13.21.

Suppose a Healthy Hospital policy is specified to state that the Physician must practice at the Hospital one week every eight weeks before any patient treatments can be scheduled. Due to some shortage in the hospital staff, that parameter is altered to one week in every six weeks. The Physician object attempts to establish a binding to the hospital scheduling object for scheduling a patient procedure. The hospital policy is analyzed with the Physician practices, based on the hospital policy parameters that have been changed dynamically. Let's assume the Physician has not practiced at the hospital within the specified amount of time. Then the binding between the hospital scheduling and the Physician objects is denied (dynamically) and results in an error stating "InvalidPolicy." What is important is that neither the hospital scheduling object nor the Physician object requires

Binding Contract
•EIRs and Causality Roles
•Binding Type (Related to Interface Type)
•QoS
•Transparency Specification
•Actions:
 Instantiate/Delete Interfaces,
 Start/Stop Flows,
 Change QoS,
 Change Interface Location,
 Monitor Events
 ...
•Binding Rules (Policies)

FIGURE 13.21 Binding Contract

change in any way. The determination to grant the establishment of a binding is parameterized in the policies of the objects involved in the binding.

A binding is the result of a sequence of events to establish a connection between two (or more) object interfaces. Binding is an agreement of how that connection is to function, based on a contract, the engineering interface reference templates, channel template, and binding template.

A particular instantiation of an interface is bound across only one binding. However, an interface can be instantiated more than once, and use different bindings. This may be desirable to communicate to different objects using the same interface specification.

The elements that form the Binding Model are discussed in this section and include:

◗ Binding types

◗ Binding object

◗ Binding establishment and behavior

◗ Channel configuration and behavior

13.9.1   BINDING TYPES

There are three types of binding specified in the computational viewpoint. One is implicit binding, and the other two are explicit. The explicit binding is either primitive or compound. A binding may or may not make use of a channel. So a further refinement is to identify a local binding or a distributed binding. Much of this is covered in Chapter 6, "Separation of Concerns: Using RM-ODP Viewpoints," and minimally repeated here for completeness.

Implicit binding is used only for operation interfaces. It assumes the pre-existence of the server object interface for use by the client. A binding is established between the client interface and the existing server interface. The binding behavior is "implicit," in that there is no need to establish a binding based on negotiated behavior.

Explicit primitive binding is used for most bindings. The behavior associated with the binding is defined to perform the binding establishment. Any type of interface can make use of the explicit primitive binding.

Explicit compound binding is used for multiple objects to interact, using possibly different interface types. This binding is associated with a computational binding object, to manage the bindings.

Local binding is the creation of a binding between objects that does not require the use of a channel. This occurs for simple bindings, say within a cluster, so that the full configuration of channel objects is not necessary. However, a local binding can also be used if one of the channel objects requires a binding to a local object, perhaps in support of a distribution transparency or an ODP function. In any event, a channel is not required, though the object interfaces being bound are any set of objects local to the cluster.

Distributed binding is the creation of a binding between distributed object interfaces that requires the use of a channel for transparent interaction. A distributed binding is used in a node-to-node communication, within a domain or across domains, or in support of intra-node distributed objects, such as objects that span different capsules. The ODP Node Management function is involved in a distributed binding. It must allocate the resources for the channel, and enable the communication of engineering interface references, used in binding decisions.

A view of how all of this is put together is shown in Figure 13.22.

WARNING

The concept of a local versus distributed binding in RM-ODP is addressed in the standard. However, the concept is not consistent. In particular, if an object in a channel (e.g., the binder object) needs to communicate with an ODP function object (e.g., the Relocator object), it may use a local binding or a distributed binding. This is not made clear. The rule is that the objects in a local binding are in the same cluster, but channel objects do not address a cluster or the ODP function objects, which may or may not exist in the same cluster. So, the type of engineering binding is not clear, and is therefore an architectural decision.

13.9.2 Binding Object

The computational binding object is an intermediate object specified to manage the bindings between two (or more) objects. To do so, it must interact between pairs of interacting objects; it receives a request for binding from object A, establishes a binding to object B, and transfers the messages between the objects.

The binding object is typically used for complex bindings, especially if the interacting objects use different types of interfaces. The binding object is, thus, a binding control object. It makes sure the binding is established, in accordance with the behavior defined. It makes sure that the type of binding and the type of channel agree with the type of interfaces to be bound. A stream interface, for example, is bound to a channel that communicates flow interactions to another object, or set of objects, across a receiving stream interface. Thus, a binding object is used to manage multiparty bindings. It can also be used to manage multimedia interactions to the same object. In this case, separate interface streams can be defined, one for audio, one for video, one for a high-resolution televised video, and all managed in the same binding to the target object for processing. The binding object is responsible, therefore, for managing and ensuring the QoS specification, the configuration of the objects in the binding, the number of bindings, and the originating and target object interfaces involved in the binding.

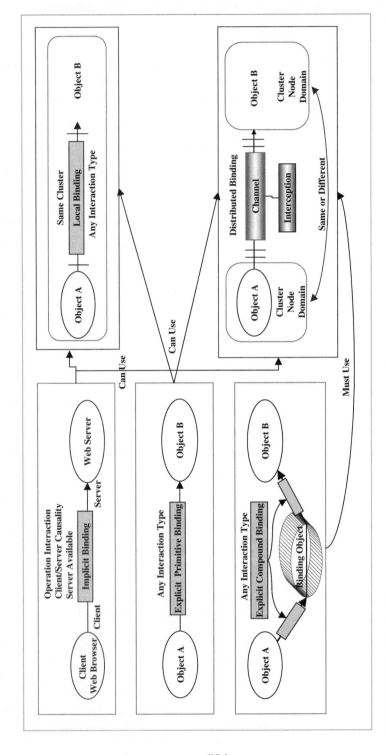

FIGURE 13.22 Binding Types

Figure 13.23 shows a partial example of a multimedia multiparty computational binding using the binding object. In this example, an operating room object offers a video teleconference center set of interactions to multiple parties, to perhaps participate in some surgical procedure. These interactions are specified in separate interface signatures. The binding object is used. One interface provides a flow interaction one-way to the physician and one-way to the hospital, for a two-way conversation. One interface provides a flow interaction to support video. Each receiving object receives one type of interface, but separate interactions to an audio/video consumer: one is a flow in a stream interface; the other is the audio in a stream interface.

The binding object manages the multiparty binding. It ensures that the video is delivered to all viewer objects (the Physician objects in the figure). Likewise, it ensures the audio consists of two one-way flows, possibly in the same interface specification, or possibly as separate interface specifications (which is shown), supporting two-way conversation across all objects. The binding object manages the configuration of objects. It also manages QoS issues such as the coincidence of audio and video to each receiving party, a priority of an audio interface response from one of the Physician objects, appropriate resolution of the image, and the complexity of multiple interfaces to be bound to the same object (Physician). Hence, they originate and terminate at different interface reference points (shown by the small black circles).

A control interface is usually specified for a binding object to control the other objects, such as security audit of the use of an interface, or to perhaps define and manage a QoS for the interface. Other actions can be provided through this interface, such as management of the binding itself, or a security authorization

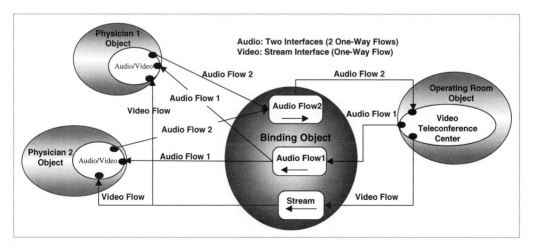

FIGURE 13.23 Multimedia Multiparty Computational Compound Binding

policy. The control interface template for the binding object specifies the actions provided across this interface, and their expected behavior.

There are many uses for the binding object. It can multiplex, combining multiple streams into a single binding, or multiple voice streams in a single binding. It can be used simply to manage a QoS property of an interface binding between two objects. A binding object also supports dynamic binding, where objects enter and leave a binding dynamically. The binding object can support dynamic subscription services, or dynamic subscribers to a subscription service, without knowing ahead of time all the statically defined interfaces that may be bound over time. The uses for the binding object are limited only by the architectural needs and ingenuity.

The binding object maps onto either a channel, a binder in a channel, or a separate engineering object in the engineering viewpoint. This is one of the ambiguities in RM-ODP. Further, the emerging standard on Computational Protocol Support for Computational Interactions [ISO-CP] and Interface References and Bindings [ISO-IRB] both address the use of a binding object, but map it differently in the engineering viewpoint. The architect needs to be aware and specify what is wanted in the architectural specification.

13.9.3   BINDING ESTABLISHMENT AND BEHAVIOR

To establish a binding requires the EIR and template for each interface, the binding template, and the channel template and channel. The *binding establishment* is a series of actions that ensure that the behavior of the binding is in agreement with both ends, and the initial steps to setup the channel are accomplished. A UML metamodel of binding behavior elements is shown in Figure 13.24. Some of these concepts are discussed in later sections.

The behavior of the binding can be either implicit or explicit. *Explicit* behavior is where two or more objects interact directly. *Implicit* behavior is where a third object establishes the binding, used by two or more other objects. Actually, the object establishing the binding may also participate in the binding, but not necessarily. Implicit behavior might be associated with a DBMS server, for example, where the binding to the server is established for use by multiple client objects.

A difference between explicit and implicit behavior relates to when the binding is to be terminated. It may be acceptable to terminate the explicit binding between two object interfaces. However, terminating an implicit binding may require determining if the binding is being used by other interfaces, or if the third object desires to keep the binding active, or some other criteria. This entire behavior for the implicit binding case is captured in the contract.

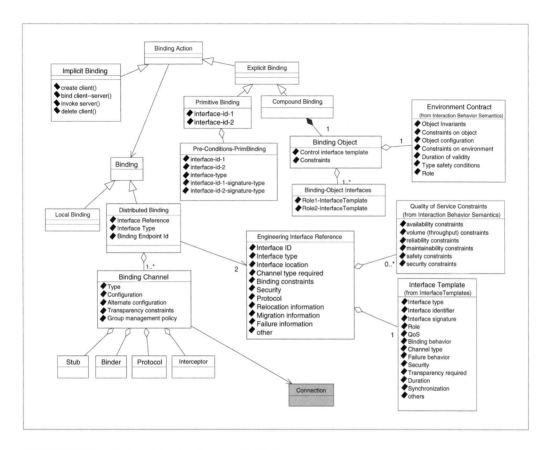

FIGURE 13.24 Binding Behavior Elements in UML

A binding may be established between two object interfaces or more than two. For example, if an object is replicated, the same interface from all replicas is bound in the same binding, to maintain the state of the replica objects. As another example, multimedia binding may be used to communicate audio and video streams across the same binding. In any case, the behavior of the binding must be established and agreed to among all objects with interfaces participating in the binding.

First, an object initiates a binding request. It identifies its role in participating in the binding. It also identifies one or more recipient objects in terms of the roles assumed, and an engineering interface reference to define the interface of each object to participate in the binding. If there is agreement to the causality roles assumed by each object and the interfaces to support the roles, then the appropriate interfaces are established in each object, a binding is established to connect the interfaces, and an object is identified (or instantiated) to enforce and manage the binding behavior. This is, in essence, is how a binding is established.

To determine the identities of the objects with which an object wants to interact, the infrastructure needs to support a means of object discovery and, in particular, the object's engineering interface references for the interfaces to be bound. This can be accomplished through a Trader, a naming service, an interface repository, or hard-coded into the originating object.

Once a binding is created, a binding endpoint identifier is provided to the object using the binding. This identifier is unique within the naming context. It is useful for the object to select the binding among possibly many that it is involved with. The form of the binding identifier is not defined in RM-ODP; this is a specification the architect provides.

Once accomplished, binding establishment includes the following steps (not necessarily in this order):

▶ Ensure the node provides the resources to instantiate the object interfaces and instantiate a channel.

▶ Ensure the node provides the infrastructure objects to manage the binding. Some of this is managed by the binder object in the channel; some of this is managed by the ODP function objects, depending on the distribution transparencies selected.

▶ Ensure that the interfaces to be bound are of the same type: operation, stream, or signal.

▶ Ensure that the causality roles assumed by each end are complementary. That is, if one end assumes the role of "client," the other end must assume the role of "server."

▶ Ensure that the behavior specification of each end is compatible. That is, if one end requires, through a policy, that the response time be within a certain timeframe, the other end must provision for this QoS constraint. This is called establishing the behavior between two objects. It includes:

    – Instantiating the contract between the objects, to include the policies to be applied.

    – Possible negotiation to reach a common view of the processing behavior. In this case, a separate binding may take place to exchange pertinent policy rules, and to conduct the negotiation.

    – Determine which interface template to instantiate for use in the binding.

    – Establish the rules for binding termination, as specified in the contract.

    – Ensure the types of the parameters in the interface signatures match. Part of binding establishment includes type matching and type resolution. Each interaction is typed and has typed parameters. Each interface is typed. In order to bind across distributed systems, mediation of the typing contexts may be required. Sometimes, types can be dynamically queried in the system. Sometimes, typing systems make this part of the static definition. However types are discovered, mediation may be required. This is part of the job of the interceptor and, as such, greatly enhances interoperability across disparate systems.

▶ Ensure that the causality role assumed by the initiator permits the initiator to execute the interaction. This is part of the role specification, as well as part of the permitted actions in the policy.

▶ Ensure that the transparencies required in the binding are provided on both ends, with appropriate infrastructure objects.

▶ Create a binding endpoint identifier to the binding for use by the object to designate that particular binding of its interface.

▶ For a distributed binding, create an appropriate channel, of the correct type, and of the correct behavior as determined by the engineering interface reference templates, binding template, and channel template. These must all be compatible. This is the topic of the next section.

Once all of these actions are accomplished, the result is a binding that behaves in accordance with the contractual behavior among the objects involved. That is, the binding and the behavior of the binding are all established and agreed to among the objects involved in the binding. The light grey lines in Figure 13.25 illustrate the relationship between the binding specification and establishing a binding. This figure expands upon the previous figure showing a binding object. In this example, the binding object is shown as a separate engineering object that initiates two channels in support of the complex binding needs, specified in the computational viewpoint. Interceptors are shown to manage any mediation required across domains, which is addressed in a later section of this chapter. To focus on the binding models and their configuration of objects, the interface icon (a cross-bar icon) is not shown.

There is no relationship between the causality roles assumed by the object and which object initiates the binding. Even in the client/server case, either the client object or the server object can initiate the binding. There is, however, a relationship between the participating objects in the binding and their causality roles. The roles determine what interactions the objects can participate in. But the binding is not concerned with these interactions. That is, the binding is the conduit to communicate the interactions, but is at a different level of abstraction from the interaction.

The contract and the type of binding (implicit or explicit) determine terminating a binding. If a failure occurs for which there is no fault tolerant mechanism (see Chapter 16, "RM-ODP Fault Tolerant Framework"), the binding is deleted in accordance with the terminating behavior in the contract. If the initiating or terminating object requests an end of the interaction, or if either interface is deleted, the binding is deleted for the explicit binding case.

Trading is a special case of binding. The Trader acts as the third object to receive a request for a service from an object (object A), and to provide information about an interface for use of another object (object B). Hence, the Trader imports an interface identifier with certain criteria or properties of a service from object B, and exports that interface identifier to object A that meets the criteria requested. A binding can then be established between the identified interfaces of object A and object B, to support the interaction requested.

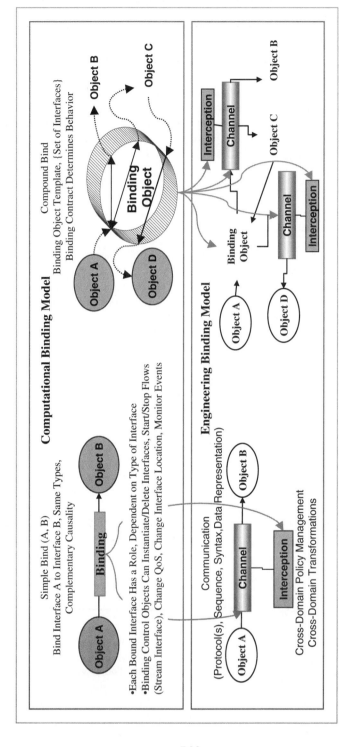

FIGURE 13.25 Computational and Engineering Binding Models

13.9.4 CHANNEL AND CHANNEL BEHAVIOR

A channel is the mechanism used for distributed binding. A channel consists of the following objects: stub, binder, protocol, and sometimes an interceptor. A channel is the conduit that establishes the communication between endpoints. As such, a channel is normally constructed as pairs of these objects. A discussion of the channel is provided in Chapter 6, "Separation of Concerns: Using RM-ODP Viewpoints." The discussion is augmented here.

13.9.4.1 Channel

A channel can be initiated by any engineering object, whether or not it participates in the channel. The channel is actually created by the nucleus of the node, through the use of the Node Management function. The properties of the channel are defined in a channel template, to include the type of interface it can support, the configuration of objects in the channel to support the interface binding, and possibly alternate configurations in support of some required property (such as encryption). RM-ODP does not explicitly define the form of a channel template, but Figure 13.26 provides some of the elements for such a template.

The channel establishes the connection to enable communication of the interactions. To do so, it transfers data, engineering interface references, and possibly cluster templates, between interacting engineering objects. This is the expected behavior to be negotiated and agreed upon for the binding to be established.

A single channel supports one type of interface: operational, stream, or signal. Different channels are required for different interface types. Multiple interfaces of the same type, however, can be bound in the same channel, but a mix of interface types is not allowed. An overview of a stream channel configuration is shown in Figure 13.27.

The distributed interface binding can be used to establish all manner of connections: FTP, support for SQL queries, e-mail, remote procedure calls, the full seven-layer Open Systems Interconnection (OSI) communication suite, or some

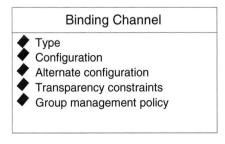

FIGURE 13.26 Channel Template Elements

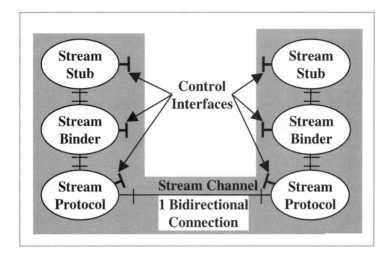

FIGURE 13.27   Stream Channel Configuration

other kind of connection. Actually, the distributed interface binding is very similar to the concept of a software architecture connector. Clearly a client/server connector is a connection of operational interfaces. An event connector includes a stream connection, with additional behavior. Pipe and filter connectors are either signal or stream interface connection. In essence, the software architecture connectors can be mapped onto the three types of interfaces and associated channels, using particular methods of connection for that type.

The behavior of the channel is managed in part through the control interfaces provided by each of the stub, binder, protocol, and interceptor objects. These control interfaces are optional, dependent on the specification.

13.9.4.2   Stub

The *stub* object provides the support to the interacting object. It is cognizant of the structure of the interaction (message) and packaging it for communication. It is the stub that must initiate the process of communicating to support distributed binding and, thus, communication of the interaction. It provides marshalling and unmarshalling of parameters, and conversions in the messaging data.

The stub can interact with one or more channels, or one or more basic engineering object interfaces. It may provide a control interface. It provides access transparency to the communication mechanism. The stub also supports multicast of results from the communication, providing the results to each of the basic engineering objects involved in the binding. The stub also supports multiple objects that wish to use the same channel.

The stub interacts with some of the ODP function objects as well, especially those that provide the functions for security, storage, trading, relocation, migration, and engineering interface reference tracking. The stub can also perform additional value added capabilities such as maintaining an audit trail of activity, notification of a failure to the basic engineering object, security authentication, etc.

The stub interacts with the binder object in the channel. The stub, perhaps in support of multimedia, may interact with more than one binder in a channel: one for each binding behavior, or for different interaction types (e.g., different flow types). The interface template associated with the basic engineering object's use and the channel template determine which binder to use.

In addition, the stub object may in fact interface to different binder objects in different channels. Hence, the stub not only supports the objects that are bound to the channel, but may participate in more than one channel.

13.9.4.3   Binder

The *binder* object maintains the integrity of the binding and coordinates the communication across the channel. The binder object interfaces to a stub object, a protocol object, and may provide a control interface. The binder packages the message into the structures needed by the protocol object. The binder also supports encryption and de-encryption, and auditing of the use of the channel. The binder object communicates with its peer binder object at the destination.

The binder object monitors failures in the binding, notifies the appropriate infrastructure object of any failures, and attempts to re-establish a broken binding by instantiating a new binder object. If this cannot be accomplished, the binder will attempt to establish a new channel for use.

To accomplish these actions, the binder performs bind, unbind, control, monitor, etc., to maintain that communication mechanism, to extract the message from the communication protocol for use by the object, and to provide some level of translation that might be required, such as from one format of a parameter to another.

The binder is able to interface with more than one protocol object, in the case where multiple protocols are managed in the channel. This is useful to manage different destinations or different protocols in case one endpoint is unavailable.

It may also directly interface to an engineering object, or to an ODP function object, such as the Trader, Replicator or Relocator object. If the distributed binding is local to the node, a protocol object may not be needed.

13.9.4.4   Protocol

The *protocol* object provides the structure and transfer syntax of the communication protocol. It performs any protocol-specific actions required, including the formatting of the message into the protocol format to communicate.

The protocol object provides an interface to the binder object. It may also provide an interface to an ODP function object (e.g., storage), and may also provide a control interface. It also communicates with one or more protocol objects at the distributed end of the connection of the same or different type. If the remote protocol object is of a different type, an interceptor is needed. The interceptor object (covered in "Interaction Framework" on page 509) is used between two protocol objects to mediate differences in protocol formats.

A protocol object is associated with a specific communication domain, defined by a set of interworking protocol objects. If protocol objects are in different communication domains, naming conflicts may arise in terms of interface identifiers, names of interfaces, and so forth. In this case, an interceptor object is used to mediate the different naming contexts in order to complete the channel establishment.

The protocol object can interface with more than one protocol object at the remote end, perhaps to manage multiple transmissions. RM-ODP does not specify how this is accomplished; it relies instead on the choice of a technology viewpoint protocol mechanism that may in fact support this capability.

An interworking reference point is associated with any interaction point between protocol objects, between a protocol object and an interceptor, and between interceptor objects. All control interfaces are programmatic reference points. These reference points form conformance test points for interoperability and software composability. See Chapter 11, "Architecture Analysis and System Conformance Evaluation," for more detail about these reference points.

The communication action is assumed to be part of whatever technology chosen for the protocol, such as a Remote Procedure Call (RPC) connection.

13.9.4.5   Channel Flexibility

Each of these objects (stub, binder, and protocol) may have a set of interfaces, discussed above and shown in Figure 13.28. Each of these objects can interface to different objects. The flexibility of the channel object interfaces provides multiple channels, different channels, multiplexing of object interfaces, and all manner of different kinds of connections.

The stub, binder, or protocol objects can be basic engineering objects with separate channel structures. A binding can exist from any of the stub, binder, protocol, or interceptor objects to another object outside the channel. This is the mechanism to support some of the ODP functions, such as Migration, Replication, and Relocation.

Sometimes it is desirable to specify a distributed binding for multiple interface types. In this case, multiple channels are required, one for each type of interface connection. This can all be coordinated through a basic engineering object, reflecting the capabilities of the binder object, or the stub object of a channel since the stub is able to support different channels, and can be specified to also handle

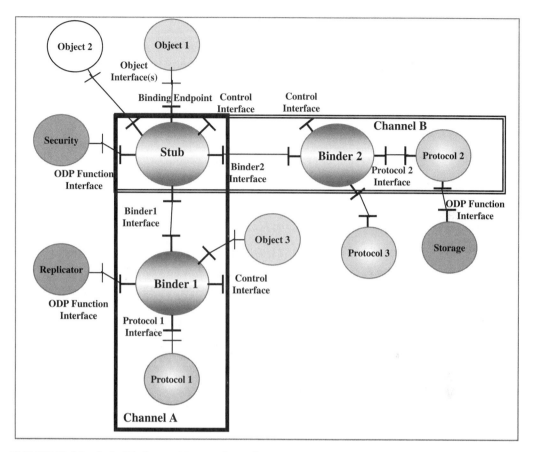

FIGURE 13.28 Stub, Binder, and Protocol Interfaces

different channel types. To accomplish this, however, the stub must be provided with interface information such as the type of binder to use, and the type of channel to manage.

To support a collaborative workspace of multimedia communication requires the specification at both the computational and engineering viewpoints. The computational objects that provide the capabilities must be identified:

▶ Multimedia manager, such as the binding object

▶ Operational interfaces

▶ Stream interfaces

The engineering structure must then be specified to instantiate two types of channels: one for the operational interface connections and one for the stream interface connection. How the different channels are managed is an architecture decision. The same stub object can manage both. A control object can manage both. Or a separate basic engineering object can manage both.

Figure 13.29 shows an overview of the configuration of computational and engineering objects for this capability, as well as a mapping from the computational to the engineering configurations. The computational objects correspond to separate basic engineering objects, which in this example are shown as replicated. The "Data Server" computational object is decomposed into a DBMS server, with associated channels. Notice that the DBMS server may use the same stub object for connections to its client objects. However, separate binder objects are probably used to maintain the integrity of the channel connection to each client, for better stability.

The configuration of the channel objects may appear simple. Coupling the ability for the channel objects themselves to connect to multiple channels provides flexibility of architecture decisions, and allows a great deal of variation in the interaction framework, to support all manner of multiuser, multicast, multimedia connections.

Coupled with the interception framework, these capabilities also support interaction across a domain, and across federations of domains. For an excellent discussion on the subject of multimedia supported by RM-ODP, see [Blair-98]. Further discussion of techniques to realize simple and complex bindings can be found in [Otway-95].

RM-ODP does not fully explain the rules for distributed binding. For example, it is not clear if the engineering objects that comprise a channel always exist, sometimes exist, or under what circumstances. The rule is that a channel consists of at least two of each of the stub, binder, and protocol objects. The configuration of the channel is determined by the channel template in conjunction with the engineering interface reference templates. But at the same time, RM-ODP states that the configuration of a channel is defined in a channel template, without further explanation. If a distributed binding is created in support of two objects in the same capsule, then the protocol objects may not be required. In fact, perhaps only a single stub object is required. Further, each of the channel objects optionally provides an interface for binding to a control object. But where that object exists is not clear. Is it in the same node? Does it matter? What is the nature of the binding to that object from the channel objects? The answers must, so far, be architectural decisions.

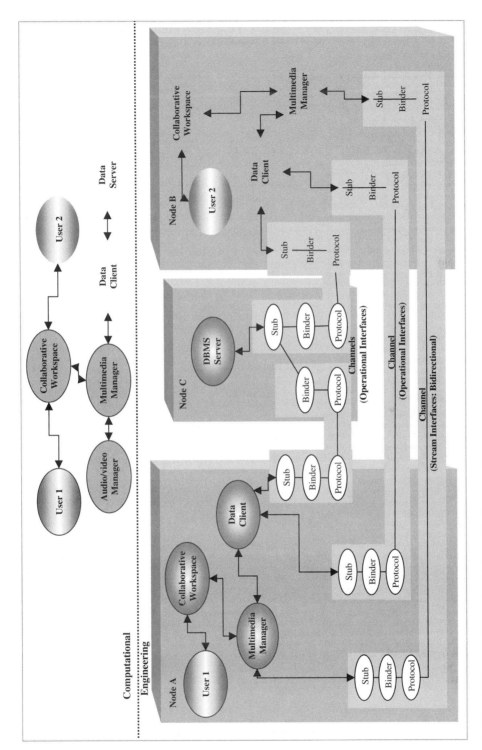

FIGURE 13.29 Collaborative Multimedia Configuration

547

13.10   INTERCEPTION FRAMEWORK

Interception is a powerful concept that supports cross-domain interaction. It provides the ability to dynamically determine if the interaction can be accomplished, observe QoS characteristics, mediate transformations required, support negotiation of services, support negotiation of policies, and so much more.

The *interceptor* is an object in a channel between protocol objects crossing different domains. There are three kinds of interceptor structures, shown in Figure 13.30. The structure showing channel 1 is used to translate simple formats, such as protocol formats. The structure showing channel 2 is used to mediate across more complex domains. Sometimes the cross-domain situation requires multiple channels and multiple interceptors, as shown by the structures showing channels 2 and 3.

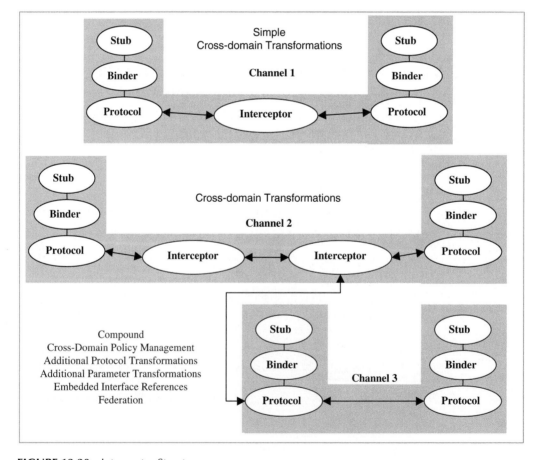

FIGURE 13.30   Interceptor Structures

Almost always, different domains have differences in policies, procedures, contexts, and so forth. Interception is about negotiating those differences to some agreed upon contractual context so that objects in the different domains can interact.

Current technology, however, is limited in the capabilities provided for such an object. Often, interceptors are used merely to transform one protocol to another, or to transform one naming convention to another. Current work in several communities, including the Object Management Group, is adding to the capabilities of this object in order to better support QoS across systems, negotiation across domains for security reasons, and so forth. In this section, the full capability of the interceptor is described in terms of an interception framework of concepts and rules.

A domain consists of a common management policy across the objects in that domain. A domain is able to distinguish interactions that occur within its domain and those that occur outside its domain. The key concept here is that of a single management policy that applies to all objects that make up the domain. If that management policy is about naming, it is a naming domain. If that management policy is about security, then it is a security domain.

Domains are classified in terms of:

▶ Technology: Particular technologies are used and managed within the domain, such as communication protocols, data formats, distributed middleware.

▶ Administrative: Particular policies for security, management, resource control are defined.

▶ Application or business: Particular rules of engagement are defined, dealing with environment constraints.

Examples of different types of domain include:

▶ Technology: Naming domain, where the naming context is used to assigning names or identifiers, define the form of the name, and define the scope of the name

▶ Technology: Addressing domain, where the addressing context is used to assign a logical and physical address to a user, a domain, a node, an interface, and whatever else is addressed in the system.

▶ Administrative: Security domain, where the policy of security is enforced, and access control mechanisms are defined.

▶ Technology: Distribution middleware domain, where the use of one technology is defined (e.g., Common Object Request Broker Architecture (CORBA), message-oriented middleware (MOM), relational DBMS, object DBMS).

▶ Technology: Type domains, defining different methods of type and type management.

- ▶ Administrative: Management domain, where the rules of system management are defined.
- ▶ Administrative: Accounting domain, where the rules of accounting are defined.
- ▶ Application: Business domain, where all rules of engagement in accordance with business activities are defined.

In cases where a channel crosses a technical or organizational domain, there may be a need for additional checks or transformations to match the requirements on the separate sides of the boundary. These functions are performed by interceptors, which form part of the channel. An object may participate in different domains (e.g., naming, security, administration, and technology), depending on the architecture decisions. Therefore, to interact with another object may require interception across one or more domains.

In cases where multiple middleware systems are used, the appropriate interceptors need to be defined. Examples of interceptors are bridges such as a CORBA-DCE bridge, or a CORBA-MOM bridge, or a CORBA-RMI bridge. Within each of these bridges, additional bridges may be required to facilitate mediation of naming, protocol formats, message formats, and the like.

It is most likely, especially in large-scale systems, that there are multiple domains in which an object must behave. One domain may be an enterprise-wide system management (ESM) domain that includes all objects in the system. Another domain may be defined as a special security domain, in which a subset of objects exists. Another domain may be a naming domain that provides unique names and identifiers for objects and object interfaces. The result could look like Figure 13.31.

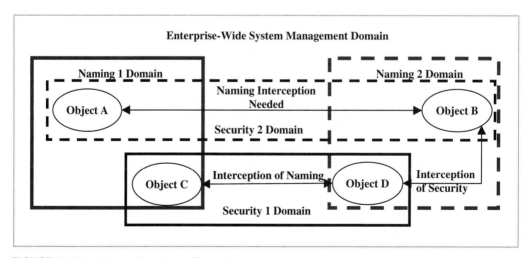

FIGURE 13.31 Interception Across Domains

The following table shows the domains each object is a member of. In order to interact, each object in the interaction must belong to the same set of domains, not just one of them. For every difference in domain, an interception is required. The "X" designates that the object is a member of the domain.

	DOMAIN				
	ESM	Naming 1	Naming 2	Security 1	Security 2
Object A	X	X			X
Object B	X		X		X
Object C	X	X		X	
Object D	X		X	X	

If object A wishes to interact with object B in this figure, naming interception is needed to mediate the potential different naming contexts and policies. However, neither ESM nor security requires interception. Similarly, object C and object D can interact only with naming interception. Object B and object D can interact with security interception. In fact, in this figure, no object can interact with another without some interception. It is very important to define the domains of objects in a system, to offset the required interception.

Interception is a process that instantiates and inserts interceptors in the binding when crossing domain boundaries. These interceptors perform the negotiation and transformations needed to enable or deny a binding and provide auditing capabilities.

Negotiation is the process of reaching agreement between the parties involved, as defined by a contract. Dynamic negotiation is still state of the art. However, minimal negotiation is available in products today, where a choice of parameters is offered, and one is selected in agreement. Complex negotiation, say for a full security policy, requires human intervention.

A *contract* is a series of statements that reflect agreement among the parties. Generally, a contract exists for the duration of the interaction. A duration may also be associated with a contract, as may actions in case of contract violation, such as terminating the interaction. The contract defines the relationship between the domains so that interaction can be accomplished.

There are different scenarios to accomplish interception in a system. Consider Figure 13.32, where object A is in domain A, and object B is in domain B. This figure refines Figure 13.31 to the configuration of objects that take part in the interception between object A and object B.

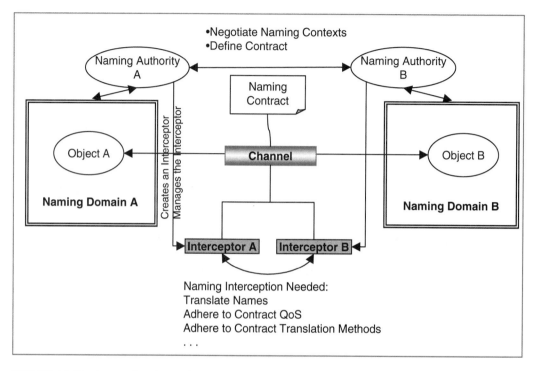

FIGURE 13.32   Interaction Across Naming Domains

One possible scenario for interception is:

▶ The type of domain is identified (e.g., naming, administration, security).

▶ The domain control object (domain authority) is identified for both domains.

▶ A binding is established between the two domain authority objects, for the purpose of negotiation.

▶ The domain authority objects exchange information to arrive at a common agreed upon contract for interaction.

▶ If the contract requires transformation of data, the domain authority object in each domain establishes an interceptor object for use in the channel to accomplish this (one for each end of the channel). How this is actually accomplished is particular to the design.

▶ The binding between object A and object B now contains two interceptor objects.

▶ The interaction commences, and the interceptors perform the required transformations, in accordance with the established contract between the domains. In some cases, only one interceptor object is needed, if the domains are simple format translators.

▶ Once the interaction is completed, the binding can be deleted, as can the interceptor objects.

Interception permits or denies a binding according to compatibility checks: contracts and policy rules, type, name, interface reference identifier, quality of service requirements, protocol types, and so forth. The interceptor enables dynamic negotiation and mediation of cross-domain contract rules, QoS specifications, and negotiation of services across domains. It is this engineering language concept that can provide the underlying mechanism for federation and any required mediation across domains (see Chapter 15, "Federation").

To achieve interception, the language used to describe aspects of interaction must be compatible. That means the following must be such that each domain authority can interpret the particular aspect:

▶ Interface signature, interaction signature, and properties of the interaction must be specified in a common language.

▶ Types must be described in a common language.

▶ Naming must be described in a common language.

▶ Declarative quality of service requirements, in a common language.

▶ Language of contracts and policies (semantics) should be defined. This is by far the most difficult to achieve and is still state of the art.

If interception cannot be automated due to insufficient commonality of description, then human intervention is required for the interaction to occur.

The following are possible steps to achieve interaction:

▶ Detect the need to cross domain boundaries and initiate an interaction between domain authority objects to define an inter-domain contract.

▶ Determine what parameters need transformation, in accordance with the contract established between the domains.

▶ Define the mechanism to achieve the transformation.

▶ Perform the action of transformation with the following possible alternative outcomes:

   – Reject because the transformation cannot be accomplished.

   – Do nothing because there is no need for a transformation.

   – Transform the protocol, if necessary.

   – Transform the parameters detected, using a simple mediator if possible.

   – Transform the parameters using an interceptor.

▶ Create a means of transforming the interface reference, if necessary. This is most likely due to a difference in distributed middleware, wherein interface reference forms are completely different.

▶ Maintain an audit trail monitoring the activities of interception.

Again, interception technology is emerging, but not quite in hand. For an excellent discussion of the different aspects of interception, see [Hoffner-95].

13.11   BEHAVIORAL SEMANTICS FRAMEWORK

Behavioral semantics permeate the Interaction Framework. To achieve end-to-end interaction correctness for interoperability requires not only the specification of behavior, but also the agreement to that behavior across all parts of the interaction. That is, interoperability is enabled by the end-to-end correct behavior of interaction.

Semantics means "meaning." Behavior means "constrained action(s)."

13.11.1   BEHAVIOR

Behavior is specified through several mechanisms, as shown in Figure 13.33: a contract between objects, an environment contract between an object and the environment in which it interacts, policy rules about what can and cannot happen, roles, preconditions and postconditions that must be true for an interaction, templates that define the behavioral details of an element, interface reference templates that constrain the type of binding, constraints of quality of service, temporal constraints, type constraints, invariants that must always be true for a specified duration, and so forth.

The framework addresses the behavior expected of all aspects of interaction; i.e., relationships among objects, behavior associated with interfaces, binding behavior, and interception behavior. It is very important to capture semantics for an object, interface, and the interactions associated with these concepts.

For example, QoS constraints include temporal, availability, reliability, maintainability, safety, and security constraints. Temporal constraints include

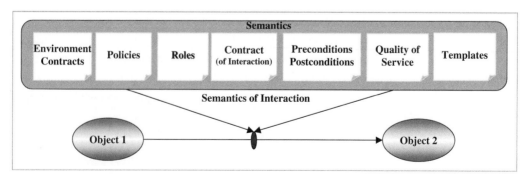

FIGURE 13.33   Behavioral Semantics of Interaction

real-time, sequential, non-deterministic, or concurrent constraints. The environment contract includes QoS, constraints on time and space (location), constraints that invalidate the contract, duration of validity, persistence, safety, transparencies, and policies.

RM-ODP provides the ability for expressing interaction in terms of interfaces, binding, contracts, and semantics. Chapter 8, "Composition and Semantics: Quality Composition Minimizing Architectural Mismatch," provides more detail on environment contract, contract, policy, and templates. An overview of these elements, and their relationship to interaction, is presented in this section.

13.11.2   POLICY

Part of the specification includes capturing the policies that constrain (or enable) the actions among the objects. That is, a policy will define what is allowed, what is permitted, and what is prohibited for an action. Figure 13.34 provides a UML metamodel of a policy.

A policy constrains the behavior of the interaction. For example, if a policy specifies that a certain quality of service must be met for a particular interaction, the interface template specifies this QoS specification. Then, whenever the inter-

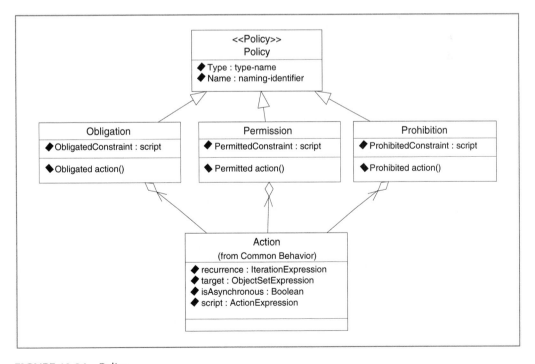

FIGURE 13.34   Policy

face is instantiated using this template, the parameterization of the QoS required is also instantiated.

Policy constraints are associated with a community and the roles in the community, with computational behavior, with ODP functions, with management, and with just about any entity in the specification.

Consider, as an example, that one policy the Federal Aviation Administration (FAA) environment contracts with an airline community is "passenger rights are to obtain a reserved paid-for seat on the airplane." No matter what community is involved (e.g., United Airlines reservation system, US Airways reservation system, Delta reservation system), all must abide by the guaranteed reservation (a QoS property) policy of the FAA. The environment contract, then, provides some of the interoperability constraints for the behavior of the system. Policy is discussed in depth in Chapter 14, "Policy Framework."

13.11.3   CONTRACTS

A contract is an agreement to provide or not provide something, as defined by the specification of the rules that constrain the cooperation between objects. It's a promise, an obligation of fulfillment, by all objects participating in the contractual behavior.

Recall from Chapter 8, "Composition and Semantics: Quality Composition Minimizing Architectural Mismatch," a contract consists of temporal properties, QoS properties, one or more policies, duration, conditions of type safety, and so forth. It includes what the object may be obligated to do, what the object is permitted to do, and what the object must not do. It addresses what can be expected across the interaction. The interface template and the object template capture these behaviors.

Figure 13.35 provides a UML metamodel of the elements of a contract, an environment contract, and the relationship with a policy.

The *environment contract* addresses the rules of behavior between an object and its environment, including the environment in which it interacts. The environment contract specifies the behavior of the binding and interception. That is, every interaction occurs in an environment. The environment of an interacting object is the binding, the other object, and the infrastructure supporting the binding. As such, each object that engages in an interaction defines the environment contractual behavior expected. This is an agreement between the object and its environment of what each is expected to provide.

In the case of interaction, the environment contract establishes the QoS expected from the object and the QoS expected from the environment, along with a promise to provide the resources from the environment to fulfill that QoS, as an example. The QoS language for expressing QoS on the interface is the current focus of an emerging standard [ISO-QOS]. Another type of environment constraint may be the length of time for an interaction across the interface, or the resources available for use by the object.

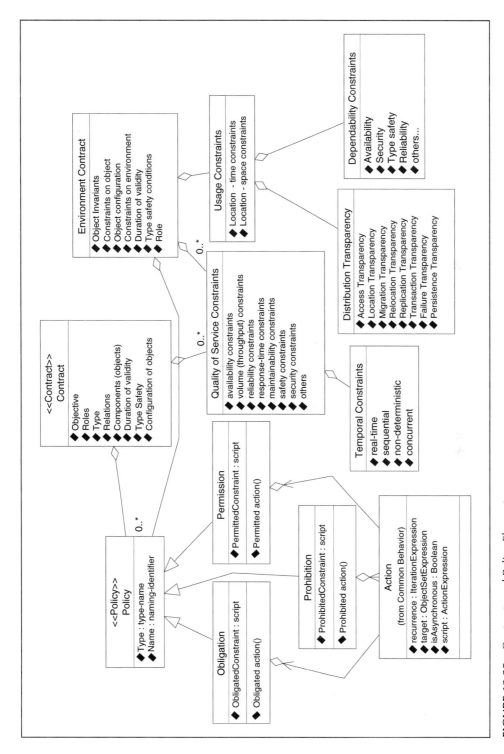

FIGURE 13.35 Contracts and Policy Elements

In addition to an environment contract, each interaction is characterized by a *contract*. Recall that a contract is an agreement among the set of objects that are involved in the interaction, and the contract specifies and controls their behavior. A contract between objects, then, includes the specification of the roles the objects assume, quality of service attributes, the behavior of an object that would violate the contract, and span of time over which the contract is valid.

Once again, RM-ODP provides the reasoning to specify the behavior between two interacting objects, though it does not provide the actual structure for doing so. This structure is for the architect to define, and may be subject to emerging standards to achieve openness. Current work on the expanded enterprise language [ISO-EntVP] is defining the framework for specifying policies, and the current work on the QoS Framework [ISO-QOS] is defining the framework for specifying QoS properties. Chapter 12, "Enterprise Business Specification," Chapter 17, "Quality of Service Model," and Chapter 18, "Frameworks and Other Methods of Architecture," cover more details.

As another example, a constraint may be the rule to order incoming interactions according to a timestamp. The constraint in this case consists of both sequentiality and temporal properties. Another constraint may be to notify an object of a particular transaction. In this case, the result may be to assign a thread to an incoming request across which the Event Notifier can notify the object of an incoming request. This supports asynchronous publish/subscribe messaging, for example.

A contract may be *implicit*, in which case some of the elements in the contract are not explicitly defined. This all depends on the support provided by the environment. For example, a client object is not permitted to access the operations permitted to a server object, such as administration. This is a "prohibition" on the interaction between the client and server. This prohibition is usually not explicitly specified in the contract.

Rather, the construction of the interaction signature provides the full set of interactions for an object assuming the causality role of server, and a subset of interactions for an object assuming the causality role of a client.

On the other hand, an *explicit* contract specifies the details required for a behavior. For example, explicit specification in a contract might include the role that is assumed of an interfacing object, and perhaps the QoS parameters associated with dependability offered by an object across the interface. The contract would explicitly specify the actions that invalidate the contract, and cause termination of the interface, such as attempting to access a service (e.g., update authorization codes) across the interface that is not associated with the role (e.g., client access) of the interface.

13.11.4   TEMPLATES

Templates, recall, are patterns to instantiate an entity. Each fully defines the structure and semantics of that entity. In the case of interaction, the object template specifies the behavior of the object, as well as *all* interface templates that can be instantiated for the object. The role captured in the object template is an identifier for its behavior. The role in the interface template is the causality role. Figure 13.36 provides an overview of the elements in some of the templates discussed.

The object template includes the set of permissible activities for the object, and the policies that apply. A computational object can:

▶ Instantiate other object templates, subject to the rules of the environment contract specification

▶ Instantiate interface templates

▶ Establish an interface identifier

▶ Initiate/respond to signals

▶ Produce/consume flows

▶ Initiate/respond to operation invocations

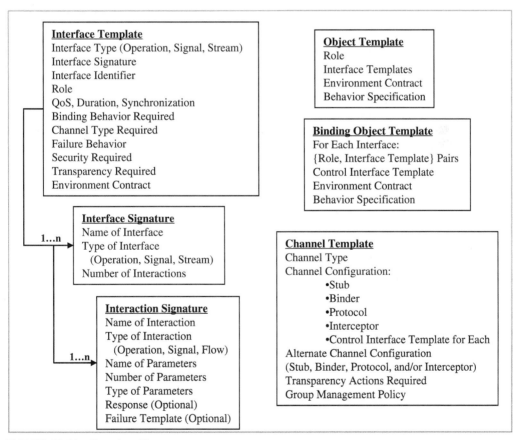

Interface Template
Interface Type (Operation, Signal, Stream)
Interface Signature
Interface Identifier
Role
QoS, Duration, Synchronization
Binding Behavior Required
Channel Type Required
Failure Behavior
Security Required
Transparency Required
Environment Contract

Object Template
Role
Interface Templates
Environment Contract
Behavior Specification

Binding Object Template
For Each Interface:
{Role, Interface Template} Pairs
Control Interface Template
Environment Contract
Behavior Specification

Interface Signature
Name of Interface
Type of Interface
    (Operation, Signal, Stream)
Number of Interactions

1...n

Channel Template
Channel Type
Channel Configuration:
    •Stub
    •Binder
    •Protocol
    •Interceptor
    •Control Interface Template for Each
Alternate Channel Configuration
(Stub, Binder, Protocol, and/or Interceptor)
Transparency Actions Required
Group Management Policy

Interaction Signature
Name of Interaction
Type of Interaction
    (Operation, Signal, Flow)
Name of Parameters
Number of Parameters
Type of Parameters
Response (Optional)
Failure Template (Optional)

1...n

FIGURE 13.36 Template Elements

▶ Initiate operation announcements

▶ Initiate/respond to operation terminations

▶ Bind interfaces

▶ Access and modify its state

▶ Delete itself

▶ Delete its interface(s)

▶ Spawn, fork, join activities

▶ Get a computational interface identifier for a Trader

▶ Test if one computational interface signature is a subtype of another computational interface signature

Each interface template defines the interface and all of its interactions, along with the behavior of the interface in accordance to the role assumed by the object. The interface template specifies the name of the interface, type of interface, the constraints applied due to any object or environment contract, QoS parameters that must be honored, and behavior that defines any pre- or postcondition action. Each interface is associated with a causality role that captures the behavior of the interface. For example, a computational interface may include the algorithms and rules for implementation of real-time latency computation.

An interaction template defines the interaction in the interface. Each interaction template defines the parameter count, and names and types of parameters. In the case of the operational interface, the termination type and associated parameter information is included, for each possible termination allowed. In each interaction template, the roles are defined. When instantiated, one of the causality roles is assigned to interface.

A binding object template is a special case of an object template. It includes the same elements as the object template, as well as the (interface template, causality role) pairs for all interfaces to be bound. Along with the set of interface identifiers to be bound, the binding object template is used to specify the parameters and actions of the binding object. The preconditions (behavior) to be met for the binding are:

▶ Role for each interface is the same type (operation, stream, signal)

▶ Role for the interface to be bound is complementary

▶ Role is a subtype of the interface signature

The binding object template also includes one or more control interface templates, to be used by the objects interfacing to the binding object. Part of the behavior specified for the binding object includes a policy on the use of the control interface, and a set of actions available on that interface. These actions, as constrained by the policy, may include:

▶ Monitor the quality of service

▶ Measure the quality of service

▶ Change the quality of service

▶ Monitor the use of the binding

▶ Monitor changes to the binding

▶ Authorize changes to the binding

▶ Change the membership of the binding

▶ Change the pattern of communication

▶ Delete the binding

13.11.5 SEMANTIC BEHAVIOR

Semantics are specified in terms of the three information viewpoint schemata: static, dynamic, and invariant.

Semantic behavior may result in one or more additional computational objects and interactions. For example, if fault tolerance is a constraint, often identified as "no single point of failure" in requirements specifications, then the computational objects performing failure detection, analysis, and recovery may be defined in the computational language, and further refined into engineering constructs in the engineering language, in order to realize the stated constraint.

Sometimes constraints are manifested as preconditions: actions that must happen before an interaction can take place. In these cases, some additional computational object may be required to monitor certain actions, or perform certain actions, to ensure the precondition is met. For example, it may be a precondition that a security monitor be initiated prior to any application interactions commence. A computational object "initiate the security monitor" may be defined, and further refined in the engineering specification.

Semantic behavior generally results in constraints on the interaction that must be observed and managed (such as a requirement to bind to a control interface), additional objects to perform some action (e.g., a security monitor, or a control agent), or additional objects and interactions, especially in support of interception.

The semantics contained in many of the constructs shown in Figure 13.37 are also specified in the information viewpoint. An example of some semantic constructs associated with computational interaction are shown in Figure 13.37.

A contract exists for all interactions. *The contract includes specification for what is to be expected and the behavior that violates the contract.* A contract can be composed of multiple contracts. Each component contract is a refinement of some aspect of the composition. For example, a contract can specify the correct security and QoS behavior of objects within the domain. A refinement of that contract can specify, perhaps, a less restrictive behavior for a subset of the objects in the domain, and their interactions. One subcontract can specify that there is no need for enhanced security to establish the authorization of certain objects within the same domain. Another refinement can establish that the QoS expected for a set of object interactions in the domain is less than for certain interactions. Each of these contracts are refinements of the "parent" domain contract. This is exemplified in Figure 13.38.

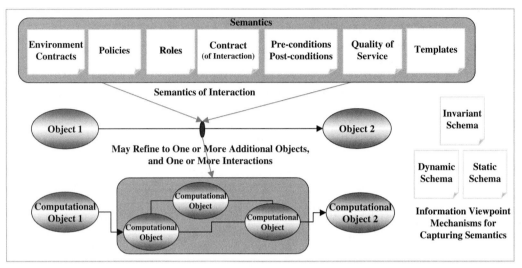

FIGURE 13.37   Computational Interaction and Semantics

A contract can be a dynamic specification, where an object can terminate the contract. The contract constraints are applied to the objects engaged in the interaction, and the interaction building blocks (interface, binding, and interception). With the capability for dynamic contract specification, interception across domain boundaries becomes feasible; the domain-specific contract information is exchanged, negotiated, altered, and results in a new (dynamic) contract for use to enable cross-domain interaction.

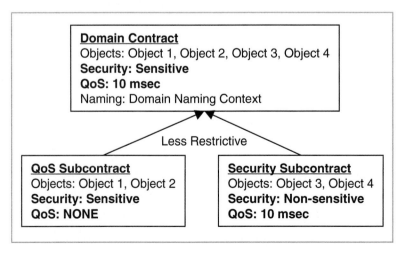

FIGURE 13.38   Contract Composition Example

In crossing domain boundaries, several contracts may be required to provide end-to-end correctness and interoperability. The collection of contracts may be considered a cross-domain contract, and refinements address the nature of the individual domain boundaries being crossed. For example, if domain A and B each have different naming domains and technical domains, a single cross-domain contract can establish the need for interception of naming and technology. Subcontracts can be specified for the naming interception, and for the technology interception. Perhaps a subcontract can also be established for a different QoS. Hence, a contract may be a composition of several contracts, which collectively define the behavior of interaction.

Composition of behavior results in a new behavior, determined by the behaviors being composed and the way they are composed. Care must be exercised in composing behaviors so that constraints on the original behavior do not lead to indeterminate behavior of the composition. "Behavior is inherent in objects and compositions of objects and there is a need to specify behavior independently of implementations. Such behavior specifications must be composable." [Thompson-98]

The semantic constructs that affect interaction are represented in Figure 13.39. This figure shows the interface template, binding object template, interface signature, EIR, interface identifier, and the binding endpoint identifier that were discussed in previous sections. These templates define the semantics and syntax of the objects or interfaces to be instantiated.

To achieve interoperability across a system of components, the system architect must address the profile of all necessary interfaces to support each of the subsets of interactions between objects of one application with the objects of another application, in the external environment of communicating object interactions. This is one reason why software architecture is complex. The architect must consider the system of interaction building blocks, as addressed in the Interaction Framework, across objects in subsets of interactions in order to achieve an interoperable system.

13.12   SUMMARY

Interoperability is complex; it deals with much more than an interface, and an interface is much more than a protocol. To achieve interoperability, there must be end-to-end correctness of interaction, both syntactically and semantically.

The focus of interoperability should be on interaction among components, and interaction captures multiple levels of abstraction for interworking between/ among components. Such an Interaction Framework that provides structure and semantics of interworking with multiple levels of abstraction was addressed as a pattern of reasoning in this chapter.

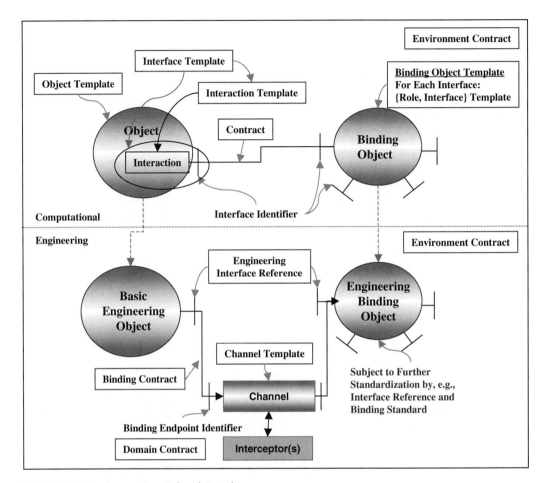

FIGURE 13.39   Interaction-Related Templates

Interaction deals with identification of action between objects as a result of a relationship required, each interface that provides the conduit of the interaction, the binding that provides the conduit of the interfaces, the interception that deals with mediation across domain boundaries to enable interaction, and the semantics associated with all of this.

Software architecture is defined to address components, connectors, and styles or constraints. An Interaction Framework defined in terms of multiple levels of abstraction along with well-defined concepts and consistency rules, such as from RM-ODP, is useful to adequately address issues of interoperability and semantic behavior. From these abstractions, definition of high-level abstract aspects of interaction, as well as low-level protocols, composition of interfacing and binding, analyses of behavior, composition of behavior, and specification of interaction properties, at the appropriate level of abstractions, can be accomplished.

To achieve end-to-end correctness in interaction requires a focus not only on the actions associated with interaction, but on the building blocks that support communicating interaction, and on the end-to-end semantics associated with them. In this chapter, these building blocks were discussed in terms of patterns of reasoning for:

▶ Relationship Framework—that captures the relationship among objects that result in defined interactions

▶ Interfacing Framework—that specifies the form, content, and actions associated with the interface that glues together sets of interactions

▶ Binding Framework—that specifies the connection of interfaces to enable communication of interactions

▶ Interception Framework—that specifies the actions required to enable cross-domain interactions

▶ Behavioral Semantics Framework—that specifies the semantics associated with correct behavior

It is through the computational specification for interaction that the interaction aspects of the system are addressed. It is the consistency of the computational and engineering specifications that provides further definitions of these interactions into engineering constructs of interfaces, bindings, and communication mechanisms.

However, capturing the semantics of interaction, identifying a categorization of concepts to be associated with each level of abstraction, and associating invariants with those properties has not yet been explicitly formalized. That is, the semantics discussed are patterns of reasoning for what must be specified; RM-ODP has not yet defined how to specify the semantics in an open language for support across ODP systems.

Current work in QoS framework, policy, contracts, federation, and interception will provide a great deal of specificity in these areas. The capabilities of this framework can provide support for further definition of interaction in the pursuit of software architecture connector and style semantics.

F O U R T E E N

POLICY FRAMEWORK

This chapter revisits policy from the Reference Model of Open Distributed Processing (RM-ODP), and then discusses the emerging work for a policy framework to support policy specification. Covered in this chapter are:

▶ What a policy is defined to be and why policy is important to the business enterprise

▶ What RM-ODP currently specifies for policy

▶ Examples of using policy in a system

▶ The emerging policy framework for specifying a policy, from the work in [ISO-EntVP]

▶ Current tools for representing a policy

▶ A study on the use of UML and OCL, using the Healthy Hospital case

---

14.1   WHAT IS A POLICY

Policy-based systems have the intelligence the business needs to manage the actions of the role-based objects, and management and use of the resources in the system. This is derived from the fact that a policy is initially defined in the enterprise specification: the business specification. A policy is a set of rules that govern the behavior of something. *Policy* is defined as "a definite course or method of action selected from among alternatives and in light of given conditions to guide and determine present and future decisions; a high-level overall plan embracing the general goals and acceptable procedures of a government body [or business]; a writing whereby a contract of insurance is made." [Webster's]

"…policies need to be made explicit because their monitoring and enforcement will require actions by the system implemented, and the correctness of these actions can only be guaranteed if there is a well defined framework for the description of concepts such as ownership, right, objective, authority, delegation and policy." [Linington-98]

In the real world, a policy is used to guide the actions of an organization. For example, a state regulation policy for medical equipment may state that all radiology equipment in a hospital must be inspected and granted a safety certificate. In this case, the policy must be enforced, or the hospital may lose its accreditation. So a policy is a set of statements, coupled with either explicit or implicit actions on violation of a policy.

POINT

Policy statements express constraints on the actions that constitute behavior.

In the system world, a policy is also a set of rules to constrain the actions of the system. A policy needs to be stated in such a manner that the system can interpret the statements and act accordingly. A policy specification is derived from policy as specified in the enterprise specification, and further refined in the remaining viewpoint specifications. That is, a policy is first a business rule. It is refined into mechanisms that define the effect of a policy on objects and interactions. It is further refined into engineering mechanisms that detect, manage, and enforce a particular policy on an interaction among objects. The policy specification, then, is a collection of all of these specifications. This is represented in Figure 14.1.

Specifying a policy is not as straightforward as it seems. Part of the problem is how to define a policy that has enforcement associated with it; part of the problem is how to define a policy that a system can operate on, without human intervention; and part of the problem is how to negotiate for relaxing a policy. One of the problems faced by a business is how to specify one or more policies as applied to the roles involved in the business. Another problem is how to manage such a business and guarantee that its actions are in agreement with the policy specification.

RM-ODP defines the fundamental aspects of a policy. The emerging work on the Enterprise Viewpoint extensions [ISO-EntVP] furthers the definitions, and is being used to develop a policy framework for use in automated systems. RM-ODP uses policy to define much of the behavior of a system, so it is important to be able to specify such policies for a system. The motivation for specifying a policy, then, includes the ability to:

▶ Precisely define what behavior applies to actions, to facilitate precise system implementation.
▶ Manage the system resources in accordance with the business rules.
▶ Facilitate the implementation mechanisms for enforcement of the policy.
▶ Enable consistency checks on the policy statements throughout the architecture specification.
▶ Enable conformance testing of enterprise behavior to a policy specification.

Policy

Is a Set of Rules

Represents Business Rules or Objectives

Expressed as One or More Statements

Permission
Obligation
Authorization
Prohibition

Applies to:
•Community Scope
•Set of Roles
•Single Role
•Assignment of Objects to Roles
•Processes
•Interactions
•ODP Functions

Part of:
•Environment Contract
•Community Template
•Template

Is Composable

Static or Dynamic

Has a Type/Subtype

Specified as Sum of:
•Enterprise, Computational, Engineering Specifications
•Constraints in Information Specification

Actions in Case of Violation

FIGURE 14.1 Policy Specification Elements

14.2   REVISITING RM-ODP CONCEPT OF POLICY

The focus of policy in RM-ODP is primarily in the enterprise viewpoint. An enterprise community is specified by a community template that defines the roles, and policies that govern the behavior of the objects fulfilling those roles. The purpose for a community policy is to achieve some specified objective. It sets forth a set of actions to determine decisions appropriate for the business.

For example, a hospital business objective may state that a patient record be current. In terms of a policy statement, a particular quality of service (QoS) would be specified for each organization that deals with a patient, and in each organization, a further policy statement may state that it is an obligation for the organization agent (e.g., a radiologist) to record all patient activities within a QoS time (e.g., 24 hours).

Each policy applies to a role (e.g., radiologist), an interaction (recording treatment results on a patient), and represents what is permitted, obligated, or prohibited for that role. Since a given role can be assumed by one or more objects, a policy can apply to one or several objects.

Policy is defined in RM-ODP in terms of deontic logic. That is, it is defined in terms of obligation, permission, and prohibition that determine the allowable behavior. Deontic logic speaks to "ought to do" instead of "must do." However, deontic logic considers only a static picture and does not take into account the interactions of objects in a dynamic, changeable state.[1] [Linington-98] The work on the Enterprise Viewpoint standard is expanding the specification of policy beyond deontic logic.

For example, a particular policy in a hospital is "access to the electronic medical record should be determined by an internal particular individual's job description and 'need to know.' All other access is prohibited." The "need to know" agents are those internal to the hospital; no one external is allowed access. Over time, the "need to know" is changed to "someone else," and the ability to support electronic medical record access is enhanced by appropriate security firewalls. So the policy changes to "access to the electronic medical record should be determined by secure access to a protected Web-enabled server" and the list of "need to know" agents includes any external physician practice authorized to practice at the hospital. The policy changes to "obligated to enable access to the Web server from an external authorized agent."

Systems are dynamic since things change over time. Policy is dynamic in that obligations, for example, can be applied at different points in time such as new obligations introduced into the system, through some external administration capability.

---

1. Problems of deontic logic can be found in [deontic-role], for those interested in exploring logic.

Dynamic policy statements, or statements that change dynamically, can introduce conflicts in the policy that must be negotiated and resolved. For example, given the above policy that no one other than authorized internal agents may access a patient's record, assume a policy is put in place that states "it is permitted that the pharmacist provide prescription orders to an external pharmacy through electronic fax or e-mail." This is in conflict with the hospital policy, which states that only internal agent access is allowed. Which policy takes precedence? The architect needs to indicate which and what action to take in case a policy is violated in some way.

To manage and enforce a policy generally requires extra objects in the specification. What the policy says is what should or needs to happen. What the policy does not say is that there needs to be a role specified to enforce the policy in the system. This is for the architect to specify. Notice, however, that once an enforcer role is specified, it is the policy that designates assignment of an object to a role, including the enforcer role.

Not directly stated in RM-ODP, but being defined in [ISO-EntVP], is the concept that policies may have types and subtypes, and are composable. It is quite useful to specify a high-level set of policy statements in the enterprise specification, and refine these statements into specific policy statements as applied to a set of objects in the engineering specification. In other words, a policy is an <X>. This concept was used in the Chapter 16, "RM-ODP Fault Tolerance Framework." In the case of a hospital, for example, the radiologist policy may be a subtype of the hospital policy.

The focus now will concentrate on what is meant by role, behavior, permission, obligation, and prohibition.

14.2.1   ROLE

Role is one of the foundation concepts in the RM-ODP standards, as discussed in Chapter 8, "Composition and Semantics: Quality Composition Minimizing Architectural Mismatch," and Chapter 12, "Enterprise Business Specification."

Role is defined as a unique identifier that characterizes some behavior. A role can be a composite object template parameter, which is a property of one of the component objects of the composite object. [RM-ODP-2] What this means is that the role identifies some defined behavior that can be assumed by an object, agreeing to provide this behavior. A *behavior specification* is a set of actions, and indications of epoch for these actions (which are constraints). [RM-ODP-2]

An example of a role-based system is the Healthy Hospital, where a billing agent assumes the role of billing and a physician assumes the role of physician, both as specified in the duties and actions of the roles. In this example, the patient is a role, assumed by a real person, not part of the "system," but must interact with the system. Hence, roles are defined not only for objects of the system in the business, but also for objects that are real-world persons, machines, etc., that interact with the system. In the case of policy, although policy applies to any object, enforcement of a policy on a real-world entity is difficult or impossible. But what the architect can do is to define the policy to include actions to take in case of a violation of the policy. So if a human patient, for example, does not show up for an appointment, the scheduling and billing policies may indicate "obligated to bill the patient for 'no show,'" a consequence of some action not taken by a human.

A role does not stand alone. The relationships, which are the inter-working of the objects that assume the role, are also specified. Each role includes a specification of the policies that apply. For example, the specification of the radiologist role in Healthy Hospital may include an action to bill the patient. A policy "obligated to submit a bill to the patient" would be specified.

One object may assume a role for a particular duration, go away, and another object then assumes that same role. A role includes the policy defining the behavior of the object assuming that role. And policies affect the interworkings of objects in certain specified roles. That is, RM-ODP separates the specification of behavior and interaction from the actual instantiation of an object in the system.

This approach enables the following: An application is developed that satisfies the actions and behavior specified by the role. It is part of the system, assuming that role. Now, technology advances so that a commercial product can replace the application. The product is determined to satisfy the behavior specified by the role. Without changing the architectural specification, the newer product can plug into the system, and the developed application can be removed from the system, because both act in accordance with the specifications of *the role*. That is, a newer technology can be evaluated against a role specification, and then plugged into the system, without change to the architecture specification.

Sometimes it's useful if more than one object can assume a role. For example, a role can specify a persistent storage management system, and the behavior associated with this role. In one part of the system, an Oracle® product assumes the "storage-role"; in another part of the system, a Sybase™ product assumes the "storage-role." The specification is the same for both, and unbundled from both products. The assignment of the role to a database management system object, and then the instantiation of the object enables multiple choices to happen, and multiple occurrences of the same role to exist. These are all unbundled in the architectural specification and, therefore, facilitate change.

The objects fulfilling roles can be very dynamic. Some roles allow the object to change a policy. A nursing example is shown in Figure 14.2. Nurse Jane is assigned to a patient. Nurse Jane is logged on the system. Nurse Jane is reassigned someplace else, and Nurse Joe takes over that patient's care. Nurse Joe logs on to

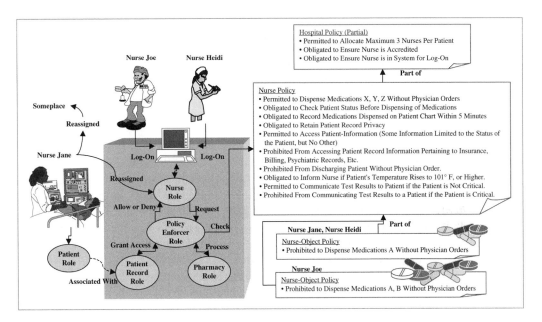

FIGURE 14.2 Nurse Policy Example

the system, and is associated with the role of "a nurse" to take care of the patient. Of course, the system must be informed of the reassignment of Nurse Jane for this to validly occur, so this reassignment action is a precondition of a nurse role reassignment action.

As another example, a nurse role may include an action to dispense medication to a patient, to record any such medication, and to retain patient privacy. The nurse policy, associated with these actions and others, might state:

▶ Permitted to dispense medications x, y, z without physician orders

▶ Prohibited to dispense medications a, b, c without physician orders

▶ Obligated to check patient status before dispensing of medications

▶ Obligated to record medications dispensed on patient chart within five minutes

▶ Obligated to retain patient record privacy

▶ Permitted to access patient-information (some information limited to the status of the patient, but no other)

▶ Prohibited from accessing patient record information pertaining to insurance, billing, psychiatric records, etc.

▶ Prohibited from discharging patient without physician order

▶ Obligated to inform nurse if patient's temperature rises to 101° F, or higher

▶ Permitted to communicate test results to patient if the patient is not critical

▶ Prohibited from communicating test results to a patient if the patient is critical

In both example cases, the policy remains the same. There is no need to change the policy, or the definition of the role. Only the object that assumes the role changes. This is one of the primary benefits of unbundling a role, policy, and object instance in the architecture specification.

Alternatively, a hospital policy may direct that more than one nurse, to some specified limit, may take care of a single patient. In this case, the precondition the system evaluates is a count. Perhaps when Nurse Joe takes over, he is able to dispense additional medications with a physician's order, due to some enhanced accreditation. So the policy may be dynamically changed in this area. Perhaps Nurse Heidi is assigned to the patient as well, and is allowed to dispense the same medications as Nurse Jane. But now, Nurse Heidi and Nurse Joe are dually taking care of the patient. The policy associated with each differs as to the medications each is allowed to dispense. So, in this case, perhaps a subpolicy is specified that is applicable to the object that assumes the role, adding additional constraints or enabling additional actions, and the main nurse policy continues to apply to all objects. Hence, it is possible to create new role-based object instances dynamically, and change, enable, or disable policies dynamically, and to dynamically modify the membership of the community.

A role is further refined into computational interactions and engineering bindings. The policies are further refined. So a policy that defines the behavior of a nurse and a patient in the enterprise specification, would be refined to constrain the messaging and binding associated with the interactions of "access records," or "get medications," or "record dispensing of medications." That is, the policy is refined to the interaction specification in the computational viewpoint, introducing an enforcement object, perhaps, and then further refined in the engineering viewpoint into interfaces between the enforcement object, the channel, and the protocols that constrain the exchanges of messages between the objects. The interface specification and channel specification, in this case, are based on the specification of rules constraining the possible responses on receipt of a message based on the preconditions that the nurse did (check the physician order, match the order to the request for a medication from the pharmacy) or did not do (recorded the medication dispensed in more than five minutes).

A policy, therefore, must include definitions for when the policy is applicable (e.g., when a nurse logs on the system), what information must be available for the policy to use (patient record, physician order, etc.), defining the decision process of what to do if a policy is violated (reject request), defining the decision process of how to evaluate adherence to the policy (policy enforcer), and defining all invariants, preconditions, and postconditions that must be adhered to for the policy to be effective.

14.2.2 PERMISSION

Permission allows something to happen. Permission only means that the action is not prohibited. Permission is the absence of a prohibition. It says there is no rule that prohibits the action. Permission is very weak in RM-ODP. It can only be strengthened by the architect who strengthens permission enforcement, permission is normally totally without force.

> Permission: There is not an obligation for x not to happen,
> for some action x: ~O ~ x

A permission is defined by:

▶ A role that permission applies to
▶ An interaction that permission applies to
▶ A target role in the interaction

There is no violation associated with a permission, so there is no exception handling required.

In RM-ODP, there is no such authority role that grants permission, because permission is the concept of "having permission," not necessarily being granted the right to exercise that permission. For example, a nurse *has the permission* to dispense certain medications to the patient, and the example in Figure 14.2 indicated a policy enforcer to allow this. But that policy enforcer need not be part of the system for permissions, and hence the system may in fact not allow the nurse to obtain the medications from the pharmacy to dispense. This is okay in RM-ODP; this may not be okay in a real system. So the architect must decide how to specify the act of granting permission to the role "having permission." The architect can further strengthen permission by specifying an obligation on the policy enforcer to allow the nurse to obtain the medications. That is, if A is permitted to do X, then A can elect either to do X or not. If A elects to do X, then the policy enforcer is obligated to allow A to do X. Accomplishing X is handled somewhere else in the system (e.g., the pharmacy role to request medications, and issue an order to provide the medications, and managing the stock inventory of ordered medications).

14.2.3 OBLIGATION

"However, analysis of obligations implied by the granting of permissions is clearly an area where the branching trees of consequences from our various actions rapidly become intertwined, and some level of conflict or inconsistency in the obligations that result is inevitable." [Linington-98]

Obligation requires something to happen. It is a rule.

> Obligation: That x can happen for some action x: **O x**

An obligation is defined by:

▶ A role that obligation applies to
▶ An interaction that obligation applies to
▶ A target role in the interaction
▶ A violation exception action to take

Obligation is fundamental to the community. It is the means by which the business rules are specified as constraints on the actions. The question of whether there is an authority to enforce the obligation is not addressed in RM-ODP. This is a decision of the architect, as was shown in the policy enforcer role in Figure 14.2. Sometimes an obligation includes accounting and charging for the use of resources.

In the case of joining two or more communities into a federation (see Chapter 15, "Federation"), obligation has a somewhat different meaning. In this case, an obligation is not obligatory, but rather a negotiable part of the policy between the communities in the federation. That is, the communities agree to the policy between them (to allow them to federate), and some policy enforcer then, and only then, enforces whatever obligations they have agreed to. If a particular obligation in one policy is not agreed to as an obligation, but rather as a permission, then the federation policy may well change the obligation to a permission. For example, if a physician policy has a statement of "obligated to access the patient records" and the hospital policy has a similar policy statement of "permitted to access the patient records," then the joining of the physician community and the hospital community into a federation may result in a joint policy that says "physician is permitted to access the patient records."

14.2.4 PROHIBITION

Prohibition expresses something that must not happen. A prohibition is a rule.

> Prohibition: There is an obligation that x not happen, for some action x: **O ~x**

Similar to a permission, a prohibition is defined by:

▶ A role that prohibition applies to
▶ An interaction that prohibition applies to

▶ A target role in the interaction

▶ An authority role that enforces the prohibition

In this case, a violation of a prohibition must accompany an action to be performed. There needs to be a policy enforcer for this case.

What this means is that an object that has a prohibition policy applied to it (e.g., the nurse is prohibited from dispensing certain medications without a physician's order), the object cannot play part in the action identified (e.g., dispensing certain medications). The system must provide a policy enforcer to make sure prohibition is handled in accordance with the policy statement. That is, if A is prohibited from doing X, then A can never be allowed to do X. The policy enforcer is obligated to deny A to do X.

Looking closely at these policy concepts, one can see that the strength of "must" or "required" or "must not" is not there. Deontic logic does not provide the strength of real-world practice of policy; it defines permission, obligation, and prohibition as "allowable." It does not include stronger concepts such as authority, rights, valid claim, violation, ability, capability, power, and force of law. Therefore, policy is weakly defined in RM-ODP. And the architect needs to include in the architecture specification a stronger emphasis on policy enforcement to overcome this weakness, if desired.

The next section will first show the use of a policy, though there have been examples elsewhere in the book, followed by the policy framework from both RM-ODP and the new work on the enterprise language.

14.3   EXAMPLES OF POLICY USE

An example of the use of policy for Healthy Hospital is discussed above. Another example is fault tolerance, discussed in Chapter 16, "RM-ODP Fault Tolerance Framework."

Another example is discussed here. From an engineering specification, a policy manager and a policy enforcer might be required. For example, Figure 14.3 represents a policy management engineering design. The objects A, B, C represent, perhaps, applications that request a distributed binding. The objects X and Y represent the destination application or service of the binding. A policy statement is shown, possibly stored in a persistent store for access by the policy manager object. The policy statements specify a QoS and a subject of that statement. The policy manager interacts with the interceptor of the channel to direct policy nego-

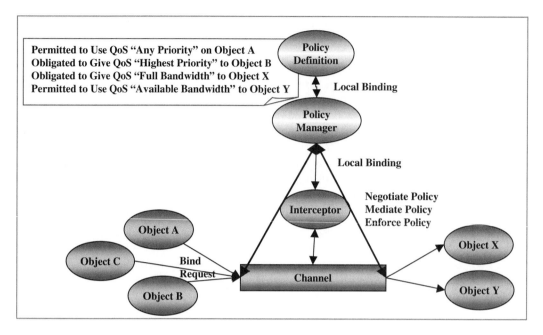

FIGURE 14.3 Policy Management Example

tiation, mediation, and enforcement as required. In essence, the policy manager manages the policies for the channel, in this example, and the interceptor takes appropriate action in the channel to accomplish it.

In the runtime system of this example, object A requests a binding to object X. Because of the policy statement that any priority is assigned to object A in the use of the channel, but full channel bandwidth is assigned to object X, the result is a dedicated channel between objects A and object X. The policy statements about both objects are not in conflict, but the result gives more QoS to object A.

Now, object B requests a binding to object X. According to the policy, that binding must result in the highest priority given to object B, and full bandwidth for object X. The policy statements are not in conflict. The result of enforcing this particular binding achieves a dedicated channel for the binding, as in the binding between object A and object X. Notice in these two cases, neither object B or object C are able to use the channel for the duration of the interaction between object A and X.

If object A requests a binding to object Y, the result is that object A is allocated any priority, and the bandwidth of the channel is sharable. This results in a reusable channel by object C. If object B requests a binding to object Y, the result is "highest priority, shared bandwidth." This is in some conflict, because if the purpose of prioritization is to get something through, sharing the bandwidth may deny the QoS. In this case, the architect should specify an appropriate negotiable action, such as delaying any other lower priority connections in the channel.

Although this example used the QoS for bandwidth and priority, other QoS properties could also be specified (e.g., security, traffic flow binding routed through another channel tracking of resource utilization, or some other service). These actions are driven by the behavior specified in the policy.

The policy can only be an architectural specification. However, if the form and parameterization of any policy are specified, a dynamic runtime definition of a policy can be created by an administrator adhering to the form and parameterization to be used by the system. In either case, the policy manager and interceptor play the roles discussed in the management and enforcement of the policy.

Notice that this example is similar to policy-based networking (PBN), where the objects in the example represent network elements. But also notice that PBNs are not the only place where policy management is important.

14.4   POLICY FRAMEWORK FOR SPECIFYING A POLICY

The emerging policy framework from the work on an enhanced Enterprise Viewpoint [ISO-EntVP] is powerful and flexible, and accommodates not only the business needs, but also the dynamic nature of a system. In this section, details about this policy framework are presented, and related to those of the RM-ODP standard. When the Enterprise Viewpoint standard work is completed, it will supercede some of what RM-ODP currently states; this is primarily in the definitions of permission, obligation, and prohibition. The Enterprise Viewpoint will also greatly enhance the policy work of RM-ODP and, finally, will be considered a part of the RM-ODP suite of standards. The status of this standard is currently at Committee Draft. It is expected to be at Draft International Standard status by publication of this book.

The RM-ODP enterprise language emerging work does not yet include a policy specification language (a notation for specifying policies). The augmentation of the deontic statements to RM-ODP is a step forward, but there are still some policy concepts not yet included; e.g., the concept that a role prohibits some action with respect to another role (security prohibits access attempts by an unauthorized object), versus the concept that a role cannot perform some action (security is prohibited from granting access to an unauthorized object).

14.4.1　CONCEPTS

The work on formulating a policy framework is focused on the enterprise viewpoint.

A *policy* is a set of obligation, prohibition, permission, and authorization rules on the interactions between objects. Policy is used to define actions in relation to a stated purpose. [ISO-EntVP]

This is an enhancement to RM-ODP. At present, two additional policy statements are being added to RM-ODP. *Authorization* means that some rule must not be prevented from happening. This is an empowerment. *Violation* means a rule of a policy statement has been breached. This is much like a failure.

A community specification includes structure and behavior of the community. A policy is directly related to the fulfillment of an objective of the community. The enterprise specification includes policy statements regarding the system, and policy statements of environment contracts.

With respect to the policy part of the community specification, policies that apply to the processes in a community include:

▶ Policies that allocate objects to roles
▶ Policies that govern the activities of a role
▶ Policies that govern the interaction of objects
▶ Policies associated with the environment contracts of the objects in the community
▶ Policies that govern resource creation, usage, and deletion by objects fulfilling roles

14.4.2　POLICY RULES

A policy that applies to a community applies to every role in that community. If a role-based object, such as object X in Figure 14.4, interacts with a role-based object in its environment (object Y), the policies that apply to that environment also apply to object X. So in this case, the behavior of object X is governed by the policy for community A plus the policy for community B.

Furthermore, when an object assumes a role, it assumes the policies associated with that role. The policy of the community includes specifying the population of objects in the community (that is, it governs what objects can assume what

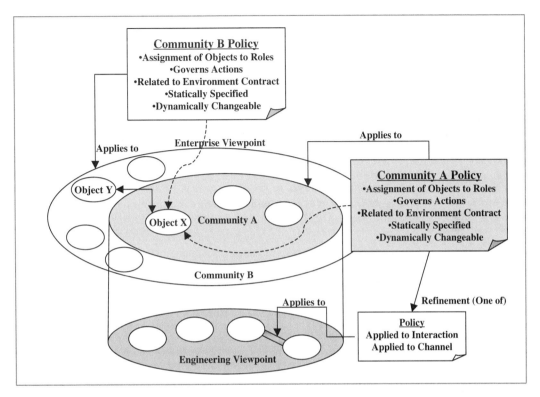

FIGURE 14.4   Communities and Policies

roles). It may be that not all roles are allocated to an object, for some reason. Perhaps the nurses are on strike, and the hospital community's nurse-role cannot be filled. The policy framework rules state that the community is still responsible for the policy of the role, as it affects the rest of the system (e.g., dispensing of medications).

Currently, there are no rules for specifying relationships between roles. However, progress is being made, and such rules are expected to be included in the Enterprise Viewpoint standard.

A role can be assigned dynamically, or dynamically changed (as was discussed in "Role" on page 571 in the example about Nurse Jane and Nurse Heidi). Since a role is part of a community, the policy of the community establishes the constraints on these dynamic actions, and any behavior permitted to accommodate this dynamic nature. For example, if the nurses are on strike, the hospital policy should contain a statement permitting some other person (or system entity) to assume the nurse-role, such as a doctor, or a nurse who has been loaned from another hospital and is only temporarily registered to the hospital. Then the role can be assumed by an object that may not meet the precise type properties specified, but can meet the dynamically changed properties.

14.4.3 Environment

The environment of the community plays a part in the definition of the policies of the community. First, the policies of a community (e.g., community A) must be defined within the context of its environment, which is either an implicit or explicit community (e.g., community B). The definition of the "inner community" policy must not conflict with or be inconsistent with the definition of the policy of "outer community." The state in which the hospital exists, for example, has its own medical policies. The hospital (an inner community in this example) policy cannot conflict with these, nor can it "weaken" any of the state (an outer community) policies. This is the sense in which the inner community policy cannot conflict with or be inconsistent with the outer community policy. In essence, a role associated with a community is subject to the policies of the community, and any other policy that applies from the environment of the community.

A policy can apply to all members of a community, to a set of roles within the community, to a single role, or to an action. For example, the hospital policy applies to all roles in the hospital community. The state regulation policy applies to the admission agent, billing agent, and radiologist roles. The admission policy applies to the admitting agent role. The billing policy that a patient is billed after the insurance company payment is received is a policy on the action.

14.4.4 Policy Refinement

Further policies also apply in all viewpoint specifications. In this case, the policy is a refinement of the enterprise policy, as shown in Figure 14.5. A policy as defined in the computational viewpoint is associated with the objects and interactions in that viewpoint. A policy defined in the engineering viewpoint is associated with the objects, their interfaces, their bindings, the channel, and any of the ODP functions. In this example, the patient record policy from the enterprise viewpoint is refined into the security policy (for access control) in the computational viewpoint, as well as the security interaction policy in the engineering viewpoint. The use of the replica and storage policies reflect that certain ODP functions come into play to achieve the 24 × 7 access to patient records, and the persistent storage of the patient records. And these functions are associated with policies as well, refined from the original enterprise policy.

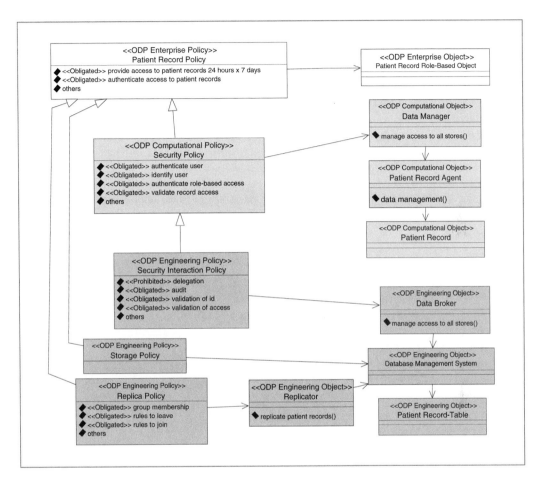

FIGURE 14.5   Example Policy Refinement

There is also a concept of a policymaker that owns the enterprise object subject to that policy. However, this has not been fully defined. Furthermore,
since an enterprise object may be affected by more than one policy, it is not
defined which policymaker is the owner. Hence, this topic is not addressed
here.

14.4.5 PERMISSION, OBLIGATION, PROHIBITION, AUTHORIZATION, AND VIOLATION

Let's now revisit the constraints of permission, obligation, and prohibition, and add in a discussion about authorization, new to the policy framework. In the following definitions, the normal font indicates the policy concepts from both RM-ODP and the new policy framework. The italicized items are concepts or rules added by the new framework.

14.4.5.1 Permission

Permission is defined as above, but what has been added is the concept of an authority that grants the permission.

> Permission: There is not an obligation for x not to happen,
> for some action x: $\sim O \sim x$

A permission is specified by the following:

▶ A role that permission applies to
▶ An interaction that permission applies to
▶ A target role in the interaction
▶ *A predicate describing the behavior*
▶ *An authority that grants the permission*

14.4.5.2 Obligation

An *obligation* is now defined as a requirement of a behavior that must be achieved by some defined behavior. [ISO-EntVP] This changes the definition of RM-ODP, and makes it stronger. It now says that if the action does not happen, it is contrary to the obligation rule and a stated violation action then takes place.

> Obligation: There is an obligation on the action, x,
> to happen, as authorized: $A (O x)$ or $A x$

An obligation is defined by:

▶ A role that obligation applies to
▶ An interaction that obligation applies to
▶ A target role in the interaction
▶ *A predicate describing the behavior*

> ◗ *An authority that grants the permission*
> ◗ A violation exception action to take

The authority enforces the constraints of the policy (an obligation on a policy enforcer role), whereby permissions are granted and prohibitions are enforced. The enforcement of obligations, permissions, and prohibitions, performed by the authority, is itself an obligation. So the authority assumes a special kind of obligation—it must accomplish the task.

An authority role needs to know certain information about an obligation. This includes:

◗ Conditions when it is active (e.g., applies to hospital community roles) and when it is inactive (e.g., patient privacy rights)

◗ Duration of when it applies (as long as the patient is a patient of the hospital)

◗ The situation under which the obligation has been fulfilled (retrieving a patient record by an authorized role-based object)

◗ The condition when the obligation is violated (an obligation applies to a role that is denied service)

◗ The action to take on a violation (notify the hospital administrator)

All of these can be expressed in terms of behavior associated with the interactions between the policy enforcer role-based object and the user role-based object that assumes the obligation; between the policy enforcer and the target of the policy enforcement (e.g., the patient record); and any other object that participates in fulfilling the obligation.

The predicate on behavior refers to the way in which obligations are or can be expressed. (Again, there is yet no policy language to explicitly define how to express an obligation.) An obligation can be expressed as active and the conditions to make it active (a patient has arrived is the condition, and the obligation to admit the patient is the policy that has become active); the determination conditions that an obligation is satisfied (the patient record has been updated to reflect the admission); and the violation condition that an obligation was not met or is unachievable (24 hours have elapsed and the patient radiology record is not updated).

14.4.5.3 Prohibition

Prohibition is defined as above, but what has been added is the concept of an authority that disallows the set of objects to take part in the prohibited action. Prohibition is defined by:

◗ A role that obligation applies to
◗ An interaction that obligation applies to
◗ A target role in the interaction
◗ A violation exception action to take

▶ *A predicate describing the behavior*

▶ *An authority that enforces the prohibition*

Prohibition: There is an obligation for the action, x, not to happen,
as authorized: **A(O ~x)** or **A ~x**

If the action happens, this is contrary to the prohibition rule and some stated violation exception action takes place.

14.4.5.4   Authorization

An *authorization* is new. It is defined as a requirement that the stated behavior must be allowed to occur and not be prevented from occurring. [ISO-EntVP]

Authorization: There is an authority to make the action, x, happen: **A x**

An authorization means that no object is able to deny an action that is the target of a policy statement. No other object can interfere with the policy statement on that action. For example, Nurse Heidi is permitted to dispense certain medications. If Heidi chooses to dispense those medications, neither the pharmacy nor any other object can stand in the way of Heidi's permission, because it was authorized. If an object does prevent Heidi from obtaining the medications to dispense, for example, then a violation occurs, and whatever action is designated in such a case becomes active (e.g., the pharmacist is issued a termination notice).

14.4.5.5   Violation

Violation is new. It is defined as a condition wherein an action does not adhere to a rule. [ISO-EntVP]

Violation: The authorized action, x,
breached a rule resulting in a failure exception, f: **V f**

A violation means that some policy rule (an obligation or prohibition rule) was broken, either because an object prevented an authorized action from happening, or an object did not perform something in accordance with the policy statement, as authorized, or an action that was not to happen did happen. Any denial of an authorized service is a violation. For example, if an object that is prohibited from something performs the action anyway, a violation has occurred. If Nurse

Heidi did not record the medications dispensed with five minutes, she violated the policy. The force of the violation comes in the action taken on a violation. In the case of Nurse Heidi, this may mean a negative comment is placed in her record.

These are the possible policy statement constraints (or empowerments), with the force of authority and violation action: permission, prohibition, obligation, and authorization.

14.4.6 POLICY ENFORCEMENT

Policies can be enforced. A continual monitoring of the policies is performed to ensure that they are properly enforced—that what can and must be done is, and that what can not and must not be done isn't. The architect determines the mechanisms to do this, probably much like the fault tolerant Control object discussed in Chapter 16, "RM-ODP Fault Tolerance Framework."

Not all policies need to be enforced, but some do. Access control to the system is one such policy to be enforced, and the enforcement is some software that always receives a request to log on and checks the appropriate authorization for the user before granting or denying access. For example, the continual monitoring that any action associated with a physician order must be done in accordance with policy. Otherwise, either some action is not performed on the patient that may be critical, or someone has overridden the physician order, which also may be critical for the patient. This form of policy enforcement is generally used when the consequences of a policy not being followed are high, or trust is low on adherence to the policy, or if some preventative measure can be applied to correct the situation immediately. As an example of a preventative measure, an alarm is sent to the hospital administrator to notify that object of the action of the pharmacy agent who overrode the physician order (e.g., dispensing the incorrect medication). Continual monitoring of policy has consequences of additional complexity in the system and possibly additional performance requirements on the system, so selecting and specifying which policies or which parts of a policy should be enforced is important.

Another form of enforcement is to assume everything works fine, but instead detect noncompliance, and then institute some action to record, report, and correct the action. This type of enforcement is cheaper to implement and doesn't impact the performance of the system as much. So, it is a good method to use if the consequences of a violation of a policy are not severe or life-threatening. It's also a good method to use if everything generally works well, and there is little reason to suspect that a policy will be violated. An example of where this might apply is the part of the hospital policy that says "Permitted to allocate a maximum of three nurses per patient." If two nurses are allocated to a patient, this may be okay. If four nurses are allocated to a patient, only then a notification to the hospital administrator may be needed.

The enforcement actions to architect should be assessed against the business objectives, the risk, and the performance cost on the system.

The enforcement of a policy may lead to how a policy should be organized. Since a policy can be a composition of other policy components, the architect should look at splitting policy statements into subpolicies to better manage them in the enforcement in the system. For example, since permission is not obligated, the hospital policy dealing with permissions may be a separate component of the hospital policy. Likewise, since obligation is important, and comes with a violation action, these may be aggregated into a separate component policy that is part of the hospital policy. Perhaps a policy enforcer role is specified that ensures the obligation rules are enforced, taking an appropriate obligation action if a violation occurs. This enables better policy management in the system, and still maintains the consistency of the policy specification of the system. Figure 14.6 shows an example using the hospital policy. The hospital policy is shown as a composite of separate policies. The policy enforcer is a role that enforces the obligation rules

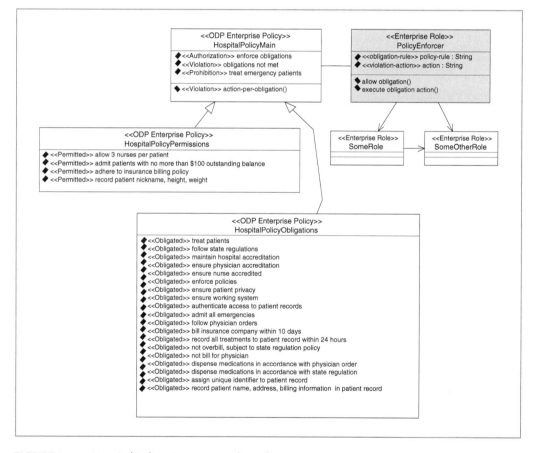

FIGURE 14.6   Hospital Policy Composition for Enforcement

wherever those rules apply between other roles. The policy enforcer invokes the appropriate obligation-specific action if an obligation rule is violated. There are other methods of specifying enforcement; this is only an example.

Finally, the policy framework identifies some of the consistency rules associated across the viewpoints, as shown in Figure 14.7. These are itemized below:

▶ Enterprise viewpoint policies govern the invariant, static, and dynamic schemata of information objects.

▶ Information objects are constrained by the policies of the community, policies related to objects in the community, policies related to an object in the community, interactions between objects, and an action associated with a policy.

▶ Enterprise policies restrict the behavior of computational objects.

▶ Enterprise policies constrain the behavior of an engineering interaction in the channel (on the stub, binder, and protocol objects).

▶ An enterprise policy may correspond to an engineering interceptor which implements it, at an administrative domain boundary or otherwise.

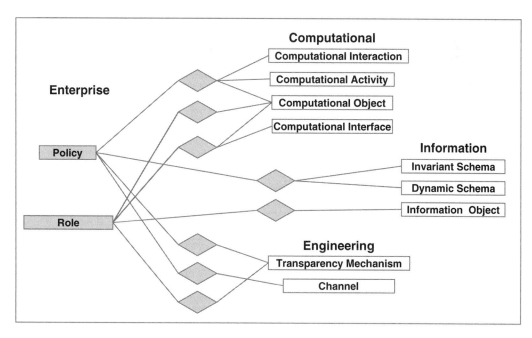

FIGURE 14.7 Policy Consistency Rules

14.4.7   CONSISTENCY

Once again, the enterprise viewpoint work is ongoing. More specific consistency rules are expected to be defined. Currently, Figure 14.7 provides an overview of the correspondences between the enterprise policy and computational, information, and engineering concepts. For example, a policy corresponds to a computational interaction, activity, and object. As was stated, a policy affects these computational constructs. Policy corresponds to statements in the invariant and dynamic schemata of the information viewpoint, where constraints are specified. A policy affects the transparency mechanisms as well as the channel. What is not represented in this figure is how a policy is enforced. Since there are several different methods of enforcement, it is left to the architect to define the correspondences for a particular architectural specification. As the policy framework becomes more defined in the Enterprise Viewpoint standard, a pattern of reasoning for policy enforcement may also be defined.

Some of the work to be accomplished, either in the standard or elsewhere, is the ability to determine consistency and appropriate relationships of multiple policies. As has been shown in Healthy Hospital, the different organizations that make up the Hospital community may each have one or more policies. These different organizations include hospital, admission, billing, insurance, physical therapy, pharmacy, radiology, physician, patient (bill of rights), and so forth. How the statements in the policies are interrelated, and are not in conflict, is currently a manual process. If this becomes an automated checking process based on some consistency rules associated with the permissions, obligations, prohibition, and authorization, then relationships across behavioral constructs becomes possible. This enables specifications of many types of relationships in better support of the real-world entities such as supply chain, business transactions, legal contractual relationships, and author/publisher relationships, not to mention medical enterprise relationships.

14.5   TOOLS TO REPRESENT A POLICY

Some tools are emerging to directly specify a policy. One such capability is a specification language for a policy that is built on top of the formal object-oriented specification language Object-Z [Steen].

The Australian Distributed Systems Technology Centre (DSTC) is building a role-based framework of a notation and tools for specifying obligation and authorization policies in an organization. This tool is called the Imperial College Role Framework (ICRF) [ICRF]. The tool is role-based. It provides structured management in a large distributed system. It allows for policy to be specified for a domain of objects, for policy specifications to be grouped into roles that achieve the dynamic policy management properties previously discussed, and for analyzing policy conflicts where policies are specified in multiple communities.

A Design by Contract [Meyer-97] Java™-based tool, called iContract [iContract], is freely available and provides the explicit specification of "software contracts" by means of class invariants and method pre- and postconditions. Although this tool is not exactly applicable to RM-ODP policies, it nevertheless provides the architect with a means of representing the correspondences of an enterprise policy and the information viewpoint schemata.

The Unified Modeling Language (UML) tool is used in a special way. These enhanced UML methods to express a policy make use of Object Constraint Language (OCL) [OCL1 and OCL2]. Policy statements can be realized as constraints on the associations (relationships) among the objects, defined in OCL. OCL can explicitly capture the constraints of policies, except for temporal constraints, and then be attached to a UML model in some way, such as a note or an association class. An RM-ODP UML/OCL profile has been proposed that uses certain UML and OCL concepts to model distributed systems and policies. [EDOC-UML, EDOC-UMLb] Work is rapidly progressing to represent policy in a standard way in UML/OCL. In addition to OCL, UML can be coupled with tools such as iContract.

How these constraints are processed requires further refinement of the UML diagrams. UML does not provide constructs that directly support the modeling of RM-ODP. The draft profile for Enterprise Distributed Object Computing (EDOC) consists of a mapping from RM-ODP concepts onto a set of UML concepts. Other work in representing policy in UML can be found in [Linington-99], [Aagedal], and [EDOC 99]. With respect to policy, the UML/OCL representations here are derived from these works, and augmented for purposes of the example.

The OCL notation includes set-based constraints and expressions of attributes and methods results. The constraints have a formal syntax and semantics, resulting in precision. Each constraint is defined in a context relating to a specific UML element in a UML model. OCL statements can be directly associated with the UML model by attachment, or can be provided in a separate closely related specification.

Mechanisms of representing policy in UML include [Linington-99]:

▶ Specify the policy as a class
▶ Specify cardinalities of associations
▶ Specify in OCL:
  – Constraints
  – Pre/postconditions applied to actions
  – Invariants
  – Prohibiting noncompliance as an OCL constraint
▶ Use each of the parameters of the policy as constraints on the relationships among the objects assuming roles: in the class diagram, the collaboration diagram, or a state diagram where temporal properties can be made explicit.

▶ Include control objects to represent management and control of actions for policy enforcement.

Returning to the Healthy Hospital example, the Hospital community function can be represented in an RM-ODP–founded UML and OCL model. This community is represented as a class with the stereotype *ODP Community*. Roles associated with the community are represented as a class, with the stereotype *ODP Enterprise Role*. An object that assumes a role is represented as a class, with the stereotype *Enterprise Object*. A policy for the community is a class that is associated with the community class and the role class, with a stereotype *ODP Enterprise Policy*. A policy can be a subset of another policy, which is represented by a generalization in UML. Finally, the environment contract policy is also represented as a policy, but with the stereotype *Environment*. This is represented as a part of the community policy, though more appropriately, it should be as another association on the community class and the role class. This is a limitation in UML; only one association class can be associated on the association between two classes.

A policy may constrain the occurrence of a specific step or multiple steps in a process or result in additional objects in the system model. This may result in additional steps, creation of processes, or termination of processes. The proposal from Open-IT, Ltd. group [EDOC-UML] has suggested that policy be represented in UML as a constraint on the objects assigned to the roles, thereby combining all the policy rules into a single class called "a policy for X."

Although this approach appears on the surface to be a good one, some problems in the use of UML render this approach questionable. UML does not allow multiple association classes to the same association, which is problematic. UML does not allow an association class to be associated with more than one association, again problematic. Hopefully, the EDOC work will determine the best approach.

Figure 14.8 shows an enterprise view of how a hospital policy relates to other policies in the Healthy Hospital community, and how roles relate. Some possible parameterization of the policies is shown.

The rules associated with the associations among the objects reflect aspects of the radiology policy shown in the Figure 14.8. That is, one mechanism of representing policy in UML is to specify the policy as a class, and to use each of the parameters of the policy as constraints on the relationships among the objects assuming roles in the collaboration diagram or a further refinement in a state diagram where temporal properties can be made explicit.

Sometimes policy rules, such as "notify authority on violation," result in extra processing by one or more role-based objects or the introduction of additional objects in the model, such as enforcer. Sometimes policy rules result in management role-based objects to manage and control actions of other objects affected by the policy rules, such the policy enforcer role-based object that manages and enforces the policy in the system.

Figure 14.9 shows one possible computational class diagram of the some of the role-based objects, and the introduction of the policy enforcer object to manage the policies.

Figure 14.10 extends Figure 4.9 to a collaboration diagram to show one computational viewpoint of objects that perform radiology actions, as constrained by the policy rules. This figure shows the objects that are part of the radiology capability. Further, the policy enforcer is shown. It enforces the radiology policy not only on the function of the radiologist, but also on the binding and the access to the databases. In UML, these are represented as classes. The object name of an instance of the class is not shown. Some objects are persistent, mostly in terms of the data stores. Some are static, primarily the policies. This is due to the policy framework that a policy may change. They are, after all, responsible for admitting a patient, updating the patient record, maintaining equipment safety, and constraining all manner of activities in the hospital community. The radiology policy is shown in the gray UML class instance. This figure shows what might be, with respect to policy effects and policy management.

In addition, OCL represents the rule (policy) as an invariant or precondition, and applies the OCL invariant to the collaboration diagram, shown in Figure 14.10. OCL can be used for expressing some of the ODP concepts of obligation, permission, and prohibition (policy rules).

A permission can usually be modeled as a precondition in OCL that evaluates to true.

There are two possible ways of representing prohibition in OCL: represent it as a precondition that is forced to evaluate to false; or represent it as a "not" on the object receiving the message. The problem is that OCL allows preconditions to be applied to the originating object, not the receiving object. This is a current limitation in OCL.

An obligation is a complex case, because obligation may be associated with a temporal context and needs to be associated with actions of objects performing them. This means that explicit statements of actions that allow or lead to an obligation, when the obligation is fulfilled, and violation conditions must be specified. It is difficult to specify such temporal constraints in OCL. It is possible to use OCL statements and apply them to the collaboration diagram of UML. The results of this approach are shown in Figure 14.11.

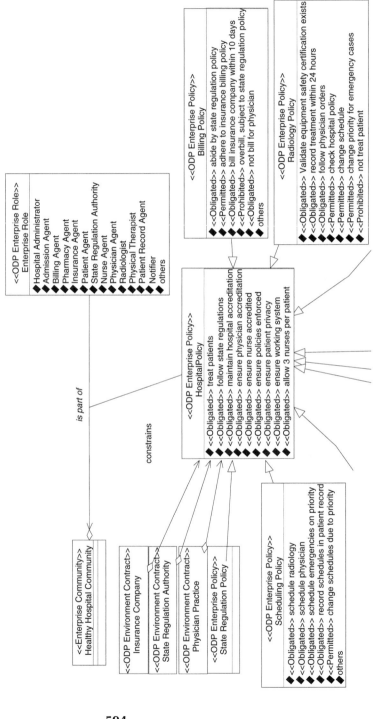

594

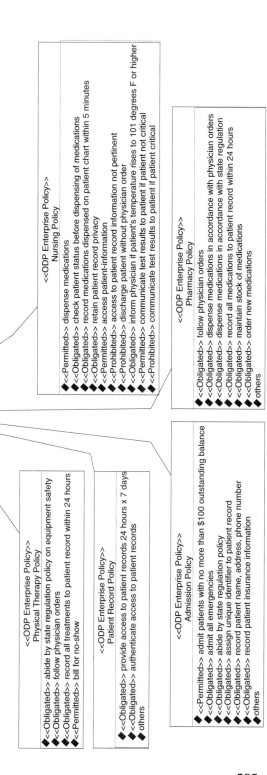

FIGURE 14.8 UML Hospital Policy—Top-Level Class Diagram

595

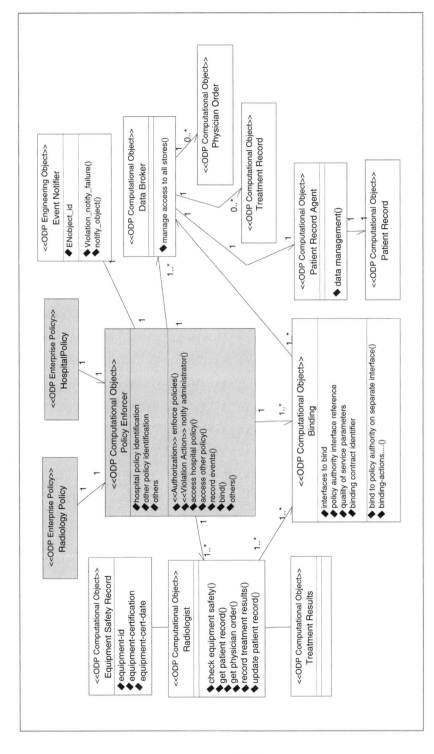

FIGURE 14.9 Computational Example of Policy Enforcement

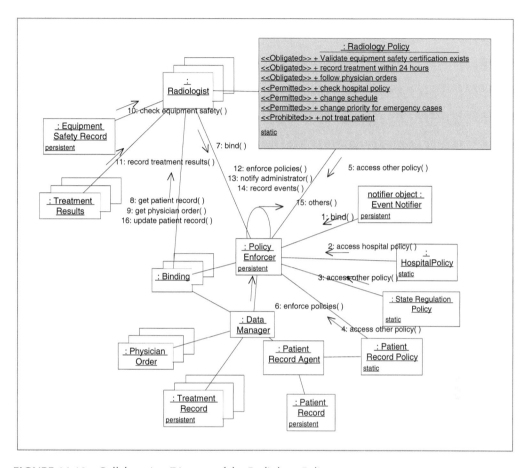

FIGURE 14.10   Collaboration Diagram of the Radiology Policy

An example of OCL to represent the policy obligation rule of *follow state regulation for equipment safety* is:

```
-- comment: Bind Radiologist to Policy Enforcer first
Object of Policy Enforcer::bindto(control-interface-ref:Radiologist)


-- comment: Policy rule: obligated to validate equipment safety
   certification exists
Equipment Safety Record::check(equipment-certification:Equipment
   Safety Record)
self.check-equipment-safety(equipment-certification) = self.equipment-
   safety-record.oclIsTypeOfBoolean=true AND today—self.check-
   equipment-safety(equipment-cert-date) <= state-requlation-policy
   (period-of-frequency-check)
```

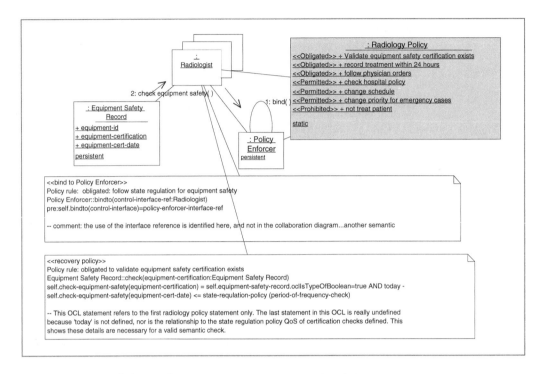

FIGURE 14.11   Radiology Policy Representation in UML Using OCL

In creating an OCL rule, one might discover that additional relationships in the UML should be shown to adequately semantically cover the constraint. Such is the case in validating the certificate of safety example for some radiology equipment. It's not enough to know the certificate exists; it must be validated to be current, within the rules of the state regulation policy. Since this was not shown previously, the OCL shown in Figure 14.11 indicates that a relationship between the radiologist and the state regulation policy should be included, and that the state regulation policy should include a QoS timeframe when equipment checks are required. This is just an example of the sorts of things the architect needs to consider, which may cause an update to the specification.

OCL can explicitly capture the constraints of policies, except for temporal constraints, and then be attached to a UML model in some way, such as a note or an association class. Work is rapidly progressing to represent policy in a standard way in UML/OCL. In addition to OCL, there are other emerging tools to represent contracts and policies, such as iContract based on Design by Contract™ [Meyer-97].

Additional use of OCL can be found in Chapter 16, "RM-ODP Fault Tolerance Framework."

14.6   SUMMARY

Policy is currently of great interest to business practices. Policy represents the constraints on the actions of the business, or some empowerment of the business. Examples include legal policies, state regulation policies, security policies, and business policies. Policy is generally captured in books.

Policy is an important system property of a distributed system to enable a robust, reliable, and stable system that supports the business objectives and business rules. Many are working diligently to provide a way of expressing policy in their systems, without guidance of how to capture a business objective in terms of a policy. If an architect can specify a policy for use in a system, that system can operate on a changeable policy dynamically. If the policy can be captured in an open manner, negotiation of policy between businesses is possible, which leads to the ability to federate or to enter into a virtual enterprise relationship, dynamically.

In the hospital case, a set of rules for all on paper might be stated as the following:

> *"The Healthy Hospital is dedicated to protecting a patient's rights to privacy, especially online. Patient information includes all identifiable personal and financial information. All information gathered is used solely to book an appointment with Healthy Hospital. It is not shared with any other organization, ever. For your safety, we use Digital Certificate technology."*

This chapter has provided a policy framework to capture what is written on paper into automated capabilities that enforce the written word.

RM-ODP, enhanced by the new work on the Enterprise Viewpoint, provides a policy framework based on an object model. The policy framework consists of precise terminology, an enterprise viewpoint method of relating a business objective to a policy, an enterprise method for associating policy with business roles, rules for structuring a policy specification, rules to enable a proper system specification of policy, and behavioral semantics in the use of enhanced deontic logic (permission, prohibition, obligation, and authorization) to accommodate the authorization and enforcement needed for policy. All these aspects were discussed at some depth in this chapter, supported by extensions to the Healthy Hospital case study.

Policy statements express constraints on the actions (the rules) that constitute behavior. A policy may constrain the occurrence of a specific step in a process, or multiple steps, or result in additional objects in the system model. This may result in additional steps, creation of new objects and associated processes, or termination of processes. Because system capabilities expand over time and individual job responsibilities change, it is prudent to periodically revisit the policies of the system for possible change. Preferably this is accomplished through administration, and the system operates accessing policy rules dynamically.

Currently, the policy framework does not yet provide a specification language for use. This is expected to emerge and, in fact, a reference to some emerging work was provided in this chapter.

In addition, a focus on how certain policy behavior can be specified and achieved in an object-based system, using the constructs of UML and OCL, was shown. However, limitations in both UML and OCL still prevent full behavioral semantics to be specified and associated with a single vendor toolkit…though we are getting closer. Today, there is no standard methodology to do so. Instead, there are emerging "patterns" for accomplishing the UML/OCL representation of policy. Although OCL was used in this chapter, other tools provide similar capabilities, as identified in this chapter.

Today, there is no standard methodology to capture the constraints of policy. Instead, there are emerging "patterns" for accomplishing the UML representation of policy. Software engineering to capture the appropriate aspects of policy is still required. Policy parameters can be realized as constraints on the associations (relationships) among the objects, defined in OCL. How these constraints are processed requires further refinement of the UML diagrams. OCL can explicitly capture the constraints of policies, except for temporal constraints, and then be attached to a UML model.

The architect has a great deal to consider in specifying policies that are pertinent to the business objectives and follow the business rules, and are refined into objects and processing to realize the enforcement of these policies. The policy framework provides these capabilities.

A policy specification, then, results from the specification of the enterprise language that initially captures policy, through the computational and engineering specification that identifies the mechanisms to realize the policy behavior. Representing policy in UML+OCL, even with its limitations, or in UML plus some other semantic contract tool (e.g., iContract), in conjunction with the computational and engineering aspects of the policy mechanisms, is very important to achieve a good description that includes some of the behavioral semantics of policy. Work is rapidly progressing in this area to not only represent RM-ODP in UML/OCL, but policy specifically. Some references that provide excellent discussion of policy are [EDOC-97, EDOC-98, EDOC-99, JP-WORDS, JP-ISORC, ECOOP-97a, ECOOP-97b, ECOOP-98a, ECOOP-98b].

FIFTEEN

FEDERATION

In this chapter federation is discussed, both in terms of what it is, how the Reference Model of Open Distributed Processing (RM-ODP) provides some help, and what is required but not part of RM-ODP. This chapter discusses:

▶ What is federation

▶ Why federation is important

▶ What considerations need to be addressed to achieve an automated federation

▶ What are the RM-ODP constructs for use in support of federation

▶ Where technology to support federation is today

15.1   WHAT IS FEDERATION

Large distributed systems tend to span different distributed domains. A domain can be organizational such as a business unit; administrative, such as a naming domain; and technical, such as a message-oriented middleware (MOM) domain. Each of these domains has its own control authority providing management of policies, control of resources, control of access, and possibly quality of service (QoS) constraints. Each domain provides this control to support different needs, different constraints, and different reasons for processing. Yet the need for flexible distributed processing, across networks of business systems, requires agreement among the control authorities of the different domains to create a federation. This is because of business' ever changing dynamic cross-organizational needs, with each unit possibly using different technologies that span different administrative boundaries. A federation enables collaboration, coordination, interoperability, and sharing among different domains, while the barriers for sharing that exist across technical, administrative, or organizational domains are alleviated.

Federation, as a noun, is a community of a collection of multiple domains that come together to share resources while retaining their autonomy over the resources. It is actually a configuration of components from separate domains that come together (federate) to share. A federation can consist of all members from a domain, or some members. That is, a federation may not include all members from a particular domain. In the general non RM-ODP case, a federation can exist independently of any active objects participating in the federation.

To federate, as a verb, means the action of federating a configuration of components together, resulting in a possible additional state, "federating," for those components. RM-ODP allows the use of an establishing behavior to define the establishment of a federation. The architect defines the actions and constraints associated with "to federate;" RM-ODP does not indicate what the establishing behavior is.

Autonomy means that each domain retains its management and sharability control over the resources it offers for sharing. That is, a domain determines the entity to be shared, identifies those peer components in the domain that may participate in the federation sharing of that entity, and retains its freedom to modify the state of the shareable entities. [Heimbigner-82, Heimbigner-85, Heimbigner-94] The result of a federation is to extend the information or services of any single object because of the ability to include into its other object resources within the federation.

But to achieve autonomy requires the ability to dynamically negotiate, to dynamically enter and leave the shared environment, and to bridge across differences in domains (e.g., naming, administration, and communication).

A top-level view of federation is presented in Figure 15.1. In this figure, a component from one domain desires to share a service or data or both with a component in the other domain. There are other components in each domain that are not part of the sharing. A federation, shown by the gray dashed line box, is created of the components that wish to share, a control component to manage the federation, and a policy that defines the constraints on the federation. Although this appears to be a simple case of sharing, remember that there are possible differences in technologies and administrations to be negotiated and intercepted (translated).

Federating requires a number of mechanisms to achieve a federation. Services to be shared need to be identified, discovered, and negotiated. Differences in technologies in the domains, such as communication protocols, need to be negotiated and mediated. Differences in administration policies, such as security or

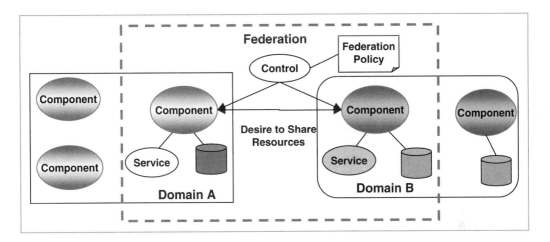

FIGURE 15.1 Federation of Two Domains

naming, need to be negotiated. And the use of resources by a component of one domain needs to be made known to a component of another domain providing the resource. Furthermore, each domain component in the federation retains ownership and control of its resources.

That is, each domain:

▶ Determines what resources to share, and with what specific domain(s)

▶ Determines how it will use resources made available to it from other domains

▶ Uses its own infrastructure and is not forced to use a common infrastructure

▶ Has the freedom to dynamically change any part of its association with the federation (enter, leave, etc.)

▶ Has the freedom to dynamically manage creation, deletion, and sharability of the resources it offers, including removing them from sharing

▶ Continues to participate in its own domain independent of the federation

▶ Is able to participate in multiple federations

SIDEBAR

ORIGINAL FEDERATION WORK

The work in federation began in 1980. Its concepts were explored, and the basis for a federation was put forth to the RM-ODP committee. [Putman-94] The current work in federation still adheres to this original work. *Federation* was originally defined as: a collection of components that come together into a loose confederation in order to share and exchange information. [Heimbigner-82] These components must be:

- Autonomous: control data sharing, control data viewing, engage in cooperative activity, and support structural evolution
- Willing to engage in controlled and partial information and transaction sharing
- Able to describe itself

In the enterprise viewpoint, RM-ODP addresses federation in terms of a community, where the enterprise objects are different domains. RM-ODP defines community, federation, and domain as:

▶ *Community* is a collection of interacting objects whose purpose is to fulfill an objective, which is a contract defining how the objective can be met.

▶ *Configuration (of objects)* is a grouping of objects that can potentially interact.

▶ *Federation* is a community. The community is distinguished by a common <X> relationship. As a community, the community defines an objective, which is the set of resources that are shareable with other domains in the federation. Each <X> domain that forms the federation can be autonomous with respect to entering or leaving the federation, and with respect to sharing its resources, as defined by the establishing behavior for the federation.

▶ *<X> Domain* is a set of objects with a <X> relationship to a controlling object that may or may not be part of the domain. [RM-ODP-2 and RM-ODP-3]

A domain is a set of objects under the control of a separate object, which may not be part of the domain, but rather associated with it. That is, the control object may exist outside the boundary of the domain. Different types of domains are allowed, denoted by the construct "<x>". For example, the health insurance company can be a domain where the insurance policies are set by some management authority. A hospital can be a separate domain, and a patient identification service (PIDS) can be a naming domain for patient identifications, where some naming authority controls the policy for naming. A domain may be a specific security management domain where access controls are specified. A domain can also be a technology domain where common choices of software or hardware are specified.

The controlling object is the object that is authorized to enforce the policies. For example, in a naming domain, the naming authority object determines allowable component membership in the domain, and an allowable name for a patient identification, perhaps denying entrance to the domain by all other components that do not adhere to this policy.

What RM-ODP defines as a federation is a community of domain-specific objects with the behavior of autonomy and the actions to participate with other domain-specific objects.

In RM-ODP, a federation is a community of domains where each domain (<X>) is considered as an object. A federation is not an action: to federate. The establishing behavior for an <X> federation is a set of actions with constraints, which tells how the federation is established. Though RM-ODP federation is not an object, per se, one could define a composite object that consisted of the domains in the federation: <X = composite objects>.

In general a federation can live independently of any objects participating in the federation for sharing. That is, even if there are no objects currently part of a federation, the federation exists with a defined controlling object. This facilitates pre-establishment of a federation wherein future domains or components of domains can enter and leave, dynamically.

A federation can exist across domains of the same type. For example, one kind of domain is a hospital domain. Several hospital domains can federate, though their security policies are perhaps different. For example, Healthy Hospital protects its patient records through the use of user identification and authentication. Another hospital, call it ABC, is not so diligent. It allows open access to its patient records. A patient record from the ABC hospital can be shared by Healthy Hospital, because the security policies are not in conflict. However, a patient record from Healthy Hospital cannot be shared by ABC unless the security policies are negotiated; either ABC enforces the security of Healthy Hospital or Healthy Hospital allows open access to the patient record or some intermediate solution. When a patient record is allowed to be shared from one hospital with another hospital, this is crossing the domain boundaries of the two hospitals. The two domains are of the same type (hospital), but the security domains are of different types.

A federation can exist across domains of different types. For example, one kind of domain is a physician-practice domain. Sharing a file from Healthy Hospital to a physician results in crossing a domain of type hospital and a domain of type physician. The two domains are of different types, and presumably the security domains are of the same type in this example. Some examples of different domains include:

- Naming domains
- Addressing domain
- Policy domains
- Trading domains
- Service provider domains, such as telecommunication, hospital, financial
- Administration domains
- Organizational (business) policy domains
- Database management systems domains
- Servers that manage a particular technology (e.g., Web servers)

- ▶ Environments, such as component-based framework environments
- ▶ ODP systems
- ▶ Component-based frameworks
- ▶ Technology domains, such as protocols, distributed object computing environments, operating systems
- ▶ Any set of components involved in information sharing

The key is that each domain is different because of the policies or technologies used in the distributed systems, not necessarily because the type of domain is different. The specification of federation in RM-ODP includes specifying the nature of the interaction between different domains, along with the policies that define the constraints of this interaction.

Figure 15.2 shows what federation provides, for the case of sharing the typical information about patients across different medical domains. This example uses some of the current work in the Object Management Group's (OMG) CORBAmed on PIDS. [OMG-PIDS]

In this example, the patient visits a particular physician associated with a group practice. Here, the patient fills in the group practice's particular form of patient identification managed by the "Patient Record" component. The patient's records are associated with this form of patient identification. The patient is then sent to the hospital, where a different form is required, with essentially the same type of information.

The hospital has chosen to share its records on the patient with the referring group practice. In order to facilitate sharing of patient information managed by the

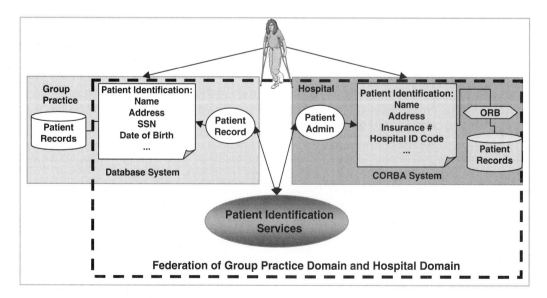

FIGURE 15.2   Federation of a Group Practice and Hospital Domains Example

Patient Admin component and the patient's hospital records, a federation is established between the group practice and the hospital. The group practice is allowed access to the hospital's patient record. The group practice domain, however, chooses not to share the patient's records with the hospital.

In this simple case, the form of the patient record is made consistent through the use of the PIDS specification. The Patient Admin component of the hospital and the Patient Record component of the group practice provide the necessary mediation between how a patient record is retained and the form required by PIDS to facilitate sharing. The hospital uses a Common Object Request Broker Architecture (CORBA)-based technology system, while the group practice uses a direct access database system.

The federation requires access through the Patient Record component of the group practice and Patient Admin component of the hospital. A component is shown in the federation that provides the PIDS services. Bridging across differences in naming, technologies used, and administration is required. In actuality, the federation service (based on PIDS) consists of an architecture that involves several components in the federation, to manage domain naming, correlate identifications, manage access control, and enable search and retrieval services. In any event, the federation enables the patient information and records from one domain to be made available to another domain, for purposes of sharing. This is an example of a federation of different types of business domains, and different types of technology domains.

15.2   WHY FEDERATION IS IMPORTANT

Across many organizations, strategies for sharing, interoperability, and collaboration are being formulated. Organizations are engaged in mergers, and as such their information systems need to work together. No longer is it viable for organizations to practice isolation and succeed.

Likewise, the distributed processing systems in these organizations need to collaborate. Expanding the scale of distributed systems today is often accomplished by federating smaller scale systems to achieve a wider span of resource sharing, resulting in networks of cooperating systems instead of a single, very large-scale stovepipe system.

This trend towards more interconnected, diverse, distributed systems means that ways are needed to federate the systems leveraging the work of different organizations and their distributed computing components.

Further, each distributed system itself is typically governed by an administration policy, and thus an explicit administration domain. In the business world today, there are many organizations that need to share information, processing, or some resource. What is important is that each organization, although needing to enter into a shared environment, needs to also retain its autonomy over its own domain resources. Retaining autonomy means that the object does not relinquish control over its resources. It means that the organization decides what data or information from its domain it will share; what hardware and software assets will participate in the federation; what processing will be shared; and what services will be shared.

The results of the federation are resources that are shareable across the objects that enter into the federation: that federate. In this way, the resource assets of one domain extend the capabilities of another domain in the federation.

Consider, for example, the three domains shown in Figure 15.3. Each domain is independent. When domain A and domain B enter into a federation,

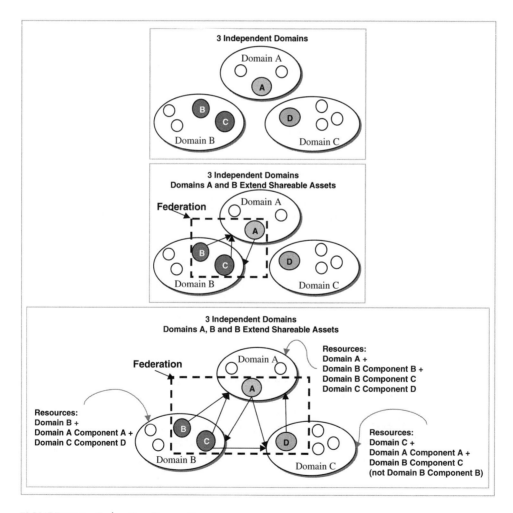

FIGURE 15.3   Federation Perspective

each designates the shareable assets. For example, domain A offers component A for sharing; domain B offers components B and C for sharing. This is shown in the middle figure. Domain A has extended its resources by the shareable components from domain B. The last figure shows the three domains entering a federation. Each domain extends its resources by those components offered for sharing by another domain. Notice that Domain B component B is not offered to Domain C for sharing, though it is still part of the federation. This represents the case where the domain retains its autonomy of what will be shareable by what other domain. This is the nature of federation.

Federation enables one component to extend its resources by engaging in a shared environment with other federated domains. And yet, by the concepts and rules of a federation, each domain in the federation retains autonomy over its shareable resources. The concept of federation applies not only to software-based distributed processing systems, but also to virtual enterprises of different business organizations that come together to achieve a common goal, sharing human, financial, or computing resources to accomplish that goal. But they relinquish no authority or control over their own resources. It is vital to our industry that we understand, engage in, and extend the technologies in support of the precepts of federation—organizationally and with our distributed processing systems. Federation alleviates the often required common technology-based infrastructure to share, allowing heterogeneous infrastructures to remain while allowing sharing and extension of usable assets. [Putman-97]

Many "virtual enterprises" are emerging to enable the sharing of resources: cross-Department of Defense (DoD) command and control domains; cross-DoD logistics domains; cross-finance banking domains; cross-health-care treatment centers; and international consortia. In OMG, as another example, a special task force is emerging to address international collaboration in support of Command, Control, Communications, Computer, and Intelligence (C4I) activities, all based on the use of CORBA.

These virtual enterprises are working out the details of what it means to federate and how to accomplish it, in order to share and yet retain autonomy over shareable assets, policies, and infrastructure mechanisms. One example of a virtual enterprise that federates to share assets comes from the National Industrial Information Infrastructure Protocol (NIIIP) Technology Reinvestment Program for which there are four separate prototypes. [NIIIP-96, Goldschmidt-98] Another example is from the DoD Modeling and Simulation Office (DMSO) High-Level Architecture (HLA) work, which federates simulation models. [HLA-96]

15.3   CONSIDERATIONS FOR A FEDERATION

To federate requires a common understanding of federation, an understanding of boundary differences, an agreement to federation approaches, and a uniform engineering approach to achieving it.

There are a number of processes involved in establishing the cooperation (establishing behavior) between domains needed for federation; e.g., negotiation, arbitration, contractual behavior.

Negotiation is a process of reaching an agreement that is acceptable to each domain, with respect to the item being negotiated, such as an obligated QoS. RM-ODP addresses negotiation as an establishing behavior through which information is exchanged to reach a consensus on future permitted behavior. The mechanisms for negotiation are not, however, described in RM-ODP, though some mechanisms are specified in CORBA version 3.0.

A contract establishes the agreement between the parties, and carries with it the obligations of each domain, the duration of the agreement, and possibly agreement to arbitration in the case of choices or failure. Arbitration is defined by policy and the control object(s) that perform the process of arbitrating.

A policy affecting the interaction between objects in a federation may be a compromise of the policies of each domain of the interacting objects. An arbitrator can be designated to resolve these kinds of differences, as directed by an arbitration policy on the objects in the federation. Termination of the agreement may also be part of the contract. The process of interaction or exchange needs to be defined as well. Often, this will include agreement to overcome differences in the interfacing mechanisms, and interfacing and binding agreements.

Specification of federation originates in the enterprise viewpoint. Considerations to be addressed to overcome differences in a number of areas are listed below. How the RM-ODP concepts aid in federation are noted.

▶ Administration and management of policies, including those of security, ownership, and creation/destruction of resources. RM-ODP enterprise and information viewpoints aid in this.

▶ Naming context differences to include different naming schemes, different naming authorities, and different naming formats. Naming applies to everything: objects, parameters, interface references, data, etc. The main RM-ODP support is the Naming function, defined in the emerging standard [ISO-Naming], which is focused in the information, computational, and engineering viewpoints.

▶ Semantic behavior differences that may include quality of service constraints, temporal constraints, use of distribution transparency constraints, and others. The support for this is the information viewpoint.

▶ Addressing context differences to include different forms of addressing, the scope of the addressing context, and the content of the address.

▶ Infrastructure differences to include the communication protocol differences, transparency mechanisms, and channel type differences. The engineering viewpoint mechanisms aid in this.

▶ Interfaces, service properties, and services for use. This includes how to specify the service offered, the behavior of an object and interface, the interface signature, and the failures. Both the information and computational viewpoints provide support for this.

▶ Type differences, which need a common model for describing type and for understanding what transformations are possible. The main RM-ODP support is the Naming function, and emerging type repository standard [ISO-TR], which is focused in the information, computational, and engineering viewpoints.

▶ Accounting, which includes any policy for billing. RM-ODP does not provide direct support for this. But the architect can use the viewpoints to define billing needs.

Almost always there will differences in the policies, administration, information, procedures, and mechanisms used in each of these areas that a successful federation will need to solve. Figure 15.4 provides an overview of the considerations that should be addressed to federate: to realize a federation for cooperation between domains.

Processes involved in the act of federating include:

▶ Negotiation—Contracts that are established for each community should be negotiated. Naming, addressing, typing, and administration are policies that also need to be negotiated. Domains that need to interoperate through the federation generally need to negotiate the conditions for interoperation of their components. Negotiation is a fundamental process in establishing a federation.

▶ Management—Management of a community (a federation is itself a community) is crucial to the overall management of the components and their interactions in the federation. Management of the shareable resources establishes, in part, the obligation of the federation to ensure domain autonomy. Management of the federation enables the federation to exist independent of active components in the federation, to manage the joining and departure of components, and to manage the overall infrastructure of the federation in support of autonomous sharing. Federation management is defined by a federation policy.

▶ Interception—Federating needs to address the boundaries (generally dissimilar) to be crossed. This requires a means to remove the dissimilarity so that sharing can be accomplished, such as transforming differences. Mediating is generally required to support differences in policies or format technologies (such as data format differences, data meaning differences, protocol differences). The interceptor of the engineering viewpoint supports mediation across domains.

▶ Established contractual contexts—To federate, each domain needs to identify its sharing strategy, meaning its sharing capabilities offered by a component to components in other domains. A federation contract is needed to establish the semantic context of the federation; e.g., what role a domain assumes, what policies are in force, and behavior. The federation contract also needs to establish the role the federation plays in the interaction among federated components; how the federation objects will support the management, negotiation, and interception activities for the federation; how failure will be handled; how obligations and prohibitions will be authorized; and how QoS will be managed across the federated domains.

A federation can exist only for the duration of components associated with it, or exist independent of active interacting components. That is, the architect can define a federation to live only as long as there are components in it. Alternatively,

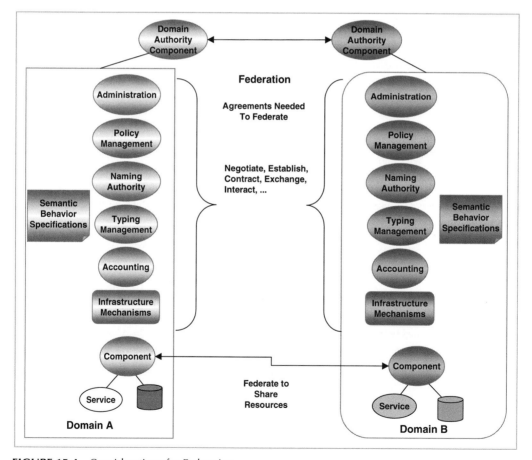

FIGURE 15.4   Considerations for Federation

the architect can define a federation to exist independently of existing active components. In this latter case, due consideration should be given to the actions of federation establishment and termination. That is, what causes a federation to be established and how needs to be defined. For example, a federation may be established as a system consisting only of a controlling component along with associated components to provide policy management. Whenever another system is established in a community, part of its establishment is to enter into a federated agreement. Further, the architect also needs to define what causes a federation to be terminated. For example, a federation may be terminated whenever the communities of interest are terminated, whenever an administrator (user) terminates the federation, or whenever a failure in policy is detected. How a federation is to be established and terminated needs to be specified by the architect.

The federation policy should address the use of distribution transparency mechanisms. Masking the complexity of these capabilities, through the distribution transparencies, is needed to enable rapid federated component sharing and lower maintenance costs of the systems involved in the federation, and of the federation itself. For example, it is preferable if a system infrastructure provides the federation capabilities rather than each component in the system. Then, as a component wishes to enter (or leave), a federation is managed by the infrastructure, transparently. Further, the maintenance of such a solution is lower because the capabilities of entering and leaving a federation are localized to the system infrastructure, not each component.

15.4 RM-ODP Constructs for Use in Specifying a Federation

Establishing a federation needs to address the constructs and rules for the federation. These are really up to the architect to define. The constructs of RM-ODP facilitate the creation of a federation, as shown in Table 15.1. Once again, RM-ODP does not define the establishing behavior to federate; it only defines what a federation is and some of the rules that govern a federation. The architect specifies federation establishment and termination, and how negotiation, arbitration, policy definition, and management are achieved. The use of the RM-ODP viewpoint concepts aid the architect to specify a federation.

Some of the constructs and rules for consideration exist, and are based on a great deal of work that was discussed in the early days of RM-ODP, coupled with the author's own work in the area, and the work of [Hammer-79, Heimbigner-82, Heimbigner-85, Heimbigner-94, ISO-Trading, ANSA-Fed-94, ANSA-FedM-94, HLA-96, NIIIP-96].

TABLE 15.1   Use of Viewpoints to Federate

FEDERATING CONSIDERATIONS	VIEWPOINT
Policies, contracts, behavior, roles, domains, for each object that enters into a federation	Enterprise
Semantics relating to federation: federation contract and federation policy	Enterprise and information
Mechanisms to establish a federation, mechanisms to terminate a federation, mechanisms to define arbitration and management	Computational and engineering
Mechanisms for negotiation of federation policies prior to binding	Engineering
Interception across domains for mediation and negotiation	Engineering

Federating can be made simpler by eliminating the autonomy aspect. Federating can be made simpler by negotiating all needs beforehand, either through design constructs or human service-level agreements. Automating a federation is still state of the art, in that a number of dynamic capabilities are not technologically feasible, such as dynamic negotiation of policies. What is presented here is what RM-ODP provides in support of establishing a federation, and the properties of such a federation. But technologies such as negotiation are appearing rapidly, as are policy negotiation techniques.

POINT

Other than RM-ODP, there is no standard today that addresses a general model for establishing a federation.

There is an important difference between the federation and interoperation. Interoperation is about sharing in a mutually agreed-upon manner. It takes the perspective that there are two objects involved, and that the interoperation lives only as long as the objects are active in the interoperation. There is no focus on autonomy, but rather on the bridging, with appropriate mediation, of the technologies to enable the full profile of interfaces to be bound. These interfaces could include anything from application programming interfaces through transfer protocols, along with data access and representation. Federation, on the other hand, focuses on the agreements, on the resources to be shared, on the objects that participate in the federation (two or more), and on retaining the rights over those resources. Further, a federation usually lives independently of the federated components in it. Domains can come and go in a federation, remain dormant, and then activate some request or provide a shareable component. There may be many shareable components available to the domain, dynamically changing as components enter into and leave the federation, as controlled by the domain. Clearly, a federation should be able to interoperate, but the interoperation may in fact be accomplished by a proxy object instead of actually physically binding two objects together. Federation, then, is a richer, more functional, more long-lived capability that embodies the concepts of cooperation, interoperation, integration, persistence, and dynamism.

15.4.1   Enterprise Viewpoint

The need for and establishment of a federation is specified in the enterprise viewpoint. Enterprise objects that assume roles with respect to the federation are also specified in this viewpoint, as are enterprise objects that provide shareable resources. RM-ODP, as extended by the new enterprise viewpoint standard [ISO-EntVP], defines federation to a point. Additional roles are needed in a federation, as identified in much of the research on the subject.

15.4.1.1   RM-ODP and Enterprise Viewpoint Standard Definition

A *federation* is a type of community that has a type, as defined in this chapter. It has at least two core roles that are members of the federation. The members of the federation are <X> domains, as controlled by their <X> controllers. The objective of the federation is to facilitate the sharing of the control among the controllers of the <X> domains. [ISO-EntVP]

The federation members must be domains of the same type. Because everything can assume multiple types, at a different level of abstraction (a refinement of this level of abstraction, actually), the domain may be of a different type. For example, at the above level of abstraction, the domain type may be "hospital," whereas at a refined level, wherein the sharing is further defined, the domain type may be "patient record in an Oracle® database" in domain A, and "patient record in a Sybase™ database" in domain B. Figure 15.5 shows what this definition means.

15.4.1.2   Federation Contract

The objective of a community is expressed as a contract. The contract of a community creates a context in which there is an obligation on the objects to accept the rules. In the case of a federation, there is a federation contract. That contract is an obligation on the objects that join the federation, in addition to any other domain-specific contract that might apply to them.

The federation community contract is used to define the bounds of the federation community, and describe the relationships between objects in the federation. The contract defines the roles of the federation, and the actions of those roles. It can define how long the contract is valid (e.g., for the duration of the federation), what quality of service characteristics must be adhered to, and what behaviors will invalidate the contract (e.g., an attempt to access a resource that is prohibited from access).

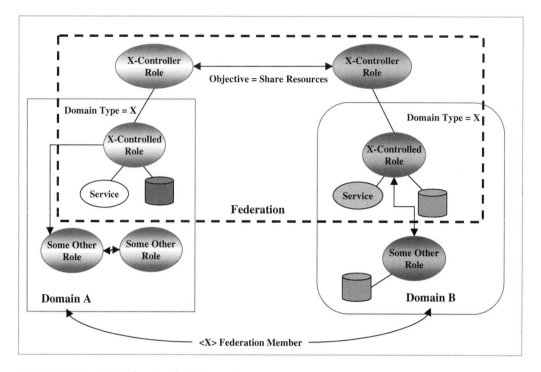

FIGURE 15.5   <X> Federation from Enterprise Viewpoint

The contract for a federation captures:

▶ Type of the federation community (e.g., naming)
▶ Objective for the federation
▶ Processes to fulfill the objective
▶ Enterprise roles and actions associated with the role
▶ Indications of duration
▶ Indications of what invalidates the contract
▶ Structure and behavior of the roles in terms of:
    – Relationship between the roles
    – Actions
    – Policies that apply to the roles
▶ QoS specifications on the access to the shared resource

Establishing the federation contract, then, establishes the federation. It is at this point that the federation can be considered a composite object; that is, a composition of the domain objects that engage in the federation.

The concept of negotiation is the agreement of the contracts representative of the domain of objects. But the actions for negotiation are left undefined in RM-ODP. The actions for establishment, termination, monitoring, and control of the federation are also left undefined in RM-ODP. It would seem appropriate that a federation is defined by a template that consists of those federation-specific components that participate in the instantiation, management, and termination of the federation. However, neither RM-ODP nor the enterprise viewpoint emerging standard address this.

15.4.1.3 Federation Policy

Federation policy defines the constraints on the roles assumed in the federation, and the configuration of the roles to objects in the federation. It specifies the obligations, prohibitions, permissions, and authorizations for each role. (Recall that a policy is part of a community contract.)

The object that assumes the federation control role is defined to manage and enforce the federation policy for all objects in the community. The role of the object is to manage the negotiation of policies across the federated domains, through a defined interaction with the object that assumes the negotiation role, and to ensure the adherence of policies by the objects in the domain. The actions to federate need to be specified. These actions include establishing a federation, negotiating policy, terminating a federation, joining a federation, leaving a federation, and managing a federation.

The federation policy applies to the the objects in the federation. For example the control object is obligated to ensure resource sharing has been permitted by a sharing policy established by the domain offering the shared resource. A domain object may, as another example, be prohibited from sharing of a resource from another specific domain. The naming object is obligated to resolve differences in naming contexts before any interaction to share resources can be permitted, as another example.

15.4.1.4 Roles

Some of the enterprise roles that should be required include:

- Management control role for the federation policies
- Management control role for the resources to be shared
- Service offerer role of federated resources
- Negotiation role for negotiating differences in policies
- Mediator role to resolve naming differences across different naming authorities
- Mediator role to resolve type differences
- Mediator role to resolve security differences

▶ Billing management role to bill for the use of shared resources (if required by the system)

▶ Possibly a trading role to match service requests with service offers

The domain that enters a federation may desire to have a domain-specific control object that acts as a bridge or gateway into the domain. This is a domain-specific decision, but the domain should protect its resources by ensuring proper access to those resources (using a security role), and may be required by the federation policy to perform certain transformations.

The federation contract establishes the federation community, and directs its operation through the policies that apply to the objects in the federation.

Figure 15.6 shows an overview of the federation roles described above. In this figure, the role is represented as a rounded box in the federation community. A domain-specific control object for each domain is shown; each interacts with the federation control object for all actions associated with the federation.

Now that some of the federation-specific roles have been addressed, the roles of the objects that offer a resource for sharing and the roles of the objects that

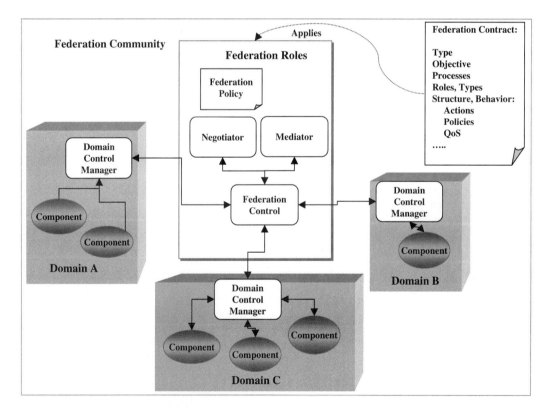

FIGURE 15.6   Possible Federation Roles of a Federation

access the shared resource and the policies associated with these roles need to be addressed as well. RM-ODP does not address this case further, though the architect needs to.

15.4.1.5   To Federate

The architect uses the enterprise viewpoint to specify the actions to federate, relating them to roles. These are further refined in the computational viewpoint. The establishing behavior *to federate* is not discussed in RM-ODP. That is, *to federate* the following actions may be pertinent, though these are not described:

▶ Establish a federation by establishing the contract for a community representing the federation.

▶ Terminate a federation. The action of termination should be specified in the federation contract.

▶ Entering a federation is defined as part of the federation policy. Domain objects may enter if the criteria established in the policy is met. An example is that the domain must be of a certain type (e.g., "hospital," and the objects are obligated to agree to a particular naming context, such as patient identification service) while in the federation.

▶ Leaving a federation is defined as part of the federation policy, as well as any preconditions or postconditions. For example, an object may leave a federation only after it relinquishes all shared resources used (a precondition).

▶ Negotiation is defined in terms of a role. How negotiation is accomplished is an architect's decision.

▶ Locating a resource for use is important to establish a shared resource capability. Perhaps a Trader will be used to maintain a dictionary of shareable resources for discovery.

▶ Resource access, once a resource has been located, is possible through the Trader, or a data broker manager.

▶ Registration of a resource for sharing establishes the resource for discovery. How the resource is registered and where a resource is registered and exists are the architect's decisions.

▶ Adding a resource is similar to registration of a resource. The metadata associated with adding a resource should include any specific restricted use of that resource by another domain.

▶ Removing a resource.

▶ Changing the shareability of a resource means that the offerer of the resource may choose to change the metadata associated with the specified domain that can use the resource, or open the resource for full federation sharing.

For a federation, a minimal trading functionality in support of the components may be necessary. In addition, federation should provide a means of message passing, information sharing, and transaction sharing. Operations associated with sharing in a federated environment [McLeod-91] should include:

▶ Discovery of information
▶ Identification of information
▶ Resolution of familiar information and desired (remote) information
▶ Sharing of information
▶ Transmission of information in an agreed-upon manner
▶ Negotiation of capability and information

15.4.1.6 Composition and Dual Membership

Federation can be composed into a "larger" federation. That is, given a collection of federations, each federation may form a component in a "larger" composite federation.

From the point of view of the component, it can be a part of many federations in addition to its domain. Many components can come together into a federation, or enter and leave while others enter and leave. A composition of different federation components can be created. Figure 15.7 shows what this means. Federation is represented by dashed boxes. Federation 1 is a federation of hospital domains. Federation 2 is a federation of physician domains. Federation 3 is a federation of insurance domains. The reasons for federations 1, 2, and 3 are not shown. Federation 1 and Federation 2 can form a composite federation by using PIDS for sharing of patient information. Federation 3 can enter this federation to share billing and patient information. This composite federation is a federation of the all three federations, with a federation control object managing the composite federation.

In RM-ODP, federation is a technique to be used for scaling of systems, where each system is a specific technical domain. One federation can cross different technical domains. Another federation can cross different organizations in a business. The constructs of RM-ODP enable compositions of federations, and compositions of policies, to achieve a higher level of federation across organizations. However, care must be exercised that the policies do not conflict with each other.

Let's look at PIDS specifically. Perhaps a patient is to be identified in different domains. Ordinarily, "Jane" may be identified in one format in one domain, and a different format in a different domain, each with a different set of parameters (e.g., name, Social Security number, date of birth, address, phone number, or some combination). Translating different data formats for every domain can result in a large number of translations and interfaces.

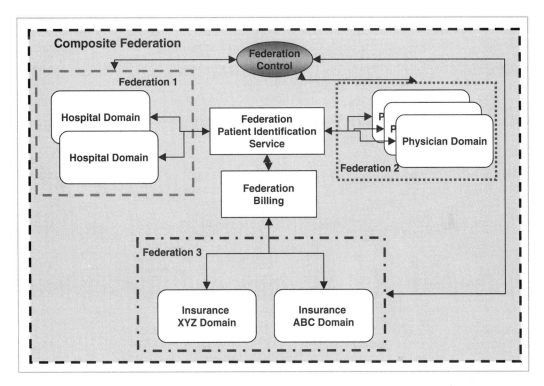

FIGURE 15.7 Composition of Federations

Alternatively, each domain can make use of a common patient identification service business object (e.g., CORBAmed's PIDS) that provides a common manner of expressing patient information using a common naming context. Each domain needs to translate into and out of PIDS for their domain-specific naming, or alternatively adopt PIDS internal to the domain. In any event, PIDS forms a common form of federating patient identification services across multiple domains.

The domains can be structured into different federations, each using PIDS, as shown in Figure 15.8. For example, one federation could be a hospital system, ancillary organization systems, and all physician practice systems that share patient records, using PIDS to access them. Another federation could be another hospital system with its ancillary systems (e.g., billing) and physician practice systems. Each federation allows the actions of query, list, present, and access of patient identification services.

Federating the federations then yields a larger community (Health Care Provider Organization) of shareable patient-related resources, across multiple hospitals and physician practices, and possibly other systems such as clinics, treatment centers, or trauma centers. This is, in essence, the architecture for PIDS, where each federation is statically defined by the PIDS services and interfaces, as well as the naming context for the PIDS.

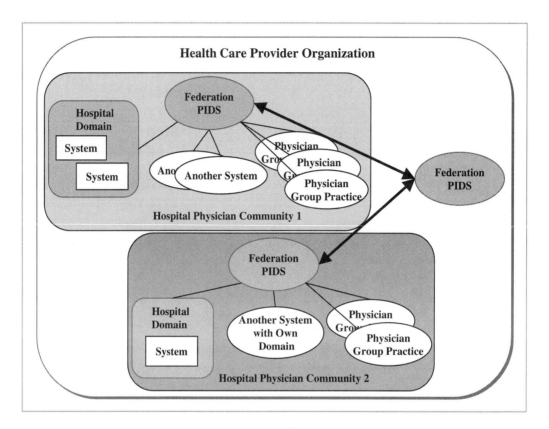

FIGURE 15.8   Domain and Federation Reference Model for PIDS

15.4.2   INFORMATION VIEWPOINT

In the information viewpoint, the rules that apply to the services are defined. These are reflective of the constraints of the policies. An example of such a statement, derived from a similar example in the Trader [ISO-Trading] specification, is:

> ***Federation Name Matching Constraint***
> *A constraint on the matching criteria imposed by the naming policy of the federation. Applying these constraints may be represented by set intersection.*

Federation policies, contracts, and enterprise roles that provide a federation, are all specified in the information viewpoint. No detail is provided in RM-ODP. Hence, the architect decides how best to use the information specification.

The actions provided by the federation, and in support of the federation, are captured and fully defined as part of the invariant, dynamic, and static schemata. Hence, the actions of negotiate, enter, and leave are captured, probably in the dynamic schema. This schema explicitly defines what can and cannot be done. All actions are constrained by the federation policies. An example is:

```
Withdraw — withdraw a resource from the federation.
```

Purpose:
The resource is withdrawn from Inventory and from the set of resources to be shared.

Constraints:
The action must be initiated by the owner of the resource.
If the preconditions are not met, the state of the federation remains unchanged.
The Withdraw operation succeeds or fails based on the preconditions.

Failure:
A failure based on resource in use will return an error ResourceInUse.

Preconditions:
The resource supplied must exist in the federation Inventory.
The resource is not in use.

The policy relationship between domains in the federation and the federation will be stated as constraints on the actions of the objects from the domains, and possibly captured as part of the invariant schema.

The behavior to be established for the federation can be specified in the invariant schema:

- Duration of the object entering into a federation interaction
- Rules regarding entering and leaving the federation
- Duration of the federation
- Rules regarding federation termination (e.g., if no more objects exist in the federation)
- The degree of autonomy each domain has over the ability to share the resources of the federation

The relationships among the roles of the federation and what resources the domain will share with other domains in the federation are probably defined in the invariant and dynamic schemata.

15.4.3   COMPUTATIONAL VIEWPOINT

The computational viewpoint addresses the decomposition of the federation into the computational objects and their interfaces. The actions identified in the enterprise viewpoint, subject to the constraints of policy, are defined in terms of interface and interaction signatures. A full computational viewpoint specification is not provided here, because it is based on a particular architecture, and because RM-ODP has nothing to add. However, some of the constructs for possible use are highlighted.

In this specification, the actions identified in the enterprise viewpoint are refined. Interactions that need to be addressed include transferring information (and access) onto a third component; and retrieval of the resource, transformations required, and management necessary to automate the processing. Management operations for a federation are defined. Entering the federation and withdrawing from the federation are some additional interactions to be defined. How a federation is established and terminated is also specified from this viewpoint. The interface templates for all such actions are specified.

Where policies constrain the interactions, a policy object can be defined and identify the cases where adherence or violation of the policy generates certain results. For example, a federation policy type, used in different operations, could include:

```
enum FederationPolicyIndicatorType {FP_TRUE, FP_RULE, FP_STR,
   FP_OBJECT};
union PolicySpecificationType switch (PolicyIndicatorType) {
   case FP_RULE: RuleConstructType Construct;
   case FP_STR: string Rule; // for conveying an entire rule to be parsed
   case FP_OBJECT: InterfaceIdentifierType policyObjectIdentifier ;
   // case for indicating TRUE, with value FP_TRUE
} ;
```

Since a policy constrains the interactions, the specification for an operation can contain a criteria representative of the policy element. A "withdrawCriteria" criteria can be defined, for example, that is of type Rule. The interface signature that contains, for example, the withdraw-a-resource operation could be defined as:

```
void withdrawOffer (
      in ResourceIdType ResourceId)
raises (BadResourceIdentity, ResourceInUse, SystemError);
//for some type associated with the resource, and some unique id.
```

This component request would, for example, generate an operation to the federation control object, such as:

```
SomeType Withdraw (
    in someType componentInfo,
    in ResourceIdType ResourceId,
    in Rule withdrawCriteria,
    in …other parameters…
) raises (BadResourceIdentity, ResourceInUse, SystemError);
};
```

For each action defined in the enterprise and information viewpoints, and each policy, such resultant operations are defined in the computational viewpoint. In addition, all possible errors are explicitly defined.

Figure 15.9 provides an overview of some of the interactions that would need to be refined in the computational viewpoint specification, to enable domain A and domain B to share resources. This figure shows the enterprise viewpoint of what a federation community might consist of in terms of the roles the objects would assume, as well as some of the policies that are defined in the information viewpoint but constrain the interactions defined.

In this figure, domain A supplies both a service and data for use. It provides the federation with the interface references to these services. Domain B can negotiate for the use of the service and data of domain A. Once it is agreed, domain B can directly access the shareable resource through the interface reference provided, or through the federation community designated component. How a domain accesses a shared resource is one of the interactions refined in the compu-

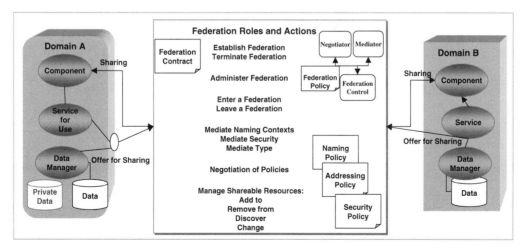

FIGURE 15.9 Possible Computational Consideration for Federation

tational viewpoint and whose behavior is captured in the federation policy. Also shown are services and other data private to the domains, that are not subject to sharing in the federation.

The complexity of domains entering into a federation may require a need for a new transparency, the federation transparency. Although the use of it would be specified in the engineering specification, the requirement for its use is specified in the computational specification.

RM-ODP originally considered federation transparency as one of the selective distribution transparencies. It was eventually not included in the standard principally because it was not sufficiently defined by member body representatives. Nevertheless, since one is able to include additional transparencies, it is worth noting some of the concepts that were included regarding federation transparency, which are discussed in the engineering viewpoint.

15.4.4   ENGINEERING VIEWPOINT

RM-ODP does not explicitly address the engineering viewpoint aspects of federation. The engineering viewpoint constructs are used as normal.

Interception is the principal mechanism in RM-ODP to accomplish federation. This is accomplished through the use of the interceptor object in the channel, to mediate between differences, and its associated policy that defines the actions of the interceptor.

A federation from the engineering viewpoint should address the services of:

- Type interceptors
- Naming context interceptors
- Communication interceptors
- Policy interceptors
- Message passing
- Transaction management
- Access control
- Etc.

A policy drives the actions of the interceptor. It should include the behavior that governs the engineering interface references across the different management domains; that is, what is permitted, prohibited, and obligated to happen. These are constraints that apply in the computational viewpoint, and are used to determine binding constraints. This policy may include:

- The interface is prohibited from binding if the management policy of the domain prohibits access from other domains.

⬤ The interface is permitted to bind if the object is allowed to be shared across domains.

⬤ The interface is allowed to bind if the naming contexts are known.

Interceptors are like mediators between domains. They permit or deny the binding in the channel, based on the contract associated with each domain. Where the technologies are different between the domains, the interceptor performs the needed protocol conversions, name translations, and use of different transparency mechanisms such as for access. Only a single interceptor is needed in this case for each technology boundary that is accessed.

Where the interaction is across management domains, however, two interceptors are required. An interceptor for each domain provides for the adherence of the management policies of its domain, protects the domain from unauthorized access, etc. The interceptors of the two domains can communicate information to facilitate transformations required to federate. To accomplish translation between the domains, the interceptors of each domain may interact before an object binding takes place, communicating the exchange of information regarding security access permissions, checking policy information to ensure there are no mismatches, etc. The object interaction can then be accomplished where the interceptor then transforms any required protocols or names. Alternatively, an interceptor may invoke other engineering objects to provide the actual transformations. This is an architect's decision. Once the transformations are accomplished, the channel can then facilitate communication of other objects across the domains. That is, the transformations set up the ability for further successive object communications (federation) across the domains.

Federating across different management domains is more involved than federating across technology domains. As such, the mechanisms for federation may include the same actions as crossing technology domains (or may not, if the two domains happen to use the same technologies), in addition to the mechanisms for crossing other kinds of domains. The mechanisms may include more than one channel, to negotiate among the interceptors. How all of this is accomplished is not addressed by RM-ODP.

Figure 15.10 depicts the two types of interceptor configurations: crossing a technology domain boundary and a management domain boundary. This figure also depicts the use of a single channel to establish the interaction among basic engineering object 1 and basic engineering object 2 for crossing a technical domain boundary. A single channel is also depicted to establish the interaction between basic engineering objects 3 and 4 for crossing a management domain, which needs to not only address differences in management policies, but may also need to address the differences in formats, much like crossing technology domains. This is one pattern of reasoning. The architect may choose to use a single channel to access the objects in different domains.

In RM-ODP, federating Traders is a special case. The interceptor may need to set up access to an initial Trader in its domain with a Trader in the other domain.

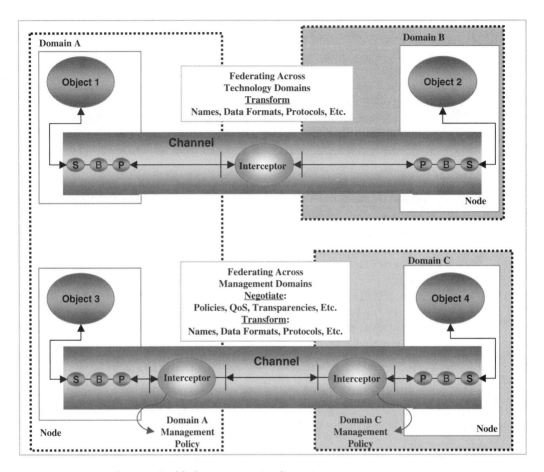

FIGURE 15.10 Federation-Enabled Interceptor Configurations

From this point on, objects that wish to access the Trader for importing and exporting of services are transparently connected with the Traders in both domains. The Trader object itself then manages the federation requests for access to services, and provisions for access to those services. Alternatively, the interceptor in one domain can be designed to be the Trader of the domain, in addition to its other federation responsibilities. Again, this is an architect's decision.

Just remember that federation is a requirement; interception is a mechanism. Federation requires more than interception, e.g., a global naming capability.

Federations may include a Trader in each domain. If the traders need to be linked across the federation, some action should occur to enable this. The Trading standard [ISO-Trading] discusses the capability of Trader federation as a hierarchy of Traders. This is one approach. Another approach is to build a Trader into the interceptor. RM-ODP merely identifies some ways to accomplish this, but none are required.

In RM-ODP, each object can offer a management interface for use in policy management. The object that enforces and manages the policy of the domain can be the initial object interaction with its counterpart in the federated domain. The negotiation and establishment of an agreement to share resources is then accomplished, prior to actual resource sharing. Once accomplished, the objects in each domain can engage in the process of resource sharing. This is represented in Figure 15.11.

Federation transparency, as was originally defined, addresses crossing boundaries that are dissimilar. The application developer need not be concerned with the domain in which a resource (data or service) needs access to. This transparency enables the use of the engineering viewpoint interceptor construct to be included in the binding between objects in different domains. If the boundary to

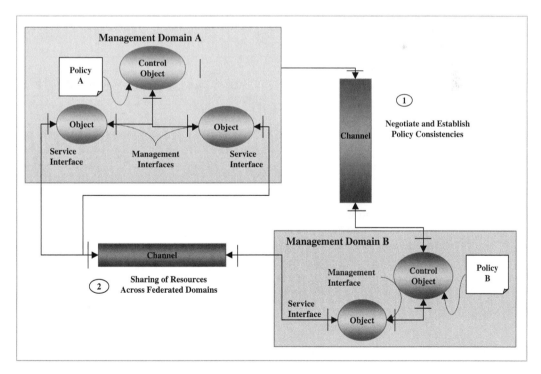

FIGURE 15.11 Federation Policy Management Design Choice

be crossed consists of differences in technologies, the interceptor performs the translations to cross the boundaries. Alternatively, the interceptor can interact with a separate proxy object located in each domain that acts in the role of a translator object, managing the transformation of the objects in its domain. If the boundary to be crossed consists of differences in administration of naming, policy, permission, etc., then the interceptor may well act in the role of a firewall or guard, to ensure that permissions and issues of policy adherence are met.

RM-ODP does not discuss what actions are performed for negotiation, what information is to be exchanged, what mechanisms are used to ensure adherence to the behavior, where to specify that a federation contract should be established before a binding contract, etc. RM-ODP does not discuss how an interceptor manages to translate across domains, or how the interceptor or an engineering object enforces a federation interface reference management policy. These are constructs for the architect to select and use.

What is important to realize is that RM-ODP provides essential basic constructs for use, along with a minimal pattern of reasoning. The constructs of RM-ODP lend themselves to specification of the policies, contracts, behavior, and roles for each object that enters into a cross-domain interaction. But the architect still has to architect the use of these constructs, with explicit detailed information, in order to realize a federation.

15.5   WHERE TECHNOLOGY IS TODAY

Establishing a federation requires agreement. To reach an agreement in computer systems, one can establish it from an organizational perspective, isolate the shareable entities, and expose the open interfaces to those entities. Generally, this agreement is captured on paper as a contract. The computer systems are not involved in establishing or negotiating the agreements. Rigidly defining what is shared, isolating those assets to a shared environment, generally constrains the autonomy of the organizations. Control is given up to whatever organization is set up to manage the shared environment. An organization that desires to change the shareable assets in some manner will need to enter into further organizational agreements, through whatever process is established.

Distributed object policy management and enforcement is a subject of much discussion today. It has to do with:

▶ How one enforces an object to do anything
▶ How one can perform negotiation

▶ How one finds the management object of a domain and the interface to use to negotiate cooperative management policy

▶ How one can accomplish sharing without incurring a large performance impact

▶ How one monitors the actual sharing of resources

▶ And so forth

The discussion and figures in this chapter provide a simplified view of the problems to be solved, focused mostly on the mechanisms available for use from RM-ODP. Engineering and architecture are still required.

RM-ODP provides the initial foundation for achieving federation, but not the complete framework. Federation has been identified and described in the Trading standard for federating Traders [ISO-Trading], and the new standard for naming [ISO Naming] and federating naming contexts. Some of the concepts in RM-ODP are not expanded well enough for use, such as capturing "scope" in the enterprise viewpoint. But work is progressing in the emerging enterprise viewpoint [ISO-EntVP] standard to expand these concepts. However, the use of federation across these standards remains inconsistent and incomplete.

What is needed is a reference model for federation along with the mechanisms to achieve and maintain federation, in a consistent manner. This was originally proposed to ISO in September 1994 [Putman-94], but was tabled as "for further study."

Other than the RM-ODP constructs presented here, there is no standard today that addresses a generic framework for realizing federation. There are no defined mechanisms for defining a federation contract, policy enforcement, or even open dynamic negotiation and arbitration, though CORBA 3 is initiating these concepts. These technologies are being investigated today, but are not yet in hand. And certainly, there is no standard that can provide a well-defined framework or pattern for reuse.

Work to further the mechanisms to achieve federation is occurring in Defense Advanced Research Projects Agency (DARPA): work on federated environments in [Heimbigner-94], work in Modeling and Simulation through the High Level Architecture (HLA) [HLA-96], and work in OMG. Some of these federations are accomplished statically by predefining all the rules, concepts, and domains that can participate in the federation. But more and more, dynamic capabilities are emerging to facilitate dynamic federation. The dynamic mechanisms of policy management, negotiation, and interception are important for a federation to be dynamically formed and operational.

It should be clarified that, to date, technology is not yet capable of capturing and processing the semantic information required for federation. Nor is technology yet able to enable dynamic negotiation of this information. Nevertheless, technology is moving closer to enabling federation dynamically. The OMG CORBA Version 3.0 specification provides more functionality in its Interoperable Object

Reference (IOR) that will eventually enable QoS parameterization. The emerging work on dynamic negotiation [Wise-98] through the use of process language and process centered environment technologies is moving closer to dynamic negotiation capabilities. It's only a matter of time before CORBA, HLA, process languages, and other technologies emerge to provide federation across domains and dynamic policy negotiation.

15.6   SUMMARY

Federation is concerned about collections of distributed objects that come together into a logically centralized domain of focus such that the information or services of any single object is greater because of the ability to include into its schema the schema of any other object within the federation. Federation extends the resources of a domain to those of other domains in the federation while retaining the autonomy of each domain. Federation is a basic capability needed to support the dissimilar distributed systems collaboration across emerging virtual enterprises and organizational mergers.

Federation continually applies to areas within RM-ODP: interworking, trading, type management, and naming repository, to mention a few. Federation forms a foundation for interworking across different distributed system domains. The new work item on ODP Naming addresses the need for federation of identifier spaces in a global ODP environment. The ODP Trader function includes federation of Traders. Federation of type repositories is being addressed, as is federation of naming authorities.

RM-ODP provides some constructs for use in defining a federation community. The enterprise viewpoint captures the objectives, policies, and scope for a federation. The information viewpoint captures the semantics of the working of the federation. The computational viewpoint refines the components and interactions in realizing a federation. The interception mechanisms of the engineering viewpoint provide the communications ability in support of federation.

Different management policies may exist across the federated domains. The specification to support federation should include the definition of policies that control the interactions in the federation in relation to the specific domain, to enable sharing and interoperability across different domains. Each domain retains its authority and autonomy to control resource sharing and management. The specification for a federation should address the mechanisms to realize federation. This specification will result in the need for one or more interceptors in the engineering specification, to negotiate under the constraints of the policies for federating.

The policies that need to be defined for federating include things such as:

- ▶ Rules that define the allowable domains to federate
- ▶ Rules that define the interaction between the domains
- ▶ Domain naming rules

RM-ODP carries this no further. However, to achieve a robust federation, other policies need to be specified. Some of these include naming policy; negotiation policy; security policy; reporting failures in QoS guarantees; resource sharing policy, and others. Some work is provided in OMG on a dynamic negotiation facility. [OMG-Negot]

The architect still has much to engineer and specify. Support for dynamic negotiation, arbitration, billing, policy management, and a federation framework for interoperability have yet to emerge from research or RM-ODP.

RM-ODP FAULT TOLERANCE FRAMEWORK

In this chapter, the Reference Model of Open Distributed Processing (RM-ODP) fault tolerance (FT) framework is discussed, along with how to use it. This chapter addresses:

▶ What is FT

▶ Why is FT important

▶ What considerations must be addressed to achieve reliability, dependability, and availability

▶ What is the RM-ODP FT pattern of reasoning

▶ How to represent an FT policy in the Unified Modeling Language (UML), using the Object Constraint Language (OCL) for more precision

16.1   WHAT IS FAULT TOLERANCE

Fault tolerance is concerned with the failure identification, analysis, and appropriate action to recover, to the extent possible, the system to a reliable stable state. A system is said to be fault tolerant if it can recover from a failure. FT is about providing a dependable transparent infrastructure for reliable application and infrastructure objects, with graceful degradation if recovery is impossible.

A failure occurs when what is observed to happen does not match what is expected to happen, or what is expected to happen does not occur. An example of the former is a software component that does not provide the expected response or quality of service (QoS). An example of the latter is a software component that hangs with no response. Failure can occur anywhere, such as in the application, in the infrastructure components, in the network, in an interface, in an interface binding, or in hardware. The RM-ODP model for failure does not distinguish where a failure may occur, but rather what constitutes a failure.

A *fault* is a condition that may result in errors in an object. [RM-ODP-2]

To assign a fault there must be a specification of what is expected to happen: a contract between an object involved in the failure and an object observing the behavior.

The various kinds of mismatches between what happens and what is expected to happen are the failure modes. Examples of failure modes include:

▶ Unexpected behavior—Something happens that is not expected to happen

▶ Nonoccurrence behavior—Something is expected to happen and does not

▶ Incorrect behavior—Something is expected to happen, something does happen, but the behavior of what was supposed to happen does not match what did happen

▶ Crash behavior—An object does not respond to all subsequent inputs (multiple nonoccurrence behaviors) until the object restarts

To provide FT, a failure must be detected and must be recovered. To detect a failure, expectations of correct behavior or deviations from correct behavior must be specified, and an object must observe these behaviors. An example is a specified set of expectations of the correct behavior of the (group of objects involved in) binding between a client object and a server object. To determine FT, each failure mode is analyzed to determine if the engineering objects can detect and tolerate the behavior. A contract between objects is the means of defining correct behavior, and essential to FT.

To determine a failure requires a failure model. The RM-ODP failure model for FT deals with the defined concepts of failure, fault, error, and stability, and one or more levels of abstraction.

The failure model further defines the levels of abstraction. One level addresses the failure or error. Another level addresses the group of objects subject to a failure or error, along with the fault tolerant detection and analysis tasks, to determine what level of FT to apply to the group of objects. Another level addresses the actions to restore the state of the failed fault group to a (more) stable state.

The model allows for either a single object to observe an event of another, or for some more global object to observe the events of a multiple grouping of objects. Recall that an object can be a composite object, and thus be composed of a number of objects.

16.2 IMPORTANCE OF FAULT TOLERANCE

FT is important to maintain operations with the least amount of interruption and impact. In the event of a failure, one needs to be able to recover the system to its operational state in the least amount of time and impact to the operational applications and infrastructure objects.

The need for an integrated open system architecture for fault tolerant dependable processing is driven by three technology trends:

1. Applications are dependent on complex large heterogeneous distributed middleware components.

2. Distributed processing systems are constructed from multiple middleware environments requiring dependability of execution.

3. Application developers should not be involved in developing the complexities of fault-tolerant systems; these should be transparent to the application developer.

Modern systems, including information systems and embedded systems, must function within an environment of objects or components whose characteristics are usually impossible to specify precisely. Examples of such impossible-to-specify environmental characteristics include existing legacy systems with which the given system must interface. These legacy systems are not necessarily considered open systems, and as such may not include the fault-tolerant mechanisms identified in this chapter. However, the legacy system can be considered to be a single component in the environment of an ODP system, so that if it fails, it has minimal impact on the ODP system that interacts with it. To accomplish this feat, there needs to be software interacting with the legacy system (e.g., a wrapper) that protects the rest of the system from failure. Unless the legacy system itself already has a fault-tolerant mechanism, it is impossible to automate it. Human involvement will be necessary to restore the failed legacy system to a stable state.

Fault-tolerant mechanisms require additional infrastructure mechanisms to achieve. The decision to include FT is typically made when the system must be available and reliable, even at the expense of other properties such as simplicity or high performance. Often this is the case for large critical systems that must be always available, such as Defense Command and Control, medical, and air traffic control; for embedded systems that have timing constraints, such as medical, satellite, signal processors, and ground-based systems; for enterprise systems, such as Command and Control, logistics, financial, and medical; and for communications systems such as telecommunication (or telephony) and network systems. In short, almost any type of system may require dependable computing. If this is the type of system being architected, the architect should consider the aspects of fault tolerance.

To achieve a dependable system requires that system to be recoverable from a failure. Consider a client/server role-based system of interacting objects. These objects can fail in any number of ways:

▶ The client may fail.

▶ The server may fail.

▶ The communication mechanism may fail.

▶ A violation of what is expected may be attempted from the client or server.

▶ A support object in the infrastructure may fail, causing a failure in one or more groups of objects of interest.

The perspective of an application failure and an infrastructure supporting the application failing is shown Figure 16.1. Any infrastructure mechanism (component, object, interfaces between objects, binding, communication, or platform) or an application component may fail. The RM-ODP modeling concepts are

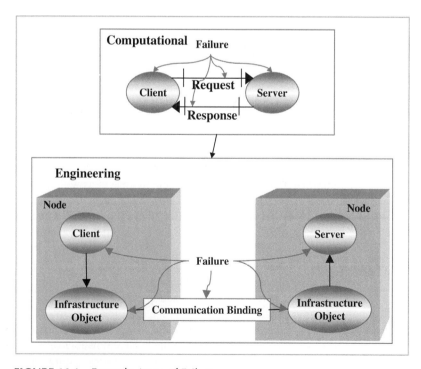

FIGURE 16.1 Example Areas of Failure

generic and can be used to describe all such failures, as addressed in the remaining parts of this chapter. Semantic behavior plays an important part of the specification of any system. When a failure is detected, it must be analyzed to determine the reason for the failure, based on a violation of some defined behavior.

16.3   CONSIDERATIONS TO ACHIEVE RELIABILITY, DEPENDABILITY, AND AVAILABILITY

Reliability addresses the expectations of continuity of service, measures associated service with service delivery as expected, and the ability of an object to perform as expected for a specified period of time. *Reliability* is the property that a failure is quantified as mean-time-to-failure (MTTF). An interruption in the processing of the system is quantified as a mean-time-to-repair (MTTR).

Failure is a behavior that violates the specified behavior. So, a system that causes a service interruption is a failure. There are degrees of reliability, depending on the MTTF.

Considerations to achieve reliability include testing to ensure certain failures do not happen (such as design failures). However, testing does not achieve a high degree of reliability. It is possible to achieve a high degree of reliability by:

▶ Replication

▶ Design by contract [Meyer-97]

▶ Precise behavior specifications

▶ Formal methods

These are methods addressed by the RM-ODP FT framework.

Availability is the ratio of accomplishing a service in the elapsed time to do so. It can be computed as MTTF / (MTTF + MTTR). Availability addresses the predictability with respect to the readiness for usage, the expected fraction of time a system is able to perform its capabilities, and the degree of accessibility to an object.

Dependability is a measure of predictability that a service will deliver as expected.

16.4   RM-ODP FAULT TOLERANCE PATTERN OF REASONING

Distribution transparency, the RM-ODP functions, and behavior defined by policy and schema comprise the general RM-ODP pattern of reasoning of FT for the architect to use.

RM-ODP defines a failure model in a generic, technology-independent manner. This model defines a failure, error, and fault, and their relationships. This model is defined in terms of objects and their relationships realized through interactions and behavior. Dependable systems are supported by such a failure model.

In addition, semantics are defined by the architect based on events with defined expectations on value, location space, time space, and actions to take when a failure is detected.

To accomplish this formidable task, however, well-defined concepts are crucial in understanding what is meant by failure, fault, error detection, and FT. When a failure is detected, it must be evaluated against some defined possible failure mode: an action that is observed and does not adhere to what is expected to happen.

16.4.1 FAULT TOLERANT MODEL

There are a number of defined concepts in RM-ODP that are used to provide the model for fault tolerance.

A *group* is a collection of objects that have some relationship, either structural or behavioral. This is the first basic concept used. It enables discussion of a collection of objects by defining the properties that cause them to be addressed as a single entity (group). An example of a group is an address group. This is a group where the objects are addressed in the same way.

A *replica group* is a group where each instance of the group is identical (or cloned). In RM-ODP, a replica group consists of corresponding objects across a set of replicated clusters. Each object in the cluster forms a replica group with its cloned object in the replicated clusters. A replica group across replicated clusters is shown in Figure 16.2. In this figure, there are three replicated clusters. Within each cluster, there are two objects. The group of all object A across all three clusters forms one replica group; the group of all object B across all three clusters forms another replica group.

A *fault group* is a special group where the objects are treated as a single entity in case of some fault. That is, the group as a whole may fail if some fault occurs, or may be collectively reactivated to a previously stable state.

A *fault-tolerant replication group* is a group of objects that participates in a sequence of defined interactions providing fault tolerance in the case of some faults.

Failure is the condition when the expected behavior, as defined by a contract, is violated in some way or does not adhere to the specified behavior. [RM-ODP-2]

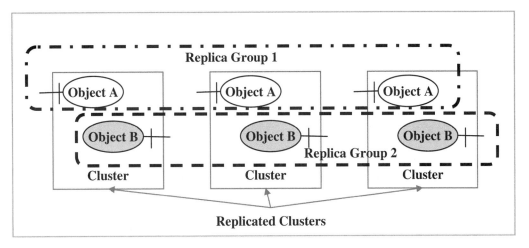

FIGURE 16.2 Replica Groups and Replicated Clusters

The ways in which an object fails are called *failure modes*. These can consist of *omission failure* when an expected interaction does not happen, a *persistent omission failure* which amounts to a crash, some *incorrectness* due to an untimely behavior (timing failure), or a *noncompliance* behavior with respect to the specification. A failure can be consistent only if all the objects perceive the failure in the same way. Here is where a group becomes important: all the objects perceive the failure in the same way, and are handled in the same way.

An *error* is considered an object state that may lead to a failure. Hence the infrastructure designer can decompose the object into objects that behave in such a manner as to possibly prevent an error from causing a failure.

A *fault* is a situation that may cause errors in an object. For example, a fault may be introduced as a design fault, and later in execution lead to a failure. When the fault actually produces an error it is called an *active fault*, which can only be determined by detecting an error. A fault can be part of an object state that may cause an error, or a result from an interaction or interference with the environment of the object. A fault may be temporary or permanent.

As shown in Figure 16.3, there is a tight causal dependency among fault, error, and failure in RM-ODP:

▶ A fault can lead to an error (when it is active).

▶ An error can lead to a failure (unless some fault tolerant behavior is introduced).

▶ A failure happens when an error affects the correct behavior of the system components.

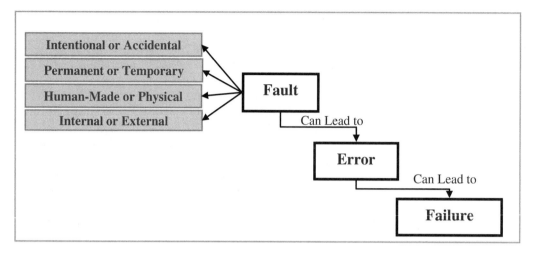

FIGURE 16.3   Fault, Error, and Failure Dependencies

A fault can be intentional or accidental. That is, a fault may be the result of a design error, or created deliberately. A fault can be human-made or physical. A physical fault may result from a hardware failure. A fault can be permanent or temporary. An example is a design error that always produces an error, or a temporary inability to bind to an interface. Finally, a fault can be internal or external. An internal fault is a part of the object state that causes an error. An external fault is a result of some interaction or negative impact from the environment.

Finally, *stability* is defined as that property of an object that prohibits it from exhibiting a particular failure mode.

To achieve FT, the system must be able to detect a failure and to recover from it. To accomplish this, the system must analyze a current state of the configuration of interacting objects and determine what failures cannot be tolerated within well-defined bounds (or behavior). This determination is then compared with specific defined policies that capture the behavior that cannot be tolerated, and the action to take by the infrastructure to recover:

▶ A failed object is recovered to a stable state in its environment.

▶ A set of failed objects (e.g., in a cluster) are collectively recovered to a stable state in their environment.

▶ A failed object is recovered to a stable state and moved to a stable environment.

▶ A set of failed objects are recovered to a stable state and moved to a stable environment.

▶ A bound interface that has failed is recovered to a stable binding, either in the same channel or a separate channel.

▶ An event history of recovered actions is made persistent.

▶ Notification to failed objects that have been recovered is performed.

RM-ODP provides several mechanisms that can support the detection of a failure, alternative ways to achieve recovery, and the semantics associated with what must happen. That is, RM-ODP identifies what objects are affected, and what behavior must be exhibited upon failure. It describes what objects detect a failure in the infrastructure, what mechanisms must be in place to capture the required actions on failure, and how these mechanisms are transparent to the application developer. It suggests mechanisms to provide the application with more dependability than may be offered by, for example, Common Object Request Broker Architecture (CORBA), Distributed Computing Environment (DCE), or some other infrastructure mechanism. In fact, the emerging Fault Tolerant CORBA [FT-Corba-1] uses some of these mechanisms to achieve FT in an Object Request Broker (ORB).

The FT patterns of reasoning are captured in the computational viewpoint addressing objects and their interactions, the information viewpoint for capturing the fault tolerant policies and schemata and associated semantics, and the engineering viewpoint for defining the fault tolerant infrastructure and communication mechanisms across nodes or in an open manner. The engineering viewpoint mechanisms include the RM-ODP functions and associated policies, as well as the distribution transparencies and associated schema. Chief among the RM-ODP functions for FT are the Replication, Checkpoint/Recovery, Migration, Management, and Relocation functions. Chief among the distribution transparencies for fault tolerance are failure, replication, and migration transparency.

There are different engineering viewpoint patterns to achieve FT. One requires a duplicate instance of an object (replication) that acts in conjunction with its duplicate, resulting in the same state. Another is to periodically provide a checkpoint of the objects for FT, retain the checkpoints, and recover the object to a previously checkpointed state.

Detecting a failure is part of both mechanisms, and requires a mechanism to check on the well being of the objects and their interfaces, and to be notified of any failure that occurs. This mechanism requires that each object subject to FT provide a special interface that is bound to a control object. The control object then manages the state of objects, detects faults, detects errors, and detects failures. This control object also initiates, or actually performs, the mechanisms to recover. Recovering from a failure can therefore include any of:

▶ Invoke a replica object to take over the processing, deactivating the failed replica.

▶ Restore an object to a previous checkpoint state, either in the same environment or a different environment, and ensure all interfaces are similarly restored.

▶ Restore the communication binding, if it failed, and restore the bound interface to a new binding, transparent to the receiving object.

▶ Ensure the transparency of these mechanisms through actions and statements of policy.

▶ Record all such event histories.

All of these mechanisms and their actions must be defined by policies for FT. The FT policies identify the objects to be addressed, the constraints on the actions, an indication of validity for which the policy holds, and possibly other properties.

16.4.2　FT Semantics

Semantic behavior plays a very important part of the specification of any system. RM-ODP provides a roadmap of how to specify the necessary behavior for interacting objects. In order to specify the mechanisms of fault tolerance, one must use the semantics concepts that constrain the actions of these mechanisms. The principal concepts include template, contract, policy, schema, and an environment contract. (See Chapter 8, "Composition and Semantics: Quality Composition Minimizing Architectural Mismatch," for more details.)

To recap from previous chapters, a *contract* in RM-ODP defines the behavior of a set of objects. It includes QoS properties, duration of validity, behavior that violates the contract, and includes one or more policies. A *policy* defines the permitted, obligated, and prohibited rules of interacting components related to a specific purpose, such as a failure policy. A *template* defines the object or interface. It includes statements of expected behavior, in terms of constraints and rules associated with the specified actions.

Of particular importance to FT, the FT object and interface templates that are used for the FT mechanisms specify the fault-tolerance–specific activities. For example, one FT mechanism might be an object that performs checkpoint on other objects. The template for this checkpoint object might specify that it provides an interface for use by any other object to allow it to perform the checkpoint action.

An example for a checkpoint object template, and one of its possible interface templates, is shown in Figure 16.4. In this figure, types are associated with the template entities. An interface reference is associated with the checkpoint interface. An object template includes the interface templates of all interfaces it uses, or offers to another object for use. An interface template for the actions associated with the checkpoint object is shown. The constraints associated with the checkpoint object interface are identified in this figure. This is only an example. The architect will no doubt include more specificity.

For a system to be able to detect an error, the system must determine what failures cannot be tolerated within well-defined bounds (or behavior). This determination is then compared with policies, capturing the behavior that must occur, cannot occur, and is permitted to occur, along with the actions to be taken by the infrastructure mechanisms to recover from failure.

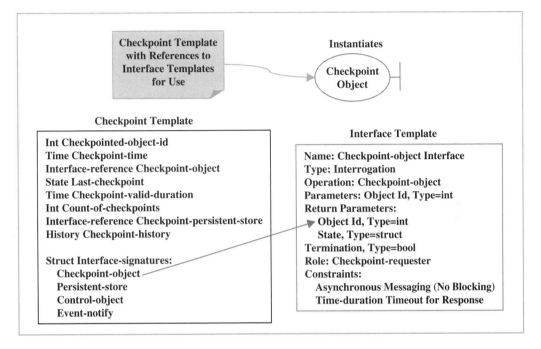

FIGURE 16.4 Example Checkpoint Object Template and an Interface Template

Fundamental to the FT model, a *contract* defines the correct behavior and the actions to take on failure. It includes roles an object may assume, duration of validity, behavior that violates the contract, and one or more policies.

Policies play a very important part of the FT model. All of the FT policies define permitted, obligated, and prohibited rules. In FT, some of the policies include a checkpoint/recovery policy, a dependability policy, a replication policy, and so forth, depending on the choice of mechanisms to enable fault tolerance. Any of the FT policies specify:

▶ The objects to be addressed

▶ The constraints on the actions; these include:

– The required behavior, such as each object subject to FT must provide an interface for a control object, and must allow itself to be checkpointed to a particular state

– The permitted behavior, such as any of the previous five checkpoint states can be used to recover an object to a stable state

– The prohibited behavior, such as a certain failure mode is not allowed to occur

◗ An indication of validity for which the policy holds

◗ Possibly other properties

Specification of contracts and policies provides a means to describe failure modes. This allows the behavior of failure detection mechanisms to be stated, as well as the behavior of the mechanisms that enforce FT expectations. These result in model constraints that reflect what failures can and cannot be tolerated, what actions to perform under failure, and what results to be recorded and notified to objects that are identified.

As an example, Figure 16.5 shows an overview of a possible checkpoint/recovery policy. This policy would be associated with the Checkpoint/Recovery object in the infrastructure. Notice that the policy is stated in terms of "obligated," "permitted," and "prohibited." The architect can specify any such policy in whatever language is deemed appropriate. In this example, the policy is represented as a note that would be associated with a class in a UML collaboration diagram.

The contract between objects is crucial in setting expectations. Present technology allows only very weak contracts (e.g., interface definition languages only define signatures). Stronger contract representations will allow better failure detection mechanisms to be built. Strong policy representation is emerging through such tools as iContract. For FT, each target object of FT focus must provide a management control interface for use in a number of FT actions.

> ### : Checkpoint/Recovery Policy
>
> + Obligated to Checkpoint in Time Interval "T'"
> + Permitted to Use Last Checkpoint for Recovery
> + Permitted to Use Persistent Store
> + Obligated to Make Checkpoints Persist
> + Obligated to Perform Recovery on Failure
> + Obligated to Initiate Recovery on Notification
> + Permitted to Use Location A for B or Recovery
> + Obligated to Notify Control Object of Recovery
> + Prohibited From Not Checkpointing Object
> + Obligated to Checkpoint State, Types, Bindings, Interfaces
> + Obligated to Checkpoint Designated Objects

FIGURE 16.5   Example UML Note for Checkpoint/Recovery Policy

16.4.3   RM-ODP Mechanisms for Use in Support of Fault Tolerance

In RM-ODP, the general fault-tolerant mechanisms comprise distribution transparency, the RM-ODP functions, a Failure Control object[1], policies that define the behavior of the ODP functions, and schema that define the permitted states of the transparency objects.

In a fault-tolerant system, fault management needs to address the following:

▶ Identification of objects subject to fault tolerance

▶ Fault detection, to include detecting where the fault exists, and identifying associated failure modes

▶ Fault notification to inform all appropriate objects of a fault, as defined by a policy

▶ Fault analysis to determine the actions to take, based on the failure mode detected and policy that determine the action

▶ Fault recovery (to the extent possible), which addresses recovery of one or more objects to a stable state, restoring bound interfaces as needed, and movement of one or more object to a more stable environment

A pattern of reasoning to provide fault tolerance for an object or a group of objects typically includes:

▶ Checkpoint and recovery of the subject objects

▶ Replication, to provide a backup of the object, allowing it to be restored from a given state, thus enhancing stability

▶ Control, to manage the state of objects, detect faults, detect errors, and detect failures, and to invoke the mechanisms to restore the objects to a stable state

Other architectures also describe similar patterns of reasoning, and specify the interfaces and semantics associated with the pattern of reasoning. The Fault Tolerant CORBA 3.0 provides such a specification. [FT-Corba-1, FT-Corba-2]

RM-ODP provides additional patterns of reasoning as well. FT can be accomplished by mechanisms to relocate the object and its interfaces to a more stable execution environment; and cooperation of the objects through an interface that enables their state to be assessed, enables the state to be checkpointed, and enables the object to be notified of a recovery in order to take some additional action. In addition, RM-ODP describes a pattern or reasoning for migrating an interface that is bound to a channel. In this case, the binding is restored, transpar-

---

1. RM-ODP identifies and specifies a control object for controlling a number of things. For FT, such an object is required. Whether this object is distinguished from other potential control objects, or is part of an object's actions, is a decision not addressed by RM-ODP. This chapter has named the control object for FT the "Failure Control object," which is not a term used in RM-ODP.

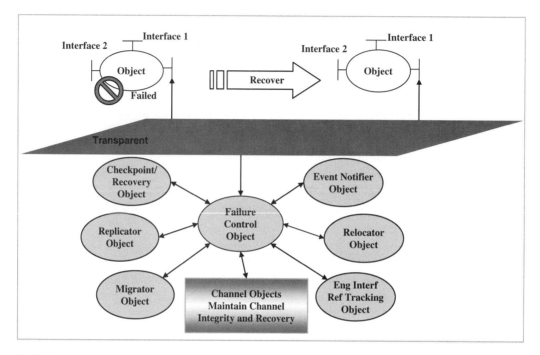

FIGURE 16.6   Overview of ODP Functions Supporting FT Mechanisms

ently to the objects affected by the failure and any object interface part of the binding. All of these mechanisms and their actions are defined by policies for fault tolerance.

RM-ODP addresses all of these, as well as distribution transparencies to hide the complexities of achieving FT from the application developer. Figure 16.6 provides an overview of the principal objects involved in FT, to recover an object and its interfaces, which is made transparent to the object affected.

16.4.4   ODP FUNCTION MECHANISMS

The pattern of reasoning for the processing in the infrastructure is described as part of the ODP functions. The relationship and use of the ODP functions in support of FT is shown in Figure 16.7. Each of these functions is highlighted in this section. See Chapter 9, "RM-ODP Functions," for a more detailed discussion of each of the functions.

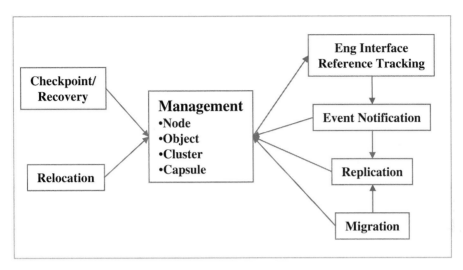

FIGURE 16.7   ODP Function Support for Fault Tolerance

Chief among the RM-ODP functions for fault tolerance are Checkpoint/Recovery, Replication, Migration, Relocation, Deactivation/Reactivation, Notification, Engineering Interface Reference Tracking (EIRT), and Management functions. These functions interrelate to provide different aspects of FT—from fault detection through fault recovery. Each function is driven by a specific policy, which is highlighted in the discussion. The infrastructure Failure Control object coupled with the ODP function objects provide the functionality required to detect an error or fault, and to recover from a failure to the extent possible.

16.4.4.1   Failure Control Object

To provide for the stability of the object, every object for which FT is designated must provide a control interface for use by a control object. In this chapter, this is identified as a Failure Control object. This object is principal in detecting a failure, analyzing the failure in terms of failure modes, analyzing what action to take as directed by the various policies and schema involved, and invoking the appropriate ODP function object, in accordance with the distribution transparencies defined, to attempt the recovery of a failed object. That is, this object initiates the actions to use a replica object as backup, or migrate and relocate objects and interfaces; deletes the unstable object, interfaces, and channel in use; and recovers the object and interfaces to a stable environment.

A Failure Control object monitors subject objects, detects failure, analyzes the failure, and invokes the appropriate infrastructure objects to inform, record, and recover a failure. This object can consist of one or more objects, as defined by the architecture, can be replicated across multiple nodes, or exist only within a single node, as per the architecture specification. RM-ODP does not dictate a particular architecture; rather, it defines what needs to be done, how to specify choices of actions, and what interactions need to occur to restore the system to a stable state. The architectural decisions must address if there are timers that designate duration of validity for a policy (that directs what must be done), and whether there are one or more instances of an FT object in a node, or across nodes (federated).

Cross-domain FT can be federated through the Failure Control object actions. These actions would be associated with the control object of each domain associated with the federation. As such, the actions address the federation policies, the scope of the domains, the rules of interaction, and uses of the channel for mediation and negotiation across the domains. More about federation can be found in Chapter 15, "Federation."

16.4.4.2   Checkpoint and Recovery

The Checkpoint and Recovery function is used to provide a stable state of an object or a group of objects, as defined by a checkpoint/recovery policy. Use of this function is generally associated with other functions, such as the cluster manager function. A policy defines what constraints are placed on actions, and under what conditions, to perform checkpoint and recovery.

To checkpoint an object or a group of objects requires the Failure Control object to coordinate the actions of checkpointing, determine the stability of the object state before it is checkpointed, coordinate the checkpoint of all objects in a replica group, checkpoint the state of each object in replicated clusters, and so forth.

It may be that the environment in which a group of objects is active becomes unstable. In this case, the action desired, and specified by the architect, may be to move the objects to a stable environment. ODP functions allow for a previous checkpoint to be used to establish the group of objects in a new environment, almost imperceptible to the objects being moved. To do this requires other functions. The Migration function moves the object. The Recovery function recovers the object. The Reactivate/Deactivate function activates the moved objects, and deactivates their previously unstable cluster. As can be seen, the ODP functions interrelate in support of failure recovery.

The policy may state that a history of all interactions and associated object states be retained. In this case, the Failure Control object records this information to a persistent store, using the ODP Storage function. The policy may state that the object subject to recovery is to be notified of recovery. In this case, the Failure Control object uses the ODP Notify function to inform the object of a recovery. The purpose for this is to allow the recovered object to re-execute previous interactions that perhaps were not captured by the checkpoint actions because they may have occurred after the checkpointed state. In addition, the Failure Control object may perform the checkpoint actions and recovery actions in the infrastructure, or may interact with another object to do so. This is dependent on the architectural specification of the composition of the Failure Control object.

16.4.4.3 Replication

The Replication function is about cloning an object and all of its interfaces. The resultant group of replicated objects is referred to as a replica group. The Replication function ensures that the replica group performs in the same manner as the original entity, to include participating in all interactions. A replica policy defines the membership of the replica group, which object can change the replica group, rules for when an object can enter (be cloned) as a single atomic action, or leave the group, and where replica objects are placed. Though the replica objects are placed in clusters, these clusters may span distributed nodes. Herein is a reason to consider an open system approach to FT.

The Replication function is important in many FT solutions today. In these cases, when a failure occurs, one of the replicas is designated to be activated in place of the failed object, and the failed object deactivated. If there are more than two replicas, then the policy must indicate which replica is to be activated.

The FT CORBA specification services in support of FT are similar to RM-ODP FT patterns of reasoning, using the replication mechanism. A representation of the FT CORBA is provided in Figure 16.8.

The objective for FT CORBA is to provide an interface standard supporting the functionality of fault-tolerant applications such that the clients of these applications will be largely insulated from such details as management of redundant copies (replication), failure masking (transparency), and recovery. That is, in terms of RM-ODP, replication and failure transparency are the principal mechanisms in this standard.

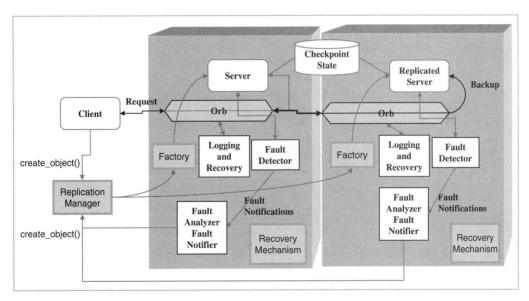

FIGURE 16.8 FT CORBA

The FT CORBA includes passive and active replication, automatic and application-controlled FT, and strong replica consistency when needed. Checkpoint provides persistent store. The details of the interface signatures, the policies, and the operations in support of each component in the infrastructure are defined in the FT CORBA standard.

In FT CORBA, the client interfaces with the replication manager to create an object. The replication manager instantiates, through the object factory, a primary server and one or more replicated servers. Each server uses the persistent storage retaining the checkpoint state of the primary server.

A single replica manager manages each FT domain and interprets policies. FT CORBA creates replica object groups (groups of identical objects), and organizes them into fault tolerance domains. [FT-Corba-3]

The replication manager object, like the Fault Tolerant control object, manages groups of objects. If a fault is detected, the backup server is instantiated to take over the client requests. Logging of all such faults is provided in each server location.

FT CORBA details the engineering structure and interfaces to address specifics and also provides the mechanisms for monitoring of faults, checkpoint/recovery actions, fault analysis, fault notification, logging, and management of recovery operations. A notification service is available for use, but it is not required.

Most of the mechanisms defined in [FT-Corba-2, FT-Corba-3] have a counterpart in RM-ODP, as shown in Table 16.1. There are differences, though, in the details. RM-ODP does not define a specific structure (such as a specific Interface Description Language), but rather leaves this to the architect. What occurs in terms of actions and behavior are defined in RM-ODP, and seem to be the same as in the FT CORBA. The mechanisms identified for a server replica (in case of a failure) are unique to the FT CORBA proposal, and do not correspond with the RM-ODP FT framework. The mechanisms to specify the engineering constructs of this capability, however, such as interface binding conditions, are similar to the RM-ODP constructs. The concepts, rules of structure, and behavior of the FT CORBA and RM-ODP FT framework are surprisingly similar. Table 16.1 summarizes some of the consistencies between FT CORBA and RM-ODP.

TABLE 16.1 Consistencies Between FT CORBA and RM-ODP

FT CORBA CAPABILITY	RM-ODP FT MECHANISM
Active replication	Replication function, replication transparency
Automatic and application-controlled FT	Dependent on the policies
Strong replica consistency	Replication function
Replica manager for FT domain	Replicator object and Failure Control object
Replica object groups	Clusters of replica objects
Manager object	Failure Control object

TABLE 16.1 Consistencies Between FT CORBA and RM-ODP (Continued)

FT CORBA CAPABILITY	RM-ODP FT MECHANISM
Fault notification	Event Notification function
Management of recovery operations	Checkpoint/Recovery function; failure transparency
Monitoring of faults	Failure modes defined in policies, Failure Control object
Checkpoint/recovery	Checkpoint/Recovery function; failure transparency
Logging of events	Event histories
Activation	Deactivation/Reactivation function
Object references	Engineering interface reference
Checkpoint and persistent store	Checkpoint/Recovery function with persistent store; Persistence transparency
Replication policies	Replication policy, replication schema
Object replica reference	EIRT function
Notification service	Notification function
Detected failure in the communication	Binder action
Cross-domain replication	Part of federation and interception

16.4.4.4 Event Notification

The Event Notification function manages events. When a failure event occurs, this function notifies the appropriate Failure Control object of the event, as defined by an event notification policy, and possibly both the capsule and cluster manager objects. In addition, the Failure Control object can use this function to notify recovered objects of the act of recovery. The policy addresses behavior in terms of which object can create event histories, which objects are notified, when notifications occur, and associated persistence and stability of event histories.

16.4.4.5 Engineering Interface Reference Tracking

The ODP EIRT function maintains information about the interfaces of an object, and manages the information about the use of all object interfaces. In RM-ODP, an engineering interface reference is a logical reference to an interface. The principal use of this function for FT is to track the stability of the binding of interfaces, determine when the binding has failed, and notify the manager object of such failure, as directed by an EIRT policy. It is here that the group manager object can begin the process of recovery. The policy for the EIRT function defines the actions that take place. If an interface is relocated, the EIRT function manages the new location information, and associates it with the old location, for a specified period of time.

Figure 16.9 shows the ODP function mechanisms that could be included in an architecture specification, if Checkpoint/Recovery, Replication, and Notification are used as part of the FT mechanism. Each function is represented as an engineering object in this figure, such as the Migrator object for the Migration function. The object performs the actions specified in the ODP function. The gray "schema" is shown. These schemata are used to constrain the function if a particular transparency is involved.

WARNING

A policy is associated with an ODP function. A schema is associated with an RM-ODP transparency. RM-ODP does not make clear why one is a policy and one is a schema, or how a policy and schema are related. When the ODP Relocation function is specified, for example, a replication policy constrains the Replication object. If replication transparency is also specified, a replication schema constrains the actions associated with the transparency-related objects, such as the Replication object. How the replication policy and replication schema are related, which takes precedence, and so forth, are not discussed in RM-ODP.

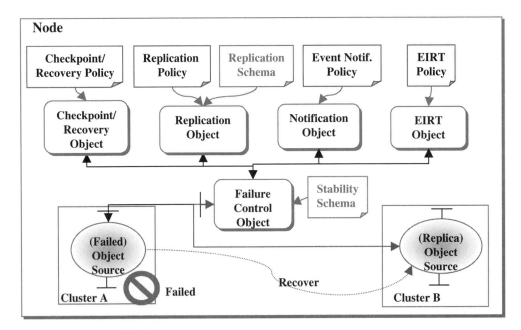

FIGURE 16.9   Use of Checkpoint/Recovery and Replication for Fault Tolerance

In the case of the FT Control object, the stability schema is associated with the failure transparency constraints. The replication schema is associated with the Replicator object. It details some of the constraints associated with replication transparency. Figure 16.10 provides an overview of the kinds of information to be specified in the shown policies and schema.

16.4.4.6 Deactivation and Reactivation

The RM-ODP Deactivation function is used to delete an object group (which can be a replication cluster or a replica group). To do this, it first determines a checkpoint of each object in the group, makes the combined checkpoints persistent, and then deletes the object group. This function can also reactivate an object group to the same environment or a different more stable environment, or even a different node. These actions are governed by a policy that defines when the object group is to be deactivated, when they should be reactivated, which checkpoint (of possibly several) should be used (e.g., the last one), and when the group of objects should be reactivated.

16.4.4.7 Migration

The Migration function enables the movement of an object or a cluster. This function is very important to move an object to a stable environment. If a cluster is to be migrated, all objects of that cluster are migrated, as well as all interfaces of those objects. A migration policy defines the migration rules. If migration transparency is involved, a mobility schema constrains the actions of the Migration object.

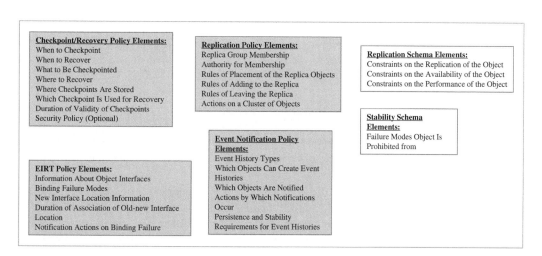

FIGURE 16.10 Policy and Schema Elements for Checkpoint/Recovery and Replication

Migration is an alternative method to use for FT, instead of Replication. Moving an object is different from activating a replica, which must always maintain a copy of the object and its interfaces. Instead, the Migration function:

▶ Creates a new cluster in a stable environment

▶ Instantiates the object template in the new cluster, and all other objects in that cluster

▶ Instantiates the object interfaces

▶ Binds the new object (and all other objects in the cluster that form a failure replica group) to the Failure Control object

▶ Deactivates the old (failed) cluster

▶ Activates the recovered (new) object to the checkpoint state, as specified by the Checkpoint/Recovery object, as well as all other objects in the cluster

The object itself is not moved, but the object template is re-used. Hence, a duplicate copy of the object is not needed, and therefore, the extra system resources to maintain a copied object are not necessary. Notice that the use of migration for failure recovery requires the use of the Failure Control object, any objects it depends upon such as the Event Notification and EIRT function objects, as well as the Checkpoint/Recovery object, the Deactivate/Reactivate object, and possibly other engineering objects.

Figure 16.11 provides an overview of the use of the Migration object, and supporting objects, to provide failure recovery, along with some of the policy and schema elements for Deactivation/Reactivation and Migration objects.

16.4.4.8   Relocation

The ODP Relocation function provides the ability to relocate a bound interface. With FT, the recovery is focused on the bound interface. Replication, on the other hand, defines actions associated with a specified interface, not one that is actively participating in a binding. Only the Relocation function recovers a bound interface.

The function must maintain the mapping of the old location to the new location of those object interfaces it relocates. The function may, therefore, make use of other ODP function objects to do so, such as the EIRT function object, which maintains a persistent store of interface locations and includes a mapping of the old location to the new location.

A relocation policy defines communication monitoring rules and the channel rules for repairing a failed binding in the channel. That is, to repair a binding means to re-establish a new binding, or channel, restore the interface bindings, and make this all transparent to the interfaces that were bound. This is much like repairing a broken browser binding, without affecting the state of the browser or making it aware that the connection has been interrupted or repaired.

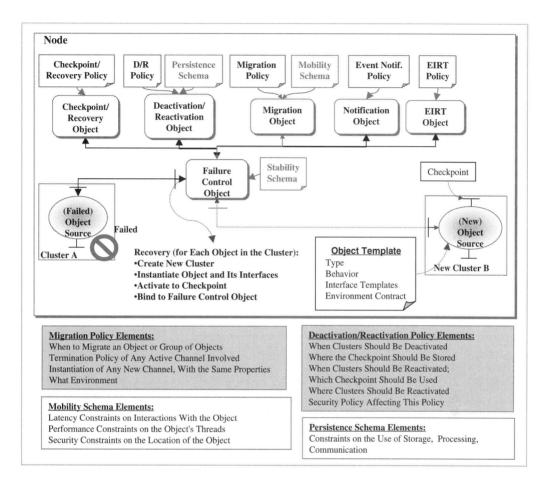

FIGURE 16.11 Migration for Fault Tolerance

As such, the channel binder object may interact with the Relocator object, and by policy, obtain the engineering interface references for use in repairing the binding. Figure 16.12 provides an overview of the use of the Relocation object to support FT, along with the additional policy and schema elements pertinent to the Relocator object. Once again, the schema is a set of constraints on the Relocator object, associated with the relocation transparency.

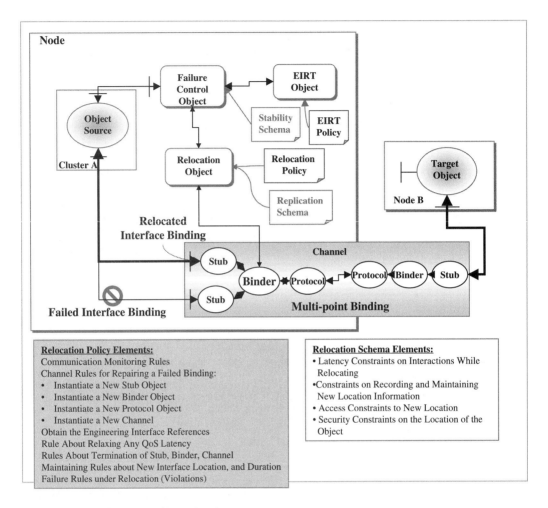

FIGURE 16.12   Relocation for Fault Tolerance

16.4.4.9   Management

The Object management function object (i.e., the Failure Control object) uses a required management interface of all objects to enable checkpoint of the objects. The Object manager is also used to delete an object through this special interface.

There are two other manager objects that play a part in FT: the Cluster manager and the Capsule manager. The Cluster manager object provides the checkpoint, recovery, and migration capabilities for the objects in its cluster, as well as deletion of the entire group of objects. A cluster management policy defines the actions that allow the checkpoint function to act on each object in the cluster.

In similar fashion, the Capsule manager object manages the group of clusters. It is used to checkpoint or recover a group of objects within its environment. To accomplish this, it uses a management interface to each designated object. The Capsule manager object can also delete any of the clusters in its environment, or itself (and all clusters within its environment). It too is directed by a policy.

16.4.5   TRANSPARENCY MECHANISMS

Transparency plays an important role in FT. The transparency mechanisms of RM-ODP are realized through the use of the ODP functions, the Failure Control object, the channel objects, and possibly objects that realize a particular transparency. (See Chapter 10, "Hiding System Complexities: Distribution Transparencies," for more information about the distribution transparencies.) Some of the distribution transparencies are used to mask the intricacies and complexities of FT computation from the application developer. Of course, the architect is very much aware of the complexity, and must specify the mechanisms of the system to support the computation.

Of importance to FT are the following:

▶ Failure transparency hides the failure and recovery of an object, or object group. This is the principal transparency supporting FT.
▶ Replication transparency hides the use of a replicated group of objects to support an interface.
▶ Persistence transparency hides from an object the deactivation and reactivation of objects (including the object itself).
▶ Migration transparency hides from an object and interacting objects changes in the location of that object.
▶ Relocation transparency hides changes in the location of a bound interface from other interfaces that may be bound to it.
▶ Access transparency hides the details of invocation and data representation in order to support interactions between objects, within or across heterogeneous systems.
▶ Location transparency hides the details of name and address used to locate interface information and bind to interfaces.

The transaction transparency does not play a role in FT.

16.4.5.1   Failure Transparency

Stability is the objective in this transparency. Failures can result from a number of things. Examples include failure to bind, failure to meet a QoS capability, failure due to some security restriction, failure to respond to an invocation, failure to locate an interface reference, etc. When an object is involved in a failure, the object may be made aware of the mode of failure.

When a failure is detected, failure transparency hides the mechanisms and details from the application developer to recover (to the extent possible) to a stable state.

Failure transparency specifies the ODP functions to use. The Replication function is used to clone an object for use as a backup in case of failure. The Checkpoint and Recovery function is used to checkpoint an object (or object group), and the checkpoint is made persistent. The Migration object is used to relocate the object, and the Relocator object is used to move or relocate any currently bound object interfaces. Relocation transparency is required if the cluster is relocated.

The mechanisms and metadata required are summarized below:

Mechanisms

▶ The object and its state must be visible to an object responsible for failure transparency (the Failure Control object).

▶ The interfaces of the object must be known, as well as the information about the interfaces (metadata).

▶ Checkpoint and recovery actions must be applied to the object.

▶ The object must provide an interface for use by the failure transparency object (i.e., Failure Control object).

▶ The Failure Control object either uses or is refined into other objects for failure management: management objects, Event Notification object, Relocator, Migrator, Replicator, etc.

Metadata

▶ The engineering interface reference provides the metadata needed about the interfaces of the object.

▶ The failure modes that are visible to the object and will be notified to the object must be specified in the object template or contract specification. Types of such failure modes include violation of security, violation of QoS, violation of an interface operation, etc.

▶ A stability schema for failure for an object is specified. It defines the failures the object is prohibited from. An example is the failure to perform an operation in an interface. It also defines the actions to take under each of the failure modes. An example is to notify the object of the failure and failure mode, and to recover the object to a previously checkpointed valid state.

▶ A persistence schema is specified that defines constraints on the use of storage, processing, and communication.

▶ A replication schema is specified that defines constraints on the availability of the object, and constraints on the performance of the object being replicated.

▶ A mobility schema for migration is specified that defines latency constraints on the interactions with the object, performance constraints on the object's threads, and security constraints on the location of the object.

16.4.5.2 Replication, Relocation, Migration, Persistence, Access, and Location Transparencies

Replication transparency is used to replicate an object or group of objects, into a replica group. To accomplish replicating the object, the engineering infrastructure must include a Replicator object that performs the actions of the ODP Replication function. Those actions may either replicate the object or the object replica. The replica object can serve as a backup and to take over should one of the replicas fail. These actions are constrained by the replication schema, and the Replication function policy must contain a specification of the allowable actions to occur for an object or cluster.

The relocation transparency requires all the support infrastructure mechanisms for the ODP Relocation function. A Relocator object must be included in the infrastructure to support moving the object's interfaces to a more stable state. Changes in the location of an object are notified to all Relocator objects. The communications mechanism may be required to exchange additional information to ensure the validity of the new binding upon relocation. If there has been a failure detected, the channel binder object involved in the communications mechanism is required to validate the engineering interface references for the interfaces that were bound, and re-establish the communication binding if necessary. If the communications is subject to a failure, the Relocator object will restore the object (or object group).

The migration transparency also requires all the support infrastructure mechanisms for the ODP Migration function. A Migration object must be included in the infrastructure to support moving the object to a more stable state. A mobility schema is defined to include the latency constraints on the interactions, performance constraints on the object threads, and security constraints on the new location of the object. The Migration function infrastructure object is charged with coordinating the location of an object in support of the schema constraints. In addition to this schema, the Migration function is bound by a migration policy. This policy, like other policies, defines what must be to accomplish migration of an object or object group.

The persistence transparency is based on the Deactivation and Reactivation ODP function. This function coordinates the object group according to a persistence schema that defines the constraints on the use of processing, storage, and communications capabilities in the infrastructure. To accomplish persistence transparency requires an object that performs the Deactivation and Reactivation function, is constrained by the deactivation/reactivation policy for this function, and uses the Relocator object to enable the reactivation of an object's interface.

The function policy defines when an object is deactivated, reactivated, what actions are to be performed, and how long the policy is valid.

The location transparency allows an object to identify and use an interface without identifying the location of that interface. The infrastructure provides the mapping between the engineering interface reference, interface template, and physical location. The access transparency enables the binding between appropriate interfaces, and the communication mechanisms, to support object interaction. The communications mechanisms of RM-ODP are specified as separate objects, and in this case, provide the actions to support data representation conversions, marshalling and unmarshalling of parameters, and use of a canonical data representation. They also support these actions across domain boundaries.

16.5   FAULT TOLERANT MODEL IN UML AND OCL

Representing the fault tolerance constructs in the Unified Modeling Language (UML) is somewhat difficult. The UML functional behavior can be represented, but the constraints associated with policy or schema are difficult to represent. Furthermore, since policy is most likely a composition of other policies, the representation in UML using an enterprise viewpoint is currently being investigated. [EDOC-UML, EDOC-UMLa]

One mechanism of representing policy in UML is to specify the policy as a class, and to use each of the parameters of the policy as constraints on the relationships among the objects assuming roles in the collaboration diagram or a further refinement in a state diagram where temporal properties can be made explicit.

Based on current work coupled with extensions provided by this chapter, Figure 16.13 shows a possible way to represent policy in the enterprise viewpoint, and shows some possible RM-ODP parameterization of the checkpoint/recovery policy. The Checkpoint/Recovery function is represented as an enterprise class, *Enterprise Object*, fulfilling some role, *Checkpoint/Recovery*, in the system. These roles identify the processing that the system must accomplish, constrained by policy. A policy may constrain the occurrence of a specific step in a process, or multiple steps, or result in additional objects in the system model. This may result in additional steps, creation of processes, or termination of processes.

One way to represent policy is as an association class that constrains the object assigned to a role. [EDOC-UML] Though such a class is represented in the figure, the extension is to allow a composition of policies. In this figure, the concept of a dependability policy is shown, which may be decomposed into a checkpoint/recovery policy, and many of the other policies discussed in this chapter. Some representation of the policy elements is also shown. The actual specificity is for the architect to define; RM-ODP provides the pattern of reasoning for re-use, not the explicit details.

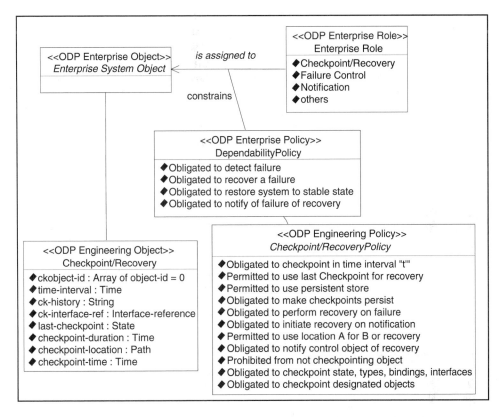

FIGURE 16.13 UML Enterprise Viewpoint Representation of Policy Example

Finally, a Recovered object is the object that results from an FT recovery action. For a UML representation, it is an instance of the same UML class of the failed object; the "Object of FT," but may be relocated to a different location, different processor, or even different node. This is dependent on the recovery policy and on checkpoint/recovery in particular.

Sometimes policy rules, such as "permitted to use a persistent store," require another object in the system, such as CheckpointStore. Sometimes policy rules, such as "permitted to capture failure event" or "permitted to notify recovered object of a failure," result in extra processing by one or more objects or additional objects in the model, such as Event Notify. Sometimes policy rules result in management objects introduced in the model to represent management and control of actions, such the Failure Control object that manages fault detection, recovery initiation, event history, and so forth. In addition, constraints, such as those expressible in the OCL [OCL1, OCL2], represent the rule (policy).

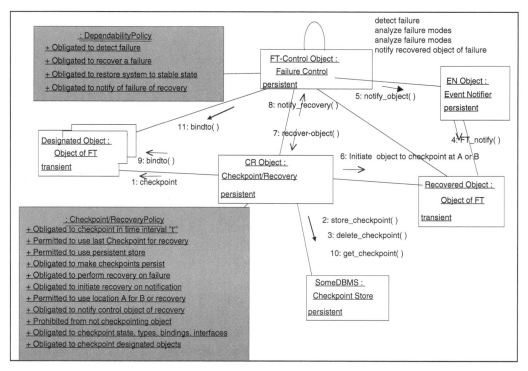

FIGURE 16.14 UML Collaboration Diagram for Replication Recovery

Figure 16.14 provides a view of a portion of the Checkpoint/Recovery and Replication functions and policies in terms of a UML collaboration diagram. This figure shows one computational viewpoint of objects that realize checkpoint and recovery actions, constrained by the policy rules. The figure shows the infrastructure objects Failure Control, Checkpoint/Recovery, Checkpoint Store, and Event Notifier for FT. In UML, these are represented as classes. The name preceding the colon is the object name of an instance of the class for purposes of the collaboration diagram. In the gray UML note box are the policy rules for checkpoint/recovery, as associated with the specific objects. This figure shows what might be the policy rules associated with the Failure Control object. Multiple policies can be represented on the same diagram, since each policy is associated with one or more specific object(s). This is only an example.

OCL statements can be used to more precisely define the semantics of policy, as discussed in Chapter 14, "Policy Framework." It is possible to use OCL statements and apply them to the collaboration diagram of UML.

An example of OCL to represent the policy obligation rule "all designated objects should be checkpointed" is:

```
Object of FT::bindto(ck-interface-ref:Checkpoint/Recovery)
pre: self.bindto.control-interface= ck-interface-ref
<<invariant>>
Object of FT
self.control-interface->forAll(control-interface, c:Checkpoint/
   Recovery) | control-interface.bindto() = c.ck-interface-ref)
```

An example of OCL to represent the permitted rule "recover an object to the last checkpoint" is:

```
Checkpoint/Recovery::recover-object (last-checkpoint:
   Checkpoint/Recovery)
self.recover-object(last-checkpoint) = self.recovered-object(state)
and self.recovered-object.OclIsTypeOf(Object of FT) -- is true
```

An example of OCL to represent the prohibited rule "cannot checkpoint designated object" is:

```
Object of FT
Collection->select(object-id:Object of FT | not (ckobject-id:
   Checkpoint/Recovery = 0) -- where ckobjbect-id=0 means empty
```

UML notes are not true UML model elements. They require manual repetition in all UML models that require these notes. UML model consistency does not address the content of the notes, or that they are even consistent across models. Hence, the semantics of the policy rules are purely English text and not subject to UML model analyses.

Figure 16.15 provides an example of the use of OCL for some of the checkpoint/recovery policy constraints, and shows how they might be attached to the UML diagram as notes. Nevertheless, since the purpose of these UML models is to communicate an architecture and design, the notes will suffice until UML vendor products begin to incorporate OCL, or some other mechanism to capture semantic constructs, into their object model. The UML diagram, though less detailed than the previous figure, represents the same elements as Figure 16.14.

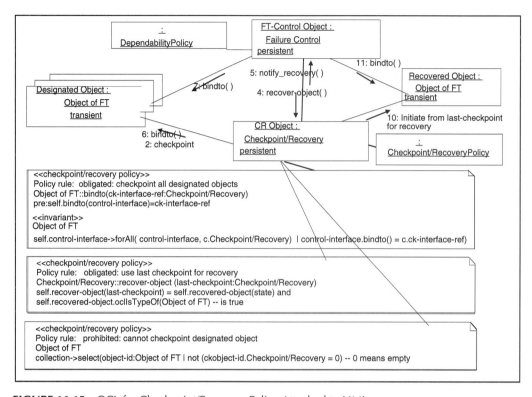

FIGURE 16.15   OCL for Checkpoint/Recovery Policy Attached to UML

16.6   SUMMARY

FT is an important system property of a distributed system that enables a dependable, reliable, and accessible system. Achieving FT is very difficult, but the ability to do so is enhanced by a well-founded framework (RM-ODP) and a rigorous well-founded specification focused on the fault tolerant semantics and mechanisms.

To achieve FT requires a number of additional infrastructure mechanisms and associated policies for governing the actions of those mechanisms. Part of the contribution from RM-ODP is a pattern of reasoning for a fault tolerant framework that consists of precise terminology, precise concepts for FT based on a failure model, different mechanisms of infrastructure services, levels of abstraction in addressing FT mechanisms, and policies to govern the behavior of the system. An overview of the patterns for choice in specifying FT of a system are summarized in Figure 16.16.

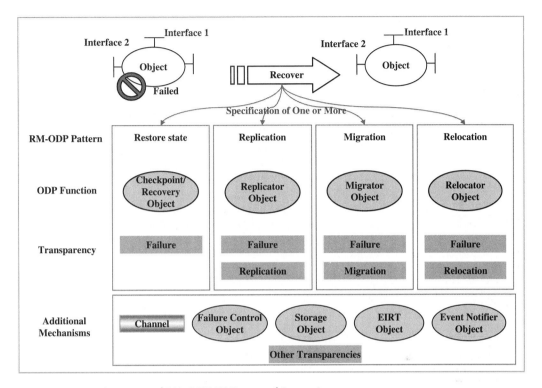

FIGURE 16.16   Summary of RM-ODP FT Pattern of Reasoning

One RM-ODP FT pattern is the use of checkpoint/recovery. In this case, the designated object subject to FT is repeatedly checkpointed. If a failure occurs, the object is recovered to one of its checkpoint states.

Another RM-ODP FT pattern is the use of replication. In this case, the designated objects subject to FT are replicated. If a failure occurs, one of the replicas takes over. This is the nature of the FT CORBA specification.

Another RM-ODP FT pattern is migration. In this case, a failed object and its interfaces are moved to a more stable environment, and reactivated through the defined object and interface templates.

Another RM-ODP FT pattern is relocation of bound interfaces. In this case, if a communication binding fails, the binding is either restored or a new channel created. Though there may be degradation of performance in relocation, the affected bound objects are not made aware of the recovery.

Another RM-ODP FT pattern is to use some combination of the previous patterns.

In most of the FT patterns, failure transparency is used to hide the complexities of FT from the application developer. If the relocation FT pattern were specified, the relocation transparency would be specified. If the replication FT pattern were specified, the replication transparency would also be specified. If the migration FT pattern were specified, the migration transparency would be specified.

Policy represents the rules that constrain the actions of the FT mechanisms. There are emerging "patterns" for representing policy in UML. In addition, policy parameters can be represented in OCL as constraints on the relationships among the UML classes or objects in a collaboration diagram.

The new FT CORBA proposal is very similar to the FT framework of RM-ODP. Extra engineering designs are included in the FT CORBA proposal, whereas precise general concepts and structuring rules (as is the case for a general reference model) are included in RM-ODP. As such, additional semantic behavior is captured in RM-ODP that currently is not defined in the FT CORBA proposal.

Achieving FT is difficult, but the ability to do so is enhanced by a well-founded framework (RM-ODP), a good representation tool (UML with a semantic tool such as OCL), and a good architectural specification of the mechanisms to achieve FT in a system (e.g., FT CORBA).

SEVENTEEN

QUALITY OF SERVICE MODEL

Quality of service (QoS) is important in realizing the expectations of users, applications, and real-time systems. There are two views to QoS. One deals with end-to-end messaging and communication in support of (generally) real-time systems. Another equally important view is end-to-end capability as required by an end user or application. The difference is that the latter may result in the need for a real-time system, but ordinarily not. The former generally results in a real-time system.

In this chapter the following are discussed:

▶ Purpose of QoS

▶ What is QoS

▶ Meeting QoS in an architecture specification

▶ Emerging QoS reference model is addressed, though much work is still needed in this area

▶ Some work in the area of QoS

The information in this chapter pertaining to the QoS reference model for RM-ODP is current. However, much work is ongoing in this area, especially by [ISO-QoS]. An excellent discussion of the importance of QoS can also be found in [Sluman-97].

17.1   PURPOSE AND MOTIVATION

Users of a system generally expect a certain quality of performance of that system. From the user's perspective, this is end-to-end. They don't care so much if a certain part of the system fails to deliver some performance, as long as the system as a whole provides the expected level of performance. Fault management, for example, is set up to make sure the system has no single point of failure, so that the user can, for the most part, continue to use the system, because the system will recover itself to a stable state. The user does not expect to know anything about this; it just happens.

Sometimes a business will desire a certain quality from a service it either commissions or buys, such as a network service. If that service fails to meet the expectations of the business, chances are the business will either buy/commission something else, or build it. For example, users today often are encouraged to participate in electronic commerce using the Internet services. If they discover that the end-to-end service is not what they anticipated, they are likely to go to a different e-commerce service. Sometimes it isn't the problem of the e-commerce application but rather the Internet service provider. In either case, the stakeholder will just look somewhere else to get the expected QoS.

In some cases, QoS is critical. Department of Defense military services rely on thresholds for when some information is provided (timeliness), as well as the level of believability in that information (accuracy). Satellite systems, both military and commercial, rely on an assured QoS to perform their function (e.g., managing visual contact of a target, or providing communications of a critical nature). The medical industry relies on critical QoS, especially in medical equipment, such as magnetic resonance imaging (MRI) machines, which must interleave the images and cannot tolerate missing or out-of-sequence images. In some applications, QoS is so critical that its failure can result in loss of life. An example of this last point is the accuracy of information to decide to issue a destruct sequence on a satellite launch vehicle so that its destruction does not affect the population on the ground. Another example of this last point is the criticality of timeliness in cases of emergency where an emergency room issues an automated request for blood from a blood bank, or a "stat" request to a surgeon.

QoS is a measure of some quality of service desired or required of a system or a part of the system. QoS permeates all parts of the system involved in providing that quality, from the business requirement through the network capabilities. Further, the QoS is additive with respect to certain qualities requested (e.g., timeliness). That is, if end-to-end timeliness of a certain value is required, every component involved in the end-to-end processing adds to the time to complete the processing. The total sum of time must then be less than or equal to the required timeliness quality property requested.

Often, QoS is a measure associated with real-time systems, a threshold of time within which a certain action must be performed. This is traditionally an a priori set of design and sizing decisions. QoS in this case deals with end-to-end connection and achieving messaging within a certain time. But QoS also applies from the business perspective, meaning end-to-end user supported service quality. Support for not only real-time QoS but also end-to-end QoS is the type of QoS model that is being formulated now.

An example of a business requested end-to-end QoS is depicted in Figure 17.1 (a modification of Figure 1.5 page 9). Here there are three business user communities, at different locations across the country. They are linked together through networking, some kind of server or servers, and processing. The image, perhaps generated by the satellite, needs to be provided within a certain amount of time, perhaps five seconds, at each location. This is an example of an end-to-end user QoS requirement with alternative architectural decisions, depending on the risk involved.

In order to achieve the five-second QoS requirement, the architect must closely analyze the choices involved to make this happen. Suppose this QoS is not of a critical or life-threatening nature. The timeliness aspects of QoS could be architected to ensure an end-to-end delivery of five seconds, but with reduced performance of resources, or ensure an end-to-end delivery of five seconds "most of

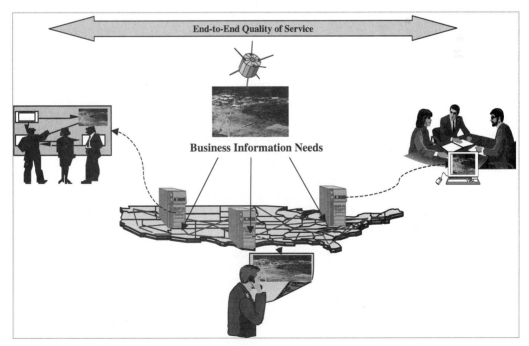

FIGURE 17.1 End-to-End User Required QoS Example

the time," resulting in a smaller loss of performance. Perhaps the satellite image is stored in a data store that is replicated to all sites. Perhaps five seconds is a desire, but not an absolute requirement. Or perhaps in order to achieve the five-second delay, the architect needs to specify a real-time system. RM-ODP doesn't provide the solution for this—only the architect's engineering skills can do so. RM-ODP provides, however, the open capability of specifying the QoS required across the communication, from the satellite down-link to each receiving site.

17.2   QUALITY OF SERVICE EXAMPLE

QoS is based on several things, some of which are mutually exclusive. These things include, but are not limited to, user requirements, system requirements, bandwidth requirements, local area network (LAN) and wide area network (WAN) QoS and latency, and coexistence with other network applications. For example, our Healthy Hospital can have two very important data and videoconferencing projects:

1. Remote consultation and diagnosis of high-resolution computed axial tomography (CAT) scans sent from another hospital

2. Streaming video for training sessions

Requirements for the first project include higher priority for data transfer than all other applications and a data rate of 40 MBit/sec with no errors. The second project's requirements include a data rate of 10 MBit/sec with a maximum of four simultaneous classes being broadcast, no interruption of the data stream, but a minimum number of dropped packets are allowed, data traffic is considered medium priority, and a voice latency of no more than 10 milliseconds. The existing network is a 100 Mbit ethernet and average network usage is 30 percent of the total bandwidth.

In the example, several conflicting requirements exist. First, CAT scan traffic can use up to 40 MBits/sec, four simultaneous class sessions can use a total of 40 MBits/sec, and average network traffic is 30 MBits/sec. The total amounts of traffic required exceeds the existing 100 MBit/sec capacity of the network; in other words, the pipe isn't big enough for all the existing data requirements. Does the architect specify bigger pipes or enforce data priority requirements? Or is the QoS not of a critical nature, so whatever can be achieved in resolution is "good enough?"

Second, transmission of the CAT scans takes priority over all other traffic. Yet, the steaming video, though medium priority, cannot be interrupted. What should happen if a CAT scan transfer is required when student classes are in session?

When developing an architecture, requirements similar to the above may need to be incorporated and conflicting priorities resolved.

The need for QoS permeates the fundamental need of end-to-end functional performance of a system that is pervasive throughout the system. QoS often is at the heart of integration needs.

17.3 WHAT IS QUALITY OF SERVICE

QoS is a set of requirements that address a quantifiable property of quality, defined independently of the means with which it is represented or controlled, and that affect the behavior of one or more objects. QoS is an abstraction of the non-functional behavior of a system. A QoS property is a measurable value. It can be specified in a contract, or measured after some event.

RM-ODP defines QoS as:

Quality of service is a group of quality characteristics that are requirements placed on the behavior of one or more objects. QoS can be measured, parameterized, reported, and observed after an event has taken place. QoS is specified in a contract. [RM-ODP-2]

Examples of QoS include a maximum value of something (four hours to record a physician consultation); a threshold (the inventory of medication cannot go lower than five units); a rate of transfer across a communication channel; a latency; the probability of a system failure; "quick" response time in accessing a database; issues of security; issues of human safety; etc. However, to express the need for QoS across heterogeneous systems and to achieve end-to-end QoS across those systems requires a language for QoS. It must consist of well-defined terms, rules that relate the terms, and rules that relate the structure of the terms. Further, the form of the specification of the language constructs, and the manner in which the QoS parameters are typed and parameterized with a value needs to be agreed to. This is often called an abstract syntax, and is used to define the language to communicate. In this way, when one system requires a threshold of five units, a receiving system will understand this request. To date, the only work attempting to achieve such a language is the International Organization for Standardization's (ISO) QoS reference model [ISO-QoS], which is addressed later in this chapter.

Such a language also enables dynamic negotiated and managed QoS. If, for example, a particular resource is consumed to near capacity, an automated management object may be architected to:

▶ Inform an administrator of a suboptimal level of resource availability

▶ Dynamically reprioritize the use of the resource according to critical QoS needs

▶ Dynamically change to the use of a backup resource

▶ Dynamically negotiate the QoS requirements to a lesser capability

▶ Some combination

Distributed systems today are heterogeneous and widely distributed. It is not reasonable to expect that all systems are real-time based. Static approaches to achieving QoS are acceptable for small closed systems, but do not scale to federations of systems. The need to share resources while achieving required or desired QoS necessitates the need for dynamic management of QoS across the systems. And the need to associate a QoS request with a criticality factor better facilitates dynamic management. Though it is expected that bandwidth on demand and self-adapting and intelligent networking will soon be possible, the need of resources always seems to precede the ability to provide the necessary resources. Consider multimedia use of resources, coupled with required quality of resolution; today's systems cannot support arbitrarily large amounts of requests for such material. Therefore, systems are needed that can evaluate a QoS need, negotiate that need, and manage the resources to provide the needed QoS. Some architectural techniques to provide dynamic management of QoS include resource reservation, reprioritization, filtering based on criticality needs, intelligent networks that can allocate higher quality bandwidth or resolution channels, and mobility to backup resources.

As an example, consider Figure 17.2, which shows a user sending a multimedia message consisting of voice, music, and video (of a dog named "Truffles"). Normal bandwidth with normal resolution can be used, but a higher resolution channel is preferred to better capture the animation. Intelligent, adaptable, and dynamic communication will soon be able to accomplish this, if it has not already. Nevertheless, the application or user needs to be able to request a higher degree of quality in the service of e-mail, in this example.

17.4   MEETING QOS IN ARCHITECTURE

Meeting the requirement for QoS most likely involves actions throughout the system, even those parts of the system that have no direct bearing on providing a QoS. This includes network connections, interactions with a database, an application interaction with the infrastructure, presentation to an end user, modification of requirements, and just about any aspect of the system.

All the parts of the infrastructure that support the pertinent messaging capabilities must support the specified QoS. In some cases, this may be so critical as to lock in guaranteed QoS at the design stage. In this case, performance requirements are predetermined. Both hardware and software are evaluated to meet those

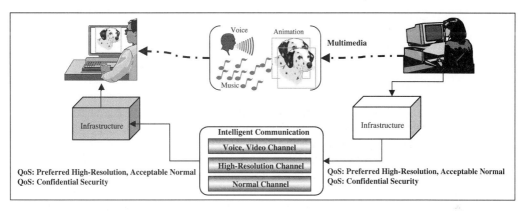

FIGURE 17.2 Quality of E-Mail Service Example

performance requirements, based on predictions or actual measured performance. Real-time controls are probably used. Once the system is operational, no further controls are used to manage the QoS. If the system does not meet the designed-in QoS, it becomes unacceptable, or fails.

Though this meets the critical real-time requirements of a system, it is insufficient for meeting end-to-end business requirements. The user should be able to specify an expected QoS on the performance of some activity, such as sending and receiving e-mail within two hours. The extensive use of the Internet has intensified, not diminished, the QoS expected by the end user. Blending multimedia transmissions into multiple simultaneous receiving sites requires management of the networking capabilities to achieve a QoS. Process control of manufacturing equipment needs QoS relating to accuracy, and possibly timeliness, safety, and security. These QoS requests are better suited to dynamic management of QoS, and dynamic allocation of resources to accommodate a QoS.

Dynamic QoS management enables systems to:

▶ Respond to changes in QoS

▶ Negotiate for better performance or whatever can be achieved

▶ Manage resources, negotiation for resource reservation and control

In the distributed heterogeneous system environment, QoS is a challenge. It requires an open systems solution, whether the QoS is statically defined or dynamically managed. QoS can affect all decisions regarding the architecture of a system and, as such, achieving QoS across non-open distributed processing systems is still state of the art.

Alternatively, using RM-ODP provides an open system method of handling QoS requirements. One such method is the use of the viewpoints. Another is understanding the impact of a QoS requirement on the constructs in each viewpoint. Still another is specifying a QoS capability that is associated with an open reference model, such as [ISO-QoS]. The systems can still be heterogeneous, but their interactions and behavior are specified and implemented in an open manner using a QoS-specific form of language. This enables QoS across distributed heterogeneous systems.

For example, a requirement that all sites must receive the message, no matter what, may result in a requirement for fault tolerance across all systems in the communications path. As another example, a delay requirement may so affect the guaranteed throughput and storage requirements of a system as to require a real-time technology solution set. As another example, QoS is always affected by distribution. Software that has a QoS constraint might need to be engineered onto the same node to achieve that QoS, instead of being distributed across nodes.

The use of the RM-ODP viewpoints facilitates the decisions made for an architecture. For example, a QoS requirement for quick access to the patient record, specified in the enterprise viewpoint, could result in QoS on a computational data manager object to either negotiate for access to the patient record, or include a priority capability that allows the data manager to pause current access in order to allow immediate access. The priority does not replace the timeliness QoS request, but rather aids in dynamic resource allocation. As such, a QoS requirement puts additional constraints on the architect's choices: fault tolerance or not; real-time or not; prioritization or not; where; etc.

Not every system need provide dynamic QoS management. Sometimes, the design approach is the most cost-effective method, especially when the criticality of the QoS is known. Nevertheless, it is important to find a way to discuss QoS among stakeholders and architects, provide a language to define the QoS needs (e.g., what does "quick" mean?), define patterns of reasoning of how to architect QoS capabilities for system reuse, and to know how to evaluate and test for conformance to a QoS requirement. The model of QoS discussed in this chapter provides a common language of understanding across the stakeholders and architects, and across systems that must meet QoS requirements, facilitating federation of heterogeneous distributed systems that achieve an end-to-end QoS requirement.

Some of the challenges to be solved in providing a QoS model include:

▶ How can a QoS need be expressed?
▶ How can a QoS be provided in a dynamic way?
▶ What kinds of tools are needed?
▶ How can end-to-end QoS be achieved across unknown environments?
▶ How does a user convey his QoS needs or requirements to the infrastructure services?
▶ How can the system meet those needs?
▶ How can differences between user needs and services offered be negotiated?
▶ How does the system inform the user if something goes wrong during use of the end-to-end QoS?

▶ What kind of remedial actions might the user take?

▶ What tools are needed?

In RM-ODP [RM-ODP-2, RM-ODP-3], QoS are constraints of a variety of elements, not merely timeliness. Figure 17.3 shows a metamodel in UML of some of the QoS constraints. QoS is usable throughout an RM-ODP specification, but no language is provided to parameterize QoS properties. The emerging work from ISO [ISO-QoS] is providing the necessary reference model for use in specifying QoS of an ODP system.

An application must be able to define its QoS needs to the system. To enable the appropriate QoS processing by the system, QoS constraints must be specified in all relevant aspects of the architecture of that system: QoS policy statements, semantic behavior constraints associated with object interactions, contracts associated with interfaces, binding constraints, channel constraints, etc. For example, an application that requires a higher level of security must be able to inform the system infrastructure services of this request. To achieve true end-to-end application and messaging QoS, a number of constructs should be in place and work together. The include all or some of:

▶ Application request of QoS—the application needs a method of requesting a QoS from the infrastructure, dynamically.

▶ QoS policies for resource usage, channel usage, threading, protocol usage, priority, reservation services, etc.—QoS policies can be architecturally defined and either statically or dynamically used.

▶ Dynamic QoS management—If dynamic QoS is specified by the architect, the actions to be performed need to be specified. The QoS "manager" in this case is also associated with a QoS for monitoring the QoS needs. That is, this object must have guaranteed, high priority access; accuracy of information;

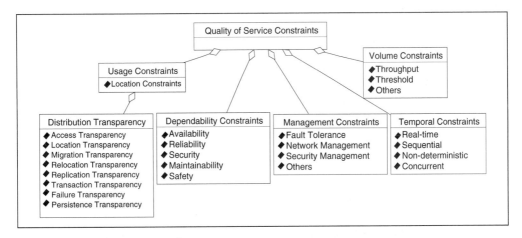

FIGURE 17.3 RM-ODP QoS Elements

etc.; in order to detect a QoS request; monitor the resource usage; and manage resource utilization. The latter point may require the object to interrupt an interaction in order to reprioritize the use of the resources.

▶ Binder-aware QoS specifications—These specifications would enable the appropriate choice of channel objects that give a higher QoS, such as more security or faster throughput.

▶ Protocol-aware QoS specifications—These specifications would enable the appropriate communications capabilities.

▶ Network QoS control—This would support the communications.

▶ Operating system QoS control—This would be especially useful for supporting real-time systems, or for allowing priority interrupts for reprioritization.

Note that a reservation model that reserves a resource for use may be needed to assure a QoS capability in the system. Resources required to support a QoS need to be reservable through a reservation model that allocates the needed resources for binding, associated with the QoS. How resource reservation is accomplished is not discussed here, however.

To achieve QoS in a system, the architect needs to carefully select the appropriate technology viewpoint solutions: the right operating system, the right network, and the right channel objects.

The following discussion looks at the RM-ODP constructs and the emerging component standards [ISO-QoS], [QoS-framework], and [QoS-framework2]. The discussion will address the constructs for a system to provide applications with quality control over their use of resources and resource allocation, their use of channel capabilities, and their need for quality multimedia flows. The application should be shielded from knowledge of how the infrastructure will provide these control qualities. As such, the infrastructure needs to provide transparency constructs that enable the application's QoS. This, in turn, off-loads the application with the complexity of details of how to design the QoS mechanisms. Also addressed are some mechanisms for dynamic QoS allocation of resources. Not addressed are the means of evaluating the performance of products for selection, the network or operating system choices, the database management system choices, etc. There are such products today: real-time and near-real-time operating systems; high-bandwidth networks; dynamically allocated high-bandwidth networks; and so forth, that can be chosen for a given system.

17.5   EMERGING QoS REFERENCE MODEL FOR RM-ODP

QoS is complex. Enabling QoS requires a correct parameterization of the QoS requirements so that both the application and the infrastructure elements agree on the semantics. Policies establish the rules for achieving QoS in a system.

There are two standards addressing QoS. The work of a QoS framework [QoS-framework, QoS-framework2] specifies the concepts and relationships that address QoS in OSI: the reference model for communication. It discusses general concepts of QoS and relations among the concepts. Its focus is on communication and messaging. ISO established a working group to formulate a related model for ODP, since distributed processing aspects of QoS differ from communication aspects. This is the QoS reference model for RM-ODP [ISO QoS].

The OSI QoS model is focused on service offering, service access points, and service-level agreements, and is based on a layered approach owing to the nature of the OSI reference model (seven layers). The ODP model, on the other hand, provides a focus on objects that interact across a binding. Communication in ODP is considered an enabler for interaction, not the purpose of ODP. The constraints on the ability to interact and the ability to bind two or more interfaces consistute part of the semantic behavior. This is where QoS fits in. ODP is concerned with issues of distribution, functional behavior, semantic behavior, and dynamism. The concept of a service in OSI is very different from the concept of a service in ODP, as well as the concepts of semantic behavior. ODP focuses on end-to-end distributed processing; OSI focuses on end-to-end communication. The needs of distributed processing systems must be specified to include QoS, and supported by appropriate communication systems, OSI or otherwise. To do so requires the ability to specify the requirements for QoS from the business needs through the choices of technology, and to makes choices of interaction, binding, and communication based on those requirements. All of this requires a common language to speak "QoS-ese." This is, in essence, what the QoS reference model addresses: requirements, behavior, distribution, and dynamism relating to QoS needs.

The ISO QoS work also discusses how QoS can be managed, specified, and parameterized. Once the ISO QoS standard, which uses the QoS framework standards, is completed, it will become Part 5 of RM-ODP. These extensions address the parameterized specification of QoS, and the pattern of reasoning to make use of the QoS concepts in an architecture specification. The actual concepts and their definitions used in the ISO QoS come from the QoS framework standard [QoS-framework], and will be provided to some extent in this chapter.

17.5.1 FOUNDATIONS

The reference model for QoS focuses on specifying QoS in an ODP system. "It must be possible to express QoS requirements and, to meet the needs of emerging applications (particularly those that offer multimedia services), QoS must come to be a pervasive aspect of the specifications of ODP systems." [ISO-QoS] Its objective is to provide a reference model addressing requirements, behavior, and relations among objects requiring QoS. The focus is on QoS statements addressing predictability, uncertainty, control adaptation, and binding aspects in a distributed environment, not on the measured behavior. The standard is to support an object's request for a QoS, and for ODP systems to deliver the requested QoS. The ODP system may be statically or dynamically defined, which is an architectural decision based on cost effectiveness. So, for example, the ODP system can make use of a real-time infrastructure rather than a non-real-time one, negotiate adequate allocation of shared resources (e.g., communication), discover additional servers offering services at the required QoS, adapt to changes in available QoS, etc. [ISO-QoS]

The QoS reference model approach "foresees the embedding of QoS management functions into the concept of interfacing and binding." [deMeer] The reference model takes the approach of defining properties about QoS, and addresses how those properties are fulfilled. The property set defined by [ISO-QoS] includes:

▶ QoS is a behavioral property that affects the functioning of the system.

▶ QoS can be ensured at certain epochs.

▶ QoS can be negotiated.

▶ QoS is associated with a metric to be measured and monitored.

▶ QoS, like everything else in RM-ODP, is composable.

The concepts defined for QoS include QoS management, which provides the actions of monitoring, administration, control, and general management of a QoS property. What is accomplished by QoS management is defined in a policy that affect the actions, stemming from the original enterprise contract that captured the original user requirements in the enterprise specification.

Another concept is a QoS *characteristic* that can be quantified. This is a property that is not dependent on the representation or control. That is, this is a property to be achieved, but that may not ever be measured as such in use. So, this property is considered an approximate value. There can be an acceptable threshold or range of values that are associated with such a characteristic. These bound what can be observed in a conformance test. For example, a delay of retrieving a patient record could be expressed as a QoS characteristic of one second, and associated with a threshold not to exceed two seconds. Alternatively, the QoS requirement of one second could be associated with a probability that in 98 percent of the cases, this value is achieved. Conformance testing in the latter case is more difficult, however.

There are other commonly used QoS characteristics that affect the interactions between or among objects. These include the following, with a small description of the term: *Delay* is some time that is generally associated with a transfer. A *jitter* is some time interval associated with a transfer delay. An *error probability* is the probability of a failure. *Throughput* is the rate of transfer of a message or some data. *Availability* is a measure of the mean time to failure, or alternatively, a percentage of time that a service is usable (available). *Reliability* is the mean time between failures. Both availability and reliability are addressed in Chapter 16, "RM-ODP Fault Tolerance Framework." *Integrity* is defined as the probability of survival. *Precedence* is a priority. *Confidentiality* is the probability of being safe from unauthorized access.

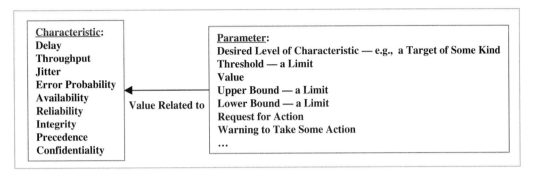

FIGURE 17.4   Relating QoS Characteristics and QoS Parameters

These characteristics define the kind of QoS. But to communicate a QoS between objects on the same system, or across different systems, the characteristic needs to be parameterized. A QoS *parameter*, then, is a value associated with a QoS characteristic, where a QoS characteristic may include one or more QoS parameters and a QoS parameter may relate to one or more QoS characteristics. Some examples of the mapping of a QoS characteristic and QoS parameter are shown in Figure 17.4. A QoS characteristic, then, is similar to the concept of a template for a QoS.

How a QoS specification is used is shown in Figure 17.5, which provides a view of the relationship between QoS characteristic and QoS parameters, as perhaps used in an interaction between the radiologist and the data manager managing the patient records. All of the QoS classes are shaded gray. In this figure, there is one QoS class that has been repeated and not duplicated, with the identical QoS characteristic-parameter relationships: QoS Emergency 3 and 4. Due to a limitation in UML, the class, which is related to the interaction between the radiologist and the data manager, can only be related to one association. Since there are two associations to the data manager, there is a dual set, not duplicated, because duplication of an association class still cannot be associated with more than one association. QoS Consistent and QoS Availability of Record are duplicated. These QoS classes depict the QoS characteristics (e.g., precedence, delay, and jitter), and their parameters.

Other concepts address how a QoS is parameterized, used, monitored, and so forth. Figure 17.6 provides an overview of these additional concepts, from [QoS-framework].

QoS information is a general term. It either refers to a QoS requirement or QoS data. A QoS requirement is a manageable requirement for some QoS, such as a threshold. It is expressed as a QoS parameter. QoS data is information used by a QoS mechanism, such as the results of an inquiry about a QoS across an interaction, or a warning that a QoS had degraded. So, a requirement relates directly to a QoS characteristic, whereas data is about a QoS characteristic used for management purposes. A relationship diagram pertaining to this discussion may also be found in Figure 17.6.

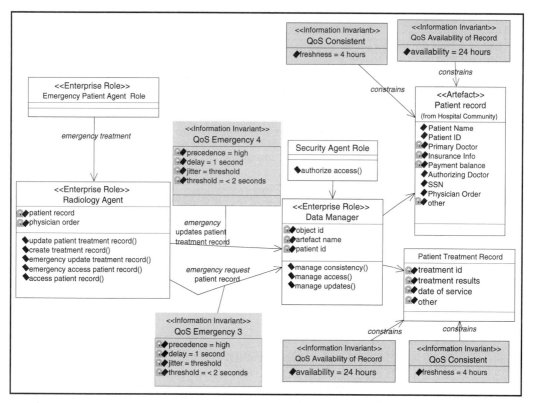

FIGURE 17.5   Example of QoS Characteristics and Related QoS Parameters

In Figure 17.6, each object has a QoS context, which will establish the QoS across the interaction. A QoS mechanism supports the management actions regarding the QoS across the interaction. It establishes a contractual behavior between object 1 and object 2, controls the QoS across the interaction, and so forth. The QoS mechanism can also observe and inquire about the QoS. When doing so, the parameterized data is observed, from which some measure can be evaluated to determine if the contracted QoS is within limits. If not, the QoS mechanism is set up to act according to a QoS policy, which may reduce the QoS across the interaction and notify the objects of the degradation in service; or modify some condition to establish the right QoS (such as reprioritizing the use of a communication channel so that object 1 and object 2 receive a higher priority), manage the infrastructure resources allocating more if needed, or abort the interaction. It is the QoS mechanism that supports dynamic QoS.

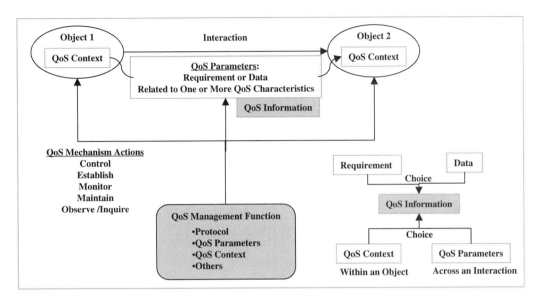

FIGURE 17.6 QoS Concepts

Dynamic means that the objects in the system requiring some QoS can negotiate for an acceptable level of QoS. Sometimes one object (object 2) cannot meet a preferred required QoS characteristic of another object (object 1). But object 1 may have an established range in its parameterization of the QoS that object 2 can meet. For example, the data manager of Figure 17.5 may be able to meet the QoS delay of two seconds for the radiologist, but not the preferred one-second delay. So it's important to specify thresholds in a QoS requirement. Sometimes dynamic negotiation requires a QoS mechanism to initiate negotiation among the objects and adapt the QoS to a level (possibly degraded) acceptable for the interaction. This requires that the bounds of the QoS characteristic be statically defined.

Static means that the parameters are either specified in the architecture or at design time. In either case, the parameters are "locked in." These parameters also remain constant (invariant) over the lifetime of the object or interaction to which the QoS characteristic applies.

QoS parameters, whether dynamic or static, affect the choices of technologies, such as the operating system, the database management system, the network, and so forth. They also affect the configuration of infrastructure objects to support the QoS, and the environment in which an interaction takes place. There are patterns of reasoning for different QoS characteristics, applicable in each of the viewpoints. These are addressed in the next section.

In addition to the concepts discussed, the QoS foundation also consists of what is meant by a QoS relation. In Figure 17.6, an arrow is shown from a QoS context of object 1 to object 2, which relates the QoS parameters in the interaction. What exactly does this mean? It is a QoS relation, and there are several aspects to this relation that must be met.

A QoS is met when the environment of the object agrees to an expected QoS needed by an object, and the object agrees to provide a certain QoS itself. Hence, a contract is formed between the object and its environment that establishes the contractual behavior between the object and its environment, in terms of obligations. If one or the other cannot provide the QoS or does not obligate to providing it, the interaction cannot take place. How a contract comes into being is either defined statically, or through dynamic negotiation. Figure 17.7 takes the UML portion of the diagram relating to the radiologist and the interaction with the data manager, and shows how the contract results from agreements between the radiologist and its environment (the data manager and all mechanisms that enable the interaction). Notice that the UML did not indicate the QoS offered by the radiologist. If the radiologist requires a patient record, it is an obligation on the radiologist to be available to receive it, with sufficient resources to receive it. Often, this sort of QoS is implied, but should be stated.

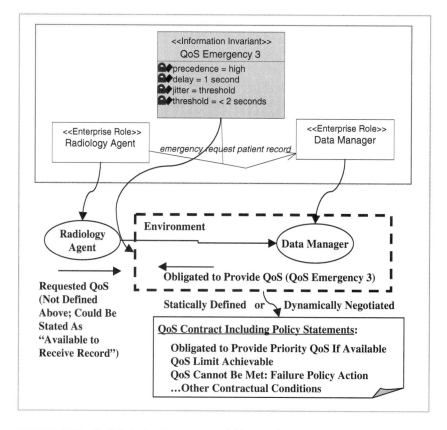

FIGURE 17.7   QoS Relation Between an Object and Its Environment

17.5.2   Using the RM-ODP Viewpoints

Recall that the viewpoints are nested. Therefore, in specifiying a particular part of the architecture, the architect may wish to consider that part as an enterprise, defining the scope, policies, and purpose of that part. The architect may then proceed to fully define that part in terms of the remaining viewpoints. As will be discussed, the engineering specification is the most complex. It may benefit the architect to specify the dynamic negotiation mechanisms in the engineering viewpoint as a full subsystem, including all the viewpoints. On the other hand, there may be such specifications for reuse, in which case the architect needs only to plug them into the specification being created.

As will be shown, there is still much left to specify in the use of the RM-ODP viewpoints for a QoS reference model. The discussion below captures what is current, with the understanding that this is evolving all the time, resolving many of the inconsistencies and ambiguities identified in the following section.

A word about QoS policy is in order here, as it applies to several viewpoints. QoS policies address what must be done to assure a certain QoS, and what should be done if that QoS is not provided. Such a policy is particular to the QoS needs. Resource reservation may facilitate some of the QoS requirements. Such a capability would be provided by a QoS management object. Further, this management function may take action if a certain QoS cannot be achieved, and this is defined in the policy. QoS policies apply in every viewpoint specification, though the refinement details vary. And the information viewpoint invariant schema captures all such policies for use in any of the viewpoints.

17.5.2.1   Enterprise Viewpoint

QoS requirements are specified in the enterprise viewpoint. These include requirements on the environment, and the expectations of the environment in supporting the required QoS. The specification is in terms of an environment contract that contains QoS statements, as represented in Figure 17.7.

Some of the QoS requirements apply to the enterprise object, and some apply to the enterprise interaction. RM-ODP provides a top-level description of QoS and enterprise interaction, which are enhanced by [ISO-QoS].

For QoS to be specified on an interaction, the enterprise interaction specification must include a definition the objects that participate in the interaction, the purpose of the interaction, the information exchanged to express any QoS applicable, and recovery actions.

Some of the QoS requirements overlap with those of RM-ODP, some are new, and some appear to be a subcategory of those shown in Figure 17.3. The QoS requirement, enhancements, and applicability are shown in Table 17.1.

TABLE 17.1   QoS Object and Interaction Requirements

QOS REQUIREMENT		APPLICABILITY	
RM-ODP	**ISO-QOS**	**OBJECT**	**INTERACTION**
Volume			
Temporal			
Dependability	Availability, reliability, safety	X	
	Security: preserve the integrity and confidentiality of the information	X	
Management			
Usage			
Distribution transparency		X	
No category	Capacity: performance, storage, etc.		
No category	Information: freshness, precision		X
No category	Timeliness (e.g., delay)		X
No category	Precedence (e.g., priority)		X
No category	Accuracy (e.g., error probability)		X
No category	Capacity (e.g., throughput)		X
	Others defined by the architect: physical handicaps, special needs, recording resolution (e.g., televised, audio, music)	either	either

There are a few things to notice here. One is that the RM-ODP QoS requirements are not fully addressed. Another is that "Capacity" has two meanings (not distinguished in [ISO-QoS], except by example and applicability). And another is that the areas described as "no category" may in fact be a subset of one of the RM-ODP categories, but this is not discussed in [ISO-QoS].

For each affected object and interaction, the enterprise specification will contain:

▶ QoS requirements specified in terms of QoS characteristics and some notion of the QoS parameters, such as a metric for delay (e.g., one second to access a patient record), a dependability metric that the system will be available (e.g., mean time to failure = one hour per week), currency of information (e.g., retrieved information shall be current to within one day), an implicit requirement relating to multimedia (e.g., assurance of synchronized audio and video), or others.

▶ Limits or thresholds that allow for dynamic negotiation, and that can be associated with one or more of these parameters.

▶ QoS parameters about information, such as currency (or freshness), consistency, availability, and so forth.

▶ If an enterprise object is involved, all actions that are to be performed to assure a contracted QoS, or to perform some function on failure, are defined.

The architect needs to refine these requirements into computational and engineering constructs that support the required QoS. Speed may refine into constraints on the channel, or a dedicated channel to achieve throughput and capacity. Availability may refine into the need for fault tolerance, or perhaps replication of that part of the system that needs to be available. Information currency may refine into controls that manage updates in accordance with the QoS time, or possibly data replication to ensure the data is always current, and hence accurate. Synchronization of multimedia streams may result in the need for a binding object with a control manager to manage or negotiate for the allocation of needed resources, and dedicated channels to ensure the streams have available bandwidth or appropriate resolution, or dynamic alternate routing capability to locate and use a sufficient channel. This capability would support, for example, the example of Figure 17.2. Dynamic alternate routing based on specified quality of service is how the telephone system works, by the way.

17.5.2.2 Computational Viewpoint

QoS in the computational viewpoint specification is addressed in terms of the QoS requirements of the objects and their interfaces. These are captured as part of the object template and interface template.

Since the computational viewpoint is a distribution-independent view of the functional components of a system, this viewpoint will need to address any of the mechanisms needed to achieve a QoS, and the QoS applied to those mechanisms as well.

The granularity of the QoS requirement, from the enterprise viewpoint as refined in the computational viewpoint, may be further refined into one or more QoS characteristics. So, for example, an enterprise QoS that requires availability may be refined into a replication transparency, to achieve that availability. Speed of delivery, as another requirement from the enterprise viewpoint, may translate into throughput. The patterns of reasoning that refine an enterprise QoS requirement into a computational QoS characteristic are not yet defined in [ISO-QoS], except by example.

Some of the QoS requirements apply to an object and some to an interaction in the computational specification. The QoS characteristics associated with an object could include availability, safety, security, reliability of processing, capacity, and processing time. Some QoS requirements on the objects may be one or more transparencies, such as failure, migration, replication, and others. Some apply to the information within an object and include freshness, precision, confi-dentiality, integrity, and consistency with respect to other information in other objects.

A round-trip speed of delivery QoS requirement may require an operation (client/server) interaction. But to support the QoS requirement, each part of the operation may be associated with a portion of the QoS value, enabling adequate monitoring and dynamic change as needed. That is, an enterprise QoS requirement may be split into several QoS characteristics, each associated with some part of the interaction, and the processing of each end of the interaction. It all depends on the QoS requirement.

Some of the QoS requirements result in QoS characteristics such as jitter, delay, throughput, security, precedence, error probability, and others.

QoS on an interaction affects the environment of the interaction, as well as the objects involved in the interaction. It can also affect the binding object, if it is involved. So the relative impact of a QoS requirement on an interaction is greater than that on an object. As discussed above, a QoS associated with an interaction must negotiate with the environment to achieve a contractual relationship between the object initiating the interaction and its environment (to include object on the other end of the interaction). This is one very good reason why a binding object may be used in all interactions requiring a measure of QoS; the binding object can act in the role of the QoS management function.

Finally, as is the case in the enterprise viewpoint, a QoS requirement on an object or an interaction requires the architect to specify the QoS characteristics applicable to each, the values associated with the characteristic, the computational objects that participate in the QoS-related interaction, and recovery actions. Though this is similar to the enterprise specification, it is more refined in detail in the computational specification.

17.5.2.3   Engineering Viewpoint

There is little provided for this viewpoint from [ISO-QoS] at this point in the work program. However, RM-ODP provides some of the constructs for doing this, and the following discussion reverts back to RM-ODP. Some of the constructs the architect will need to specify.

The engineering specification is a refinement of the computational and enterprise specifications to a level of detail where the QoS characteristic is applied. For example, if any of the distribution transparencies are required, the computational object becomes a basic engineering object, that is affected by the selected transparency. The infrastructure support for the transparency is specified. This topic is covered in Chapter 10, "Hiding System Complexities: Distribution Transparencies."

QoS is enabled through the mechanisms of the engineering viewpoint, while providing the capability transparently to the application developers. This is a non-trivial task that requires careful analysis and engineering.

QoS will be specified from the business or application. Neither should need to design and implement the decisions of binding, concurrency, message queues, choice of protocols, etc. Instead, they should parameterize the needed QoS in such a way as to enable the infrastructure to understand the semantics, and dynamically determine what it needs to do to provide the required QoS.

The choice of protocol to use can and should be dynamic; that is, the ability to select a particular protocol is provided in the infrastructure, and allocated as needed at runtime. The choice of protocol is determined by the parameter associated with the application interface template, that then relates to the engineering interface reference template in the engineering specification. What this also enables is the infrastructure to be re-engineered with new protocols that provide better QoS as they emerge through different products, or for the implementation team to construct new and better QoS-enabling protocols, without impact or change to the applications. All of this is predicated on using an appropriate QoS framework to clearly and unambiguously provide QoS parameterization that can be used by the applications and understood by the infrastructure.

Some of the options to specify for engineering QoS in an architecture specification are:

▶ Resource allocation, such as a buffer size to limit the size of a message
▶ Concurrent (executing at the same time) processing, defining the number of tasks that can execute at the same time, which can also include only one
▶ Concurrent messaging to define the maximum number of messages to be processed concurrently. An invariant here could be that the concurrent messaging specification may not exceed the concurrent processing specification.
▶ Multiplexing, defining the maximum number of multiplexed transport connections
▶ Channel allocation, defining the sole usage of a channel or the shareability of that channel, and the associated limits
▶ And more

A system that provides different levels of QoS will support access to the same service and creation of bindings with different levels of QoS. That is, the system provides end-to-end QoS through dynamically offering the mechanisms appropriate for the QoS request. Of course, the architect can specify the system be implemented in such a way as to always provide a single level of QoS, but this is restrictive to any future evolution of the system. To enable different levels of QoS, the server side must be able to offer multiple levels, and multiple binding interface endpoints (one for each level). Hence, QoS places requirements on the mechanisms needed for each node involved in end-to-end communication in the system.

When support for multiple binding interface endpoints to the same service is provided, the complexity to determine which binding interface endpoint to use is masked by the infrastructure. That is, it is transparent to the application how the determination is made, as are the mechanisms required to select a particular binding interface endpoint. All the application developer needs to know is to invoke a particular standard interface reference, which in turn encapsulates the necessary parameters for the QoS for that application. The infrastructure uses these parameters to distinguish which binding interface endpoint is appropriate.

One of the object request brokers in use today is DIMMA (Distributed Interactive Multimedia Architecture). Not only does it provide the normal Object Request Broker (ORB) capabilities, it also supports QoS across the bindings. [Dimma-98]

QoS across a communications channel requires that the protocols provide a particular quality of service. This could be accomplished by including in specification all possible variants of a protocol, each providing a specific QoS. In this case, the application's request for a specific QoS communication would require the infrastructure to bind with a specific protocol-type. But this has an overhead on the infrastructure to dynamically load a specific protocol, and on the management of a suite of similar protocol variants. Sometimes the choice of channel and protocol is reflected in the way a message needs to be packaged, requiring separate formatters for different kinds of QoS. For example, the choice of sending music over a low-capacity network may require the recorded music to be formatted into a smaller package (e.g., 5 MB instead of the recorded 16 MB). Though the essence of the music is transmitted, and the receiver can obtain the package better (i.e., it's smaller), there is degradation of the quality of the music. This may be okay, but what it requires on the sending side is a capability to format the high-resolution music into a low-resolution packet for interchange.

A QoS model (such as being defined by [ISO-QoS]) is used that, among other things, defines a generic QoS capability. When an application binding request is received by the binder (or some other engineering object), the protocol for communication is chosen, and the QoS characteristic is parameterized to relate to the protocol-specific QoS. That is, the protocol object dynamically handles the required QoS requested. To accomplish this, the protocol mechanisms must understand the QoS parameterization semantics, and provide dynamic QoS mapping onto capabilities that are protocol specific.

Some of the ORBs provide some of this capability by including a value-added Internet Interoperability Protocol (IIOP) that provides this, or a transparent alternative associated with the ORB. DIMMA [Dimma-98] is one such ORB.

Providing QoS with all the "extra" infrastructure constructs does not necessarily equate to a degradation in performance of the system. Certainly, that is always possible, depending on how the infrastructure is architected. However, with careful architecture, using the constructs of RM-ODP, the opposite has been shown to be true. Remember that RM-ODP enables the architect to dynamically allocate resources within the constraints of the QoS needs. So, instead of guessing at a static QoS capability in a system, the architect can specify the capability to support different levels of QoS in the system and dynamically allocate them as the application request is received.

17.5.2.4 Information Viewpoint

In RM-ODP, the information schemata capture the semantics of processing, including the QoS characteristics. However, this is inconsistent with the direction of [ISO-QoS], and as such will not be further discussed here. Again, this emerging standard is expected to resolve many such issues before becoming final.

17.5.2.5 Technology Viewpoint

As stated above, the technology viewpoint specification contains those products and technologies that formulate the system. In the case of QoS, the selection criteria may include meeting a particular tested and validated characteristic, such as delay, or throughput across a network. There are many such evaluations, especially for real-time systems. However, once again, the topic of QoS addresses not only end-to-end communication, but also end-to-end application interaction. As such, real-time constraints may not apply at all, enabling a wider choice of technologies and products.

DIMMA's ORB provides such a dynamic QoS capability. In [Dimma-98] the performance results were provided. They realized an ORB, using dynamic QoS allocation of resources, that resulted in a 2–3 times faster ORB than the popular ORB against which they compared it, executing on a 167 MHz Sun™ Ultra™ 1 with 128 MB memory. With a multithreaded high-QoS performance channel (dynamically allocated), their ORB was tested to execute at 600 microseconds compared with approximately 1700 microseconds for the other ORB. Other tests were conducted, with variations in the allocation mechanisms. These are captured in [Dimma-98].

The message here is that the architect can achieve good performance results for support of QoS by using the RM-ODP constructs (which DIMMA does), dynamically allocating QoS capabilities, and selecting the appropriate technologies for the infrastructure.

17.5.3 SOME AMBIGUITIES AND INCONSISTENCIES

The set of parameters relating to the characteristics, and how that mapping is achieved, are yet to be fully defined. At times, reference is made to a characteristic across the interaction, when in fact the reference should be to the parameter(s) associated with a characteristic. QoS measures those things that can be observed by the QoS mechanism, to determine the status of a QoS interaction, or to manage something about it. However, a QoS measure is defined in terms of a set of values associated with a characteristic [QoS-framework], but this set appears to be the set of parameters [ISO-QoS]. Hence, this is an inconsistency across these two standards. This is principally based on the focus of each standard: QoS framework is focused on OSI communication, while the QoS reference model is focused on ODP. As discussed above, a clash in the meaning of "service" and the relationship between a measured value and a requirement will need to be worked out in further editions of [ISO-QoS].

QoS context, data, QoS information, and QoS requirement are not clear in [QoS-framework]. Some terms are left undefined (e.g., the concept of a QoS data context). Some are poorly defined (e.g., QoS data is that QoS information that is not a QoS requirement, which does not say what QoS data is). Some are contradictory (e.g., QoS context is retained by an entity, and yet contains QoS information to be managed, by an external entity). More work in this area will hopefully resolve these problems.

There are statements of QoS, such as a QoS offer. However, it is not made clear which entity provides an offer, and what the contents of that offer include: a QoS requirement, characteristic, or parameter. It would appear that the purpose of a QoS offer is similar to a Trader in that what is offered is from the target object to the requesting object, but it is not clearly stated.

The QoS policy is defined as a set of rules to establish the QoS characteristics and functions used for management. This is more like an RM-ODP contract than a policy, or a template establishing the behavior. A QoS contract is an obligation on the environment and the object requesting a QoS. This is more like an RM-ODP policy statement than a contract. The two concepts of policy and contract seem to be reversed to those in RM-ODP.

The concept of a composition of QoS relations adds the meaning of composite behavior with respect to QoS to the concepts in RM-ODP. However, in order to accomplish this, it requires that the components expose their requirements to the environment, and the environment obligations to the component. That is, encapsulation is broken. Composing QoS relations, where each component relation is exposed, ends up being a large overhead in the composition, since every single component needs to expose its behavior and its environment's behavior. Perhaps the committee formulating the standard will take another look at this important concept (composition) and determine how the behavior of the composition can be better defined.

The QoS use of the enterprise viewpoint does not make use of the concepts in the enterprise viewpoint, with respect to the QoS characteristics. In particular, as shown in Table 17.1, there are elements in RM-ODP that are not addressed in [ISO-QoS], and the categories of RM-ODP are not used to categorize those in [ISO-QoS]. Further, the QoS characteristic is "explained," often by example, rather than defined, resulting in such ambiguities as the QoS characteristic "capacity" being used in two different ways.

The use of the information viewpoint as described is inconsistent with RM-ODP. [ISO-QoS] suggests that the QoS applies to the schemata of the information viewpoint, not addressing how the information specification captures the semantics of QoS for an architecture.

This discussion reflects the work that has been done to date. The QoS reference model standard is in draft form, meaning that it is recognized that more work needs to be accomplished. Hopefully, these sorts of inconsistencies and ambiguities will be resolved in the future issuance of the standard, but they remain unresolved today.

17.6 WORK IN THE AREA

There has been a great deal of work in the area of QoS. Thus far, most of it has dealt with end-to-end communication (or messaging), such as the work from [Quorum]. Other work, such as that of the OMG CORBA messaging [Corba3-messaging] service, provides for dynamic QoS. The DIMMA ORB [Dimma-98] specification provides for application control and management of resources through the use of QoS parameters. And there are many others, principally working in the area of real-time QoS, or QoS issues of timing (only).

With respect to DIMMA, resource reservation is allowed. A binding manager intercedes with the application to manage the QoS across a binding. And all of this is transparent to the application.

In addition, the Internet Engineering Task Force (IETF) is focusing on QoS-based routing, and producing a variant of a QoS framework. Some of this important work can be found at the [IETF-QoS] Web site.

The Defense Advanced Research Projects Agency (DARPA) has initiated some work in QoS, called Quorum. [Quorum]

There is a worldwide QoS special interest group, QoSIG, open to anyone working in the area of QoS, which is accessible through e-mail. [QoS-email]

The International Workshop on QoS is into its eighth annual conference, focusing on developments of QoS in distributed systems. [IWQoS]

The Quality of Service Forum is promoting QoS in standards as well as products. [QoS-Forum]

Work on a quality objects framework can be found at [QUO].

17.7 SUMMARY

In this chapter, a discussion was provided that shows the importance of QoS. QoS applies to real-time systems, across an end-to-end messaging and communication capability. But QoS also applies to user requirements for end-to-end services that are associated with a less stringent QoS.

RM-ODP specifies a basic set of capabilities to support QoS requirements. Under the RM-ODP initiative, work is progressing in defining a QoS framework and reference model that will fully define what a QoS requirement means, how it relates to a parameter, and how values are associated with a parameter, at all view-points. With this, the architect can specify the required QoS in a language that is understood. After all, what exactly a QoS property such as "throughput" really means is only currently defined in the real-time area. But throughput also applies to the ability to access data, and the ability to interact with another application, and the ability to specify the multimedia audio, video, music, and televised informa-tion interaction.

To achieve a QoS requirement and to achieve the ability to evolve the system to more capable products will generally require dynamic negotiation and manage-ment of QoS. In this way, neither the architect nor design needs to specify a priori what the "anticipated" QoS needs to be. Rather, a preferred value, with a range of acceptable qualities of service, can be specified, and dynamically negotiated. The overhead and impact on system performance for such dynamism has been shown, at least in one case, to be non-existent.

With the capability of a well-defined reference model for QoS and products that support the definition of this reference model, systems can begin to provide end-to-end QoS capabilities, be they real-time requirements or application-level end-to-end requirements.

ARCHITECTING FRAMEWORKS, ARCHITECTING HEURISTICS, AND CONCLUSIONS

EIGHTEEN

FRAMEWORKS AND OTHER
METHODS OF ARCHITECTURE

There are several frameworks or methods of architecture that can be selected for architecting a system. Indeed, many of these are in practice today. This chapter provides a comparison of some of the well-known methods of architecture with the Reference Model of Open Distributed Processing (RM-ODP):

▶ Zachman Enterprise Framework model

▶ Department of Defense (DoD) Command, Command, Control, Communication, Computers, Intelligence, Surveillance, and Reconnaissance (C4ISR) framework

▶ Unified Modeling Language (UML) as an architecture framework, with some about the 4+1 Model Views upon which UML is based

▶ New draft IEEE P1471 Architectural Description standard

18.1   ARCHITECTURE METHODOLOGY SELECTION CRITERIA

One of the decisions an architect makes is what approach to take in the specification of an architecture. Sometimes, an approach has gained a great deal of backing from the user community such that the architect may think the approach must be the only correct method of specifying an architecture. Sometimes, an approach has an altogether different objective: a uniform repository of architectural artifacts, independent of how well those artifacts define a part of the architecture. How can an architect choose? What should an architect use for criteria in selection? There are no clear-cut answers to these questions and, furthermore, it all depends on the objective of the architect and the resources available to specify an architecture. This chapter provides a set of criteria for those architects desiring to specify, not merely represent, an architecture.

A precisely defined architecture is recognized as a critical part of the successful development of a system in support of a business need. The architectural definition of a system can range from a loose definition of concepts used to define the distributed processing aspects within a domain, to a precise definition of concepts. This is a dimension of definitiveness. The architectural definition of a system can also range from an informal specification that is not based on formal description techniques to a formal specification founded on formal description techniques (FDT) (e.g., Z, SDL, LOTOS, ESTELLE). This is a dimension of formalism. Another dimension is the completeness of the architecture specification, meaning whether it is a part of the system or the entire system. A good specification is precise. A better specification is precise and formal. A complete specification can be either a full system specification, or a part of the system specification, as long as it's precise and formal. A view of these dimensions is shown in Figure 18.1.

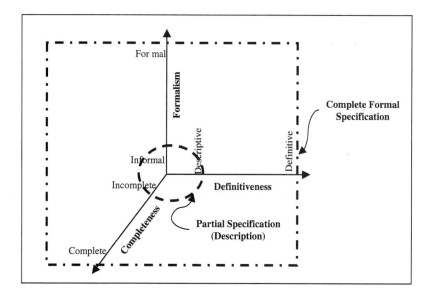

FIGURE 18.1   Dimensions of Specification

The more precise the architectural definition, the less is left open for interpretation. The less left for interpretation by either the stakeholder or the implementer, the more accurate the resultant system will be with respect to the needs of the business as prescribed by the architecture. A formal specification can be challenged and defended because of its formal underpinnings in mathematics. Sometimes the architect only needs to specify a part of a system, perhaps a high-risk part; sometimes the architect needs only to specify the interaction details of part of the system, without the full specification of the part. These are choices made by the architect, depending on the desires of formality, correctness, completeness, and budgetary constraints, to allow for full, precise, formal specification.

Many architectural frameworks are founded on "views." Furthermore, a more precise architecture provides explicit definition of the implicit decisions often left during the implementation. A more precise architecture provides the ability to conduct analysis of the architecture for tradeoff and performance decisions, as well as the ability to create a valid simulation of the architecture to determine if the system performs in accordance with the business need. This analysis becomes more accurate, versus more notional, when the degree of precision and formalism of the architectural specification increases.

The term *framework* (of an architecture) is meant to be a structure for investigating an architectural problem or building a specific approach to architectural concerns that are related to each other through the rules of the structure.

 NOTE The RM-ODP framework is defined to support an architecture specification addressing integration, portability, interworking (interoperability), and of course distribution. [RM-ODP-2]

Framework is not defined in RM-ODP, though the whole is considered a framework. What must be included in a framework that is used to relate a modeling language to the ODP concepts is defined as follows:

- An *entity* is some concrete or abstract thing being modeled.
- A *term* is used to refer to any kind of entity.
- A *sentence* contains terms and predicates.
- A *predicate* refers to a relationship between entities.
- A *proposition* is some fact that can be asserted or denied.
- A sentence is used to make a proposition about the entities.

A framework for use in an ODP architecture must relate the syntax of the modeling language (text, graphic notations, natural language, etc.) and the chosen model concepts (entities, propositions relating to the entities, and levels of abstraction) to the concepts of RM-ODP. [RM-ODP-2]

RM-ODP provides viewpoints of a system (each of which is a model), defining in a consistent manner the concepts and rules for use in each view and allowing for abstractions and composition within each view. Each of the five viewpoints is a total view of the system, from different perspectives. When the framework is based on formalisms, such as predicate calculus, this kind of framework produces a precisely defined architecture specification.

POINT Many architectural frameworks are founded on "views." Often there are published works that discuss whether one set of views is better than another. Some published works equate all of RM-ODP to its set of five viewpoints (only), and then continue to compare these five viewpoints to another set of views. At this point, it should be apparent that RM-ODP is much more than five separate viewpoints, and that, in fact, the five viewpoints are interrelated through consistency of concepts, rules, and terminology.

The discussion to follow will provide a discussion of RM-ODP in relation to each architectural framework presented, from the perspective of the whole of RM-ODP, not merely five viewpoints of "things." An architecture framework, shown in Figure 18.2, can help the architect to create an architecture of a system. How well a framework provides these criteria results in how well-defined the architecture of the system is. The architecture framework can be a collection of architectures that specify architectural perspectives of the architecture of the system, such as the architecture of the enterprise, or the architecture of the security aspects of the system. In terms of the RM-ODP architecture framework, the architecture specification of a system consists of the set of architecture specifications from each of the five viewpoints. That is:

$$\text{Architecture specification} = \sum_1^5 \{\text{enterprise, information, computational,}$$
$$\text{engineering, technology}\} \text{ specifications}$$

In selecting a method of architecture, the framework criteria can be used. These criteria will be referred to in the subsequent sections to discuss the relationship between a certain method and RM-ODP. Some of these criteria lend themselves to representations that facilitate communication among stakeholders and architects (such as visual graphic tools). Some of these criteria are pertinent to the specification of an architecture, such as the specification language. The architect decides upon the objective of presenting the architecture. This results in either a definition (specification) or a description (representation) of the architecture. In either case, the architecture framework must include the definition of its concepts

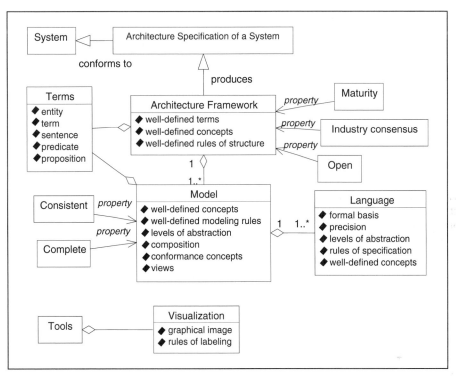

FIGURE 18.2   Architecture Framework

and a specification of any associated rules. For example, a framework may use an underlying object model, as is the case with UML. In this case, the object model must be fully specified, and any concepts provided to the modeler must be fully defined and consistent with the rules. In the case of UML, for example, the concepts of aggregation, class, etc. are fully defined and consistent with the underlying object model. Without definition of the concepts and rules of the framework, the architect will have to *interpret* the meaning of the concepts, and hence the meaning of the framework method, which in turn could result in misinterpretation and assiciated erroneous models. If the model is erroneous, the presentation of the architecture is then erroneous as well, resulting in an inadequate and often inaccurate presentation of the architecture.

There are different kinds of frameworks. One can be an architectural framework, one can be an analytical framework, one can be a description framework, and so forth. There is no hard and fast rule about a framework. A good discussion of some different kinds of frameworks can be found in [Ansa-arch-frwmk]. In the following discussion, some of the more popular architectural frameworks are presented. The stronger the framework, the more precise the architecture. As such, the criteria chosen for discussion represents more precision and formalism in the architecture specification, but not necessarily a full system specification. A complete precise and formal specification of a part of a system is considered to adhere to all the criteria.

18.1.1   FRAMEWORK META-CONCEPTS

A framework for use in specifying an architecture provides well-defined terminology and well-defined distributed processing propositions (concepts and rules). Using the distributed processing propositions, the framework enables the architect to define the constituent parts of a domain-specific system, how they function, and how they semantically behave. The framework enables the architect to specify relationships among the elements of the system both within their environment as well as interacting with their environment. The architect is able to express different kinds of relationships among the elements of the system. Recall that a system can be as large as an enterprise system of systems, or as small as a major component of a system.

18.1.1.1   Open

The method should be open, supported by an open committee that anyone can participate on for a nominal fee, and provide a fully published product of its results. Chapter 1 discusses *open* in more detail.

18.1.1.2   Maturity

The method should be proven through practical use in specifying an architecture of a system, which is proven by a system implemented from that specification.

18.1.1.3   Industry Consensus

The method should be supported by various industries. Only through maturity and industry consensus is an architecture technique *proven*.

18.1.2   MODELING METHODS

A well-formed architectural specification is a conceptual model of a system. The modeling method should be capable of defining the modeling structure, elements, and relationships that relate to those of a system, from the perspective of the model of that system. If not, the architect will need to create this metamodel.

The modeling method should enable models of different views that relate to the different perspectives of the system being modeled. The ability to use the views or viewpoints fully or partially should be supported. The modeling method should be capable of expressing multiple levels of abstractions, in order to separate the complexity (e.g., number of considerations, difficulty of an entity) into simpler entities for specification. Composition should also be supported by the modeling method. The modeling method should support the ability to express asymmetric relationships among the system elements. Lastly, the modeling method should handle the specification of behavior, sameness, quality, classification methods, and failure.

The architecture methods to be discussed all provide a separation of concerns in terms of a set of viewpoints or views. Many of these methods are founded on an object model, with well-defined specific object-model concepts. Some of these methods provide some degree of consistency across the views, by sharing model relations (classes, attributes, properties, etc.). Some of the methods claim that a formal architecture specification can be a representation of interrelated viewpoints, which is arguably not the case.

18.1.2.1 Completeness

The modeling method should provide a complete architecture of the system or part. Any aspect of distribution should be addressed by the method, including functional and semantic behaviors.

18.1.2.2 Consistency

The modeling method should support consistency across all parts of the modeling framework, in terms of its concepts and propositions. The modeling method should allow the architect, with support from the method, to define consistency across all models that constitute the architecture of the system. Without consistency, the models of the system become separate models with little or no provable assertions. Consistency is needed across levels of abstraction, composition, and viewpoints, especially to test for conformance, perform analytical studies, and make propositions that are true or false.

18.1.2.3 Conformance

The modeling method should support the ability to define conformance testing criteria (of the implementation to the architecture specification). Otherwise, the "architecture specification" may or may not specify the architecture of the resultant system—no one will know for sure without provable tests. Some models provide compliant test criteria to ensure the architecture model is compliant with the modeling method.

18.1.3 SPECIFICATION LANGUAGE

The general specification language provides precision and formalization, either directly, through the use of a formal description technique, or through a language founded on an FDT. The use of the FDT allows propositions about entities of the model to be well-founded. The form of the modeling language is not important as long as it is well-defined and precise, allowing for levels of abstraction. A specification language that is not formal is considered by some not to be a specification language at all. However, some relaxation of this is given here, to allow for the cases where a language used by an architect also precisely defines the concepts used. The formal language is much better since it comes with precision. The informal language requires more work on the part of the architect. An informal language that is not precise is unacceptable as a specification language, because there is no "definition." And that is what a specification is attempting to achieve: a definition of how the system is to behave, minimizing misinterpretation.

Representation languages are not specification languages, unless the representation language is founded on a formal language. This is generally the case. Once again, a representation language used in a precise way can suffice for an architectural specification.

18.1.4   TOOLS

The method should be supported by tools for use by the architect in specifying the architecture of a system.

18.1.4.1   Visualization

The visualization of an architecture is a graphical image of an architecture or some part of an architecture. A graphical representation often facilitates human communication of architectural concepts. The use of a visualization capability (or tool) should include rules of labeling the icons of the image, to make clear to the reader what is being represented. This is generally an architect's task.

An architecture specification can be represented through a graphical image. To accomplish this, however, a consistent mapping of the specification concepts and rules to the concepts and rules of the representation model is required. What often happens is that the representation model is mistaken for the specification model, which is not the same.

18.2   ARCHITECTURE METHODS

The architect selects an architecture method to use from the several that are available. The choice is dependent upon the objective of the architect, as well as programmatic considerations of cost, schedule, performance, and available resources.

In general, the architect needs to address several mappings to architect a system. Figure 18.3 provides an overview of the following discussion. First, the business domain consists of domain-specific terminology, such as hospital and admitting agent from the medical domain. These should be well-defined terms. Terms for distributed processing, concepts of how the terms are used, and rules for relating one concept to another all need to be well-defined. For example, what is an interface? What is a control object? What is an entity of software (e.g., object, component, module)? What is a failure? How do these relate? RM-ODP provides these terms for specification. Not all architecture methods do, however.

The architect also needs to define and use architecture concepts. For example, what is abstraction? What do levels of abstraction mean? What is a view? How is a view used? What are valid views and their objectives?

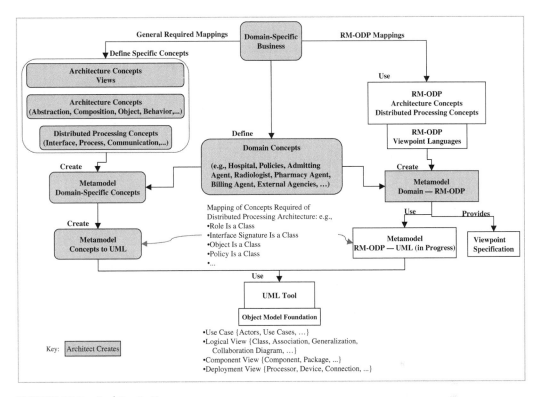

FIGURE 18.3 Architect's Concerns

The architect needs to map the domain-specific terms onto the terminology of distributed processing when architecting. For example, a billing system is a software component, an admitting agent is a role, a hospital is a community, etc. Once all of these terms, concepts, and rules are well-defined, and the mapping of the domain language onto that of distributed processing is accomplished, the architect can use well-defined concepts to architect the system.

As an aid in doing so, the architect may choose to use a modeling language tool that provides visual representation, such as a UML vendor tool. UML has its own language (e.g., Use Case, logical view, aggregation, connection). Furthermore, this language is based on a specific UML object model, as defined by the UML specification. The architect needs to map the concepts of the domain-specific distributed processing architecture onto the concepts of UML in order to use UML. For example, how does the architect use UML to represent the admitting agent or the hospital policy? One method is to represent both as a class. Another method is to represent the admitting agent as a Use Case actor, and a hospital policy as a class. However this is accomplished, the architect needs to be concerned with consistency and completeness in the use of the UML tool, for whatever is represented.

Why use RM-ODP when there are so many frameworks that are capable of specification and representation (see Chapter 7, "Architecture Specification and

Representation"), and since UML provides so much functionality? One reason is that RM-ODP provides much of the definition and mapping work that the architect would need to generate. Another is that RM-ODP modeling languages are provided and founded on distributed processing concerns that are well-defined. Another is that RM-ODP is founded on predicate calculus (formalism). This framework provides foundational models that permeate all the methods of architecture. This framework results in an architecture specification. Another reason is that in recognizing the importance of visual aids, work is progressing to map all of RM-ODP onto UML constructs for the architect to use.

In this section, several architecture methods are presented and discussed in terms of what the method is, what its intended usage is, and how it matches the criteria above. A notional value of zero to five is assigned to each criteria for each method. Five represents a maximum match, one represents a very small match, and zero represents no match. Furthermore, not all possible architecture methods for selection by the architect are addressed here; only some of the more popular ones. And the architect may choose to use more than one method. Whatever method is used, and whatever tools are used for visualization (there are more than those for UML), the architect's task remains that as shown in Figure 18.3, depending on how well each framework already provides some of the definitions and mappings required.

18.2.1   ZACHMAN FRAMEWORK

The Zachman Framework was created by John Zachman in 1987 [Zachman-a], and then updated in 1992 [Zachman]. It was created to provide an enterprise-wide framework of concerns about a system, in terms of descriptive artifacts. "The Framework as it applies to Enterprises is simply a logical structure for classifying and organizing the descriptive representations of an Enterprise that are significant to the management of the Enterprise as well as to the development of the Enterprise's systems." [Zachman-97] It presents different levels of abstraction, in terms of a classification scheme of artifacts, about the system and the enterprise, while maintaining a holistic view of the enterprise. "It is a comprehensive, logical structure for descriptive representations (i.e., models, or design artifacts) of any complex object and is neutral with regard to the processes or tools used for producing the descriptions." [Zachman-97]

18.2.1.1   Zachman Framework Overview

The Zachman Framework is based on a set of views, formulated in terms of aspects and perspectives. The framework is defined as a table of columns representing aspects and rows representing perspectives. Each cell is an artifact of interest, or a model, defined by the intersection of the row (perspective) and column (aspect). A model may span more than one cell, or a cell may be defined by more than one model. In this case, the model describes those aspects (columns) of the system from those perspectives (rows) that it spans. The collection of models that form a complete row (perspective) across all columns (aspects) represents a view of the complete system from that perspective. The framework can be used as a baseline (or as-is) description of a system, as well as a description of a target system. The essence of the framework is depicted in Figure 18.4.

The *perspectives* consist of Scope (a description of the overall view of perhaps a planner), Business Model (from the stakeholder's view, reclassified as the Enterprise Model), System Model (a logical conceptual model from the designer's view), Technology Model (a physical model from the implementer's view), Detail Description (from a subcontractor's view of representation), and Actual System. The *aspects* consist of data (what it is made of), function (how it works), network (where the entities are), people (who does what), time (when things happen), and motivation (why choices are made). Each row constitutes a model of a view of the enterprise. Figure 18.1 also shows some examples of what might be part of each cell for the enterprise model and the system.

Each column addresses a dimension of a software system. There is no order to the columns or importance or layers assumed. Each of the columns is unique, not necessarily related to other columns. The collection of models from the same

Aspects						
Perspectives Data (What)	Function (How)	Network (Where)	People (Who)	Time (When)	Motivation (Why)	**Model Type**
Objectives/ Scope	Business Entities	Business Processes	Business Locations	Major Orgs	Major Bus Events	Goals, Success Factors	Contextual
Enterprise Model	Bus Entity Bus Relation	Business Process Model	Business Locations	Organiz. Unit	Master Schedule	Business Plan	Conceptual
System Model	Data Model	Appl Arch	Distributed Sys Arch	Human Interface Arch	Process Structure	Business Rules Model	Logical
Technology Model	Physical Data Arch	System Design	System Arch	Presentation Arch	Control Structure	Condition, Action	Physical
Detailed Representation	Data Definition	Program	Network Arch	Security Arch	Timing	Rule Specif	Out-of-Context
System	Data	Function	Network	Organ- ization	Schedule	Strategy	Functioning Enterprise
	Entity/ Relation	Process, I/O	Node, Link	People, Work	Time, Cycle	End, Means	

Model Elements Per Column

FIGURE 18.4 Zachman Framework

column all relate to the same aspect. It is not clear if a model to represent an aspect (column) is the same throughout the cells, with different levels of detail, or different models. This may be an architect's decision.

Each row is a unique view from a user perspective. Rows depict and display various levels of detail of some aspect. Different models are generally used for the different cells within a row (e.g., a logical data model using entity/relationship diagram for the data model, or a network protocol model for the network architecture). The collection of cell artifacts across a row represents a model (asserted to be complete) of the system from that user viewpoint and all relate to the same perspective.

All cells need not be filled with a descriptive artifact; this depends on the objectives of the enterprise system. If an artifact in a cell is missing, there should be a good reason why. Furthermore, the user can add a new perspective (row) or a new aspect (column) to the framework. If this is done, the entire related column cells for a perspective and the entire row cells for an aspect should define the models or artifacts to be created.

18.2.1.2   Zachman Framework Meta-Concepts

The precise definition of the terms shown in Figure 18.4 are not in hand. It is not clear whether the definition of these terms is notional or fully defined. The Zachman Framework rules of usage are not explicitly stated, other than to suggest that all the cells in the framework should be completed by the associated artifact (e.g., model or document). However, examples of using the framework are provided in [Zachman].

The Zachman Framework was one of the original architecture frameworks. It is a generic framework, meaning that it can apply to manufacturing or an automated system architecture. It has been used in several different reference architectures, such as the Federal Information Technology Architecture Conceptual Model [FedITA], and proposed for others such as the OMG Object Management Architecture [Shelton]. Several methodologies are compared to the Zachman Framework to ensure more complete coverage of the elements to be considered for an enterprise architecture. As such, its maturity level is high.

Zachman Framework has achieved industry consensus as a good framework for capturing the representations of an enterprise architecture. But current work is superceding this framework, especially in the areas of specification. It has not achieved consensus as a specification tool. Then again, it wasn't designed to provide a means of architectural specification. It was designed to provide a classification scheme for information systems architecture, "for organizing knowledge and forming a basis for constructing more complex theses." [Zachman]

Since this framework was specified by Zachman and Sowa, published by IBM, and not subject to change by anyone other than the authors, it is considered a published closed specification, not an open one.

18.2.1.3 Zachman Framework Model/Views

Views are discussed, but the actual model method for the cells is not. Again, this is a framework of artifacts to represent an enterprise architecture, not a methodology of how to achieve those artifacts (e.g., models).

The views are from the users involved in the creation of the system: planner, stakeholder or owner, designer, implementer, subcontractor. In other words, each cell is a view of some aspect of the architecture for some user, and each row is a view of the system for a given user. Each cell provides a model or artifact to capture the aspects of that part of the view. All models (or other artifacts) in a row collectively provide a complete model of an architecture from the perspective of that row. Figure 18.5 provides an overview of a few such models.

Many of the aspects of an enterprise architecture are depicted in the framework. But the specification is left for the architect. Semantic behavior, and how that behavior affects the functioning of the components and their interactions, is not addressed.

Furthermore, the relation between one cell and another is not defined. That is, the consistency of the artifacts is not addressed. There is no discussion as to the consistency from one cell to another, or from one row to another, or from one column to another.

There is no discussion of conformance.

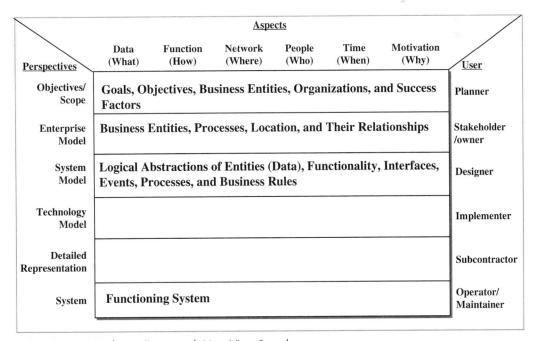

	Aspects						
Perspectives	**Data (What)**	**Function (How)**	**Network (Where)**	**People (Who)**	**Time (When)**	**Motivation (Why)**	**User**
Objectives/ Scope	**Goals, Objectives, Business Entities, Organizations, and Success Factors**						Planner
Enterprise Model	**Business Entities, Processes, Location, and Their Relationships**						Stakeholder /owner
System Model	**Logical Abstractions of Entities (Data), Functionality, Interfaces, Events, Processes, and Business Rules**						Designer
Technology Model							Implementer
Detailed Representation							Subcontractor
System	**Functioning System**						Operator/ Maintainer

FIGURE 18.5 Zachman Framework User View Sample

18.2.1.4   Specification Language

There is no formal specification language required. Many of the concepts are not defined. The degree of completeness of (part of) a system is left to the architect to discover and define. As such, this framework falls short of a good specification technique.

18.2.1.5   Tools

Each cell can be supplied by a visual representation from some tool. The framework itself is presented visually. However, the framework does not explicitly provide a visual representation of a model in one of the cells.

Some tools exist to support the Zachman Framework, and to augment its capabilities by providing a degree of consistency and traceability across some of the cells.

Visible Advantage™ is a tool that supports the business aspects of the Zachman Framework, linking the business component and process to the logical data model. [Visible] The tool is also promoted to "specify physical information system designs based on the data model" [Visible]. Another tool is called the Universal Model [Visible] for enterprise architecture development. It is claimed to be based on an object-oriented model, and supports enterprise engineering.

18.2.1.6   How RM-ODP Enhances Zachman Framework

The Zachman Framework provides a list of considerations for architecting an enterprise system. The terms used are not precisely defined. "There isn't a clean separation between 'policy,' 'mechanism,' and the allocation of the 'policy' onto the 'mechanism.'" [Tockey] RM-ODP provides the specification formalism, the viewpoint languages, how to specify quality of service, how to achieve different "ilities" and performance, how to achieve transparencies, and other distributed processing concerns. The concepts of the interaction framework discussed in Chapter 13, "Interaction Framework: Interoperability," are not delineated in the framework. The concepts of communities within an enterprise are not precisely defined.

In essence, RM-ODP provides precision, semantic behavior, levels of abstraction of a component, levels of abstraction of behavior, composition, and much more. The Zachman Framework is a good tool to see much of the complexity of an enterprise system and to organize a presentation of different views of the system for conversation. RM-ODP provides the missing precision and formalisms for specification of the models in each of the cells, and the semantic behavior and relationships to actually architect such a system, focusing not only on semantics but also on the relationship among the parts of the system and how the system interacts with its environment.

The RM-ODP viewpoints do not cleanly map to those of the Zachman framework. Figure 18.6 provides a possible view of the computational viewpoint

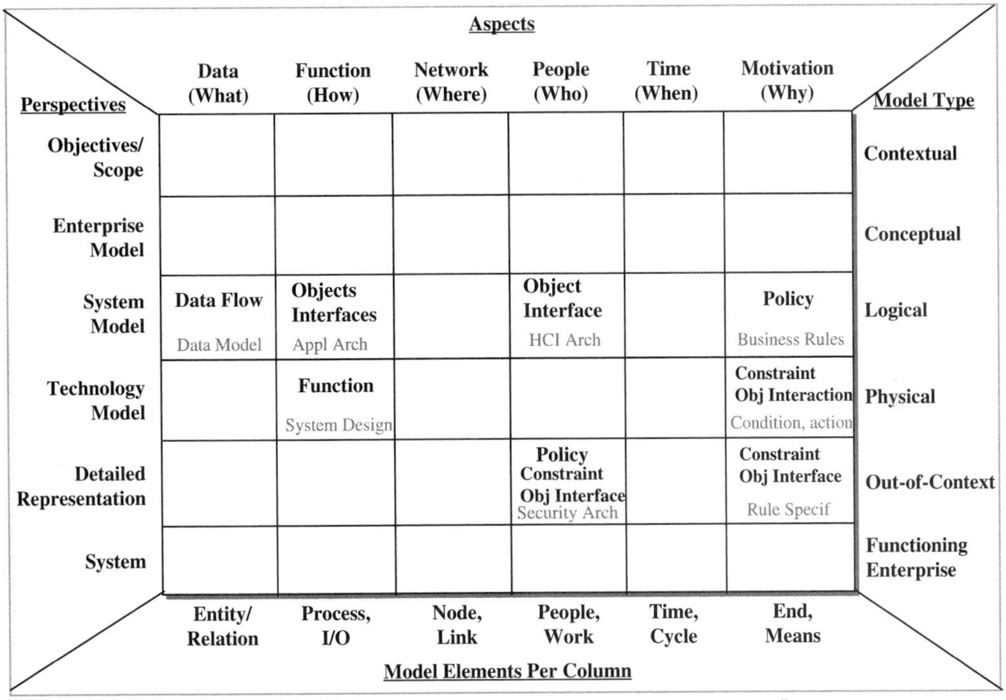

	Aspects						
Perspectives	**Data** (What)	**Function** (How)	**Network** (Where)	**People** (Who)	**Time** (When)	**Motivation** (Why)	**Model Type**
Objectives/ Scope							Contextual
Enterprise Model							Conceptual
System Model	**Data Flow** Data Model	**Objects Interfaces** Appl Arch		**Object Interface** HCI Arch		**Policy** Business Rules	Logical
Technology Model		**Function** System Design				**Constraint Obj Interaction** Condition, action	Physical
Detailed Representation				**Policy Constraint Obj Interface** Security Arch		**Constraint Obj Interface** Rule Specif	Out-of-Context
System							Functioning Enterprise
	Entity/ Relation	**Process, I/O**	**Node, Link**	**People, Work**	**Time, Cycle**	**End, Means**	

Model Elements Per Column

FIGURE 18.6 Computational Viewpoint Perspective of Zachman Framework Cells

mapping to the cells of the framework. The light gray words in each cell represent the framework, while the black words in the same cell represent the computational viewpoint elements. Missing, however, are the constructs of binding, the relationships of an interaction and interface, different types of interfaces, and so forth. Presumably, these would be left to the modeler using the framework to define, as needed. The business rules of the framework are mapped to policy and constraints of the computational viewpoint. These mappings should be considered partial and possible mappings, since the meaning of the terms used in the framework is not in hand. But again, the framework provides a description, and a view of some of the concerns of the system within the enterprise. It is not intended to provide a prescription for a specification of an architecture of that system.

18.2.1.7 Architecture Support and Selection Criteria Evaluation

The focus of the Zachman Framework is a set of views from which to architect a system. A perspective of how much the Zachman Framework supports the work of the architect is shown in Figure 18.7. The gray boxes reflect what the architect needs to do, whereas the white boxes reflect what the Zachman Framework provides.

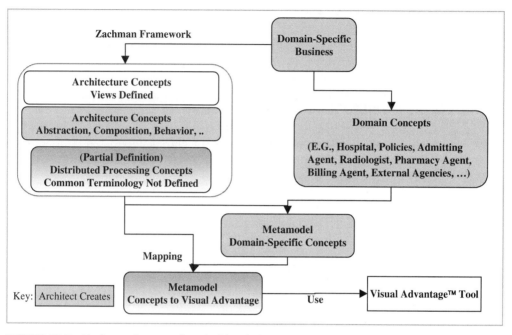

FIGURE 18.7   Zachman Support of an Architect's Concerns

In terms of the selection criteria for the architect, Table 18.1 provides a notional view of how well the Zachman Framework matches the criteria.

TABLE 18.1   Criteria for Zachman Framework

CRITERIA	NOTIONAL VALUE
Defined meta-concepts	1
Open	2
Maturity	4
Industry consensus	3
Modeling methods	2
Completeness	3
Consistency	0
Conformance	0
Specification language	1
Tools	3
Visual representation	2

18.2.2 DoD C4ISR

The U.S. Department of Defense (DoD) promotes the use of a framework called the Command, Command, Control, Communication, Computers, Intelligence, Surveillance, and Reconnaissance (C4ISR) Architecture Framework. This framework consists of a number of mandatory and optional artifacts, that represent some aspect of the system architecture. It is primarily used to align representation methods, rather than specification methods. It is used in comparing an aspect of one system's architecture to another system's architecture for purposes of reuse and interoperability. This framework is expected to level the representation methodologies across the DoD programs, to provide a common representative view of the architectures of the systems across DoD and the U.S. Federal Government.

18.2.2.1 C4ISR Architecture Framework Overview

The C4ISR Architecture Framework addresses the enterprise objectives, business processes, and architecture products of systems within a mission operation. The framework is a structured set of architecture products that provide different architectural views of the system in the context of the mission operations. The use of the framework is to capture the architecture of the system in a common, unified way so that comparisons of architectures can be accomplished, requirements for interoperability can be determined, and possible reusable processes and system alternatives can be detected.

The framework consists of:

- Three architecture views: operational, systems, and technical
- Common architecture products (or artifacts)
- Prescription of the required and optional architecture products
- Prescription of the minimal content of an architecture product (what it must contain)
- Guidelines for determining the purpose, scope, characteristics to be captured in the architecture, and architecture products to be built
- Common reusable building blocks as defined by other DoD frameworks (such as a common infrastructure of services and products for reuse)

The Operational Architecture View is defined as a "description of the tasks and activities, operational elements, and information flows required to accomplish or support a military operation." The Systems Architecture View is defined as a "description, including graphics, of systems and interconnections providing for, or supporting, warfighting functions." The Technical Architecture View is defined as "the minimal set of rules governing the arrangement, interaction, and interdependence of system parts or elements, whose purpose is to ensure that a conformant system satisfies a specified set of requirements." [C4ISR]

Clearly, the C4ISR Architecture Framework is more than a set of representation artifacts. It attempts to guide the development of an architecture in terms of what should be captured and described, what can and should be reused, and how to present the architecture in a way that benefits the entire DoD enterprise. Figure 18.8 provides an overview of the C4ISR Architecture Framework elements. The kinds of information represented in each architecture view are highlighted in each view box. The words on the arrows between the different architecture views represent the manner in which the framework provides consistency among the different views. The architecture products result from each of the views, plus the general information artifacts.

Figure 18.9 provides an overview of the artifacts from this framework. The gray boxes represent those that are required. The remaining white boxes represent those that are optional. A full discussion of each of these artifacts is not provided here, but can be found in [C4ISR].

The framework prescribes certain information to be contained in each architecture product. Sometimes the information is defined by a template for use. Sometimes the template is very detailed, especially for data attributes. Many times, however, a definition of the terms is not provided. Furthermore, the framework does not prescribe a particular tool for use in representing one of the architecture products, such as the logical data model, though it may prescribe a standard for use such as Integration Definition for Information Modeling

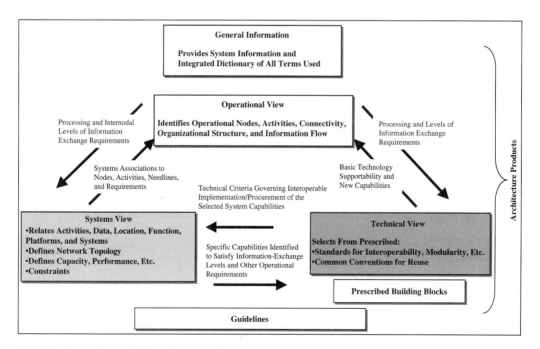

FIGURE 18.8   DoD C4ISR Architecture Framework Overview

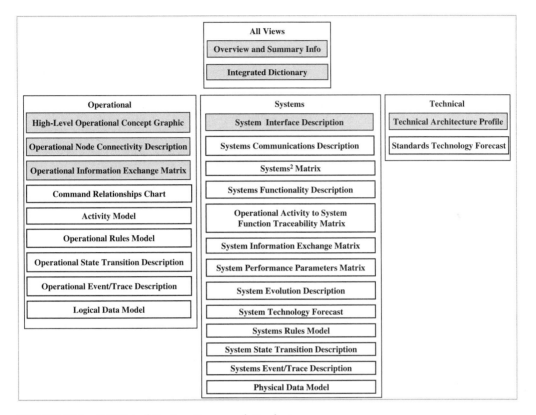

FIGURE 18.9   C4ISR Architecture Framework Products

(IDEF1X) [IDEF1X]. This is the nature of DoD business: it cannot promote a particular vendor. Therefore, the tool used to provide a graphical representation is left to the architect to decide. One thing missing from C4ISR is a prescription of what metamodel to use in conjunction with a tool, or what information is required to be captured by the tool. The result is that each architect can determine the degree of specificity in the use of the tool. C4ISR prescribes little about this.

Each of the required framework products is discussed below. Figure 18.10 provides notional examples of what these products might look like, and an optional SV-2 product.

From the Operational View, the representation of the High-Level Operational Concept Graphic (called OV-1) is often a graphical representation using an office automation graphics package, such as Microsoft PowerPoint® or Visio® Professional from Visio Corporation. The only content requirement is that the graphic contain "the missions, high-level operations, organizations, and geographical distribution of assets." [C4ISR] The Operational Node Connectivity Description (OV-2) depicts a graphic showing "operational nodes and elements, the needlines between them, and the characteristics of the information exchanged." [C4ISR]

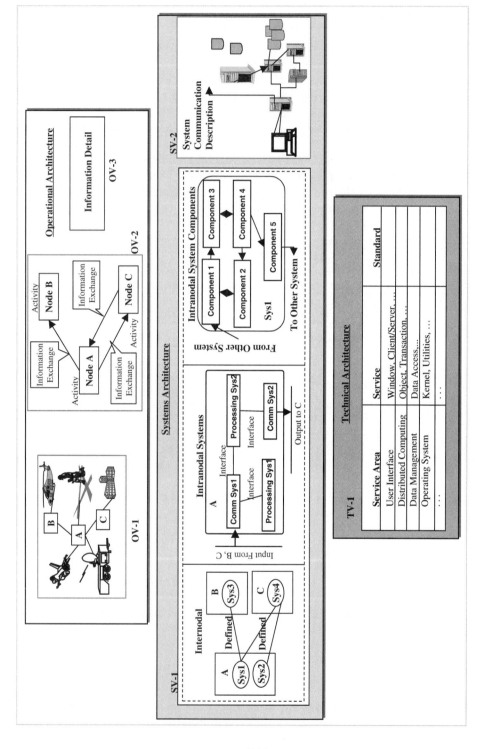

FIGURE 18.10 Architecture Product Examples

Note that in C4ISR, an operational node depicts an operational entity that performs a mission, which is clearly not the same as the RM-ODP node, which is similar to a computer system. The Operational Information Exchange Matrix (OV-3) is a table, or spreadsheet, or relational database that contains information exchange requirements (IERs). The requirement is that the matrix contain "who exchanges what information with whom, why the information is necessary, and in what manner. IERs identify the elements of warfighter information used in support of a particular activity and between any two activities. The node of the producing operational element and the node of the consuming operational element are identified. Relevant attributes of the exchange are noted." [C4ISR] The attributes that are included depend on the decision of the architect and the nature of the information. There are no requirements. The objective of this product is to better understand the information needs of the system and the DoD enterprise. What is meant by many of the terms in the quoted requirements is not defined, though in the above examples the following are defined: attribute, organization, mission, IER, and information.

From the Systems View, the representation of the System Interface Description (SV-1) provides a link between the Operational and Systems Views. For each node in the Operational Architecture, that node must be represented in the Systems Architecture showing the systems within the node and their interfaces to other nodes. This product is a graphic and/or text description of "the interfaces between systems nodes, between systems, and between the components of a system." [C4ISR] The system interface is a representation of communications between two systems or components, depicted graphically with annotated information about the communication (e.g., TCP/IP). The details of the interface are captured in the Systems Communications Description product, which is not required. This product provides a graphic and/or text description of the physical aspects of the information transfer among nodes, as well as descriptive information about the communication elements and services, to include location of routers, particular communication paths, satellite connections, encryption methods, etc.

From the Technical View, the Technical Architecture Profile (TV-1) provides a set of technical standards that apply to the architecture, where they apply, and how they will be implemented. This is called a profile of standards. The profile can be time-phased to depict the current and future use of standards and technologies.

18.2.2.2 C4ISR Framework Meta-Concepts

In general, some of the key concepts are defined, but not all. In essence, the framework provides a common methodology for describing certain architecture parts, with guidelines on how to provide these representations. Some of the definitions include [C4ISR]:

▶ *Architecture*: "The structure of components, their interrelationships, and the principles and guidelines governing their design and evolution over time." This definition is taken from [IEEE STD 610.12].

▶ *Operational Architecture*, defined above

▶ *Systems Architecture*, defined above

▶ *Technical Architecture*, defined above

Some terms are defined throughout the document. For example, *rules* are defined as "statements that define or constrain some aspect of the enterprise." The glossary list of defined terms consists of "Attribute, Communications Medium, Data, Data Element, Data-Entity, Format, Functional Area, Information, Information Exchange Requirement, Link, Mission, Mission Area, Needline, Network, Node, Operational Element, Operational Node, Organization, Platform, Process, Requirement, Role, Service, System, System Element, System Function, Systems Node, Rule, Task." [C4ISR]

There are only seven mandatory architecture products for the C4ISR Framework, as shown in Figure 18.11. All of these products have been previously discussed.

This framework is defined by a DoD-based task force, with input from federal agencies. As such, it can be considered a published specification, through committee consensus, but a closed committee.

View	Reference	Product	Description
All Views (Context)	AV-1	Overview and Summary Information	Scope, Users, Environment, Analytical Findings
All Views (Terms)	AV-2	Integrated Dictionary	Definitions of All Terms Used and Some Rules
Operational	OV-1	High-Level Operational Concept Graphic	High-Level Organizations, Missions, Configuration, Connectivity, etc.
Operational	OV-2	Operational Node Connectivity Description	Operational Nodes, Activities, Connectivity, Information Flow Between Nodes
Operational	OV-3	Operational Information Exchange Matrix	Information Exchanged Between Nodes Plus Attributes of Message Type, Quality, Quantity, Level of Interoperability
Systems	SV-1	System Interface Description	Node-Node Interfaces, Node-System Interfaces, System Components and Interfaces
Technical	TV-1	Technical Architecture Profile	Standards That Apply

FIGURE 18.11 Required C4ISR Products

C4ISR Framework was one of the main architecture methods in DoD. It has been used in several different mission architectures. As such, it is somewhat mature within DoD.

The C4ISR Architecture Framework Version 2.0 was developed by the MITRE Corporation and DoD to ensure that federated architectures are developed in accordance with uniform templates and taxonomies to enable them to be integrated and compared. Many organizations outside of DoD are applying the framework successfully, including several components of the Interoperability Clearinghouse, incorporating framework products into the Treasury Information System Architecture Framework, and coordinating with industry, e.g., The Open Group Architecture Framework (TOGAF). In addition, the Carnegie Mellon University Software Engineering Institute has used the framework products in their manual on how to construct and analyze scenarios for architecture evaluation. The Australian Ministry of Defence is examining the framework for their use. However, to date this framework is mostly applicable to U.S. federal government agencies.

18.2.2.3 Modeling Methods

C4ISR does not define or promote modeling for the framework. That is, it does not define abstraction, composition, behavior analyses, semantic behavior specification, and so forth, for modeling with the framework. Only certain parts of the framework identify the use of a model as an artifact. Such models include an activity model, business process model, logical data model, and a physical data model. However, this does not constitute a model of the entire architecture from a given view, since there is no defined modeling method for a view.

The architecture products are graphic images, text, relational databases, spreadsheets, or models. Templates are provided to represent, notionally, the content of these products. The mapping of the concepts of a modeling tool to the concepts of the architecture is not addressed.

In terms of completeness, many of the aspects of an architecture are depicted in the framework. But the specification is left for the architect. Some semantic behavior is addressed, such as rules in the Operational Rules Model. Some of the operational rules relating to relationships are a part of the Integrated Dictionary. Some action rules are associated with the operational business processes, and contain integrity constraints (which are invariants). Dynamic behavior is addressed in the System View, dealing with the timing and sequencing of events for system performance as part of the Systems State Transition Description. The Systems Rules Model describes the constraints on business processes or systems functionality derived from some aspect of the system architecture or design or implementation.

Consistency across the architecture views is not truly addressed. A notion of consistency, as it applies to a node, is identified between the operational and system views. But in general, consistency is not addressed. Relationships among the concepts, and rules of structure, are minimal. The prescription of the content for each architecture product does not always contain defined terminology. The structure of an interface relative to a logical structure or signature, a binding, or a communication protocol are not separately defined. The types of interfaces, components of a system or node, concepts such as interception and others are not defined. The framework does not provide a specification mechanism for generating an architecture, nor for rules that associate distributed processing elements with each other. The framework does not address distribution properties such as security, reliability, transparency, though it does address interoperability. Some semantic behavior is not addressed, such as policy or a set of invariants that may apply across more than one system or node. How one security policy, for example, affects the system in one node versus another node governed by a different security policy is not addressed.

There is no conformance of a system to the architecture, there are only conformance criteria for the use of C4ISR in an architecture representation.

18.2.2.4   Specification Language

It is suggested in some places that a formal language be used to represent some of the rules. Otherwise, there is no specification language identified for each view. Therefore this framework falls on the dimensions of informal, little prescribed definitiveness, and an incomplete system (or part) specification if only the mandatory aspects of each view are used.

18.2.2.5   Tools

The C4ISR Architecture Framework requires products that are a result of a tool, such as a activity model, or logical data model. However, the framework is intentionally vendor-tool-independent. Vendor products exist to provide the framework products, but no specific vendor is required. Some of the vendor tools that could be used include:

▶ Ptech FrameWork—This tool provides many of the C4ISR Architecture Framework products. This tool provides the templates for building the framework models, and can link the models. The tool can output to HTML, word processing, spreadsheets, and project management tools. It can also generate code, and provide model validation.

▶ netViz—This tool provides a graphical representation of communications network design supported by a database that can be imported by the user into another database. The diagrams are linked. They can represent operational nodes, linking them to the systems at the nodes. The tool can also be used for the IERs.

▶ Sterling Software's COOL™ tools—These tools provide graphical models of business processes, supporting some of the framework models (activity, logical data model, etc.). A companion tool can generate code as well.

- ❯ Any spreadsheet or relational database vendor product
- ❯ Any graphic editor product, such as Microsoft PowerPoint or Visio
- ❯ IDEF vendor tools

Most products can be provided by a visual representation from some tool.

18.2.2.6   How RM-ODP Enhances C4ISR Architecture Framework

RM-ODP can enhance the C4ISR Architecture Framework in a number of ways. The framework defines a good set of representation products. In some cases, terms are defined for use. Some semantic behavior is specified in terms of rules and what is termed "integrity constraints" that amount to invariants. And there are three views.

What is missing that RM-ODP can add is precision in terminology, consistency across distributed processing terms, levels of abstraction concepts throughout, explicit focus on distribution, explicit focus on semantic behavior, and a means of specifying the enterprise through well-defined concepts of community, domain, federation, role, policy, objectives, and scope.

Although three views are defined in the framework, they seem to be intertwined with the concept of three different architectures. The consistency across the elements of each view (or architecture) is not sufficient to provide a well-formed architecture. This could be improved by more precision in terminology, and addition of rules of structure that carry forward through all the views. Clearly, a distinction also needs to be made between "architecture" and "view." It is difficult to compare the RM-ODP viewpoints and the C4ISR architecture views because of the interpretation required of the terms in C4ISR. However, a notional comparison is provided in Figure 18.12. There is overlap, to be sure, but there are concepts in *each* of the RM-ODP viewpoints not addressed in the C4ISR architecture views. Some of those concepts are highlighted in the previous section. There are many places where parts of a C4ISR view architecture product can relate to some concept in one of the RM-ODP viewpoints, in which case a line is shown between the C4ISR architecture product and the RM-ODP viewpoint.

Concepts pertinent to distributed processing, such as capturing the interface signature, the structure of an interface signature, how policy affects an interaction, quality of service and where that is traced in the interactions and binding, and so forth could enhance the framework in specifying an architecture. Methods of achieving transparency, and many of the ilities, could be added from RM-ODP.

Each Operational and Systems View goes into more detail than may be necessary from the stakeholder who is designated to provide the products of that view. The Operational View reflects many of the computational viewpoint aspects, while also trying to describe the enterprise viewpoint aspects. Sometimes these get mixed and confused. Likewise, the System View reflects many of the computational and engineering viewpoint aspects and some technology aspects, even though there is a Technology View. Perhaps creation of more views in line with RM-ODP can better separate the areas of concern in addressing the architecture of a system.

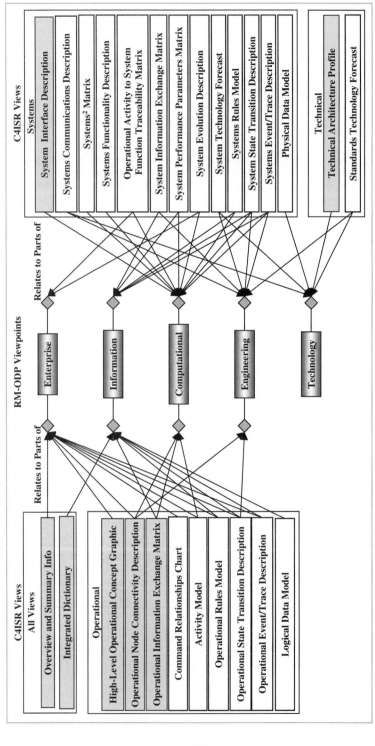

FIGURE 18.12 C4ISR Framework Views Related to RM-ODP Viewpoints

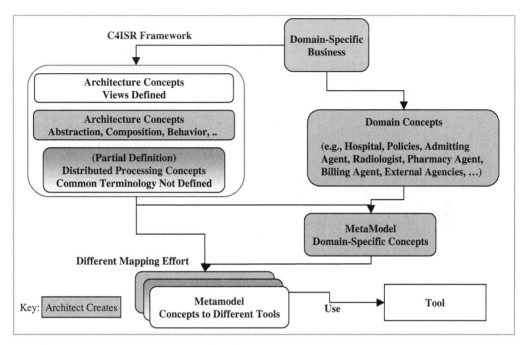

FIGURE 18.13   C4ISR Support of Architect's Concerns

18.2.2.7   Architecture Support and Selection Criteria Evaluation

The focus of the C4ISR Framework is a set of views from which to architect a system. A perspective of how much the C4ISR Framework supports the work of the architect is shown in Figure 18.13. The gray boxes reflect what the architect needs to do, whereas the white boxes reflect what the C4ISR Framework provides. The mapping effort is dependent on which representation is used in C4ISR. Some are more fully defined than others are. Where definition and metamodels are not defined, the architect needs to do so.

In terms of the selection criteria for the architect, Table 18.2 provides a notional perspective of how well the C4ISR Framework matches the criteria.

TABLE 18.2   Criteria for C4ISR Framework

CRITERIA	NOTIONAL VALUE
Defined Meta-Concepts	3
Open	3
Maturity	3

TABLE 18.2   Criteria for C4ISR Framework (Continued)

CRITERIA	NOTIONAL VALUE
Industry Consensus	3
Modeling Methods	2
Completeness	3
Consistency	2
Conformance	0
Specification Language	1–2
Tools	4
Visual Representation	4

18.2.3   THE UNIFIED MODELING LANGUAGE (UML)

The UML provides a framework of views, structured as Use Case, logical view, component view, deployment view, and activity view. The foundation for UML is an object model. Much about UML has already been discussed in this book. In fact, UML has been used many times to represent aspects of RM-ODP in this book. In this section, an overview of UML as an architecture framework is provided.

18.2.3.1   Overview of UML Models

The 4+1 View Model of [Kruchten] was a principal foundation for UML. It consists of five views addressing stakeholders concerns plus scenarios, all of which constitute the 4+1 View Model. The scenarios model, which now result in Use Cases, becomes the fifth view. The model includes notations and formats for each view, all founded on an object model. Figure 18.14 provides an overview of the 4+1 View Model.

The four views are related to the Rational Software Corporation's Rational Rose® products and implementation of UML. A notion of this mapping consists of:

1. The Scenarios relate to the Use Case view. They describe the use of the system as a collection of actors and the related transactions they can perform.

2. The Logical View is the object model and relates to UML packages, classes, and relationships.

3. The Process View addresses concurrency and synchronization. Concurrency relates to the UML class specification and synchronization relates to state and activity diagrams in UML.

4. The Development View describes the software modules and their relationships, in terms of the development environment. This relates to the class specification, collaboration diagram, sequence diagram, and the component view.

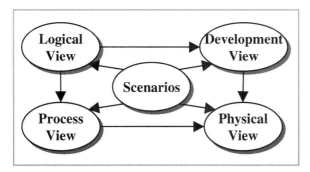

FIGURE 18.14 4+1 View Model

5. The Physical View maps the software onto the physical nodes in the system and the distribution aspects. This relates to the UML deployment view.

These views do not necessarily cleanly map onto the UML models. Therefore, this section will address UML as defined today.

The UML diagrams include static structure, Use Case, Sequence, Statechart, Collaboration, Activity, and Implementation. [UML-1.3] UML also includes the Object Constraint Language [OCL1] used to define constraints. However, many vendors do not include this aspect of UML in their tool offering.

18.2.3.2 UML Meta-Concepts

UML provides a well-defined set of modeling concepts, founded on an object model. The structure, elements, and relationships of the entities of UML are well-defined. It is an excellent method of architectural description, and it provides concepts that can be used for the modeling of a system.

With respect to distributed processing concepts, however, it is argued that UML provides more of a design perspective than an architecture perspective. Certain concepts are not part of the language of UML, such as binding, behavior, interaction, interface signature, etc. For example, it is difficult for the architect to express levels of abstraction using UML. The architect needs to provide the mapping of such distributed processing and specification concepts onto the use of UML.

UML does not directly provide well-defined distributed processing propositions (concepts and rules). The modeling constructs enable the architect to define a metamodel to model the constituent parts of a system, how they function, and how they behave, singly and collectively, within and with their environment, but these are not UML concepts.

Throughout this book, limitations in the use of UML have been noted. In addition, the use of UML for a variety of distributed processing concerns has been shown. The ongoing work of [EDOC-UML, EDOC-UMLb] and others is expected to provide a general RM-ODP underpinning to UML for use by an architect of any domain.

The UML specification is a product of the Object Management Group (OMG) consortium. Any company can join OMG for a fee. The specification is a result of a committee consensus. As such, it is an open specification.

UML is a relatively mature specification. UML is always evolving. However, the main constructs are solid. The enhancements to UML are generally semantic behavioral enhancements, and additional functionality.

Different vendors' tools that provide UML modeling and visualization are at varying levels of maturity. To date, no such tool provides the full UML specification capabilities, which includes OCL.

Industry consensus abounds, but it's harder to pin down an accurate answer on what it should be used for. Many believe the use of UML is architecting! It's not, of course, but it has gained widespread acceptance. Remember, UML is a language to describe whatever the architect chooses to describe, using whatever precision the architect chooses. Further, UML is aimed more at design and implementation than at architectural specification. Because of the implementation aspects of UML tools, the vendor ensures that the result of a UML description can be encoded in one of several programming languages: C, C++, Java™, COBOL, and IDL (an interface description language). As such, support for architectural specification to include composition, decomposition, abstraction, refinement, different views (superimposed onto the UML models), etc., are not supported by UML. And it is generally recognized that UML is difficult to use to appropriately represent semantic behavior. Nevertheless, UML is a good tool to use to represent an architecture, as long as the architect uses the tool wisely.

18.2.3.3   UML Modeling

Modeling addresses the ability of abstraction, composition, views, objects, behavior, and so forth. UML is object-based, and as such provides modeling constructs that support objects, classes, types, encapsulation, etc. UML also provides classification and strong typing mechanisms. UML provides models from different predefined views: Use Case, logical, component, and deployment. Models from these different views relate to different perspective of the architecture of a system.

UML does not directly support multiple levels of abstractions or composition. UML does not adequately support the specification of behavior, sameness, or quality. In addition, the handling of failure is not clearly provided. The architect needs to define how the use of UML will accomplish these modeling methods.

UML coupled with OCL models do not provide a complete specification of a system, for a variety of reasons. The principal reason is the specification of time and invariants in OCL. In addition, the capability of specifying multiple interfaces, policy, contracts, constraints of policy on an interaction, and so forth are not yet part of the UML specification.

Consistency across the models is provided, but consistency across certain uses of UML is not. In particular, the use of annotated notes, especially if used to represent some semantics or constraints, are not part of the model and there is no effort to ensure that such notes are represented in other related models. This remains a manual task of the architect. The consistency provided by UML tools is generally syntactic and arises from the correct use of the UML object model.

Conformance is not addressed. However, UML compliance is provided, ensuring the model generated from UML complies with the standard (as interpreted by the UML vendor product).

18.2.3.4 Specification Language

UML itself is a specification. However, it does not provide a specification language for an architecture of a system. In terms of the dimensions of specification, UML is not based on formalism, but does define its concepts and rules of structure. Although completeness is left for the architect, a model check will identify inconsistencies and incompleteness of the use of UML. If the model is without error, code can be generated. However, not all constructs used in UML are evaluated in the model checks (e.g., notes).

18.2.3.5 Tools

There are many UML-based tools. Not all tools cover all aspects of UML, however. Some "UML tools" add vendor-specific constructs, which may be beneficial to some organizations. However, such constructs are generally not part of the UML specification, and as such model exchange across different UML vendors is at risk.

18.2.3.6 How RM-ODP Enhances UML

The principal enhancement that RM-ODP provides to UML is that of behavior specification. In addition, RM-ODP provides the architect with architecting methods for use, which can be mapped to UML. RM-ODP viewpoints provide the distributed processing concepts. RM-ODP and the metamodel work of mapping RM-ODP to UML [EDOC-UML, EDOC-UMLb] will provide an architecture specification coupled with a modeling language that has widespread use, and tools that enable visualization. The ongoing work at OMG in providing a synergy between RM-ODP and UML will greatly offload the work of the architect, while providing an architecture specification and visualization capability.

18.2.3.7 Architecture Support and Selection Criteria Evaluation

The focus of the UML is a set of object-modeling constructs and views from which to architect a system. A perspective of how much the UML supports the work of the architect is shown in Figure 18.15. The gray boxes reflect what the architect needs to do, whereas the white boxes reflect what the UML provides.

In terms of the selection criteria for the architect, Table 18.3 provides a notional view of how well UML matches the criteria.

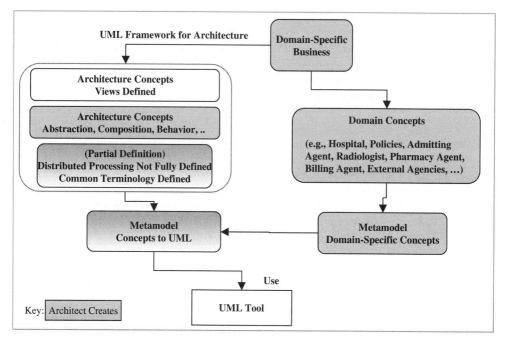

FIGURE 18.15   UML Support of an Architect's Concerns

TABLE 18.3   Criteria for UML

CRITERIA	NOTIONAL VALUE
Defined meta-concepts	3
Open	4
Maturity	4
Industry consensus	5
Modeling methods	3
Completeness	3
Consistency	4
Conformance	0
Specification language	3
Tools	5
Visual representation	5

18.2.4   IEEE P1471

IEEE Recommended Practice for Architectural Description is a not-yet-approved IEEE-recommended practice standard, identified as P1471.1, hereafter identified as P1471. This work is the product of the IEEE Architecture Working Group (AWG), which began its work in 1995. This standard addresses architectural description of software-intensive systems.

The IEEE Software Engineering Standards Committee (SESC) chartered the AWG to produce a standard with the following goals [IEEE AWG-97]:

▶ Define the direction for incorporating architectural thinking into IEEE standards.

▶ Develop a framework (terms, concepts, and principles) for software systems architectures.

▶ Examine IEEE standards for architectural relevance.

▶ Produce an action plan for future IEEE activities in this area.

The P1471 framework, then, is the set of terms, concepts, and principles for an architectural description. In particular, this standard claims that the framework presented is a *conceptual framework* to present the content and structure of an architectural description of a system.

18.2.4.1   Overview of IEEE P1471 Architecture Description Standard

An architectural description documents an architecture. Its purpose is to facilitate conversation among stakeholders and the architecture team by capturing the products of an architecture during the process of system development. Figure 18.16 provides an overview of the P1471 framework.

The standard identifies the need for architecting to be a part of the system lifecycle: development, operation, and maintenance of a system. However, the standard does not prescribe a lifecycle to use. This is left to the architect.

The architectural description is defined in terms of a fundamental set of terms, conformance criteria to the P1471 standard, necessary information to define a viewpoint, and the requirement to use one or more views to describe the architecture. Each view is a realization of a viewpoint template, in part or in whole. A viewpoint is a pattern or template that defines certain prescribed properties, but the standard does not prescribe any particular viewpoint or prescriptive properties of a viewpoint. One of the properties of a viewpoint described includes one or more descriptive or modeling techniques that can be used by a view. Another property is a list of stakeholders addressed by the viewpoint. A view, then, identifies a subset of the viewpoint properties, those stakeholders and concerns it will address and the description techniques to be used. A viewpoint is considered a template from which to generate a specific view of a specific system. As such, viewpoints are reusable artifacts, and views may or may not be reusable depending on the system.

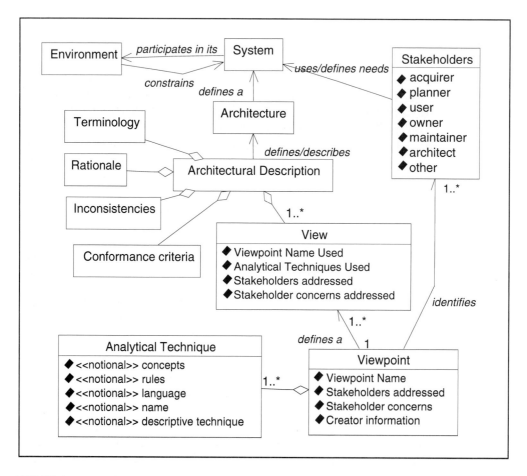

FIGURE 18.16   IEEE P1471 Overview

Thus, the architectural description of a system:

▶ Is based on the terminology of P1471

▶ Identifies the stakeholders and their concerns

▶ Identifies the viewpoint templates used

▶ States any known inconsistencies across architectural descriptions

▶ States a rationale for the architecture

▶ Defines one or more views of the whole system:

  – Each view originates from exactly one viewpoint

  – Each view defines the viewpoint stakeholders

- Each view defines the viewpoint set of concerns
- Each view defines the viewpoint analytical techniques used

Some viewpoints are provided as informational, not prescriptive. These include structural, behavioral, physical interconnect, and link bit error rate. In previous versions of this standard, other viewpoints were addressed: data, management, distribution, capability, and security.

As an example, the *structural viewpoint* suggests (not prescribes) a focus on components, connectors, roles, and other properties. This viewpoint is to provide a description that addresses things such as the computational elements of a system, their interfaces, and how they connect. The architect may elect to use this viewpoint or not. If selected, the architect is encouraged to provide the elements identified, using one or more identified descriptive techniques. The result is a *structural view* of the system of concern.

As will be discussed below, P1471 lacks the precision necessary for a full architectural specification. It leaves most of this to the architect of the system. It provides a guide of what is important to capture in the process of architecting a system to meet the stakeholders concerns. As such, it helps the architect to scope the problem, converse with the stakeholders through common viewpoints, and provide flexibility in the viewpoints chosen for a particular architecture.

18.2.4.2 IEEE P1471 Framework Meta-Concepts

A fundamental goal of the P1471 standard is to provide common terminology and concepts for unifying the use of any architectural description mechanisms. Part of P1471 provides "a conceptual framework and vocabulary for talking about architectural issues of systems." [Sachs] The standard provides a number of definitions of terms and concepts used through its framework. It defines some key terms, all quoted from [IEEE-P1471]:

▶ An *architecture* as "the fundamental organization of a system embodied in its components, their relationships to each other and to the environment and the principles guiding its design and evolution"

▶ An *architectural description* as a "a collection of products to document an architecture"

▶ A *view* as a representation of "a whole system from the perspective of a related set of concerns"

▶ A *viewpoint* as a "a specification of the conventions for constructing and using a view"

Other terms defined include acquirer, architect, architecting, lifecycle model, system, and system stakeholder. It also bases several of its terms on other IEEE standards.

This is (or will be) an open published standard from IEEE, a national standards body. Participation on this committee is open to any IEEE member. At its maximum level, the AWG consisted of around 30 members. Review of this standard included over 125 international reviewers.

As stated above, this is a relatively new standard from IEEE. It attempts to capture and document some of the work of ISO RM-ODP. Normally, IEEE standards are extensions or enhancements to international standards, as are those originating from ISO or ITU-T.

Industry consensus has yet to be determined. Some have begun to use P1471, as in applications from individual companies (e.g., Rational, IBM), and some consortia such as The Open Group. These groups are mostly at the stage of considering the use of P1471.

18.2.4.3   IEEE P1471 Modeling

As noted above, P1471 provides an architectural description of a system. It is claimed that this architectural description "is a model used to present the structure and behavior of the whole system...It shows how the system fulfills the needs in the context of its environment...It identifies major system components, their interconnections and dependencies, and the limits within which they must operate." [Sachs] According to [Sachs], P1471 also provides "architectural methods and processes...Techniques for architectural review and analysis." This amounts to an architectural specification of some dimension, but the standard does not prescribe this.

It is suggested that each of the viewpoints provide one or more analytical techniques (models, analytical tools, documentation, etc.) as part of its template specification. Each viewpoint template should consist of a viewpoint name, the stakeholder community addressed, the concerns of the stakeholder community addressed, the concepts and rules for modeling that defines a view, and author information that created the viewpoint template.

Another example of a viewpoint template technique is the use of Acme [Acme] as a technique for a *structural viewpoint* [Hilliard]. This particular technique is precise and based on formalism. If the architect chooses to define or reuse such a template, the architectural specification is more precise. However, a structural template technique can also be defined as a set of PowerPoint charts, with some labeling. This would address some aspects of a structural viewpoint, and be less precise. And P1471 does not explicitly define the techniques for use in such templates.

P1471 explicitly excludes the definition of the architecture description language for modeling, the views required in the architectural description model, and provides no formal consistency or completeness criteria.

There is no clear separation between an architecture evaluation and an architecture description. The standard asserts, as an example, that the architectural description will allow one "to predict the quality of systems whose architectures conform to the architectural description." [IEEE-P1471] This statement is arguably true only if the viewpoint analytical method is based on precise terminology and formalism. The former deals with a definition of an architecture, whereas the latter deals with how well the architecture is documented. If the architecture definition is poor, because the viewpoint specifications are insufficient, but the documentation from those viewpoints is high, then that architecture description would achieve a high degree of conformance with this standard. These two concepts are intertwined in the standard. The standard appears to base its precise definition of an architecture on the precision of the architecture viewpoint templates, which it does not require or specify.

Though this is a good framework for an architectural description of a system, the lack of consistency across the viewpoints and choice of views to represent the architecture requires the enterprise program manager to force a common use of these artifacts across all systems in the enterprise if the systems are to interoperate. Furthermore, since the choice is variable for each system, the chances of interoperability across heterogeneous systems are small. It is claimed that this flexibility of choice lends itself to a system that can evolve. This is arguable. One can always add to a system, but one cannot always integrate a change into a system or interoperate with another system as an afterthought. Again, precision and formalism lend to precision in change (the where, how, the analysis of the result), whereas ad hoc informal methods are more difficult to facilitate a change in a system.

The standard requires all known inconsistencies be documented. However, there is no attempt to unify the methodology of distributed processing architectural specification through a precisely defined language. In other words, this standard does not provide a metamodel of distributed processing for use in defining inconsistencies. And these inconsistencies can appear in modeling techniques chosen, terminology, viewpoints selected, views generated, and any number of ways. As a result, this standard is not an architectural description of a unifying or open set of systems.

P1471 provides compliance checking criteria of an architectural description to P1471. These criteria include the identification of the stakeholders and their concerns, the viewpoints defined and used, the architectural views used to represent the architecture, rationale, and known inconsistencies. P1471 does not specifically address conformance of a system implementation to the architecture description.

18.2.4.4 Specification Language

There is no formal specification language in P1471. Some terms are defined, but not all. Completeness of a description of (part of) a system is left to the architect.

18.2.4.5   Tools

Since a viewpoint definition includes any analytical technique, most representation tools can be used. For example, a structural viewpoint can include an architectural description language, or a UML tool, or a document. This is defined by the creator of the template.

However, there is no tool that is focused solely on P1471.

18.2.4.6   How RM-ODP Enhances IEEE 1471 Architecture Description

One of the appendices of P1471 attempts to relate the standard to RM-ODP. It claims that RM-ODP provides a definition of viewpoint (which it does) but not a definition of view (which is also true, in the strictest sense). However, the viewpoints of RM-ODP can be somewhat related to P1471 viewpoint templates, and the use of the RM-ODP viewpoints related to a set of P1471 views. Furthermore, P1471 attempts to suggest a list of concepts addressed in each of the RM-ODP viewpoints. This list is incomplete, and does not address all of the foundational aspects of RM-ODP.

RM-ODP can enhance P1471 with precise terminology. In one place, for example, P1471 addresses the term *environment* as a context. No further definition is given. It suggests that the environment influences the architecture of a system, but does not elaborate how. RM-ODP can provide precision of the treatment of an environment to P1471.

The RM-ODP viewpoints and associated languages, coupled with the foundations of the object model, rules of specification, and rules of structure, can be considered separate viewpoint templates for P1471. Then the P1471 standard becomes the documentation vehicle for the use of RM-ODP, providing a formal, open, and consistent foundation to P1471.

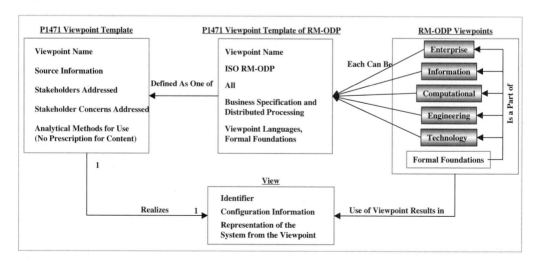

FIGURE 18.17   IEEE P1471 Views with RM-ODP Viewpoints

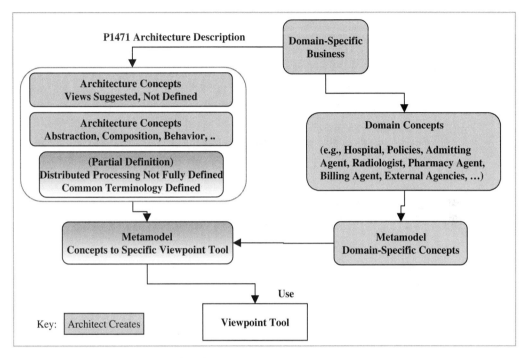

FIGURE 18.18 P1471 Support of Architect's Concerns

18.2.4.7   Architecture Support and Selection Criteria Evaluation

The focus of P1471 is a set of views from which to architect a system. A perspective of how much the P1471 architecture description supports the work of the architect is shown in Figure 18.18. The gray boxes reflect what the architect needs to do, whereas the white boxes reflect what the P1471 provides.

In terms of the selection criteria for the architect, Table 18.4 provides a notional view of how well the P1471 Framework matches the criteria.

TABLE 18.4   Criteria for IEEE P1471

CRITERIA	NOTIONAL VALUE
Defined meta-concepts	2
Open	4
Maturity	2
Industry consensus	2

TABLE 18.4   Criteria for IEEE P1471   (Continued)

CRITERIA	NOTIONAL VALUE
Modeling methods	0–4*
Completeness	0–3*
Consistency	2
Conformance	0
Specification language	1–3*
Tools	0–4*
Visual representation	0–4*

(*) Since no viewpoint is required, there are no modeling methods required, or associated tools and visual representations of the viewpoint techniques. The degree of specification is totally dependent upon the viewpoint templates defined and chosen by the architect.

18.3   SUMMARY

Architecture practice today generally encompasses the use of a specific architecture framework, especially if that framework enables a visualization of the architecture artifacts. Some of the popular frameworks used include the Zachman Framework, the DoD C4ISR Architecture Framework, the UML as an architecture framework, and the emerging draft IEEE P1471 standard. This chapter discussed the usefulness of each of these frameworks from the perspective of specifying the architecture of a distributed processing system.

Any framework for use in specifying an architecture needs to provide certain functionality, some of which includes:

▶ Architecture concepts for supporting the architecting process

▶ Architecture concept of views or viewpoints

▶ Distributed processing concepts that support the architecture of a distributed processing system

Some of the architecture frameworks are a result of committee consensus, and some are the result of a particular company. Some are mature, some are not. Some have widespread industry acceptance, some do not.

Properties of the architecture framework concepts that are important to consider when selecting a framework include completeness, consistency, and the ability to specify conformance properties. Properties of the distributed processing concepts include openness, level of maturity, and industry acceptance. Each must provide well-defined terminology, concepts, and rules, to ensure the architect understands how the framework will guide the architecting of the system.

Modeling methods of an architecture framework are important to consider. Any such modeling method needs to support multiple views, multiple levels of abstraction, composition, and the ability to represent the architecture and distributed processing concepts.

RM-ODP provides all of this, plus separate viewpoint languages. Each language supports the viewpoint specification of a system. The collection of all such specifications results in the architecture specification of a system.

Views have become a major aspect of an architecture framework. The intent of a view is to capture the focus of related concerns of a system, leaving other concerns to other views. This provides a means of separating the complex task of architecting a system into doable parts. But the parts need to be cohesive so that they collectively specify a system, instead of stovepipe parts specifying some aspect of a system that collectively do not work together. In terms of RM-ODP, a viewpoint provides the concepts and structure for any system specification from that viewpoint. The use of that viewpoint, and refinement of the architecture concepts of that viewpoint, is considered a view of the system.

In some frameworks, there are many kinds of views; e.g., data view, distribution view, physical view, component view, logical view, enterprise view, system view, and others. Often these views are orthogonal, meaning that one does not address the concerns of another. For example, a data view might consist of the data schema, data flow, and operations on the data, but not distribution, functional use, constraints (such as access control), or quality of service (such as resolution). Some frameworks prescribe the use of a view, but do not define the views to use. This is left to the architect. Some suggest the architect define and use a view (any view will do). Some provide a set of views from which the architect can select for the architecture of the system. Some of the views are precisely defined, but most are not. Architecture practice today makes possible the use of many different inconsistent views. There is no agreement on what views are necessary and minimal for a system architecture across the enterprise, except for RM-ODP, which has achieved international agreement.

The architect must perform additional tasks when using a tool. Namely, defining how the architecture, distributed processing, and domain-specific concepts can be represented in the tool. Most of the frameworks do not provide a model of its concepts in the concepts of a tool (a metamodel) for use by the architect. For example, how the architect depicts a component, or a connector of varying types, or constraints, is a matter of choice in the use of most tools. But the architect should choose, and should make those choices explicit, resulting in a mapping from the concepts of the framework, coupled with domain-specific terms and concepts onto the constructs of the tool.

Evaluating the choice of framework to use for architecting is not easy. This chapter presented a set of criteria and architect's concerns to use to evaluate the frameworks. There are other criteria one could use, but the ones chosen were those important for specification.

NINETEEN

ARCHITECTURE HEURISTICS
AND CONCLUSION

Architecting is one of the major "undiscovered" processes. With the trend toward complex systems that span international boundaries, the need for a solid approach to architecting is critical. Modern technology is such that one can accomplish a great deal in a system. On the other hand, technology choices are so plentiful that they complicate the decision of how to construct the system.

The Reference Model of Open Distributed Processing (RM-ODP) defines the standard reference model for distributed, software systems architectures, based on object-oriented techniques, an ontology of distributed processing, rules of specification, rules of structure, rules of conformance testing, rules of consistency, and viewpoints to aid in separation of concerns. This has all been accepted at the international level by the International Standards Organization (ISO) and the International Telecommunications Union (ITU). Figure 19.1 provides a final overview of all that RM-ODP addresses.

RM-ODP is a reference model for distribution, interoperability, portability, and semantic behavior. RM-ODP is based on precisely defined terms and concepts forming the foundations for open distributed processing. It applies to software intensive architectures, across a heterogeneity of components. It addresses business specifications, as well as federation of autonomous domains. RM-ODP also provides techniques to delay choices of technology and products, while specifying what the system is to do.

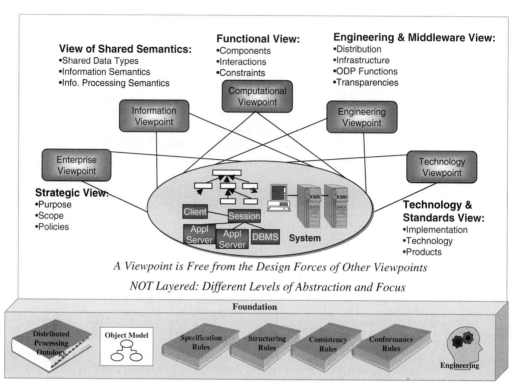

FIGURE 19.1 Overview of RM-ODP

RM-ODP consists of well-defined techniques for abstraction, composition, structuring, and conformance testing. It provides an ontology for expressing the functioning, behavior, problems, and requirements for heterogeneous organizations and systems, and provides a focus on externally observable behavior (semantics) rather than just the internal structure (application functionality). RM-ODP supports, through its formal semantic definition, "what-if" analyses including effective tradeoff analyses.

RM-ODP enables communication among architects, designers, implementers, and stakeholders (customers, users, program managers, business domain experts, etc.). It provides a consistent architecture specification across levels of abstraction, with an explicit manner of specifying system behavior, conformance testing of the system implementation to architecture, and full system construction lifecycle focus, or any subset, as desired. It provides techniques for software distribution, interoperability, reusability, portability, and composibility. RM-ODP serves as an enabler for seamless integration of disparate applications/components over multiple, dissimilar systems. As an enabler, it also permits dynamic (re)configuration of functions/objects to provide a service. And it enables transparent sharing of resources/services across the enterprise.

RM-ODP is equally applicable to a system of systems, a single system, or a software component in the system. The reference model supports alternative selections of technologies and products for the system, prescribing none in particular, but providing criteria for use in selecting the technologies that best meet cost, schedule, and performance.

RM-ODP provides a separation of distributed system concerns into five viewpoints, coupled with viewpoint language addressing the concepts, structuring rules, and terms associated with the viewpoints. In addition, the consistency across these viewpoints supports evolutionary growth and technology infusion, as well as program management of a distributed architecture team in formulating an architecture specification.

RM-ODP also provides 24 specific ODP infrastructure support functions for reuse, as well as eight reusable selective and optional distribution transparencies. The underlying foundation for all of RM-ODP is an object-based model, unique in the object-oriented world.

19.1 SUMMARY OF THE CONTENTS OF THE BOOK

The book provided a tutorial of RM-ODP. How to use RM-ODP in creating an architecture specification of a system, coupled with techniques of specification, differences in representation and specification, patterns of reasoning for addressing distributed system concerns, and possible choices of frameworks for representation were covered in this book.

The approach to using RM-ODP was addressed. Key properties such as interoperability, dependability, integration, composability, scalability, transparency, behavior specification, policy management, federation, and conformance testing from the principles of RM-ODP were provided.

Key features addressed in this book included the following:

▶ How to manage the architecting process in the lifecycle of system
▶ How to create a business specification
▶ How to understand and use the concepts of distributed processing
▶ How to understand and use the techniques of architecting
▶ How to specify an architecture
▶ How to understand and specify behavior
▶ How to provide the right level of detail in an architecture specification
▶ How to ensure the implementation conforms to the architecture specification
▶ How to specify non-functional properties of a system (the "ilities")
▶ How to use RM-ODP

Many organizations are using RM-ODP to define their business specifications, their information system, information system semantics, and full distributed processing system architecture. RM-ODP has been in use in a number of industries and consortia. These include:

▶ Consortia

– The Object Management Group (OMG), where RM-ODP is a required part of all requests for proposal of OMG services, and is used as the general object model in the upcoming revised Object Management Architecture guide

– The Telecommunications Information Network Architecture (TINA) telecommunications consortium

– Australia's Distributed Systems Technology Centre (DSTC)

▶ Industry

– Telecommunications industry companies: AT&T®, Lucent Technologies®, Nortel Networks®, GTE®, and others

– Financial industry, such as Merrill Lynch[SM], Morgan Stanley[SM], and others

– Manufacturing industry, such as the work in product data

– Health industry, such as specific health care companies, and specific health care services such as patient identification services

– Geographical systems

▶ Government agencies

– U.S. Department of Defense health domain

– United Kingdom logistics

– United Kingdom C3I interoperability

– Norway C2

– Australia C2

– United Kingdom air traffic control

▶ And others

The principles of RM-ODP were discussed, both at an introductory level and in depth. Each chapter provided an introductory discussion of the topic, a progressively in-depth discussion of the details specified by RM-ODP, and an introductory-level summary of what was covered. RM-ODP is not easy. It is a hard study. Specification is not easy. But then, developing distributed systems (of systems) is not easy either; it is very easy to get it wrong, and requires good techniques and engineering skills to get it right.

The author of this book was privileged to have been a member of the RM-ODP standard committee from the beginning, and continues today to help formulate some of the emerging supporting RM-ODP standards, such as the Enterprise Language.

A medical case study was used throughout the book, producing an increasingly detailed specification. This medical case study is based on actual experience from the author. In addition, many metamodels were provided to represent the concepts of RM-ODP. All of these metamodels are contributions from the author. The techniques of using RM-ODP in conjunction with specification techniques are based on actual practice as well as contributions from the author's own work.

19.2   CONCEPTS OF ARCHITECTURE

The purpose of an architecture is to address the support of the business objectives. In terms of an ODP system, an architecture defines the functionality and behavior that the system must be architected to achieve, such as reliability, security, and performance. The role of the architect is to communicate and explain the needs of the customer to the system builder, and to track the conformance of the system to the architecture as specified. This role is satisfied by an architecture specification, which is a result of the architecting process.

Architecture is much more than a design template or pattern. It must address capabilities for:

▶ Defining and comparing system components
▶ Rules for design integrity
▶ Abstraction of components, interfaces, and behavior
▶ Composition of components, interfaces, and behavior
▶ Acknowledge distribution issues, and address them
▶ Guidelines for making choices

All of this requires engineering, semantics, and well-formed rules for analysis and design.

Successful architecture specification is achievable through the use of the unprecedented foundation of RM-ODP. The use of the foundation, coupled with a language for distributed processing concerns, enables an architect to create a valid architecture specification of a distributed processing system. As an international standard, RM-ODP goes a step further in defining these architecture specification techniques to result in an open system, thereby enhancing the capabilities of interoperability and federation.

RM-ODP is the result of a depth of thinking that permeates every aspect of architecting. Viewpoints provide the mechanism to separate concerns into achievable specifications. The viewpoints of RM-ODP are necessary and sufficient to cover every aspect of open distributed processing. This is a result of using the foundations of abstraction, composition, modeling, and a language of distributed processing, tailored to the viewpoint concerns. Consistency across the viewpoints is provided both in terms of specific correspondences of viewpoint concepts, as well as rules for the architect to achieve additional consistency. Without consistency of the viewpoints or views of a system, the result is often a stovepipe, independent, non-cohesive set of views that represent something, but is generally not a single system. The system implemented from the architectural description, in this case, can lead to an unwanted system, a system that does not solve a business problem, or a system that simply does not work.

By applying the proven techniques of RM-ODP in a domain-specific manner, an organization can construct its own architecture specification, based on a solid foundation of architecting techniques. This book provided a guide for the architect to construct a software systems architecture using RM-ODP specification techniques that meet the objectives of the business.

19.3	HEURISTICS TO REMEMBER

Architecting techniques were provided in this book. Many heuristics apply to the process of architecting, to create an architecture specification of a system that works. Some of these heuristics are repeated here, with the knowledge that many more could be added to this list. These heuristics reflect the process of architecting a system from parts into a whole. The result is a well-formed architectural specification that works, can be analyzed, tested, and implemented into a working solution.

19.3.1 ARCHITECTURE OF A SYSTEM ADDRESSES MUCH MORE THAN STRUCTURE: IT ADDRESSES CAPABILITIES IN SUPPORT OF THE BUSINESS. CONVERSING BUSINESS NEEDS AMONG STAKEHOLDERS AND ARCHITECTS IS CRITICAL.

A system is not an end; it is a tool to provide a solution to a problem in the business. An architecture specification needs to reflect the needs of the business, how the system operates in conjunction with the business, and how the system solves the problem for which it was created. The use of the Healthy Hospital case study showed how a system for a hospital can be architected to support the business of the hospital, and the business of interaction with the external domains of insurance, physician practices, and state regulation authorities. The enterprise business specification techniques showed how the language in the domain of medical care is used to formulate such an architecture, while enabling communication among the stakeholders and the architect.

19.3.2 SCOPE THE PROBLEM TO BE SOLVED AND THEN SIMPLIFY.

Attempting to architect a large, complex problem is difficult if not impossible without techniques that enable focused, composable solutions. The problem can be scoped through the concepts of community and domain. From there, the techniques of RM-ODP are applied to each such community in the problem to be solved. Because of the consistency of the concepts, the resultant parts will fit together. This was shown using the Healthy Hospital case, separating the hospital into one community, and the insurance company, for example, into another community. Architecture specifications for each community proceeded independently, but were linked together through the concepts of federation and cross-domain interception and interaction, all founded on reusable patterns of reasoning provided by RM-ODP. With the use of abstraction and composition, the architect can simply focus on a problem to engineer, leaving the details to another refinement.

19.3.3 An architecture specification specifies how the system will solve a business problem. An architecture specification specifies how the system will interact in the business.

An architecture specification of a system must always consider the problem to be solved (the scope and objectives) in the domain of the business (community), interacting with external businesses, and constrained by business rules (policies and contracts). The concepts of RM-ODP provide the specification of an architecture that addresses these heuristics.

19.3.4 The architecture specification is a model of the system.

The architecture specification is a model; it is not the system itself. That is, a model of a system follows well-defined concepts and rules. Models of a system are important for a number of reasons: communication among all persons involved in the development of the system; simulation of some aspect of the system prior to development to determine expected behavior, or some other criteria; analysis of some aspect of the system for determining a choice of a particular pattern of reasoning, a particular architecture pattern, a particular design pattern, etc.; criteria for selecting system products, technologies, standards, code to implement, etc.; performance prediction and possible change of some performing characteristic of the system; and analysis of conformance of the developed system to the architecture. The original statement of the problem from the stakeholders may not be the right problem to solve. Modeling enables the architect to make choices, based on refining a choice to a point that is valid or invalid, and cycling back to a better choice if necessary. Through modeling, the solution can iterate to what the stakeholder wants, and the architect is able to deliver. This book provided many modeling techniques and examples using the Healthy Hospital case study. One such example was the realization that a data manager object was needed to manage access and quality of service, instead of direct access to all data sources from all users of the system, as was originally presented in Part One.

19.3.5 SPECIFICATION IS NOT REPRESENTATION. USE AVAILABLE REPRESENTATION TOOLS, BUT USE THEM WISELY.

A specification is a definition of what is wanted. A representation is a description that provides a warm fuzzy feeling of what can be accomplished. But a warm fuzzy feeling is neither a solution nor a definition. The use of examples is another form of representation. They cannot replace a specification: they tend to be over specific, using techniques of "color" to represent some semantics (sort of); they tend to not address semantic behavior explicitly (i.e., by definition); and they tend not to cover all aspects of the problem.

Architecture specification means definition: functional capabilities, semantic behavior, and components and their interactions. A representation is a presentation of, for example, two boxes with a line between them in a drawing. Architecture specification addresses the meaning of each box, and the meaning of the line between two boxes, and much more. There are many tools available for representing an architecture, and these tools are very useful for discussing the architecture with others. Such a tool is not sufficient for an architect to further the architecture, or an implementer to implement, or a tester to test. The architect should make use of such tools, but wisely. Often, added notations to the tools are required to explain the meaning of some part of the specification (such as a constraint). Often these tools help to visualize a decision, with the knowledge of what is meant by the parts. Numerous examples of Healthy Hospital were represented using the Unified Modeling Language (UML), and these were generally augmented with notations to show some constraint. The knowledge to do this is part of the job of architecting.

19.3.6 THERE ARE THREE DIMENSIONS OF SPECIFICATION, RESULTING IN A SPECTRUM OF A FULL ARCHITECTURAL SPECIFICATION TO A MERE ARCHITECTURAL REPRESENTATION.

There are three dimensions of specification, depending on what the architect requires. These dimensions are formalism, definitiveness, and completeness. The more formal, fully defined, and complete a specification, the better the end product. The informal, less defined, and partial specification of a system is a representation because it lacks specificity. Nevertheless, an architect can elect to use a representation technique and fully define all aspects of its use, and completely define some part of the system. Though this is not a formal specification based on mathematics, it provides a degree of specificity to offset misinterpretation, and to enable better analyses.

Representations are very useful means of communicating, notionally, with different stakeholders, such as the use of the general modeling language, UML. What then is required is a mapping of the model concepts and rules from the specification model to the concepts and rules of the representation model. What often happens is that the model representation language is mistakenly taken as the model of specification.

But a representation does not take the place of specification.

19.3.7 KEYS TO SUCCESSFUL ARCHITECTING ARE THE METHODS OF ABSTRACTION, COMPOSITION, AND GOOD THINKING.

Abstraction and composition enable a complex problem to be focused on parts at varying levels of detail. Composition addresses some software in the system as a coarse-grained object, focusing on the aspects of how that object interacts in the system, and the semantics of that object. Decomposition addresses the parts of the composition to enable the architect to provide more and more detail. The only way composition works is through the rules of composition and consistency that tie the specifications of the parts together. Abstraction enables the architect to focus on coarse-grained multiple parts, not necessarily composed, to address some capability of the system. Subsequent levels of abstraction enable the architect to further refine the capabilities. Once again, the specification of the parts fits together through the rules of abstraction and consistency.

Good engineering skills and thinking permeate the use of abstraction and composition. A good architect is one who can use precise concepts in the construction of an architecture specification, abstraction techniques to define the parts of the architecture, thread in domain-specific business needs, and use good engineering skills in the process. No clearly defined process for architecting is in hand. Today most architecture approaches are ad hoc. But RM-ODP provides a defined set of techniques for accomplishing this task. The architect needs to know when to use these techniques and how. Examples of Healthy Hospital were discussed at various levels of abstraction throughout the book, sometimes addressing a composition and its parts, such as the admitting agent and its components that provide general admission and scheduling.

19.3.8 VIEWPOINTS ARE AN AID, NOT AN END UNTO THEMSELVES. CONSISTENCY ACROSS VIEWPOINTS IS CRUCIAL TO A WELL-FORMED ARCHITECTURE SPECIFICATION.

RM-ODP provides a reference framework, grammars, methods of abstraction and composition, and separation of concerns of a system to achieve an architecture specification of a system. There is a lot of work ongoing in trying to scope the need for a large-scale system to a (set of) architecture(s). Some attempts are struggling with separation of concerns for architecting a system, and approach this step either in terms of "views" or provide no effective separation at all. Some attempts are struggling with the ability to analyze an architecture, or determine conformance of a system implementation to its architecture. Using the current approach of separating the architecting process into "views," the correspondences across these ad hoc views usually does not work. That is, the current conformance (checking that the implementation conforms to the behavior of the architecture) approach is in research, at best, with view integration as an afterthought. In contrast, RM-ODP has the depth of thinking for a separation of concerns that accounts for cross-domain view integration. It provides a framework for this separation, using viewpoints, as well as separating out certain decisions (e.g., product decisions) until later. But the viewpoints are an aid to the use of the techniques and formalisms of architecture specification; a viewpoint does not stand alone. It is a mechanism to focus on a set of issues. The architect still needs to apply the methods of abstraction, composition, structuring, and modeling.

19.3.9 CONSISTENCY ACROSS MODELS OF AN ARCHITECTURE SPECIFICATION GENERALLY REQUIRES A FORMAL LANGUAGE UNDERPINNING. THIS ENABLES ANALYSIS POSTULATES TO BE ASSERTED, SIMULATION TO BE ACCURATE, AND CONFORMANCE TESTING.

RM-ODP is based on formalisms in predicate calculus that enable assertions to be made about the constructs in an architecture specification. These statements can be challenged and defended because they are precise. Such a foundation enables analyses, simulation, and conformance testing founded on mathematical principles. Architectural semantics clarifies the concepts provided. Correspondences across constructs in each viewpoint can be formally asserted. This in turn enables a set of consistency rules to be well-founded. This in turn provides a single architecture specification of a system, instead of independent views on a system. And a single architecture specification is essential to provide a distributed system that works.

19.3.10 TOP-DOWN, BOTTOM-UP, OR SIDEWAYS—ITERATION AND SPIRALING ARE KEYS TO SUCCESSFUL ARCHITECTING.

Incremental specifications, with the expectation of spiraling back for changes, is the best approach to architecting. A complex problem cannot be solved all at once. It requires an incremental approach. As the architect knows more about a solution, that knowledge is folded back into the specification. How an architect determines when to drill down into a part to more fully specify it, or to address all parts at a coarse-grained level, is an individual decision. It doesn't matter how an architect approaches the specification of an architecture, as long as the system functionality and semantic behavior are well-defined. Using the techniques of RM-ODP enable composition, abstraction, and separation of concerns to accomplish this, all consistently tied together to formulate a single architecture specification. The key is to specify, so as to define what is wanted. A best-practice approach is to start with a business specification to understand the problem to be solved. After that top-level understanding is accomplished, the architect can approach the definition of the parts of the system top-down, bottom-up, or sideways. To scope the problem to be solved by the system in support of Healthy Hospital, an overview of the top-level components of the system was presented in Chapter 1. The technique of iterative refinement was presented throughout the book using various levels of detail of Healthy Hospital. Sometimes a particular part of the system was presented in great detail, leaving the rest of the parts for further detail.

19.3.11 SPECIFYING SEMANTIC BEHAVIOR IS CRUCIAL. IT ENABLES INTEROPERABILITY, INTEGRATION, AND COMPOSABILITY, MINIMIZING MISMATCH.

All relationships between objects deal with the semantics of behavior, independent of the functionality of the relationship and the means of realizing or representing the interactions of the relationship. Interoperability, integration, and composability are concerned not with functionality of the parts, but with the behavior of the parts. What is to be interoperable, integrated, or composed is a matter of functionality. How it is to be interoperable, integrated, or composed is a matter of semantic behavior. And semantic behavior and open interaction are the enablers. Several chapters in this book addressed semantic behavior, composition, and an interaction framework for interoperability. Throughout the book, emphasis was placed on the need to specify the semantic behavior. RM-ODP focuses on semantic behavior, and provides a rich framework for the specification of semantic behavior in an explicit, rigorous, and uniform manner.

19.3.12 OPEN SYSTEMS ENABLE INTEROPERABLE SYSTEMS AND FEDERATION OF SYSTEMS.

Current businesses depend upon a plethora of complex computer systems that must work together to support a business. Typically, these systems are built from multiple architectures, multiple designs, different vendor products, and different versions of those products, across all aspects of a computer system. Computer systems are generally developed in parts and possibly placed on different computers. These dissimilar software parts need to interact together in order to enable the construction and execution of the single business system, whether that system is a single computer or a group of computers, to be able to share information in support of business needs. What is meant by *open* is the use of published concepts, rules, and interfaces, which can be used by any other software entity and combined in a system of such software entities. Openness supports interoperable distributed processing across heterogeneous environments of computers and software, that are composed into a single system or a federation of systems.

19.3.13 A LANGUAGE OF DISTRIBUTED PROCESSING IS NEEDED TO ARCHITECT A DISTRIBUTED PROCESSING SYSTEM.

Constructing distributed processing systems is not easy. The concepts to do so need to address the concerns of distribution: interoperability, portability, remoteness, mobility, concurrency, heterogeneity, evolution, scale, autonomy, failure recovery, quality of service, security, and many others. These are concerns of distributed processing, and a language defining terms and rules for focusing on distributed processing is needed. This language is used to communicate among the stakeholders of the system: the business customer who wants and pays for the system; the user who uses the system; the architect who architects the system; the designer who provides a detail specification of the system; the implementer who selects products or develops code to realize the system; the tester who tests the system to be sure it's conformant to the architecture; the re-engineer who wants to use current technology advances in the system; and the maintainer who needs to understand how the system works. That is, the terms of distributed processing must be well-defined and precise, such as distributed processing, architecture, system, interface, binding, composition, component, client, server, and so forth. They do not need to be redefined—they need to be reused.

19.3.14 DISTRIBUTION TRANSPARENCY IS A KEY ENABLER FOR MANY "ILITIES."

Distribution transparencies help a system achieve reliability (continuity of service), availability (how often the service is ready for use), fault tolerance (recoverability from failure), integrity (correctness), enhanced performance, decreased latency, and other system properties. It is very difficult for every application to develop all the details required to achieve these ilities across a distributed system. In fact applications alone cannot provide these properties (e.g., reliability) because they need to take the infrastructure into account as well. The RM-ODP transparency mechanisms enable the "ilities" by localizing to the infrastructure explicit capabilities to provide management of the system under failure, replicating components of the system for more assured availability, ensuring the integrity of a binding across a channel, and controlled management of a variety of changes (e.g., movement of a software component, replication of an object, relocating an interface, etc.), and much more. The mechanisms of RM-ODP are both general purpose and explicit, in order to enable enterprise-wide interoperable transparencies.

19.3.15 DISTRIBUTED SYSTEM ARCHITECTURE SHOULD ADDRESS CONSIDERATIONS OF POLICY, FAULT TOLERANCE, QUALITY OF SERVICE, FEDERATION, AND CONFORMANCE TESTING.

Distributed system architecture should address considerations of policy, fault tolerance, QoS, federation, and conformance testing. These are aspects of any distributed processing system to be considered. And all of these are formalized, to varying degrees of maturity, with RM-ODP.

19.4 EMERGING TECHNOLOGIES

Emerging research capabilities will arrive as technology specification and products in the marketplace, and will generally be founded on solutions to semantic behavior specification: the key. No longer is it viable to focus solely on functional capabilities. There are products in the marketplace today that can provide just about any functional capability desired. The problem is that they do not plug together. There are too many mismatches to contend with, and some cannot be resolved.

Users want the functionality, but users want that functionality in terms of a system, since the whole is greater than the parts. Products that provide value-added functionality, but do not open enough details to plug with other products, are not desirable. Users tend to shy away from such choices, and select more intelligent products that can provide both added functionality and composition.

Architecture is emerging as a discipline, generally founded on the use of formalisms. The problem with this is that communicating among the stakeholders and the architect is difficult at best. Stakeholders are expert in the business domain, not necessarily in information technology. Architects are expert in information technology, not necessarily in mathematical formalisms. So though these techniques are available to the architect for use, they are also generally unusable in the real world. The use of RM-ODP provides both a language of distributed processing, tailorable to the language of the business domain, for use by the architect. And the creators of RM-ODP already provided the formal specifications of RM-ODP so that the architect need not use these formalisms directly.

Many aspects of a distributed system are being actively pursued. Some of these include:

- Dynamic federation
- Negotiation of semantic behavior
- Policy management
- QoS parameterization for dynamic management and control
- Reliable systems based on open systems constructs

◗ Enterprise-wide open systems

◗ Composable parts founded on precise semantic behavior specification

◗ Semantic behavior specification tools

◗ Architecture specification visual tools

◗ UML tools to represent constraints and distributed object computing

Computers, memory, sensors, communication devices, and navigation devices are all becoming commodities. Combinations plus software are being composed into systems. Many concepts now in research will emerge into enormous capabilities for selection. Such concepts include network services that allow software systems to act as appliances; they just plug into the network for services and communication, that just magically, transparently, happens.

Integration and interoperation will rapidly improve through the use of open system standards and reusable software components. Composability of software components will be enabled, as solutions of the specification of semantic behavior for such will enable dynamic plug and play.

Federating systems will soon be possible, dynamically, through emerging techniques in negotiation. Supporting federation, policy management, and negotiation techniques are now emerging in terms of specifications for use by the architect. Dynamic negotiation is available today in limited functionality, but more capable dynamic negotiation, using the semantic behavior specification of software and policy, is not far away.

Speech, gesture, three-dimensional virtual reality, holography, and "just-in-time," coupled with high-resolution digital streams, are emerging to provide a rich user interface. Infrastructure support for these capabilities, in terms of functionality, dynamic specification of behavior, and QoS assurance, are all being addressed in current research.

Enterprise-wide security of systems is available today in pieces. Architecting the pieces into an enterprise-wide system solution remains elusive. This is one area of active research as well.

19.5   SOME WARNINGS

RM-ODP is exceedingly precise and terse. It is definitely not a quick read, nor a long read, but rather an extensive study. Part 2 is the foundational content for all open distributed processing, and this is accomplished in a mere 22 pages! As such, a definition is interleaved with other definitions to the extent that understanding one concept may require understanding the entire 22 pages. A definition may contain some familiar terms, but generally those terms are further defined somewhere else, causing the reader to thread through a great number of definitions.

The object model defined is object-based. There are major differences between object-oriented and this model. In this model, an object is an abstract entity; may have multiple interfaces; may assume multiple roles; may assume multiple types; and is instantiated through an explicitly defined object template that captures not only syntax but also semantics.

RM-ODP composition techniques are powerful. They enable anything to be composed: objects, interfaces, and semantic behaviors. As was shown in several places, a policy that specifies a business rule can be decomposed into separate policies that apply to different objects and interactions. On the one hand, the business rules are discussed with the stakeholders to assure their correctness and completeness. On the other hand, these business rules are composed and decomposed into parts that define the semantic behavior affecting the working of the system. The trace from the business rule to the implementation of that rule is inherent in the specification and composition techniques of RM-ODP.

As pointed out throughout the book, there are some ambiguities, inconsistencies, and incorrect statements made in RM-ODP. They are not of great consequence, as they tend to relate to some detail, rather than the major concepts. However, the architect using RM-ODP needs to be aware of these, and ensure that additional definition is included in the architecture specification that relates to these ambiguities.

Some of the frameworks for distributed processing are now being developed. Included are the enterprise viewpoint enhancements for specifying a business, the policy framework, and the quality of service reference model. What was provided in this book was a discussion of the current work.

19.6 COMPARISON WITH OTHER ARCHITECTURE APPROACHES

There are many architecture approaches today: Zachman [Zachman], the U.S. Department of Defense (DoD) C4ISR [C4ISR], the new Institute of Electrical and Electronics Engineers (IEEE) standard on architectural description [IEEE-P1471], and others. Many of these architecture practices make numerous inconsistently defined views possible; some are more precisely defined than others. A wide spectrum of different views exists across these approaches, leaving the architect in a quandary as to what to do. Some of these views are data, physical, development, performance, distribution, administration, and security. These are good views to focus on a topic of distributed processing, but are insufficient to define a specification for distributed processing. For example, a data view captures the data flow, data model, schema, etc., of a system, independently from any other concern such as security, distribution, failure recovery, and others. And the data view is not consistent with any other view. That is left to the architect to determine, if possible.

Most of these approaches do not address the process of architecting, using formalized techniques, such as abstraction and composition. Most of these approaches do not address consistency rules or conformance rules to enable a single architecture specification. Most of these approaches do not provide a stable, precise set of terms. Some do not even define any of the terms used. Some rely on products from a representation technique, such as UML or Microsoft Power-Point® charts, without any specified consistency. This results in a collection of representations that may have little to relate to each other. None of these approaches have achieved international acceptance.

A formal architecture specification may be represented as a set of interacting viewpoints having roles and actions, as long as the viewpoints are consistent and correspond with each other. Viewpoint objects should be modeled using a language that addresses distributed processing, not a language that addresses graphical representation. A primary benefit in using a set of standard viewpoints and approaches, such as provided by RM-ODP, is a specification. That specification can then be represented in a variety of ways to different audiences, each with their own concerns, while knowning that a single cohesive specification of the system is in hand. Additional discussion of this topic can be found in [Malveau].

19.7   WRAPPING UP

There are large gaps in the theory and practice of software architecture and engineering. Much is published about the representation of a software architecture, such as the UML, but little is available about the specification for a software architecture. RM-ODP is a well-established international standard for addressing all levels of software architecture. It is a principal contributor to the building blocks required for developing and specifying a software architecture. However, few outside the academic communities, standards communities, and the Defense Advanced Research Program Agency (DARPA) know much about these advancements.

RM-ODP provides an architecture reference model for use in specifying an architecture of a system:

▶ Viewpoints: enterprise, information, computational, engineering, and technology, to separate concerns and simplify the specification of heterogeneous, distributed systems

▶ Transparencies, to hide the complexities of distribution

▶ Functions, to provide infrastructure services

▶ Semantics, to define the behavior of the system, component, object, interface

▶ Composition, to enable levels of abstraction resulting in a specification of a system of systems to a single component

Software engineering methods of domain engineering, process modeling languages, and well-formed patterns of reasoning aid in the specification of an architecture. The software systems architecture work that is emerging, and is focused either at the component level or at the systems level, provides a key resource for others, which is enhanced by the architecting techniques provided by RM-ODP. By applying the proven techniques of RM-ODP for what makes a good architecture, readers will be able to build their own tailored architectures, with an understanding of the underlying principles and without hundreds of iterations. By using the RM-ODP specification constructs, associated languages, patterns of reasoning for architecture designs, semantic behavior, and conformance abilities, this book provides readers with the ability to architect their specific systems based on the RM-ODP specification foundations, and specify architectures that work.

Once an architecture is defined, it can be represented in all manner of different representation languages. This book presented these great ideas from RM-ODP, from architecture specification techniques, from modeling techniques, and explained what they all mean, and how to use them for practical benefit.

Complementary RM-ODP–based standards are evolving in the International Organization for Standardization (ISO) and by influence on other bodies (e.g., OMG). These include Naming, Trading, Enterprise Language (extensions), Computational Interfaces, Engineering Interfaces and Binding, Type Repository, and a QoS reference model.

How do enterprise systems engineers approach the process of architecting their system(s)? Generally, an architecture is first scoped to a specific domain of interest. How do enterprise systems engineers construct a cost-effective solution for their system(s)? Generally, by identifying common reusable artifacts of their domain, reused within the system(s) of the domain, and reusing architectural patterns that work. How is this accomplished? Today, no clearly defined process has reached the general public. Most of the approaches are ad hoc. Lessons learned from domain-specific RM-ODP architectures in practice provide a solution to the process of architecting to create a valid architecture specification of a system.

This book provides guidance to the user to construct software systems architecture from an RM-ODP perspective, conveying the principles of RM-ODP (at both an introductory and in-depth level) so that further reading and application of the standard is enabled. Discussion was provided that related RM-ODP to other framework approaches, and the techniques available in the software architecture arena. Practitioners of RM-ODP have found that the standard is extremely beneficial in guiding architecture definition and providing standard terminology and principles for distributed object applications and infrastructures from an enterprise perspective. This book provided the approach to using the RM-ODP foundations in architecting and specifying a distributed processing system that addresses such key properties as interoperability, dependability, portability, integration, composability, scalability, transparency, behavior specification, quality of service, policy management, federation, and conformance validation.

Some lessons learned in the pursuit of architecting, from many who have participated in construction of large-scale architectures, include:

▶ Architecting requires good engineering skills, coupled with specific architecting skills in the language of distributed processing systems.

▶ Architecture is key to achieving interoperability. Standards on the interface are not enough.

▶ An open system is key to interoperability and information sharing.

▶ An open architecture specification is key to heterogeneous interworking software systems at any size.

▶ Architecture is key to achieving a well-performing system. It doesn't just happen.

▶ Architecture is key to achieving evolvability to new technologies, scalability to increased resource requirements, flexibility to adapt to change. These characteristics need to be constructed into the plan of the system.

▶ Architecture is key to achieving a more fault-tolerant system, i.e., one that knows what to do in case of failure. The alternative of allowing a failure to happen, and then checking out the design to see what went wrong is unacceptable in mission-critical systems today (e.g., your telecommunication system that must "get the call through").

▶ Architecture is key to enabling the complexities of a system to be hidden from the end user and application using the services of the system.

▶ Architecture is key to enabling a choice of "better, cheaper, faster" benefits of a system development.

▶ A specification is a precise definition.

▶ Architecting is the construction of an architecture specification of a system, along with appropriate choices of the degree of specificity.

▶ Architecting is both a science and an art. The science aspect is gaining ground, especially with tools of specification such as those provided by RM-ODP.

▶ The architect needs to identify the degree of variability to support, to help in evolving architectures.

▶ One size does not fit all; that is, there may be more than one architecture relevant for a system.

The key benefits of using RM-ODP analyses are robust and reusable software architecture and design. Further, the analysis proponents claim that these benefits are teachable and repeatable. This is a cost-effective, useful result, rarely found in other practices that can create robust, reusable software; software interfaces; or even know about best practices for architecture analysis.

In summary:

▶ RM-ODP has solved any number of architecture problems, but many do not know of, or about, this standard. It is complex, and can only be popularized by describing it in a digestible, clear manner.

▶ RM-ODP has solved any number of architecture reuse and cost-effective problems, but many do not know of, or about, this process. It is complex, and can only be popularized by describing it in a digestible, clear manner.

▶ Architecture is a prime topic in systems engineering.

▶ Specification techniques are necessary to architect effectively.

▶ Architects can specify better systems through the use of RM-ODP and engineering.

▶ This book can set the stage for a number of tools that will become available from the vendor community (such as an RM-ODP language description tool, in line with the architecture description languages; an RM-ODP architecture assistant; a tool to capture and specify semantic behavior; etc.).

Specifying an architecture of a system, supported by the RM-ODP, narrows the gap of "architecting and the search for the Holy Grail." There is little in the literature about RM-ODP, and certainly not a book dedicated as a tutorial of this subject and a focus on the use of RM-ODP. There is little in the literature about the specification techniques used to create an architecture specification. This book detailed what RM-ODP is about, discussed how to use it, provided patterns of reasoning for specifying the architecture of a system, provided techniques of specification, and provided a case study to exemplify the concepts of RM-ODP, and to show how they might be used.

GLOSSARY[*]

<X> Domain: A set of objects with a characterizing <X> relationship, and with a control object that may be part of the domain or outside it. The control object determines the membership of the domain, and administers policies across the membership in the domain. [RM-ODP-2]

<X>-Federation: A typed community. The community is distinguished by a common <X> relationship. As a community, the community defines an objective, which is the set of resources that are sharable with other domains in the federation. Each <X> domain that forms the federation can be autonomous with respect to entering or leaving the federation, and with respect to the sharing its resources, as defined by the establishing behavior for the federation. [RM-ODP-3] The members of the federation are <X> domains, as controlled by their <X> controllers. The objective of the federation is to facilitate the sharing of the control among the controllers of the <X> domains. [RM-ODP-3, ISO-EntVP]

<X> Relationship: <X> is a relationship. It refers to or characterizes either the common behavior or the structural relationship among objects. [RM-ODP-2]

---

[*] The RM-ODP definitions are paraphrased from [RM-ODP-2 and RM-ODP-3]. Verbatim text is not quoted to honor the copyrights of ISO 10746-2 and ISO 10746-3 (parts of RM-ODP) as directed by ANSI on behalf of ISO. The reader is encouraged to obtain the standard from ISO for the exact wording of these terms.

<X> Template: A specification of the characteristics of a set of <X>s (anything of a type) such that an <X> can be instantiated from it. A template may include the specification of parameters to be bound at instantiation time, or another template to be instantiated. [RM-ODP-2]

Abstraction: The process of rendering something into a more general model. Abstraction is either a verb or a noun: the result of abstracting. A general model simplifies what is to be addressed, by hiding or encapsulating details not to be addressed until later. [RM-ODP-2]

Access transparency: Hides the details of accessing another object, within or across heterogeneous systems. This includes hiding how the object is invoked, any data formats between the objects, and the interfaces required. [RM-ODP-3]

Act of commitment: Establishing a contract with a party (any party, the agent, or the principal) that agrees to abide by the rules of the contract. [ISO-EntVP]

Action: What an entity does. It is an occurrence or a happening. [RM-ODP-2]

Active fault: When the fault actually produces an error, which can only be determined by detecting an error. [RM-ODP-2]

Activity: An ordered set of actions, where each action is determined by the preceding actions. An activity is a directed graph of these actions that has a single starting point and does not cycle back. It is a sequence of one or more actions. [RM-ODP-2]

Actor role: An identifier for a behavior, realized by the set of interactions it participates in with other object roles; a role that initiates and responds to actions. [ISO-EntVP]

Administrative domain: Defines particular policies for security, management, and resource control.

Agent: The enterprise object that is subject of a delegation. The agent can be a human or an ODP system or a part of an ODP system. [ISO-EntVP]

Announcement: A one-way operation interaction that the client object uses to request something of a server object. The client expects no response and the server does not respond. [RM-ODP-3]

Application management: The management actions of applications. [RM-ODP-2]

Application or business domain: Where particular rules of engagement are defined, dealing with environment constraints.

Architecting: The process of creating an architecture specification. It is both a science and an art.

Architectural model of a system: Specification of an architecture that relates the system concepts and behaviors to the users of the system in the domain in which it participates, and to the designers who will implement the model into a system that serves the purpose of the domain. It consists of precisely defined rules and concepts that address all aspects of the system, from functional to nonfunctional to semantic behavior. It defines the rules to construct the system, in the language of distributed processing.

Architectural specification: Definition of the structural elements (software entities) and elements that support their interworking by which a system is composed. A precise definition of the behavior of the interworking relationships among the software entities is also part of the architecture specification. A well-formed model.

Architectural style: A set of constraints on the structure of an architecture and on the connectors between components. [Shaw-96, Mehta-99]

Architecture: The concepts and rules that define the structure, semantic behavior, and relationships among the parts of a system; a plan of something to be constructed. It includes the elements that comprise the thing, the relationships among those elements, the constraints that affect those relationships, a focus on the parts of the thing, and a focus on the thing as a whole. [RM-ODP-2]

Architecture mismatch: Deals with the inability to combine or compose components of an architecture based on adverse behavior.

Artefact role: A role that is used by actor roles as a resource, and does not perform any action. [ISO-EntVP]

Atomicity: That all actions of the transaction are considered as a single atomic action. If a transaction fails in any way, all preceding actions that comprised the transaction are undone (rollback). [RM-ODP-2]

Authorization: That the behavior required and stated must not be prevented from happening: it must be allowed to occur. This is an empowerment. [ISO-EntVP]

Autonomy: Where each domain retains its management and sharability control over the resources it offers for sharing.

Availability: Measure of the mean time to failure, or alternatively, a percentage of time that a service is usable (available).

Base class: The class of the template if additional properties are added. The derived and base classes form an inheritance hierarchy, where the arcs define the derived class relation. [RM-ODP-2]

Basic engineering object: An engineering object that corresponds to a computational object and requires the services of the local or distributed infrastructure to perform its function. [RM-ODP-3]

Behavior: A set of actions and indications of epoch for these actions (which are constraints). Constraints define the dependencies that exist between actions. The actions are also constrained by the object's environment. [RM-ODP-2]

Behavioral compatibility: That one object can replace another object because the objects behave the same. The criteria for determining this are that if a second object replaces an object, the environment of the object detects no change. [RM-ODP-2]

Binder: An engineering object in a channel that maintains the integrity of the binding and coordinates the communication across the channel. [RM-ODP-3]

Binding: A contract between two or more object interfaces that is the result of agreed-upon behavior. [RM-ODP-2] It enables two objects to communicate.

Binding behavior: Behavior established between two or more interfaces. [RM-ODP-2]

Binding contractual context: A contract establishes the behavior of the binding. [RM-ODP-2]

Binding endpoint identifier: The identifier of a binding of the basic engineering object, which may be involved in more than one binding. [RM-ODP-3]

Binding establishment: Series of actions that ensure the behavior of the binding is in agreement with both ends, and the initial steps to setup the channel are accomplished. [RM-ODP-2]

Binding object: An intermediate object between two or more objects interfaces that manages the interface binding of the objects involved in an interaction. [RM-ODP-3]

Binding precondition: Prior to binding, the identifiers of all interfaces are known by the object performing the binding. [RM-ODP-2]

Capsule: A grouping of clusters that form a single unit of processing (such as a software module). [RM-ODP-3]

Capsule manager: Manages a single capsule. [RM-ODP-3]

Causality: Categorization of roles of interacting objects that are associated with the type of interaction. As such, causality constrains the behavior of the objects while they are interacting. [RM-ODP-3]

Causality role: The name of each end of the interface for the object participating in the interactions of that interface, which corresponds to the causality assumed by the object.

Chain of actions: An ordered sequence of actions. [RM-ODP-2]

Channel: A configuration of four engineering objects (stub, binder, protocol, and interceptor objects) that provides a binding in support of interaction between basic engineering objects. [RM-ODP-3]

Class: The set (possibly zero) of all members that satisfy a specific type, in which case each entity is a member of that class. [RM-ODP-2]

Class hierarchy: Where the arcs denote the subclass relation. [RM-ODP-2]

Client object: An object that requests a service be performed by another object. [RM-ODP-2]

Cluster: A grouping of objects from the computational specification to be treated as a single unit. [RM-ODP-3]

Cluster manager: Manages a specific cluster. [RM-ODP-3]

Communication: The way in which information is transferred from one object to another. This transfer of information can include a single interaction, or more interactions. The transfer can be direct between two or more objects, or include one or more intermediate objects. [RM-ODP-2]

Communication interface: A protocol object interface, which is bound to either another protocol object in the channel, or an interceptor in the channel, at a point called the interworking reference point. [RM-ODP-3]

Communication management: The management actions of the objects that support communication. [RM-ODP-2]

Communications domain: Interworking protocol objects. [RM-ODP-3]

Community: A collection of interacting objects whose purpose is to fulfill an objective, which is a contract defining how the objective can be met. [RM-ODP-3, EntVP]

Community contract: A contract of a community that forms the agreement of the behavior of the community within and with its environment. [ISO-EntVP]

Compliance: Where the specification corresponds to another specification. [RM-ODP-2]

Compliance testing: A set of tests to test a standard (e.g., an ODP standard) to RM-ODP, which generally occurs during the standardization process. [RM-ODP-2]

Component: An entity that is part of a composition and assumes a component type. [RM-ODP-2]

Component: The locus of computation and state. Each component has an interface specification that defines its properties. [Shaw-94]

Component or component composition standard: A standard that forms the specification of the interrelationships and use of a set of components to achieve some distributed processing capability. [RM-ODP-2]

Composite object: The composition considered as an object, where its members are objects. [RM-ODP-2] The concept of "composite policy" or "composite behavior" is being defined now.

Composition: A configuration of related entities (e.g., objects) that results in a new entity (e.g., an object) at a different level of abstraction. That is, a composition is a grouping of two or more entities that can be referred to as a single entity at a different level of abstraction from its component entities. [RM-ODP-2]

Computational interface template: An interface template that specifies a signal, stream, or operation interface (which consists of one or more signal, flow, or operation interactions, respectively). The computational interface template is specified in terms of an appropriate interface signature, along with its behavior specification and an environment contract specification. [RM-ODP-3]

Computational name: Unique identifier of an object, interface, interaction, or parameter. [RM-ODP-3]

Computational viewpoint: Viewpoint on a system that focuses on objects, interfaces, and enablers for distribution; partitions the system into functional modules that perform the capabilities of the system and are capable of being distributed throughout the enterprise. [RM-ODP-3]

Concurrency: Executing in parallel with another software entity in a distributed system.

Confidentiality: Probability of being safe from unauthorized access. [RM-ODP-3]

Configuration of objects: A grouping of objects that can potentially interact. [RM-ODP-2]

Conformance: Where the implementation corresponds to the specification. [RM-ODP-2]

Conformance assessment: The determination of consistency either by testing (conformance) or by model checking (compliance). Ensures that the implementation of the system corresponds to the architectural specification. [RM-ODP-2]

Conformance point: Reference point that can be used to test conformance related to the architecture specification of an observable behavior of an implementation. [RM-ODP-2]

Connector: The locus of relations among components. Connectors mediate interactions among components; each has a protocol specification that defines its properties, to include rules about the types of interfaces it is able to mediate, assurances about properties of the interaction, rules about order in which things happen, and commitments about the interaction. [Shaw-96, Mehta-99]

Consistency: Relation across the models of a specification that produces no conflicts among the properties across the models. In terms of an architecture specification, consistency means that the relations among key concepts in each model are linked together to provide a cohesive specification. [RM-ODP-2]

Consistency (of a transaction): That the transaction will always produce the same result, preserving invariance.

Consumer object: Target object of the exchanged information. [RM-ODP-2]

Contract: A specified agreement to some behavior common to a configuration of objects, that thus tells the environment the behavior to expect; an agreement to provide or not provide something, as defined by the specification of the rules that constrain the cooperation between objects. It's a promise, an obligation of fulfillment, by all objects participating in the contractual behavior. It define the constraints, to include the policies. [RM-ODP-2]

Contracting party: An object that agrees to a contract. [ISO-EntVP]

Contractual context: The knowledge that a contract is in place among a set of objects and defines the behavior of those objects. [RM-ODP-2]

Controlling object: An object that manages the behavior of the community of objects, with respect to the relationship of the domain. [RM-ODP-3]

Correspondences: Consistency statements of concept relationships. [RM-ODP-2]

Creation: Instantiation that results from some action. For example, an object's interface may be "created" at a point in time when that interface is to be used. [RM-ODP-2]

Cross-domain interaction: The ability for two or more different domains to interact across their domains.

Declaration: The establishment of the contract.

Decomposition: The dual to composition. It is the specification of the composed entity (e.g., object), which means a specification of all of its constituent entities (e.g., all of the objects that form the composition). [RM-ODP-2]

Delegate: Entrust to a party the authority to enforce a contract, policy, or to perform some function. [ISO-EntVP]

Delegation: The act of delegating. [ISO-EntVP]

Deletion: The act of removing or destroying something that was instantiated, such as an object or interface. [RM-ODP-2]

Dependability: Measure of predictability that a service will deliver as expected.

Derived class: The set of all instances of a template that have resulted from some incremental modification of that template; forms an inheritance hierarchy, where the arcs define the derived class relation. [RM-ODP-2]

Description: Rules about describing or presenting, not about specifying or defining.

Designers: Term used to mean any architect, system designer, developers, implementer, tester, administrator, or maintainer of the system.

Distributed binding: A binding that involves a channel, and the objects that make up the channel. A distributed binding is most often associated with interconnection between nodes. [RM-ODP-3]

Distributed processing: Processing performed by hardware and software entities that are physically separated. The software processing by the computer system can be distributed within the computer system, across multiple distributed computing systems, or both.

Distributed processing system: System composed of separate processing systems, that interwork together for the purpose of sharing information and processing.

Distribution: Different locations, whether the software are next to each other, or across the world.

Distribution: The ability to place objects in different spaces and to locate them.

Distribution transparency: Capability that masks (or hides) the consequences of distribution and associated behavior from a user, application developer, or system developer. [RM-ODP-2]

Dividing action: Is the separation of a chain into two or more chains; it is the reverse of a joining action. [RM-ODP-2]

DSSA: Domain-Specific Software Architecture. Software architecture for a family of systems that includes behavioral requirements for applications in the domain, a domain model, an infrastructure to support the DSSA, and a process to instantiate and refine the DSSA. This is an architectural framework for a specific class of problems.

Durability: That a transaction is stable, in that the effects of the transaction are reversible and persistent.

Dynamic schema: All the actions that allow a state or structure change of one or more information objects. [RM-ODP-3]

Enabling behavior: The behavior that characterizes a particular set of objects by the establishment of the contract, which may apply differently to the different objects. [RM-ODP-2]

Encapsulation: Property of hiding the details; internal processing of an object is hidden, and the only access to an object is through an invocation of the interfaces offered by the object.

Engineering interface: An engineering interface that corresponds to a computational interface. [RM-ODP-3]

Engineering interface reference: The identifier of an engineering object interface, used for purposes of binding and management. [RM-ODP-3]

Engineering interface reference management domain: A naming domain for engineering interface reference identifiers (names). [RM-ODP-3]

Engineering interface reference management policy: A policy (permissions, prohibitions, and obligations) that applies to a federation of engineering interface reference management domains. [RM-ODP-3]

Engineering object: An object only in the engineering viewpoint that corresponds to an infrastructure specific capability. [RM-ODP-3]

Engineering viewpoint: Viewpoint on a system that focuses on the distributed interactions between objects in the system, and provides the mechanisms to support distribution. [RM-ODP-3]

Enterprise object: An object in the enterprise that assumes a role. [RM-ODP-3]

Enterprise viewpoint: Viewpoint on a system concerned with the policy, scope, and purpose of the system; takes the perspective of a business model. [RM-ODP-3]

Entity: Any abstract or concrete thing. [RM-ODP-2]

Environment (of an object): All those elements or entities not part of the model of the object, leading to the ability to specify what an object expects of its environment, and what constraints the environment places on the object. [RM-ODP-2]

Environment contract: A contract formulated between an object and its environment, which constrains the environment as well as the object within that environment. This contract addresses such things as quality of service, resource usage, and management and other constraints. The environment constraints describe the requirements of the environment to support the behavior of the object, and the behavior required of the object to be a member of the environment. [RM-ODP-2]

Epoch: Defined period of time. [RM-ODP-2]

Error: An object state that may lead to a failure. [RM-ODP-2]

Error probability: The probability of a failure.

Establish behavior: Behavior that results from an instantiated contract template between objects. [RM-ODP-2]

Evaluation: The act of assigning a value to something.

Event: An observable invocation on an object that coordinates the flow of control among objects.

Explicit binding: Behavior where two or more objects interact directly across an interface of any type. [RM-ODP-3]

Explicit compound binding: A binding that makes use of the computational binding object to bind two or more object interfaces. [RM-ODP-3]

Explicit primitive binding: An explicit binding defining constraints and actions (behavior) associated with the binding of an interface, of any type. [RM-ODP-3]

Extensibility: The capability for an entity to migrate or change with newer technology, or new requirements.

Failure: The condition when the expected behavior, as defined by a contract, is violated in some way or does not adhere to the specified behavior. [RM-ODP-2]

Failure modes: Ways in which an object fails. [RM-ODP-3]

Failure transparency: Hides the details that something has failed in the system, and the act of recovery. [RM-ODP-3]

Fault: A condition that may result in errors in an object. [RM-ODP-2]

Fault group: Special group where the objects are treated as a single entity in case of some fault. [RM-ODP-3]

Fault tolerance: The ability to recover from failure of individual software entities, possibly resulting in reduced functionality; concerned with the failure identification, analysis, and appropriate action to recover, to the extent possible, the system to a reliable stable state. A system is said to be fault tolerant if it can recover from a failure. [RM-ODP-3]

Fault tolerant replication group: A group of objects that participates in a sequence of defined interactions providing fault tolerance in the case of some faults. [RM-ODP-3]

Federate: The action of federating a configuration of components together, resulting in a possible additional state, "federating," for those components. RM-ODP allows the use of an establishing behavior to define the establishment of a federation.

Federation: Community of a collection of multiple domains that come together to share resources while retaining their autonomy over the resources. It is actually a configuration of components from separate domains that come together (federate) to share. [Putman-94, Putman-97]

Flexibility: Ability for an entity to adapt to different situations.

Flow: An ordered set of one or more interactions that are communicated one-way from a producer object to a consumer object. [RM-ODP-3]

Forking action: A dividing action that enables the chains to rejoin later. [RM-ODP-2]

Framework (of an architecture): A structure for investigating an architectural problem or building a specific approach to architectural concerns that are related to each other through the rules of the structure. As per [RM-ODP-2], support to create an architecture specification addressing integration, portability, interworking (interoperability), and of course distribution.

Group: A set of objects with a specified structural or behavioral relationship (called a characterizing relationship). [RM-ODP-2]

Head activity: The initial action in an activity. [RM-ODP-2]

Heterogeneity: Dissimilarity. Software entities and systems can be developed from different technologies, different vendor products, or different versions of the same product.

Identifier: An unambiguous name in a naming context. [RM-ODP-2]

Implicit binding: An operational interface (only) between a client and a server. [RM-ODP-3]

Information viewpoint: Viewpoint on a system that is concerned with the information content of the system, and the semantics about the processing of the system (its semantic behavior). [RM-ODP-3]

Inheritance: The classes can be arranged in an inheritance hierarchy according to derived class relationships. [RM-ODP-2]

Initiating object: Starts a communication. [RM-ODP-2]

Instance: The <X> that satisfies the type. [RM-ODP-2]

Instantiation: To create an instance of a specific template. [RM-ODP-2]

Integration: The seamless property of one cohesive cooperative set of information and processing. To integrate a set of software means presentation, behavior, and software functionality is consistent, and acts as a single system.

Integrity: The probability of survival.

Interaction: An action that involves one or more objects and their environment(s) at an interface; set of services that are offered across a single interface, and are linked to another object with a binding. [RM-ODP-2]

Interaction point: Location where an object interacts with its environment. It is a location where there may be one or more interfaces. [RM-ODP-2]

Interception: Process that instantiates and inserts interceptors in the binding when crossing domain boundaries. [RM-ODP-3]

Interceptor (of a specific type): An engineering object in a channel between protocol objects crossing different domains that manages any policy enforcement and transformation required across a specific type of domain. [RM-ODP-3]

Interchange conformance reference point: A reference point used to test the access methods and formats of physical media to ensure interoperable information across systems that use physical media: access, record, transfer, and use. [RM-ODP-2]

Interface: The behavior of an object along with constraints at a subset of the object's interactions constrained by the circumstances for when they occur. An interaction is associated with a single interface. [RM-ODP-2]

Interface identifier: Unique unambiguous name for an interface in a naming context; used to select for use. [RM-ODP-3]

Interface signature: Set of interaction templates for an interface; structures the information about a specific type of interface, for use by other objects. It identifies the type of interface, the type of interactions, and for each interaction, the interaction template. [RM-ODP-2]

Interface type: The semantics of the object's behavior and state associated with an interaction with another object. The semantics are associated with the interactions in the interface and constraints on those interactions and on the binding. [RM-ODP-3]

Internal actions: Actions within an object. [RM-ODP-2]

Interoperability: To exchange and use information in a mutually understandable manner between objects; exchange can be one-way. Interoperability is about agreement.

Interrogation: An operation interaction that consists of two one-way interactions: one to request, one to respond. [RM-ODP-3]

Interworking: The communication and exchange of information between two or more systems. [RM-ODP-2]

Interworking conformance reference point: Reference point used to test for interoperability between systems implementations. [RM-ODP-2]

Introduction: Instantiation that it is not a result of an action of an object. For example, a policy may be introduced into a part of the system. It is not created by an object. [RM-ODP-2]

Invariant: "A logical predicate that must remain true during some scope; a scope might be the lifetime of a managed relationship or the execution of a relationship management operation." [ISO GRM, ITU-GRM]

Invariant schema: Set of predicates that must always be true for one or more information objects for some specified period of time or an interval. [RM-ODP-3]

Invocation: Interrogation that enables a client object request. [RM-ODP-3]

Isochronicity: A sequence of actions that are equally spaced in time and are unique. This type of activity is associated with voice media. [RM-ODP-2]

Isolation (part of ACID property): Where a transaction's internal states are separate from other transactions and invisible to them.

IXIT (Implementation Extra Information for Testing): That extra information associated with the conformance test point to use in observable behavior during testing, and to define what observable behavior is expected. [RM-ODP-2]

Jitter: Some time interval associated with a transfer delay. [ISO-QOS]

Joining action: Where an action is shared between chains (two or more) and results in a single chain. [RM-ODP-2]

Liaison: Relationship that results from enabling a behavior in accordance with the contract established that defines the behavior of the liaison. [RM-ODP-2]

Local binding: A binding that does not require a channel. [RM-ODP-3]

Location (time or space): A specification of an interval of arbitrary size in time or space when or where an action can occur, in terms of a specified. [RM-ODP-2]

Location transparency: Hides the details of a name and physical address used to locate some information and to interface to it. [RM-ODP-3]

Managed role: Object role being managed. [RM-ODP-2]

Management information: Information relevant to the management of the objects. [RM-ODP-2]

Managing role: Object role that performs the management actions. [RM-ODP-2]

Migratability: Ability to change the object configuration, replacing the object reference point with another reference point while the object is active. [RM-ODP-2]

Migration transparency: Hides the details that an object has moved to some other location. This transparency enables other software objects in the system to continue to interact with the moved object, as though it were still in the same place. [RM-ODP-3]

Mobility: Change in location of information, software entities, processing, and even hardware. [RM-ODP-3]

Model: Represents the system from a set of concerns or foci on the system. A model can be a document, a representation in a visual tool, or some other artifact. A system, then, is typically represented by a set of models, each addressing some particular area of concern.

Modularity: Ability to componentize a system or application into sub-elements that can be considered individually.

Modularization: Breaking up the areas of concern into parts.

Multicast interaction: Involves a sender and multiple recipients of a message, and associated constraints. [RM-ODP-3]

Multiple inheritance: Where several base classes are involved in a hierarchy. [RM-ODP-2]

Name resolution: Process that can discover a named entity given an initial name and naming context. [RM-ODP-2]

Naming action: Action where an entity is given a name from the name space. [RM-ODP-2]

Naming context: Relation between a set of unique names in a name space to the entities that are named. A name space is a set of unambiguous terms used as names. [RM-ODP-2]

Naming domain: The set of all entities that are named from the same naming context by a name authority object.

Naming graph: Directed graph associating a naming context and an association between a source naming context and a target naming context. [RM-ODP-2]

Negotiation: The process of reaching agreement between the parties involved, as defined by a contract.

Node: The computer and operating system. [RM-ODP-3]

Notification: An interaction initiated by a managed role based object. [RM-ODP-2]

Nucleus: Similar to an operating system. [RM-ODP-3]

Object: A model of something; it is not a concrete instance of a class, as is often the case in object-oriented (OO) languages. It is defined by state and behavior. It changes state as a result of some internal or external action. The state of an object is unique. [RM-ODP-2]

Objective: A statement for an enterprise community: Why the system is required and what it will do. [RM-ODP-3, ISO-EntVP]

Objectives: The purpose of the business. [RM-ODP-3, ISO-EntVP]

Obligation: A requirement of a behavior that must be achieved by the occurrence of the defined behavior. [RM-ODP-2, ISO-EntVP]

ODP functions: Capabilities needed to support ODP systems and the distribution transparencies. [RM-ODP-3]

Omission failure: When an expected interaction does not happen. [RM-ODP-3]

Ontology: "A formal and declarative representation which includes the vocabulary (or names) for referring to the terms in that subject area and the logical statements that describe what the terms are, how they are related to each other, and how they can or cannot be related to each other." [KSL]

Open: "Completely free from concealment: Exposed to general view or knowledge." [Webster's]

Open: The use of published concepts, rules, and interfaces, which can be used by any other software entity, and combined in a system of such software entities. Openness supports interoperable distributed processing in heterogeneous environments of computers and software.

Open system: System that is designed to enable portability of the software, and to allow other software entities to interoperate with it across dissimilar software and systems, whether or not the software entities are on the same computer or reside on different computers.

Operation: An interaction between a client object and a server object, which is either an interrogation or an announcement. [RM-ODP-3]

Operation interface type: An interface where all the interactions are operations. [RM-ODP-3]

Operational-type interaction: A template that is sufficiently defined to instantiate the client/server interface. [RM-ODP-3]

Owner: An object that models a real person with authority to control something. [ISO-EntVP]

Party: An object that models a real person. [ISO-EntVP]

Perceptual conformance reference point: Reference point used in the testing at user interfaces in communications ports that represent external boundaries to the system. [RM-ODP-2]

Permanence (part of ACID property): State in which changes are durable (stable).

Permission: The action is not prohibited; the behavior that is allowed to occur. [RM-ODP-2, ISO-EntVP]

Persistence: A characteristic that an object continues to exist despite changes in time, location, or context in which the object was established. [RM-ODP-2]

Persistence transparency: Hides that an object continues to exist in the system, even if the object is deactivated and then reactivated in the system. [RM-ODP-3]

Persistent omission failure: A crash. [RM-ODP-3]

Policy: A set of obligation, prohibition, or permission rules that either constrain or enable actions, as related to a purpose. [RM-ODP-2]

Policy: "A definite course or method of action selected from among alternatives and in light of given conditions to guide and determine present and future decisions; a high-level overall plan embracing the general goals and acceptable procedures of a government body [or business]; a writing whereby a contract of insurance is made." [Webster's]

Policy: A set of obligation, prohibition, permission, and authorization rules on the interactions between objects; used to define actions in relation to a stated purpose. [RM-ODP-2, ISO-EntVP]

Polymorphism: The ability for one instance of one type to be treated as an instance of another type.

Portability: Ability to be used in multiple locations in the distributed processing system. As such, portability allows that software entity to be used in different locations, in different environments, and on different computing resources. [RM-ODP-2]

Postcondition: Predicate that must be true and occur after an action. [RM-ODP-2]

Precedence: Priority.

Precision: How well something is defined; not how well something is detailed.

Precondition: Predicate that must be true prior to an action, and that results in success for that action to occur. [RM-ODP-2]

Prescription: Establishes a rule.

Principal: The party that delegates. [RM-ODP-3]

Process: A collection of steps that together form a task of the business. Objects can participate in the process at specified intervals, not necessarily only from the beginning. [ISO-EntVP]

Producer object: Source object of some information exchanged. [RM-ODP-2]

Programmatic conformance reference point: Reference point used in the usual notion of testing the behavior of software interfaces. [RM-ODP-2]

Prohibition: The behavior that must not occur. [RM-ODP-2]

Protocol object: An engineering object in a channel that provides the communication mechanism to achieve interaction; it provides the structure and transfer syntax of the communication protocol. [RM-ODP-3]

Publish: "To make generally known; to disseminate to the public; to produce or release for distribution; to issue the work of (an author)." [Webster's]

Quality of service (QoS): A group of quality characteristics that are requirements placed on the behavior of one or more objects. QoS can be measured, parameterized, reported, and observed after an event has taken place. QoS is a property that can be quantified and is not dependent on the representation or control; a measure of some quality of service desired or required of a system or a part of the system. QoS is specified in a contract. [RM-ODP-2, ISO-QOS]

Recoverability (part of ACID property): Atomic transactions.

Reference model: A formal definition of architecture and design practices that are general purpose. It provides the ability to transform abstract visions into concrete specifications. It provides the ability to simplify the discussion of relationships among entities. It provides a durable framework to structure decision making about an architecture. It guides the choices made in an architecture, that then guide the choices made in an implementation.

Reference Model for Open Systems Interconnection (RM-OSI): Seven-layer stack framework for additional standards addressing aspects of telecommunications.

Reference point: Point at an interaction used as a conformance testing point to observe some behavior. [RM-ODP-2]

Refinement: The dual of abstraction. It is a process that addresses the detail abstracted away, providing a more granular detailed specification. [RM-ODP-2]

Relationship: "A collection of ... objects together with an invariant referring to the properties of the ... objects." [ISO GRM, ITU-GRM]

Reliability: The property that a failure is quantified as mean-time-to-failure.

Relocation transparency: Hides the details that an interface has changed location, even if that interface is being used. [RM-ODP-3]

Remoteness: Distance from each other in location, where communication may be local or remote.

Replica group: The resultant group of replicated objects. [RM-ODP-3]

Replication transparency: Hides the existence of copies of the software object in the system. [RM-ODP-3]

Representation: "1: one that represents: as a : an artistic likeness or image b (1) : a statement or account made to influence opinion or action; 2: the act or action of representing." [Webster's]

Representing: "1: to bring clearly before the mind; 2: to serve as a sign or symbol of; 3: to portray or exhibit in art; 4: to serve as the counterpart or image of; 7: to describe as having a specified character or quality; 9: to serve as a specimen, example, or instance of; 11: to correspond to in essence." [Webster's]

Responding object: An object participating in the communication, but not the initiating object. [RM-ODP-2]

RM-ODP (Reference Model of Open Distributed Processing): Standard for modeling object-based distributed processing architectures that separates concerns and simplifies the specification of heterogeneous, open distributed processing systems.

Role: A unique identifier that characterizes some behavior. A role can be a composite object template parameter, which is a property of one of the component objects of the composite object. What this means is that the role identifies some defined behavior that can be assumed by an object, agreeing to provide this behavior. [RM-ODP-2, ISO-EntVP]

Scale: Over time, additional users, additional distributed processing, and additional resources may be added to the distributed processing system to accommodate the increasing demands of the organization. In addition, some action in time may require that the distributed processing system dramatically increase its resource and processing capability, or re-prioritize its available resources and processing (e.g., surge of activity based on war, or on determining a cause of failure that needs an immediate response).

Scope: Set of roles and associated behavior. [ISO-EntVP]

Semantic behavior: The specification of allowable actions with a set of constraints (invariants, preconditions, postconditions, etc.) on what is to be accomplished and when those constraints may occur.

Server object: An object that performs a requested service. [RM-ODP-2]

Sharing: Ability to share resources, such as data repositories, metadata stores, or data.

Signal: A one-way interaction between an initiating object and a responding object. [RM-ODP-3]

Signal interaction: Single direction atomic shared action. [RM-ODP-3]

Signal interface: A type of interface consisting of only signal type interactions. [RM-ODP-3]

Software-intensive system: One where the software is the central part of the system and its operation.

Spawn action: An action that is not a forking action where each divided chain is a separate chain, and can interact independently. [RM-ODP-2]

Specification: "1 : the act or process of specifying; 2 a : a detailed precise presentation of something or of a plan or proposal for something—usually used in plural b : a statement of legal particulars (as of charges or of contract terms); also : a single item of such statement."

Specification: A precise definition.

Specification language: Language to express a specification that is based on mathematical formalisms. This does not mean the specification language used consists of mathematical symbols, but rather is founded on such precision.

Specifying: "1: to name or state explicitly or in detail; 2: to include as an item in a specification." [Webster's]

Specifying: The process of writing things down in a well-defined, precise manner using the language of the subject matter (e.g., for a system, using the language of distributed processing).

Stability: That property of an object that prohibits it from exhibiting a particular failure mode. [RM-ODP-2]

Stakeholder: Term used here to represent any customer, user, owner, administrator, acquisition authority, or program manager.

State (of an object): The condition of an object that determines its behavior: the set of constrained actions and their constraints in which the object can participate. [RM-ODP-2]

Static schema: The state and structure of one or more information objects at some point in time. [RM-ODP-3]

Stream interaction: Single direction sequence of messages of a specific type, such as a data stream. [RM-ODP-3]

Stream interface: A type of interface from an object assuming the role of producer to an object assuming the role of consumer consisting of only flow type interactions. [RM-ODP-3]

Stub: An engineering object in a channel that provides interpretation and support of the interactions in the channel to the basic engineering object, such as marshalling and unmarshalling of parameters. [RM-ODP-3]

Subactivity: Proper subset of the activity, and if it includes one action that eventually will fork-join, the subactivity must include these fork-join actions of the parent as well. [RM-ODP-2]

Subclass: The set of all entities that satisfy a subtype relation. [RM-ODP-2]

Subdomain: Subset of the membership of a domain. [RM-ODP-2]

Substitutability (called behavioral compatibility in RM-ODP): Where one object can be substituted for another and one interface to be substituted for another, as long as the environment cannot detect a difference, a set of criteria are met, and a template type captures the design for substitutability. [RM-ODP-2]

Subtype: Where every property that satisfies an entity of that subtype also satisfies an entity of its parent type. [RM-ODP-2]

Superclass: The set of all entities that satisfy a supertype relation. [RM-ODP-2]

Supertype: The parent type. [RM-ODP-2]

System: An entity that is a whole or a configuration of parts or a part. Therefore, a system can be a component, a subsystem, a system of interest, or a system of systems. [RM-ODP-2]

Systems approach to architecture: Focuses on the system as a whole.

Technology domain: Particular technologies are used and managed within the domain, such as communication protocols, data formats, distributed middleware.

Technology viewpoint: Viewpoint on a system addressing where to apply the technologies and products of choice, and allow the conformance testing of the system implementation against its architectural specification. [RM-ODP-3]

Template: A specification that contains sufficient detail of an entity to instantiate it. More than one instance can be instantiated from the same template. [RM-ODP-2]

Template class: The set of all things that satisfy the template type. Each template defines only one template class. [RM-ODP-2]

Template type: Predicate in the template that defines the requirements for instantiations of the template. [RM-ODP-2]

Terminating behavior: Ends a liaison, as identified in the contract. [RM-ODP-2]

Termination: Interrogation that enables a server to respond to a client request. [RM-ODP-3]

Thread: Chain of actions that has at least one object participating in all the actions. [RM-ODP-2]

Throughput: The rate of transfer of a message or some data. [ISO-QOS]

Trace: History of an object's interactions, generally used by some capability in the system to record a history of the object. The result is a finite sequence of the object's interactions. [RM-ODP-2]

Trading: The interaction between exporting and importing objects, where exporting objects offer services that can be requested by importing objects, as determined by a third object (Trader). Exporting is the specification of an interface identifier to a required service. Importing is the specification of an interface identifier that matches a required service enabling a binding behavior to be established. [RM-ODP-2]

Transaction: An activity that maintains a consistent set of object states, in accordance with the dynamic and invariant schemata. [RM-ODP-3]

Transaction transparency: Hides the coordinated activities of software objects in support of any transaction. A transaction is classified by the properties atomicity, consistency, isolation, and durability (ACID). [RM-ODP-3]

Transparency: The ability to hide some aspects of the processing of the system. [RM-ODP-3]

Type: A conceptualization of a property of one or more entities. Type applies to at least an object, interface, and action. A specification can associate type with other entities (e.g., a domain). In RM-ODP, the phrase "<X>" designates the collection of entities that has a type. Type is a predicate: a set of conditions and constraints that can classify an object, and are evaluated for an object. [RM-ODP-2]

Type hierarchy: Where the arcs denote the subtype relation. [RM-ODP-2]

Type of interface: An interface that consists only of a set of specific typed interactions. [RM-ODP-3]

Type of template: Pattern of templates, such as object templates, interface templates, interaction templates, binding templates, channel templates, and so forth, which are instantiated from its template. [RM-ODP-2]

Unbinding behavior: Terminating a binding. [RM-ODP-2]

Viewpoint (on a system): An abstraction of a set of concerns on a system derived by using a set of concepts and rules of structure. [RM-ODP-2]

Violation: A condition wherein an action does not adhere to a rule. [ISO-EntVP]

Virtual enterprise: "Consortium of companies or organizations which come together to share resources (cost, personnel, equipment) to achieve common objectives, foster collaborative efforts, and share engineering and information, while retaining autonomy over those resources." [Putman-97]

Visibility (part of ACID property): Isolation of transactions from one another.

Acronyms

ACID	Atomic, Consistent, Isolated, and Durable
ADL	Architectural Description Language
ANSA	Advanced Network Systems Architecture
ANSI	American National Standards Institute
API	Application Programming Interface
AWG	IEEE Architecture Working Group
B2B	Business-to-Business
BEO	Basic Engineering Object
C2	Command and Control
C3I	Command, Control, Communications, and Intelligence
C4I	Command, Control, Communications, Computer, and Intelligence
C4ISR	Command, Control, Communication, Computers, Intelligence, Surveillance, and Reconnaissance

CAT	Computed Axial Tomography (CAT Imaging)
CBD	Component Based Development
CBF	Component Based Frameworks
CDC	Centers for Disease Control
CFO	Chief Financial Officer
CORBA	Common Object Request Broker Architecture
COTS	Commercial Off-The-Shelf
DARPA	Defense Advanced Research Projects Agency
DBMS	Database Management System
DCE	Distributed Computing Environment
DIMMA	Distributed Interactive Multi-Media Architecture
DLL	Dynamic Link Library
DMSO	DoD Modeling and Simulation Office
DoD	Department of Defense
DSSA	Domain-Specific Software Architecture
DSTC	Distributed Systems Technology Centre
EDOC	Enterprise Distributed Object Computing
EIR	Engineering Interface Reference
EIRT	Engineering Interface Reference Tracking
EJB	Enterprise JavaBeans™
EO	Engineering Object
EOB	Explanation of Benefits
FAA	Federal Aviation Administration
FDT	Formal Description Technique
FEDERAL ITA	Federal Information Technology Architecture
FIPS	Federal Information Processing Standard

FT	Fault Tolerance
GRM	General Relationship Model
HLA	High Level Architecture
HTML	Hypertext Markup Language
HTTP	Hypertext Transfer Protocol
IDEF	Integration Definition for Information Modeling
IDL	Interface Definition Language
IEC	International Electrotechnical Committee
IEEE	Institute of Electrical and Electronics Engineers
IER	Information Exchange Requirements
IETF	Internet Engineering Task Force
IIOP	Internet Interoperability Protocol
IP	Internet Protocol
IRB	Interface Reference and Binding
ISO	International Organization for Standardization
IT	Information Technology
ITU	International Telecommunications Union
IXIT	Implementation eXtra Information for Testing
JTC1	Joint Technical Committee 1
LAN	Local Area Network
LOTOS	Language of Temporal Ordering Specifications
MMC(S)	Multimedia Conferencing (System)
MOD	Ministry of Defence

MOF	Meta Object Facility
MOM	Message-Oriented Middleware
MRI	Magnetic Resonance Imaging
MTS	Message Transaction Service
MTTF	Mean-Time-To-Failure
MTTR	Mean-Time-To-Repair
NIIIP	National Industrial Information Infrastructure Protocols
OCL	Object Constraint Language
ODMA	Open Distributed Management Architecture
ODP	Open Distributed Processing
OMA	Object Management Architecture
OMG	Object Management Group
OMT	Object Modeling Technique
OO	Object-Oriented
ORB	Object Request Broker
OSI	Open Systems Interconnection
OTS	Object Transaction Service
PBN	Policy-Based Networking
PC	Personal Computer
PIDS	Patient Identification Service
QMF	QoS Management Function
QoS	Quality of Service
RFI	Request for Information
RFP	Request for Proposal

RMI	Remote Method Invocation
RM-ODP	Reference Model of Open Distributed Processing
ROI	Return on Investment
RPC	Remote Procedure Call

SDL	Specification and Description Language
SESC	IEEE Software Engineering Standards Committee
SSA	Software Systems Architecture

TCAS	Tactical Collision Avoidance System
TCP	Transmission Control Protocol
TINA	Telecommunications Information Network Architecture
TOGAF	The Open Group Architectural Framework
TP	Transaction Processing
TRP	Technology Reinvestment Program

UCC	Uniform Commercial Code
UK	United Kingdom
UML	Unified Modeling Language
URL	Uniform Resource Locator

VDB	Virtual DB (Database)
VTC	Video Teleconferencing

W3C	World Wide Web Consortium
WAN	Wide Area Network
WG7	Working Group 7
WWW	World Wide Web

X.400	Electronic Messaging
X.500	Directory Services
XMI	Extensible Markup Language Interchange
XML	Extensible Markup Language
Y2K	Year 2000

REFERENCES

[1] [Aagedal]   Jan Oyvind Aagedal and Zoran Milosevic, *ODP Enterprise Language: UML Perspective*, ENTERPRISE DISTRIBUTED OBJECT COMPUTING (EDOC) '99 PROCEEDINGS (Sep 99).

[2] [Abd-Allah-95]   A. Abd-Allah, *Composing Heterogeneous Software Architectures*, USC-CSE TR 95-502 (Apr. 13, 1995).

[3] [Abd-Allah-96]   A. Abd-Allah, *Composing Heterogeneous Software Architectures, Doctoral Dissertation*, CENTER FOR SOFTWARE ENGINEERING, UNIVERSITY OF SOUTHERN CALIFORNIA (August 1996) (accessed at sunset.usc.edu/TechRpts/dissertation.html).

[4] [Acme]   David Garlan, Robert T. Monroe, and David Wile, *Acme: An Architecture Description Interchange Language*, PROCEEDINGS OF CASCON '97, Ontario, Canada (November 1997).

[5] [Adage]   L. Coglianese and R. Szymanski, *DSSA-ADAGE: An Environment for Architecture-based Avionics Development*, PROCEEDINGS OF AGARD '93 (May 1993).

[6] [Aesop]   David Garlan, Robert Allen, and John Ockerbloom, *Exploiting Style in Architectural Design Environments*, PROCEEDINGS OF SIG-SOFT '94: THE SECOND ACM SIGSOFT SYMPOSIUM ON THE FOUNDATIONS OF SOFTWARE ENGINEERING, ACM PRESS (December 1994).

[7]   [Andersen]   E.P. Andersen and T. Reenskaug, *System Design by Composing Structures of Interacting Objects*, PROCEEDINGS OF THE EUROPEAN CONFERENCE ON OBJECT-ORIENTED PROGRAMMING (ECOOP) (1992).

[8]   [Ansa-arch-frwmk]   David Iggulden, Owen Rees, Rob van der Linden, *Architecture and Frameworks*, APM.1017.02, ANSA (Oct. 25, 1994).

[9]   [Ansa-Fed-94]   Mike Beasley, Jane Cameron, Gray Girling, Yigal Hoffner, Rob van der Linden, Gomer Thomas, *Establishing Co-operation in Federated Systems*, ICL SYSTEMS JOURNAL (Vol.9, Iss.2, November 1994).

[10]   [Ansa-FedM-94]   Yigel Hoffner, *Management of Object-Based Federated Distributed Systems*, ARCHITECTURE PROJECTS MANAGEMENT LTD., APM.1018.01 (Oct. 25, 1994).

[11]   [BEA-TP]   BEA WebLogic® and BEA Tuxedo® (accessed at www.bea.com).

[12]   [Blair-98]   Gordon Blair and Jean-Bernard Stefani, *Open Distributed Processing and Multimedia*, Addison-Wesley (1998).

[13]   [Boasson]   Maarten Boasson and Edwin de Jong, *Software Architecture for Large Embedded Systems*, Hollandse Signaalapparaten, The Netherlands (1997) (accessed at boasson@signaal.nl and edejong@signaal.nl).

[14]   [Boehm-81]   Barry Boehm, *Software Engineering Economics*, Prentice Hall (1981).

[15]   [Boehm-88]   Barry Boehm *A Spiral Model of Software Development and Enhancement* IEEE COMPUTER (Vol. 21, #5, May 1988, pp. 61–72).

[16]   [Boehm-92]   Barry W. Boehm and William L. Scherlis, *Megaprogramming*, PROCEEDINGS OF THE DARPA SOFT WARE TECHNOLOGY CONFERENCE (Apr. 1992).

[17]   [Boehm-97]   B. Boehm et al., *Developing Multimedia Applications with the WinWin Spiral Model*, PROCEEDINGS, ESEC/FSE 97, Springer Verlag (1997).

[18]   [Boehm-98]   B. Boehm et al., *Using the Win Win Spiral Model: A Case Study*, IEEE COMPUTER (July 1998).

[19]   [Boehm-99]   B. Boehm, D. Port, *Escaping the Software Tar Pit: Model Clashes and How to Avoid Them*, ACM SOFTWARE ENGINEERING NOTES (Jan. 1999).

[20]   [Boehm-2000]   Barry Boehm, Chris Abts, A. Winsor Brown, Sunita Chulani, Bradford K. Clark, Ellis Horowitz, *Software Cost Estimation with Cocomo II*, 1/e, Prentice Hall (2001), ISBN 0-13-026692-2.

[21] [Booch-98] Grady Booch, James Rumbaugh, Ivar Jacobson, *The Unified Modeling Language User Guide*, Addison-Wesley (1998).

[22] [Bursell-98] Michael Bursell, Richard Hayton, Douglas Donaldson, Andrew Herbert, *A Mobile Object Workbench*, APM Ltd Poseidon House, Castle Park, Cambridge CB3 0RD United Kingdom (1998).

[23] [C2] R. N. Taylor, N. Medvidovic, K. Anderson, E. J. Whitehead, Jr., J. E. Robbins, K. A. Nies, P. Oreizy, and D. L. Dubrow, *A Component and Message-Based Architectural Style for GUI Software*, IEEE TRANS. SOFTWARE ENGINEERING (Vol.22, No.6, June 1996).

[24] [C4ISR] *C4ISR Architecture Framework, Version 2.0*, DoD C4ISR ARCHITECTURE WORKING GROUP (Dec, 18 1997).

[25] [CItech] (accessed at www.semanticintegration.com).

[26] [Clarke-96] Edmund M. Clarke and Jeannette M. Wing, *Formal Methods: State of the Art and Future Directions, Report by the Working Group on Formal Methods for the ACM Workshop on Strategic Directions in Computing Research*, ACM COMPUTING SURVEYS (Vol. 28, No. 4, December 1996, pp. 626–643). Also CMU-CS-96-178.

[27] [Corba3-messaging] OMG, *CORBA Messaging*, OMG TC DOCUMENT ORBOS/98-05-05 (May 18, 1998).

[28] [Corba-OTS] OMG, *Object Transaction Service 1.1*, OMG TC DOCUMENT ORBOS/96-12-06 (Nov 1997).

[29] [Cornily-99] Jean-Michel Cornily, France Telecom, Development Branch, CNET, electronic mail (1999).

[30] [DAIS] DAIS ORB (accessed at www.peerlogic.com/products/dais/f_dais.htm).

[31] [deMeer] Jan de Meer and Abdelhakim Hafid, *The Enterprise of QoS*, MIDDLEWARE '98 CONFERENCE (1998).

[32] [deontic-role] J-J Ch Meyer, R.J. Wieringa and F.P.M Dignum, *The role of Deontic Logic in the Specification of Information Systems*, Chapter 2 in LOGICS FOR DATABASES AND INFORMATION SYSTEMS, Eds J Chomicki and G Saake, Kluwer (1998).

[33] [Dimma-98] D. I. Donaldson, M. C. Faupel, R. J. Hayton, A. J. Herbert, N. J. Howarth, A. Kramer, I. A. MacMillan, D. J. Otway, S. W. Waterhouse, *DIMMA—A Multi-Media ORB*, APM Limited Poseidon House, Castle Park, Cambridge, CB3 0RD, United Kingdom (1998).

[34]   [DSTC-TM]   DSTC type management at
(accessed at www.dstc.edu.au/AU/research_news/odp/typemgmt/).

[35]   [Easy-WinWin]   (accessed at sunset.usc.edu/research/WINWIN/index.html, and
www.GroupSystems.com/).

[36]   [ECOOP-97a]   Haim Kilov and Bernhard Rumpe, *TUM-I9725,* ECOOP '97 WORKSHOP ON
PRECISE SEMANTICS FOR OBJECT-ORIENTED MODELING TECHNIQUES (May 1997).

[37]   [ECOOP-97b]   Haim Kilov, Bernhard Rumpe, and Ian Simmonds, *TUM-I9737,* OOPSLA
'97 WORKSHOP ON OBJECT-ORIENTED BEHAVIORAL SEMANTICS (WITH AN EMPHASIS ON
SEMANTICS OF LARGE OO BUSINESS SPECIFICATIONS) (September 1997).

[38]   [ECOOP-98a]   Haim Kilov and Bernhard Rumpe, *TUM-I9813,* SECOND ECOOP WORK-
SHOP ON PRECISE BEHAVIORAL SEMANTICS (WITH AN EMPHASIS ON OO BUSINESS SPECIFICA-
TIONS) (June 1998).

[39]   [ECOOP-98b]   Haim Kilov, Bernhard Rumpe, and Ian Simmonds, *TUM-I9820,* SEVENTH
OOPSLA WORKSHOP ON BEHAVIORAL SEMANTICS OF OO BUSINESS AND SYSTEM SPECIFICA-
TIONS (Aug. 1998).

[40]   [EDOC-97]   IEEE, *Proceedings of First International Enterprise Distributed Object Computing Workshop*, EDOC '97 (1997).

[41]   [EDOC-98]   *Proceedings of the Second International Enterprise Distributed Object Computing Conference*, EDOC '98 (Nov 1998).

[42]   [EDOC-99]   *Proceedings of the Third International Enterprise Distributed Object Computing Conference*, EDOC '99 (Sep 1999).

[43]   [EDOC-UML]   OPEN-IT Ltd. supported by SINTEF, Geco Schlumberger, Economica, *A
UML Profile for Enterprise Distributed Object Computing, Version 1*, OMG UML/99-10-19
(Oct 25, 1999).

[44]   [EDOC-UMLb]   Fujitsu Limited and Genesis Development Corporation, *UML Profile for
Enterprise Distributed Object Computing, Version 1.0,* OMG DOCUMENT AD/99-10-08 (Oct.
25, 1999).

[45]   [Edwards-94]   N.J. Edwards, *An ANSA Analysis of Open Dependable Distributed Computing*, ICL SYSTEMS JOURNAL, Hewlett-Packard (1994).

[46]   [Egyed]   Egyed, A. and Medvidovic, N. *A Formal Approach to Heterogeneous Software
Modeling*, PROCEEDINGS OF FOUNDATIONAL ASPECTS OF SOFTWARE ENGINEERING (FASE),
Berlin, Germany (2000).

[47] [Egyed-99] Egyed, A. and Medvidovic, N. *Extending Architectual Representation in UML with View Integration*, PROCEEDINGS OF THE 2ND INTERNATIONAL CONFERENCE ON THE UNIFIED MODELING LANGUAGE (UML), Fort Collins,CO (Oct. 1999).

[48] [ESTELLE] ISO/IEC 9074, *Information Processing Systems—Open Systems Interconnection—ESTELLE—A formal description technique based on an extended state transition model* (1989).

[49] [FedITA] DoD, *Federal ITA Conceptual Model, Draft* (June 25, 1998) (accessed at www.itpolicy.gsa.gov/mke/archplus/cmodel.htm).

[50] [FDT] ISO/IEC TR 10167, I*nformation Technology —Open Systems Interconnection - Guidelines for the application of Estelle, LOTOS and SDL* (1991).

[51] [Flexinet] Richard Hayton, Andrew Herbert, Douglas Donaldson, *FlexiNet — A Flexible Component Oriented Middleware System*, ANSA, in SIGOPS (1998) (accessed at www.ansa.co.uk/Research/FlexiNet.htm).

[52] [Fowler-97] Martin Fowler with Kendall Scott, *UML Distilled Applying the Standard Object Modeling Language*, Addison-Wesley (1997).

[53] [FT Corba-2] OMG, *Joint Revised Submission Fault Tolerant CORBA*, OMG ORBOS/99-10-05 (Oct. 25, 1999).

[54] [FT-Corba-1] OMG, *Fault Tolerant CORBA Briefing*, ORBOS/99-08-27 (Aug. 16, 1999).

[55] [FT-Corba-3] OMG, *Fault Tolerant CORBA Joint Revised Submission*, ORBOS/ORBOS/99-11-04 (Nov. 16, 1999).

[56] [Gacek-97] Cristina Gacek, *Detecting Architectural Mismatches During Systems Composition*, USC TECHNICAL REPORT USC-CSE-97-506, CENTER FOR SOFTWARE ENGINEERING, UNIVERSITY OF SOUTHERN CALIFORNIA (July 8, 1997). (http://sunset.usc.edu/TechRpts/Papers/usccse97-506/usccse97-506.ps).

[57] [Gacek-98] C. Gacek and B. W. Boehm, *Composing Components: How Does One Detect Potential Architectural Mismatches?* WORKSHOP ON COMPOSITIONAL SOFTWARE ARCHITECTURES, MONTEREY, CA (Jan. 1998).

[58] [Gacek-99a] Cristina Gacek, *Detecting Architectural Mismatches During Systems Composition*, USC, PH.D. THESIS (computer science) (Dec. 1998).

[59] [Gacek-Boehm] Cristina Gacek and Barry Boehm, *Composing Components: How Does One Detect Potential Architectural Mismatches?*, OMG-DARPA-MCC WORKSHOP ON COMPOSITIONAL SOFTWARE ARCHITECTURES. (no date).

[60] [Garlan-95]   David Garlan and Dewayne Perry, *Introduction to the Special Issue on Software Architecture*, IEEE TRANSACTIONS ON SOFTWARE ENGINEERING (Apr. 1995).

[61] [Garlan-95a]   David Garlan, Robert Allen, John Ockerbloom, *Architectural Mismatch: Why Reuse Is So Hard*, IEEE SOFTWARE (Nov. 1995).

[62] [GenLedger-98] Stanford Software International Ltd and the OMG Domain Contributing Members of the European Union's COMPASS Project; Economica AS and Real Objects Ltd., *Revised Submission, OMG's Finance DTF's RFP 4 (General Ledger Facility), ISO RM-ODP Computational Viewpoint Specification of the OMG General Ledger (GL) Facility Revision 3.11*, OMG DTC DOCUMENT FINANCE/98-12-03 (Dec. 21, 1998).

[63] [Goldschmidt-98]   Art Goldschmidt, Paul Horstmann, and John Laurentiev, *Exploiting Enterprise Java Beans for the NIIIP Virtual Enterprise*, EDOC '98 (Nov. 1998).

[64] [Gruber]   Tom Gruber, *What is an Ontology* (Sep. 1997) (accessed at www-ksl-svc.stanford.edu:5915/doc/frame-editor/what-is-an-ontology.html).

[65] [Hall-97]   Anthony Hall, *Keynote Address*, REQUIREMENT ENGINEERING 1997 CONFERENCE.

[66] [Hammer-79]   M. Hammer and D. McLeod, *On database management system architecture*, MIT LAB. FOR COMPUTER SCIENCE, MIT/LCS/TM-141 (Oct. 1979).

[67] [Hayes-Roth-95]   Barbara Hayes-Roth, Karl Pfleger, Phillippe Lalanda, Phillippe Morignot, and marko Balabanovic, *A Domain-Specific Software Architecture for Adaptive Intelligent Systems,* IEEE TRANSACTIONS ON SOFTWARE ENGINEERING (Apr. 1995).

[68] [Heimbigner-82]   D. Heimbigner, *A Federated Architecture for Database Systems*, UNIVERSITY OF SOUTHERN CALIFORNIA PH.D. THESIS (Aug. 1982).

[69] [Heimbigner-85]   D. Heimbigner, and D. McLeod, *A Federated Architecture for Information Management*, ACM TRANSACTION ON OFFICE INFORMATION SYSTEMS (July 3, 1985).

[70] [Heimbigner-94]   D. Heimbigner, *Infrastructure for Federated Software Environments*, NIST PRESENTATION (Mar. 1994).

[71] [Herring-97]   Charles Herring, Zoran Milosevic, Simon Kaplan, *Selecting Distributed Object Technologies in the Presence of Uncertainty: An Experience Report on C4I Enterprise Modelling* (1997).

[72] [Hilliard]   Rich Hilliard, *Using the UML for Architectural Description*, PRESENTATION TO ISIS 2000.

[73]   [HLA-96]   DOD, *High Level Architecture Federation Development and Execution Process (FEDEP) Model, Version 1.0* (Sept. 6, 1996).

[74]   [Hoare]   C.A.R. Hoare, *Mathematical Models for Computing Science* (Aug. 1994).

[75]   [Hoffner-95]   Yigel Hoffner, Ben Crawford, *Federation and Interoperability*, ARCHITECTURE PROJECTS MANAGEMENT LTD., APM 1514.01 (Oct. 1995).

[76]   [Holmes-94]   John E Holmes, DERA, UK, *MCI [Methods for C3I Interoperability]: the RM-ODP in Practice* (1998).

[77]   [Holzmann]   Gerald Holzmann, *The Model Checker SPIN*, IEEE TRANSACTIONS ON SOFTWARE ENGINEERING (Vol. 23, No. 5, May 1997).

[78]   [iContract]
(accessed at www.reliable-systems.com/tools/iContract/documentation/documentation.htm).

[79]   [ICRF]   Emil Lupu, Zoran Milosevic, and Morris Sloman, *Use of Roles and Policies for Specifying, and Managing a Virtual Enterprise*, DISTRIBUTED SYSTEMS TECHNOLOGY CENTRE, UNIVERSITY OF QUEENSLAND, QLD 4072, AUSTRALIA (1999).

[80]   [IDEF1X]   National Institute of Standards and Technology, *Integration Definition for Information Modeling (IDEF1X)*, FIPS PUB 184, GAITHERSBURG, MD.

[81]   [IEEE-P1471]   IEEE AWG, *Draft IEEE Recommended Practice for Architectural Description IEEE P1471/D5.2* (Nov. 99).

[82]   [IEEE AWG-97]   IEEE AWG, *Toward a Recommended Practice for Architectural Description*, BRIEFING TO THE SIGADA WORKSHOP, SOFTWARE ARCHITECTURES IN PRODUCT LINE ACQUISITIONS: ENGINEERING OR WITCHCRAFT?, SALEM, MA (June 12, 1997).

[83]   [IEEE-610-12]   Institute of Electrical and Electronics Engineers, *IEEE Standard Glossary of Software Engineering Terminology*, IEEE STD 610.12-1990, PISCATAWAY, NJ (1990).

[84]   [IETF-QoS]   (accessed at www.ietf.org/html.charters/rtfm-charter.html and www.ietf.org/html.charters/intserv-charter.html).

[85]   [ISO GRM]   ISO/IEC 10165-7, *Information Technology—Open Systems Interconnection—Management Information Systems—Structure of Management Information —Part 7: General Relationship Model* (1995).

[86]   [ISO IDL]   ITU-T Recommendation X.920 | ISO/IEC 14750-1, *Information Technology—Open Distributed Processing—Interface Definition Language*.

[87]   [ISO Naming]   ISO/IEC 14771, *Draft IS Text for ODP Naming Framework* (1998).

[88]   [ISO-CP]   ISO/IEC JTC1/SC7 N1978, *FCD 14752—Information Technology—Open Distributed Processing—Protocol Support for Computational Interactions* (Aug.25, 1998).

[89]   [ISO-EntVP]   ISO/IEC JTC1/SC7/WG17, ISO/IEC 15414 I ITU-T Recommendation X.911, Initial Committee Draft, *Information Technology—Open Distributed Processing—Reference Model—Enterprise Language*, CD 15414 (Jan. 28, 2000).

[90]   [ISO-IRB]   ISO/IEC FCD14753 ITU-T Draft Recommendation X.930, *Open Distributed Processing—Interface References and Binding* (Sept.1998).

[91]   [ISO-QOS]   ITU-T Recommendation X.905 I ISO/IEC 15935 ISO/IEC JTC1/SC21 Open Systems Interconnection, Data Management and Open Distributed Processing, *Open Distributed Processing—Reference Model—Quality of Service*, Committee Draft (1999).

[92]   [ISO-TR]   ITU-T X.960, ISO/IEC 14769, *Information Technology—Open Distributed Processing—Type Repository Function* (June 1999).

[93]   [ISO-Trading]   Draft Rec. X.9tr I ISO/IEC DIS 13235, *ODP Trading Function* (June 20, 1995).

[94]   [ITU-GRM]   ITU/T X.725, *Information Technology—Open Systems Interconnection—Structure of Management Information: General Relationship Model* (Nov. 1995).

[95]   [IWQoS]   (accessed at www.fokus.gmd.de/research/cc/tip/employees/jdm/private/SC-IWQOS/home.html).

[96]   [Jackson-2k]   Daniel Jackson and Martin Rinard, *The Future of Software Analysis*, IN FUTURE OF SOFTWARE ENGINEERING, Ed. Anthony Finelstein, ACM Press (June 2000).

[97]   [Jackson-96]   Daniel Jackson and Jeannette Wing, *Lightweight Formal Methods*, IEEE COMPUTER (Apr. 1996).

[98]   [Jacobson-99]   Ivar Jacobson, Grady Booch, James Rumbaugh, *The Unified Software Development Process*, Addison Wesley (1999).

[99]   [JP-ISORC]   Janis Putman, *Model for Fault Tolerance and Policy from RM-ODP Expressed in UML/OCL*, ISORC PROCEEDINGS (Mar. 2000).

[100]   [JP-WORDS]   Janis Putman, *General Framework for Fault Tolerance from ISO/ITU Reference Model for Open Distributed Processing (RM-ODP)*, WORDS 99, Monterey (Nov. 1999).

[101]   [JTS]   Java Transaction Service (JTS) (accessed at java.sun.com/products/jts).

[102]   [Karamanolis-98] Christos Karamanolis and Jeff Magee, *Construction and Management of Highly Available Services in Open Distributed Systems*, DISTRIBUTED SYSTEMS ENGINEERING (Vol. 5, pp. 29–45, 1998).

[103]   [Kiczales]   Gregor Kiczales, John Lamping, Anurag Mendhekar, Chris Maeda, Cristina Videira Lopes, Jean-Marc Loingtier, John Irwin, *Aspect-Oriented Programming*, PROCEEDINGS OF THE EUROPEAN CONFERENCE ON OBJECT-ORIENTED PROGRAMMING (ECOOP) (June 1997).

[104]   [Kilov-93]   Haim Kilov and Laura Redmann, *Specifying Joint Behavior of Objects: Formalization and Standardization*, IEEE COMPUTER SOCIETY, PROCEEDINGS OF THE 1993 SOFTWARE ENGINEERING STANDARDS SYMPOSIUM (Sept. 3, 1993).

[105]   [Kilov-94]   Haim Kilov, James Ross, *Information Modeling: An Object-Oriented Approach*, Prentice Hall (1994).

[106]   [Kilov-97]   Haim Kilov, INTERNATIONAL STANDARDS DEFINE SEMANTICS: RM- ODP AND GRM BRIEFING (June 6, 1997).

[107]   [Kilov-98]   Haim Kilov, *Business Enterprise Modeling*, Prentice Hall (1998).

[108]   [Kilov-99]   Haim Kilov and Michael Guttman, *Distributed Computing Architecture Advisory Service: ISO Reference Model of Open Distributed Processing: An Informal Introduction*, VOL. 2, NO. 4, CUTTER CONSORTIUM (1999).

[109]   [Kramer]   Reto Kramer, *iContract — The Java™ Design by Contract™ Tool*, CAMBRIDGE TECHNOLOGY PARTNERS (Jan. 20, 1999).

[110]   [Kruchten]   Philippe Kruchten, *Architectural Blueprints—The "4+1" View Model of Software Architecture*, IEEE SOFTWARE (Vol. 12, No. 6, Nov. 1995).

[111]   [KSL]   Stanford Knowledge Systems Laboratory's Network Services, Stanford University, (May 7, 2000).
(accessed at www-ksl-svc.stanford.edu:5915/doc/frame-editor/what-is-an-ontology.html).

[112]   [Leveson-95]   Nancy Leveson, *Safeware System Safety and Computers*, Addison-Wesley (1995).

[113]   [Leveson-96]   Nancy G. Leveson, *Software Engineering: A Look Back and A Path to the Future*, University of Washington (Dec. 14, 1996).

[114]   [Linington-98]   Peter Linington , Zoran Milosevic , Kerry Raymond, *Policies in Communities: Extending the ODP Enterprise Viewpoint*, PROCEEDINGS OF 2ND INTERNATIONAL WORKSHOP ON ENTERPRISE DISTRIBUTED OBJECT COMPUTING (EDOC) '98 (Nov.1998).

[115]   [Linington-99]   Peter Linington, *Options for Expressing ODP Enterprise Communities and Their Policies by Using UML*, PROCEEDINGS OF 3RD INTERNATIONAL WORKSHOP ON ENTERPRISE DISTRIBUTED OBJECT COMPUTING (EDOC) '99 (Sept. 1999).

[116]   [Liskov-94]   Barbara H. Liskov and Jeannette M. Wing, *A Behavioral Notion of Subtyping*, ACM TRANSACTIONS ON PROGRAMMING LANGUAGES AND SYSTEMS (Nov. 1994).

[117]   [Liskov-99]   Barbara H. Liskov and Jeannette M. Wing, *Behavioral Subtyping Using Invariants and Constraints*, TO APPEAR IN FORMAL METHODS FOR DISTRIBUTED PROCESSING: AN OBJECT ORIENTED APPROACH, Eds H. Bowman and J. Derrick, Cambridge University Press. Also CMU-CS-99-156 (July 1999).

[118]   [LOTOS]   ISO/IEC 8807, *Information Processing Systems—Open Systems Interconnection—LOTOS—A formal Description Technique Based on the Temporal Ordering of Observational Behavior* (1989).

[119]   [Malveau]   R. C. Malveau and T. J. Mowbray, *Software Architecture Bootcamp: A Field Manual*, Prentice Hall (2000).

[120]   [MARS]   Douglas Isbell, Mary Hardin, Joan Underwood, *MARS Climate Orbiter Team Finds Likely Cause of Loss*, PRESS RELEASE 99-113, NASA (Sept. 30, 1999).

[121]   [McLeod-91]   D. McLeod, *Semantic Heterogeneity in Federated Database Systems: Identification, Resolution, and Interconnection*, USC (1991).

[122]   [Medvidovic-2000]   N. Medvidovic and R. N. Taylor, *A Classification and Comparison Framework for Software Architecture Description Languages*, IEEE TRANSACTIONS ON SOFTWARE ENGINEERING (IN PRESS).

[123]   [Mehta-99]   Nikunj R. Mehta, Nenad Medvidovic, Sandeep Phadke, *Towards a Taxonomy of Software Connectors*, USC-CSE-99-529.

[124]   [MetaH-93]   Pam Binns and Steve Vestal, *Formal Real-Time Architecture Specification and Analysis*, TENTH IEEE WORKSHOP ON REAL-TIME OPERATING SYSTEMS AND SOFTWARE, New York, NY (May 1993).

[125]   [MetaH-96]   S. Vestal, *MetaH Programmer's Manual, Version 1.09*. TECHNICAL REPORT, HONEYWELL TECHNOLOGY CENTER (April 1996).

[126]   [Mettala-92]   Erik Mettala and Marc Graham, *The Domain-Specific Software Architecture Program*, TECHNICAL REPORT CMU/SEI-92-SR-9, CARNEGIE MELLON UNIVERSITY (June 1992).

[127]   [Meyer-2000]   Bertrand Meyer, *Beyond Objects: What to Compose*, SOFTWARE DEVELOP-MENT MAGAZINE (Mar. 2000).

[128]   [Meyer-2000-2]   Bertrand Meyer, *Rules for Component Builders,* SOFTWARE DEVELOP-MENT MAGAZINE (May 2000).

[129]   [Meyer-97]   Bertrand Meyer, *Object-Oriented Software Construction*, Prentice Hall (1997).

[130]   [Mezini]   Mira Mezini and Karl Lieberherr, *Adaptive Plug-and-Play Components for Evolutionary Software Development,* PROCEEDINGS OF THE CONFERENCE ON OBJECT-ORIENTED PROGRAMMING: SYSTEMS, LANGUAGES, AND APPLICATIONS (OOPSLA) (Oct. 1998).

[131]   [Miller-97]   Joaquin Miller, *OMA Object Models and the ODP Object Model* briefing, MCI Systemhouse (1997).

[132]   [Milosevic]   Zoran Milosevic, *Enterprise Aspects of Open Distributed Systems*, PH.D. THESIS SUBMITTED TO THE DEPARTMENT OF COMPUTER SCIENCE, UNIVERSITY OF QUEENSLAND, AUSTRALIA (Oct. 1995).

[133]   [MoF]   OMG, *Meta-Object Facility 1.3*, MOF 1.3 (ad/99-06-05) (June 1999).

[134]   [Moormann-97]   Amy Moormann Zaremski and Jeannette M. Wing, *Specification Matching Software Components*, ACM TRANSACTIONS ON SOFTWARE ENGINEERING AND METHODOLOGY (Oct. 1997).

[135]   [MQS]   IBM, MQSeries product suite (accessed at www-4.ibm.com/software/ts/mqseries/).

[136]   [NIIIP-96]   DARPA, *NIIIP Reference Architecture: Concepts and Guidelines* (1995–1996).

[137]   [Nutt-92]   Gary J. Nutt, *Open Systems*, Prentice Hall (1992).

[138]   [OCL1]   OMG, *UML Object Constraint Language Specification, Vers 1.1*, DOCUMENT OCL-97-08-08 (Sept. 1, 1997).

[139]   [OCL2]   J. Warme and A. Kleppe, *The Object Constraint Language: Precise Modeling with UML*, Addison-Wesley (1999).

[140]   [OMG MOF]   OMG, *MOF Model & Interfaces with errata*, RTF/97-10-02 (Oct. 1997).

[141]   [OMG-Negot]   OMG Electronic Commerce Domain Task Force, Negotiation Facility Final Revised Submission, ec/99-038-01 (Mar. 1999).

[142]   [OMG-PIDS]   OMG, *CORBAMed: Healthcare Domain Specifications, Version 1.0*, COR-BAMED-99-03-01 (Mar. 1999).

[143]   [OMG-RFP-97]   OMG, *Request For Proposal*, ab/98-03-02 (1998) (accessed at ftp://ftp.omg.org/pub/docs/ab/98-03-02.doc).

[144]   [OMG-UML-97]   OMG, *Unified Modeling Language, UML Semantics, Vers. 1.1*, ad/970804 (Sept.1997).

[145]   [OMG-UML-ODP]   OMG, *Relationship of the Unified Modeling Language to the Reference Model of Open Distributed Computing, Vers 1.1.2* (Sept. 21, 1997).

[146]   [OMG-XMI-98]   OMG, *XML Metadata Interchange*, ad/981005 (Oct. 1998).

[147]   [OSI]   ITU-T Recommendation X.200 (1994) I ISO/IEC 7498-1, *Information Technology—Open Systems Interconnection—Basic Reference Model* (1994).

[148]   [Otway-95]   Dave Otway, *The ANSA Binding Model*, APM-1392-01 (Jan. 10, 1995).

[149]   [Putman-94]   Janis Putman, *Federation in RM-ODP*, CONTRIBUTION TO X3T3 (Sept. 1994).

[150]   [Putman-97]   Janis Putman and Stephen Strong, *Technology Enabled Virtual Enterprises of Stakeholders and Systems,* paper and briefing, CALS '97 (1997).

[151]   [QoS-framework]   ITU-T Recommendation X.641 (1997) I ISO/IEC 13236, *Information Technology—Quality of Service—Framework*, (1998).

[152]   [QoS-framework2]   ITU-T Recommendation X.642 I ISO/IEC 13243, *Information Technology—Quality of Service—Methods and Mechanisms* (in final stages).

[153]   [QoS-email]   (accessed at www.fokus.gmd.de/research/cc/tip/employees/jdm/private/jdmQoSIG.html).

[154]   [QoS-Forum]   (accessed at www.qosforum.com).

[155]   [QUO]   (accessed at www.dist-systems.bbn.com/tech/QuO/quorelease.html).

[156]   [Quatrani-98]   Terry Quatrani, *Visual Modeling with Rational ROSE and UML*, Addison-Wesley (1998).

[157]   [Quorum]   *Dynamic Response to Mission-Critical Applications* (accessed at www.darpa.mil/ito/research/quorum/index.html).

[158] [Rakotonirainy-97] Andry Rakotonirainy, Andrew Berry, Stephen Crawley, Zoran Milosevic, *Describing Open Distributed Systems: A Foundation*, Proceedings of the Thirtieth Annual Hawaii International Conference on System Sciences: Software Technology and Architecture (1997).

[159] [Rapide] D. C. Luckham and J. Vera, *An Event-Based Architecture Definition Language*, IEEE Transactions on Software Engineering (Sept. 1995).

[160] [Raymond-95] Kerry Raymond, *Introduction ICODP '95 briefing*, CRC for Distributed Systems Technology (Feb. 1995).

[161] [Rechtin-97] Eberhardt Rechtin, Mark Maier, *The Art of Systems Architecting* (Systems Engineering Series), CRC Press (1997).

[162] [RM-ODP] International Organization for Standardization, *Basic Reference Model of Open Distributed Processing,* ITU-T X.900 series and ISO/IEC 10746 series (1995).

[163] [RM-ODP-1] *ITU-T Recommendation X.901 | ISO/IEC 10746:1: Information Technology —Open Distributed Processing—Overview and Guide to Use* (1996).

[164] [RM-ODP-2] *ITU-T Recommendation X.902 | ISO/IEC 10746-2: Information Technology—Open Distributed Processing—Reference Model: Foundations* (1995).

[165] [RM-ODP-3] *ITU-T Recommendation X.903 | ISO/IEC 10746-3: Information Technology—Open Distributed Processing—Reference Model: Architecture* (1995).

[166] [RM-ODP-4] *ITU-T/CCITT X.904, ISO/IEC 10746-4: Information Technology—Open Distributed Processing—Reference Model: Architecture Semantics* (1995).

[167] [Rumbaugh-91] James Rumbaugh, Michael Blaha, William Premerlani, Frederick Eddy, William Lorensen, *Object-Oriented Modeling and Design*, Prentice Hall (1991).

[168] [Rumbaugh-96] James Rumbaugh, *OMT Insights: Perspectives on Modeling*, Journal of Object-Oriented Technology, SIGS Books (1996).

[169] [Rumbaugh-99] James Rumbaugh, Ivar Jacobson, Grady Booch, *The Unified Modeling Language Reference Manual*, Addison Wesley (1999).

[170] [Rutt-93] *Comparison of the OMG and ISO/CCITT Object Models*, Report of the Joint X/Open/NM Forum/OMG Taskforce on Object Modelling (Tom Rutt, ed, 1993).

[171] [Sachs] Ira S. Sachs, *Recommended Practice for Architectural Description, IEEE Standard P1471*, Briefing from High Performance Technologies, Inc. (Dec. 9, 1999).

[172] [SADL] M. Moriconi, X. Qian, and R. Riemenschneider, *Correct architecture refinement*, IEEE TRANSACTIONS ON SOFTWARE ENGINEERING (21(4), pp. 356–372, April 1995).

[173] [SDL] ITU/T RECOMMENDATION Z.100, *CCITT Specification and description language (SDL)* (Mar. 1989) (accessed at www7.itu.int/publibase/itut_rec/ItutAllBySeries.asp?serie=Z).

[174] [Sec-A] ITU-T RECOMMENDATION X.811 | ISO/IEC 10181-2, *Information Technology—Open Systems Interconnection—Security Frameworks for Open Systems—Authentication* (1995).

[175] [Sec-AC] ITU-T RECOMMENDATION X.812 | ISO/IEC 10181-3, *Information Technology—Open Systems Interconnection—Security Frameworks for Open Systems—Access Control* (1995).

[176] [Sec-Arch] CCITT RECOMMENDATION X.800, *Security Architecture for Open Systems Interconnection for CCITT Applications* (1991).

[177] [Sec-Au] ITU-T RECOMMENDATION X.816 | ISO/IEC 10181-7, *Information Technology—Open Systems Interconnection—Security Frameworks for Open Systems—Audit* (1995).

[178] [Sec-C] ITU-T RECOMMENDATION X.814 | ISO/IEC 10181-5, *Information Technology—Open Systems Interconnection—Security Frameworks for Open Systems—Confidentiality* (1995).

[179] [Sec-Frmwk] ITU-T RECOMMENDATION X.810 | ISO/IEC 10181-1, *Information Technology—Open Systems Interconnection—Security Frameworks for Open Systems—Overview* (1995).

[180] [Sec-I] ITU-T RECOMMENDATION X.815 | ISO/IEC 10181-6, *Information Technology—Open Systems Interconnection—Security Frameworks for Open Systems—Integrity* (1995).

[181] [Sec-K] ISO/IEC 11770-1, *Information Technology—Security Techniques—Part 1: Key Management Framework* (1994).

[182] [Sec-NR] ITU-T RECOMMENDATION X.813 | ISO/IEC 10181-4, *Information Technology—Open Systems Interconnection—Security Frameworks for Open Systems—Non-Repudiation* (1995).

[183] [SELECT-98] *User Guide for SELECT Enterprise Version 6*, SELECT SOFTWARE TOOLS, (Mar. 1998). Additional information at www.selectst.com.

[184] [Shaw-94] Mary Shaw, *Procedure Calls Are the Assembly Language of Software Interconnection: Connectors Deserve First-Class Status*, CMU-CS-94-107 (Jan 1994).

[185] [Shaw-95] M. Shaw, R. DeLine, D. V. Klein, T. L. Ross, D. M. Young and G. Zelesnik, *Abstractions for Software Architecture and Tools to Support Them*, IEEE TRANSACTIONS ON SOFTWARE ENGINEERING (Apr. 1995).

[186] [Shaw-96] Mary Shaw and David Garlan, *Software Architecture: Perspectives on an Emerging Discipline*, Prentice Hall (1996).

[187] [Shaw-97] Mary Shaw, Robert DeLine, and Gregory Zelesnik, *Abstractions and Implementations for Architectural Connections*, PROCEEDINGS, 1996 (THIRD) INTL. CONFERENCE ON CONFIGURABLE DISTRIBUTED SYSTEMS (ICCDS96) (June 15, 1997).

[188] [Shelton] Robert E. Shelton, President & CEO, Open Engineering Inc., *Adapting Zachman for Business Objects*, PRESENTED TO OMG OBJECT- REFERENCE MODEL SUBCOMMITTEE (June 1997). More information at www.openeng.com.

[189] [Shlaer-88] Sally Shlaer and Stephen J. Mellor, *Object-Oriented systems Analysis: Modeling the World in Data,* Yourdon Press (1988).

[190] [Sluman-97] Chris Sluman, Jeremy Tucker, J. P. LeBlanc, Bryan Wood, *Quality of Service (QoS) Green Paper* (June 1997).

[191] [Steen] Maarten W. A. Steen and John Derrick, *Formalising ODP Enterprise Policies*, PROCEEDINGS OF 3RD INTERNATIONAL WORKSHOP ON ENTERPRISE DISTRIBUTED OBJECT COMPUTING (EDOC) '99 (Sept. 1999).

[192] [Szyperski-98] Clemens Szyperski, *Component Software: Beyond Object-Oriented Programming*, Addison-Wesley (1998).

[193] [Thompson-98] Craig Thompson, Bryan Wood, Sandy Tyndale-Biscoe, Joaquin Miller, Chris Sluman, Haim Kilov, Paul Rabin and Robert Shelton, *Reference Model Extension Green Paper*, OMG ORMSC/98-05-02 (May 26, 1998).

[194] [TINA-97] Telecommunications Information Network Architecture Consortium (TINA-C), *Baseline Service Architecture, Version 5.0*, (June 16, 1997).

[195] [TOGAF] The Open Group, *The Open Group Architectural Framework (TOGAF)*, Version 5, Document Number: I900, (Dec. 1999).

[196] [Tracz-94] Will Tracz, *Collected Overview Reports from the DSSA Project*, LORAL FEDERAL SYSTEMS (NOW LOCKHEED MARTIN FEDERAL SYSTEMS), OWEGO, NY (Oct. 1994).

[197]   [Tracz-94a]   Will Tracz, *Domain-Specific Software Architecture (DSSA) Frequently Asked Questions (FAQ)*, LORAL FEDERAL SYSTEMS, OWEGO, NY (July 94).

[198]   [Tockey]   Steve Tockey, *An Introduction to the Zachman Framework,* OMG DOCUMENT ORMSC/97-06-08 (June 1997).

[199]   [Tyndale-Biscoe]   Sandy Tyndale-Biscoe, Paul Ravenhill, John Bull, Robert van der Linden, *Results of the Pilot Enterprise Description Project*, DRA, United Kingdom (no date).

[200]   [Tyson-96a]   Kevin Tyson, *Reliable Distributed Object Computing in the Financial Services Domain, briefing*, ENTERPRISE ENGINEERING ASSOCIATES (Mar. 1996).

[201]   [Tyson-97a]   Kevin Tyson, Enterprise Engineering Associates, and Chuck Alvarez, J. P. Morgan & Co., *Event Management Architecture Large Scale Distributed Systems, briefing,* (May 1997).

[202]   [Tyson-97b]   Kevin Tyson and William Frank, *The Business of Objects is Business, briefing,* ENTERPRISE ENGINEERING ASSOCIATES (Oct. 1997).

[203]   [Tyson-98]   Kevin Tyson, *Applying Object Technology in Finance* (1998) (accessed at www.enteng.com).

[204]   [UCC]   Robert N. Corley and Peter J. Shedd, *Fundamental of Business Law*, Prentice Hall (1990).

[205]   [UML-1.3]   Object Management Group, *OMG Unified Modeling Language Specification, Version 1.3* (June 1999).

[206]   [UML-4Keeps]   (accessed at www.adexperts.com).

[207]   [UML-Rose-Realtime]   (accessed at www.rational.com/products/rosert/index.jtmpl).

[208]   [UniCon]   Mary Shaw, Robert DeLine, Daniel V. Klein, Theodore L. Ross, David M. Young, and Gregory Zelesnik, *Abstractions for Software Architecture and Tools to Support Them*, IEEE TRANSACTIONS ON SOFTWARE ENGINEERING (Apr.1995).

[209]   [VDB]   Enterworks, Inc., Virtual DB (accessed at www.enterworks.com).

[210]   [Vestal-94]   Steve Vestal, *Mode Changes in Real-Time Architecture Description Language*, PROCEEDINGS OF THE SECOND INTERNATIONAL WORKSHOP ON CONFIGURABLE DISTRIBUTED SYSTEMS (Mar. 1994).

[211] [Visible] Alan Perkins, VP, Consulting Services, Visible Systems Corporation, 201 North Union St, Alexandria VA 22314 USA, Phone: +1-703-739-2242 Fax: +1-703-739-0074, (accessed at www.visible.com).

[212] [Webster's] *Merriam-Webster Dictionary* (accessed at www.m-w.com/dictionary.htm).

[213] [Wing-95] Jeannette M. Wing, *Hints to Specifiers*, CMU-CS-95-118R, CARNEGIE MELLON UNIVERSITY (May 22, 1995).

[214] [Wing-95] Jeannette M. Wing, *Hints to Specifiers*, Chapter 5 in TEACHING AND LEARNING FORMAL METHODS, Eds Dean and Hinchey, Academic Press, pp. 57–77 (1996) . Also available as CMU-CS-95-118R (May 1995).

[215] [Wing-98a] Jeannette M. Wing and John Ockerbloom, *Respectful Type Converters*, IEEE TRANSACTIONS ON SOFTWARE ENGINEERING (Nov. 1998). Also CMU-CS-98-130.

[216] [Wing-98b] Jeannette M. Wing, *A Symbiotic Relationship Between Formal Methods and Security*, PROCEEDINGS FROM WORKSHOPS ON COMPUTER SECURITY, FAULT TOLERANCE, AND SOFTWARE ASSURANCE: FROM NEEDS TO SOLUTION, CMU-CS-98-188 (Dec. 1998).

[217] [Wing-98c] Jeannette M. Wing, *Formal Methods: Past, Present, and Future*, KEYNOTE ADDRESS AT ASIAN '98, MANILA, THE PHILIPPINES (Dec. 10, 1998).

[218] [Wing-99] Jeannette M. Wing and John Ockerbloom, *Respectful Type Converters For Mutable Types*, FOUNDATIONS OF COMPONENT BASED SYSTEMS, Eds G. Leavens and M. Sitaraman, Cambridge University Press (in press). Also CMU-CS-99-142, June 1999.

[219] [WinWin] Barry Boehm, *WinWin Reference Manual: A System for Collaboration and Negotiation*, USC (1998). Tool available at sunset.usc.edu/Tools.html.

[220] [Wise] A. Wise, *Little-JIL 1.0 Language Report*, University of Massachusetts (Apr. 1998).

[221] [Wright] R. Allen and D. Garlan, *The Wright Architectural Specification Language*(Sept. 24, 1996) (accessed at www.cs.cmu.edu/afs/cs/project/able/ftp/wright-tr.ps).

[222] [Wright-a] Robert Allen and David Garlan, *Formalizing Architectural Connection*, PROCEEDINGS OF THE 16TH INTERNATIONAL CONFERENCE ON SOFTWARE ENGINEERING (May 1994).

[223] [Z] J.M. Spivey, *The Z Notation: A Reference Manual, International Series in Computer Science, Second Edition,* Prentice Hall International (1992).

[224] [Zachman]   J. F. Sowa and J. A. Zachman, *Extending and Formalizing the Framework for Information Systems*, IBM SYSTEMS JOURNAL (Vol. 31, No. 3, IBM Publication G321-5488, 1992).

[225] [Zachman-97]   John A. Zachman, *The Framework For Enterprise Architecture: Background, Description and Utility* (1997).

[226] [Zachman-a]   John A. Zachman, *A Framework for Information Systems Architecture*, IBM SYSTEMS JOURNAL (Vol. 26, No. 3, IBM Publication G321-5298. 914-945-3836, 1987).

BIBLIOGRAPHY

[1] [ADML] MCC, *ADML Documentation, Version 1* (2000)
(accessed at www.mcc.com/projects/ssepp/adml).

[2] [Allen-97] R. Allen and D. Garlan, *A Formal Basis for Architectural Connection*, ACM
Transactions on Software Engineering and Methodology (1997).

[3] [ANSA] Nigel Edwards, Owen Rees, *A Model for Failures in Dependable Systems*,
APM.1143.01 (1994).

[4] [ANSA-89] Advanced Networked Systems Architecture, *An Engineer's Introduction to the
Architecture*, Architecture Projects Management Limited, United Kingdom, (1989).

[5] [Ansa-EventMgmt] John Warne, *Event Management for Large-Scale Distributed Systems*,
APM.1633.01 (1995).

[6] [ANSA-Intro] Advanced Networked Systems Architecture (ANSA), *An Engineer's Introduction to the Architecture*, TR.03.02, Architecture Projects Management Limited (1989).

[7] [AOP] Workshops on Aspect-Oriented Programming (AOP) at ECOOP '97, '98 and '99, and
ICSE '98.

[8]   [ASN-90]   ISO/IEC8824, *Open Systems Interconnection Specification of Abstract Syntax Notation One* (ASN.1) (1990).

[9]   [Baniassad]   Elisa L.A. Baniassad and Gail C. Murphy, *Conceptual Module Querying for Software Reengineering*, PROCEEDINGS OF THE INTERNATIONAL CONFERENCE ON SOFTWARE ENGINEERING (ICSE 20) (1998).

[10]   [Bass-98]   Len Bass, Paul Clements, Rick Kazman, *Software Architecture in Practice* (SEI Series in Software Engineering), Addison-Wesley (1998).

[11]   [Berry-94]   A. Berry and K. Raymond (eds), *The DSTC Architecture Model*, DSTC TECHNICAL REPORT (1994).

[12]   [Bershad-90]   B. N. Bershad, T. E. Anderson, E. D. Lazowska and H. M. Levy, *Lightweight Remote Procedure Call, ACM Transactions on Computer Systems*, 8(1) (1990).

[13]   [Booch-91]   Booch, G., *Object-Oriented Design with Applications*, Benjamin/Cummings, RedwoodCity, CA,(1991).

[14]   [Brooks-87]   F. Brooks, *No Silver Bullet*, IEEE COMPUTER, (20)4 (1987).

[15]   [Brown-98]   William Brown, Raphael Malveau, Hays McCormick III, Thomas Mowbray, *Anti-Patterns Refactoring Software, Architectures, and Projects in Crisis*, John Wiley & Sons, Inc. (1998).

[16]   [Buschmann-97]   F. Buschmann, R. Meunier, H. Rohnert, P. Sommerlad, M. Stal, *A System of Patterns*, John Wiley & Sons (1997).

[17]   [Carzaniga-98]   A. Carzaniga, E. Di Nitto, D. Rosenbloom, and A. L. Wolf, *Issues in Supporting Event-Based Architectural Styles*, PROCEEDINGS OF THE THIRD INTERNATIONAL WORKSHOP ON SOFTWARE ARCHITECTURES, Orlando, FL (1998).

[18]   [Clements]   Paul C. Clements, *From Domain Models to Architectures*, WORKSHOP ON SOFTWARE ARCHITECTURE, USC Center for Software Engineering, Los Angeles (1994).

[19]   [CMIP-91]   ISO/IEC 9596, *Information Technology Open Systems Interconnection Common Management Information Protocol Specification. International Standard* (1991).

[20]   [Coad-98]   Peter Coad with David North and Mark Mayfield, *Object Models Strategies, Patterns, & Applications*, *Second Edition*, Yourdon Press, Prentice Hall (1997).

[21]   [Colouris-94]   G. Colouris, J. Dollimore and T. Kindberg, *Distributed Systems: Concepts and Design*, *Second Edition*, Addison-Wesley (1994).

[22]   [Cook-99]   J. E. Cook and J. A. Dage, *Highly Reliable Upgrading of Components*, PROCEEDINGS OF THE 21ST INTERNATIONAL CONFERENCE ON SOFTWARE ENGINEERING, Los Angeles, CA (1999).

[23]   [Crowcroft-95]   Jon Crowcroft, *Open Distributed Systems*, Artech House (1995).

[24]   [Cugola-98]   C. Cugola, E. Di Nitto, and A. Fuggetta, *Exploiting an Event-Based Infrastructure to Develop Complex Distributed Systems*, PROCEEDINGS OF THE 20TH INTERNATIONAL CONFERENCE ON SOFTWARE ENGINEERING, Kyoto, Japan (1998).

[25]   [Dashofy-99]   E. M. Dashofy, N. Medvidovic, and R. N. Taylor, *Using Off-the- Shelf Middleware to Implement Connectors in Distributed Software Architectures*, PROCEEDINGS OF THE 21ST INTERNATIONAL CONFERENCE ON SOFTWARE ENGINEERING, Los Angeles, CA (1999).

[26]   [Dean-95]   T. R. Dean and J. R. Cordy, *A Syntactic Theory of Software Architecture*, IEEE TRANSACTIONS ON SOFTWARE ENGINEERING, 21(4) (1995).

[27]   [DeLine-99]   R. DeLine, *Avoiding Packaging Mismatch with Flexible Packaging*, PROCEEDINGS OF THE 21ST INTERNATIONAL CONFERENCE ON SOFTWARE ENGINEERING, Los Angeles, CA (1999).

[28]   [DII COE] DISA, *Defense Information Infrastructure (DII) Common Operating Environment (COE) Integration and Runtime Specification (I&RTS), Version 2.0* (1995).

[29]   [DiNitto-99]   E. Di Nitto and D. S. Rosenblum, *Exploiting ADLs to Specify Architectural Styles Induced by Middleware Infrastructures*, PROCEEDINGS OF THE 21ST INTERNATIONAL CONFERENCE ON SOFTWARE ENGINEERING, Los Angeles, CA (1999).

[30]   [DistibApplSvs]   John Brenner (ed), *Distributed Application Services (Open Framework)*, Prentice Hall, ISBN 0-13-6320518-0.

[31]   [Douglass-2000]   Bruce Powel Douglass, *Beyond Objects: Components, States and Interfaces, Oh My!*, SOFTWARE DEVELOPMENT MAGAZINE (2000).

[32]   [Edwards-97]   Jeri Edwards, Deborah DeVoe, *3-Tier Client/Server at Work* (1997).

[33]   [Eeles-98]   Peter Eeles, Oliver Sims, OMG, *Building Business Objects*, John Wiley & Sons Computer Publishing (1998).

[34]   [Ellis-98]   W. J. Ellis, R. F. Hilliard II, P. T. Poon, D. Rayford, T. F. Saunders, B. Sherlund, R. L. Wade, *Toward a Recommended Practice for Architectural Description*, FROM THE IEEE ARCHITECTURE WORKING GROUP READING ROOM (accessed at www.pithecanthropus.com/~awg/browsing_library.html).

[35] [Ezran-98] Michel Ezran, Maurizio Morisio, Colin Tully, *Practical Software Reuse: The Essential Guide*, European Systems and Software Initiative SURPRISE Project (1998).

[36] [Gamma-95] E. Gamma, R. Helm, R. Johnson, and J. Vlissides, *Design Patterns: Elements of Reusable Object Oriented Software*, Addison Wesley Longman (1995).

[37] [Geneva-98] Rapporteur Of Working Party 4/4 Question 14, *Status Document for X.770—ODMA Notification Dispatch Function—Geneva* (1998).

[38] [Hamilton-97] G. Hamilton (ed.), *JavaBeans API Specification, Version 1.01*, Sun Microsystems (1997).

[39] [Heineman-98] G. T. Heineman, *Adaptation and Software Architecture*, PROCEEDINGS OF THE THIRD INTERNATIONAL WORKSHOP ON SOFTWARE ARCHITECTURES, Orlando, FL (1998).

[40] [Herbert] Andrew Herbert, *The Challenge of ODP*, APM 1016 (1993).

[41] [ICL-94] Guangxing Li, Dave Otway, *An Open Architecture for Real-Time Processing*, ICL SYSTEMS JOURNAL, Vol.9 Iss.2 (1994).

[42] [IDEF0] National Institute of Standards and Technology, *Integrated Definition for Function Modeling (IDEF0)*, FIPS PUB 183, Gaithersburg, MD.

[43] [IEEE-610-5] Institute of Electrical and Electronics Engineers, *IEEE Standard Glossary of Data Management Terminology*, 1990, IEEE 610.5, Piscataway, NJ.

[44] [ISO-ALS] ITU-T Recommendation X.207 | ISO/IEC 9545: *Information Technology—Open Systems Interconnection—Application Layer Structure* (1994).

[45] [ITU-X770-98] Status Document for X.770-ODMA Notification Dispatch Function, ITU-Telecommunication Standardization Sector, Temporary Document 52-E (WP4/4) STUDY GROUP 4 (1998)

[46] [JTA] DISA, *Department of Defense Joint Technical Architecture, Version 2, Draft* (1997).

[47] [Kazman-97] R. Kazman, P. Clements, L. Bass and G. Abowd, *Classifying Architectural Elements as a Foundation for Mechanism Matching*, PROCEEDINGS OF COMPSAC 97, Washington, D. C. (1997).

[48] [Kilov-97] Haim Kilov, *International Standards Define Semantics: RM-ODP and GRM, briefing* (1997).

[49] [Kilov-email] Haim Kilov to Fred Cummins. Personal communication. (Feb. 2, 1999).

[50] [Krieger-98] David Krieger, Richard M. Adler, *The Emergence of Distributed Component Platforms*, IEEE COMPUTING (March 1998).

[51] [Lamping-93] J. Lamping, *Typing the Specialisation Interface*, PROCEEDINGS OF OOPSLA '93, CONFERENCE ON OBJECT-ORIENTED PROGRAMMING, SYSTEMS, LANGUAGES AND APPLICATIONS, ACM Press (1993).

[52] [Lamport-78] L. Lamport, *Time, Clocks and the Ordering of Events in a Distributed System*, COMMUNICATIONS OF THE ACM, 21(7) (1978).

[53] [Manola-99] Frank Manola, *Providing Systemic Properties (Ilities) and Quality of Service in Component-Based Systems, Draft,* Object Services and Consulting, Inc. (1999).

[54] [Meseguer] José Meseguer and Carolyn Talcott, *Formal Foundations for Compositional Software Architectures Position Paper*, OMG-DARPA-MCC WORKSHOP ON COMPOSITIONAL SOFTWARE ARCHITECTURES (no date).

[55] [Miller-87] J.S. Miller, *MultiScheme: A Parallel Processing System Based on MIT Scheme*, MIT/LCS/TR-402 (Sept. 1987).

[56] [Milosevic-95] Z. Milosevic, *Enterprise Aspects Of Open Distributed Systems*, BSEE(HONS), MSC, PH.D. THESIS SUBMITTED TO THE DEPARTMENT OF COMPUTER SCIENCE, THE UNIVERSITY OF QUEENSLAND (Oct.1995).

[57] [Mowbray-94] Thomas Mowbray, Ron Zahavi, *The Essential CORBA Systems Integration Using Distributed Objects*, John Wiley & Sons (1994).

[58] [Mowbray-97] Thomas Mowbray, Raphael Malveau, *CORBA Design Patterns*, John Wiley & Sons (1997).

[59] [Neumann-94] B.C. Neumann, *Scale in Distributed Systems*, READINGS IN DISTRIBUTED COMPUTING SYSTEMS, IEEE Computer Society Press (1994).

[60] [ODMA-99] ITU-T Q.14/4 Draft Rec. X.704, *Status Document For Systems Management and Open Distributed Management Architecture (ODMA)—Viewpoint Notations* (Jan. 1999).

[61] [OMG-97] OMG, *CORBAservices: Common Object Services Specification, Revised Edition* (Mar. 1995). OMG Document formal/97-05-03.

[62] [Oreizy] Peyman Oreizy, Nenad Medvidovic, Richard N. Taylor, David S. Rosenblum, *Software Architecture and Component Technologies: Bridging the Gap*, INFORMATION AND COMPUTER SCIENCE, UNIVERSITY OF CALIFORNIA, IRVINE (no date) (accessed at www.ics.uci.edu/pub/arch).

[63]   [Oreizy-98]   P. Oreizy, N. Medvidovic, and R. N. Taylor, *Architecture-Based Runtime Software Evolution,* PROCEEDINGS OF THE 20TH INTERNATIONAL CONFERENCE ON SOFTWARE ENGINEERING, Kyoto, Japan (Apr. 1998).

[64]   [Orfali-96]   R. Orfali, D. Harkey, and J. Edwards, *The Essential Distributed Objects Survival Guide*, John Wiley & Sons (1996).

[65]   [Orfali-98]   Robert Orfali and Dan Hartley, *Client/Server Programming with JAVA and CORBA, Second Edition*, John Wiley & Sons Computer Publishing (1998).

[66]   [Perry-87]   D. E. Perry, *Software Interconnection Models*, PROCEEDINGS OF THE 9TH INTERNATIONAL CONFERENCE ON SOFTWARE ENGINEERING, Monterey, CA (May 1987).

[67]   [Perry-92]   D. E. Perry and A. L. Wolf, *Foundations for the Study of Software Architectures*, ACM SIGSOFT SOFTWARE ENGINEERING NOTES (Oct. 1992).

[68]   [Perry-97]   D. E. Perry, *Software Architecture and its Relevance to Software Engineering*, INVITED TALK. SECOND INTERNATIONAL CONFERENCE ON COORDINATION MODELS AND LANGUAGES, Berlin, Germany (Sept.1997).

[69]   [Rectin-91]   Eberhardt Rechtin, *Systems Architecting, Creating and Building Computer Systems*, Prentice Hall (1991).

[70]   [Robbins-98]   J. E. Robbins, N. Medvidovic, D. F. Redmiles, and D. S. Rosenblum, *Integrating Architecture Description Languages with a Standard Design Method*, PROCEEDINGS OF THE 20TH INTERNATIONAL CONFERENCE ON SOFTWARE ENGINEERING, Kyoto, Japan (Apr. 1998).

[71]   [Roodyn-99]   N. Roodyn and W. Emmerich *An Architectural Style for Multiple Real-Time Data Feeds*, PROCEEDINGS OF THE 21ST INTERNATIONAL CONFERENCE ON SOFTWARE ENGINEERING, Los Angeles, CA (May 1999).

[72]   [Rosenblum-97]   D. S. Rosenblum and A. L. Wolf, *A Design Framework for Internet-Scale Event Observation and Notification*, PROCEEDINGS OF THE SIXTH EUROPEAN SOFTWARE ENGINEERING CONFERENCE, Zurich, Switzerland (Sept. 1997).

[73]   [Schmidt-94]   D.C Schmidt, *Reactor: An object Behavioral pattern for Concurrent Event Demultiplexing and Event Handler Dispatching*, PROCEEDINGS OF PLOP '94, pp 529–545, (1994).

[74]   [Sefika-96]   Mohlalefi Sefika, *Design Conformance Management of Software Systems: An Architecture-Oriented Approach*, PHD THESIS, UNIVERSITY OF ILLINOIS AT URBANA-CHAMPAIGN (July 1996).

[75] [Stavridou-98]   V. Stavridou and R. A. Riemenschneider, *Provably Dependable Software Architectures*, PROCEEDINGS OF THE THIRD INTERNATIONAL WORSHOP ON SOFTWARE ARCHITECTURES, Orlando, FL (Nov. 1998).

[76] [Steyaert-96]   P. Steyaert, C. Lucasclucas, K. Menskimmens, *Reuse Contracts: Managing the Evolution of Reusable Assets,* OOPSLA'96, (1996).

[77] [Su-95]   Stanley Y. W. Su, *Object-oriented Knowledge Base Management in a Virtual Enterprise Environment*, University of Florida (May 1995).

[78] [Tarr]   P. Tarr, H. Ossher, W. Harrison and S.M. Sutton, Jr., *N Degrees of Separation: Multi-Dimensional Separation of Concerns*, PROCEEDINGS OF THE INTERNATIONAL CONFERENCE ON SOFTWARE ENGINEERING (ICSE 21) (May 1999).

[79] [Taylor-96]   R. N. Taylor, N. Medvidovic, K. M. Anderson, E. J. Whitehead, J. E. Robbins, K. A. Nies, P. Oreizy and D. L. Dubrow, *A Component- and Message-Based Architectural Style for GUI Software*, IEEE TRANSACTION ON SOFTWARE ENGINEERING, 22(6) (1996).

[80] [Tracz]   Will Tracz, Loral Federal Systems, *Domain-Specific Software Architecture (DSSA) Frequently Asked Questions (FAQ)* (no date).

[81] [Tyson-96]   Kevin Tyson, Enterprise Engineering Associates, and Chuck Alvarez, J. P. Morgan & Co., *Introduction to RM-ODP, briefing*, DECORUM '96 (Mar.1996).

[82] [Tyson-97]   Kevin Tyson, Enterprise Engineering Associates, *Introduction to RM-ODP Part 3, briefing*, OMG document number ORMSC/97-06-07 (June 97).

[83] [Vlissides-95]   John Vlissides, James Coplien, Norman Kerth (eds.), *Pattern Languages of Program Design*, Addison Wesley (1995).

[84] [Vlissides-98]   John Vlissides, *Pattern Hatching Design Patterns Applied*, Addison-Wesley (1998).

[85] [Walker]   Robert J. Walker, Elisa L.A. Baniassad, and Gail C. Murphy, *An Initial Assessment of Aspect-oriented Programming*, PROCEEDINGS OF THE INTERNATIONAL CONFERENCE ON SOFTWARE ENGINEERING (ICSE 21) (May 1999).

[86] [Wood-97]   Bryan Wood, *ODP Functions and CORBA Services*, Background material for Green Paper on ODP functions and Object Services, OMG document 97-03-04 (March 1997).

[87] [Wood-98]   Bryan Wood, Open-IT Ltd, *Report from the SC33 Berlin Meeting* (Feb. 1998).

[88] [XML] Object Management Group, *XML Metadata Interchange (XMI)*, Proposal to the OMG OA & DTF RFP 3: Stream-based Model Interchange Format (SMIF). OMG Document ad/98/10-05 (Oct. 1998).

[89] [Yellin-94] D. M. Yellin and R. E. Strom, *Interfaces, Protocols, and the Semi-Automatic Construction of Software Adaptors*, PROCEEDINGS OF OOPSLA '94, Portland, OR (Oct. 1994).

[90] [Zachman-96a] John A. Zachman, *The Framework For Enterprise Architecture: Getting Beyond the 'Legacy'* (May 1996).

[91] [Zachman-96b] John A. Zachman, *The Challenge Is Change* (May 1996).

WORLD WIDE WEB SITES

RM-ODP

Official RM-ODP site: http://www.itu.int/ITU-T/com7/index.html

ISO site: http://www.iso.ch:8000/RM-ODP

ISO online: http://www.iso.ch/welcome.html

RM-ODP papers and work: ftp://ftp.dstc.edu.au/pub/arch/RM-ODP

DSTC site for RM-ODP: http://www.dstc.edu.au/AU/research_news/odp/ref_model

http://enterprise.Systemhouse.MCI.com

JTC1: http://www.jtc1.org

ITU: http://www.itu.int

ITU standards: http://www.itu.int/ITU-T/com7/index.html

NCITS: http://www.ncits.org

RM-ODP parts: http://enterprise.Systemhouse.MCI.com

RM-ODP parts: http://www.opennc.org/public/arch/rm-odp.htm

RM-ODP STANDARDS WORK

Enterprise Viewpoint work: http://enterprise.Systemhouse.MCI.com/WG7/current.htm

ANSA Research: http://www.ansa.co.uk

ANSA documents: ftp://ftp.ansa.co.uk/phase3-doc-root

DSTC Architecture Unit:
http://www.dstc.edu.au/AU/ http://www.cutter.com/consortium/index.html

DSTC Enterprise Distributed Computing: http://www.dstc.edu.au/AU/research_news/arch_model

Trader: http://www.objs.com/survey/trader-reference-model.html

Type management work at DSTC: http://www.dstc.edu.au/AU/research_news/odp/typemgmt

Work on policy: http://enterprise.shl.com/policy/contributions.html

Work on interaction and architecture:
http://www.dstc.edu.au/cgi-bin/redirect/rd.cgi?http://archive.dstc.edu.au/RDU/reports/GIA

Use of RM-ODP papers: http://www.dstc.edu.au/cgi-bin
redirect/rd.cgi?http://archive.dstc.edu.au/AU/staff/zoran-milosevic.html

ICL home page: http://www.icl.com

QoS ballot comments:
http://forum.afnor.fr/afnor/WORK/AFNOR/GPN2/ZH70/PUBLIC/07n2059.pdf

ARCHITECTURES

Architecture sponsored by Barry Boehm at the University of Southern California:
http://sunset.usc.edu/Soft_Arch/SwArch.html

Papers on composability from CMU:
http://www.cs.cmu.edu/afs/cs/project/compose/www/html/Publications/1.html

Architecture papers from SEI: http://www.sei.cmu.edu/architecture/bibpart1.html

Architecture papers from UCI: http://www.ics.uci.edu/pub/arch

Architecture papers from University of Colorado: http://www.cs.colorado.edu/users/serl

World Wide Institute of Software Architects: http://www.wwisa.org

http://www.enteng.com

OMG site: www.omg.org

OMG UML and MoF: http://www.omg.org/uml

OMG OMA Guide official site (membership to OMG required):
http://www.omg.org/cgi-bin/members/doclistm.pl

OMG documents: ftp://www.omg.org/pub/docs

OMA Guide work: http://enterprise.shl.com/omwg

Kevin Tyson's page: http://www.exit109.com/~kpt

Daniel Jackson's papers: http://sdg.lcs.mit.edu/~dnj/publications.html

TINA-C: http://www.tinac.com

PIDS from Los Alamos National Laboratory: http://www.acl.lanl.gov/TeleMed

ESPRIT work: http://www.cordis.lu/esprit/home.html

DISGIS Web site: http://www.disgis.com

COMPASS Web site: http://www.compassgl.org

OBOE Web site: http://www.dbis.informatik.uni-frankfurt.de/~oboe

ISO TC211 Web site: http://www.statkart.no/isotc211

Open Geodata Consortium Web site: http://www.opengis.org

ADL Rapide: http://poset.stanford.edu/rapide

Survey of ADLs at CMU: http://www.cs.cmu.edu/~spok/adl/adls.html

Software architecture by the SEI http://www.sei.cmu.edu/architecture/sw_architecture.html

NIIIP: http://www.niiip.org

The Open Group Architectural Framework (TOGAF) work at:
    http://www.opengroup.org/public/arch

Software Development Magazine: http://www.sdmagazine.com

Zachman Framework information: http://www.ies.aust.com/~ieinfo/zachman.htm

C4ISR: http://www.c3i.osd.mil/org/cio/i3/AWG_Digital_Library/index.htm

IEEE P1471: http://www.pithecanthropus.com/~awg

Federal ITA: http://www.itpolicy.gsa.gov/mke/archplus/cmodel.htm

IETF QoS: http://www.ietf.org/html.charters/rtfm-charter.html and
    http://www.ietf.org/html.charters/intserv-charter.html

IWQoS: http://www.fokus.gmd.de/research/cc/tip/employees/jdm/private/SC-IWQOS/home.html

QoS Forum: http://www.qosforum.com

QoS e-mail: www.fokus.gmd.de/research/cc/tip/employees/jdm/private/jdmQoSIG.html

QUO: http://www.dist-systems.bbn.com/tech/QuO/quorelease.html

DARPA Quorum: http://www.darpa.mil/ito/research/quorum/index.html

TOOLS AND PRODUCTS

WinWin: http://sunset.usc.edu/Tools.html

Easy WinWin: http://sunset.usc.edu/research/WINWIN/index.html and
    http://www.GroupSystems.com

Select tools: http://www.selectst.com

Peerlogic DAIS ORB: http://www.peerlogic.com/products/dais/f_dais.htm

Rational ROSE products: http://www.rational.com

ADML: http://www.mcc.com/projects/ssepp/adml

EiffelBase library: http://eiffel.com/products/base

APM FlexiNet: http://www.ansa.co.uk/Research/FlexiNet.htm

SPIN: http://netlib.bell-labs.com/netlib/spin/whatisspin.html

iContract: http://www.reliable-systems.com/tools/iContract/IDEs/VAJ/VAJ.htm

Virtual DB www.enterworks.com

Oracle products: www.oracle.com

Sybase products: www.sybase.com

Sun RMI: http://www.sun.com/research/forest/opj/docs/api/java/rmi/server/package-use.html

Sun Java™ and other software: http://www.sun.com/products-n-solutions/software

Little-JIL process language: http://laser.cs.umass.edu/Little-JIL.htm

BEA WebLogic® and BEA Tuxedo®: www.bea.com

MQSeries" product suite: http://www-4.ibm.com/software/ts/mqseries

Real-Time QoS work: http://www.darpa.mil/ito/research/quorum/index.html

Visible tool for Zachman Framework: http://www.visible.com

Ptech tool: http://www.ptechinc.com

Sterling Software Cool products: http://www.sterling.com/cool/index.asp

NetViz: http://www.netviz.com

DSSA

http://www.sei.cmu.edu/arpa/dssa/DSSAexp.html

http://www.sei.cmu.edu/arpa/evo/dssa-sum.html

http://www.teknowledge.com/dssa

http://www.ai.mit.edu/projects/adage/adage.html

XML

http://www.w3.org/XML

http://www.w3.org/DOM

INDEX